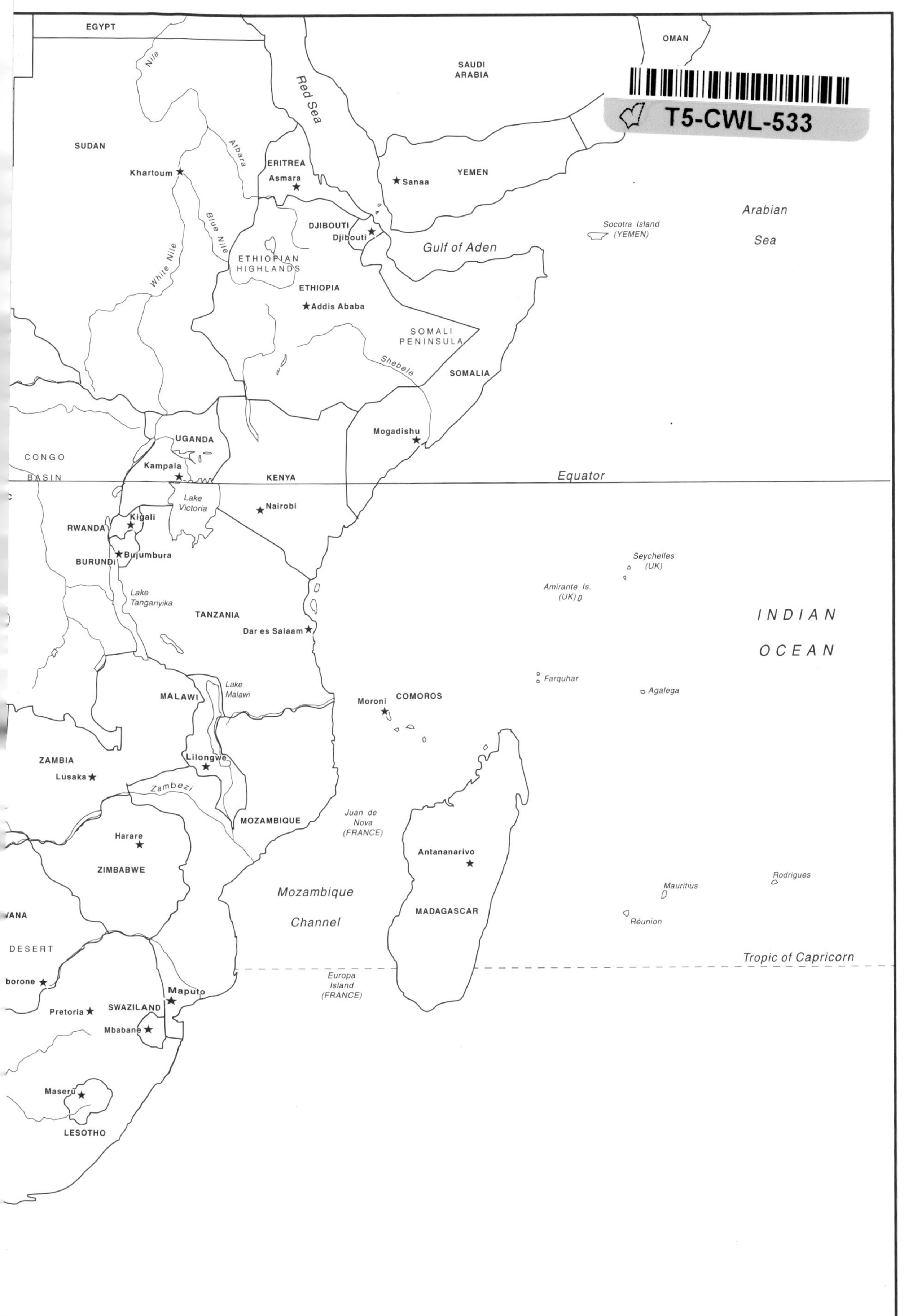
EGYPT
OMAN
SAUDI ARABIA
Nile
Red Sea
SUDAN
Atbara
ERITREA
Khartoum
Asmara
Sanaa
YEMEN
Arabian Sea
Blue Nile
DJIBOUTI
Djibouti
Socotra Island (YEMEN)
Gulf of Aden
White Nile
ETHIOPIAN HIGHLANDS
ETHIOPIA
Addis Ababa
SOMALI PENINSULA
Shebele
SOMALIA
UGANDA
Mogadishu
CONGO BASIN
Kampala
KENYA
Equator
Lake Victoria
Nairobi
Kigali
RWANDA
Bujumbura
BURUNDI
Seychelles (UK)
Amirante Is. (UK)
Lake Tanganyika
TANZANIA
INDIAN OCEAN
Dar es Salaam
Farquhar
Agalega
Lake Malawi
MALAWI
Moroni
COMOROS
ZAMBIA
Lilongwe
Lusaka
Zambezi
Juan de Nova (FRANCE)
MOZAMBIQUE
Harare
Antananarivo
ZIMBABWE
Rodrigues
Mauritius
Mozambique Channel
MADAGASCAR
Réunion
DESERT
Tropic of Capricorn
Europa Island (FRANCE)
Maputo
Pretoria
SWAZILAND
Mbabane
Maseru
LESOTHO

The Greenwood Encyclopedia of
World Popular Culture

General Editor

GARY HOPPENSTAND

Volume Editors

MICHAEL K. SCHOENECKE, North America

JOHN F. BRATZEL, Latin America

GERD BAYER, Europe

LYNN BARTHOLOME, North Africa and the Middle East

DENNIS HICKEY, Sub-Saharan Africa

GARY XU and VINAY DHARWADKER, Asia and Pacific Oceania

THE GREENWOOD ENCYCLOPEDIA OF WORLD POPULAR CULTURE

SUB-SAHARAN AFRICA

Gary Hoppenstand
General Editor

Dennis Hickey
Volume Editor

GREENWOOD PRESS
Westport, Connecticut • London

Library of Congress Cataloging-in-Publication Data

The Greenwood encyclopedia of world popular culture / Gary Hoppenstand, general editor ; volume editors, John F. Bratzel ... [et al.].
p. cm.
Includes bibliographical references and index.
ISBN-13: 978-0-313-33255-5 (set : alk. paper)
ISBN-13: 978-0-313-33316-3 (North America : alk. paper)
ISBN-13: 978-0-313-33256-2 (Latin America : alk. paper)
ISBN-13: 978-0-313-33509-9 (Europe : alk. paper)
ISBN-13: 978-0-313-33274-6 (North Africa and the Middle East : alk. paper)
ISBN-13: 978-0-313-33505-1 (Sub-Saharan Africa : alk. paper)
ISBN-13: 978-0-313-33956-1 (Asia and Pacific Oceania : alk. paper)
1. Popular culture—Encyclopedias. 2. Civilization, Modern—Encyclopedias. 3. Culture—Encyclopedias. I. Hoppenstand, Gary. II. Bratzel, John F. III. Title: Encyclopedia of world popular culture. IV. Title: World popular culture.
HM621.G74 2007
306.03—dc22 2007010684

British Library Cataloguing in Publication Data is available.

Library of Congress Catalog Card Number: 2007010684
ISBN-13: 978-0-313-33255-5 (Set)
ISBN-10: 0-313-33255-X

ISBN-13: 978-0-313-33316-3 (North America)
ISBN-10: 0-313-33316-5

ISBN-13: 978-0-313-33256-2 (Latin America)
ISBN-10: 0-313-33256-8

ISBN-13: 978-0-313-33509-9 (Europe)
ISBN-10: 0-313-33509-5

ISBN-13: 978-0-313-33274-6 (North Africa and the Middle East)
ISBN-10: 0-313-33274-6

ISBN-13: 978-0-313-33505-1 (Sub-Saharan Africa)
ISBN-10: 0-313-33505-2

ISBN-13: 978-0-313-33956-1 (Asia and Pacific Oceania)
ISBN-10: 0-313-33956-2

First published in 2007

Greenwood Press, 88 Post Road West, Westport, CT 06881
An imprint of Greenwood Publishing Group, Inc.
www.greenwood.com

Printed in the United States of America

The paper used in this book complies with the Permanent Paper Standard issued by the National Information Standards Organization (Z39.48–1984).

10 9 8 7 6 5 4 3 2 1

To Joseph Farkas
A Good Life, and a Life of Goodness

CONTENTS

FOREWORD

POPULAR CULTURE AND THE WORLD

GARY HOPPENSTAND

Popular culture is easy to recognize, but often difficult to define. We can say with authority that the current hit television show *House* is popular culture, but can we say that how medical personnel work in hospitals is popular culture as well? We can readily admit that the recent blockbuster movie *Pirates of the Caribbean* is popular culture, but can we also admit that what the real-life historical Caribbean pirates ate and what clothes they wore are components of popular culture? We can easily recognize that a best-selling romance novel by Danielle Steel is popular culture, but can we also recognize that human love, as ritualistic behavior, is popular culture? Can popular culture include architecture, or furniture, or automobiles, or many of the other things that we make, as well as the behaviors that we engage in, and the general attitudes that we hold in our day-to-day lives? Does popular culture exist outside of our own immediate society? There can be so much to study about popular culture that it can seem overwhelming and ultimately inaccessible.

Because popular culture is so pervasive—not only in the United States, but in all cultures around the world—it can be difficult to study. Basically, however, there are two main approaches to defining popular culture. The first advocates the notion that popular culture is tied to that period in Western societies known as the Industrial Revolution. It is subsequently linked to such concepts as "mass-produced culture" and "mass-consumed culture." In other words, there must be present a set of conditions related to industrial capitalism before popular culture can exist. Included among these conditions are the need for large urban centers, or cities, which can sustain financially the distribution and consumption of popular culture, and the related requirement that there be an educated working-class or middle-class population that has both the leisure time and the expendable income to support the production of popular culture. Certainly, this approach can encompass that which is most commonly regarded as popular culture: motion pictures, television, popular fiction, computers and video games, even contemporary fast foods and popular fashion. In addition, this approach can generate discussions about the relationship between popular culture and political ideology. Can popular culture be political in nature, or politically subversive?

Can it intentionally or unintentionally support the status quo? Can it be oppressive or express harmful ideas? Needless to say, such definitions limit the critical examination of popular culture by both geography and time, insisting that popular culture existed (or only exists) historically in industrial and postindustrial societies (primarily in Western Europe and North America) over the past 200 years. However, many students and critics of popular culture insist that industrial production and Western cultural influences are not essential in either defining or understanding popular culture.

Indeed, a second approach sees popular culture as existing since the beginning of human civilization. It is not circumscribed by certain historic periods, or by national or regional boundaries. This approach sees popular culture as extending well beyond the realm of industrial production, in terms of both its creation and its existence. Popular culture, these critics claim, can be seen in ancient China, or in medieval Japan, or in pre-colonial Africa, as well as in modern-day Western Europe and North America (or in all contemporary global cultures and nations for that matter). It need not be limited to mass-produced objects or electronic media, though it certainly does include these, but it can include the many facets of people's lifestyles, the way people think and behave, and the way people define themselves as individuals and as societies.

This six-volume *Encyclopedia of World Popular Culture*, then, encompasses something of both approaches. In each of the global regions of the world covered—North America, South America, Europe, the Middle East, Sub-Saharan Africa, and Asia—the major industrial and postindustrial expressions of popular culture are covered, including, in most cases, film; games, toys, and pastimes; literature (popular fiction and nonfiction); music; periodicals; and radio/television. Also examined are the lifestyle dimensions of popular culture, including architecture; dance; fashion and appearance; food and foodways; love, sex, and marriage; sports; theater and performance; and transportation and travel. What is revealed in each chapter of each volume of *The Greenwood Encyclopedia of World Popular Culture* is the rich complexity and diversity of the human experience within the framework of a popular culture context.

Yet rooted within this framework of rich complexity and diversity is a central idea that holds the construct of world popular culture together, an idea that sees in popular culture both the means and the methods of widespread, everyday, human expression. Simply put, the commonality of national, transnational, and global popular cultures is the notion that, through their popular culture, people construct narratives, or stories, about themselves and their communities. The many and varied processes involved in creating popular culture (and subsequently living with it) are concerned, at the deepest and most fundamental levels, with the need for people to express their lifestyle in ways that significantly define their relationships to others.

The food we eat, the movies we see, the games we play, the way we construct our buildings, and the means of our travel all tell stories about what we think and what we like at a consciously intended level, as well as at an unintended subliminal level. These narratives tell others about our interests and desires, as well as our fundamental beliefs about life itself. Thus, though the types of popular dance might be quite different in the various regions of the world, the recognition that dance fulfills a basic and powerful need for human communication is amazingly similar. The fact that different forms of popular sports are played and watched in different countries does not deny the related fact that sports globally define the kindred beliefs in the benefits of hard work, determination, and the overarching desire for the achievement of success.

These are all life stories, and popular culture involves the relating of life's most common forms of expression. This *Encyclopedia of World Popular Culture* offers many narratives about many people and their popular culture, stories that not only inform us about others and how they live, but that also inform us, by comparison, about how we live.

INTRODUCTION

POPULAR CULTURE IN SUB-SAHARAN AFRICA

DENNIS HICKEY

The world of African popular culture is seemingly infinite in its richness, complexity, and creative possibility. A Kenyan master of world literature tells the tale of a mythical (though depressingly familiar) African tyrant who borrows a fortune from the "Global Bank" to build a tower to the heavens as a tribute to his monumental ego; a Malian musician sits down with an American folk and blues artist and cuts a CD that blends the sensibility of the West African town and savanna with its lineal descendant, the musical artistry of Memphis, New Orleans, and the Mississippi Delta; craftsmen in Botswana use their ingenuity to fashion toys out of wire for the enjoyment of children and tourists, while an Ethiopian artist in a studio in New York uses her talent to help define a new genre of fine art. Soccer fans in Cameroon cheer on their national team, the Indomitable Lions, to another victory, while dedicated young runners in Ethiopia and Kenya train hard for their chance at Olympic gold and glory. A Nigerian writer tells the story of a young Elvis impersonator who struggles to make ends meet on the hard streets of Lagos, while in South Africa a puppet troupe performs a series of sketches that serve as an educational tool in the fight against AIDS; video film producers in Nigeria, operating on a shoestring budget, turn out a product that blends everyday Nigerian concerns with the entertainment formats of American television; a powerful new literary voice—a writer from a West African family born in Washington, DC—portrays the horrific existence of a child soldier, while another important novelist speculates on what would happen when the quest to build a casino in the "new" South Africa runs up against the haunting legacy of an anti-colonial rebellion that happened a century and a half before.[1] These examples represent just a small portion of the vast tapestry of intellect, action, and creation that is African popular culture, a vivid and living expression of the dynamism of its people and a gift to the world.

It is ironic that even today Africa is approached and explained in terms of its supposed "isolation." Throughout the rest of the world, Africa is still seen through the distorting lens of the symbolic conventions that were formed decades, even centuries ago: savannas teeming with wildlife, picturesque villages and "primitive" customs, tribal peoples living in pure and holistic mindsets and spaces, oblivious to the wider social, political, and economic forces that shape their lives, effectively detached from the world beyond their own village, lonely outsiders cut off from the global village that is fast becoming our common home in the early stages of the twenty-first century.[2] True, much of the continent is badly in need of all-weather roads of asphalt and concrete to strengthen the sinews of its economic progress, but in relation to the rest of the world, the pathways of thought and expression, invention and adaptation, identity and consciousness have been well and heavily traveled over generations of the African past—and, as the contributors to this volume clearly demonstrate, from a cultural and intellectual standpoint the traffic has been, and continues to be, heavy in both directions.

A Very Brief History of the End of Africa's "Isolation"

When Africans reflect on their history, they cannot be faulted if they wish that their ancestors *had* enjoyed greater isolation and autonomy from the aggressive interventions of the outside world. While scholars continue to debate the numbers, the most credible estimate is that the Atlantic slave trade, after 1600, took 11 million or more people from the continent and landed 10 million of them alive in the Western Hemisphere.[3] The willing participants in these dreadful transactions—the Europeans who initiated and directed them and their African collaborators who were essential to an operation on this scale—caused untold human suffering and disrupted internal possibilities and processes of political unification and constructive economic development. While the Atlantic slave trade extended over roughly four centuries (peaking in the eighteenth century) and was particularly intensive in its impact, the East African slave trade with the Persian Gulf region and southwest Asia extended over a millennium and tore a comparable number of people from the continent. This destructive phenomenon proved equally persistent, and an intensification of this trade during the nineteenth century caused considerable disruption in parts of Eastern and Central Africa. In fact, while many who are familiar with the major themes of the African diaspora are well aware of the slave revolts that were staged in such places as Haiti, Jamaica, and South Carolina, fewer know that one of the most significant slave rebellions in history occurred in the salt flats near Basra in what is now Iraq, in the ninth century AD. In retrospect, it should not be surprising that the people of Africa have had such a great cultural influence on the rest of the world, since, for ages, their people, and their genius, were the continent's greatest export.

The Slave Trade and the New World

Tragically, the slave trade, in its various regional manifestations, provided the foundation for the first extensive episode of cultural exchange between the peoples of Sub-Saharan Africa and the rest of the world. In particular, after the demographic collapse of Native American populations as a result of disease and the impact of conquest, this part of the world was repopulated by newcomers from two continents—from Europe, whose settler populations arrived free from the specter of perpetual servitude, and from Africa, whose captives arrived in slave ships and would have to wage long struggles to gain their freedom. The African contribution to the forging of this "new world" went far beyond the incalculable value of their labor: Africans and their descendants also played a vital role in shaping the cultural landscape of the post-Columbian world, on the one hand through the development of their own vibrant and distinctive subcultures, and on the other through the fusion of their creativity with the mainstream cultures of these emergent American societies. In every aspect of culture and the arts, from the plantations of antebellum Alabama and Mississippi to the cane fields and hills of Cuba and

Jamaica, from Harlem to Rio de Janeiro, from the jazz and blues clubs of Chicago to the gospel music that resounded within the churches of the rural American South, through a multiplicity of artistic expressions and genres, African slaves and the generations that followed them, unfree and then free, played—and continue to play—a profound role in defining the linguistic, musical, literary, artistic, and expressive universe of the Americas.

European Conquest and African Response

Throughout the period of the Atlantic slave trade the European presence in Africa was largely confined to the coast (southern Africa being the major exception). By the late nineteenth century, with the passing of the Atlantic slave trade and the sharpening of economic and political rivalries among the nation-states of Western Europe, a quest to acquire overseas colonies emerged as a central objective of the ruling elites in London, Paris, Brussels, and Berlin. The territories and natural resources of Africa south of the Sahara were now seen as attractive targets, and during the last two decades of that century that entire expanse of the continent was conquered and reduced to colonial status (with the exception of Liberia in the west and Ethiopia in the east). Britain, France, Belgium, and Germany were the primary aggressors, with Portugal holding on to its colonial outposts from an earlier era and Italy joining in the division of the spoils.

With the culmination of the "scramble for Africa" between 1880 and 1900, the second major period of cultural exchange between Africa and the rest of the world began. Although the inherent dynamic of this power relationship—Europeans as rulers, Africans as the ruled—empowered the voices and ideologies of the colonizers over those of the colonized, the peoples of the continent proved remarkably resilient in defending their cultural autonomy and accepting these external influences on their own terms. In its own way, the transformative impact of colonial economies, with their focus on cash crop cultivation and mining, had an impact every bit as profound (and ultimately more extensive) than the overseas slave trades. Nevertheless, despite these powerful influences, African popular culture during the colonial period stands as a testimony to the human capacity to borrow and accept what is useful while refusing to surrender that collective identity (and will to freedom) that is the very anchor of our dignity, no matter what part of the world we call home. For example, the gospel of the European Christian missionaries, stressing meekness and submission and emphasizing personal guilt and redemption, soon became transformed in the hands of literate Africans into an abiding source of hope and endurance, and, in a number of places around the continent, the African faithful went on to hone this belief system into a powerful ideology of liberation. Also, while the introduction (and imposition) of European languages tended to disadvantage Africans and African modes of expression within the schoolroom, the courtroom, the workplace, and the corridors of power, it often provided them with a *lingua franca* in large, sometimes vast, areas where one was previously lacking, and whether it was the written word from the pen of a member of the intelligentsia or the spoken word of an urban labor organizer or rural freedom fighter, the people of the continent, once again, were able to turn an instrument of the colonizer to their own advantage. Moreover, during the relatively short period of European colonial domination—indeed, it is sometimes forgotten that, in most of the continent, this lasted less than a century—Africans did not passively accept European cultural forms and content, but they used these avenues of expression to encode and preserve their own collective values and memories and to express their hopes and yearnings for survival; for the future of their families and their people; for their personal dreams and aspirations; and, most emphatically, for their freedom.

Recent History

The 1960s marked the beginning of a new era in the history of the continent. During this decade the great majority of African colonies achieved their independence, and although the struggle would go on in certain parts of the continent—Portugal was slow to relinquish its African possessions, and the apartheid system in South Africa would not give way to majority rule until the early 1990s—Africans had taken the first crucial step toward gaining control over their political and economic destiny (a quest that continues, albeit in different form, up to this day). African popular culture both encouraged and reflected the triumph of what one writer has called "the first dance of freedom,"[4] and when, in many instances, the new African regimes failed to live up to their rhetoric and promises, artistic expression provided a potent outlet for political protest, especially when no other means of dissent were available short of violence and revolution.

African nations continue to struggle with a host of daunting economic problems, ranging from the need to provide their people with functional **Transportation** systems (a situation described here by Fred Lindsey) to the urgent priority of combating the AIDS epidemic (analyzed by Ulrike Schuerkens in her chapter on **Love, Sex, and Marriage**). Nevertheless, in the era of globalization and a world financial order that has disadvantaged Africa and, some would argue, reduced it to a new state of dependency, the cutting edge of African popular culture – its literature, its art, its music, its theater—remains as sharp and uncompromising as ever as a tool of political protest.

THE CULTURAL GENIUS OF AFRICA

Throughout the period of European colonialism in Africa, the West continued to benefit from—and liberally draw upon—the cultural genius of Africa. Figures as diverse as Pablo Picasso and Elvis Presley derived their inspiration from African (and African diasporan) models. Ironically, while artists and entertainers from Europe and North America were glad to embrace and adapt African models as a source of innovation within their own cultural universe, Western audiences have always been far more reluctant to accept the reality and dynamic of change within Africa itself. It is not surprising that many outside the continent have had a hard time coming to terms with the modernity and fluidity of African popular culture (or, to be more accurate, African popular *cultures*). Still, as the contributors to this volume forcefully demonstrate, Africans have never stood still: in domains of popular expression seemingly as far afield as **Fashion and Appearance** (surveyed by Martha Donkor), **Games, Toys, and Pastimes** (described by Eva Nwokah and Clara Ikekeonwu), **Food and Foodways** (considered by Fran Osseo-Asare), and **Architecture** (evaluated by George William Kofi Intsiful), Africans have continued to build on what is best in their past without turning their back on the rest of the world.

The Nature and Reality of Tradition

Indeed, a basic theme confronted by the contributors to this volume, both explicitly and implicitly, is the nature and reality of "tradition." The Western approach to Africa—yesterday, and today—has been characterized by an obsession with this concept, a quixotic pursuit rendered all the more futile by centuries of determined outside intervention in the African cultural sphere. The very concept of tradition is highly problematic, even within the precolonial context, and a number of the contributors to this volume provide valuable (if contrasting) perspectives on this issue. Ubong Samuel Nda (**Theater and Performance**) suggests that African cultures once existed in a "pure state," and while Matthew Evans Teti (**Art**) also argues strongly for the cultural integrity of the pre-colonial African world, he stresses that this phenomenon was rooted in diversity rather than uniformity. Speaking of the work of local artisans, Teti notes that, historically, "even though only a few miles may separate two centers for ceramic production, potters from both locales may dig their clay from different sources, throw their pots in a different manner, and fire their wares using different techniques." Moreover, he notes that "proximate groups may also display variations in the style and meaning of the arts they produce" ("Art," this volume). Unfortunately, as Teti points out, in large measure these local nuances have been, and are being, sacrificed in the crucible of Western demand for "traditional" African artistic commodities, a phenomenon which has led to the consolidation of broad regional styles and the production of art and craftwork geared solely toward the export market—an aspect of what historians Eric Hobsbawm and Terence Ranger have called the "invention of tradition."[5]

Taking a cautionary view of the concept of tradition (as it is applied in the present day), Gary Baines, in the **Music** chapter, warns us that its misapplication can result in a distorted and oversimplified view of African life and culture. He cautions against those in his field who argue for

> an essentialist understanding of identity which regards cultures as hermetically sealed entities that exist in time warps. . . . [This approach] draws an unnecessarily rigid distinction between traditional and popular music, and between "tribal" areas and the cities/townships. In emphasizing the traditional–modern urban–rural dichotomy, these musicologists tend to overlook the degree of cultural exchange that has occurred throughout Sub-Saharan Africa. ("Music," this volume)

The Future of African Culture within Globalization

In any event, while many in the West will continue to demand a cultural product from Africa that is rooted in an imaginary past, Africans, without abandoning their roots, will continue to live and create in a complex present even as they move toward an increasingly globalized future. In urging African writers to write in their own language, Ngugi wa Thiong'o is not encouraging these artists to merely look to the past, but he is urging them instead to marshal the singular consciousness that is rooted in every language to deal with the challenges of the present. Also, it is indeed paradoxical that, while cultures are formed collectively, in the final analysis they are lived and experienced individually, and individual Africans, like people all over the world, will confront each new day with the unique sensibility provided by their own particular array of ideas, influences, and memory. In this regard, categories such as urban and rural, modern and traditional, and local, regional, national, continental, and global are essentially meaningless, if convenient, frames of reference that obscure a more complex and fascinating reality.

In addition to the question of "tradition," a further issue that runs through this volume is the future of African culture and creativity within the framework of globalization. Will African artists benefit from the synergy of communications technologies, innovations in mass media, and financial and corporate integration (and reach) that are driving this phenomenon, or will they be overwhelmed and marginalized by forces every bit as intrusive as, and perhaps even more powerful than, those that shaped their world during the era of colonialism? Outside influence on African cultural production is certainly nothing new, as Teti demonstrates ("African art" as an industry aimed at Western audiences, tastes, and markets), and as Baines points out (in his discussion of the political economy of the recording industry on the African continent). The pervasiveness of American popular culture is an undeniable reality—from hip-hop music blaring out of boomboxes, to Hollywood blockbusters muscling out African films on African screens, to refugee children wearing T-shirts and caps bearing the logos of American colleges and professional sports teams (donated by Western charities). It should not be surprising that as African economies struggle, so do African artists, as well as those entrepreneurs who play an essential role in bringing the fruits of their intellectual labor to a broader audience. Charles Sugnet informs us in his piece on **Film** that, as African movie theaters continue to close for financial reasons, and foreign product predominates on the screens of those that survive, it is easier to see a major African film in Chicago, New York, or San Francisco (or on an American college campus) than it is in Abidjan, Kinshasha, or Mogadishu. And, as Ginette Curry warns us in her piece on **Literature**, far from moving boldly into the age of the Internet, most African nations are struggling just to find the resources to maintain and update the collections of books and journals in their major libraries.

Can it be concluded, then, that for African culture the prospects of globalization are uniformly negative? In fact, it would be seriously misleading to take this position, since on balance the opportunities would seem to be every bit as compelling as the dangers.

If I may be allowed a personal case in point: as I sit here composing the introduction to this volume I am listening to Angelique Kidjo of Benin singing "Tombo" on AOL Radio's African music channel (which I selected with a few strokes on my keyboard over XM Radio's Ngoma channel, which is equally available on my PC and, indeed, on my laptop). Next to my television sits a DVD of South African director Gavin Hood's version of Athol Fugard's *Tsotsi* (a film that I first saw in a movie theater in Montclair, New Jersey, and that, in future, will probably be available through my public library). And, Friday being payday, I fully intend to order my own copy of Ngugi wa Thiong'o's latest novel, *Wizard and the Crow,* from the Barnes and Noble or Borders Website. I am fully alert to the irony here: using the tools of global capitalism to order the work of one of global capitalism's more eloquent and impassioned critics. In fact, this very example illustrates both the possibilities and the perils inherent in the emerging nexus between African artistry and the process and instrumentalities of globalization.

With due respect to Thomas Friedman (who, to be fair, has much of value to say about the impact of globalization), the world is not yet "flat,"[6] and, as Bea Vidacs shows us here in her piece on **Sports and Recreation**, the playing field is not yet level between even the elite African World Cup soccer teams and their more economically privileged competitors.

Undoubtedly, the tools of globalization are opening up markets for, and levels of accessibility to, the products of African culture that were not even dreamed of a decade or two ago, but is this very process creating a new class of corporate gatekeepers (the AOLs, the Amazons, the major film production companies and media conglomerates) that are emerging as a new "eye of the needle" for African artists in search of a wider audience, not only globally but even on their own continent? Will these forces encourage talented Africans to compromise their art in order to appeal to a wider market (carrying the pattern explained by Teti to a whole new level, invading and influencing whole new genres)? Will African **Radio and Television** producers and executives continue to be overly reliant on foreign programming because of a lack of the financial and technical resources needed to produce their own (a problem that is outlined here by Ali N. Mohamed)? And, conversely, as African markets become increasingly lucrative in the decades to come, will the independent spirit of the "new breed" of African journalists and publishers—discussed in this volume by Charles Muiru Ngugi in his chapter on **Periodicals**—be overwhelmed by a tide of foreign capital and control? If the world is not yet "flat," are the creative talents in the less powerful parts of the world in danger of being flattened by outside forces that will be difficult to contain or resist?

Actually, the future of African culture—be it "popular" or more institutional in nature—is much brighter than a consideration of these very real challenges and constraints might suggest. A more optimistic analysis would suggest that African artists across all genres will find a global audience that is anxious for their particular perspectives, sensibilities, and insights; that accepts, in fact expects, that they conceptualize their work on their own terms (and in constructive synthesis with other cultural streams, a development that already can be seen in the exciting new realm known as "world music"). In fact, it must be asked whether, in decrying the influence of globalization, there is a danger of embarking on a misguided quest for "purity" and "tradition"—a reactionary trend that would ultimately prove as pointless and sterile as the essentialist mentality that preceded it.

At this point, one can only pose these questions; it is far too early to provide definitive answers. The only certainty is that African culture, in all its forms, will continue to enrich the rest of the world, in our generation and for generations to come.

THIS VOLUME

Finally, a word about the internal structure of the fourteen chapters that constitute this volume. As the editor I was confronted with a basic problem: How could I ensure that the reader was provided with a synthetic overview of a particular subject for the vast geographical area under consideration, while still allowing for a treatment of the complexities of the various regions that constituted the whole? After much reflection I instructed the authors to provide a broad introduction to their subject and to follow it up with a more targeted treatment of at least two nations within each of four regional subsections: Western, Central, Southern, and Eastern Africa. Each chapter concludes with a helpful "Resource Guide," comprising, in most cases, recommended print resources, Websites, organizations, and occasionally videos, recordings, and events. In addition, the volume concludes with a general bibliography and a comprehensive index.

Although this is an encyclopedia, it is more than a vast collection of disconnected information—the contributors have made sure of that. The authors who are represented here have provided chapters that are rich in analysis, synthesis, and perspective, and as editor, I have made no attempt to impose ideological consistency or stifle or inhibit the flow of ideas. The authors here have much to say, and irrespective of my own position on any particular issue, they have been given free reign to say it.

Any student of Africa will be aware of the difficulties here in content presentation. For example, there is no clear consensus as to which of these regions that certain of these nations should be classified in; the boundaries of the nation-states themselves were forged by Europeans, not Africans; and, beyond that, a strong argument can be made that the nations and peoples north of the Sahara cannot be logically separated from those to the south. Moreover, there was an obvious danger that larger, more populous, and more prosperous nations might be overrepresented at the expense of others. Realistically, it would take a much larger undertaking than this to provide a construct approaching a comprehensive and fully balanced portrait of the cultural riches of the African continent: perhaps the very number of volumes that constitute this entire global encyclopedia. Nevertheless, Greenwood Press is to be richly complimented for the ambitious project of producing a practical and accessible encyclopedia of world popular cultures, and, as its editor, I take full responsibility for any deficiencies that may be inherent in the structure and format of this particular volume.

NOTES

1. Ngugi wa Thiong'o, *Wizard of the Crow* (New York: Knopf, 2006), and see "Literature," this volume; Ali Farka Touré and Ry Cooder, *Talking Timbuktu*, Hannibal CD 571381 (1995), and see "Music," this volume; for wire toys, see "Games, Hobbies, and Toys," this volume; for Ethiopian artist Julie Mehretu, see "Art," this volume; for the Indomitable Lions and Ethiopian and Kenyan runners, see "Sports," this volume; for the Elvis impersonator, see Chris Abani, *Graceland* (New York: Farrar, Straus, and Giroux, 2005); for the puppet troupe, see "Theater and Performance," this volume; for video film producers, see "Film," this volume; for the plight of child soldiers see Uzodinma Iweala, *Beasts of No Nation* (New York: HarperCollins, 2005); and for the South African scenario, see Zakes Mda, *Heart of Redness* (New York: Picador, 2003).
2. Dennis Hickey and Kenneth C. Wylie, *An Enchanting Darkness: The American Vision of Africa in the Twentieth Century* (East Lansing: Michigan State University Press, 1993).
3. Lorena S. Walsh, review of David Eltis, Stephen D. Behrendt, David Richardson, and Herbert S. Klein, eds., *The Trans-Atlantic Slave Trade: A Database on CD-ROM* (EH.NET, October 2000). Accessed on the International Association of Labour History Institutions Website, http://www.ialhi.org/news/i0010_5.php. For a forceful statement on the impact of the slave trade on Africa's potential and prospects see Walter Rodney, *How Europe Underdeveloped Africa*, rev. ed. (London: Bogle-L'Ouverture Publications and Dar es Saalam, Tanzania Publishing House, 1972; repr. Washington, DC: Howard University Press, 1981).
4. Martin Meredith, *The First Dance of Freedom: Black Africa in the Postwar Era* (New York: HarperCollins, 1985).
5. Eric Hobsbawm and Terence Ranger, *The Invention of Tradition* (Cambridge, UK: Cambridge University Press, 1983).
6. Thomas L. Friedman, *The World Is Flat: A Brief History of the Twenty-First Century* (New York: Farrar, Straus, and Giroux, 2005).

ARCHITECTURE

GEORGE WILLIAM KOFI INTSIFUL

Africans in the Sub-Saharan region have over the years produced a distinctive and unique popular architecture. Such popular architecture could be attributed to the concept of the total environment—a combination of the physical and cultural attributes of the subcontinent. This concept has produced the numerous differences in building types and forms found in the subcontinent. For example, in various countries, round mud huts are found existing within a few kilometers from rectilinear buildings within the same administrative region. Environments where people live include caves, hilltops, and even bodies of water, where some have created housing settlements above the water surface and communicate by canoes and boats. In various countries, some people live in hamlets and dispersed settlements whereas others live in dense, nucleated settlements in the same areas. The concept of the total environment further explains why different peoples on the subcontinent use different materials, techniques, forms, and shapes to build their dwellings. For example, some societies live in woven palm-frond-and-timber dwellings with thatched roofs, whereas others live in mud buildings with either thatched or mud flat roofs, mainly because of the availability of materials and techniques of building production. The various interpretations of different settlement patterns, shapes, and forms by different peoples in the subcontinent can also be attributed to the same concept.

The physical elements of the total environment include climate, geology, and vegetation. Physically, Africa can be described as one gigantic plateau with a few mountain ranges and a rather narrow coastal plain. Across this land mass are numerous striking contrasts that include the Sahara, which is the largest desert in the world; the tropical rain forests of West and Central Africa, with their tall treetop canopies, over thirteen stories in height at some places; as well as some of the longest rivers in the world such as the Nile, Congo, Zambezi, and Niger. Most of Sub-Saharan Africa, however, has grassland vegetation. Physically, the climate in the subcontinent has produced a situation whereby certain building materials have been found to be more responsive than others in certain areas. For example, in the hot, dry regions of the areas bordering the Sahara, thick mud walls with very few openings (doors and windows) have been found to perform better against the large diurnal temperature ranges than other materials. Thus the intense solar heat of the daytime is absorbed by the thick walls, which slowly release the absorbed heat during the cold nights. Furthermore, the long dry spells, due to paucity of rain, mean that the mud walls can last longer and not deteriorate rapidly. The unique mud buildings on the cliffs of Dogon in Mali in West Africa also reflect the physical attributes of the total environment. Again, various parts of the subcontinent have geological formations that allow the use of rocks or stones, mud or timber for walls and thatch (thanks to the available grassland vegetation) for roofing construction purposes at different locations. This explains why stone walls are found in many parts of Africa where rocky outcrops abound and the people have developed a technology of breaking the rocks into stones for construction, sometimes without mortar as a jointing or bonding material.

The culture of the subcontinent pertains to the people and their social organization, language, religion, mode of dressing, eating habits, and other practices. Culturally, the people of Sub-Saharan Africa can be classified into hundreds of ethnic groups with their own languages, religions, and ways of life. Sub-Saharan Africa arguably has the largest number of languages in the entire world, and this has also contributed to the numerous differences that have produced various conflicts across the region as ethnicity has been allowed to be more important than it should be and some ethnic groups have seen themselves as being superior to others. Across the subcontinent, traditional African religions are practiced. It is not uncommon to find many professing Christians and Muslims still practicing or believing in a traditional African religion. One thing is common, though. Traditional African religion recognizes the existence of a supreme God who is worshipped through various media. This is because Africans believe that it is disrespectful to communicate directly with God; just as in the traditional Sub-Saharan African society one may address a traditional ruler (chief) only through a spokesperson, the supreme God is worshipped through various media or lesser objects that He has created. Thus trees, rivers, and rocky outcrops, as well as other natural phenomena that the African cannot easily comprehend, are perceived as media that can be used to address or reach the supreme God. Sub-Saharan African settlements reflect such religious beliefs, as shown by groves and other natural phenomena that are left undeveloped and perceived as sacred or hallowed ground.

Traditional beliefs are also translated into the form and shape of traditional settlements. In some societies, settlement forms or patterns reflect basic parts of the human body or religious beliefs. Certain parts of settlements are reserved for specific people or activities. In many societies the traditional ruler's dwelling is in the middle of the settlement and is close to the center of the settlement or specific buildings and activities. Furthermore, in some parts of the subcontinent, the house or palace of the traditional ruler must be the largest or most complex in the society. This is because the palace will invariably have different sections for the administration of justice, the women's wing (where all the cooking takes place), a section for traditional drums (very critical for sending out information to the community), stool rooms where the "souls" of departed former traditional rulers are kept, and other facilities. Thus any individual who goes against this trend and builds a house larger than the traditional ruler's is sanctioned by the community in one way or other.

The culture of the peoples of the Sub-Saharan African region also includes their occupation, which also reflects in the built forms across the region. Consequently, farmers in traditional societies live mostly in mud buildings with either circular or rectilinear walls and thatch, bamboo, and other roofs in local materials. Most dwellings for farmers have mud storage spaces (granaries) in the compounds where farm produce is stored. Where farming includes pastoralism, kraals or pens are part of the traditional dwellings. In traditional fishing communities, dwellings are also built using local materials and technology, and ovens for smoking fish are also constructed in mud or earth. Similarly, nomads who keep cattle, sheep, and goats live in tents that are easily demountable and portable so that they can be easily moved from one location to the next in the search for both water and pasture. Such dwellings originally were made up of sticks, which formed the framework, and hide from the animals, which were used as the "cladding" to protect the inside from the outside.

The culture of the people of Sub-Saharan Africa has also been greatly influenced by what has been described by Professor Ali Mazrui as the Triple Heritage concept: namely the indigenous, Islamic, and Western dimensions. In very simple terms, indigenous culture exists in places where there has been little or no relationship with the outside world, and some would argue that there are still some isolated communities in Africa like that. References made earlier in this chapter to traditional beliefs and building practices reflect indigenous culture.

The Islamic religion was introduced to different parts of Africa at different times and has also made a significant impact on popular architecture in the region. Islamic architecture in the subcontinent was given a major stimulus as a result of the pilgrimage to Mecca by Mansa Musa, the ruler of the then-Mali Empire in the fifteenth century. Over the years, such influences from the East—specifically Egypt and Saudi Arabia—have become part of the mainstream construction technology in many Islamic settlements in Sub-Saharan Africa. These include the crenellated mosques and the gated settlements of urban settlements in many Islamic communities across West Africa and particularly in northern Nigeria.

Additionally, the culture of Sub-Saharan Africa has been greatly influenced by Europeans who made landfall at many places, including *Edina*—known today as Elmina, literally, The Mine—over five hundred years ago in the then-Gold Coast, now known as Ghana. The gold and other items sent to Europe eventually led to wars and battles along the coast and forests and produced the Scramble for Africa, which was ultimately settled at the Berlin Conference. The activities of the Europeans have produced a peculiar situation in the region whereby international boundary lines actually pass through existing buildings. Consequently, people living in the same buildings in many countries may find themselves belonging to different countries or nationalities. Such a situation does not exist in any other part of the world. Furthermore, such European influence has also produced a situation whereby many buildings have been developed in the subcontinent in various European styles and materials and technology. Thus, many coastal settlements in the subcontinent have dwellings that were patterned after the earlier forts and castles but developed by indigenous wealthy merchants.

Over the years, Africans have made a distinctive contribution to the popular architecture of the world, and this is reflected by such popular and monumental buildings as the carved stone underground churches of Ethiopia, the Great Zimbabwe Ruins in Zimbabwe, the cave dwellings of southern Africa, the river settlements of Ganvie in Benin and Nzulezo in Ghana, the fetish houses in Ghana, as well as the numerous distinctive and enigmatic open-air markets of West Africa, where virtually everything under the sun is sold.

In many settlements across West Africa, these markets come in various sizes and forms. In some settlements, temporary sheds are erected to display the wares and in yet others, wares or goods to be sold are displayed on the ground along main streets or open spaces. Many settlements actually have specific market days during the week. The largest markets do have different sections with more permanent structures, which can be locked daily, where different goods and services are sold and exchanged. These could be described as the formal markets that are found in specific locations—sometimes zoned, sometimes not—in many settlements in sub-Saharan Africa. The largest of these open-air markets—especially the ones in Kumasi in Ghana and at Aba and Ibadan in Nigeria—are a sight to behold and certainly make a huge impression on foreign visitors.

The markets are located next to truck parks or stations where bulk-breaking of goods takes place. That is, enterprising women buy various food items in bulk and then resell them in smaller quantities to various traders (mostly women). Such enterprising women have become known as "market queens" for various food items. Large numbers of human beings pass through these markets daily, and these spaces have over the years developed a life of their own.

There are also informal markets, which take place at different sections of many settlements. These may involve people carrying various wares in containers on their heads or improvised mobile "shops" in wheelbarrows and other structures or even open spaces under trees or along pathways. These may specialize in single or multiple items for sale.

Finally, the streets in the central business districts of many urban centers in sub-Saharan Africa have been slowly but surely turned into informal open-air markets. More often than not, the metropolitan, city, or district authorities are unable to cope with cleaning up the mess created by these markets, largely because of the numbers of people involved, and refuse piles up for days or weeks in these market centers.

Other distinct buildings in the sub-Saharan African region include the townships of Southern Africa, the *zongos* of West Africa, churches, and mosques. The townships of Southern Africa were part of the efforts by the former colonial governments to keep the local people together and away from where the European settlers lived. These townships were invariably at the western end of the urban settlements created by the settler governments. Most of the buildings were a single story in height and had rather small rooms by any standard. The houses were simple and small and provided accommodation for the teeming urban poor. These townships could be described as dormitory towns, since residents had to go to the central business districts in the urban centers for various facilities and activities. It is not surprising that these townships eventually became the hotbeds for the struggle for independence in many parts of Southern Africa. Like the townships, the zongos—literally the "stranger's town"—were created on the outskirts of urban centers and originally had houses developed in locally available materials. Job seekers on their way to the urban centers from the rural areas stayed in the zongo first because of cheap rents and also literally to "acclimatize" before attempting to look for accommodation in the urban center. Many new arrivals never made it to the urban centers, and the zongos grew in leaps and bounds. Interestingly, both the townships and the zongos experience high incidence of overcrowding. Harsh realities mean that large families cannot rent more rooms, basic amenities such as toilets and bathrooms are hard to come by, and kitchens are easily converted into sleeping spaces.

In many parts of the African subcontinent, various buildings are developed and decorated by users themselves and not by contractors or real estate developers. Furthermore, in all the leading human settlements in the region, what has been referred to as "villafication" is proceeding unabated. This is a process in which individuals in the community who have improved themselves financially transform their dwelling units dramatically—sometimes beyond recognition—by demolishing the original buildings and putting up new ones in their place. This is normally done in phases. Such new dwellings sometimes have fence walls (defining ownership) and gates. Additionally, across the subcontinent, gentrification is also proceeding without limits. This is a process in which wealthy developers acquire old, traditional dwellings in the older sections of settlements for a pittance and then demolish them to be replaced with bigger houses and shopping facilities. Thus, the local people who rented rooms in the old houses are literally pushed out to find accommodation—sometimes, very far away from their workplaces. Consequently, their standard of living deteriorates.

Some of these displaced people have ended up creating their own form of shelter—with materials such as cardboard and corrugated roofing sheets—in parts of the central business districts in the major urban centers just so that they can be closer to their places of work. In most countries in the subcontinent, such people are constantly being pursued and harassed by the development officers and authorities to quit their new dwellings because they are squatters and do not have tenure on the land they have developed. Such human settlements have been commonly referred to as "slums" by some academicians and politicians, mainly because they were developed on a "do-it-yourself" basis without the involvement of professionals in the building/construction trades, and also without building permits, but such places are vibrant, colorful, and economically prosperous. These residential developments have been given various interesting names such as "Sodom and Gomorrah" and "Abuja" in Accra in Ghana and other equally intriguing names in other countries.

Just as in some townships and the zongos, places of convenience are rare in some of these residential developments, and health hazards in such places are numerous. Thus, outbreaks of diseases such as cholera and typhoid are very difficult to deal with in such settlements. Many lives are lost, and the effects of such ailments or health problems persist for years, sometimes generations, in these settlements. Aptly, such places could be referred to as exemplifying the architecture of the poor. Obviously, the harsh realities involved in daily pursuits have influenced their struggle to provide housing and shelter for themselves. Housing and shelter therefore become the dominant issues, and all other issues and considerations are placed on the back burner. These include basic hygienic issues such as the provision (or lack) of water, waste disposal, and toilet facilities as well as the presence or lack of communal spaces.

It must be pointed out at this point that, at various times under military regimes in various countries (and the subcontinent has had more than its fair share of military governments over the years), such do-it-yourself housing developments have been razed to the ground with no compensation paid, sometimes under cover of darkness but in other instances in broad daylight. Thus, illegitimate governments have over the years demolished the architecture of the poor, or popular architecture, in the name of building regulations and standards and law and order. Invariably, whenever such developments have occurred over the years, they have greatly impacted both the formal and informal economy. This is largely because many such communities have informal economic or home-based enterprises, which are destroyed. Many women prepare and sell various food items (both cooked and uncooked) and foodstuffs in their homes or neighborhoods. Such preparations may even involve members of the extended family and, in some cases, hired hands. Thus, the level of poverty in such communities is increased and the national economy suffers generally when these communities are destroyed.

Another common characteristic of the subcontinent is that all the countries in the region (except Ethiopia and Liberia) were colonized by European nations and therefore share certain common experiences. For example, virtually every country in the region has urban centers with "European" quarters, where the foreign people lived, and African quarters, which had different names across the region for the inhabitants.

Sub-Saharan Africa is divided into four regional subsections: West Africa, Central Africa, Southern Africa, and East Africa. Three countries have been selected from West Africa (because of their large population and numerous ethnic groups), whereas there are two each from the other regions. The regions and countries selected are as follows:

- West Africa: Ghana, Nigeria, and Ivory Coast
- Central Africa: Democratic Republic of Congo (DRC) and Central African Republic (CAR)
- Southern Africa: Zimbabwe and the Republic of South Africa
- East Africa: Kenya and Ethiopia

In each country and region, the popular architecture will be discussed by using a variety of critical approaches in discussing popular architecture in the sub-continent, including analyzing how such critical factors as ethnicity, race, gender, class, age, region, and sexuality are shaped by and reshaped by popular culture. In this regard, four major dimensions of popular culture will be addressed:

1. Production analysis: Who owns the buildings? Who makes these buildings? With what intentions? Under what constraints? How democratic or elitist is the production of popular architecture? How much creative expression is involved?
2. Building analysis: How do specific works of popular architecture make their meanings? How do explicit meanings differ from implied ones? How do texts consciously and subconsciously shape those who experience, see, and touch them?
3. Audience analysis: How do different groups of popular architecture consumers, or users, make similar or different sense of the same buildings?
4. Historical analysis: How have these other three dimensions changed over time? How does current popular architecture differ from that of ten, twenty, or thirty years ago? What accounts for these changes?

REGIONAL SUBSECTIONS

West Africa

Ghana

Ghana can be divided into three broad climatic regions, namely the coastal savannah, the tropical rain forest belt, and the northern savannah belt, and these each have an impact on popular architecture in Ghana. The physical and cultural attributes of each region have a direct bearing on the type of building materials and construction technology utilized. The resulting combination of the physical and cultural attributes—collectively, the total environment—means that the three regions use different sets of building materials. For example, whereas there is abundant timber in the tropical rain forest belt, the same is not true in the coastal and northern savannah belts. Similarly, certain building forms are found in certain places more than others. Forts and castles, for example, are found only along the coast, except the Kumasi Fort, which was developed by the British army after the conquest of the Ashanti Empire after the Sagrenti War in 1874. Likewise, the village of Nzulezo, which is built on stilts above a lagoon and located near Beyin in the Western Region, represents a variation that is found only in the coastal savannah climate and can be described as a solid example of indigenous architecture. In all regions, however, buildings are found that can be described as indigenous, Islamic, and Western.

Popular architecture in Ghana will be discussed along two lines: residential and commercial. Residential buildings in Ghana come in different shapes and sizes, but the majority of them—in the south and in the middle, forest belt—are rectangular houses with mud walls. Many of the people in northern Ghana, however, live in round houses with mud walls and conical thatched roofs.

One common theme running through popular indigenous residential buildings is the use of the courtyard. In all three broad climatic zones, the courtyard has been used as a generator of the floor plan. The origins of the courtyard are similar for the south and middle belts but different in the north. In the two southern climatic regions, generally, the residential building starts as one wing of the future courtyard with a row of rooms. The other three wings are added on later; sometimes one at a time, until the development is complete, but family size greatly influences the size and pace of development. In the north, however, depending on the location, a courtyard house can be developed by a family, and a series of courtyards can be added later as the extended family grows. Thus, the north tends to have more complex courtyard buildings, as sons marry and add rooms for their growing families to the original courtyard building.

Walling materials can differ from one climatic region to another. Palm or coconut fronds or bamboos are used in the coastal savannah, but mud walls, in different forms, are used in all three zones. They come as coursed mud, wattle-and-daub, and sun-dried brick walls. Across various settlements, the courtyard has been used to facilitate cross-ventilation and simultaneously provide spaces for such purposes as cooking, sleeping, and the washing of clothes. In more recent times, many people bring their television sets out to the courtyard when very important and popular soccer teams are playing and also when very popular television shows are shown, for the benefit of those who do not own television sets. In most indigenous settlements, the courtyard residential building is only of one story, and rooms open out to the central courtyard. All the rooms in the courtyard building share common cooking and toilet facilities.

The roof form of the indigenous courtyard residential building differs from one climatic region to another. Generally, roofs in the tropical rain forest belt are steeper to take care of the greater annual rainfall and are expressed in the rafter-and-purlin form as hipped or gable roofs. Materials used for these roofs in the tropical rain forest belt originally were in bamboo or thatch for the indigenous buildings, but as a result of Western influence, corrugated metal is now the preferred choice. In the northern savannah, roofs are either of the flat type and in mud or inclined and in thatch. In certain parts of the northern savannah, particularly in the Wa area, roofs have crenellations that indicate that the owner is a member of the royal family. The Wa Na's palace is a very good example of this building type. The flat mud roofs of the northern savannah belt have been described as having been influenced by Islamic architecture.

Residential courtyard buildings are developed by people for their own use. Across the various climatic zones, people build these houses for themselves using locally available materials. In most cases, there are no building plans; the indigenous peoples simply mark out the outline of the building on the ground and start the construction. Arguably, therefore, this system is very democratic. In the past, additional rooms were added as and when the need arose. In some parts of Ghana, in traditional or indigenous settlements, members of the community helped each other to build their houses through communal labor or self-help approaches. The prospective owner of the residential unit provided food and drinks for the members of the community who came in to help. Building materials were locally available and were used mainly because the people cannot afford modern or expensive materials. This is primarily because of very low income levels. In indigenous or traditional societies, creative expression is exhibited in these residential buildings through decoration of the entrances or walls by the application of different materials or paint.

Over the years, the traditional courtyard residential building has been given new interpretations and uses. Urban areas in Ghana have many Western-style buildings. In these urban centers, multilevel courtyard residential buildings in reinforced concrete, with staircases in the courtyard, have been developed. The same rectangular floor plan is repeated on different levels for the use of both the nuclear and extended family members and also for rent (income generation) for the developer(s).

Commercial buildings in Ghana also come in different shapes and forms. Every Ghanaian settlement has an outdoor market. In the rural areas, such markets can be simply a number of tables placed together for sellers to display their wares. Buyers walk through aisles to inspect, haggle, and make purchases. Sometimes, there are no physical structures for these markets and there is no protection from the elements. Generally, the markets are created by the local authorities. In recent times, various municipal and district authorities have put up large, covered sheds that are sometimes divided into cubicles that are rented out to traders as shops or stalls. Commercial buildings in the urban centers are, however, different. There are Western-style shopping centers developed along the lines of department stores with shopping arcades, for instance. Across the length and breadth of the country, however, a new commercial building form has developed. This is generally not designed by professional architects but by draftsmen. They have assumed the shape and form of the rectangular courtyard residential building, but all the rooms are rented out as shops, eating places, and drinking spots.

The majority of Ghanaians live in the rural areas. However, popular architecture in the capital and the other regional capitals is different. These urban centers display a combination of both indigenous and modern architecture. Housing styles for the poor generally rely on local materials since many parts of the urban centers were originally villages which have now become part of the metropolis by accretion. Thus, housing in Ghanaian centers could be classified into low-income, middle-income, and high-income areas. The high-income areas exhibit the latest architectural styles from around the world, since there are many Ghanaians living and working overseas who send money for such houses. Unlike what happens in the rural areas, housing development in the urban areas tends to involve all the professionals in the building industry, including architects, structural engineers, and building technologists. They are developed in zoned high-income residential areas, which, ironically, more often than not display inadequate infrastructure or building services such as roads, piped water supply, and electricity.

Consequently, Western-style glazing and building materials are employed and many people live in apartments and bungalows with both exterior and internal decoration comparable to what pertains in any city in the Western world. Many such buildings are described as mansions or villas and have swimming pools and gated entrances with intricate security systems; they can be found in certain suburbs in Accra. Concrete fence walls, sometimes very elaborate, however, hide the beauty or ugliness of these gated houses. Most people prefer the concrete fence wall to flower hedges, mainly because of a perception of better security. Other examples of residential housing communities developed by real estate developers in Accra have exotic names such as Manet Estate and Regimanuel Gray Estates. For entertainment venues, the Chinese-designed and -built National Theater in the center of Accra and the Accra International Conference Center (designed and built by Yugoslavians) are used for concerts and drama and combine effectively with the restaurants and casinos in the star-rated hotels such as La Palm, La Beach, Cresta Royale, The Golden Tulip, Novotel, and other international resorts. National sports stadiums are also found in the capital and other regional capitals.

How do specific works of popular architecture make their meanings? Across the length and breadth of Ghana, in popular indigenous architecture, buildings send out various meanings. In the Wa area in Upper West Ghana, for instance, crenellations along the walls projecting beyond the flat mud roof indicate that the occupant of the building is a member of the royal family, as mentioned previously. Similarly, the sprawling and recently renovated Manhyia Palace, with a number of courtyards, for the Asantehene—King of Ashanti—in Kumasi stands out prominently in the townscape. The number and complexity of the courtyards also give an indication of how "important" an individual is in the community. In the central business districts in the largest urban settlements, the popular craving now is for glazing and more glazing for offices and high-income houses despite the intense solar radiation during the day. The more glazing there is, the more "current" the public perceives the office or residential building to be. Meanwhile, many of the offices rely solely on mechanical ventilation.

A few modern buildings, such as the Engineering Guest House on the Kwame Nkrumah University of Science and Technology campus in Kumasi, have, however, combined both natural and mechanical ventilation—energy-efficient construction—with the use of a courtyard. To many native people, the forts and castles along the Ghanaian coast still portray the power and strength of the European colonial powers even though Ghana achieved independence from Great Britain in the 1950s. Arguably, therefore, different groups of popular architecture consumers, or users, make different sense of the same buildings based on their education, experiences, and exposure. Popular architecture in Ghana in the first decade of the twenty-first century definitely is different from that of ten, twenty, or thirty years earlier, and this can be attributed to the availability of new building materials, new building technology, and the prevailing economic conditions in the country. Consequently, different groups of popular architecture consumers, or users, will never make similar sense of the same buildings.

Nigeria

Applying the concept of the total environment to Nigeria's popular architecture means that the different land regions with their different climate and culture produce different built forms. Combine this with Africa's Triple Heritage, and the resulting popular architecture in Africa's most populous country could be described as varied. Most Nigerians live in rural areas. Most homes in rural Nigeria are built in locally available materials such as grass, dried mud, and thatch. In more recent times, roofs in asbestos, cement sheets, and corrugated metal have been used in the rural areas. In very broad terms, popular architecture in Nigeria can be classified into three styles, based on the largest ethnic groups: Hausa, Igbo (or Ibo), and Yoruba.

Hausa architecture is found mainly in northern Nigeria. For the purpose of this discussion, Hausa architecture can be seen as the traditional, dominant architecture of cities that were under the medieval Hausa states. These cities were Kano, Katsina, Bornu, Sokoto, Kaduna, and Zaria. Two major types of Hausa settlement patterns can be discerned: indigenous and Islamic (which was introduced after the Holy War [or Jihad] of Uthman dan Fodio). The latter has been described as a modification of the indigenous settlement pattern that saw a replacement of the emir's palace by a mosque adjacent to the market square. Before urbanization, however, the Hausa had lived in small agricultural communities that had relied on the extended family system with its myriad influences upon the social life of the people. Traditional religion plays a significant role in the life of the people and affects the building tradition. The Hausa house plan, however, follows the traditional African pattern with rooms arranged within or surrounding a courtyard. Hausa cities have always been surrounded by walls with gates. The walls had high battlements and moats around its outer circumference. The main square in the Hausa city is the main focal point, and the main mosque and the emir's palace are two major objects that define it. The main square is a multifunctional space that is used for religious and traditional ceremonies. The main building material used in Hausa architecture is mud, and many of the houses have both indigenous and Western motifs as decoration. In many places, modern Western materials such as aluminum or corrugated metal roofing members have replaced traditional ones.

Igbo (or Ibo) architecture is practiced in southeastern Nigeria. This is a forest zone with abundant timber and clay for building. These people live both in villages and urban centers, and the extended family is the basic unit of social organization. The extended family house layouts are grouped in compounds. Responding to the concept of the total environment, most of the building material is obtained locally. Woven raffia palm frond ribs, in square grids and poles, are used for wall construction and plastered over with clay. For the roof, a similar lattice structure is used, and raffia palm fronds serve as matting. Courtyards are prevalent, and each house is built to serve a specific purpose.

Meeting and spirit houses, which collectively form variations of ancestor houses, or cult houses associated with specific deities, are common. Such temples are primarily rectangular and square in plan, and serene locations with trees and shade are preferred. Elaborate burial chambers for departed chiefs or traditional rulers are another popular architectural form with the Igbo people. The chambers are lined with carved wood and with the corpse laid or seated in the middle of the chamber; some of the precious earthly belongings are carefully arranged within the chamber for the next life. This is reminiscent of the ancient Egyptians and the burial chambers in the pyramids.

Most finished walls have impressive smooth surfaces which have elaborate geometric patterns painted on them. House decoration is an essential component of Igbo architecture. The geology and climate of the region make this possible with the availability of clay (with a wide variety of hues) for the wall painting. Traditionally, wall painting is carried out by women, and the paintings depict the triple heritage of African architecture with images or murals of past daily experiences and the people's perception of the environment, religious themes rooted in ancestor worship, and Western images.

Yoruba architecture is practiced in southwestern Nigeria. The Yoruba people are generally urban dwellers, and generally their houses are grouped in compounds according to lineage, occupation, and position in the settlement. The center and the most important part of every Yoruba town is the king's palace. The palace grounds also have the town hall, court of justice, theater, and sports arena. The palace is walled, and the wall serves as protection, because it was forbidden to see the king and whoever did so would die. The walls had tiny windows from which the king could see everything happening in town. The king's palace reflects a hierarchy and order of the city and occupied the largest area of land, compared to all compounds, in Yoruba towns. The king's palace is also the cultural center of the town as well as its political center. The arrangement of the king's palace's courtyards and surrounding buildings closely resembles the bureaucratic structures of the king's government. The sociopolitical structure of the Yoruba people, which is based on lineages, age groups, title societies, cults, and other institutions, accounts for this. The palace is usually occupied exclusively by the king and his numerous wives and therefore has a number of courtyards. Residences of the king's advisers and elders—also with a multiplicity of courtyards—surround the palace.

Yoruba architecture was originally developed in clay adobe style with raffia and other local roofing materials; in more recent times modern building materials such as cement and corrugated metal roofing sheets are used. Such modern palaces have also been greatly influenced by an architectural style associated with the freed slaves who returned to Nigeria from Brazil *(emancipados)*. Some of the major elements of this type of popular architecture include handrails with a series of balustrades.

Across the various ethnic groups in Nigeria, the courtyard house dominates in residential building development, and the more complex and larger the courtyards, the more important the occupant of the complex. Whereas settlements in the southern regions portray evidence of the influence of European and Brazilian architecture (which were introduced along the coast), settlements in the northern regions display Islamic influences, which were introduced by people from the north who participated in the trans-Saharan trade. The colonial government introduced a new form of residential building development for the colonial civil servant—the bungalow—in all their former colonies. This bungalow has been given various new and different interpretations. It has come to be a favorite of the highly educated, high-income earners who build such structures in both the rural and urban areas. With the largesse of oil money to fall back on, numerous interpretations of the bungalow have been used for gated communities, and villafication also continues unabated across the country. The fact that Nigerians have perennially experienced power shortages has not put a damper on such development.

Commercially, Nigeria probably has more open-air markets than any other country in sub-Saharan Africa. They also have some of the largest. Virtually everything under the sun is available for sale in these markets. Shops and department stores as well as shopping centers and malls also abound in Nigeria. Popular architecture in four settlements (namely Ife, Ibadan, Lagos, and Abuja) deserve special attention.

Ife and Ibadan are two of the most important settlements in Nigeria. They not only exemplify the contradictions, complexities, and confusion of the modern, independent African state but also display the lack of self-confidence and blind copying of foreign ideas. Both Ife and Ibadan have seen myth, science, and modern education combine effectively to create settlements that are unique. Both are homes to the spiritual leadership of the Yoruba people but also homes to two of Nigeria's elite and oldest universities. The university campus at Ife was designed by British architects who conceived the main core as a square serving as the heart of the whole campus. Arguably, the campus is a modern hybrid of the traditional king's palace with multiple courtyards serving different purposes. The University of Ibadan was planned along similar lines. The university nucleus has a concentrated layout of connected buildings consisting of a ring of residential colleges around a center of teaching and administration buildings.

Lagos is the former capital city of Nigeria. It was also founded by the Yoruba people as a fishing and trading port but today is a vibrant and highly Westernized metropolitan city. Almost surrounded by lagoons, creeks, and marshes, Lagos generally suffered from inadequate infrastructural services such as drainage and good roads, which were built only in exclusive quarters reserved for Europeans. The colonial government developed Ikoyi for reserved housing, and Ebute Metta and Yaba were also developed in between the 1920s and 1930s to reduce congestion on Lagos Island. Surulele, Ajoromi, Mushin, and Ikeja were all developed in the 1950s and 1960s in Lagos for middle-class housing, while Shomolu, Bariga, and Agege were settled by migrant workers. As in other former colonies, the British left a significant mark, architecturally, in Lagos and the rest of Nigeria.

From special housing for colonial civil servants to churches and office buildings, British architectural styles were introduced to Nigeria. Superblock high-rise apartment buildings in reinforced concrete were developed in the 1950s and 1960s. The oil boom of the 1970s saw a major development in Lagos, which included the multimillion-dollar national theater, built by a joint consortium of Nigerian and European architects. The building, which has been labeled high-tech, has been very expensive to maintain, since all the major installations in it were imported from Europe. Numerous overhead bridges and high-rise office blocks were also developed, and many immigrants from the rural areas and neighboring countries also moved into Lagos. Consequently, the city's population swelled beyond manageable limits. Growing congestion and traffic jams became the order of the day. Lagos slowly but surely was becoming impossible to govern. Lack of housing, exorbitant rents, overcrowding, and numerous other urban design and development problems led to one significant conviction—Lagos could no longer remain the capital city of Nigeria. A new capital city had to be established, and this was to be called Abuja. Precisely on November 23, 1991, the capital was moved from Lagos to Abuja.

ABUJA, A MASTER-PLANNED CITY

Abuja has a very interesting history. With its site selected by Nigerian mathematicians as being an ideal location at the center of the country and being at an equal distance from all Nigerians and also satisfying the need to achieve ethnic neutrality, its development became the most ambitious urban design project of the twentieth century in Nigeria, or perhaps in Africa. Located on the Gwagwa Plains in the middle of Nigeria, Abuja is a classic example of how the International Style sought to solve socioeconomic and sociopolitical problems through the direct application of urban design and architectural solutions. It is a symbol of what Nigeria has aspired to be, but the jury is still out as to whether that has been achieved or not. The authors of the master plan for Abuja, which was conceived as a city for 1.3 million people and to be completed in twenty years, borrowed ideas from Brasilia, Chandigarh, and even older cities such as Washington, DC, and Tokyo. However, reminiscent of Brasilia and Chandigarh, the symbolic architectural manifestation of a national political ideology did not seem to fully reflect Nigerian architecture.

The spirit of place or the genus loci of the Nigerian environment appears to be unfortunately lost in the desire to develop a modern, commercially profitable capital for the *nouveaux riches*. A chance to capture and produce an authentic Nigerian urban setting seems to have evaporated. Instead, an attempt has been made to develop a futuristic city for automobiles and the elite. Like the other major urban centers, Abuja has houses for both the rich and the poor, including high-rise and expensive apartments, lavishly decorated interiors (even though most buildings have the spartan modernist look), and gated communities. The villafication of Abuja had been achieved. Entertainment venues range from elitist golf clubs to theaters, restaurants, and casinos. There is a national stadium and hotels and resorts abound in Abuja.

It must be pointed out, however, that just as in the other former British colonies, even though professional architectural bodies in Nigeria have struggled to secure a bureaucratic control to register professional architects, many buildings are conceived and constructed by people on the outside—specifically by nonarchitects. The Nigerian artist Demas Nwoko seems to have successfully mounted a challenge to the fledgling orthodoxy of bureaucratic control. He was not only commissioned but actually constructed a number of important projects, including the Dominican Chapel in Ibadan, and the Cultural Center in Benin City, which was secured through government patronage (against all expectation). Perhaps the case of Nwoko is only a manifestation of how various artists, draftsmen, and builders have immensely contributed toward the development of popular architecture in Nigeria. Popular architecture in Nigeria therefore includes architecture without architects and definitely has changed from one generation to another.

Ivory Coast

Ivory Coast (officially known as Côte d'Ivoire) can be divided into three broad climatic zones: the coastal savannah, the middle tropical rain forest belt, and the northern savannah. Combine these with the concept of the total environment, and naturally various differences in the popular architecture of the country become obvious. Add these differences to Mazrui's Triple Heritage concept, and Ivory Coast's popular architecture can further be classified as indigenous, Islamic, and Western.

Popular residential architecture in Ivory Coast comes in various shapes and forms and will be generally discussed under rural and urban settings. Due to the peculiar circumstances found in the former French colonies, largely due to the practice of assimilation, huge discrepancies exist between popular residential architecture in the rural and urban areas. This is largely because indigenous Ivorians who have attained a certain level of education and professional qualifications see themselves as and live and behave like white French citizens living in France.

The majority of Ivorians live in rural areas in small villages. Each village consists of various compounds, and each compound is made up of groups of homes that house members of an extended family. An extended family in Africa is defined as one that includes such relatives as parents, married children and their offspring, uncles, aunts, and cousins. Initially, village houses had mud walls and thatched roofs, but today, modern materials such as corrugated metal roofing sheets are used. Generally, in most traditional African settings in Ivory Coast, there is hardly any distinction between religion and government. Precisely, at the traditional level, government is often an extension of ancestor theocracy administered by elders. This situation naturally is reflected in popular residential architecture, as the house borrows from the elements that adorn the sacred houses of ancestors. Specifically, the façade of built forms across the country reflect the ritual imagery characteristic of traditional Ivorian society. Additionally, religious motifs are incorporated into traditional housing. The courtyard house is also very popular. In general terms, building forms in traditional or rural Ivory Coast, including markets and commercial buildings, can be likened to those in the three broad climatic regions in Ghana.

Popular architecture in the urban centers is exemplified by the two cities of Abidjan and Yamoussoukro. There are sharp contrasts in housing between the middle- and upper-income and poor households in the urban centers. While wealthy and middle-class people live in modern apartment buildings or in spacious villas, the urban poor inhabit densely populated districts with very few or sometimes nonexistent government services.

The city of Abidjan lies along a lagoon, and a canal connects the lagoon with the Gulf of Guinea. Abidjan proper is connected by a multipurpose bridge, Pont Houphouet-Boigny, to Treichville. Abidjan has a checkered history. It is one of the cities in West Africa that was born out of colonial French ambition. After the demise of Federal French West Africa in 1960 (due to the independence movement that swept across the African continent), Ivory Coast became France's largest trading partner in West Africa, and the port of Abidjan became the center of this commerce. Designed originally as one of the cities of a policy of building a greater France, Abidjan reflects French urban planning practices. The master plan for the city was undertaken by two French architects, and a classical *parti* is obvious in many of the buildings in the city center. Examples include the *Palais de Justice* and the *Place de la Republique.*

Numerous French architects have worked in Abidjan over the years. With its wide boulevards and numerous buildings designed in the International Style, Abidjan's waterfront certainly could be easily mistaken for a location in Europe or North America. Abidjan has many high-rise office and apartment buildings as well as numerous single-family houses. The Riviera Golf complex is a very good example of the urban architecture associated with high-class people in Abidjan. With its two golf courses, a public club house, and the Golf Hotel Residence boasting lounges, restaurants, bars, decorated waterfalls, fountains, and pools, the entire structure is constructed in reinforced concrete. With tourism being a major foreign exchange earner for the country, some buildings in the city have been designed to cash in on this sector. A hotel in Abidjan built in the Mousgoum castle style but in reinforced concrete is a clear indication of attempts at regionalism or incorporating traditional architecture into the city's landscape. Simultaneously, however, the city has overcrowded slums, particularly in the suburbs.

Like Abuja, the capital city of Nigeria, the new capital city of Yamoussoukro has a very interesting history. The hometown of the late President Felix Houphouet-Boigny, who led the country to independence from France, Yamoussoukro could be compared to the new inland capital city of Abuja in Nigeria. It was started from scratch and has become known around the world for the excesses associated with many of the buildings and facilities in the city. For example, the wide boulevards of the city are woefully underutilized, just like the university, the town hall, the golf course, and the international airport. From a population of 1,300 in 1955, the city now has a population of over 100,000. Yamoussoukro displays conspicuous consumption in a pursuit of utopia, and failures associated with other cities developed from scratch are repeated here.

The tallest Catholic church in the world, the Basilica of Our Lady of Peace (Basilique Notre Dame de la Paix) is located in Yamoussoukro. Rushed to completion in less than three years, the structure cost $200 million, but unofficial estimates range between $500 and $900 million. With a seating capacity of 7,000 and enough room for 14,000 to stand, the church, modeled on St. Peter's Basilica in Rome, has a mega-courtyard (similar to St. Peter's Square) with 276 Doric columns, capable of holding 400,000 pilgrims. Completely air-conditioned, this is the world's most expensive building to maintain because of its cooling costs. With 80,000 square feet of glass, the most ever used in a church, and tons and tons of Italian marble, the surrounding landscape mirrors the classical French gardens of Versailles. It is surely another unfortunate development in Africa's architectural growth, particularly with the death of the founding President of Ivory Coast and the ensuing political instability that has engulfed the country. In recent years, a civil war has divided the country into two, the northern and southern portions, with the north ruled by soldiers who are believed to have a support base from migrants from the neighboring countries. The civil war has to all intents and purposes affected the development of popular architecture in Ivory Coast. Commercially, the urban centers have department stores, shopping malls, and numerous grocery stores, but many of these were vandalized and destroyed in the course of the civil war.

Central Africa

Central African Republic (CAR)

In this part of the world, nature and the spirits of the ancestors play very important roles in social organization and hence architecture. Beginning with the individual and on to the extended family headed by an elder, the organization of the village very much depends on the social structure for its very survival. Thus the spirits of the ancestors shape the arts, rites, and settlement patterns. Both the visible and invisible world are represented by masks. Carved objects are also used to represent the stories of the people in different ways. Public display of valuable sacred objects is not encouraged. Most likely, this demonstrates the people's regard for such objects. Following the concept of the total environment, the people live in housing units developed in locally available materials such as mud walls and thatched roofs. In the Central African Republic, traditional society exists side by side with the modern world.

The hinterland is sparsely populated, and the country has only one real urban center, Bangui. Access to the larger outside world is only through Bangui. Bangui used to be an European settler town situated along the Ubangi River astride the rapids, but it is now a bustling city centered around the *Place de la Republique*, and along *Avenue Boganda*. The city has grown in leaps and bounds after independence, as many people have flocked to the city from the hinterland looking for jobs. Despite the fact that Bangui has seen three principal urban renewal plans (in 1946, 1967, and 1971), it still remains a highly segregated city, with foreigners and high-level native bureaucratic bourgeoisie living in the center of the city. The Government Palace, the ministries, the embassies, the European commercial areas, the army headquarters, and the residences of many of the wealthy people are also located in the city center. Other carefully planned zones are also found to the west and north of this well-established and meticulously constructed area. Most Central Africans, however, cannot afford to live in these areas. The influence of the West is very obvious, as street paintings in the capital of Bangui tell elaborate stories of the Western influence on African architecture. Thus, scenes representative of daily urban life are depicted utilizing images that are foreign to the indigenous culture.

Away from the planned center and its periphery, the city consists of spontaneously developed African *kodros* (neighborhoods). *Kilomètre Cinq* is the most conspicuous of these kodros, which has a market—Mamadou-Mbaika—that covers 14,650 square meters and has many stores owned by Lebanese, Portuguese, and Hausa merchants. The market also has dusk-to-dawn bars and dance halls, and though this section of the city is virtually off-limits to people who do not live here, it is the center of urban life for many Central Africans. It is worth noting that the city's largest and most important mosque is located in this center of African-controlled commerce. The perception of the bourgeoisie who live in the city center is that life is too dangerous in the kodros. The average Central African, however, does not seem to think so.

Democratic Republic of the Congo (DRC)

Generally, the country can be divided into three climatic zones—tropical rain forest, savannah, and highland—and these influence the built environment. Most Congolese are farmers who live in small rural villages. They live in small villages that vary in size from a few dozen to a few hundred people, and the great majority of village families farm on a small plot of land. Virtually all raise their own food, which includes cassava, corn, and rice. Some others also catch fish. Most of the people, however, practice subsistence farming, and the result is that the cycle of poverty is perpetuated. Many villagers flock to cities looking for nonexistent jobs.

In rural Congo, most of the people live in mud houses. There are two types of mud houses: those with mud bricks and others with dried mud and sticks (also known as wattle-and-daub). Thatched roof is the most popular roof form in the rural areas. However, corrugated metal roofing sheets have been introduced into the rural landscape by those who can afford them.

In the urban centers, the situation is different. Belgium had set out to create a large empire to challenge everything England and France had acquired in Africa, and Leopoldville, named after King Leopold II, was to be the center of this empire. Thus Leopoldville (now named Kinshasa) was planned like a European city, with boulevards that proceeded from major city landmarks and met at roundabouts. Public buildings take on the form of European design precedents and interestingly enough, the Museum of African Life building is actually a Renaissance building with Roman arches. Many other public buildings are in the International Style (Modernism) but with a classical *parti*. The Auditorium Lovanium at the University of Kinshasa is a very good example of this development. Similarly, there are churches built in the Gothic style, and this is exemplified by the Roman Catholic cathedral in Kinshasa.

Other public amenities, such as restaurants, cinemas, casinos, sports stadiums, shopping centers, and markets, are also found in the cities. When it comes to housing, there are attractive bungalows in the urban centers for middle- and high-income Europeans and Congolese. But many factory and office workers live in crowded areas of small, cheap houses and apartments made from cinder blocks and baked mud bricks. Such high-density housing areas, however, are avoided by foreigners and middle- and high-income natives, who have the perception that danger lurks around the next corner in these boisterous, noisy, and sometimes dirty but lively and viable environments. Commercially, the outdoor marketplaces in the high-density areas are also very busy and growing. The majority of people buy their goods from there.

Southern Africa

Republic of South Africa

The contrasting ways of life for the different peoples of the country at the urban and rural levels require that popular architecture of the country be discussed along these lines. Additionally, the injustices and inequalities created by the apartheid system and earlier oppression of nonwhites have profoundly affected the way of life of people and, particularly, their popular architecture. The architecture of South Africa draws more on European building style than on Islamic or traditional influences, taking the triple heritage theory into consideration. Officially, since the end of apartheid, the different racial groups are no longer separated by law, but nonwhites still encounter both overt and covert discrimination, and most high-paying jobs are still held by whites. This situation naturally affects architectural development in the country. It has to be mentioned that differences of all kinds still exist within each racial group and between the groups. The differing cultural backgrounds of the peoples of South Africa have certainly created contrasting ways of life, and additionally, the inequalities created by the apartheid system have impacted the lives of the people and, not surprisingly, their architecture.

Many of South Africa's blacks live in areas that were formerly called black "homelands," where they were assigned permanent residency. Not only were the farms in the homelands smaller than the white-owned ones, but the soil on homeland farms was also poor. Consequently, many black men and women looked for jobs in the cities to support their families. The homeland system was ended by the government in 1994, and today almost 50 percent of blacks live in urban areas, though many urban blacks still live in segregated neighborhoods. While some blacks have moved into formerly all-white neighborhoods, others have built makeshift shelters on empty land inside the city limits and on land along major roads leading into the cities. Mainly as a result of the years of oppression, many blacks in South Africa are poor. In 1990, barely at the beginning of the end of apartheid, the average per capita income of blacks was about one-tenth that of whites. Large numbers of blacks are unemployed, and many blacks lack adequate housing.

The situation with whites is completely different. Almost 90 percent of whites in South Africa live in urban areas. They enjoy a high standard of living, and their clothing, social customs, and homes closely resemble those of middle-class Europeans and North Americans. The comfortable and luxurious suburban sections of Pretoria, Cape Town, Durban, and Johannesburg, for example, literally overflow with white families who live in single-family homes with nonwhite servants. To highlight some of the differences among races and peoples, English-speaking whites and Afrikaans-speaking whites (Afrikaners) not only live in different sections of cities but also lead separate lives by attending different schools and belonging to different churches and social and professional bodies. Afrikaners held many important government jobs until the epochal 1994 elections, and they continue to control most of the country's agriculture, but English-speaking whites dominate business and industry.

With respect to the so-called Coloured people (offspring of different races), about 85 percent of them live in cities. They are mostly concentrated in the Western Cape and have worked for whites for generations. In the rural areas they work in the vineyards and orchards, but they also work as servants, craftsmen and craftswomen, factory laborers and servants.

South Africa's Asians, the majority of whom are Indian, live largely in cities. The majority of Indians live in the KwaZulu-Natal region, but many of them have retained most of their old social customs. Most Indians in South Africa are poor and work in factories or grow vegetables for markets in the cities, but a few are prosperous medical doctors, lawyers, industrialists, and merchants.

In the urban areas, many South Africans spend much of their leisure hours outdoors, thanks to the mild climate. On weekends and holidays, many urban dwellers troop to the beaches and visit the national parks and game reserves. Facilities such as restaurants and theaters were for many years allowed to serve only either whites or nonwhites, and new regulations permitting them to serve all races were put in place only in the 1970s and 1980s. Around the same time, sports competitions involving more than one race were also legalized, but segregation still exists in private social and sports clubs even though, officially, it is illegal.

In rural areas, many poor blacks live in traditional round houses called *rondavels.* The conical beehive roof forms are readily seen in the traditional Zulu homesteads, and a significant element of traditional South African architecture is mural painting, largely done by the Ndebele people. Thus their houses radiate bright colors in images derived from their surroundings and living patterns, and these include designs taken from alphabets, blankets, tiles, and traditional birds. Because of a need to accommodate a life in which cattle symbolize wealth, the traditional South African house has evolved to the creation of an outdoor room (or living space shared by residents and cattle) encircling the living space. This need gradually led to the development of two separate outdoor spaces: one for the people and another (called the *kraal*) for animals and agricultural products. Thus the people's intrinsic need and desire to be together was also satisfied, and this is reflected in the typical village plan.

Zimbabwe

Popular architecture in Zimbabwe closely follows the pattern in the Republic of South Africa. Perhaps the only difference is that most of the whites in Zimbabwe originally came from the United Kingdom. As in South Africa, the whites in Zimbabwe perhaps never really intended to allow Zimbabwean blacks to govern the country. Policies similar to some aspects of the apartheid system in South Africa were also pursued in Zimbabwe, and this invariably affected the development of popular architecture in Zimbabwe.

In the cities and towns, blacks tended to live in the eastern sections in areas referred to as "high-density housing areas," where the houses were smaller and generally of one story. Plot sizes were also much smaller, and tall security lights rose above these houses. When lit at night, these lights virtually ensured that no group activities could go unnoticed.

Whites, on the other hand, lived in suburbs in the western sections of the cities and towns, where plot sizes were very generous in times gone by. Thus many whites lived in Western-style, one-story family houses with swimming pools, double garages, and other amenities on plots measuring a minimum of one acre. The central business districts in the cities and towns have tall office blocks, apartment houses, shopping centers, multilevel car parks, restaurants, theaters, hotels, and casinos. For sports, cricket ovals, swimming pools, soccer stadiums, tennis courts, and golf courses were developed.

Many affluent blacks have moved into houses in the suburbs formerly reserved for whites only. This has become possible with the migration of many whites after independence and also improved and more accessible education. The influence of South Africa on the development of the popular architecture of Zimbabwe also cannot be ignored. Long before many Zimbabweans aspired to get education and jobs in South Africa, architectural forms and shapes from the southern neighbor were being copied. Bulawayo Center, a new shopping center in the city of Bulawayo and the brand-new campus of the National University of Science and Technology, also in Bulawayo, were both designed in the postmodern style by architects trained in South Africa and the United States. The demolition of "unauthorized" housing units in the cities of Harare and Bulawayo and other towns in 2005 definitely only compounded the problems associated with the development of popular architecture, because these unauthorized structures had provided residential and economic facilities to support the urban poor over the years.

In rural Zimbabwe, the story is different. Most of the people live in mud houses, and the tuck shop—a small shop similar to the kiosk of West Africa or little corner shop—happens to be the focal point. Many of the houses are roofed in thatch, and in many villages in the rural areas the people share their compounds with their cattle. This compound adds a spiritual dimension and also acts as a shrine that can be used to communicate with one's ancestors on a daily basis. This is because family members hold their meetings in these courtyards, and they believe that their ancestors are present at these meetings. Ndebele round houses found around Bulawayo demonstrate the communal and security-conscious designs very clearly, with their walls and controlled entrances. It must be emphasized, however, that traditional influences on architectural development continue to wane.

East Africa

Kenya

In the urban centers and cities of Kenya, about one-quarter of the population lives in modern houses built in cement and stone. These houses come in different sizes and styles. Houses for the working-class people are simple and inexpensive, but the wealthy people live in large expensive houses and apartment buildings. Nairobi, the capital, arguably belongs to the class of African cities such as Abidjan, Accra, Cairo, and Lagos that have large built-up areas predominantly reflective of European urban design principles. Nairobi also is a dual city of well-planned areas as well as heavily populated unplanned areas. Thus, not too far away from the well-planned areas with their hybrid Victorian-style buildings and predominantly International Style skyline with little or no reference to African culture, one finds one of the largest slums on the African continent.

In the slums, some of the urban population live in small houses with thatched roofs, walls made of mud or bundles of branches, and dirt floors, while others live in makeshift structures. Some of these people arrive in the urban centers every year from the rural areas in search of jobs. Nairobi has functional Cartesian grids that are intercepted by roundabouts at central points. This is based on a model that the colonial English city planners introduced to the colonies. Most of the buildings found in the colonial districts of Nairobi are designed in Renaissance and neoclassical styles and could be found anywhere in Europe, particularly London. Similarly, rich landlords, mainly of English origin, built Victorian houses with large yards and gardens in the suburbs. Nairobi also has a number of churches and mosques. The Jamia Mosque exhibits the strong presence of Islam in the city.

Commercially, there are shopping centers and shops. Though street vending is becoming popular, large open-air markets as seen in West Africa are not common. For recreation in the cities and towns, dance halls are common. Motion pictures are also popular, and cinema houses are also found in the cities and towns. Additionally, the cities and towns also have beautiful golf courses, hotels, restaurants, swimming pools, casinos and sports stadiums.

Most rural Kenyans live in small houses with mud walls or bundles of branches, dirt floors, and thatched roofs on small farm settlements. They raise crops and livestock for a living. While many of these rural farm families struggle to produce enough food for their own use, others grow enough to offer their extra produce for sale. Many of the farmers hold part-time jobs as blacksmiths, carpenters, shoemakers, tailors or work in other trades or on large farm estates, particularly coffee and tea plantations, owned by wealthy landowners. Culture revolves along ethnic lines, and the extended family is the center of an individual's loyalty in small village communities. A small percentage of Kenya's population are nomads who raise livestock for a living. Because they are seasonally on the move looking for pasture and water for their livestock, they live in tents that are demountable and easy to erect. Leaves and animal skin as well as bent stems tied together to form flat-roofed buildings with round corners are some of the materials used. The Masai are the best known of these nomads. Like the Masai, the Kikuyu people also build homesteads in villages. The Kikuyu homestead, however, usually consists of various unit houses belonging to members of the same ancestral lineage.

Communal labor is used to build a house, which more often than not is completed in one day. In more recent times, the Kikuyu people have adapted modern materials and technology in the construction of their buildings. For example, corrugated metal roofing sheets are slowly replacing thatched roofs. The houses, however, are usually circular in shape, and the family structure usually determines the arrangement of houses within a homestead. The homestead chief's house, or the man's house, is usually near the entrance to the compound. The senior wife's house follows a traditional pattern in terms of how things are arranged within and has a fireplace in the middle with other furniture arranged around the corners of the house. Usually, only girls sleep in the same room with the women, and boys, except when young, sleep in the men's room. Usually, there is a central courtyard for the homestead, and this is used for cooking and socialization during the hot dry seasons but is used most in the evening after sunset. This is the same place where women tell folk tales to children to teach them the traditions of their ancestors and to expose them to the laws of society, while young adult men enjoy increased contact with older men to learn the process of initiation into manhood. Film shows are very popular in the rural areas, and mobile motion-picture units deliver films on a regular basis.

Ethiopia

Historically, popular architecture in Ethiopia was deeply influenced by the Ethiopian Orthodox Church. The most dramatic expression of this influence is the famous rock-hewn churches of Lalibela.

In the urban centers of Ethiopia, nineteenth- and twentieth-century imperial politics also shaped architectural development. Though Ethiopia is the only country in East Africa not colonized by any imperial power (with the exception of a three-year Italian occupation during World War II), Britain, France, and Italy were highly involved in the country's development. For example, during the Italian occupation, both the private and the recreational quarters built for their military officers conformed to a mixed Italian and traditional Ethiopian style. The founding of the capital, Addis Ababa, by Emperor Menelik in 1896 after the battle of Adowa began the process of modernizing the nation. Official government buildings were built in the Western style, and this trend continued in the 1960s, when Emperor Haile Selassie built the headquarters for the Organization of African Unity (OAU), the Hall of Africa, in the city. Thus Addis Ababa was literally infected by the post-World War II architectural and technological movements that swept the world, and many buildings were done in this style. These include the Parliament Building, the Development Center, and the Hilton Hotel.

The city also has many modern apartment buildings and a number of skyscrapers. Interestingly, much of the country's art has a close relationship with the Ethiopian Orthodox Church. This is because, in the past, many artists had painted biblical scenes and pictures of saints on church walls. Artists and writers have over the years also been influenced by religious manuscripts with elaborate art work.

Poverty also exists in the urban centers, but generally the urban population is better off economically than their rural counterparts. Again, broadly speaking, schools, medical care, electricity, and other modern living comforts are more readily and widely available in the urban areas. It must be mentioned that the bloody Marxist revolution by the military in the 1970s impacted heavily on architectural development in Ethiopia. Construction virtually came to a standstill.

Most of the people in Ethiopia live in rural areas. Most rural Ethiopians live in villages or isolated homesteads. The majority are farmers who work the land with wooden plows pulled by oxen. Ethiopia's rural population includes nomads who raise livestock, and poverty is widespread in the rural areas. Day in and day out, large numbers of rural people migrate to the urban areas in search of jobs and a better life. Some of them have created what are referred to as slums, such as Santa Barbara in Addis Ababa, where conditions are similar to those in the rural areas they left behind. To put it simply, the lives of Ethiopian villagers remain hard and precarious.

Traditional housing is of two types. The commonest form of traditional housing for Ethiopians is the round house with walls made from wooden frames plastered with mud and topped off with cone-shaped thatched straw or the occasional metal roofing. In places where stone is readily available, people live in rectangular stone houses with the same roofing systems.

CONCLUSION

The concepts of the total environment and Mazrui's Triple Heritage of Africa have been two major linchpins around which this discussion of African architecture has revolved. As much as possible, the impact of these two forces on the development of popular architecture in the sub-continent has been discussed. The discussion, however, has revealed some similarities and contrasts in the development of popular architecture across the different regions of Sub-Saharan Africa.

In terms of similarities, the concept of the total environment has revealed that building materials utilized in locations in rural areas with similar physical and cultural characteristics in Sub-Saharan Africa are the same. In other words, similar built forms in similar building materials and technology have been utilized in these places. What remains to be more clearly appreciated is why circular forms are utilized in certain places as against rectangular ones, but this may be explained more by cultural factors such as religion, social organization, the community's history, and levels of technology. Additionally, all the African countries that were formerly colonized by Europeans have experienced similar patterns of development.

Invariably, the former colonial powers developed exclusive housing and administrative buildings for their citizens and hardly concerned themselves with improving the housing needs of the majority of the indigenous peoples who lived in the rural areas. Thus, areas that were actually developed included the capital cities and a few urban centers. Even in places where mining activities took place, housing and administrative buildings for the foreign mining staff were drastically different from corresponding facilities for the local people. An obvious similarity is the importance of the courtyard in all the regions considered. From east to west and from central to southern, the courtyard formed an indispensable part of the lives of the native people in the rural areas and was used for various activities and functions. Another obvious similarity is in the push and pull of rural and urban migration. All the urban centers of all the countries in the subcontinent, particularly the capital cities, have experienced and continue to experience rural-to-urban migration on a daily basis. Obviously, perceived attractions in the urban centers far outweigh the dangers and realities, and all the indigenous peoples of Africa do aspire to better living standards.

The development of popular architecture in Sub-Saharan Africa also illustrates some contrasts. One obvious contrast stems from the political philosophy of the former colonial power. For example, whereas the Francophone countries (colonies) were considered to be an integral part of the broader French "empire," the same could not be said of the Anglophone countries (colonies). Thus the impression is created that the former Francophone colonies were physically better developed than their Anglophone counterparts. In places where this contention does not seem to be true, for example in the former colonies of Northern Rhodesia (Zambia), Southern Rhodesia (Zimbabwe), and the Republic of South Africa, another argument is that the whites never really intended to leave those colonies, hence the long, bitter guerrilla wars with considerable loss of lives that preceded independence (in the latter two cases). Another contrast appears to be the lack of influence of Islam in the southern regions of Sub-Saharan Africa. In the development of popular architecture, the impact of Islam is the least important in the southern African countries of the four regions discussed.

In light of the foregoing discussion, the question can be asked as to whether there is anything that can be called popular architecture in Africa. The simple answer is "yes." There is popular architecture in Sub-Saharan Africa, and it is definitely not determined by the buildings designed and built by world-famous architects and construction companies. Popular architecture in Sub-Saharan Africa certainly includes some buildings designed and developed by foreigners over the years as well as buildings developed by the local peoples without any outside influence. Such buildings may be given different names by different people according to various means of classification, but one thing is certain: popular architecture in the Sub-Saharan African region certainly is appreciated and very useful to the people.

RESOURCE GUIDE

PRINT SOURCES

"The Basilica in the Bush: The Biggest Church in Christendom Arises in the Ivory Coast," *Time* 134.1 (1989, July 3).

Bourdier, Jean-Paul, and Trihn T. Minh-Ha. *Drawn from African Dwellings*. Bloomington: Indiana University Press, 1996.

Denyer, Susan. *African Traditional Architecture*. New York: Africana Publishing Company. 1978.

Elleh, Nnamdi. *Architecture and Power in Africa*. Westport, CT: Praeger, 2002.

———. *African Architecture: Evolution and Transformation*. New York: McGraw-Hill, 1997.

Frescura, Franco. *Rural Shelter in Southern Africa*. Pretoria, South Africa: Sigma Press, 1981.
Fry, Maxwell, and Jane Drew. *Tropical Architecture in Dry and Humid Zones*. New York: Reinhold, 1954.
Garlake, Peter. *Great Zimbabwe*. London: Thames and Hudson, 1973.
Gerster, George. *Churches in Rock: Early Christian Art in Ethiopia*. London: Phaidon, 1970.
Hull, Richard W. *African Cities and Towns before the European Conquest*. New York: W. W. Norton Publishers, 1976.
"Ivory Coast: A Monumental Dispute." *Time* 136.1 (1990, September 17): 61.
Judin, Hilton, and Ivan Vladislavic, eds. *Blank: Architecture, Apartheid and After*. Rotterdam, Netherlands: NAI Publishers, 1998.
King, Anthony D. "Africa 1880–1980." Pp. 193–223 in Anthony D. King, *The Bungalow: The Production of a Global Culture*. London: Routledge and Kegan Paul, 1984.
Kulturmann, Udo. *New Architecture in Africa*. New York: Universe Books, 1963.
———. *New Directions in African Architecture*. New York: Braziller, 1969.
Lawrence, A. W. *Trade Castles and Forts of West Africa*. London: Jonathan Cape, 1963.
Le Roux, Hannah. "The Post-Colonial Architecture of Ghana and Nigeria." *Architectural History* 47 (2004): 361–392.
Okoye, Ikem Stanley. "Architecture, History and the Debate on Identity in Ethiopia, Ghana, Nigeria and South Africa." *Journal of the Society of Architectural Historians* 61:3 (2002, September): 381–396.
Oliver, Paul. *Shelter in Africa*. New York: Praeger, 1971.
———, ed. *Encyclopedia of World Vernacular Architecture*. Cambridge, UK: Cambridge University Press, 1997.
Prussin, Labelle. "An Introduction to Indigenous African Architecture." *Journal of the Society of Architectural Historians* 33.3 (1974): 183–205.
———. *Architecture in Northern Ghana*. Berkeley: University of California Press, 1969.
Schreckenbach, Hannah, and Jackson Abankwa. *Construction Technology for a Tropical Developing Country*. Eschborn: GTZ, 1982.

WEBSITES

International Architecture Database. http://www.archinform.net. A database for international architecture, originally created from building projects from architecture students, this has become the largest online database about worldwide architects and buildings, and includes plans for projects mainly from Southern Africa.

VIDEOS/FILMS

The Africans: A Triple Heritage (UK/United States, 1986). Written and narrated by Ali Mazrui. BBC and PBS television series.

ART

MATTHEW EVANS TETI

The definition of "art" in Sub-Saharan Africa has always been a highly disputed topic. The basis of the dispute, which has raged in the Western art world as well as in Sub-Saharan Africa for more than a century, is further complicated because that debate centers around the definition of art itself. The very first step in understanding the art of Sub-Saharan Africa is to understand the nature of this discrepancy and its implications for the project of learning about Sub-Saharan African art.

Since before the time of the Roman Empire, the Western world has been cultivating a system of knowledge, practices, and institutions of art, which have become highly developed over the past 2,500 years. Although the processes and products of this legacy have changed drastically since Roman times, the West has developed methods of defining, evaluating, and interacting with art that adapt to the changing world. The stability of museums, libraries, universities, and governments in Western nations has ensured that we maintain a great history of artistic practice that spans hundreds of years. These institutions reinforce our notions of what art is, who makes it, how it is looked at, and what it tells us about our society. They succeed in teaching the West about its artistic heritage and reinforcing the definition of art in the present through a solid and unwavering presentation of art's past. But what happens when we apply this model to the diverse and dissimilar arts of Sub-Saharan Africa? What we find is that the West's method of defining art and its history is not well suited for telling the story of Sub-Saharan African art, which may as well be in a different language.

The inconsistency encountered when fitting Sub-Saharan African concepts of art into the aforementioned Western model is because the Western model of art is based on a historical concept. In Sub-Saharan Africa, people have been making art for just as long, if not longer, than anywhere else on earth. Therefore, it seems logical that we can look at African art and civilization and draft a timeline in the same way we account for the history of the West. In the case of art, this would mean positing a continuum of styles in which each progressed from the last, all the while keeping the history of artistic practice in mind. However, the method of looking back, recording the past, and moving beyond it that defines our notion of history has only recently become common in Sub-Saharan African society. The West has the concept of history it has because for thousands of years Western man has undertaken the project of recording the past and maintaining that record for posterity. In Sub-Saharan Africa, no such far-reaching practice was ever carried out, and thus nothing like a Western concept of history was constructed within this region of the world. This is not to say that the people of Sub-Saharan Africa have no history, but their history has been maintained and passed down in a manner different from that of the West. Barring a discussion of why Sub-Saharan African society developed in this manner it suffices to say that art, which is a concept built on history, also has completely different meanings and manifestations in Sub-Saharan Africa than it does in the West. When we attempt to learn about Sub-Saharan African art today in its popular manifestations, it is necessary for us to realize this (and other) aspects of the history of Sub-Saharan African art.

SUB-SAHARAN AFRICAN ART IN THE WEST

The best way to start to dispel Western misconceptions of Sub-Saharan African art is to focus our attention on how the West, with its unique form of art history, has tried to understand and teach its citizens about Sub-Saharan African art. When encountered with a work of fine craftsmanship from Sub-Saharan Africa, the instinct of the Western art patron or institution is to collect the object and to display it in the interest of aesthetic enjoyment and education. Our museums, art galleries, and collectors seek to understand and appreciate Sub-Saharan African objects, but when they are placed within Western systems of art and history, these objects lose a large portion of their significance.

The greatest deterrent to understanding Sub-Saharan African art objects when they are placed within a Western art-historical setting is context. Western art produced over the last few hundred years is generally intended to be viewed as a static piece of art, whether it is in a museum, in a gallery, at home, or in public. Sub-Saharan Africans, who for centuries have not had art museums, galleries, or systems of patronage similar to those of the West, never independently created art for these contexts. The Sub-Saharan African art that we find in the West that was made before 1950 is for the most part functional, which is to say that its use in the setting for which it was created is what gives it meaning. For instance, Sub-Saharan African masks were not made for display on walls or in cases. They were made for inclusion in a public ceremony in which people danced with them, acted out stories, and performed communal rites. The meaning of a mask cannot be gained by looking at it statically mounted in a museum in the West. To understand this art, we must first realize that it is not like Western art and that to gain a full appreciation of its significance we must consider its original intention.

Acquiring the knowledge necessary to place Sub-Saharan African objects within their original contexts can be extremely difficult, and this difficulty poses the major obstacle to understanding Sub-Saharan African art in the West. Not only is it nearly impossible for us to see Sub-Saharan African objects being used in the manner in which they were intended to be used; it is often hard to determine what their original context was and frequently even where these objects come from. For years, art historians in Western institutions have had to rely on very minimal firsthand evidence of Sub-Saharan African life to place the great many objects that had ended up out of context in our museums, colleges, and private collections. Many of the pieces of Sub-Saharan African art that have left the continent in the past, and many of those that leave today, carry with them no information as to their place of origin or intended usage. They have been traded, stolen, bought, and sold by people for whom this information is either inconsequential or as much of a mystery as it is to the West. Aesthetic comparison and inference have been the tools of the scholar of Sub-Saharan African art, whose background knowledge of the cultures and traditions of Sub-Saharan Africa is probably little at best. As we have already seen, Sub-Saharan African people do not share the same methods of recording history with the West; thus no thorough documentation of Sub-Saharan African forms has ever been accomplished. Granted, piecemeal accounts of Sub-Saharan African life and art exist. They have been produced by foreign travelers and scholars in Sub-Saharan Africa as well as by Africans who have accepted Western educational and socio-historical practices. These accounts lend a great deal to uniting Sub-Saharan African objects in the West with their origins, but today it remains the case that no comprehensive understanding of Sub-Saharan African life and art exists.

Reproductions or "Fakes"

Now that we have a grasp on the historical setting of Sub-Saharan African art in the West, we can begin to see how this exchange colors contemporary Sub-Saharan African artistic practices. The work of contemporary Sub-Saharan African people, as in any other society in the world, is dependent on a combination of various interrelated factors. It so happens that as outsiders, who have a history of misunderstanding Sub-Saharan African art, we can best come to understand the current situation of the arts in Sub-Saharan Africa through an understanding of our own relationships with them. Since the dawn of Western contact with Sub-Saharan Africa, we have been tremendously influential in changing their societies to mirror our own. This persuasion has not only caused the arts of Sub-Saharan Africa to look like the arts of the West, but it has caused their indigenous arts to look like Western interpretations of themselves.

Pre-colonial Sub-Saharan Africa consisted of thousands of culture groups who all maintained indigenous artistic legacies which were unique to their localized regions of the subcontinent. Hundreds of years ago, Westerners began to alter the makeup of Sub-Saharan African society through the process of colonization. The result of this process is that, today, Sub-Saharan African society functions very much like the West in terms of its economic, political, and cultural systems. Caught up in colonization was the appropriation by the West of Sub-Saharan African art. The West took the cultural objects of a myriad of Sub-Saharan African groups with little concern for their specific meanings within those societies and removed them to private collections and museums in Europe and America. At the same time, colonization replaced former cultural practices with Western notions of what art was, who made it, how it was taught to subsequent generations, and who reserved the right to own art, display it, and speak about it. The colonizers built museums, universities, and artist–patron relationships over the top of African systems of cultural heritage, threatening to destroy their very existence.

Today, little remains of the once thriving local cultures of millions of Sub-Saharan African people. The great majority of Sub-Saharan African culture groups have become so assimilated into the Western world that only traces of their former identities are still discernible in quotidian life. What does remain of their once native cultures is not protected by the societies' eldest and most revered citizens, but rather is poorly preserved by the same guardians of culture who have misunderstood and misrepresented it in the West. In Sub-Saharan Africa, museums and other art institutions have been guilty of the same abstraction and mistreatment of Sub-Saharan African cultural heritage as in the West, leaving little time left to preserve the vanishing indigenous cultures of the once unscathed African subcontinent.

Out of the estranged relationship that the imposition of Western art institutions has caused Sub-Saharan African cultures to have with their own art, a bizarre set of circumstances has arisen. As a result of the overthrow of cultural patrimony in Sub-Saharan Africa,

Africans have looked to Western histories of art to learn about the fading and extinct cultural practices of their ancestors. Tragically, the history of art told by museums and books does little more than reproduce images, which are rarely imbued with the cultural significance and contextual information that would preserve the original meaning of the works of art. Since both the West and Sub-Saharan Africa are viewing the same types of images and learning about Sub-Saharan African art from the same sources, in a strange twist of fate our cultures have come to possess the same equally deprived knowledge of the history of Sub-Saharan African art.

This homogeneity of culture, which has been enforced on Sub-Saharan Africa over the past century, is a symptom of the larger cultural and economic phenomenon of globalization. In the global market of today, it is increasingly the case that people all over the world have access to the same products and are exposed to the same culture. In a global framework such as this, cultural products are intended for vast audiences that extend far beyond the city, country, or continent of the producer. Years ago, when Sub-Saharan Africans were violently thrown into the capitalist free market of their colonizers, they adapted by producing things that appealed to the tastes of Europeans and Americans who had the means to purchase goods and services from them. Rather than satisfying the needs of their countrymen, whose resources were scarce, Sub-Saharan African producers looked elsewhere to the tastes of other nations for their patronage. In the realm of artistic production, Sub-Saharan African craftsman who had formerly fashioned objects for local culture groups began to look toward the styles that Westerners found attractive in Sub-Saharan African art. Sub-Saharan African craftsman abandoned their inherited styles of local production and instead began to reproduce cultural icons that had been esteemed in the Western art world. They came to use publications highlighting Western museum and private collections of Sub-Saharan African art to copy the cultural products of other Sub-Saharan African groups and make a profit from buyers in the West. These objects have been taken up by the Western art world, stripped of their meaning and cultural context, represented to Sub-Saharan Africans, and in turn reproduced by Sub-Saharan Africans. Objects that are produced in this manner are commonly referred to on the market as "fakes."

Given this history, there is still a debate within the global Sub-Saharan African art market about the application of the term fake and the value of such objects. People from within art institutions claim that as long as fabricated cultural products retain an educational value, they are worthy of recognition and inclusion in museums. This argument only perpetuates the system of misunderstanding Sub-Saharan African art, which Western art institutions produced in the first place by disregarding the intent of the producer, function of the object, and meaning within its society of origin. Furthermore, so-called fakes suffer a twofold misrepresentation at the hands of the forger, whose craftsmanship is equally as uninformed as its source. Sub-Saharan African art forgers have usually never seen the objects they create for commercial sale, and they frequently misjudge sizes and commit errors that are a result of not having the proper perspective of an object to create a three-dimensional representation of it. These copies are doubly inappropriate for the world's cultural institutions, because they not only are lacking their appropriate contextual significance but are not even accurate representations of the objects they emulate.

However, despite what the West thinks about the perpetuation of copied cultural products, it is a pervasive practice that today spans most countries in Sub-Saharan Africa and is probably the most thriving commercial venture in arts of those countries. Although the line between what is supposedly fake or plagiarized and what is genuine popular production is very thin indeed, there are a couple of clues to distinguishing the two camps. The term "fake" is generally reserved for a product that is produced by a cultural group other than that which originally produced the object. Because colonialism and globalization have succeeded in extinguishing multitudes of indigenous Sub-Saharan African cultures, this usually entails contemporary craftsman fashioning objects whose original function belongs to a set of extinct cultural practices. This can also involve production of an object native to, say, Southern Africa, by industrious craftsman in West African port cities.

INDIGENOUS ART FOR THE MASSES

In looking at the popularization of indigenous art it will help to first understand a bit more about the makeup of Sub-Saharan African society. In a very general sense, Sub-Saharan African civilization is made up of sociocultural groups whose members speak the same language, hold similar beliefs, and practice the same religion. In any one Sub-Saharan African nation there might be several to hundreds of such groups that coexist with one another. Within these groups, smaller divisions of people are defined by local variations of more widely held practices, such as linguistic dialects and differing styles of dress or social mores. As the Western world has encroached on the people of Sub-Saharan Africa, the identities that have broadly defined Sub-Saharan African groups such as the Yoruba or the Zulu have been threatened by the homogenization of culture under the demands of globalization and the free-market economy. Although the larger cultural entities that define the Sub-Saharan African populace have persisted to some degree in maintaining their autonomy from Western cultural branding, the individualized units that composed them are rapidly disappearing. Under the threat of cultural conquest, local Sub-Saharan African populations have congealed under the more pervasive characteristics of their more general cultural identities to save some semblance of their heritage from extinction.

In terms of artistic output, Sub-Saharan African people who share general things in common such as geographic location, language, and religion typically practice similar arts as well. More often than not, the arts that these people share are inseparable from some other part of their culture, so that it is natural for a wide variety of local groups to participate in the same tradition. However, despite trends such as this, there has historically been a tremendous amount of diversity among the individual practices of local artisans in Sub-Saharan Africa. For instance, even though only a few miles may separate two centers for ceramic production, potters from both locales may dig their clay from different sources, throw their pots in a different manner, and fire their wares using different techniques. In addition to having different processes for working with the same materials, proximate groups may also display variations in the style and meaning of the arts they produce. To the untrained eye, such as that of the distant Western museum, subtle differences between the arts of various subsets of the same larger culture group can be imperceptible, and they have led to the gloss of Sub-Saharan African aesthetics discussed earlier. This failure of the Western world to assimilate the intricacies at the basis of Sub-Saharan African art has helped to diminish unique local production in the arts in favor of the widely recognized regional styles of the larger population. Today, local variations surely still exist in many parts of the subcontinent, but overall the arts of Sub-Saharan Africa have seen the amalgamation of local specificities under broader categories of artistic production.

The coalescence of Sub-Saharan African forms described above has led to the popularization of formerly indigenous cultural and artistic features. Formerly a tradition was composed of many individual producers creating art that was similar, so that a broader trend was evidenced among the pieces. Today, normative cultural forms are increasingly dispersed from large centers of production that cater to the needs of a wider public. This is a result of the increase in social networks that technological advancement has brought about in Sub-Saharan Africa. As is all too often the case, improved systems of communication in a community evolve on the coattails of advertising. This means that the financial interests that provide communities with the ability to grow do so because they are compensated by the increased revenue that a larger, wealthier population brings them. When the producers of a certain type of artwork are faced with the "sink or swim" mentality of free-market capitalism, which requires that businesses reap ever bigger returns to stay afloat, they must expand their business to succeed. In Sub-Saharan Africa, where capitalism is the economic system of most nations, it is becoming necessary for artists and craftsmen to appeal to larger populations to stay in business. With this expansion, artists are forced to standardize their product to appeal to the widest possible market. Whereas in the past, artisans would produce work for only a handful of local culture groups who shared very specific needs, now they must produce for a highly varied public whose cultural needs may be very different from their own. So today, indigenous artistic production in Sub-Saharan Africa, which was formerly tied to the special needs of a local community, has been forced to become generic and popular to preserve the legacies of local cultures.

POPULAR ARTS IN URBAN CENTERS

Nowhere have the multifaceted, unique, indigenous populations of Sub-Saharan Africa melded into a homogeneous public better than in the urban centers of the subcontinent. Today cities such as Lagos, Nigeria, and Kinshasa, Democratic Republic of the Congo, can be counted among the world's largest. Although Sub-Saharan African metropolises may still lag behind Western capitals in terms of urban advances, they share many of the same characteristics. It is both alarming and fascinating to study the evolution of Sub-Saharan African cities, because it so closely mirrors the development of the West. As in the West, popular art arose in Sub-Saharan Africa as a symptom of the social expansion that is inherent in metropolitan living. Greater numbers of people began to share the same new experiences in the city that were distinct from their small-town lives and as a result they developed similar tastes and pleasures. Once Sub-Saharan Africans settled into urban existence, they began to have a certain amount of leisure time and expendable income. Popular art, among other categories of goods and services, arose in Sub-Saharan African cities to meet the needs of these new populations.

In Sub-Saharan Africa, as in the West, advertising has galvanized the drive to fill the empty spaces in urban existence with a flood of products for the common man. The crux of advertising in the free-market economy is the assumption that everyone in a certain demographic category has the same basic needs and thus will be interested in the same types of products. This universality of the consumer both nurtures and is in turn shaped by advertising, which becomes a constant symbol visible to the urban community as a whole. Popular art fills the exact same niche within urban populations, wherein it both reflects the aesthetic taste of the people and at the same time creates a market for its product. The alliance between popular art and advertising is so strong that, in the West, what we call popular or "pop art" plays off of the advertising industry's universal audience to create a whole new general public for fine art. In Sub-Saharan Africa, the general principle behind popular art is the same as in the West, although the development and manifestations of popular art are slightly different.

Rather than organically developing out of a natural progression of events, Sub-Saharan African urbanity was inherited in large measure from the West. Through a cycle of hundreds of years and very particular historical circumstances, the West developed its distinctive version of what we know as urban civilization. When Sub-Saharan Africa was colonized by the Europeans, they brought the concept of the great urban melting pot with them and replicated it in Sub-Saharan African cities that, up until then, had functioned in their own unique manner. Along with this urban model Sub-Saharan Africa adopted the bulk of its attributes, including the burgeoning discipline of mass advertising. Sub-Saharan Africans who were previously unfamiliar with being universal urban subjects were therefore molded into them by the likes of advertising, rather than arriving at that state of their own accord. Sub-Saharan Africa's nuanced reception of advertising culture led individuals not to completely assimilate the Western identity of generic urban consumer; rather, it enabled them to retain a subjective, personal element despite the homogenizing effect of advertising.

Inherited from Sub-Saharan African modes of advertising, popular art also retained a personal flavor that it uses to market its otherwise generic product. Even though it is mass produced for the general urban population of the growing Sub-Saharan African city, popular art more often than not wears a face that lends it a touch of humanity. Rather than using billboards, TV commercials, or other ads, and rather than selling popular art in chain stores staffed by indifferent strangers, Sub-Saharan African popular art is sold by vendors who engage the customers in interpersonal contact to sell their work. Although it may be bland and general, popular Sub-Saharan African art has the human touch of the vendor, who is synonymous with the artist or craftsman in a small-town patronage system.

In Sub-Saharan Africa, advertising itself drifts into the realm of popular art given that it is frequently imbued with the same personal feeling that appeals to individuals rather than mass-produced urban subjects. Entrepreneurs and small-business owners, who are legion in Sub-Saharan African cities, will go to great lengths to create their own advertising that has a very local significance and individual spirit that elevates it to the level of art. Rather than plastering ads all over town, these vendors and service providers can usually afford only to decorate their shop and put up one or two neighborhood signs. Their approach caters to their immediate neighbors, who undoubtedly know the entrepreneurs and are familiar with their goods and services. In this manner, Sub-Saharan African metropolises can function on a very grassroots level, where neighborhoods work like small, autonomous cities out of necessity and an inherited way of doing business. Today, the decorative signs of Sub-Saharan African urbanity are sold and collected as art when their advertising potential runs out. They are highly regarded for their stylized depictions and ardent message, albeit a capitalist one. Sub-Saharan African signs are unlike popular art in that each is an original production, but they are similar in the individualized way in which they target consumers. All across the subcontinent, the ingenuity of small businessmen has turned their ploy to attract the business of their neighbors into an art form, which has rapidly gained popularity around the world.

Tourist Art

A curious spin-off of both popularized indigenous production and urban art in Sub-Saharan Africa is what has become known as tourist art. Although the nomenclature has come to refer to a number of separate kinds of art, tourist or "airport" art is first intended for sale to visitors from outside Sub-Saharan Africa. Therefore, tourist art is only found in those regions of the subcontinent where tourists visit in large numbers. This generally means that Sub-Saharan Africa's large cities, which are the most frequent destinations of foreign tourists, are home to most of the subcontinent's tourist art trade. Tourist art is akin to popular art in its locale, but also in terms of its capitalist purpose and the degree to which the practice of reproduction has come to define this category. Tourist arts are constituted by objects that are fashioned in multiple copies, and they are sold to visitors with the same Sub-Saharan African flair for personal vending that lends the pieces a unique touch. Tourist markets are even staged in the same manner as Sub-Saharan African markets, with a wide range of art objects, fresh produce, meats, and utilitarian goods for sale in many stalls each occupied by a different vendor. Tourist markets may contain many of the same items found in any given Sub-Saharan African market, but they are organized with a particular public in mind and they are conspicuously located in areas of the city that see a lot of tourist traffic.

The main factor that distinguishes tourist art from popularized indigenous production and urban art in Sub-Saharan Africa is the taste of the audience. As previously noted, arts of this nature are defined by their appeal to a general public, whether it be an ethnic group, city, or foreign population. Their taste defines what is on the market, but also is defined by their selection of what is available to them. In the case of tourists to Sub-Saharan Africa, their taste can be broadly defined as wanting objects that are, in their minds, quintessentially African. This is to say that tourists are looking to purchase something that visually connotes Sub-Saharan Africa. It is generally the case for visitors to Sub-Saharan Africa from the West and other parts of the world that their notion of what visually signifies Sub-Saharan Africa is based on stereotypes, which are a symptom of a widespread misunderstanding of Sub-Saharan Africa throughout the world. Through this system of tourist patronage, a realm of artistic production has been defined that resembles other forms of Sub-Saharan African art, but differs in the types of product it necessitates.

As we have already seen, Western art institutions have played a major role in propagating stereotypes of Sub-Saharan African art. The wide-reaching effects of the Western, museological view of Sub-Saharan African art have shaped countless people's perception of Sub-Saharan African aesthetics. When tourists travel to Sub-Saharan Africa they expect to find and purchase objects that reflect the Sub-Saharan African art they have seen in museums, books, and galleries in the West. On the one hand, this means that the genre of tourist art is rife with objects that fit the category of fakery. These objects are produced by Sub-Saharan Africans who have been exposed to the same Western tradition of Sub-Saharan African art through the same types of sources. These people know to expect tourists to their countries to be in the market for similar objects. Therefore, they copy the indigenous forms of their own region and those of other regions of the subcontinent for sale to foreigners. This practice supports the myth that Sub-Saharan Africans are still making such objects as masks and wooden sculpture and that they sell these objects in their own markets. Although this may not entirely be a fabrication, its basis in the misinformed Western art world and not in Sub-Saharan African indigenous practice is what leads this form of art to be called fake and "touristy." On the other hand, this leads foreigners to have certain material expectations of Sub-Saharan African art that, although they may not be that far off, are certainly misconstrued. This is to say that tourists to Sub-Saharan Africa generally expect the artistic production of the subcontinent to come in certain forms such as the aforementioned wooden masks and sculpture. This extends to expectations of colorful textiles with busy prints and objects made from the "primitive" materials of earth and plant matter. Anticipation of finding such objects in Sub-Saharan African markets by tourists leads to the definition of such objects as tourist art because of the assumed audience for which the objects are created, even though they may be similar in many ways to other forms of Sub-Saharan African art.

MODERNIST FINE ART

Another remnant of colonization that colors the arts of Sub-Saharan Africa today is the popularity of modernist fine arts. This includes painting, printmaking, photography, and drawing in the Western tradition, which were integrated into Sub-Saharan African culture through colonial education systems. Forced to assimilate the beliefs and practices of their colonizers in mission schools, Sub-Saharan Africans became likewise interested in the arts of their captors. When the colonial powers at first refused to provide the Sub-Saharan Africans with artistic training, claiming that they were unfit for the fine arts, students became more interested in learning these skills and demanded to be taught. Some struck out on their own and forged careers mimicking the art that was revered by Westerners. Sub-Saharan Africans entered the Western art world in the late nineteenth century when the ideals of the Parisian Salon, which dictated the terms of beauty in the arts for centuries, were in decline. At this time, a more liberal handling of materials arose in the work of the Impressionists, which deviated from the rigid style of the Salon. For Sub-Saharan Africans, who were interpreting foreign arts of Western nations with little or no classical training, this liberated style was very appealing and caught on quickly. Sub-Saharan African artists began producing figurative studies and landscapes in Western materials which they sold to Western patrons. As the arts of the West evolved into abstraction and in turn looked to Sub-Saharan African arts for inspiration in the early twentieth century, Sub-Saharan African artists progressed right along with them.

Today, modernist-style arts thrive in Sub-Saharan Africa with many virtuosic painters, sculptors, printmakers, and photographers working on the subcontinent and in art centers around the world. In every region of Sub-Saharan Africa, Western-style arts have been incorporated into the native canon, where Sub-Saharan African artists have added their own inventions to create works similar to our modern art, but distinct enough to be worthy of mention in their own right. These artists have surpassed the simple copying of Western arts and created whole schools of practice that boast native origins, themes, and patrons. These artists have so far excelled at their trade that Sub-Saharan African variations on Western artistic traditions have won wide acclaim all over the world.

CONTEMPORARY FINE ART

As Sub-Saharan African art in the modernist style has progressed alongside Western art over the past century, it too has arrived at the progressive phase of contemporary art that is popular throughout the subcontinent today. Contemporary fine art in both Sub-Saharan Africa and the West is defined by work that has increasingly tested the boundaries of fine art in terms of its medium, presentation, and message. For instance, contemporary fine art makes use of more photographic techniques today, such as video and film, to create works that are distinct from movies in their frequent lack of narrative, characters, and dialogue. Contemporary artists also produce installations, which is a new genre of art in which objects are placed in physical spaces in a way that is sculptural, but not in the classic sense. Installations can consist of a wide variety of components, but they are usually defined by the inclusion of multiple elements, which are not fused together and which are situated in a space to produce a desired effect. Installations are typically transitory and variable, meaning that they are temporary and can be altered to fit different venues. Installations can be produced in museums or galleries, but they are just as frequently installed in other spaces, wherein the piece's meaning will rely on the space in which it is situated. They can be private or public, but installations always involve some level of manipulation that converts a space in accordance with an intended goal. With the change in materials and methods of display that has seen the rise of photo-based art, installation as well as performance art since the 1960s are a result of the changing meaning of fine art. Art today is more theoretical and less literal than in the past. New methods of creating art have been devised because the old methods are inadequate to express the feelings of our highly developed and rapidly changing society.

In the global society that we live in today, Sub-Saharan Africa and the West have reached a point where both societies are facing the same sets of circumstances, and artists from both radically different traditions are creating similar work in response to similar situations. In today's contemporary art world, many of Sub-Saharan Africa's popular artists no longer even live on the continent. They are African by heritage, and more often than not their work treats the situation of the continent on the world stage, but many successful Sub-Saharan African artists have moved to Europe or the United States to carry out their work. Although this fact speaks to the dismal social conditions of many Sub-Saharan African nations at the present time, it also speaks to the universal vocabulary of contemporary art, in which, at least, this variety of Sub-Saharan African art is relevant, respected, and really understood by the Western art world. Sub-Saharan African art has evolved a long way from its status earlier in the century with regard to the Western art world. Whether this is a good or bad outcome of its relation with the West is not for us to say. What it does allow us to do is to regard Sub-Saharan African contemporary art with an educated eye that gives us a clear window into the world of Sub-Saharan Africans and the problems they face today.

REGIONAL SUBSECTIONS

West Africa

Mali

The reception of Malian art in the West has led to the popularization of the artistic legacies of a number of culture groups from the southwest region of the country. The work of the Dogon, Bamana, and Senoufo has been widely collected by Westerners since colonial times, and the arts of these groups are well known throughout the world. Because of the popularity and proliferation the indigenous practices of these cultures have received, their cultural objects are reproduced and marketed for sale. The plentiful and readily available books on the art of the Dogon, in particular, a culture of cliff-dwelling people with an exceedingly rich iconographic tradition, leads enterprising forgers in city centers to copy their work. The work of these groups that is faked usually consists of painted and unpainted wooden sculpture and masks, which are typically figurative in human and animal forms.

One traditional type of art of the Bamana people, which has caught on throughout Mali and is popularly produced today, is the *bogolan,* or mud-cloth. A bogolan is a cotton cloth that is dyed with a plant-based dye to a deep yellow and then painted with mud. What results are fabrics with deep yellow, red, brown, black, and white colors. The decorations range from geometric patterns (most common) to abstract representations of known objects, in addition to elaborate scenic representations. Bogolans in repetitive patterns are commonly made into clothing for both men and women. Today, bogolans are sold in markets, stores, and art galleries alike to a large cross section of the Malian population. Standard geometrically patterned cloths are priced to be available to all walks of life, whereas cloths depicting people and animals generally sell for more and are treated more like visual art than utilitarian objects. Although there is a great demand among Malians for bogolan textiles, their significance has also reached a larger, global audience through prominent Western collections and museum shows. Therefore, tourists traveling to Mali are frequently on the lookout for bogolan and, indeed, tourist markets provide their fair share of the traditional fabrics to travelers.

In the major urban centers of Mali, in addition to the neighboring Francophone nation of Burkina Faso, models made from recycled materials are a particular popular art form that has arisen out of urban life and consumer culture in West Africa. Commonly conceived as toys because of their similarity with the miniature reproductions of real objects that children play with, this brand of creation consistently blurs the boundaries between commodities, kitsch, and art. The models are fashioned from all manner of discarded materials such as metal, plastic, wood, rubber, and paper, much of which comes from the packaging of consumer goods. Similar to all models, some are rugged and durable, perfect for a child's amusement, whereas others are delicately intricate and intended solely for display. The forms that the models take range from animals to boats, planes, and bikes. They are copied from the visual fabric of everyday life as well as movies, TV, and advertisements. Intentionally or not, the models engage in a compelling dialogue with the consumer culture that fuels their creation by using the market's material waste to mimic luxury possessions such as motorbikes and cars. Vespa scooters and Volkswagens constructed from used insecticide and paint cans have found their place in African homes and art galleries alike because of the relevance, resourcefulness, and skill with which they are made.

ABDOULAYE KONATÉ: A CONTEMPORARY PERSPECTIVE

Mali's most well-known contemporary artist is a man named Abdoulaye Konaté, who lives and works in Bamako. Konaté's art is a combination of painting, textile art, and installation that deals with complex issues of nationhood, religion, and personal identity. Konaté's work reflects the global status of contemporary Sub-Saharan African art, because he treats subjects both native and foreign to Sub-Saharan Africa. In works that deal with the individual's internalization of world politics, Konaté has referenced the struggle between Israel and Palestine, the breakup of the former Soviet Union, and the current tension between the United States and France.

Today, photography abounds as a medium of artistic practice all over Africa. Although the photographic work made in Africa occupies a wide range of styles, subjects, and purposes, corresponding to the vastly different practitioners who produce it, the fathers of African photography came from Mali. In Bamako during the 1960s, when Mali was gaining its independence from France, portrait photographers Malick Sidibé and Seydou Keïta established thriving commercial photography studios that catered to liberated urban Malians. The oeuvre of these two men has become immensely popular throughout Africa and the West because it captures a pivotal moment in African history with style, compassion, and an adept eye for the times. Sidibé and Keïta's photographs document and reproduce the fashion, music, and social lives of Mali's independent African youth, whose tastes are inherited with an original flavor from the French culture of their former colonizers. The men don Western attire straight out of the French New-Wave cinema, and women appear in go-go dresses made of African fabrics and high-heeled shoes. Sidibé and Keïta's work caught a last, prosaic look at a great Sub-Saharan African city transforming under the influence of the West.

Nigeria

Today Nigeria is one of the most progressive and Westernized nations in Sub-Saharan Africa, with the largest city on the continent, Lagos. In a country that has assimilated into the economic and social systems of the West with such vigor, a thriving cultural trade has developed that capitalizes on the rich heritage of the Nigerian people. Home to some of the most fascinating ancient cultures, such as the Nok and the kingdom of Benin, Nigeria's past has long been excavated to the interest of the entire world. Her relics are now very well known and reside in many prominent Western museums. With this blessing also comes the curse of forgery, which has seen Nigeria's cultural artifacts imitated for sale throughout West Africa. In the case of the Nok it is small terra cotta figures, and for Benin it is phenomenal cast brass objects, which can be found in Sub-Saharan African markets as well as with traders who distribute them throughout the West.

With free-market capitalism and the long shadow of the West extending to almost every corner of Nigeria, business interests have also inherited many of the vibrant regional cultures and transformed their cultural capital into real capital. The popular and strong local cultures of Nigeria have evolved with the imposition of capitalism, so much so that today the marketing of cultural goods has reached a massive level. Members of the Yoruba, Igbo, and Nupe, three of Nigeria's largest culture groups, so dominate the social fabric of a large segment of the Nigerian population that their formerly local arts are now filtered through the same economic system that sells consumer goods. Figurative sculpture, beaded objects, decorative arts, and textiles have all been raised to the level of popular art through the subordination of culture to market interests that is inherent in advanced capitalist countries.

All over West Africa, in cities in both Anglophone and Francophone nations (including Nigeria), the use of hand-painted signs has emerged as an artistic spin on advertising. Employed by small businessmen to appeal to neighborhood patrons, these signs are a popular product of various groups' attempt to thrive on the capitalization of culture. Sign-painting workshops have sprung up throughout the region to cater to the ongoing need for this homespun, yet popular form of artistic publicity. The most popular signs, both for their prevalence and their artistic vision, are barbershop signs. These signs display representations of popular hairstyles that are taken from TV, magazines, and movies.

In the realm of classical fine arts no Nigerian collective has fared as well over the last thirty years as the artists of the Nsukka Group. Named for their residence in and around the mostly Igbo city of Nsukka in southeastern Nigeria, the artists of the Nsukka Group have all at some point come through the University of Nigeria, Nsukka. The work of these artists is known for using traditional design principles inherited from both Igbo and non-Igbo regional cultures, and applying these principles to Western artistic media such as painting and printmaking. Artists Uche Okeke, Obiora Udechukwu, and El Anatsui are a few of the bigger names to emerge from the Nsukka school along with artist-turned-critic Olu Oguibe.

The most significant Nigerian contemporary artist is actually not even Nigerian, technically. Yinka Shonibare, a British citizen by birth, grew up in his parents' native Nigeria, where he received some of his formal training. Shonibare possesses one of the dual nationalities that are increasingly common in Sub-Saharan African contemporary art and which are a symptom of today's global culture. Shonibare critically engages his dual perspective on Sub-Saharan Africa and the West to create sculpture, installations, and photographs that deal with how cultural contact between these parts of the world has been portrayed throughout the course of history. Shonibare's most well-known work consists of Victorian and other Western garments made from stereotypically "African" wax-printed textiles, the irony being that the fabrics commonly associated with Sub-Saharan African dress are actually Dutch in origin and still predominantly made in the West.

Central Africa

Cameroon

The most widespread, popular, indigenous artistic tradition in Cameroon is that of the Cameroon Grasslands cultures. Made up of various groups who occupy the western grasslands of Cameroon, such as the Bamoum, Bamilike, Kom, and Mambila, their artistic legacy has come to stand for the art of the whole nation. The Grasslands cultures are known for various artistic forms, which have spread from their homeland throughout the northern half of Cameroon. Through the urbanization of a large region surrounding the capital of Douala, not far from the edge of the Grasslands, knowledge of the local traditions of these cultures spread rapidly. Among the varied creations of Grasslands artists, their wooden stools have received a popular reception at home and abroad. The stools have a corresponding circular base and seat, which are connected with repetitive figurative or geometric carving. Grasslands bags or *kwas* are another traditional art that has grown in popularity. Common kwas are made from grasses or bamboo fibers, which are dyed and woven into bags. Today it is not uncommon to find them sporting popular imagery, such as Bob Marley or black, red, and green pictures of the African continent. A popular pottery tradition has also developed out of the Grasslands cultures, where male potters work in workshops and mass produce ceramic wares for sale at regional markets. Throughout the Grasslands and northern Cameroon, the same styles of ceramic vessels are created by a variety of local cultures for what is today a general usage.

The cultural forms of the Grasslands people in Cameroon have become so well known and repeatedly displayed in the literature and museum exhibitions of this country that a tourist industry based on the reproduction of Grasslands ritual and royal art exists in Douala and larger Grasslands cities such as Bamenda and Bali. Masks, both wooden and beaded, figure largely into the tourist trade as do wooden figurative sculpture, elaborate pipes, and cloth hats. These objects all descend from the rich court art and patronage systems that defined the Grasslands kingdoms of the past. Today, the former Grasslands kingdoms have largely been assimilated into modern governments, but their arts are kept alive by foreign interest and tourist capital.

One of the most recognized contemporary Cameroonian artists is Barthélémy Toguo, whose works in painting, sculpture, collage, photography, installation, and performance have been well received all over the world. Toguo is another one of those global producers who applies a worldview gained through travel and residence in Sub-Saharan Africa and Europe to create art that transcends national boundaries. Toguo's art is particularly poignant when he confronts the relationship between African people and the West. In a series of works related to immigration, Toguo created large mock rubber stamps that were integrated into installations and bore messages refusing passage to Western nations. Images of transportation and global commerce frequently figure in Toguo's work along with concerns about identity formation, which are expressed through such issues as race, gender, and nationality. Both of these subjects are not Africa-specific and thus Toguo's work fits into a larger context of contemporary culture that is common throughout the world.

Democratic Republic of the Congo (DRC)

In the Democratic Republic of the Congo, hundreds of culture groups live side by side in a nation of truly massive proportions. The diversity and similarity among the cultures, their volume, and variety has made the classification of Congolese artistic traditions a mammoth task. Since the beginning of the Belgian colonization of the Democratic Republic of the Congo, much has been made of certain Congolese cultures, such as the Kongo, Songe, and Luba, but little to nothing is known of many others. Such an abundance of unknown cultural forms makes forging Congolese art relatively easy. Although popular items such as Songe masks and so-called power figures (figurative wooden sculpture in various forms) from all over the country are frequently copied for sale because of their prominence, it is just as easy for vendors to fabricate exotic objects and attribute them to the artistic tradition of a poorly documented Congolese cultural group.

One of the indigenous traditions whose arts are popular throughout the Democratic Republic of the Congo is the Kuba kingdom, a culture group comprising smaller local groups who all practice similar arts. Kuba cultures are particularly known for their embroidered textiles, which have been traded throughout the region for centuries. The well-known Kuba textiles are made from raffia, a fiber derived from the leaves of an eponymous palm tree common to central Africa. Kuba cloths have a variety of uses, including clothing and household decoration. They are known for their geometric designs, which are created in earthy shades of brown and can be quite complex.

A great popular painting tradition has arisen in the Democratic Republic of the Congo since its independence in 1960, centered around the country's two major cities, Kinshasa and Lubumbashi. Popular Congolese painting mainly takes two forms: that created on fabric in the style of Western fine art and that which is painted for the community in an indigenous tradition of mural making. The public art of muralists has been a highly influential tool for historicizing the turbulent political and cultural past of the Democratic Republic of the Congo. Whereas foreign historians and theorists committed tomes to the past, present, and future situation of "the Congo," post-independence local muralists took to the streets to portray the same subjects on the walls of buildings as a people's history or a living memory of their times. Differing slightly in tone and approach to works on fabric, murals tackle subjects as wide ranging as slavery, colonization, HIV/AIDS, political strife, comportment, and identity. They can display precise moments in history or great expanses of time through an inventive narrative strategy that overlaps multiple stories in the relation of a larger depiction of an era. One of the most popular figures to appear in urban murals from post-independence to the present is the inaugural prime minister of the Democratic Republic of the Congo, Patrice Lumumba. Prime Minister Lumumba was a popular personage all over Sub-Saharan Africa, and his image is a symbol of the African struggle for self-government and freedom.

Alongside the tradition of mural painting in the Democratic Republic of the Congo, a popular school of fine art painting developed from similar roots. Although they tackle similar topics as the muralists, the Congolese easel painters are able to take more liberty with their images, which have a private (versus public) destination and therefore a diminished audience to please. Despite their smaller audience, paintings on fabric are created in the popular fashion, which is identified by vibrant colors, cartoonish naïveté, and an innovative, formal rigueur that combines text, collage, and inherited imagery to form lush narrative panels. Frequently the works of popular painters satirize Western art forms, popular figures, and the social ills of Sub-Saharan African life such as poverty, disease and corruption. Paintings such as this function as political cartoons, which employ humor to depict social and political realities with an unabashed critical eye. This style of painting has reached such a wide Congolese audience and attracted so many artists to the genre that in 2002 the painters formed an organization called the AAPPO (Association des Artistes Peintres de style Populaire) to act as a labor and professional union. Some of the artists, such as Cheri Samba, have won acclaim throughout the world, and their paintings have earned them considerable local fame as well as a place in prominent Western collections.

Angola

In Angola, where the political instability, forced migration, scarcity of resources, and violence of an intermittent civil war plague daily life, the arts are second to survival for most citizens. However, after decades of conflict, strong nonviolent sentiments have arisen in an attempt to conceptually cleanse the nation's abundant wounds by expressing and working through people's feelings and experiences of war. In the late 1990s, Angolan artist Fernando Alvim produced a traveling exhibition that visited sites all over South Africa and consisted of art by Angolans, South Africans, and Cubans who had been affected by the Angolan civil war. The work of these contemporary artists was largely conceptually based and tackled issues of memorializing the war and archiving the physical, social, and psychological destruction that it caused. Although this work is not very accessible to an audience that was not overtly involved in the Angolan struggle, the act of reconciling the ravages of war through art is a thread shared in many African nations that are combating histories of violence.

Southern Africa

Republic of South Africa

Beaded garments have been a staple of the Zulu people of eastern South Africa since their unification by King Shaka Zulu in the early nineteenth century. Clothing such as aprons, vests, and capes, and accessories such as hats, headbands, necklaces, bracelets, anklets, and belts, are made from glass or plastic beads that are strung together by a variety of yarns and fibers and which are often fashioned in combination with pieces of cloth. In the past, beaded wear was a strong symbol of Zulu identity and served to celebrate and distinguish the Zulu from other cultural groups, while also signifying regional identities and sociopolitical status among the Zulu. Today, the regional differences that lent meaning to variations in beaded garments have largely been outmoded through the half-century-long South African battle with an apartheid government that repressed indigenous cultures and enforced cultural norms. Despite these misfortunes, Zulu cultural traditions have remained strong and have actually spread to other parts of the nation as the Zulu Empire has broken up in the twentieth century. Art and personal adornment with clear ancestry to Zulu beaded wares are popular all over South Africa today. Stripped of their original meaning, these potent cultural symbols persist and are recognized as the popular heritage of the nation as a whole.

One way in which the Zulu beading tradition lives on today is in the creation of HIV/AIDS-related art in South Africa. Plagued with one of the world's worst HIV/AIDS problems, South Africans have been particularly strong in using the arts as a method of building awareness and community support for those suffering from the HIV/AIDS virus. Beaded pins bearing the HIV/AIDS logo and beaded pictures bearing educational messages are among the ways that the Zulu tradition is popularly manifest today. The other HIV/AIDS arts take on many different popular forms, where each object is made in multiple and sold to generate profits to help victims of the HIV/AIDS epidemic, whether it is people diagnosed with the disease or orphans who have lost their families as a result of HIV/AIDS. Many of the artists who make such objects live in rural communes, which are havens for victims of HIV/AIDS, domestic violence, or other tragic circumstances. These individuals create support groups wherein they can grow and learn from their trials, and they earn money to support their community through the sale of art objects that raise awareness of their various causes. Not only is the creative project a revenue generator, it is also a vehicle for victims of violence, injustice, bigotry, and disease to express their feelings and air their grievances. The arts of rehabilitation are now a widespread phenomenon in South Africa, and the work produced by artists in duress has ensured that their cry will be heard well beyond the borders of South Africa.

One of the many popular arts that appeals to South Africa's copious tourist population is telephone wire basketry. The practice of weaving wire baskets developed from a Zulu tradition that used woven wire covers, or *izimbenge*, to decorate their earthenware beer pots. The baskets are made from PVC-covered copper telephone wire, which was previously obtained at scrap yards or through theft but is now readily available to craftsman. The patterns of the early baskets were based on Zulu beaded arts, but they gradually developed as the medium evolved into an art form. Today all manner of themes and motifs can be found decorating wire baskets, and individual craftsman strive to make their mark in the trade through innovative design and striking colors.

In addition to the myriad craft-oriented popular arts, South Africa also has the subcontinent's most vital contemporary art scene. The legacy of the apartheid government, which controlled South Africa until 1994, was disastrous to the nation, but interestingly prosperous for the contemporary art world. The apartheid government in South Africa ensured that although the African population was persecuted, the white, mainly European residents enjoyed a high level of economic and cultural advancement. When apartheid was lifted and the African population was invited into the established cultural networks of galleries, museums, and patrons, they took full advantage of the strong artistic community to make their voices heard. The violence, segregation, and exclusion that all South Africans experienced under apartheid left them with feelings of trauma, confusion, sadness, pain, and anger that found their necessary expression in the arts during the last decade. The new mediums of contemporary art were particularly well suited to give form to these feelings, and South African artists have succeeded in pushing representational boundaries to encompass the unsettling aftereffects of a repressive government.

Zimbabwe

An art form that abounds in urban Zimbabwe today and that is well known all over the world is stone sculpture. Frequently referred to as Shona Sculpture for the ethnic group that makes up a majority of Zimbabwe's population, the art of stone carving is not, nor has it ever been, the work of only one cultural group. The stone sculpture tradition in Zimbabwe grew out of a mid-twentieth century urban population of ethnic Zimbabweans and immigrants who were searching for work because the country was on the cusp of independence. This tradition is by far the most popular stone-carving tradition in Sub-Saharan Africa, and exhibitions of Zimbabwean stone sculpture have toured the world in recent years. Vigorously marketed both in Zimbabwe and abroad, stone sculpture's home today is at the Workshop School in Harare. Here Zimbabweans are instructed in their great national tradition of carving in soft stones such as serpentine, opal, and soapstone, which are native to the region. Initially Zimbabwean sculptors applied their own cultural traditions, mythology, and lived experience to create figurative and representational pieces that could be more or less fluidly inserted into their heritage. As the indigenous cultures of Zimbabwe started to fade from memory later in the twentieth century, carvers shifted their practice to the creation of figurative and abstract art that was more akin to the Western arts of the last century. Today Zimbabwean stone sculpture comes in a wide array of sizes, shapes, and intentions, which account for its diverse audience in Sub-Saharan Africa and beyond.

In Zimbabwe, as is the case for a large part of the countries in Sub-Saharan Africa, tourist art ranges from mass-produced indigenous forms and popular arts to the classic, romantic portrayals of the idyllic natural beauty that is thought to define the subcontinent as a whole. One of Zimbabwe's popular tourist art forms is the paintings in the Weya style. Weya is the name of a women's commune on the outskirts of Harare that became known in the late 1980s for the paintings its members produced as a source of additional income. Weya painting is executed in a naïve or untrained manner and usually portrays local, everyday scenes in vibrant colors applied to board. Although the women of Weya are known for their paintings, they also offer various textile arts in the same format. Today the Weya style has spread and numerous communes have sprung up with the intention of surviving on the cultural trade of their craft objects. The Weya style has also spread to different objects and can be found gracing dishware and T-shirts among other things.

Large-scale art education has, since colonial times, been a defining factor in the development of the arts of Zimbabwe. Representatives of the Church of England were the first to bring Western art education to Zimbabwe in their mission schools, which occupied rural centers such as Cyrene and Serima in the early twentieth century. Generally concerned with the creation of Christian art to decorate church buildings, these schools were significant for teaching art at all and for encouraging Zimbabwean children to make Christian art in a decidedly indigenous style. After independence, Zimbabwean educational administrators were avid about replicating the Western educational system, which resulted in the creation of art schools like the Workshop School (now called the Visual Arts Studio). In addition to adopting Western educational models for the arts, Zimbabwean schools have excelled at spreading Western-style art throughout the nation. As in the mission schools, Zimbabwean artists apply elements from the cosmology and graphic traditions of their culture groups to painting, drawing, and sculpture. Following in the modern art traditions of Europe that coincided with the birth of Western art in Sub-Saharan Africa, Zimbabwean artists tend toward the creation of representational, abstract, and expressionist works that reflect the nature of their contemporary society.

East Africa

Kenya

In the Kenyan capital of Nairobi, an interesting form of marketing transportation and spicing up the impersonal urban experience can be found in the decoration of *matatus*, or passenger buses. Used to transport commuters to and from the city, the system of matatu service has been around since the beginning of the 1980s. As the buses got nicer and competition for fares escalated, matatu owners started advertising different types of music on their buses to entice riders. They painted pictures and wrote the names of featured artists in their buses on the outside of the vehicle in imitation of commercial carriers, which bear pictures of their products and advertising slogans. Figures such as the ever-present Bob Marley, Mariah Carey, and James Brown are frequently cited as well as genres such as Reggae, Dub, Soul, and R&B. As if that was not enough, said music is usually blaring from matatu buses, making them a highly visible mark of culture's marriage with advertising in Nairobi.

After World War II and after the freedom struggle against the British, European tourism to the country developed at a steady pace. Kenyan artisans, familiar with the British through years of colonial rule, began to fashion crafts to sell to the tourists and established an industry that is famous for these products today. The Kenyans are known for the abundance of kitsch art objects that fill tourist markets in the major cities and are similarly exported to the West for sale in specialty exotic goods stores. Among these are carved wooden animals, spoons and utensils, carved soapstone animals, painted gourd objects, woven grass bags, and drums. Their production evolved from workshops in the 1960s and 1970s to factories, which produce the objects today in response to the great demand for them in Kenya and abroad.

Part of the British Empire in the mid-nineteenth century, Kenya inherited the medium of photography from their Western colonizers, which gave breath to one of the earliest Sub-Saharan African photographic traditions. Whether European photographers were engaged in studio or on-site photography, there were Kenyans involved every step of the way. More often than not the Kenyan people found themselves the subjects of the British lens in elaborately decorated studio scenes. If not, they were generally engaged in carrying the bulky equipment of early photography and assisting Europeans on safari-style shoots. It was the studio tradition that left an indelible mark in Kenyan arts, with its showy costumes and fantastic sets, the fiction of which whisked the viewer and subject to faraway places and romantic situations. Today that studio tradition, which was introduced decades ago, is still practiced in Kenya, where the desire to travel and live exciting new lives still appeals to the Kenyan youth. In coastal cities such as Mombasa, entrepreneurial photographers have set up makeshift, open-air studios with crowded, flashy backdrops in which one can have their picture taken. Equipped with bench seats and props, the studios are painted with varied backgrounds including scenes from European and African cities, tropical paradises, soaring planes, and sailing boats. Young Kenyans and tourists alike have their pictures taken with friends as souvenirs or to send to friends and family who have gone abroad.

Tanzania

In Dar es Salaam in the 1970s, a tourist art tradition developed out of the work of a painter who called himself Tingatinga. Named after the adopted moniker of their founder, Tingatinga painters produce brightly colored, stylized renderings of idyllic East African scenes, which frequently include sunny landscapes populated by the famous wildlife of the Serengeti plains. Generally very busy, Tingatinga paintings display crisp, clear colors, which are typically gradated through shading, giving them the feeling of airbrush paintings. The painters who make up the Tingatinga School have little or no artistic training but they work together at communal studios in the city and learn from their peers. There is virtually no market for Tingatinga paintings among Tanzanians and other native East Africans, but they are wildly popular with tourists.

Along the southeastern border of Tanzania, a century-old woodcarving tradition has existed amongst the Makonde people who have migrated to that area from Mozambique. Displaced from their homeland in a search for plantation work during the colonial era, Makonde carvers continued to practice their trade, although removed from the society that gave meaning to their work. After World War II ended the German occupation of Tanzania, European tourists began to travel to the area and buy Makonde sculpture, further distancing it from its significant, religious past. As the demand grew, Makonde sculpture became a popular artistic practice which employed numerous carvers throughout the region. As interest in Makonde sculpture spread, the creativity of the artists developed beyond the inherited cultural traditions handed down from the Makonde of Mozambique. Although battles over the legitimacy of Makonde sculpture have raged in the West over the last 30 years, they failed to put a stop to the active sculptural industry which has continued to expand in southern Tanzania. Today, Makonde sculptors are recognized for their innovation and skill at carving rather than their allegiance to fading sculptural traditions.

Ethiopia

Ethiopia is one of the oldest Christian cultures in the world, and the arts of Ethiopia's past and present clearly attest to the vibrant spirituality of its people. The presence of

Christianity in Ethiopia dates to the fourth century AD and the ancient kingdom of Axum. Christianity was eventually adopted by many of the people of northern Ethiopia, who practice their own strain of the Orthodox faith. The tradition of Christian iconography, which flowed into Ethiopia from Europe, has left its mark on the church itself through a rich tradition of mural painting and the liturgical art of illuminated scripture and prayer books. Over time, biblical subjects were appropriated and reproduced by the Ethiopian people. However, instead of depicting European demeanors, Ethiopians recast the Christian narrative with people who fit their own physical description. In the same way that Ethiopians made the practice of Christianity their own, they reinterpreted its iconography to reflect their own reality. Today a continuous Christian painting tradition survives in Ethiopia and enjoys considerable popularity. By far the most fascinating aspect of this legacy is the way that contemporary artists have retained the medieval style and simply substituted Ethiopian characters for European ones. Undoubtedly proud of their significant history within the Christian faith, Ethiopian artists seek to further promote and celebrate the achievements of their rich heritage. Today, paintings of biblical scenes can be found in both tourist and native markets as well as in the fine art market in Ethiopia, and they remain a powerful symbol of Ethiopian identity at home and abroad.

THE SOCIAL COMMENTARY OF GEORGE LILANGA

One of Tanzania's most visible contemporary artists is George Lilanga. Lilanga hails from the Makonde region of southern Tanzania, although he developed as an artist in Dar es Salaam, where he was influenced by the Tingatinga painters. Drawing on both of these cultural heritages, Lilanga makes paintings and sculptures that best fit under the categories of social critique and caricature. His colorful renderings of partially clothed characters with big lips, noses, and ears mock stereotypical views of Sub-Saharan Africans, while at the same time chastising Africans for playing into the cynical, hell-bound vision that much of the world has of the subcontinent. The playfulness of Lilanga's satire lends it an ease of acceptance that is not present in much of the heavy-handed conceptual art that tackles social woes in Sub-Saharan Africa. For this reason, Lilanga is more widely recognized among Western collectors who enjoy seemingly innocent social criticism over overt social protest in their Sub-Saharan African art.

The popularity of and widespread identification with Christian iconography in Ethiopia, especially in the medium of painting, has led to the advent of derivative genres over time. Familiar with the representation of biblical stories in pictorial terms, Ethiopian artists have long been dedicated to recording the history of their own lived experience in painted scenes. One of the most frequently reproduced scenes over the past century has been the famous Battle of Adowa, where in 1896 the Ethiopians defeated the Italian army to defend their independence. Some of the oldest representations of the battle attest to the direct influence of Christian painting on Ethiopian iconography and also to the confluence between religion and reality for Ethiopian artists. Two such early representations of the Battle of Adowa were painted on the walls of St. Mary Church at Läqämt and St. George Cathedral in Addis Ababa. True to its Christian inspiration, the scene at St. Mary, the oldest known depiction of the battle, features the intervention of St. George on the side of the Ethiopians in the style of a grand biblical tableau (the battle was fought on St. George's day). Often painted in a Medieval style congruent with that of the great Christian murals in Ethiopian churches, depictions of the Battle of Adowa similarly inspire feelings of pride in the Ethiopian people and their imitation of religious iconography is no coincidence. Today, scenes of Adowa, as well as portraits of the legendary Ethiopian ruler Haile Sellassie and other popular subjects, are frequently represented by Ethiopian artists, and they can also be found in markets, homes, and businesses throughout the country.

In the early 1990s, Ethiopia emerged from the socialist dictatorship of Colonel Mengistu Haile Mariam, which took a considerable toll on the social and cultural life of the country. Although the visual arts in Ethiopia were never completely compromised during Mengistu's autocratic rule, the country's art establishment was dealt a serious blow. Many contemporary artists who had been involved with the universities, those who practiced and taught a more Westernized style of art, were forced to take up residency in other countries where they were free to pursue their work. Today this art drain continues to have a considerable effect on the state of the arts in Ethiopia, although in recent years expatriated citizens have begun to return in light of a stable government and significant social improvements. Although in Addis Ababa an art market based on gallery sales to tourists is emerging, there is still a major lack of not only artists, but people skilled in the arts who can repopulate Ethiopian art schools and regenerate the contemporary art market. At this point there is virtually no government funding for the arts and few places where artists can obtain supplies.

Meanwhile, in the West, expatriate Ethiopian artists have enjoyed considerable success since the 1970s. Current surveys of African art attest to the proclivity of Ethiopian artists for traditionally Western media such as painting and installation sculpture, due in part, no doubt, to their historic ties to the arts of Europe. One Ethiopian artist of note is New York–based painter Julie Mehretu. Having lived in the United States for most of her life, Mehretu has developed a process of historical and cultural examination that she calls "self-ethnography." Through abstract canvases, Mehretu riffles through her own history and personality in an attempt to elucidate the social and cultural amalgam that is both her own heritage and that of many contemporary global subjects. Mehretu's work highlights the identity-forming effect of architecture and cartography in particular, which she considers to lie at the heart of today's globe-trotting populace.

Sudan

In Sudan, the arts have suffered greatly over the course of a devastating civil war that has lasted for more than 20 years. The war in Sudan has resulted in a formidable fissure in the country in terms of the quality of life and distribution of resources. In the northern and eastern parts of the country, one finds a relatively dense population with urban centers that support both the folk and fine arts of the citizens. The capital, Khartoum, is home to the College of Fine and Applied Arts, which since the 1960s has been the locus of the Khartoum School of artists who were all related at one time to the university. Led by expatriate figurehead Ibrahim El Salahi, the Khartoum School is known for their practice of *Sudanawiyya,* which applies Sudanese cultural practices to Western artistic styles. The Khartoum School, not unlike the Nsukka Group of Nigeria, is unique because its members have mostly all remained in Sudan to forward their tradition by teaching and cultivating younger artists. The support system fostered by the university provides Khartoum artists with a meaningful outlet for their artistic vision, which in turn keeps them from leaving their homeland. However, as is the case in many African countries today, Sudanese artists have been emigrating to the West for many years to receive more advanced training and increased opportunities. Sculptor and installation artist Amir Nour and painter Hassan Musa have both enjoyed success (in the United States and France respectively).

Although the model of the College of Fine and Applied Arts is replicated to some extent in other northeastern Sudanese cities, the place of fine art in society has changed rapidly in recent years with the increasing influence of radical Islamist politics on culture in the Sudan. Although contemporary Muslim culture is increasingly adapting its standards in light of the changing worldview that most urban citizens hold today, the repressive Sudanese state casts a long shadow over the artistic freedom of Africa's largest country. Thus far the state has been politely tolerant of Sudan's established artistic communities, but this is no guarantee that their acceptance will lead to increased or even continuing support of the fine art establishments of Sudan's urban communities.

In the meantime, what is now a relatively benign force on the arts of northeastern Sudan has had ravaging effects on the indigenous cultures of the southern and western regions of the country. Plagued by civil war, slavery, and genocide since war in the Sudan resumed in the 1980s, the culture and arts of these people are being seriously threatened along with their lives. Once home to the Bari and Dinka people, among others, southwestern Sudan is now rife with ghost towns and refugee camps that are the result of a government-supported initiative to drive the people of southwestern Sudan out of the country. The Bari, Dinka, and their neighbors are largely pastoral people who live in rural communities and survive off the land. Their arts have long consisted of earthenware sculpture, weaving, and beadwork, with a strong emphasis on personal adornment as an outlet for artistic expression. The art of these cultures is deeply tied to the lived experience, rarely resulting in what we call "art for art's sake" but, rather, art that serves to accentuate daily life by imbuing cultural products with the mark of ingenuity, beauty, and, most of all, pride. Suffering under the violence and oppression of a regime hostile to their very existence, the arts of the people of southwestern Sudan are disappearing as rapidly as the citizenry.

CONCLUSION

Surveying a continent as large and diverse as Africa is a delicate practice. In taking stock of the various histories and trends in Sub-Saharan African art, it is possible to observe common currents running through the arts of many, formerly disparate cultures. However, despite the multiple overarching themes in today's popular art of Sub-Saharan Africa, it is still pertinent to study and understand the individual trajectories that led to each current situation. Certainly we must look to the precolonial arts of Sub-Saharan Africa, which were largely functional objects with both quotidian and ceremonial purposes. Then the process of cultural dissolution that the people of Sub-Saharan Africa faced at the hands of their colonizers from the West must be considered in all its facets. Colonial domination, which lasted for more than 400 years in some Sub-Saharan African countries, destroyed indigenous culture by stealing its objects, desecrating its beliefs, and finally replacing it with Western culture. In the process of being dispossessed of precolonial society, Sub-Saharan Africa's art objects lost their cultural significance and history in many instances. Those objects and their meanings were appropriated by Western nations, who shipped African culture back to museums in the West as fast as they could conquer it. Once in the West, the art of Sub-Saharan Africa was recontextualized and reinterpreted according to Western philosophical and religious paradigms. Western art institutions, such as museums and universities, eventually began to emerge in Sub-Saharan Africa, and with their advent, the West started to reeducate the African people on the subject of their own history, art, and culture. At the base of all popular artistic production in Sub-Saharan Africa today, this narrative holds true. Every aspect of contemporary art has been touched, in some way, by the long arm of colonialism. Although this is a general fact across the subcontinent, there are nonetheless countless individual histories that have made each Sub-Saharan African artist's approach to their work unique. Each person and each society has faced their inevitable encounter with the West differently. As a result, it remains important to first look closely at this history before approaching contemporary African art.

The specific histories of Sub-Saharan Africa art are, however, easy to overlook today. Contemporary Sub-Saharan African society has become homogenized as a direct effect of the influence of Western cultural marketing. The term "popular" in and of itself refers to a marketing principle that assumes that the same basic tastes are held by a wide range of people. Popularity emerges from a reciprocal relationship in which universally appealing cultural products both shape and are shaped by the formation of a populace to enjoy them. In Sub-Saharan Africa's urban centers, this process has achieved widespread success in breaking down the individual cultural traits of a myriad of people and replacing their art with homogenized urban culture. In Sub-Saharan Africa, the traditional crafts that have adapted to popular situations and the new art forms that have emerged each trace their current cultural standing to a specific historical trajectory that makes their emergence and existence unique. For example, if Sub-Saharan African artists use trash as a popular medium, it is not because trash is an inherently African medium. Rather, the use of recycled materials in contemporary Sub-Saharan African art is a product of the failure or mismanagement of sanitation on a local level. It so happens that this particular problem is rampant in Sub-Saharan African cities and thus common to a wide range of people across cultures, but each artist's approach to the popular medium reveals a unique encounter with the urban polity. Some take a whimsical approach to garbage, fashioning toys out of cans of insecticide. Other lambaste the disease and pollution that result from poor waste management in some of Sub-Saharan Africa's largest and most developed cities. Although popular art and the homogenization of culture have achieved a level of normality in Sub-Saharan Africa, it is essential to examine the origins and mechanisms of these arts to understand an otherwise generic cultural product.

In the future it will be nearly impossible to stop the great lumbering beast of cultural imperialism from running its course all across the African subcontinent. As new generations of Sub-Saharan African urbanites come of age, more and more of the traditional cultures of their forefathers are being replaced by modernity. Even distant rural regions of Sub-Saharan Africa are beginning to emerge on the world stage in the twenty-first century with cell phones, satellite TV, and the Internet, and they have already begun to accept cultural homogeneity. The traditional Sub-Saharan African art forms that have adapted to a general audience will, however, continue to flourish. These generic cultural products remain a potent register of cultural memory for people who have seen the world of their ancestors completely turned on its head. Urban residents in Sub-Saharan Africa are an especially captive audience for traditional looking arts and crafts, which remind them of their cultural past. This market, which has outlets all over the West and increasingly in Sub-Saharan Africa, should remain strong for years to come.

The twenty-first century will also see the increased popularity of Western-style fine arts in Sub-Saharan Africa. As acculturation proceeds in the subcontinent, both historic Western media, such as painting and sculpture, and contemporary art in new media will similarly begin to appeal to a wider audience. Art galleries, boutiques, universities, museums, TV, and the Internet, which are already becoming ingrained in Sub-Saharan African culture, will usher in an even greater appeal to Western-style fine arts. As has already been the case with this transition, it is safe to predict that Sub-Saharan Africans will continue to make their own interpretations of new media arts, combining them with preexisting systems of art production, distribution, and exhibition. As with the barbers, who colorfully advertise their services in a manner befitting the West and small-town Africa alike, popular Sub-Saharan African art will undoubtedly maintain a nuanced view on Western aesthetics. Look for Sub-Saharan African artists to appear even more prominently in the international art fairs and exhibitions, while augmenting their exposure in Africa at the same time. Outside of the international art world, contemporary Sub-Saharan African art also stands to gain increased attention from private collectors outside of Africa. Major collections of contemporary African art have begun to appear in the West and on the subcontinent, and it follows that mainstream art collectors in the West will soon start to gain an appreciation for current African art rather than fetishizing Africa's cultural past the way they have been for the past few centuries.

RESOURCE GUIDE

PRINT SOURCES

Africa on the Move: Toys from West Africa. [Une Afrique en mouvement: jouets de l'Afrique de l'Ouest.] [Afrika bewegt sich: Spielzeug aus Westafrika.] Plonk & Replonk, Collection. Pierre Pfiffner, photos. With contributions by Stefan Eisenhofer, Karin Guggeis, and Jacques Froidevaux. Stuttgart: Arnoldsche, 2004.

African Arts. Los Angeles: African Studies Center of the University of California, 1967–2006.

Arment, David, and Marisa Fick-Jordan. *Wired: Contemporary Zulu Telephone Wire Baskets.* Santa Fe, NM: Museum of New Mexico, 2005.

ArtSouthAfrica. Cape Town: Bell-Roberts Publishing, 2002–2005.

Becker, Carol. "Amazwi Abesifazane (Voices of Women)." *Art Journal* 63.4 (2004, Winter): 116–134.

Bourgois, Geert G. *Legacies of Stone: Zimbabwe Past and Present.* Tervuren: Royal Museum for Central Africa, 1997.

Ewel, Manfred, and Anne Outwater, eds. *From Ritual to Modern Art: Tradition and Modernity in Tanzanian Sculpture.* Dar es Salaam: Mkuki na Nyota Publishers, 2001.

Gillow, John. *African Textiles.* San Francisco: Chronicle Books, 2003.

Harney, Elizabeth, Jeff Donaldson, and Achamyeleh Debela. *Ethiopian Passages: Contemporary Art from the Diaspora.* Washington DC: National Museum of African Art, Smithsonian Institution, 2003.

Jewsiewicki, Bogumil, and Barbara Plankensteiner. *An/Sichten: Malerei aus dem Kongo 1990–2000.* Vienna and New York: Springer, 2001.

Jewsiewicki, Bogumil, Dibwe dia Mwembu, Mary Nooter Roberts, Allen F. Roberts, Nyunda ya Rubango, and Jean Omasombo Tshonda. *A Congo Chronicle: Patrice Lumumba in Urban Art.* New York: Museum for African Art, 1999.

Jules-Rosette, Bennetta. *The Messages of Tourist Art: An African Semiotic System in Comparative Perspective.* New York and London: Plenum Press, 1984.

Kasfir, Sidney Littlefield. *Contemporary African Art.* London: Thames & Hudson, 1999.

Lamunière, Michelle. *You Look Beautiful Like That: The Portrait Photographs of Seydou Keïta and Malick Sidibé.* Cambridge, MA: Harvard University Art Museums; New Haven, CT: Yale University Press, 2001.

Nka: Journal of Contemporary African Art. Brooklyn: NKA Publications, 1994–2004.

Ottenberg, Simon. *New Traditions from Nigeria: Seven Artists of the Nsukka Group.* Washington, DC, and London: Smithsonian Institution Press and the National Museum of African Art, 1997.

Sibanda, Doreen, ed. *Zimbabwe Stone Sculpture. A Retrospective, 1957–2004.* Harare: Embassy of France and Weaver Press, 2004.

Third Text. London: Kala Press, 1987–2006.

Tribal: The Magazine of Tribal Art. San Francisco: Primedia, 2002–2006.

Wendl, Tobias, and Heike Behrend. *Snap Me One: Studiofotografen in Afrika.* Munich and New York: Prestel, 1998.

World of Tribal Arts, The. St. Peter Port, Guernsey, Channel Islands: Tribarts Ltd., 1994–2002.

WEBSITES

African Colours Network, The. *Africancoulours.* Accessed February 2007. http://www.africancolours.net/.
Art in South Africa. Accessed February 2007. http://www.art.co.za.
Fung, Karen. *African Art on the Internet.* Stanford University Library. Accessed February 2007. http://library.stanford.edu/africa/art.html.
Shaggag, Iman. *Sudan Artists Gallery.* Accessed February 2007. http://www.sudanartists.org.

EVENTS

Dak'Art: Biennale de l'Art Africain Contemporain. Dakar, Senegal. Every 2 years. Appearing for its eighth installment in 2009, *Dak'Art* attracts artists, curators, scholars, and fans from all over the world. Its focus remains Africa-specific, but its breadth spans the global experience of the African Diaspora.

Trienal de Luanda: Arte, Cultura, História, e Política Contemporânea. Luanda, Angola. Every 3 years. The first version of this international art exposition took place in 2005–2006 with events and exhibitions on a fairly small scale. Look for its much anticipated return in 2009 as a major contender among African art expos.

ORGANIZATIONS

Diversity Art Forum, Learning Resources Centre, University of East London, Docklands Campus, Royal Albert Way, London E16 2QJ, United Kingdom. http://www.uel.ac.uk/aavaa. Formerly called the African and Asian Visual Artists' Archive, this research institution houses information on African artists working in the United Kingdom from the postwar period to the present.

The Melville J. Herskovits Library of African Studies, Northwestern University, 1970 Campus Drive, Evanston, IL 60208, United States. http://www.library.northwestern.edu/africana/index.html. The largest separate library for African studies in the world, the Herskovits Library is open to the public for research on all areas of African studies. In addition to printed resources the library houses historic photographs, archives, posters, art work, and pop culture ephemera.

Musée du quai Branly, 37, quai Branly, portail Debilly, 75007 Paris, France. http://www.quaibranly.fr. A brand new museum dedicated to the cultures of Africa, Asia, Oceania, and the Americas. It is a powerhouse institution that combines the collections of the Musée des Arts Africains et Océaniens and the Musée de l'Homme, among others.

Museum for African Art, 36-01 43rd Avenue at 36th Street, Long Island City, NY 11101, United States. http://www.africanart.org/. A prominent museum of African art that hosts original exhibitions of popular, contemporary, historic, and ethnographic art.

National Museum of African Art, Smithsonian Institution, 950 Independence Avenue, SW, Washington, DC 20560, United States. http://www.nmafa.si.edu. The largest museum and archive of Sub-Saharan African art in the United States, the National Museum of African Art has an extensive collection of historic and contemporary arts. The museum features traveling and permanent exhibitions as well as public programming and they facilitate research at their facilities.

Royal Museum for Central Africa, Leuvensesteenweg 13, 3080 Tervuren, Belgium. http://www.africa museum.be. Originally built to house King Leopold's plunders from the Congo, this is the most comprehensive museum of central African art, especially that of Belgium's former colony.

WAMP Programme des Musées de l'Afrique de l'Ouest, 11 route du Front de Terre Villa No. 6, Dakar, Senegal. http://www.wamponline.org. Celebrating its twenty-fifth year in 2007, the WAMP (West Africa Museums Program) is an association of Western-style museums in West Africa that supports cultural events, exchange, and education using, among other publicity tools, blogging.

FASHION AND APPEARANCE

MARTHA DONKOR

Peoples and cultures everywhere in the world have their own sense of fashion and appearance, depicted in the clothing they wear on a daily basis and on special occasions, and also in the ways they adorn the body and hair. Yet when we refer to fashion, our attention is immediately drawn to London, Paris, Rome, and New York. These are the places where haute couture reigns, and where people look to new trends in fashion to modify local tastes. Standards of fashion and appearance are rarely, if ever, linked with Africa. But as culture-bearing people, Africans have their own unique sense of fashion that has evolved with time. And that evolution is the more interesting because of cultural diffusion. Countries on the eastern coast of Africa interacted with the people of the Arabian peninsula long before the Europeans arrived in West Africa. Both the Arabs and Europeans introduced their modes of dress in areas in which they settled, and these modes were in turn incorporated into what was already in existence. Thus, when we talk about fashion in Africa, we are talking about the blending of the fashion traditions of three continents into forms that are unique and yet universal.

Many non-Africans assume that Africa has a homogenous culture and hence do not make distinctions when thinking about fashion in Africa; but there are thousands of cultures that have reached varying degrees of material progress and hence different levels of fashion sophistication in Africa. For example, the so-called pygmies (Mbuti) in the Congo forests, who are one of the few remaining forager groups in the world, may cover only their private parts with strips of fabric. However, in the same country and among nonforaging groups the situation is entirely different. As such it is difficult, in fact impossible, to make generalizations about what people wear in Africa or what informs what they wear. Generally, Africans dress to reflect class, educational, ethnic, gender, and religious backgrounds. They also dress to make a statement. "Clothing in tropical Africa is certainly not intended to cloak one's personal feelings. In Africa you wear your heart on your sleeve. Passion, meekness, unbridled joy, deep sorrow, pride, admiration, impassioned protest—clothing reflects all these expressions."[1] Clothes and body adornment express the aesthetic, political, social, and spiritual philosophy of a group, and these are reflected in the colors, motifs, and styles that group members design their clothes in or adorn their bodies with.

Gender is an important influence on fashion in Africa. Wherever they live and whatever their educational background, women in most African countries wear a blouse over a long skirt or wrapper, over which, depending on age, one may wear a cover cloth. The head tie is a common item of African women's daily wear, even when they braid or perm their hair. Many women working in the public space as professionals do not usually put on a head tie when they wear business attire; however, on special occasions they, too, may wear the traditional long skirt/wrapper and blouse with a head tie. Pants, especially jeans, are not very popular among women, especially older women. On the other hand, men wear pants and shirts and T-shirts as daily or work wear. In rural West Africa, where people are generally nonliterate, men are more likely to wear large pieces of cotton fabric (8 to 12 yards depending on a man's size) that they wrap around the body. In rural East Africa men wear a tunic made of white muslin over pants. Among some ethnic groups there is a link between education and dress. The Akan of Ghana refer to nonliterate people as *fira tamfoo*, literally meaning "people who wear traditional cloth" whereas "literate female," *awuraba*, and "literate male," *krakye*, do not have connotations with dress. The Igbo of Nigeria also distinguish between *irosi* and *ibele*, the former referring to the ways educated people dress, and the latter to the dress of nonliterate people. However, in colonial Kenya Christian converts were referred to as *jo-nanga*—"people of the cloth"—apparently due to the dresses they got from the missionaries.

As in colonial Kenya, religion continues to influence fashion and appearance. African Muslims, similar to their counterparts everywhere, can be identified easily by dress. The women wear the veil and the men wear the traditional long, straight dress with a cap or turban. African traditional priests and priestesses wear amulets and charms on their dresses, arms, and legs, and may wear hair in locks and twists adorned with cowrie shells and other charms. These adornments distinguish them from the youth who wear hair in twists and locks as fashion.

A person's economic situation also determines what he or she wears. The quality of fabric used to make a dress and the amount and quality of embroidery in the dress usually tells whether the person wearing such dress is a person of means or a poor person. In Ghana, the Ivory Coast, and Nigeria, Hollandais, one of the line of Vlisco-manufactured textiles (also called Real Dutch Wax), is considered to be of better quality than locally manufactured prints. Akosombo and Tema, prints produced in cities in Ghana with those names by the Ghana Textiles Print (GTP) are considered to be of lower quality than Vlisco, although GTP is a Vlisco affiliate. Hollandais is "prestige" fabric, the "cloth with name" and therefore more desirable. Poor people who cannot afford Hollandais on a regular basis generally wear lower-quality, locally manufactured prints. When they manage to buy Hollandais, they use it on special occasions. In Nigeria, where lace is a fabric of choice, the type of lace that a person uses to make a dress makes a statement about the person's class background. Cheap lace gives the impression that the person is either poor or has bad fashion taste. Similarly in Kenya, the quality of accessories worn with a *kanga* distinguishes poor women from women of means. And yet in Ethiopia, locally manufactured, hand-woven cotton cloth called *shama* is desired regardless of class background.

Ethnicity accentuates gender and class distinctions in dress and appearance, especially among those individuals who still favor more traditional modes of adornment. The Maasai of Kenya can be identified by body painting, hairstyle, beaded necklaces, and the red cloth that they wrap around their bodies. The Frafra of Ghana, Mossi of Burkina Faso, and Yoruba of Nigeria wear facial marks to denote ethnic identity, whereas in Chad men, women, and children braid their hair and wear big earrings from end to end of the ear. The Karo of Ethiopia make small incisions in intricate patterns on women's bodies, especially in the abdominal area, in which they apply special ashes so that when the wounds heal, the skin is raised in patterned keloids that are considered beautiful. In Kenya, in the early 1950s, people wore hair in twists and locks to denote that they were freedom fighters, whereas in Ghana and the southeastern portions of the Ivory Coast, a person wearing his or her hair in twists and locks would have been a traditional fetish priest or priestess. It is common these days to see people, mostly young men, in these countries wear hair in locks not as a religious symbol or political statement but as a new fashion trend copied from Africans in the diaspora. Some ethnic groups in southern Sudan, notably the Dinka and Nuer, extract four lower front teeth when children of both sexes are initiated into adulthood. Among the Xhosa of South Africa, boys are circumcised during initiation rites to usher them into adulthood. Although many of these patterns and practices are no longer universal or even predominant, fashion and appearance in Africa remain diverse and rich and rooted in particular social and cultural settings.

It is also important to state that some Africans have been led to believe that light brown or fair skin tone is more beautiful than a dark hue and they have used creams to lighten their skin. Bleaching, as the practice is commonly called, has been popular among women in many African countries since the 1960s, in spite of warnings of the dangers that the practice poses. Local and international manufacturing companies such as Narrow Pharmaco, PZ, SIVOP, Labo Derma, and Skyros International manufacture hydroquinone-based products especially suited to black skin. The names of the products and the images that are used to market them draw links between beauty and light skin. Product names such as Fair and White and Peau Clair and the images that go with them depict light skin as beautiful. Although these are marketing strategies, they nonetheless attract women to bleach their bodies by spending hundreds of dollars a year on cosmetic creams and soaps. Bleaching is more popular among semi- and nonliterate women in both rural and urban areas than it is among literate women. Men seldom bleach, and the few who do are usually young men in the entertainment industry.

Apart from color, another marker of beauty for many Africans is a full body. A thin build is generally considered a sign of deprivation, disease, or poverty. But there is another functional aspect to having a strong, full body. Large proportions of African populations are subsistence agricultural workers who perform physically demanding labor. Such people need well-built bodies to perform daily survival tasks. And in the wake of the AIDS pandemic, a person looking thin may draw the wrong kind of attention and conclusion.

There is also a link between a full body and dress. The long skirt and blouse that women wear or the large piece of fabric that men wrap around their bodies looks better on a full and curvaceous body than on a slender build. That is not to say that Africans celebrate "fat." In fact, in most places, people work so hard, sometimes have so little to eat, and burn so many calories that they cannot grow fat. In other instances—as is happening in Chad, Niger, and Mauritania, where famine has led to starvation, or in Angola and Sudan, where civil war has created food shortages—people simply do not become overweight. Even then, there is a distinction between a shapely figure and a fat one, and public health education in some countries is increasingly drawing attention to the need to "stay smart." In the late 1980s and for most of the 1990s, "keep fit" clubs were in full swing for middle class people in major towns in southern Ghana. In Accra, Dimples lnn led the way by fitting a gym where patrons and club members could go for daily keep-fit exercises.

Apart from keeping their bodies in shape, Africans have used herbs and seeds as perfumes and soaps for centuries to keep their bodies clean. In West Africa women grind cloves, linseed seed, and a kind of plant stem, into a mixture that gives off a pleasant fragrance. This perfumed mixture can be put in bath water or smeared on the body.

In Burkina Faso, northern Ghana, and the Ivory Coast, women put special herbs in shea butter to improve its scent and then use it as daily body oil. Shea butter is also used as hair moisturizer and growth cream. Somali women "smoke" themselves with *unsii*, a special herbal mixture that keeps them smelling fresh for hours even when they cover their entire bodies with thick garb as part of their Islamic faith. In Ethiopia, *etari*, incense that is produced from the sap of acacia trees, is burned around the house for its pleasant smell. In Ghana, after working for hours on farms, Akan women might take the leaves of a special shrub, rub them in the palms to release the aroma, and then put them behind the ears to mask the smell of sweat. And in rural areas some married Akan women might eat roasted dry corn to keep their mouths smelling pleasant before they go to bed. In many places people continue to use cut stems of special trees to clean teeth. The sap from these trees contains ingredients that prevent tooth decay and ensure strong, white teeth. In spite of the introduction of toothpaste, many Akan continue to use plantain fiber and charcoal to clean, for dazzling white teeth and an odor-free mouth.

FASHION TRENDS ACROSS SUB-SAHARAN AFRICA

Much of what we know about fashion in Africa prior to European contact in the fifteenth century comes from accounts left behind by Arab chroniclers. Ibn Battuta, a celebrated Arab traveler and writer who visited West Africa in the fourteenth century AD, described the vestments of the kings of ancient Ghana as made of rich fabric and adorned with gold. State officials also wore the "trouser of honor," a pair of white cotton pants with a broad seat and narrow legs that increased in seat size as the official gained more royal recognition. Although Ibn Battuta did not describe daily wear for ordinary people, we are left to guess that they too may have dressed in plain white cotton clothes. And given that the peoples in West Africa engaged in trade with the peoples across the Sahara for centuries, they may have obtained some items of clothing from southern Europe, notably Spain and Portugal, to modify or improve the ways they dressed. By the late nineteenth century explorers in Nigeria were reporting that Yoruba chiefs wore layers of rich silk and velvet clothes. Chiefs also gave dresses to loyal friends and officials during annual festivals to buy their continued support. The quality of dress given to subjects matched the position of the recipient. High-ranking officials received high-quality dress.

In his book *Trade and Politics in Africa,* K. Y. Daaku observed that one of the important items of trade between Africans and Europeans was cotton cloth.[2] The seeming fascination with cotton cloth was not necessarily part of Africans' rush to consume European goods. Africans living in the Sahel, the region immediately south of the Sahara, developed the art of weaving, which also suggests that they cultivated cotton. Women spun cotton into yarn on spindles and men wove the yarn into cloth on handlooms. Strips of woven fabric were sewn together to form large pieces of cloth that people wore by wrapping them around the body. Women usually wore them in two pieces: one from the waist down to the ankle and another piece from the chest down to the waist. In the mid-nineteenth century, European travelers who pushed into the interior of what is now the Ivory Coast described indigo pits that were used to dye white cotton cloth into different hues of blue. However, in Ethiopia, woven cotton was not dyed; rather, weavers used colored thread to make a patterned layer at the selvedge. Thus, Africans took advantage of European trade and learned new ways of diversifying fashion.

Regardless of local variations in fashion, the Islamic long tunic is fast becoming the fashion statement across Africa. In spite of the emerging popularity of the tunic, often called the *boubou*, as a common form of dress across Africa, Western dress styles are more prevalent. Men from modest circumstances usually wear pants and shirts in everyday activities, but on formal occasions they revert to traditional attire, whereas women in this category seldom wear Western-style dresses. In some farming communities, however, they may wear pants and shirts as farm gear to protect their bodies from insect bites and thorns. Reflecting the legacy of colonial influence, educated men usually wear Western-style dress on formal and informal occasions, and their female counterparts combine Western and traditional attire at home and at work. It is also interesting that some Pentecostal churches forbade clergy and other functionaries to wear African dresses and accessories at church ceremonies because these were believed to depict heathenism. Although these churches may not hold the same beliefs today, their functionaries have continued the practice of not wearing African attire at church functions.

Children mostly wear Western dress, even in extremely poor areas, because of access to the secondhand clothes market and also gifts of clothing from charitable organizations abroad. Indeed, Western dress has become so entrenched in African societies that in some countries governments and fashion designers are making conscious efforts to encourage Afrocentric fashion to get people to be proud of their traditional modes of dress, a situation that may partly explain the emerging popularity of the boubou. The Ghana Broadcasting Corporation (GBC) is notable in this regard. Newscasters seldom wear Western-style suits during newscasts. The current president of Ghana was inaugurated wearing the traditional *kente* cloth. President Obasanjo of Nigeria and former South African President Nelson Mandela usually wear boubou or shirts made of African prints as proud symbols of their African background.

The dressmaking industry is fairly well developed in Africa. Tailors and seamstresses abound in cities and towns, and even in small villages there are individuals who carry sewing machines around to mend tattered clothes. Among the Akan of Ghana these people are called *oye adie yie*, literally meaning "one who makes it right."

THE BOUBOU

The long tunic worn by Muslims has become popular throughout Africa, with Christians and traditional believers of both sexes in almost all age groups wearing it in different styles. Instead of the plain white cotton gown that Muslims traditionally wear, the new fashionable outfit is made of brocade, georgette, linen, or cotton fabrics with African motifs and sewn in a variety of styles. The outfit has different names among different cultural groups, although *boubou* (*bubu*) is emerging as the generic name. In Nigeria the Hausa call the male boubou *babariga*, and the Yoruba call it *agbada*. In Ghana it used to be called *batakari* or *fugu*. Boubou may be worn as a single straight outfit, as a trouser and gown combination, shorts and shirt outfit, skirt and shirt combination, or as a four-piece outfit for men comprising trousers, straight dress, an outer flowing cover dress, and a cap. These pieces are usually elaborately embroidered. Although the shorts/skirts and shirt or trousers and gown combinations may be worn as casual wear, the four-piece attire is usually used as a formal wear. When women wear boubou, the headgear may not necessarily be made in the same material as the dress.

AFRICAN CONTRIBUTION TO FASHION

Although African fashion has had a definite presence and influence on the global fashion scene, especially since the 1960s, it has not made an overwhelming impact. One might suppose that cool and colorful cotton prints would appeal to the international community, especially in summer, but that has not always been the case. Africans in the diaspora are the main patrons of African fashion abroad and they do so to affirm their African roots. African Americans in particular are increasingly wearing dresses with African motifs as a way of establishing spiritual and cultural links with the ancestral homeland. In this regard, the kente cloth has emerged as a symbol of African identity. Priests, pastors, and students often wear the kente stole at important public ceremonies. Men also wear caps and ties made of kente and other African fabrics. The boubou has also caught on with African Americans. At African-centered cultural events African Americans wear boubou in solidarity with Africans from the continent. And, of course, African immigrant communities in Euro-American cities continue to wear traditional African outfits and support fashion shows mounted by African designers.

Some international fabric and fashion houses have also helped to popularize African textiles and dress. Vlisco, a Dutch company established in 1846 and headquartered in Helmond, Holland, manufactures high-quality textiles principally for an African market. Vlisco started exporting to Africa in 1909, after African soldiers returning from the Dutch East Indies (Indonesia) popularized batiks they brought home with them. In 1921, Vlisco became a trading partner with the United Africa Company (UAC) to sell Real Dutch Wax. Vlisco uses local motifs and traditions behind those motifs to make statements about what people wear. For example, an Akan wife who feels betrayed by her husband (perhaps for taking a second wife) may buy *obarima nye sumie*, literally meaning "a man is not a pillow." Since a pillow cushions and gives comfort, a woman who buys a fabric with that name makes an important statement about spousal trust through dress. However, not every Vlisco fabric makes such a statement. There are elegant, glossy finished fabrics called "Aura," whose designs do not have traditional symbolism but that are desired for their sheer beauty and quality. Although Vlisco markets its products to the international community, non-African patrons usually do not use the fabrics with African motifs to make clothing. They may buy them instead for quilts or for other interior decoration purposes.

Another reputable fashion house is Woodin. A British citizen with that name who lived and traded in fabrics in the Ivory Coast in the 1890s began the company and named it after himself. In 1911 he sold his business to a French textiles company that also operated on the Ivory Coast. In 1985 the company adopted Woodin as its official name. Woodin has come to represent quality and elegance in African fabrics. Unlike Vlisco, Woodin also markets ready-made dresses and T-shirts. Woodin and Vlisco have formed a marketing partnership to sell their products principally in West African countries and in South Africa. Together, the two companies are causing a fashion stir in Africa. Vlisco, however, has affiliate companies in many West and Central African countries, where cheaper versions of their acclaimed textiles are produced to cater to local pockets. Even with stiff competition from China and other East Asian countries, Vlisco and Woodin continue to be extremely popular in Africa.[3]

Apart from textile manufacturers, there are fashion designers who are leading the way in popularizing African fashion on the international scene. Designers such as Seidnaly Alphadi and Esterella (Cameroon), Farouque Abdela (Tanzania), Gigi and Sara Abera (Ethiopia), and Oumou Sy (Senegal) have burst on the fashion scene with verve and style. They combine rich African textiles and European designs in making elegant dresses for all occasions. Although international fashion houses support African designers in fashion shows, the African products have not attracted non-African patrons as much as one would wish. In other cases, trade restrictions simply limit designers without international exposure from marketing their products abroad.

REGIONAL SUBSECTIONS

West Africa

Ghana

As in many developing countries, there are few data relating to the amount of money that Ghanaians spend on fashion and appearance. And, although fitness clubs mushroomed in cities in the late 1970s and early 1980s, there is not a systematic body of data that detail the activities of these clubs and their success rates. Nonetheless, fashion changes relatively rapidly in Ghana. Geography and ethnicity appear to have the biggest impact on changes in fashion and appearance. Southern Ghana is the hub of fashion, and the Akan ethnic group, with a strong base in Kumasi, sets the pace in influencing new fashion trends in Ghana.

The kente cloth, which has been a distinctive feature of Ghanaian culture, originated among the Akan. The Akan use colorful linen thread to weave kente. Strips of woven kente are sewn together by hand. Each strip of cloth can have one or several motifs that have specific meanings. Different colors mixed with different motifs produce intricate designs that have been the unique characteristic of kente. Modern advances in technology have not changed the technique of producing kente fabrics. Authentic kente cloth is still produced on hand looms and sewn together by hand. Women do not work the loom, although they generally market the finished products. Factory-manufactured kente cloth, especially from China and the Ivory Coast, has not diminished the market for locally produced versions. Kente used to be the cloth of royalty and ceremony among the Akan. Chiefs wore it at festivals and other important state functions. Its use is widespread now, and ordinary people who can afford to buy it use it on special occasions. However, chiefs wear exclusive designs that distinguish them from other users. In combination with gold ornaments, kente exudes opulence and importance.

A significant aspect of fashion in Ghana is the rapid pace of change. There have been dramatic changes in fashion and appearance since the 1960s, and much of the change appears to have come from the Western world, especially Western Europe and lately the United States. During the latter part of the colonial era and early in the national period, educated men dressed more conservatively, wearing suits and hats just like the English colonial masters they were replacing. Educated women wore pleated dresses and skirts and blouses with shoes. They relaxed hair with the stretching comb and pulled it on top of the head in a bun. Still, many men, women, and children continued to dress in traditional ways. In the early 1960s Ghanaians were still celebrating a new sense of national pride after gaining independence from Britain in 1957. During the same period the Civil Rights movement was empowering African Americans. Ghanaians were deeply influenced by the movement because of historical association with the United States. Prominent African Americans such as W. E. B. Du Bois and George Padmore saw Ghana as their ancestral home and actually lived there for part of their lives, and died and were buried there. Similarly, the man who led Ghana to independence, Kwame Nkrumah, attended graduate school in the United States. These links were very important in exposing Ghanaians to political and social changes occurring in the United States.

Perhaps for this reason, fashion trends that accompanied the Black Power movement soon caught up with a large section of the Ghanaian population. The new trends were not necessarily restricted to educated people, although rural folks and those in the north did not exhibit the same level of fashion change as those in southern towns and cities. Men wore bell-bottomed trousers with big hooked belts, tight shirts, and high, block-heeled shoes. Women wore mini-dresses and mini-skirts, Afro wigs, and platform shoes that were called "guarantee" shoes. Women also began wearing pants for public functions, but these were urban, educated young women. Some churches did not approve of women wearing "men's clothes" and would not allow women wearing pants to participate in church rites. By the mid-1970s Afro wigs had given way to more curly ones, especially those worn by television personalities. Wigs were named after character names in a popular Sunday evening comedy show called *Osofo Dadzie*. Popular among the names were "Baby Nayooka" and "Akua Boahemaa." At the same time women were wearing the *pantalone* (French for trousers), which was in fact a new way of wearing the traditional two-yard wrapper that they held in place with a cord around the waist. Instead of wearing the fabric loose, it was sewn together as a straight, long skirt. Although pantalone became popular, it was difficult to walk in because it did not allow for enough leg movement. Quickly, dressmakers improved on the pantalone by making an opening at the back or side of the skirt. The new version was appropriately called *slit* and that has been the name to this day. The blouse that goes with the "slit" is called *kaba*, and it is this that usually determines the level of sophistication of the wearer. The more elaborate the style, the more fashionable it is assumed to be.

Wigs, guarantee shoes, and bell-bottomed trousers became less popular in the mid- to late 1970s. Indeed, men who wore "bell" (as they were called) were referred to as "colo"—short for colonial, but local parlance for old-fashioned. Straight, narrow-mouth trousers became the craze for men. Wigs gave way to perms and guarantee shoes to "pencil heels" for women. Students experimented with their own brands of fashion on college campuses, and their focus was on hair. In the mid- to late 1970s the trend was toward the "flat top," but by the 1980s "back bushy" was in vogue, and both boys and girls patronized the trend. By the early 1990s "punk" had become the new hair trend on campuses across the country, and it became so popular that it spilled into the larger society. And yet, by the close of the decade, "punk's" reign had come to an end. Male students are now wearing hair low-cut and female students wear braids or permed hair, a trend that is in tune with the ways the larger population wears hair. People in the entertainment industry, especially performers, usually wear hair in dreadlocks.

In terms of dress, batiks, also called tie-and-dye, became very trendy, and probably marked the appearance of the boubou as a "national dress" in the 1980s. The vibrant colors and glamorous patterns of batik fabrics made them particularly suitable for boubou outfits. But, as is characteristic of fashion in Ghana, batiks soon acquired a nickname. "Adwoa Yankey," the title of a song by a local musician, became the catcall for batiks and drove people away from patronizing such fabrics. By the early 1990s the fabric of choice was linen. Since the mid-90s lace and its derivatives have been very popular among fashion conscious Ghanaians, including those in the diaspora. These fabrics make elegant boubou outfits, so that even though the choice of fabric keeps changing, the styles have not changed significantly since the 1980s.

Reflecting fashion trends in Ghana, dressmaking and hairdressing are major industries, especially among female school dropouts. It used to be the practice for women to buy sewing machines not because they intended to learn sewing but to pass them down to their daughters who might learn to sew. In addition, parents demanded sewing machines from men who impregnated school-aged girls in hopes that the girls would learn to sew. And those who could afford to sent their girls to Mancell's, a premier vocational institute for girls that specialized in sewing. By the late 1970s, vocational schools for girls and young women had sprung up all over southern Ghana, and many specialized in sewing. Vocational schools are less popular now, and girls who cannot afford this type of training take up apprenticeships with more established dressmakers. Boys, on the other hand, do not go to vocational schools to learn sewing. Rather, they too learn by apprenticing themselves to master tailors. But although women generally specialize in women's fashions, men specialize in both women's and men's fashions. Women are also more likely than men to make children's dresses.

In addition to having dresses made at local dressmakers, a significant minority of Ghanaians buy clothes from boutiques. These boutiques, mainly in the large cities, cater to men, women, and children. They sell ready-made clothes imported from Asian countries as well as from Britain, France, Italy, and the United States. Designers such as St. Ossei, Kofi Ansah, and Amegashie usually sell their products abroad and in popular boutiques, such as Menleo in Accra. Others buy their clothes on the open market in major towns and cities across Ghana. At these open markets, used clothes, also called "foes," are sold at affordable prices, which makes it possible for very many people to clothe themselves fairly decently.

In spite of the high cost of living in Ghana, people spend large sums of money on clothes and other accessories to enhance their looks. Six yards of Real Dutch Wax (which is the standard for making a blouse, slit, and cover cloth for women) would sell anywhere from 400,000 to 800,000 cedis;[4] men need between 10 and 12 yards. High-quality brocade, organza, and lace fabrics are more expensive, ranging from 1.5 million cedis to 1.8 million cedis for 6 yards. Cosmetics are relatively less expensive, but because people use them in different combinations, they end up spending quite a bit on cosmetics on a monthly basis. Meanwhile the average monthly salary is ¢800,000, meaning that people cannot buy more of the high-quality, expensive fabrics. For such people, tie-and-dye, cheap imports from China and Korea, and foes from Canada and the United States fill that need.

Nigeria

Nigeria is oil rich and has a significant class of affluent people. It is also ethnically very diverse and further divided by religion. Thus, class, ethnicity, and religion influence the ways people dress in that country. Different ethnic groups have distinctive ways of dress that give them cultural identity, although generally, people dress lavishly in Nigeria. Fabrics of choice include lace, jacquard, *adire*, tie-and-dye, and *ankara*. As in other parts of West Africa women wear a blouse over a wrapper and complement it with head wear. But unlike other West African women, Nigerian women do not usually use the same fabric to make an entire outfit. They combine different fabrics in elaborate fashion to produce elegant results. For example, a Yoruba woman will wear a lace *buba*, a loose neck blouse with long sleeves, over an *iro* or wrapper, and use an *aso oke* as cover cloth and head wear. A woman may also wear the *iborun* or *ipele*, a scarf that she would tie around the neck or across the body. Young women and girls usually wear *kaba*, or straight dress. The *gele* or headgear is an essential accompaniment of Nigerian women's dress.

Men wear boubou, called agbada in Yoruba and babariga in Hausa. They also wear Western-style dress—trousers, shirts, and suits. Agbada/babariga can be worn as a four-piece outfit consisting of the *buba* (shirt), *sokoto* (trousers), *agbada* (outer gown), and *fila* (cap). The buba and agbada are usually elaborately embroidered. In the north, where there is the largest concentration of Muslims, both young and old men wear the tunic, which can be modified to reflect a person's social standing. Rich people use more expensive lace and fine cotton brocade fabrics to make their outfits and low-income people use tie-and-dye or plain white cotton. Muslim women may put the veil on top of the gele, on their arm, wear it as cover cloth, or cover their head with it.

Young southern girls and women wear dresses, skirts and blouses, and trousers and shirts. The latter is particularly gaining in popularity because of the large diasporan population. Nigerians living abroad go home and sport casual Western wear such as jeans and T-shirts and sneakers. These outfits have become popular and young people of both sexes in urban areas are increasingly wearing them. Adults and children who cannot afford new and expensive Western dresses can always buy secondhand clothes sold on open markets across the country. As well, ready-made dresses and fabrics of different qualities are also sold on the open markets. Boutiques cater to the needs of the wealthy. Multinational stores such as United African Company (UAC) and Kingsway compete with the local fashion industry. In spite of the high fashion sense, Nigeria does not have many textile mills. Aso oke, adire, and tie-and-dye are locally manufactured and relatively inexpensive. However, lace, jacquard, brocade, Real Dutch Wax, and other prints that are imported are more expensive. A yard of quality lace fabric could sell for 15,000 niara (approximately $117 U.S.); meanwhile a man would need at least 6 yards to make an agbada.

Senegal

Modern-day Senegal is the cradle of important civilizations in West Africa, where Muslim Arabs and, later, Europeans converged to do business and proselytize. The result has been a blending of the fashion traditions of the foreigners with local ones. Islam is the major religion, and Islamic dress dominates fashion in most areas; however, educated people and urban dwellers combine Islamic and Western-style dress. There are also gender and generational distinctions in what people wear. Men generally wear the straight Islamic gown and caps and women wear the traditional blouse over wrapper with a cover cloth and head wear, over which is worn a veil, if they are Muslim. Unmarried young women and girls may dress like adult women but they would not wear the veil even if they were Muslims. Young boys usually wear shorts, shirts, and T-shirts, but if they are Muslims they wear the long tunic over trousers when they go to the mosque.

In urban areas men and women are more sophisticated in their choice of fabric and styles. Cotton brocade and batiks are fabrics of choice for urban and educated people when they make boubou. Otherwise, men wear trousers, shirts, and T-shirts and girls wear dresses. Jeans and T-shirts and sneakers are not very popular with girls and young women, even when they are educated and live in urban areas.

Unlike other women in the subregion, Senegalese women generally do not engage in skin bleaching, although the strong colonial bond with France would likely make skin-lightening products readily available on the market. Women wear lots of jewelry, especially beads. Hair braiding is also very popular among Senegalese females. Young girls usually braid hair in straight cornrows, whereas adult women may spend hours doing micro-braids. In Dakar, the capital city, specialized shops catering to the tastes of the wealthy and tourists showcase imported and locally manufactured clothes and accessories. Poor urban folks and rural people buy their fashion products in open markets. The used clothing market, although vital for a great many poor people, is not as developed in Senegal as elsewhere in the subregion.

Senegal has produced some of the finest fashion designers in Africa. Oumou Sy, an internationally acclaimed fashion designer, has committed herself to producing ready-made fashions that are elegant and yet affordable. Described by the *Africa Travel Magazine* as "Senegal's Queen of Couture," Oumou Sy blends Afrocentrism with international concepts in her designs. She uses fabrics with African motifs but then designs dresses with an international appeal that make them relevant in different cultural milieu. And yet her label, Made in Africa, underscores the importance that she attaches to her African background. Unlike many African fashion designers without international exposure, Oumou Sy has successfully operated as an international designer, especially in Western Europe, where her fashion shows attract numerous patrons.

Central Africa

Angola

Angola is a country that is rich in oil and diamonds, yet about 95 percent of the population is poor, largely because of a protracted civil war that broke out in the country shortly after independence in 1975. Widespread poverty has affected the ways people dress. Before European contact nearly 500 years ago, ethnic groups in Angola dressed as other peoples in the Central African subregion. They made clothes from raffia, tree bark, and animal skins, and later from spun cotton, which was cultivated in the semiarid sections in the south of the country. Men covered their loins with cloth made from animal skin or raffia and wore bands with tassels around their ankles. Women adorned their bodies elaborately with beads and strings of cotton cloth wrapped around their legs. They too wore skirts made of raffia. By the time the Portuguese finally colonized Angola in the nineteenth century they had interacted with the people for nearly 200 years. This long contact had cultural ramifications, including the ways Angolans dressed. Some ethnic groups, notably the Ovimbundu, adopted European dress due to large-scale conversion of their members to Christianity. As well, *mestiços*, who are the offspring of Portuguese men and Angolan women, and *assimilados*, people who had assimilated into Portuguese culture, also wore Western dress.

By the late nineteenth and early twentieth centuries, Angolans had almost abandoned their traditional ways of dressing and adopted Western attire; they had also copied the dress of neighboring Africans. Unlike many African countries, Islam arrived late in Angola so Islamic influence on Angolan dress is minimal. Currently, traditional attire is usually worn at important ethnic and national ceremonies. In Luanda, the capital city, girls and women wear skirts, pants, bra tops, and T-shirts and match these with sneakers, and men wear suits, shirts, and pants. Businessmen dress casually, often in open-necked shirts over pants. In rural districts beyond the capital, the situation is different. Young people usually wear old clothes that may be donated by charitable organizations or obtained from the used-clothing market. Women wear the traditional blouse over a wrapper with a cover cloth, and cover their hair with a scarf. Women may also braid their hair. Men wear pants and shirts, but these are mostly old clothes.

A budding fashion designer, Doroteia Carvalho, made an appeal to the government to rehabilitate the textile industry to stimulate the fashion industry. The government is heeding that call and is making efforts to rejuvenate cotton production as a first step toward improving the textile industry. In the interim, fashion designers continue to import textiles from West Africa and neighboring countries. As a result, clothes are fairly expensive. And given that the majority of the people are poor, fashion is not very high on their list of priorities.

Democratic Republic of the Congo (DRC)

Nestled in the equatorial forests of Central Africa, the Democratic Republic of the Congo (DRC), formerly Zaire, is a multiethnic and multicultural country with ties to European countries dating back to 1484. Before European contact and even long afterward, Congolese wore dress made of raffia or bark. The long fiber of the raffia palm was woven together and held by a cord at the waist. In a similar way, the bark of certain trees was beaten into pulp and then held together as a skirt. The Mbuti, a foraging group that inhabited the thick forests, covered their private parts with large leaves. As with other Africans, European contact and the introduction of woven fabric changed traditional patterns of dress. Large sections of the Congolese population were converted to Christianity, and as in Kenya, converts went to church wearing European attire. Over time, traditional clothing became a thing of the past as more and more people switched to Western dress. Congolese wear traditional dress only when they are engaged in rituals or other important traditional ceremonies. In fact, the shift to Western dress was so complete that the late President Mobutu Sese Seko embarked on a drive to return the country to its authentic self. He banned the wearing of ties and jackets and encouraged men to wear patterned shirts, which were typical in West Africa. Mobutu himself increasingly wore and popularized what came to be called *abacost* (short for the slogan *À bas le costume*, "Down with the suit!"), a collarless shirt that will not permit the wearing of a tie.

That campaign of authenticity, however, did not appear to have had a major impact, because the DRC did not have textile mills and had to depend on imports to satisfy fashion needs. In fact, currently, urban Congolese and those living abroad are seen as one of the smartly dressed African peoples. In the rural areas men wear shirts and pants; in urban areas they prefer suits. Even the so-called pygmies now sell or exchange forest produce for clothes and other imported goods. Male dress in Congo is influenced by music. For adults the influence comes from soukous and rumba, and with the youth from American hip-hop.

Women's fashion is not influenced in the same way. Thanks to the availability of Vlisco Real Wax fabric, Congolese women wear the wrapper or long skirt and blouse with a head tie, a style of dress that is pervasive in Africa. Unlike their neighbors to the south, Congolese women seldom use jewelry. In the urban centers young women and girls wear skirts and blouses or jeans and shirts as daily and work wear. Children wear Western dress, mainly used clothing from abroad that can be purchased on open markets.

Southern Africa

South Africa

South Africa is culturally very diverse and exhibits a variety of fashion trends and appearance. The British and Dutch continue to dress as their European ancestors who colonized the country. So also do the East Indians (Malays) who were brought over in the nineteenth century to work on European plantations. Indian women wear *saris* and *bindia* and lots of jewelry, and men wear tunics and vests over pants, and depending on their religion, a turban, just as people dress in India. Even the so-called Coloureds—that is, the mixed-race population in South Africa—dress like Europeans. Real variation in fashion and appearance occurs among the African population, which is as diverse as the foreign groups.

Long before the Dutch and British arrived in South Africa, ethnic groups dressed as their neighbors—in animal skins and plant fiber, accentuated with beads. Chiefs dressed in the skins of the most powerful cats, especially the leopard. Men generally covered their genitals in a sheath of animal skin and wore bands of wire and beads on their arms and legs. Warriors were distinguished from the rest of the population by the feathers they wore in their headbands. Women wore short aprons of plant fiber and jewelry. Married women, however, dressed elaborately. When a Zulu girl married, she wore colored beads in her hair and around her legs and skirt to signify her new status. The highly artistic Ndebele women adorned themselves with jewels made of shells, ivory, bone, and leopard teeth, and wore colorful dresses when they married. In an earlier period an Ndebele wife would wear copper or grass rings around her neck as well as around her arms and legs when her house was completed, and the rings would be in place until her husband died. These days they are worn for a short while and then discarded because of the health problems that continued wearing posed for women in the past. Husbands provided the rings as a symbol of their affection for their wives and also to display their wealth. Such public display of affection was believed to ensure women's continued fidelity. Married Xhosa women wore, and still put on, a headscarf over which is worn a ring of assorted beads. They also adorned the body in jewelry made of similar materials as those worn by the Ndebele.

With the arrival of Europeans and the introduction of woven cloth, South Africans gradually adapted traditional ways of dress and adopted Western modes. On important traditional occasions men would wear an animal-skin loincloth and women the fiber apron, but these are much larger pieces than were worn in earlier times. The current trend is toward Western clothes, sometimes made in African prints. Men wear pants, shorts, and shirts, and in winter, jackets and blankets. Young people wear jeans, T-shirts, and sneakers as daily wear. Adult women wear dresses and aprons, perhaps as a result of working as domestics in white families. Women continue to wear lots of accessories with their dress. The continuing poverty and sickness within South Africa's black population has impacted the amount of money that people are willing to spend on clothes. Consequently, changes in fashion are slow to occur.

Zimbabwe

Like neighboring South Africa, Zimbabwe has moved beyond traditional ways of dressing and is now more Westernized in its fashion outlook. This is the result of long settlement of the British in a country that until 1975 was called Rhodesia, named after the British explorer Cecil Rhodes. British settlers in Zimbabwe acted in ways similar to their compatriots in Kenya, discouraging the Africans from wearing clothes made of animal skins or plant fiber. People wear what comes from neighboring countries, especially South Africa. Clothes are generally cheaper in Bulawayo than they are in Harare and Mutari, because of Bulawayo's proximity to South Africa. Unlike in other African countries, the secondhand clothes market is not developed, and given an unemployment rate of more than 60 percent, many poor people rely on family members in urban areas to send them worn clothes. Those without relatives in cities must save up money to buy a few items of clothing that they will use for a long time. But the poverty in the villages contrasts sharply with city life in which young people dress as youth in any Western country. They wear sneakers and jeans and T-shirts. Girls combine an African element by braiding hair, usually in micro-braids, or they may put extensions in their hair. Boys and men wear pants, shorts, and shirts. Women wear skirts and blouses and dresses for work and as daily wear. They may also wear African prints for important ceremonies. Like others in southern Africa, Zimbabwean women adorn themselves with jewelry when they dress up.

East Africa

Ethiopia

Ethiopia is an ancient country steeped in a rich tradition of fashion. Ethiopian designers take inspiration from their Abyssinian roots. The Semitic-speaking peoples of northern

Ethiopia were reputed to be master craftsmen. Their artistic technique in working cotton was passed on and became the basis for fashion in Ethiopia. *Tite*, as cotton is called, was spun into thread on spindles and was then woven into *shama*. Because individual families produced their own clothing, they designed patterns to suit their tastes. Women worked the thread, and men who were called *shemane* wove it on hand looms. Strips of woven cotton were sewn together to make a cloth. It could take between 2 and 3 weeks to make enough cloth for a dress. A distinctive feature of Ethiopian fashion was that the cotton for the main dress was not dyed, so that everybody wore white, but specially dyed yarn in different colors was used to decorate the selvedge of the fabric. The decorative pattern is called *tibeb*. This tradition has survived modern technology; but in contrast to an earlier period, when home-produced cloth was used as daily wear, these pieces are now worn on special occasions by city dwellers. Rural dwellers continue to dress in traditional ways.

Ethnic groups can be identified by the way they dress. Amhara and Tigray men and women who live in the highland areas to the north dress conservatively; they continue to wear white dress and cover their hair. Young women and girls wear a *kamish* (woven dress), *meknat* (sash of the same design as the tibeb that they wear across the midsection), and *netela* (shawl), which they wear over the shoulder. The complete outfit is called *yahager lebse*. They also wear a blanket called a *gabbi* over their dress when the weather turns cold. In the south the Oromo dress more colorfully and without the gabbi. Unlike the Amhara, who wear white, the Oromo combine several brightly colored fabrics to make their dress and the women wear necklaces and bracelets made from gold and silver on the arms and feet. The Islamized Harar to the east wear colorful dresses made of light fabrics and other silklike materials imported from neighboring Islamic states. The women also decorate their hair with jewelry.

Although home-based cloth production is still carried on in rural Ethiopia, town and city folks nowadays buy clothes from the *markato* (or *gebeya* in rural areas), open markets where buyers can select from a range of patterns to design a dress. In effect, each dress would be custom made. There are also vendors who sell ready-made dresses at the markatos. These vendors have small cubicles where clients can try on dresses. People who cannot afford expensive dresses can always buy *salvage* or used clothing at the markato or gebeya. Then there are the *suq bedereteh*, pack peddlers who carry an assortment of goods, including clothes and other fashion accessories from door to door. They make ready-made dresses available to rural folks who may otherwise not get access to the market. Popular culture is increasingly affecting the ways in which the youth dresses, especially in Addis Ababa, the capital city, but traditional Ethiopian dress remains the preferred mode for the majority of people.

Ethiopia boasts some of Africa's finest fashion designers. One of the successful designers is Sara Abera, who started her own manufacturing company and design shop in 1989 in Addis Ababa. Growing up among the Masango and Gambilla ethnic groups in western Ethiopia Sara noticed that young girls would collect large leaves from the forest and make skirts from them. She carried the inspiration she gained to school, where sewing was an integral part of girls' education. Thus began her interest in fashion design. Sara Garment Designers and Manufacturing Company produces uniforms for schools and for Ethiopian Airlines and the company also consults for the Ethiopian Leather Industries Company (ELICO). Abera also operates a boutique that sells imported fabrics to a more affluent clientele. She has more than 30 employees who were handpicked from master dressmakers in Addis and other dressmaking schools.

Guenet Fresenbet, popularly known as Gigi, is perhaps Ethiopia's most celebrated female designer. Schooled in the United States in fine art and graphic design, Gigi returned to her native Ethiopia to apply her skills instead in fashion design. Her ambition is to internationalize Ethiopian and African fashion, and in that regard she has mounted several international fashion shows. She was the first to produce a fashion magazine in Ethiopia. Like many of her contemporaries, she has moved beyond the traditional to incorporate foreign concepts in her designs. Her designs are elegant and sophisticated and yet can be worn for all occasions.

Kenya

Famous for its wildlife reserves, Kenya is perhaps Africa's most popular tourist destination. Kenya was a British settler colony and so was strongly influenced by British culture in many respects. And yet, until about the first two decades of the twentieth century, Kenyans were not dramatically affected by British modes of dress. Generally, Kenyans wore modest clothes but accompanied them with a lot of accessories. Clothes were made from animal skins and plant fiber and ornaments were mainly made from copper wire. Among the Luo, Luyia, and Gusii of western Kenya women and girls wore a short skirt made of sisal and accompanied it with beaded necklaces and decorated their arms and legs with bands of copper wire. Married women wore a tassel, called the *chieno* by the Luo, around the waist that sat at their lower back so that it looked like a tail. Young, unmarried women would wear the *chieno* when they went to the cities and towns to stop men from making amorous advances toward them. Young women also shaved hair in decorative patterns.

Married men covered their groin with goatskin, but on special occasions also wore a larger skin over the shoulder. Men of means had beads woven into goat or leopard skin that they wore as a cloak and then accentuated with jewelry, especially numerous earrings and coils of wire for the arms and legs. Warriors dressed elaborately. Their headdress was made of ostrich feathers and carved elephant tusks, and like the rest of the population, they wore several coils of copper wire on the arms and legs. Warriors painted their faces in red and white paint, and they also carried spears and shields. Another ethnic group, the Maasai, who live in southern Kenya (and also north-central Tanzania) are noted for the red cloth, the *shuka*, that they wrap around the body and the beautiful beads and other accessories that adorn their bodies. The Maasai also shave hair in beautiful patterns to initiate men into age cohorts. Women usually shave all of their hair. Both sexes also pierce their ears and stretch their lobes by putting large objects in them. Apart from beads they wear metal armbands and other accessories on their bodies. Young men in particular may cover their bodies in paint to enhance their appearance.

Kenyan traditional ways of dressing would change with increasing British presence and trade. During the first two decades of the twentieth century British settlers tried to change the ways Kenyans dressed, focusing first on the chiefs. They encouraged chiefs to wear embroidered cloaks over *kanzu*, which is white dress introduced into Kenya by Swahili-speaking peoples from neighboring Zanzibar. The sophistication of a chief's cloak depended on his position in the traditional structure (as the British perceived it). Luo and Luhya chiefs only wore kanzu and embroidered cloaks for ceremonies: in their everyday attire they wore shirts and pants similar to the Europeans. The chiefs in turn influenced their subjects so that men began to wear shirts and pants instead of a goatskin loincloth. By the 1930s kanzu had become a thing of the past in and around urban areas as men increasingly wore khaki tunics, trousers, and boots, and complemented that with a helmet. They obtained items from a booming secondhand clothes market. The symbolism of wearing Western dress was to prove their modernity and power.

Not surprisingly, missionaries focused their efforts on Christian converts. One of the goals that missionaries tried to accomplish was the preservation of Kenyan culture; however, they did not believe that people should attend church only minimally clad. Consequently, the missionaries encouraged men to wear the kanzu and women to wear a *kanga*, a two-yard piece of fabric that they wore from the top of the breast to just below the knee. Missionaries also gave converts European dresses, but that was not a practice that they could sustain. In the missionary schools they taught girls sewing so that before long women in rural areas who desired to wear Western dresses could buy them directly from mission-school dressmakers. Boys were also taught sewing, but unlike girls, they sewed only for other boys in the schools. Christian influence on Kenyan dress was seen as turning away from tradition. Converts were sometimes chased out of their homes and took shelter within the missionary compounds. Thus, in some villages, Christians lived and dressed apart from the rest of the population.

Another influence on Kenyan dress was a consequence of economic activities. White masters preferred servants who wore kanzu, and construction engineers wanted workers who wore khaki shirts and shorts. Thus it was in Kenyan workers' interest to wear Western dress if they wanted to work at certain jobs. As migrants moved from the rural areas to work in the cities, they too changed their traditional attire to Western modes. These workers would return to their villages sporting new outfits and attracting the beautiful women (to the envy of those still wearing goatskins). Some would also give their old clothes to family members still left in the village. In this way, rural Kenyan dress was gradually transformed, but this transformation did not go without challenge.

In the 1930s and 1940s a movement began to curb Western influence on dress (with the focus on women). Opponents to Western dress wanted a return to the precolonial days when Kenyans wore skins and beads. By this time, though, Western dress was firmly entrenched and Kenyans have not looked back. In the 1960s a fashion designer, Mary Kadenge, went on a quest to find a Kenyan national dress because it appeared that many Kenyans had lost a sense of cultural rootedness in fashion. Efforts to adopt *kitenge* (similar to the West African boubou) as a national dress have not been successful; however, even now, kanga remains an important fashion item for Kenyan women. Each kanga is uniquely designed with a Swahili proverb and it can be worn in several ways. It can be used as beachwear, casual wear, and evening attire with beads and other accessories. The Maasai also continue to wear the red cloth and adorn their bodies with ornaments.

CONCLUSION

The countries described in this chapter by no means represent the most elaborate forms of fashion in Africa. Rather, the selection was done to highlight the huge diversity on the continent. Although traditional modes have remained resilient, foreign influence has dramatically changed the ways in which Africans dress. From animal skins to plant fiber and homespun yarn, Africans are now wearing the most sophisticated outfits in an explosion of colors. Designers for the international market, as well as dressmakers in towns and villages, are using African prints to capture the maturing of a fashion tradition that began centuries ago with the blending of foreign trends and local traditions.

RESOURCE GUIDE

PRINT SOURCES

Adjaye, Joseph K. "The Discourse of Kente Cloth: From Haute Couture to Mass Culture." Pp. 23–39 in Joseph K. Adjaye and Adrianne R. Andrews (eds.), *Language, Rhythm, And Sound: Black Popular Cultures into the Twenty-First Century*. Pittsburgh: University of Pittsburgh Press, 1997.

Byfield, Judith. "Dress and Politics in Post-World War II Abeokuta (Western Nigeria)." Pp. 31–49 in Jean Allman (ed.), *Fashioning Africa: Power and the Politics of Dress*. Bloomington: Indiana University Press, 2004.

Daaku, K. Y. *Trade and Politics in on the Gold Coast, 1600–1720: A Study of the African Reaction to European Trade.* Oxford: Clarendon Press, 1970.

Friedland, Shirley, and Leslie Pina. *African Prints: A Design Book.* Atglen, PA: Schiffer Publishing, 1998.

Geoffroy-Schneiter, Berenice. *Africa Is in Style.* New York and Paris: Assouline, 2006.

Gillow, John. *Printed and Dyed Textiles from Africa.* Seattle, WA: University of Washington Press, 2003.

Hay, Margaret Jean. "Changes in Clothing and Struggles over Identity in Colonial Western Kenya." Pp. 67–83 in Jean Allman (ed.). *Fashioning Africa: Power and the Politics of Dress.* Bloomington: Indiana University Press, 2004.

Hendrickson, Hildi. *Clothing and Difference: Embodied Identities in Colonial and Post-Colonial Africa.* Durham, NC: Duke University Press, 1996.

Horn, Diane V. *African Printed Textile Designs.* Owings Mills, MD: Stemmer House Publishers, 1996.

"Een Leven in Kleur." Helmond, Holland: Textieldrukkerij Vlisco, 1846–1996.

Luke-Boone, Ronke. *African Fabrics: Sewing Contemporary Fashion with Ethnic Flair.* Iola, WI: KP Books, 2001.

Rabine, Leslie W. *The Global Circulation of African Fashion: Dress, Body, Culture.* Oxford: Berg Publishers, 2003.

Renne, Elisha P. "From Khaki to Agbada: Dress and Political Transition in Nigeria." Pp. 125–143 in Jean Allman (ed.). *Fashioning Africa: Power and the Politics of Dress.* Bloomington: Indiana University Press, 2004.

Ross, Doran H., Raymond Aaron Silverman, and Agbenyega Adedze. *Wrapped in Pride: Ghanaian Kente and African American Identity.* Los Angeles: UCLA Fowler Museum of Cultural History, 1998.

Van der Plas, Els. *The Art of African Fashion.* Trenton, NJ: Africa World Press, 1999.

WEBSITES

Benedictus, Leo. *"Our forefathers were very, very neat—the neatest in the world": Congolese in Tottenham.* Accessed August 26, 2005. http://www.guardian.co.us/print.

Getachew, Idrias. *Ethiopian Women in [the] Fashion World.* Accessed August 25, 2005. http://www.nilefall.com/cloth.html.

LeBlanc, Danielle, and Carlton R. Van Lowe. *Clothing as a Cultural Expression: African Fashion.* TransAfrica Forum (2000). Accessed September 8, 2005. http://www.transafricaforum.org.

Orzada, Belinda T. *African Influences of Western Apparel.* University of Delaware (1998). Accessed August 25, 2005. http://www.udel.edu/~orzada/africa.htm.

Oumou Sy: Fashion Made in Africa. Accessed February 21, 2006. http://www.culturecooperation.de/site/s330e/htm.

WEBSITES (GENERAL)

Africa Scene Magazine. Fashion section. http://www.bcscene.com/fashion.htm. A magazine of business, tourism, and investment in Africa.

Africa Travel Association. *Africa Travel Magazine.* Fashion section. http://www.africa-ata.org/et_fashion.htm. An African tourist organization's magazine, which has links to other African fashion and textile sites. Also see the ATA's Africa Styles section: http://www.africastyles.com.

Dressing You Up the African Way. http://www.ssodangi.com/index.html. A site that shows traditional African dress, especially that of the Hausa people of West Africa.

Gigi (fashion designer). http://www.yohannes.com/2-Ethiopia/ETH-Fashion-Gigi.htm. A Website featuring Gigi (Guenet Fresenbet Azimach), the fashion designer who specializes in Ethiopian contemporary fashion design.

Kikiromeo. http://www.kikoromeo.com. This is an example of an African fashion house, located in Nairobi, Kenya, that according to its Website "combines haute couture apparel with ethnic African traditional weaves."

Motherland Nigeria. http://www.motherlandnigeria.com/attire.html. Nigerian-produced Website, including a section on attire.

Safari Web.com. http://www.safariweb.com/safarimate/natdress.htm. An East African Website for the tourist industry, which includes a section on national dress.

Vlisco. http://www.vlisco.com. The site of the Dutch textile manufacturer, which makes Real Dutch Wax fabrics.

Woodin. http://www.woodin-ci.com. The Website for the prominent Ivory Coast manufacturer of textiles and fashion.

Youngman, Jeremy. *The Maasai*. http://www.masai-mara.com/mmmaa.htm. Discussion of the Maasai people in the context of the Masai Mara park.

NOTES

1. *Vlisco Newsletter* (1996): 6.
2. Daaku 1970 (in Resource Guide).
3. Vlisco and Woodin fabrics are sold in 4-, 6-, and 12-yard pieces. Women usually use "a half-piece," that is, six yards, to make an outfit. A half-piece of Java currently sells for $45.00; the same yardage of Super Wax costs $75.00.
4. Cedi (¢) is the unit of currency in Ghana. 100 pesewas equals one cedi. At the time of this writing, one U.S. dollar exchanged for ¢9000.

FILM

CHARLES SUGNET

Moving pictures came to the African continent as soon as they were invented, with Lumière showings in Cairo, Algiers, Dakar, and Lagos between 1895 and 1905, and George Mélies shooting two films in Dakar. Over the next 60 years, hundreds of features, ethnographic documentaries, and travelogues were shot in Africa for European and North American consumption, placing the spectator in the position of explorer–colonizer cinematically reenacting the colonial conquest of African spaces.[1] Often shown as shorts accompanying a fiction feature, these films diffused stereotypes about Africans that are still widely held. Colonial film units also made didactic and propaganda films for African consumption, to "teach" Africans table etiquette and proper use of soap, or to convince them they should enlist to fight Europe's wars.

Some Africans received training as technicians, but Sub-Saharan Africans under colonialism were prevented from expressing an African point of view. Film historian Georges Sadoul wrote in 1960 that "as far as I know, sixty-five years after cinema's invention, not one truly African feature film has been produced; I mean a film acted, shot, written, conceived, produced, edited, etc. by blacks speaking, of course, a black African language (not a European one)."[2] (North of the Sahara, things developed differently, with Tunisian director Chikly completing his silent feature, *The Girl From Carthage,* by the mid-1920s, and an Egyptian film industry already flourishing beforc World War II.)

This *de facto* prohibition was formalized in French Africa with a 1934 decree by minister of the colonies Pierre Laval, later executed for his collaboration with the Nazis as head of the Vichy government. The Laval decree, stipulating that anyone making film images or sound recordings in a French colony must obtain prior script approval from the lieutenant governor, remained in force into the late 1950s. It was invoked to destroy footage shot by leftist filmmaker René Vautier for *Africa 50* (1950) and to ban Chris Marker and Alain Resnais's *Statues Also Die* (1955). Senegalese director and critic Paulin Vieyra was denied permission to film in Africa: the first African-directed films, Vieyra's *Afrique Sur Seine* [Africa on the Seine] (1955) and Guinean Mamadou Touré's *Mouramani* (also 1955) ironically had to be shot in France because of the Laval decree. Belgian legislation in the Congo was more restrictive, forbidding even the admission of Africans to movie theaters. Paradoxically,

France, which forbade African filmmaking during the colonial period, began to encourage and subsidize African filmmakers after independence, whereas Belgium and Britain withdrew from film activities.

"FIRSTS" IN AFRICAN FILM

Sembène's *Borom Sarret* and *Black Girl*

It was not until 1963 that Senegal's Ousmane Sembène made *Borom Sarret* (Cart Master) a 22-minute 16-mm short regarded as the first African film. The cart master makes his living carrying passengers and freight around Dakar in his horse-drawn cart. Few of his customers can pay, and by the day's end police have confiscated the cart; the ending implies his wife will have to prostitute herself to feed their baby. *Borom Sarret*'s style and politics were influenced by Italian neorealism, especially by di Sica's *The Bicycle Thief* (1947), but it goes beyond di Sica in its portrayal of the African's interior life. In a famous 1965 encounter, Sembène attacked French filmmaker Jean Rouch for freezing Africans in an ethnographic past, charging that "you look at us as if we were insects."[3] Sembène's cart driver is not an insect, but a full human subject engaged in contemporary struggle, something new in film depictions of Africans.

Sembène's longer *La Noire de . . .* (1966), titled *Black Girl* in English, the first African feature film, won the grand prize at Carthage and was screened at Cannes. Based on a Sembène short story, *Black Girl* follows Diouana, who works as a maid for a French couple. From a formal point of view, *Black Girl* is still one of Sembène's strongest films. Claustrophobic sets and tight camera work emphasize Diouana's confinement, and artful use of black-and-white film emphasizes the Manichean racial themes. Isolated and demoralized, Diouana commits suicide, slitting her wrists in the bathtub, making a mess of the white room her mistress forced her to clean, and breaking colonial silence by speaking with her body. It is important that the first African feature film should be about a woman: African cinema has often focused on women as actors in the public sphere, and in later films Sembène developed powerful female characters. If *Black Girl* had ended with Diouana's body in the bloody bathtub, the film would be terribly pessimistic, but Sembène adds a brilliant coda: going back to Diouana's shantytown to return her few belongings and her unpaid salary, her French boss is greeted by Sembène himself in the role of a schoolteacher, becomes afraid and disoriented in the African neighborhood, and is chased away by Diouana's little brother in an African mask, demonstrating that African resistance is possible. After *La Noire de . . .* Sembène continued, with the aid of his collaborator Paulin Soumanou Vieyra, to make excellent films. (See the following Senegal section for more on Sembène's career.)

Language Politics

Sembène, who had established his artistic reputation by writing novels in French, hoped that the use of spoken African languages would give film a better chance than books to reach populations with low literacy; funders agreed to a Wolof version of his third film, *The Money Order*, but the question of what language to use in film has remained difficult all over the polylingual continent, from Senegal to Zimbabwe. Films in a European language such as French, English, or Portuguese may reach a wider public, but at the cost of falsifying experiences lived and expressed in African languages, and of depriving African actors of the expressiveness of their mother tongues.

FORTY YEARS OF FILM PRODUCTION

Borom Sarret opened the way for an outpouring of pent-up cinematic expression: fiction features, comedies, social criticism, shorts, documentaries, and videofilms. The FESPACO *Dictionary of African Cinema* takes 500 pages just to list the continent's output. African cinema's development has, however, been geographically uneven. French West Africa, with Ministry of Cooperation subsidies, has been very productive. South Africa, because of its relative wealth, had a well-developed, although horribly distorted, film industry under apartheid, and continues to be a relative giant in audiovisual production, able to export its products to the rest of the continent since the "end of apartheid" in 1993. Independence came late to Zimbabwe and to the Portuguese colonies, so the advent of national cinema there was delayed.

Over the 40 years of African cinema's history, extraordinarily good films have been made, such as Sembène's *Xala* [The Curse] (Senegal, 1974), Cissé's *Yeelen* [Brightness] (Mali, 1987), Diop Mambety's *La Petite Vendeuse de Soleil* [The Little Girl Who Sold the Sun] (Senegal, 1999), Sarah Maldoror's *Sambizanga*, Safi Faye's *Kaddu Beykat*, Écaré's *Faces of Women* [Ivory Coast] (1985), or Sissako's *Heremakono* [Waiting for Happiness], (Mauritania, 2002), but the one thing that has not emerged, despite repeated resolutions and collective efforts, is a complete, financially viable film industry located in Africa, including training institutions, production financing, postproduction facilities, and distribution.

Making Films Out of Cigarette Butts

Sembène famously coined the word *mégotage*, literally "collecting cigarette butts" (rather than *montage* or editing), to describe the way African directors make their films;[4] both Sembène and Nigeria's Ola Balogun had to mortgage their homes as collateral for production money, and Désiré Écaré sold his car to pay film costs. The early generation of African directors and technicians had to seek their training outside the continent, many in France, Germany, or the Soviet Union. Even in a relatively active country such as Senegal, not enough films were made to sustain technical crews or a cadre of professional film actors—films in Nigeria, Senegal, and elsewhere used nonprofessionals and stage actors from local theater. An "African" film would often have an African director and African actors but a European producer, cameraman, and lighting director. A crucial undeveloped area was and still is postproduction. Despite serious, expensive, and flawed efforts to build film processing labs and editing equipment in countries from Guinea to Nigeria to Mozambique, African films shot on celluloid are sent to Europe (or more recently to Morocco) for processing, editing, and sound work. This is awkward and time consuming, constitutes a huge expense in hard currency, and perpetuates African dependency.

Distribution presented (and still presents) another crucial limitation. Film distributors (many European or Syrian-Lebanese) had no motivation to interrupt a flow of Hollywood, Bollywood, and martial-arts films that made money, and African films came out too irregularly for commercial rotation. In countries where the government attempted to nationalize the theaters or to insist on a quota of African films, the distributors fought back by refusing to bring any films into the country. It has been rare for African-made films to receive normal commercial theatrical distribution in Africa, and it continues to be rare as movie houses go bankrupt and pirated DVDs circulate for a dollar or two. With the exception of large cities where a few movie theaters remain open, and of relatively affluent South Africa, African films are seen at festivals, in cultural centers, embassies, fairgrounds, or universities, and on TV or video. It is equally rare for a new African film to be funded in the usual industrial fashion, by reinvestment of box office receipts from previous films.

Subsidized *Auteurs*

African directors, especially in the Francophone countries, often received a production subsidy in return for partial ownership of the completed film. They therefore had neither the control nor the motivation necessary to commercialize their films and recover production costs. Sembène and others expressed the view that these arrangements constituted a brilliant form of cooptation: France would let directors make anticolonial films, and would even subsidize them, but the films would be the property of France, and would go into the archives rather than into commercial distribution for a broad audience. Tunisian director and critic Ferid Boughedir tartly summed up the situation: "Francophone African film exists thanks to France, and also does not exist thanks to France."[5]

After independence, filmmakers wanting autonomy turned to new states for help but were often disappointed: impoverished national treasuries could give little help, state-owned equipment was poorly maintained, and African governments impinged on artistic freedom, demanding cuts from films like Sembène's *Xala*, and banning others outright. Insofar as there was any system at all for African filmmaking, it was an *auteur* system, with an artistically committed director starting each project anew, raising money on the basis of a script, then hiring the personnel for that project only. Sometimes, as with Désiré Écaré's *Faces of Women,* shooting occurred over a period of years, as funding became available; even a successful director like Sembène could go more than 10 years between films. Frequently the *auteur*–director did not even really control the money he had raised, as funders imposed European financial, technical, and even artistic controls.

WHAT "AFRICAN CINEMA" IS

The term "African cinema" is widely used, and indeed the "Africanness" of African cinema was its chief selling point and guarantor of authenticity, but the classification has several pitfalls. One does not speak of "European" cinema, but of French, German, or Italian cinema. The notion of an "African" cinema comforts the West's ignorant assumption that the continent, with a surface area bigger than that of the United States, China, and India combined, with nearly fifty independent countries, with hundreds of languages and cultures, is somehow one big undifferentiated whole.

In fact, even determining Africa's literal geographical boundaries is difficult: Should Madagascar be included? Réunion? Scholar Ali Mazrui argues the Arabian peninsula is part of Africa, and Islam is therefore an indigenous African religion.[6] Such debates show how ideologies shape geographic imaginations. One of the major geopolitical boundaries imposed on Africa is the divide between "Sub-Saharan" Africa and something called "North Africa" or "The Maghreb," but this is very distorting with regard to cinema: early African film institutions were created in solidarity by Pan-Africanist filmmakers from both sides of the Sahara. (Despite these distortions, the conventional "Sub-Saharan" division of the continent is so widely accepted that the present volume is obliged to follow it.)

Other boundary questions are equally complex. Mauritanian director Med Hondo's first feature film *Soleil O* (1970) concerns immigrant workers from the Caribbean and Africa in France, yet it is regarded as an African film because of the director's birthplace and perhaps because of the point of view expressed in the film. Guadeloupean Sarah Maldoror's *Sambizanga* (1972), about the Angolan struggle against Portuguese colonization, and Haitian Raoul Peck's films about the assassination of Congolese leader Patrice Lumumba are similarly called African, whereas most films by white directors of the apartheid period in South Africa are not. In other words, "African cinema" is not simply a geographical designation, but an ideological formation arising from the decolonization struggle.

Film Artists as Leaders of the Revolution—Institutions, Manifestoes, and Festivals

African filmmakers came together at a 1969 Pan-African festival in Algiers and again in Tunisia in 1970 to create the Pan African Federation of Film Makers (FEPACI). Although it functioned as a professional guild, pushing for things such as better distribution and lower taxes on film receipts, FEPACI also presumed filmmakers' commitment to achieving complete African liberation. Long after the anticolonial struggles of the 1960s and 1970s, film historian Manthia Diawara still titled his chapter on FEPACI "The Artist As the Leader of the Revolution."[7]

FEPACI has overseen the Panafrican Film and Television Festival of Ouagadougou (FESPACO), which occurs every other year in Ouagadougou, Burkina Faso: starting as an informal "Cinema Week" in 1969, FESPACO became a full-fledged festival, coordinated with the already-existing Carthage Festival (JCC) held biennially in Tunisia. A related festival, called *Vues D'Afrique*, has taken place in Montreal for 20 years. Since 1990, there has been an annual festival in Milan, where FEPACI also published a bilingual journal called *Écrans d'Afrique/African Screen.* A Zanzibar festival showcases East African films, and several South African cities now have festivals.

FESPACO was crucial in keeping African films visible from the 1970s through the mid-1990s; it still matters, but seems to be lessening in importance because there are more venues for new films. Some directors try for Cannes or Toronto, leaving FESPACO as a last resort; complaints persist that the festival competition is not selective enough, because not enough good African films are submitted. (The Milan Festival of African Cinema has added Asia and Latin America in response to this dearth.) Some Anglophone directors have been active at FESPACO, but many, including Ghana's Kwaw Ansah (whose *Heritage Africa* won the grand prize in 1989), see it as a French-subsidized affair for Francophone filmmakers who can still afford to work on celluloid because France pays for it.

Social Realism and Stylistic Experiment: African Film as Art

As with early African novels like Achebe's *Things Fall Apart*, there was a pervasive postcolonial assumption that African films should be tools for nation building, and that social realism was the correct mode for this. Such assumptions, which overlook questions of representation and treat film as if it were (really) a slice of the world, can be dangerous even for realist films. Just as Achebe's novel gets assigned to students in history or anthropology classes as though it were a primary document rather than a fictional work of art, so African films are often mistakenly viewed simply as documents of African culture or politics.

Many African films, however, are self-conscious and formally innovative. Djibril Diop Mambety, for example, insisted that he preferred "stylistic research" to the "mere recording of facts,"[8] and *Touki Bouki* (1973) goes beyond the films of the French New Wave in its brilliant surreal montage, exploding the conventions of realist narrative. Parts of Med Hondo's *Soleil O* have more in common with Genet's absurdist plays than with Gorky or Sembène. Ivorian Désiré Écaré says he hates linear films, and formal innovation structures all his work. Souleymane Cissé says that he left social realism behind to make his superb *Yeelen*, part Western, part futurist sci-fi, part national epic, and part meta-film. Bekolo's *Quartier Mozart* and *Aristotle's Plot* are formal departures of a different kind, with unmatched jump cuts and direct address to the camera. Abderrahmane Sissako's *Life on Earth* and *Heremakono: Waiting for Happiness* go beyond realism in yet another direction, dissolving the boundary between fiction and documentary, creating aesthetically scrupulous poetic collages of image and sound.

Rewriting History

Long forbidden to film their own countries, African directors were eager to revise the historical narratives imposed by colonizers. Sembène returned to the World War II era with both *Emitai* (1971) and *Camp de Thiaroye* (1988), a dramatization of the brutal 1944 French massacre of African soldiers who had fought heroically against the Nazis. Med Hondo's *Sarraounia: Warrior Queen* (1986), and Ghanaian Kwaw Ansah's *Heritage Africa* also counter dominant colonial narratives. Guinea-Bissau director Flora Gomes reconstructed the liberation war in *Mortu Nega* and is determined to film the life of independence leader Amilcar Cabral. In South Africa, Mozambique, and Angola, the work of reinterpreting apartheid and colonial historiography is still very much under way: South African Zola Maseko's reconstruction of Sophiatown during the *Drum* magazine period won first prize at FESPACO 2005.

Another approach to history is what critics have called "return to the source" films, which try to recreate or invent a usable past for newly independent nations by depicting autonomous precolonial societies. Gaston Kaboré's *Wend Kuuni* [Gift of God] (1982) and Idrissa Ouedraogo's beautiful *Yaaba* (1989) are often put in this category. Both are skillfully done and engage interesting issues, but they raise the question of whether the "return to the source" (or "calabash") films represent precisely the kind of exotic, eternally primitive Africa that French funders and Euro-American viewers want to see.

African Documentaries

Documentaries are an important genre for African film and an important tool for reorienting popular conceptions of history. Cameroonian Jean-Marie Teno has retold colonial history from his 1991 *Africa, I Will Fleece You* (an effort to trace the origins of Cameroonian violence and exploitation to their roots in the colonial period) through his 2005 *The Colonial Misunderstanding* (about the role of German missionaries in the Namibian genocide, which inspired Hitler's "Final Solution"). South African Nana Mahomo's clandestinely filmed *Last Grave at Dimbaza* (1973) got the truth about the apartheid "homelands" policy out to the world. Ethiopian Salem Mekuria's *Deluge* (1995) counts the personal cost of the 1974 Ethiopian student "revolution," pitting friends and family against each other. Rehad Desai's *Born into Struggle* (2004) goes behind anti-apartheid heroics to measure the family damage done by the absence of his activist father. African filmmakers continue to tell and retell their own history through documentary productions.

Women and African Cinema

From the beginning, directors have taken what might be called progressive positions on women's rights, satirizing polygamy (in Sembène's *Xala*, Duparc's *Bal Poussière*, and a dozen others), depicting the horrors of forced marriage (Dikongue-Pipa's *Muna Moto*), insisting that daughters be educated, and denouncing genital surgery. Although male directors could sympathize with women, however, they could not speak for them. A prominent case in point: Sembène's *Xala* [The Curse, or Temporary Impotence] is consciously feminist, yet, despite placing hope for the nation's future in the protagonist's daughter, the film still equates the power of the emerging postcolonial nation with literal male potency.

Women writing and directing can carry cinema beyond such limitations, and many are doing so. Pioneering director Safi Faye's *Kaddu Beykat* [Peasant Letter] appeared in 1974, almost at the same time as Sembène's *Xala* and Diop Mambety's *Touki Bouki*, but was banned by the Senghor government. Faye has lived in Europe and has continued to film in Senegal, producing the beautiful *Mossane* (1996) and numerous documentaries. Guadeloupean Sarah Maldoror won first prize at the Carthage Festival for her 1972 *Sambizanga*, depicting the Angolan war of liberation from a woman's point of view. Fanta Regina Nacro, after making several funny feminist shorts, released her first feature, *The Night of Truth* (2004). Other established women directors from the continent include Assia Djebar (Algeria), Salem Mekuria (Ethiopia), Flora Mbugu-Schelling (Tanzania), Ingrid Sinclair (Zimbabwe), Tsitsi Dangarembga (Zimbabwe), and Moufida Tlatli (Tunisia), whose exquisite *Silences of the Palace* won first prize at Carthage in 1994. Christiane Succab-Goldman from Guadeloupe (*The Women Are Beautiful in Bamako*, 1995) and Anne-Laure Folly from Togo (*Women with Open Eyes*, 1994; *The Forgotten Women*, 1996) have made excellent documentaries about African women. Boureima Nikiema (Burkina), Soraya Mire (Somalia), and Mahamat Zara Yacoub (Chad) have all made films questioning excision.[9]

The Importance of Music

Precisely by avoiding the stasis of a narrowly defined tradition, African popular music has become the continent's most dynamic form of cultural expression, and African filmmakers have recruited the best musicians. Sembène effectively used the Star Band of Dakar (later Youssou N'Dour's world-famous Étoile de Dakar) to define the values at play in *Xala*, commissioned renowned Cameroonian saxophonist Manu Dibango for *Ceddo*, and gave superstar Fulani singer Baaba Maal carte blanche to write the music that brings audiences near tears in *Guelwaar*. Nigerian directors such as Eddie Ugbomah and Ola Balogun used juju stars King Sunny Ade, Chief Ebenezer Obey, and Sir Shina Peters. The amazing sound tracks for many of Djibril Diop Mambety's films were composed by his brother, Paris-based singer and producer Wasis Diop. Lionel Rogosin's *Come Back, Africa* features a very young Mariam Makeba, and Malian music star Salif Keita plays a soccer coach in Cheick Doukouré's *Ballon d'Or*. Abderrahmane Sissako makes exquisite use of African music, organizing his films emotionally and aesthetically around Tunisian oud player Anwar Brahem's "Barzakh," Malian Salif Keita's "Folon" [The Source], and Oumou Sangaré's "Djorolen" [Anguish].

The musical film as a distinct genre is also prominent, including Congolese Mweze Ngangura's 1987 *Life Is Rosy* with superstar Papa Wemba, Zimbabwean Michael Raeburn's 1990 *Jit*, with Thomas Mapfumo, Gai Ramaka's 2001 Senegalese *Carmen*, Flora Gomes's 2003 *My Voice*, and the 2005 hit South African musical *uCarmen eKayelitsha*.

Changes in the Context of African Film

From the 1960s until the 1980s, the phrase "African cinema" usually referred to celluloid films that benefited from subsidies and were shown in theaters. As with cinema worldwide, however, the meaning of "African cinema" has been changing in response to technological, commercial, and cultural changes. African directors are more and more likely to need the participation of networks such as Canal Plus, Arte, or M-NET in their film deals, and viewers increasingly see films on television, VHS, or DVD rather than on celluloid. These changes in the production–distribution system mean that complex international funding packages will be decided even more than before on the basis of comprehensibility and interest for international audiences.

The anticolonial, African nationalist positions of the 1970s have given way to a more ambiguous political landscape, and the audiovisual environment has also changed dramatically since independence. In most big African cities, local musicians are now making video clips, actors and technicians are involved in comedy and soap opera production for TV, and market stalls sell pirated copies of films and TV shows from all over the world. The boundary between video and cinema becomes more and more permeable, and videofilms from Ghana and Nigeria now far outnumber celluloid films produced on the continent. (See the following sections on Ghana, Nigeria, and videofilm.)

Since the 1994 end of apartheid, South Africa, with its well-capitalized media infrastructure, can now export films and TV programs to the rest of the continent and can engage in joint ventures with other Africans. Because it is English-speaking, South Africa will act as a counterweight against previous Francophone domination. No one can say for sure whether the net effects of South Africa's influence will be good or bad (see the Southern Africa section and the Conclusion for further discussion), but they are almost certain to be large and to involve the entire audiovisual domain, not only celluloid film.

REGIONAL SUBSECTIONS

West Africa

NOTE: The Karthala *Dictionary of African Cinema* lists ninety filmmakers in Senegal, forty-six in Mali, and more than a hundred in South Africa, so country-by-country discussions cannot be comprehensive: after a brief introduction and a discussion of the most important directors, a few others, including younger artists, will simply be listed.

Senegal

Abundant talent, an early start, favorable geographic position, and close relations with France helped Senegal become a leader in number of productions, successful directors, and international recognition. Government programs aided filmmakers during the 1970s, but local subsidies have dried up, the annual Dakar film festival (RECIDAK) has ceased to function, and even the flagship theater, the Paris, has closed. Senegal's directors struggle with the problems of finance and distribution that plague the rest of the continent, but they continue to make high-quality films.

Ousmane Sembène. Unlike many postcolonial intellectuals, Africa's first director did not travel to the metropole for an elite education. Instead, he learned masonry and carpentry, fought with the Free French in Africa and Europe, participated in the strike on the Dakar-Niger railway in 1947–48 (the subject of his superb novel *God's Bits of Wood*), and then became a docker in Marseilles, getting his education from the union rather than from the Sorbonne. Seeing how few Africans could read novels written in French, he went to Moscow for cinema training, becoming a filmmaker at nearly forty years of age; the two films he made after his return, *Borom Sarret* and *Black Girl*, are considered the first African films (see the previous "firsts" section).

His *Xala* [The Curse, or Temporary Impotence] (1974) is often cited as the best African film and was chosen for the British Film Institute's collection of the hundred best films for cinema's centenary. A satirical portrait of the new Dakar bourgeoisie, with a chamber of commerce that is a thinly veiled allegory of Senegal's national government, it focuses on a polygamous businessman about to take a third wife. The comic plot turns serious when it is revealed that businessman El Hadji Abdou Kader Beye got his start by swindling the family out of their village landholding and selling it: the primordial crime of property itself. Shot in Wolof and French, the film itself stages the debate about language politics, and closes with a spectacular freeze-frame of El Hadji's punishment. *Ceddo* (1976), an ambitious effort to renarrate West African history, was banned by grammatically fussy President Senghor, supposedly on grounds that Ceddo should be spelled with only one "d," but really because the final freeze-frame of a Wolof princess killing a Muslim imam was potentially explosive in a 95-percent Muslim country.

After *Ceddo*, there was a hiatus of 12 years before the appearance of *Camp de Thiaroye* (1988), while Sembène completed the script for an epic about anticolonial resister Samori Touré and Vieyra tried to raise money for it. When that failed, he went on to make *Guelwaar* (1993), *Faat Kine* (2000), and *Moolade* (2004). There may be a falling off from his earlier work, but the films of this 83-year-old giant remain extremely interesting.

Djibril Diop Mambety. Sembène's *Xala* (1974) and Diop Mambety's *Touki Bouki* [The Hyena's Journey] (1973) were shot in Dakar at nearly the same time, but moving from *Xala* to *Touki Bouki* feels like a change of universe: after Sembène's steady, deliberate camera work and solid Marxist social analysis, the viewer is suddenly bouncing down a rough road with a handheld camera on the back of a motorcycle, going fast but with no particular destination. An actor dismissed from the National Theater for "indiscipline," Mambety did not go to film school but learned on the job, with help from the French Cultural Center in Dakar, and from New Wave directors he was watching at the cine-club. After *Contras-City* (1968) and *Badou Boy* (1970), a 90-minute picaresque with vaudeville cops and Senegalese cowboys on horseback, Mambety made a masterpiece: *Touki Bouki*. Africa's answer to Dennis Hopper's biker movie *Easy Rider* (1969), the film tracks Mory and Anta, two young Senegalese with horns strapped to the handlebars of their motorcycle who want to migrate to Paris. The bohemian student Anta's short hair and sport jacket challenge Senegalese gender norms, fooling viewers into mistaking her for a man until she takes off her clothes for an ambiguous sex scene. A slaughterhouse (homage to Eistenstein's *Strike*) functions as a metaphor of what urban modernity does to rural youth. *Touki Bouki*'s disturbing imagery dispenses with conventional narrative devices, and its avant-garde sound track constantly laps sound from one scene over into another.

After *Touki Bouki*, Mambety bounced around (France, Italy, and Switzerland) without making a film for more than 15 years, until director Idrissa Ouedraogo lured him back behind the camera in 1989. One result was *Hyenas* (1992), a miraculous adaptation of Durrenmatt's *The Visit of the Old Woman*, which turns the Swiss play into an allegory of the murderous effects of IMF and World Bank policy in Africa. Mambety's early death in 1998 interrupted a planned series of shorts called *Stories of Little People*, but *Le Franc* (1994) displays Mambety's love of Keaton and Chaplin, and the posthumous *The Little Girl Who Sold the Sun* (1999) is his best film since the challenging *Touki Bouki*, and much more accessible. It follows a handicapped, homeless 12-year-old girl who decides that "what boys can do, girls can do too," and sets out to be a newspaper seller. Without sentiment or false hope, the film shows that despite her marginality, she is living a full human life and is in possession of a rich oral culture.

Other Filmmakers. Safi Faye, a Senegalese pioneer, made the banned *Peasant Letter* (1975) about rural discontent. Her beautiful feature *Mossane*, delayed by financial and legal difficulties, appeared at last in 1996. Ababacar Samb Makharam, FEPACI's first secretary-general, made *Kodou* (1971) showing how an afflicted girl is helped by a traditional healing ritual, and *Jom, or the History of a People* (1981), an excellent feature applying Senegalese concepts of dignity and self-respect to a factory strike and a labor action by maids. Mahama Johnson Traoré took on risky subjects such as the oppression of women (*Diankha-bi*, 1969) and the mistreatment of children in Koranic schools (*Njangaan*, 1975). Ben Diogaye Beye's *A Man, Some Women* (1980) investigates the impact of polygamy and Senghor's family code legislation on different social classes. Moussa Bathily's twelve films include *Certificate of Indigence* (1981), about a rural woman whose baby dies while she is waiting for the paperwork that would allow the child to be treated. Mansour Sora Wade won first prize at Carthage in 2002 for *Ndeysaan! The Price of Pardon*, a lovely portrayal of legends in a foggy fishing village. Moussa Sene Absa's more than a dozen films include *Twist Again at Popenguine* (1993), about rival village clubs devoted to their rock 'n' roll idols, *Tableau Ferraille* (1997) with music star Ismaël Lô playing the lead, and *Madame Brouette* (2004).

Mali

Mali nationalized its film industry in 1962; the National Cinematographic Office ran production and distribution until it collapsed in the early 1990s. Only a handful of theaters remain, but changes since the 1991 ouster of dictator Moussa Traoré, including the appointment of filmmaker Cheikh Oumar Sissoko as minister of culture, have improved the cinema climate.

Souleymane Cissé. Souleymane Cissé, a cinephile from childhood and one of the greats of African film, studied with Mark Donskoi in Moscow a few years after Sembène. With French funding, he was able to make *Den Muso* [The Young Girl,] (1975), the first banned Malian film, about a mute teenage girl raped by her boyfriend. Four years later, Cissé won the grand prize at FESPACO 1979 with *Baara* (Work), a film about factory workers and an idealistic young engineer. Then, in a feat that no one has repeated, his next film, *Finye* [The Wind] (1982), won first prize both at Carthage (1982) and FESPACO (1983). With its story of a student revolt put down by a military dictator, *Finye* hit dangerously close to the Traoré dictatorship. Cissé says he knew he had reached a limit with realism: he would either have to change filmic modes or leave the country. That change opened the way to *Yeelen* [Brightness] (1987), simultaneously a "back to the source" film tapping precolonial African practices and a futuristic sci-fi epic. The story turns on a violent father–son conflict in a powerful family of magicians: young Nianankoro's father Somo sees him as a rival and would destroy the world to kill him. Without a grand budget or digital special effects, Cissé films the landscapes of Mali to brilliant effect (including the Dogon plateau, which can suggest John

Ford's Monument Valley) and he knows just when a close-up will add poetic power to his imagery. The silent dignity of Nianankoro and his mother in the face of near-certain catastrophe is unlike anything in Western cinema. In a final, high-noon confrontation, Soma and Nianankoro morph into various totem animals and then unleash the power of the Koré wing, the power of light. Cissé accomplishes this by opening the aperture on his camera until whiteout is achieved; the sound track resonates apocalyptically with what sounds like a nuclear explosion.

Read as political allegory, *Yeelen* is about Traoré's dictatorship and the rising youth movement that will overthrow him, but it is also a film about film itself, and much of *Yeelen*'s magic (the whiteout, animals walking backwards, etc.) is in fact the magic of cinema. In addition to going back to African sources, Cissé is also taking on John Ford, George Lucas, and the Kubrick of *2001, A Space Odyssey*. In place of their Hollywood resources, Cissé has only his camera, his wits, and his dense knowledge of the place he comes from, which turns out to be plenty. (After *Yeelen*, Cissé made the ambitious Pan-African 1997 *Waati*, which was not as well received.)

Other Filmmakers. A few years behind Cissé chronologically, and educated in France rather than in Moscow, Cheikh Oumar Sissoko drew attention for *Finzan* [Dance of the Heroes] (1989) a daring investigation of forced marriage and female circumcision. Then his *Guimba the Tyrant* (1995) won first prize at FESPACO, drawing on Malian performance traditions of *koteba* and *baro* for its lush portrayal of a feudal Malian dictator's overthrow. *Guimba* shows frankly how beautiful artistic traditions such as *bogolon* (mud-cloth) and griotic praise singing can be props for tyranny. Westerners, and some Africans too, are inclined to romanticize griots, but Guimba's griot is a slippery flatterer, a tyrant's PR man. Sissoko's *Battu*, based on Aminata Sow Fall's novel 1979 *The Beggars' Strike*, was delayed by disputes about artistic control, but has been released.

Adama Drabo made *Ta Dona* [Fire!] (1991), about a forester's struggles to protect Mali's environment, and the hilarious *Taafe Fanga* [Skirt Power] (1997), in which a village woman finds a mask that gives all power to women. Abdoulaye Ascofare's *Faraw! Mother of the Sands* (1996) is a rare feature in the Songhai language of eastern Mali and Niger, chronicling a rural mother's determination to make an independent living and avoid prostituting her daughter to foreigners. Jose "Zeka" Laplaine's *Macadam Tribu* [Blacktop Tribe] (1996), a Congolese director's fast-paced look at life in a popular quarter of Bamako, is more urban, less directly political, and less concerned with Bambara culture than most representations of Mali. Christiane Succab-Goldman's *Bamako Women Are Beautiful* (1995) is a Guadeloupean's look at impressive Malian women from different social classes and occupations.

Guinea-Conakry

Because of Sékou Touré's defiance of De Gaulle, Guinean filmmaking did not receive Cooperation subsidies and postproduction in France. Instead, Guinea created Syli-Cinema in 1958 to nationalize production, and fought the distributors for control of the country's twenty-eight movie theaters. With aid from the Eastern Bloc, Guinea built facilities for production of black-and-white 16-mm film and could produce its own weekly newsreel at a time when other countries still depended on France for processing and editing.

Despite Mamadou Touré's pioneering 1953 short, *Mouramani*, and Mohamed Lamine Akin's 1966 fiction feature, *Sergeant Bakary Woolen*, Syli-Cinema made mostly documentaries or propaganda until 1982, when it produced two striking features: *Amok*, about the Soweto uprising, starring Miriam Makeba, Robert Liensol, and the great Senegalese actor Douta Seck; and *Naitou: The Orphan,* an oral tale directed by veteran Moussa Diakité, with music and dance by the world-renowned National Ballet of Guinea.

Cheik Doukouré, actor-turned-writer-and-director, appeared in thirty film and television productions between 1972 and 2002, including high-quality films such as Merzak Allouache's *Salut Cousin* [Hey Cousin] (1996), and Raoul Peck's *Lumumba* (2000). He co-wrote and acted in *Black Mic Mac* (1986), a landmark French film that treated African immigrants sympathetically, and introduced Sotigui Kouyaté, Félicité Wouassi, and Isaac de Bankolé to an international audience. He has since directed *Blanc d'ébène* [Ebony White] (1992), *Le Ballon d'or* (1994), and *Paris According to Moussa* (2003). Mohamed Camara started as an actor in films such as *Black Mic Mac* and *Camp de Thiaroye* (1988) before writing, directing, and acting in the French-produced *Dakan* [Destiny] (1997), one of the first African films centered on a homosexual relationship. David Achkar made the unusual docufiction *Allah Tantou* [The Grace of God] (1991), about his father Marof Achkar, Guinea's ambassador to the United Nations, who was sent to a horrible death in Sékou Touré's notorious Camp Boiro. Mama Keïta, Achkar's friend and colleague, director of the experimental *Ragazzi* (1990) and *Choose Yourself a Friend* (1996), made a short tribute, *David Achkar, a Shooting Star* (1998), after his friend's early death, and directed *Le Fleuve* (2003), based partly on Achkar's script. Gahité Fofana directed the lively *Temporary Registration* (2001) about a French-born African looking for his father in Guinea; his *Early in the Morning* (2005) is based on the true story of an Ivorian youth who repeatedly hid in the landing gear of jets bound for Europe.

Mauritania

Riven by conflict between Moors and blacks, Mauritania has almost no film infrastructure; most filmmakers born in Mauritania live elsewhere. Despite this dismal situation, Mauritania has contributed two outstanding directors, Med Hondo and Abderrahamane Sissako, to African cinema. (Sidney Sokhona, a FEPACI activist from Mauritania, also made three good films during the 1970s.)

Med Hondo, an important first-generation director active in FEPACI, grew up on the edge of a Sarahan oasis, trained as a chef in Morocco, worked in France as waiter, docker, fruit picker, cook, and even as Swiss cheese delivery man. His painful work experiences went into *Soleil O* (1970), an aesthetically startling and emotionally powerful film about immigration, titled after a slave song. His next film, the 190-minute *Les Bicots Nègres Vos Voisins* [Your Arab and Nigger Neighbors] (1974), won first prize at Carthage and Toulon for its sharp criticism of the new slavery imposed on African immigrants; migrant workers played themselves and helped create the script. After making a black musical, *West Indies* (1979) in an effort to "free the very concept of musical comedy from its American trademark,"[10] Hondo directed the historical epic *Sarraounia: Warrior Queen*, depicting the queen's resistance to colonization and winning first prize at FESPACO in 1987.

Abderrahmane Sissako was born in Mauritania, grew up mostly in Mali, and resides in France. After film training in Russia, he brought *October* (1993), an exquisite black-and-white film about an African student parting from his Russian lover, to Cannes. Sissako's next two films, *Sabriya* (1997), shot in Tunisia for the "Africa Dreaming" series, and *Rostov-Luanda* (1997), shot in Angola, confirmed that he would not be confined to any national category.

While working on *Rostov-Luanda*, Sissako was invited to make a film for an Arte-TV series on the millenium. Starting from the packaged excess of European consumption in a basement Monoprix department store in Paris, Sissako ascended into the light of Sokolo, his father's village in Mali, to produce *La Vie Sur Terre* [Life on Earth] (1998), a gorgeous docufiction film on the connectedness and disconnectedness between Africa and Europe, undergirded with perfectly chosen quotations from Césaire's *Discourse on Colonialism* and *Return to My Native Land*. Without sentimentalizing poverty and suffering, the film shows Sokolo's genuine beauty and contemporaneity; perfect acoustic music from Brahem's *Barzakh* and from Salif Keïta's *Folon* hold everything together, as Sissako makes the boundary between fiction and documentary disappear.

La Vie Sur Terre announced the arrival of an extraordinary filmmaker, and Sissako's next effort, *Heremakono* [Waiting for Happiness] (2002), more than confirmed this, winning first prize at FESPACO 2003. Shot near the port of Nouadhibou (at last, a film set in Mauritania by this "Mauritanian" director!), *Waiting for Happiness* is a great immigration film, even though no one actually moves to Europe. One man makes a difficult trip to the coast by bush taxi, hoping to stow away on a ship; after many cups of tea and much discussion, he decides to go back home. Another immigrant has his photo taken with a cheesy studio backdrop of the Eiffel Tower and says goodbye, but his dead body washes on shore the next morning. Like Sokolo, Nouadhibou is what Europeans would call remote, and yet intimately connected to the global web: a perfectly modern railway runs from the iron mines of the interior to the port, big ships hover ominously offshore, and rusting wrecks litter the coast. A homesick Chinese merchant selling watches completes the logic of globalization. The central figure, Abdallah, a future filmmaker come to say goodbye to his Mauritanian mother before departing for Europe, is also displaced and alienated: he cannot even speak Hassanyia, the local language and his mother's tongue. Is anyone really at home anywhere? Can anyone ever really leave home? What does it mean to live in Africa, but to have been convinced that Europe is better? *Heremakono* treats these questions with humor, tenderness, and slow attention. *Waiting for Happiness* films through colored cloths over and over, suggesting that reality is partially veiled and that efforts to seize it directly will fail. Sissako's latest, *Bamako* (2006), stages a trial of global financial institutions in the courtyard of an extended Malian family, so that viewers hearing the abstract arguments of the attorneys and judges are also watching the concrete effects of the global economy on residents of the courtyard; the film's handling of questions about who gets to speak on these issues is nothing short of brilliant.

Guinea-Bissau and the Cape Verde Islands

(See the following Southern Africa section for Lusophone Angola and Mozambique.)

Guinea-Bissau and Cape Verde fought Portuguese colonialism together under the leadership of Amilcar Cabral, reaching independence in 1974 as a single nation. However, Cabral's assassination and the perception that the movement was too controlled by mestiços from Cape Verde caused a division into separate countries; since then, there has also been a devastating 1998 civil war in Bissau, destroying the infrastructure.

Although his talented colleague Sana Na N'Hada has made several shorts and the 1994 feature *Xime: A Bad Son*, the history of cinema in Guinea-Bissau is largely the story of Flora Gomes's career. Trained in Cuba, he completed his first feature, *Mortu Nega* [Those Whom Death Refused], in 1988. Financed by the new state's Cinema Institute, *Mortu Nega* has all the ingredients of a well-made national liberation story, with heroic guerrilla fighters and amazing solidarity among the peasants carrying munitions along forest paths. However, a female leader named Diminga (played by the formidable Bia Gomes, who has appeared in all of Gomes's films) pushes the film beyond masculine heroics and left orthodoxy to question women's roles and evoke specifically African social and religious forces.

After *Mortu Nega*, Gomes made his best received film, *Udju Azul di Yona* [The Blue Eyes of Yonta] (1990), investigating the question of what national independence means to the next generation through a confrontation between the youthful Yonta and Vicente, a former guerrilla leader who now drives a Volvo station wagon and, in these puzzling "postcolonial" times, runs a fish-processing business to provide jobs for former comrades. Yonta's charming younger brother, pointedly named after Amilcar Cabral, wants to be a soccer star in Portugal, not a political hero in Africa, and Yonta herself seems more concerned with fashion than with social justice. Yet she has the last word when she demands of Vicente: "Didn't you fight your revolution so I would be free to make choices for myself?" Gomes has moved even further from social realism with his ecomystical *The Tree of Souls* (1996) and with *Nha Fala* [My Voice] (2002), a witty musical shot in Cape Verde with music by Manu Dibango, and Senegalese-French actress Fatou Ndiaye playing a young woman who has to break a family taboo to become a singer.

Ivory Coast

With a vibrant capital city and money from cocoa production, Ivory Coast was an early and steady producer of film and television, especially comedies; but a civil conflict dividing the North and South along a *de facto* line has put the economic and cultural future of the country in doubt. In contrast to Senegal and Mali, where production in African languages such as Wolof and Bambara has been a point of pride, many Ivorian films are made in French, perhaps because Ivory Coast is more Frenchified, or perhaps because it does not have a single hegemonic African language that would reach a broad national audience.

Timité Bassori, one of the first African graduates of France's cinema institute (IDHEC), directed the 1964 short *Sur La Dune de la Solitude*, a contemporary version of the myth of the goddess Mamy Wata, and 1969's feature-length *The Woman with the Knife*, a Freudian image that influenced Diop Mambety's *Touki Bouki*. Working alongside Bassori was Henri Duparc, who went on to make the polygamy comedy *Bal Poussière* [Dancing in the Dust] (1988), one of Ivory Coast's best-known films. Broadly comic, it sides with the women; the plot is arranged so that the arrogant husband gets to watch his own cuckolding. More recent Duparc features include *Princess Street* (1993) and *Une Couleur Café* (1997).

Ivorian television also produced Georges Keita's *Korogo* (1964), a 2-hour adaptation of the foundational Ivorian myth of Queen Pocou. Another important early production is Kramo Lanciné Fadika's *Djeli, A Tale of Today* (1981), the first Ivorian film to win the grand prize at FESPACO for its story of two students forbidden to marry by the Mande caste system. Roger Gnoan Mbala also worked with Ivorian TV and directed *In the Name of Christ*, which won the grand prize at FESPACO 1993: a small-time drunk nearly drowns himself in a river, but emerges thinking he is Christ's cousin sent to save his people, and will stop at nothing, even crucifixion.

Another early graduate of IDHEC is Désiré Écaré, an Akan from the country's southeast corner, who sold his car to make his first film, *Concerto for an Exile* (1967), and persuaded fellow student Henri Duparc to act in it: *Concerto* is an avant-garde film that takes its musical metaphor seriously. His next, *A Nous Deux, France* [It's You and Me, France] (1970) recounts a historical episode in which a planeload of Ivorian women sent by the President to Paris as brides for the country's elite instead became liberated and did as they pleased. The film, with music by Memphis Slim, was banned in Senegal because it made fun of Senegalese poet–President Senghor's sexist poem "Femme noire, femme nue" ("Black woman, nude woman").

After working as a civil servant, raising hogs, and running a bar–restaurant in Ouagadougou, Écaré finally had enough money to start shooting *Visages de Femmes* [Faces of Women] (1985), one of the few films that delivers on all the talk about oral tradition. Starting with a village dance, the film moves to a women's chorus singing about adultery, the song becomes filmic narrative, and viewers see a complicated tale of unhappy women and village affairs, featuring a cruel husband who tells his wife "I own your shit," and a watery 10-minute sex scene in the mangrove swamp, probably the most explicit in African cinema. *Visages* won awards at Cannes and at FESPACO 1987, played commercial theaters in Paris, and was distributed on video by New Yorker Films.

Philip Brooks and Laurent Bocahut made *Woubi Chéri*, a 1998 documentary about the urban subculture of transvestite and transgender males, including an introduction to the terms they use to describe themselves, and a spectacular scene of gay males dancing in African women's boubous and head ties. Hanny Tchelley, star of *Bal Poussière*, launched a production company and a festival of short films in Abidjan in 1997, showing work by promising women such as Isabelle Boni Claverie.

Burkina Faso

Because Burkina hosts FESPACO and its associated institutions, cinema now has a high profile there. At independence, however, the country had so few film directors that a Frenchman named Serge Ricci dominated film output until Mamadou Djim Kola directed the country's first feature, with government funding, a 1971 drama about marriage taboos, *The Blood of the Pariahs.* A turning point came in 1977 with the establishment of a National Cinema Center (CNC) and the appointment of Gaston Kaboré, a filmmaker with a graduate degree in history, as its head. In 1982, the CNC produced Kaboré's well-received *Wend Kuuni* [Gift of God], which set the pattern for a certain kind of pastoral Burkinabe village film. Kaboré won first prize at FESPACO 1997 for *Buud Yam*, a sequel in which the grown-up Wend Kuuni traverses spectacular African locations in search of a healer to save his dying sister. Kaboré has had a large institutional impact as well, serving as secretary-general of the directors' association FEPACI from 1985 to 1997; his most recent venture is a private film school in Ougadougou called Imagine, to replace the defunct CINAFRIC school started by FEPACI.

Another leading figure in Burkinabe cinema is Idrissa Ouedraogo, one of the most prolific and versatile directors in Africa, who received his training at CINAFRIC. Ouedraogo's 1989 *Yaaba* [Grandmother] is an aesthetically perfect village film about a boy who befriends an outcast old woman the adults regard as a witch. In the same year (1989) Ouedraogo released *Tilai: A Question of Honor,* in which a polygamous father marries his son's fiancée, calling tradition radically into question. Ouedraogo has made many other features, including *Samba Traoré* (1992), which starts with a gas station robbery, and *Kini and Adams* (1997), a buddy movie shot in Zimbabwe in English. He has also been busy with television, doing anti-AIDS spots and a series of episodes from the animal fables of Leuk the Hare.

Dany Kouyaté, son of actor Sotigui Kouyaté, made *Keita: Heritage of the Griot* (1994), a film version of the medieval Sundiata Epic about the origins of the Mali empire; his recent *Ouaga Saga* (2004) is very different, a contemporary tale of young Africans getting along in an urban neighborhood. Pierre Yaméogo's *Laafi: Everything's Fine* (1990) tells how corruption prevents a good student from getting his scholarship, and *Moi et Mon Blanc* (2003) follows a Burkinabe student and his French buddy as they both try to find stable ways to make a living. Fanta Regina Nacro, also trained at CINAFRIC in Ouagadougou, made several sexy, funny shorts that reflect women's point of view, before releasing her first feature, *The Night of*

Truth (2005). Numerous other Burkinabe women are working in television or short film, such as Cyra Touré, Valérie Kaboré, Suzanne Kourouma-Sanou, Franceline Oubda, Cilia Sawadogo (who lives in Canada and does animated films), and Boureima Nikiema, who made *My Daughter Will Not Be Excised* (1989).

Niger

Niger's cinema connections probably started with the colonial accident that sent French filmmaker Jean Rouch there as a highway engineer during World War II. Rouch cast Oumarou Ganda in the lead role as "Edward G. Robinson" in his fiction film *Moi, un Noir* [Me, a Black] (1958) and invited Ganda to collaborate on scripting this film about the scruffy lives of young laborers. Ganda became a pioneering director with *Cabascabo* (1968), about an African veteran returning home from Indochina, and won the grand prize at FESPACO 1972 for *Le Wazzou Polygame* (1970), about a hypocritically pious Muslim lecher. Niger's other pioneer is Mustapha Alassane, a multitalented animator, visual artist, and sometime mechanic who has made sixteen films, including the famous *FVVA: Femmes, Villa, Voiture, Argent* [Wives, Villa, Car, Money] (1972), a satire of male chauvinism connecting polygamy with corruption.

Ghana

After independence, Nkrumah's government nationalized production and distribution, building processing facilities that were used mostly for newsreels, documentaries, and propaganda films directed by foreigners. After Nkrumah's overthrow, directorship of the Ghana Film Industry Corporation (GFIC) was taken on by Sam Aretey (director of Ghana's first feature, *No Tears for Ananse*, 1968), whose policy was co-production with Europeans: few Ghanaian features were made between 1966 and 1986. The great exception is independent Kwah Ansaw's blockbuster, *Love Brewed in an African Pot* (1980), about a woman who loves a poor mechanic, but is harassed to madness by the rich lawyer her father wants her to marry. The film was wildly popular in Anglophone Africa, making a healthy profit. Ansaw followed up with *Heritage Africa* (1987), the first film from an Anglophone country to win the grand prize at FESPACO. Today he heads a foundation and directs for his TV station in Accra. Remaining a cultural nationalist and Nkrumaist, he says the Ghanaian film industry has "gone to sleep," and does not like what he sees in Ghanaian and Nigerian videofilms, which he says distort black people's lives as badly as Hollywood does.

Another Ghanaian veteran is the German-trained actor and director King Ampaw, who co-produced with a German company to make two popular features during the 1980s: *Kukurantumi, The Road to Accra* (1983), and *Juju* (1986). Anglo-Ghanaian John Akomfrah works from London, where he co-founded the black Audio Film Collective. His films include *Handsworth Songs* (1986), which won the John Grierson award for social documentary; *Testament*, which was screened at Cannes in 1988; and *The Last Angel of History* (1996), which opened a rich vein of speculation about black music, technology, and Afro-futurism.

Nigeria

With rich natural resources and an internal market of well over a hundred million people, Nigeria should have been a leader, but civil war, military coups, massive corruption, and recent economic decline have rendered state film institutions ineffective. After 40 years of public investment, Nigerian Film Corporation (NFC) director Berndan Shehu says that Nigerian film is "still in the developmental stage," and the NFC indeed has released only one feature, Shehu's own *Kulba Na Barna* [Blaming the Innocent] (1992). Of perhaps fifty film houses remaining in Lagos, fewer than ten show celluloid rather than videofilms; cinemas continue rapidly to be transformed into churches, mosques, or storage depots.

With few exceptions, the history of Nigerian film is a history of brave individuals rather than organized institutions. Like Ghana, Nigeria was left at independence with some equipment that had belonged to the Colonial Film Unit; it also had the first functioning national television station on the continent, established in 1959, before independence. Segun Olusola, the director of national television, claimed his 1970 *Son of Africa* as the first Nigerian feature, but critics renamed the Nigerian-Lebanese co-production "Daughters of Lebanon" because of all the Lebanese actors and belly dancers! A rival "first" was a 1971 film adapation of *Kongi's Harvest* by Nobel Prizewinner Wole Soyinka, produced by U.S-trained film entrepreneur Francis Oladele, directed by African-American actor Ossie Davis, and starring Soyinka in the lead role; however, Soyinka himself denounced the film as untrue to the screenplay he had written. (Soyinka later wrote and directed the 1984 political feature *Blues for a Prodigal*, which was banned by the government.) Oladele tried another literary adaptation with 1972's *Bullfrog in the Sun*, a film version of Achebe's novels *Things Fall Apart* and *No Longer at Ease*, but the film's German director, foreign cast, and extensive treatment of the Biafran war (not even mentioned in either of the Achebe novels) made it a disappointment.

During the same period, Ola Balogun directed *Amadi* (1975), the first Igbo-language film, and then *Adjani-Ogun* (1976), the first of his successful Yoruba theater films; Duro Ladipo's already famous popular troupe provided the acting and the great music. Balogun continued to try new things such as *Muzik Man* (1976), a musical comedy in pidgin English, and the caustically satirical *Money Power* (1982), starring juju musician Shina Peters. Like Ghana's Kwah Ansah, Balogun is less than enthusiastic about the videofilms that have replaced cinema. Actor, scriptwriter, producer, and director Eddie Ugbomah made most of his thirteen celluloid features in English and on contemporary subjects. *The Rise and Fall of Doctor Oyenusi* (1977) fictionalizes a band of thieves who terrorized Lagos; *Oil Doom* (1981) depicts the downside of the Nigerian oil boom; and the controversial *Death of the Black President* (1983) fictionalizes the assassination of President Mohamed Murtala in 1976.

A number of films have been made in northern Nigeria in the Hausa language, starting with Adama Halilu's 1963 *Mama Learns a Lesson* and his 1971 *Child Bride*. Perhaps the best of the Hausa films is Saddik Tafawa Balewa's 1991 *Kasarmu Ce: The Land Is Ours*, a skillful and daring story of how corruption and phony religious leadership go hand in hand. With excellent scenario, acting, and camera work, Balewa makes important rural issues such as land tenure, water rights, and the price of fertilizer entertaining without oversimplification.

Ngozi Onwurah, an Anglo-Nigerian living in London, has done several films about gender, race, and body image, including *The Body Beautiful* (1991) and *Monday's Girls* (1993), about the Niger Delta custom of encouraging girls to put on weight before marriage. In addition to making documentaries for BBC and Channel 4, Onwurah has contributed shorts to the Women Make Movies compilation *White Men Are Cracking Up* (1996) and to the South African Zimmedia/M-Net collection *Mama Africa* (2002).[11]

The Arrival of Videofilm. Videofilms took over Ghanaian production in the 1980s and later came to dominate Nigerian production. By 1990, Ghana's industry was virtually all video, and by 2000, independent Ghanaian producers were completing thirty to fifty features per year, sometimes shown for a small admission fee in video parlors or converted movie theaters, but more often rented or sold for home viewing. The advent of chains such as Ghana's TV3 and South Africa's M-Net created more outlets for broadcasting videofilm.

Filmmakers interviewed for the 2001 French documentary *The Audiovisual Industry in Ghana* say they prefer video because it saves the enormous cost of sending celluloid to Europe for processing. Celluloid, they say, is for FESPACO or Cannes, but video is the way to reach African viewers who want "to see Ghanaians playing in Ghanaian stories." The videofilms sampled in the documentary, such as *One Flesh* and *Ghost Tears*, show manifestly low production values, but grip viewers with melodramatic family situations and use plenty of *juju* or African magic.

As Nigerian celluloid dried up in the early 1990s, videofilm production grew to its current level of 250–700 titles per year, depending on how you count. A popular film can sell 50,000 to 100,000 copies at perhaps $2 each. Promoters of Nigerian videofilm have been working to put Nigerian video, its stars, and its awards on the global map of movie hype, coining the term "Nollywood." At first, the technical quality of these videos, made cheaply in a few days, was terrible: at one early showing, the audience was so angry at the wretched quality of the projection that they destroyed the hall. Quality has improved, but poor lighting, problems with sound recording, and written-on-the fly scripts remain common.

Tunde Kelani, the cameraman for many Yoruba films on celluloid, has become a successful producer–director, starting with films such as *Ayo Ni Mo Fi I & II* [I Want Joy]. Igbo businessmen soon saw an investment opportunity in producing videos in Igbo and in English, and had a hit with Kenneth Nbue's *Living in Bondage* (1992), about a Lagos man who joins a cult of wealthy businessmen by sacrificing his wife. Other notable videofilms include *Violated I & II*, by female writer and director Amaka Igwe, and Zeb Ejiro's *Domitilla, The Story of a Prostitute*. In both content and style, these films are closer to soap opera melodramas or *Dallas* than to celluloid film, with family conflict, sexual intrigue, occult magic, ostentatious houses, and those ubiquitous objects of desire: Mercedes automobiles. Once all the goods have been ogled, there is often an old-fashioned moralizing conclusion; the hero of *Living in Bondage*, for example, ends up saved by prayer, because a born-again prostitute he once tried to sacrifice brings him into a revivalist Christian group. It is ironic that videofilms, incontestably a popular form produced by Nigerians for Nigerian consumption, depend so heavily on Western influences and incite such a desire for Western consumer goods.

Critics inside and outside Nigeria initially reacted negatively to videofilms' low production values and crass materialism, but as the video phenomenon has grown, it has gotten sympathetic attention, with festivals in New York and Los Angeles screening selections of videofilms. California Newsreel now distributes Kelani's *Thunderbolt*, a relatively well-made video that engages larger issues of ethnic reconciliation along with the melodrama and juju.

A genuinely popular film industry, with good distribution in Africa, independent of both European funding and African government support, has been a dream since the beginning of African cinema in the 1960s, and videofilms have enough of these attributes to deserve open-minded examination. However, the positive attention so far given to videofilms seems largely of two types: crass hype by interested parties who want to expand the market for Nigerian videos, and serious, even brilliant analysis by academics such as Brian Larkin, Onookome Okome, and Jonathan Haynes, who read the films more as documents than as artistic creations. As Haynes puts it, so far the videofilms' "claims on scholarly attention are perhaps more sociological than political or purely aesthetic."[12]

Central Africa

Angola: Coming Back after the Wars?

The first Angolan film is probably *Sambizanga* (1972), shot before independence by an extraordinary woman from Guadeloupe, Sara Maldoror. Traveling with Angolan writer and MPLA (Popular Movement for the Liberation of Angola) leader Mario de Andrade, she saw that film could reach illiterate populations. Given a Soviet scholarship, she studied film with Mark Donskoy in Moscow in 1961–62, at the same time Sembène was there. After Moscow, she lived in Morocco and Algeria, worked as Gillo Pontecorvo's assistant on *The Battle of Algiers* (1966), and made *Monangambee* (1970), a prizewinning short about the Angolan conflict. After spending 3 months with Cabral's guerrillas to film *Guns for Banta* in the bush of Guinea-Bissau with an Algerian crew, she set out to make *Sambizanga,* based on Luandino Vieira's novel *The Real Life of Domingos Xavier*. Angolan villager Maria searches the prisons of Luanda, looking for her construction worker husband, who has been arrested for supporting independence. With community help, she finds the prison, but he dies under torture. Despite this gruesome outcome, the film is not pessimistic: it depicts Maria and Luanda's poor coming to consciousness and joining a popular struggle, and ends with a clandestine party where militants inspired by Domingos' death plan to attack the prison. (The analogy with *The Battle of Algiers*, where temporary defeat serves as inspiration for a later victory, is striking.) *Sambizanga* won the grand prize at the Carthage Festival in 1972.

After the creation of Angolan TV in 1975, directors such as visual artist Antonio Ole and poet Rui Duarte de Carvalho alternated TV production with occasional film features. Ole made cultural documentaries, such as his 1977 film about the band Ngola Ritmos (the same band playing in the final scene of *Sambizanga*) and his 1980 *In the Path of the Stars*, a poetic tribute to poet Agostino Nehto and Angola itself. Duarte made the fiction feature *Nelsita* (1982), adapting two oral tales about drought in Southeastern Angola to contemporary issues. The quest for a distinctive Angolan style was cut short when the ruinous civil war shut down film production. By 2000, it had been thirteen years since the last locally produced film, both Ole and Duarte had ceased filmmaking, and the theaters of downtown Luanda were all closed.

Since then, with Jonas Savimibi's death and what seems really to be the end of the civil war, the Angolan government and the European Union are trying to revive national cinema. For some countries, only three films a year would be a disaster, but for Angola, the three features produced in 2004, the first Angolan films in 20 years, constitute a renaissance. Each is the director's first feature, each was a very long time in preparation, and each is directly concerned with the legacy of Angola's wars. *Hero* (2004) by Zeze Gamboa, shows a veteran amputee seeking work in a Luanda of political corruption where even a veteran's prosthesis can be stolen for the black market; it won the World Cinema prize at Sundance and was selected to lead off the New Directors series at MOMA. *Hollow City* (2004) by Maria Joao Ganga follows a 12-year-old rural war orphan as he drifts around a lively but menacing Luanda. *The Canhoca Train* (2004) by Orlando Fortunato recreates a colonial episode where a railroad car carrying prisoners uncoupled from the train, leaving them to survive in the forest. Not only Portugal and France, but also Tunisia and Morocco, collaborated in the production of this continent-spanning film project.[13]

Cameroon

Despite long-running dictatorships, Cameroon has stayed culturally lively; film production remains intermittent, but includes some excellent titles. Cameroon's first feature is probably

Jean-Pierre Dikongué Pipa's *Muna Moto: Child of the Other* (1975), which won the grand prize at FESPACO for treating the common problem of forbidden marriage with poetic flashbacks and exceptional lyricism. Another Cameroonian pioneer is Daniel Kamwa, who made an impression with his 1973 short *Boubou Cravate* [Boubou or Tie], and followed up with *Pousse Pousse* (1975), a comedy about a delivery driver trying to raise dowry money to get married. *Pousse Pousse* was popular, but critics cited it as an example of just the kind of unthreatening, light fare that European funders like to support. Emile Bassek Ba Kobhio, from a slightly younger generation, started with two strong features, *Sango Malo* (1991) and *Le Grand Blanc de Lambarène* (1994), a fictionalized life of that ambiguous figure, Albert Schweitzer. His *Silences of the Forest,* about an educated African (played by Eric Ebouaney) who tries to help the Pygmies, came out in 2003.

Among recent filmmakers, the standout is Jean-Pierre Bekolo, whose brilliant *Quartier Mozart* won the Prix Afrique en Création at Cannes in 1992. *Quartier Mozart* uses jump cuts, Spike Lee–style direct address to the camera, terrific pacing, and a vibrant hip-hop sound track to represent an urban neighborhood where style is the residents' only defense against poverty and degradation. Instead of dignifying Cameroon's police state with a serious response, Bekolo cartoons it in the person of Mad Dog, a policeman who gives traffic tickets to the handicapped in their little wagons and who cannot control his household, much less an entire country. Invited by the British Film Institute (BFI) to contribute to cinema's centenary celebrations, Bekolo created *Aristotle's Plot* (1996), a funny, self-critical reflection on what a truly African cinema should be. A *cineaste* (quickly dubbed "Sillyass") finds the local movie house taken over by gangsters who watch only the likes of Schwarzenegger and Van Damme. In the name of authentic African cinema, Sillyass calls the police and has them kicked out, but then his slow "calabash films" bore everyone. To make a good African film, Sillyass and the gangsters will have to cooperate. Sillyass thinks he's an innocent aesthete, but Bekolo insists that all parties in the film industry are complicit with the neocolonial state. His recent feature, *Les Saignantes* (The Bloodettes, 2005), turns to sexually explicit sci-fi dystopia to portray his home country.

Jean-Marie Teno made the fiction feature *Clando* (1996), but is best known for his excellent documentaries, including *Africa, I Will Fleece You* (1991), *Head in the Clouds* (1994), *Chief* (1999), and *The Colonial Misunderstanding* (2005). *Chief* starts from a dramatic event captured spontaneously on video: a crowd wants to beat to death an adolescent boy caught stealing chickens. After putting down the camera and intervening to save the boy's life, Teno sets out to answer the question: why is it that in Cameroon, if you steal a chicken they kill you, but if you steal the whole nation, they put up statues in your honor? His quest to understand the cult of the chief takes Teno to the jail cell of resistant journalist Pius Njawe, and to the city hall where women getting married must pledge that their husband will be "chief" of the family.

Democratic Republic of Congo (DRC)

Belgian colonizers controlled filmmaking tightly in the racist belief that Africans were not "mature" enough for cinema; their Film and Photo Bureau made simple short films with few characters and strict chronological order (no flashbacks or foreshadowing) to propagandize Africans. The Belgians left no Congolese trained to run an independent film industry, and Mobutu's dictatorship did little to develop a national cinema and much to suppress any kind of truth-telling: Thierry Michel's excellent documentary, *Mobutu, King of Zaire* (1999), shows how masterfully Mobutu warped the audiovisual landscape of the country to support his rule. Since Mobutu's fall, civil war, chaos, and financial collapse have made filmmaking nearly impossible, so that many Congolese directors live or work in exile.

Among those who have had success, Mweze Ngangura stands out: audiences found his 1987 *La Vie Est Belle* [Life Is Rosy], a musical starring singer Papa Wemba, delightful, and his 1998 comedy, *Pièces D'Identités* [Identity Cards], won the grand prize at FESPACO. He has switched to video for a recent feature, *The Governor's New Clothes* (2005). Two other "Congolese" films were made by Haitian Raoul Peck, who lived in Kinshasa as a child. The first, *Lumumba, Death of a Prophet* (1991), an excellent documentary about the rise and assassination of Lumumba, pays special attention to the power of mass media. Peck returned to his subject for the feature *Lumumba* (1999), made with a broader audience in mind. After two superb shorts, *The Checkerboard* (1996) and *Article 15 bis* (1999), Balufu Bakupa-Kayinda released the feature *Afro@Digital* (2003), continuing the exploration of African techno-futurism opened by Akomfrah's *Last Angel of History.* In addition to *Macadam Tribu* (see previous Mali section), Jose "Zeka" Laplaine has made *Clandestine* (1996), a wonderful comic short about an illegal immigrant who gets into Europe for a few minutes, then happily returns to Africa, and two fiction features, *Paris XY (2001)* and *The Garden* (2004).

Gabon

Omar Bongo, Gabon's president since 1968, for a time favored cinema to improve the country's image and gave production support to some films during the1970s. Since then, government support has slowed, but Henri-Joseph Koumba Bididi has completed two fiction films including *The Elephant's Balls* (1999), about a politician obsessed with his impotence, and Leon Imunga Ivanga's first feature, *Dolé* [Money] (1999), a study of urban youth in Libreville, won the grand prize at Carthage and best screenplay at FESPACO.

Chad

Chad has not been known for film, but that is changing. Mahamat Saleh Haroun, based in France, claims Chad's first fiction feature with his 1999 *Bye Bye, Africa*, a reflection on cinema itself that mixes 35-mm footage with Beta SP video, and has directed a second feature, *Abouna: Our Father* (2003). Issa Serge Coelo made *Daresalam* [Let There Be Peace] (2000), whose alternation of military struggle and civilian life recalls earlier nation-building epics such as Algeria's *Chronique des Années de Braise*. With spectacular battles on camelback, the film narrates the defeat and reintegration of Chadian rebels into society. However, Coelo's declaration of peace and national unity was premature: oil exploitation and dictatorship continue to incite civil conflict in Chad. Mahamat Zara Yacoub showed her courageous documentary about excision on Chadian national TV and withstood the uproar the film created.

Southern Africa

Zimbabwe

Because of Ian Smith's white settler regime, Zimbabwe did not achieve independence in the 1960s, but suffered apartheid and protracted guerrilla war until 1980. An English-speaking country with a spectacular landscape, great shooting weather, and a relatively good national infrastructure, post-independence Zimbabwe attracted overseas productions and was a prime choice of shooting locations for films set in a not-yet-free South Africa. The Southern

African festival in Harare became a hopeful 1980s gathering place. Because of the collapse of the Zimbabwean currency starting in the 1980s, and the more recent rifts between Robert Mugabe's government and the West, it has become progressively more difficult to make feature films in Zimbabwe. A significant proportion of Zimbabwe's fiction film output consists of didactic films signed by Zimbabwean directors but produced by development organizations such as John and Louise Riber's Media for Development Trust, which can access U.S., British, Scandinavian, and Canadian development money and which maintains significant artistic control.

Michael Raeburn's musical *Jit*, made 10 years after independence in 1990, is often identified as Zimbabwe's first feature film. The romantic comedy is propelled by superstar musician Oliver "Tuku" Mtukudzi playing himself and providing great Zimbabwean music. Although concerned with the lives of Zimbabwean blacks, the film treads lightly over social and political issues and offers a tidied-up version of daily life in the townships (called "high-density suburbs" in the local euphemism). Raeburn, born to British parents in Cairo and trained in Paris, also filmed Doris Lessing's novel *The Grass Is Singing*, with stars Karen Black and John Kani. A passionate Mugabe supporter during the struggle, he made *Rhodesia Countdown* (1962), satirizing white Rhodesians and welcoming national liberation. In 2003, he released *Zimbabwe Countdown*, joining the chorus of calls for Mugabe's exit: it won first prize at the Milan festival.

Directed by Godwin Mawuru and advertised by Media for Development Trust (MDT) as "Zimbabwe's second feature film," *Neria* (1992) concerns a widow whose brother-in-law insists on a customary right to marry her, taking over property and children. Neria is a modern woman who knows her rights, goes to court, and gets everything restored to her by a kindly old British judge in a wig. The didactic film seems designed to teach women how to do this, but there are problems with the scenario, including the improbability of expecting justice for black women from the very system that oppresses them. As arts policy advocate Tafataona Mahoso puts it, "the story becomes very problematic, since it associates modernity, city life, and the law and courts with the liberation of women. . . . the role of these in perpetrating gender oppression is not even hinted at."[14] Despite its shortcomings, the film was a sensation in Zimbabwe: the villain is very villainous; the happy ending is satisfying; Oliver Mtukudzi is again on hand with excellent music; and many people came for the fun of seeing Jesesi Mungoshi, wife of famed writer Charles Mungoshi, play a budding feminist.

Novelist Tsitsi Dangarembga (*Nervous Conditions*) directed the Riber-produced 1995 AIDS drama *Everyone's Child*; a superb writer, she is also credited with work on the screenplay. The film is well intentioned, and its portrayal of urban orphans' twilight world is excellent, but the plot tends toward melodrama, and the resolution (rural community recognizes its errors and takes the AIDS orphans back) seems didactically imposed. The acting is sometimes flat, perhaps because of the choice (imposed by MDT) to film in English rather than in Shona. Dangarembga has since written and directed the very different *Karé Karé Svako* [Mother's Day] (2003), based on a folk tale about a husband who eats his wife in a time of hunger, only to find that the maternal principle is more powerful than he thought.

Since *Everyone's Child*, Riber has directed some MDT films himself, including the much-heralded *Yellow Card* (2000), about how a soccer star comes to accept responsibility for the child he has begotten. Preaching male as well as female sexual and parental responsibility is an improvement over earlier MDT productions such as *More Time* (1993) and *Consequences* (1988), which seemed to put the burden of sexual responsibility exclusively on women. MDT's website proclaims it the largest distributor of African films north of the Limpopo, and *Yellow Card* used a sort of distribution blitzkrieg, including video showings all over rural Mozambique. Even for those who find it dubious that an American couple with European and North American funding should intervene in African art and morality, MDT's distribution methods warrant further study.

Among Zimbabwean films, Mahoso praises Simon Bright's *Mbira: Spirit of the People* (1990) for its "extensive and sensitive research on music, African metaphor, and symbolism in Zimbabwe. . . . the film does not have to lecture its audience. It simply invites their participation. The audience enters the space which the film has cleared for them." He also appreciates Chaz Maviyane-Davies' *After the Wax* (1992) for its densely poetic compression of almost 600 years of African history, asserting that its metaphoric style avoids the "excessive literalness so typical of the 'development' film."[15]

MDT's work is controversial, but perhaps the most controversial Zimbabwean film has been Ingrid Sinclair's *Flame* (1996), telling the stories of two women guerrillas whose battle names are Flame and Liberty. Flame is raped by her commander but puts the audience through improbable changes of sympathy by later agreeing to be his lover and bearing his child. The most telling scenes occur when impoverished Flame visits Liberty in Harare after the war and sees for herself the vast wealth gained by people who took no risks for independence. While the film was still being shot, groups of Zimbabwean "veterans" objected to it, and the police confiscated the footage on grounds that it was both subversive and pornographic to depict a national hero committing rape. Eventually, the government allowed Sinclair to finish the film, which was appreciated by international audiences. The wounds it depicts have obviously not yet healed, and the future of Zimbabwean cinema, like the future of Zimbabwean society, is uncertain.

Mozambique: The Birth (and Death) of Cinema

Very soon after independence, President Samora Machel established a National Institute of Cinema, whose main project, as shown in Margarida Cardoso's beautiful and heartbreaking 2003 documentary *Kuxa Kanema, the Birth of Cinema*, was the production of 10-minute newsreels in both 35mm (for showing in urban theaters) and 16mm (for rural projection from roving vans) film. Brazilian cinema novo director Ruy Guerra, of Mozambican origin, came back in 1978 to direct the Institute, which grew to have 250 employees. French filmmakers Jean-Luc Godard and Jean Rouch also came to Mozambique to try new ideas: Rouch experimented with lightweight Super 8 technology, and Godard advocated giving out video cameras and teaching people to use them. Sympathetic foreigners from Cuba and Brazil came to train Mozambicans of all classes and geographical regions. Small, impoverished Mozambique surpassed most African countries in its ability to shoot, process, and edit film. Kuxa Kanema produced 400 newsreels, but the war and Machel's 1986 death in a suspicious plane crash took their toll, and an electrical fire in 1992 finished off the National Institute of Cinema. Cardoso's documentary shows large parts of the building open to the sky and a few employees waiting for retirement.

Fiction film was not a priority, but features did get made, including Ruy Guerra's 1979 *Mueda: Memorial and Massacre*, a fictional account of the 1960 Portuguese massacre of 600 villagers, and Jose Cardoso's 1985 *The Wind Blows from the North.* Since the Institute's demise, many directors work with Ebano Multimedia, which co-produced Licinio Azvedo's documentary about a ghost village, *Marraacuene: Two Banks of the Mozambican River*, and Brazilian director Sergio Rezende's fictional *A Child from the South* (1991). Margarida Cardoso's documentary ends elegiacally, with shots of a TV set tuned to CNN in a Mozambique now dominated by television. Mozambicans, she says, "are deprived of an image of themselves" and invited to dream a televised dream, a "dream that people will never be able to attain."

Republic of South Africa

Because of its mineral wealth and connections with global capital, South Africa has been a regional media power for more than a century, despite the stigma of apartheid. I. W. Schlesinger, an American who moved to South Africa, founded African Film Productions, which dominated South African cinema from 1913 until it was taken over by 20th Century Fox in 1956. Schlesinger's career prefigures two tendencies: first, South African cinema has been more industrially organized and more producer driven than the cinemas of West and Central Africa, where individual directors strive to realize artistic visions; and second, although South African cinema never had a large enough audience base to challenge Hollywood, there has been a remarkable circulation of capital, technology, actors, subjects, and images between the two cinemas.The first movie about Zulus was shot in the United States in 1908 by D. W. Griffith. Schlesinger's 1916 feature-length *De Voortrekkers* (also known as *Winning a Continent*), an epic, racist celebration of the Boers' 1838 ox wagon trek and brutal conquest of the Zulus, is a South African version of Griffith's *Birth of a Nation* (1915), and it in turn probably inspired the American film *Covered Wagon*. American gangster films helped define the style of South African gangsters, called "tsotsis" (apparently a corruption of the American "zoot suit"). These connections are not accidental but arise from similarities between two white settler societies.

Censorship. In addition to subsidizing the films it favored, the apartheid government censored both domestic and foreign films. Mild material such as *The Autobiography of Miss Jane Pitman* was banned for black viewers, and quality films such as *The Battle of Algiers*, *Last Tango in Paris*, and *Seven Beauties* were banned altogether because of political or sexual content. Domestic filmmakers had to accept the censor's changes, and some films such as actor Gibson Kente's *How Long?* were confiscated and never released. Other films such as *Come Back, Africa* and *Mapantsula* (discussed herein) had to be shot clandestinely. Broadcast television was not permitted until 1976.

Perhaps the height (or the nadir) of subsidized apartheid film was Jamie Uys's *The Gods Must Be Crazy* (1980), which offers a "Bushman" (San) named N!Xau as a Noble Savage in a leather loincloth, disturbed by a Coke bottle dropped from an airplane. The film's "ethnographic" voiceover narration frankly classifies N!Xau and his family ("the little people") as less than human, part of the flora and fauna of the Kalahari Desert. This thin, low-budget vehicle was a box office success in South Africa and became one of the highest grossing films in Japan, France, Canada, and Sweden, and a success in the United States. So attractive was its racist fantasy of childlike preindustrial simplicity that it ran literally for years in some places.

Few films presented urban black life, and when they did, black life was almost always produced, written, and directed by whites. *Jim Comes to Jo'burg*, also known as *African Jim* (1949), is a case in point, with an escapist plot where an improbably glamorous nightclub takes the place of the townships, and the starving protagonist makes it as a singer. Yet by actually valuing the culture of urban blacks, the two British immigrants who produced the film were able to present a showcase of musical talent white South Africa knew nothing about, including performances by Dolly Rathebe, the African Inkspots, and the amazing Jazz Maniacs. Black, "Coloured," and Indian audiences rushed to buy tickets, breaking previous records set by the American musical *Stormy Weather*, and women in the townships styled their hair like Dolly Rathebe's.

Come Back, Africa (1959) constitutes an extraordinary exception to South African media rules. Lionel Rogosin, a wealthy leftist director from New York, came to South Africa seeking a subject for his next film and met *Drum* magazine writers Bloke Modisane, Lewis Nkosi, and Can Themba, who initiated him into the life of the famous mixed-race neighborhood Sophiatown. Modisane and Nkosi wrote the script, and various *Drum* figures appeared in the film, as did a very young Mariam Makeba. One of the triumphs of the anti-apartheid movement was that, without possessing a national territory, black South Africans such as Miriam Makeba, Hugh Masekela, and Abdullah Ibrahim created an internationally recognized black South African culture.

Come Back, Africa is of enormous value simply for its documentation of black life in Johannesburg at the end of the 1950s. The film does much more, however, than document poverty and victimization. Its title is a translation of the ANC political slogan, "*Mayibuye i-Afrika*," which might also be translated as "Take Back Africa," and the film shows undefeated black intellectuals and artists discussing cultural issues in their own space. *Come Back, Africa* won an award at the 1959 Venice Film Festival, and opened in the United States in 1960, just as images of the brutal 1960 Sharpeville massacre circulated through world media.

Cracks in Apartheid's Screen. Lionel Ngakane, a founder of FEPACI who had been both an actor and an assistant director on *Cry, the Beloved Country*, directed the short *Jemima and Johnny* (1966) and several documentaries from exile in London. Nana Mahomo, living off and on in exile, clandestinely filmed *Last Grave at Dimbaza* (1973), whose secret footage showed the systemic aspect of apartheid violence and the viciousness of the "homelands" policy. Some white directors, such as Jans Rautenbach, Ross Devenish, and Manie van Rensburg, also questioned the apartheid system.

Cry, White Season! Hollywood Enters the Fray. Almost too late, Hollywood suddenly found the anti-apartheid struggle interesting material for mass appeal movies, including Richard Attenborough's *Cry Freedom* (1987: Steven Biko seen through Donald Woods's eyes); Chris Menges's *A World Apart* (1988: Ruth First's life and death); Euzahn Palcy's *A Dry White Season* (1989: André Brink novel about an Afrikaans teacher improbably just discovering the evils of apartheid); and John Avildsen's silly *The Power of One* (1992: ultimate insult from the director of *Rocky* and *The Karate Kid*—an English-speaking white boy singlehandedly leads South African blacks to freedom, with John Gielgud, Morgan Freeman, and Winston Tshona participating in the farce). Many of these films felt obliged to give the presumedly white audience a white guide with whom to "identify." After apartheid's fall, Hollywood's invasion of South Africa gathered steam: witness Juliette Binoche as Antje Krog covering the TRC in 2004s *In My Country* (also known as *Country of My Skull*).

Apartheid's Panic: Mapantsula (1988). During the mid-1980s, a white film editor named Oliver Schmitz teamed up with Thomas Mogotlane, a black writer and actor who had been arrested for his work with Gibson Kente. Dispensing with the white guide character, Mogotlane created a scenario centered on a black gangster named Panic. They showed the authorities a dummy script implying the film would be a gangster entertainment, but the real subject was Panic's conversion by the ANC from freelance criminal revolt to organized political revolution. Schmitz, who had been a newsreel editor in Germany, made sure *Mapantsula* showed a pervasive awareness of media images as weapons of struggle. Outside South Africa, the film won numerous awards and contributed to the worldwide mobilization against apartheid.[16]

William Kentridge: Animations of History. Fine artist William Kentridge, whose father was part of Mandela's legal defense team, invented a unique new kind of animated film: instead of drawing hundreds of cells (or having a computer draw them) the way most animators do, Kentridge does a charcoal drawing, photographs it, erases parts of it, redraws, and reshoots, creating a moving picture that bears traces of its past. One might almost say that Kentridge has found a way to draw history. During the crucial late 1980s and early 1990s, he completed eight short animations in the "Drawings for Projection" series. The connections and transformations they make visible are breathtaking. In *Mine* (1991), businessman Soho Eckstein is having breakfast in bed: he pushes the plunger of his coffeemaker and it goes down through the blankets, through the bed, and into the ground, revealing black miners at work, miners in holocaust-like showers, miners sleeping like corpses in narrow stalls, and ultimately miners in a classic slave-ship configuration, all connected directly to his wealth and comfort. In other Kentridge movies, Sharpeville-like demonstrators lie dead on the ground, newspapers full of lies flutter down and cover them, and they become features of Johannesburg's landscape, piles of mine tailings waiting for resurrection. *History of the Main Complaint* (1996) reflects white responses to the Truth and Reconciliation Commission (TRC): Soho Eckstein feels unwell, enters a clinic for tests, is pronounced OK, and goes back to the amnesiac state of denial that is normal in white South Africa.[17]

The "New" South Africa. Mandela's 1990 release from prison and the 1994 elections occurred amid rapid media change. The old subsidy system was replaced by the National Film and Video Foundation (NFVF). South African TV chain M-Net's "New Directions" series offered production funds to younger African directors and started acquiring rights to numerous African films. Catalyst Productions assembled a collection of shorts called *Africa Dreaming*, distributing them widely through cable, satellite, and video sales, and *Mama Africa* did the same. The first Sithengi Market, not so much a film festival as deal-making convention, was held in Cape Town in 1996 and has become an annual affair. (There had always been South African film festivals, but only for those willing to flout the ANC's cultural boycott.)

As formal apartheid crumbled, black writers and directors no longer needed the screen of a white collaborator. Ramadan Suleiman, a theater activist who had left the country to study filmmaking in Europe, returned to shoot *Fools* (1987), based on Njabulo Ndebele's influential novella of the same name. Advertised as "South Africa's first all-black feature film," *Fools* depicts the renewal of township schoolteacher Zamani (played by Patrick Shai) whose despair has sunk him into alcoholism, cowardice, and lechery. Suleiman's second feature, *Zulu Love Letter* (2004), about a woman journalist suffering aftereffects of apartheid and hesitating to appear before the TRC in a country that only wants to forget its history, won the European Union Prize and the Best Actress Prize at FESPACO 2005.

Another award-winning all-black feature production of the transition period is Ntshaveni Wa Luruli's Soweto comedy *Chikin Bizness: the Whole Story* (1998), which won Best Film at the Montreal Festival, and both Best Screenplay and Best Actor at FESPACO 1999. Wa Luruli, who has a doctorate in scriptwriting and directing from Columbia, has completed a second feature, *The Wooden Camera,* about a boy who finds a video camera and disguises it as a toy so that he can film life in Cape Town's huge Khayelitsha squatter camp.

Zola Maseko, who studied film in England, won Best Documentary at FESPACO for *The Life and Times of Sara Baartman* (1998), an analytical history of the so-called Hottentot Venus, a woman who was exhibited nude in London and Paris, was dissected by Georges Cuvier, and her brain and genitals displayed at the Musée de l'Homme in Paris. (A 2003 sequel records the return of Sara's remains to South Africa for burial.) Maseko is devoted to reinterpreting the past, and his historical recreation of *Drum* magazine won first prize at FESPACO 2005, although there was controversy about his use of an African-American lead actor (Taye Diggs) and his opinion that African film should aspire to be like Hollywood.

Four of the twenty films in the 2005 FESPACO feature competition were from South Africa, which continues its international success. *uCarmen eKhayelitsha*, a remake of Bizet's opera sung in Xhosa, won the top prize at the 2005 Berlin Festival. *Yesterday* (2005), an AIDS drama in Zulu, was nominated for the Best Foreign Language Film Oscar, and Gavin Hood's film version of Athol Fugard's 1980 gangster novel *Tsotsi* won the foreign language Oscar in 2006. Tehobo Mahalatsi's 1999 *Portrait of a Young Man Drowning* won the Short Film category at Venice. Sechaba Morojele, Lionel Ngakane's nephew, won Best Short at the 2004 Pan African Festival in Los Angeles for *Ubuntu's Wounds* (a skeptical treatment of the TRC). Zulfah Otto-Sallies' *Raya* (2000) and *Project 10: Through the Eyes of My Daughter* (2004) have been well received.

Before concluding all is well in South African cinema, however, one should listen to young Morojele's complaint, in *Chimurenga* magazine, that white producers still decide what films will get made, and that they declare there is no longer a market for political films like his.[18] Ethiopian director and critic Haile Gerima expresses similar reservations, recounting his trips to Zimbabwe and South Africa during the 1980s and 1990s, where it seemed that whites with capital and training acquired under apartheid were still blithely in charge, where commercial considerations reigned, and where it was difficult for young black filmmakers to tell their stories in an appropriate film language. Aware that South African capital and technology will affect the whole continent's media, Gerima puts the question strongly:

> It is from South Africa that Hollywood plans to dominate the rest of Africa. . . . The latter is actually taking place on a small scale through outfits such as M-Net. The technological hype in South Africa seems to be organized on the basis of delivery, distribution, and dissemination, rather than on creating a South African cultural identity.[19]

Gerima is hopeful, but he puts his hope in the young students such as those at the Newtown Film and Video School, who must unlearn Hollywood forms and vocabularies to tell their African stories. Elsewhere on the continent, directors and writers welcome the changes in South Africa, but also worry that the media giant may sweep away some of the hard-won progress they have made since a short film called *Borom Sarret* put African film on the map of world cinema.

East Africa

Ethiopia

Haile Selassie's regime, the Mengistu Haile Mariam dictatorship, and wars with Eritrea have pushed many Ethiopian directors and critics to work in exile, where they have nonetheless managed a significant contribution. Haile Gerima has produced several important features, including *Harvest 3000 Years* (1976), his study of exploited Ethiopian peasants, *Bush Mama* (1976), the story of an urban African-American woman's struggles, *Sankofa* (1993), a brilliant fictional essay on the Atlantic slave trade, then and now, and *Adawa: An African Victory* (1999), a reconstruction of Menelik II's 1896 victory over the Italians. Gerima, who left Ethiopia at the age of 21 to study theater in the United States, and has long taught at Howard University, was strongly affected by black nationalism and Frantz Fanon; he identifies himself as a third-world filmmaker. In addition to writing and directing his own films, he founded a distribution company called Mypheduh Films, and has pioneered innovative distribution techniques (particularly for *Sankofa*) in an effort to bypass corporate circuits. Gerima is an active member of FEPACI, and a passionate defender of third-world interests whenever film criticism, theory, or infrastructure are discussed.

Yemane I. Demissie, who also attended UCLA's School of Theater, Film, and Television, directed *Tumult* (1996), an elegant black-and-white feature about a young Ethiopian involved in a failed coup who learns a profound lesson about class relations when he has to take refuge with family servants. Salem Mekuria, who works with Boston public television, has produced several documentaries, including the superb *Deluge* (1995), a history of the 1974 revolution in Ethiopia that combines public sources with family photos and letters to give a detailed and moving account of the personal cost of these brutal political events. Ermias Woldeamlak's more recent short, *The Father* (2000), which treats this same period in a compressed and intense fictional form, has received wide video distribution.

Kenya, Tanzania, and Uganda

From *Out of Africa* to *Nowhere in Africa* to *The Constant Gardener*, East Africa has long been a scenic favorite of U.S. and European directors. Foreign producers continue to use the area for location shooting, and Nairobi is a media capital in its own right, producing advertising spots, documentaries, music videos, television series, and videofilms. The Pan-Afro-Arab Festival inaugurated in 1981 in Mogadishu disappeared with the 1991 outbreak of Somalia's civil war, but other festivals have taken its place, notably the Zanzibar International Film Festival, which for 10 years has shown films from all of Africa and the Dhow countries, a regional gesture toward the Indian Ocean islands and Bollywood itself. The top prize at the first Zanzibar Festival in 1998 went to *Maangamizi: The Ancient One*, co-directed by Tanzanian Martin Mhando and American Ron Mulvihill, a film about two women that dramatizes the relationship between Western psychiatry and African epistemologies. Other notable films from the region screened at Zanzibar include *Nalaika Is Going* (2002), a videofilm about a young domestic worker made by Kenyan Albert Wanadogo, and a controversial short, *Surrender* (2000), by Caroline Gilbert, about the close relationship of two Tanzanian men.

Kenyan Ann Mungai has made more than ten films, including the fiction feature *Saikati* (1992), in Masai and Swahili, about a woman's efforts to avoid both forced marriage and prostitution. Wanjiru Kinyanjui's *The Battle of the Sacred Tree* (1994) is a German production in Swahili about a woman's struggle for emancipation in a rural milieu dominated by patriarchal religions. German-educated Tanzanian Flora M'bugu Schelling had an international success with her poetic 1992 documentary *These Hands*, about a group of women stone breakers.

CONCLUSION

No Film Industry, Just Excellent Films

The lack of a film industry infrastructure has made life difficult for African filmmakers and reduced the number of productions, but it may have had positive results as well. Since nearly every film results from the artistic vision, creative engagement, and determination of a single director (who is often also the writer), there are very few routine films, shot just to make a buck or to keep a studio busy. The quality and seriousness of the films is very high, much higher than that of Hollywood's average product, and issues such as wealth disparities, government corruption, suppression of women, or youth marginalization are addressed directly. Ghanaian philosopher Kwame Anthony Appiah has described the situation this way: "Despite the overwhelming reality of economic decline; despite unimaginable poverty; despite wars, malnutrition, disease, and political instability, African cultural productivity grows apace: popular literatures, oral narrative and poetry, dance, drama, music, and visual art all thrive."[20] The films of African cinema's first 40 years constitute an extraordinary accomplishment, achieved against the odds by tenacious creativity.

South African Film Summit

In April 2006, South Africa's Ministry of Arts and Culture and the National Film and Video Fund (NFVF) hosted an African film "summit" in Johannesburg to plan responses to the changing conditions of audiovisual production and distribution. That a South African ministry could organize and host such a summit signals a major shift in the center of gravity of African cinema and its institutions, away from French influence and the brand of *auteur* cinema practiced in Africa since 1963.

Documents distributed by NFVF before the summit were heavy with business jargon and the names of bureaucratic entities, but terms such as "art," "culture," "director," or "screenwriter" were rare. One paragraph spoke of "providing a new mandate for FEPACI to act within the NEPAD (New Partnership for African Development) context and addressing the capacity requirements of FEPACI that are necessary to carry out the new mandate." The prose is opaque: perhaps it means FEPACI will be provided with new funds and new powers, but it more likely means that FEPACI, with its liberationist past and its mixed management record, will either be absorbed into a new entity or bypassed by a new institutional configuration.

South Africa's *Mail and Guardian* and *Africultures* magazine[21] reported that after hearing the summit's account of his organization's failures, FEPACI Secretary General Jacques Béhanzin resigned, and three new officers were chosen, one from Gabon, one from Nigeria, and one from South Africa. FEPACI's directorate, bilingual for the first time in its history, will be housed in South Africa for the next four years. News reports also confirm that the "Expected Output" referred to in the planning documents was indeed delivered by the summit in the form of the Tshwane Declaration, reflecting the summit's desire for an "audiovisual industry" in its call for the African Union (AU) to establish an African Audiovisual and Cinema Commission and create a fund to promote cinema and television in Africa. Approved documents will be presented to the culture ministers of AU countries for continent-wide binding legislation to regulate audiovisual industries, but it is hard to imagine all the governments of the AU agreeing to the same legislation or refraining from interference in artistic expression.

Since 1963, numerous bodies have adopted pious resolutions about African cinema without much effect, and the Tshwane declaration may or may not join those other expressions of good will in the archives. Whatever happens to the summit's resolutions, however, major shifts in the structure of African cinema will continue to occur in response to technological changes and to post-apartheid South Africa's entry into the continent's cultural industries. It is far too early to evaluate the net effect of these changes, but it seems probable there will continue to be a small group of *cineastes* who will go to extraordinary lengths to make artistically excellent films, with or without government approval, with or without an audiovisual industry, and with or without celluloid.

RESOURCE GUIDE

PRINT SOURCES

Andrade-Watkins, Claire. "Portuguese African Cinema: Historical and Contemporary Perspectives 1969 to 1993." *Research in African Literatures* 26.3 (1995, Fall): 137–150.

Appiah, Kwame Anthony. "Is the 'Post' in 'Postcolonial' the 'Post' in 'Postmodern'?" p. 440 in Anne McClintock, Aamir Mufti, and Ella Shohat (eds.), *Dangerous Liaisons: Gender, Nation, and Postcolonial Perspectives*. Minneapolis: University of Minnesota Press, 1997.

Arenas, Fernando. *After Independence: Globalization, "(Neo)-colonialism," and the Cultures of Lusophone Africa*. In press.

Bakari, Imruh, and Mbye Cham, eds. *African Experiences of Cinema*. London: British Film Institute, 1996.

Balogun, Françoise. *The Cinema in Nigeria*. Enugu, Nigeria: Delta Publications, 1987.

Balseiro, Elizabeth, and Ntongela Masilela. *To Change Reels: Film and Film Culture in South Africa*. Detroit: Wayne State University Press, 2003.

Barlet, Olivier. *African Cinemas: Decolonising the Gaze.* London and New York: Zed Books, 2000. (Barlet's French magazine, *Africultures*, carries nonacademic reports on African films and video; some contents available in English on the Internet.)

Bickford-Smith, Vivian, and Richard Mendelsohn, eds. *Black and White in Colour: African History on Screen.* Oxford: James Currey, 2007.

Boughedir, Ferid. *Afrique noire: Quel cinéma?* Paris: Actes du colloque, Université Paris X Nanterre, 1981.

Diawara, Manthia. *African Cinema: Politics and Culture.* Bloomington: University of Indiana Press, 1992.

Écrans d'Afrique/African Screen. Bilingual journal of African cinema based in Milan; has ceased publishing, but back issues are available in many libraries. Special issues on individual directors can be very useful.

Eke, Maureen, Kenneth Harrow, and Emmanuel Yewah, eds. *African Images: Recent Studies and Texts in Cinema.* Trenton, NJ: Africa World Press, 2000.

Ellerson, Beti. *Sisters of the Screen: Women of Africa on Film, Video, and Television.* Trenton, NJ: Africa World Press, 2000.

FESPACO/L'Association des Trois Mondes. *Les Cinémas D'Afrique: Dictionnaire.* Paris: Karthala, 2000. (Excellent reference book; usable even if you do not speak French.)

Givanni, June, ed. *Symbolic Narratives/African Cinema: Audiences, Theory, and the Moving Image.* London: British Film Institute, 2000. (Based on the 1995 London conference, *Africa and the History of Cinematic Ideas.*)

Gugler, Joseph. *African Film: Re-Imagining a Continent.* Oxford: James Currey Publishers, 2003.

Harrow, Kenneth, ed. *African Cinema: Postcolonial and Feminist Readings.* Trenton, NJ: Africa World Press, 1999. (Overlaps but not identical to *Research in African Literatures* special issue.)

Haynes, Jonathan, ed. *Nigerian Video Films*, revised and expanded edition. Athens: Ohio University Press, 2000.

Hennebelle, Guy, and Catherine Ruelle. Interview of Djibril Diop Mambety in "Cinéastes d'Afrique noire." *Afrique Littéraire et Artistique* 49 (1978, 3rd Qtr., Special Issue).

Interview with Med Hondo. *Écran 79* (1979, June 15): 25.

iris: a journal of theory on image and sound 18 (1995, Spring). (Special issue on "New Discourses of African Cinema.")

Malkmus, Lizbeth, and Roy Armes. *Arab and African Film Making.* London, UK, and Highlands, NJ: Zed Books, 1991.

Mazrui, Ali. "Where Is Africa?" Pp. 23–39 in Ali Mazrui, *The Africans: A Triple Heritage.* Boston: Little, Brown, 1986.

Moorman, Marissa. "Of Westerns, Women, and War: Re-Situating Angolan Cinema and the Nation." *Research in African Literatures* 32.3 (2001, Fall): 103–122.

Nganang, Alain Patrice. "Of Cameras, Trains, and Roads: French Colonial Conquest in Practice." *Black Renaissance/Renaissance Noire* 5.1 (2003, Spring).

Pfaff, Françoise. *Twenty-Five Black African Filmakers: A Critical Study, with Filmography and Bio-Bibliography.* New York: Greenwood Press, 1988.

———, ed. *Focus on African Films.* Bloomington: University of Indiana, 2004.

Research in African Literatures 26.3 (1995, Fall). (Special issue on African cinema edited by Kenneth Harrow.)

Sadoul, Georges. "Cinema: Le marché africain."*Afrique Action* 29 (1960, May 1): 27.

Shohat, Ella, and Robert Stam. *Unthinking Eurocentrism: Multiculturalism and the Media.* London and New York: Routledge, 1994.

Thackway, Melissa. *Africa Shoots Back: Alternative Perspectives on Sub-Saharan Francophone African Film.* Bloomingtom: University of Indiana Press, 2003.

Ukadike, Nwachukwu Frank. *Black African Cinema.* Berkeley: University of California Press, 1994.

———. *Questioning African Cinema: Conversations with Filmmakers.* Minneapolis: University of Minnesota Press, 2002.

VIDEOS/FILMS

Boughedir, Ferid. *Caméra d'Afrique* (1983). A 95-minute documentary history of African cinema's first 20 years, with copious extracts from the essential films and interviews with important filmmakers.

AFRICAN FILM DISTRIBUTORS

NOTE: Many African films are distributed on video via normal commercial circuits and can be found at local rental shops. Others can be rented or bought through Netflix, Facets Video, Amazon, and other common online dealers; a persistent Internet search will often turn up an economical way to find a desired film. (Watch out for differently translated film titles, and search by director's name as well.) Most university libraries have some African films, and others can be obtained through interlibrary loan. The sources listed herein, however, specialize in African or third-world film, and their Websites can be excellent sources of information.

Art Mattan Productions, 535 Cathedral Parkway, Suite 14B, New York, NY 10025, United States of America. Tel: 1-212-864-1760; Fax: 1-212-316-6020. Website: http://www.africanfilm.com/festival.

British Film Institute, London. www.bfi.org.uk. Film books, videos, and information. Videos purchased here are likely to be zone 2 in PAL format and require some technical work to play on American equipment.

California Newsreel, 500 3rd St., Suite 505, San Francisco, CA 94107, United States of America. Tel: 1-415-284-7800; Fax: 1-415-284-7801. Orders:1-877-811-7495, or Fax: 1-802-846-1850. Email: contact@newsreel.org. Website: http://www.newsreel.org.

Film Resource Unit, PO Box 11065, Johannesburg 2000, South Africa. Tel: +27-11-838-4280/1; Fax: +27-11-838-4451. Very good collection, including some Francophone films with English subtitles at reasonable prices. Website: http://www.fru.co.za.

First Run/Icarus Films, 32 Court Street, 21st Floor, Brooklyn, NY 11201, United States of America. Tel: 1-718-488-8900; Fax: 1-718-488-8642. Email: mailbox@frif.com.

International Movie Data Base. http://www.imdb.com. Does not sell films, but has copious information about all films and directors, including many African ones; has recently begun charging for advanced searches.

Kino International, 333 W. 39th St., Ste. 503, New York, NY 10018, United States of America. Tel: 1-212-629-6880, or 1-800-562-3330; Fax: 1-212-714-0871. Email: contact@kino.com. Website: http://www.kino.com. (Distibutes Souleymane Cisse, Ferid Boughedir, and others.)

La Mediathèque des Trois Mondes, 63 bis rue Cardinal Lemoine, Paris 75005, France. Tel: 011-33-1-42-34-99-00; Fax: 011-33-1-42-34-99-01. Website: http://www.cine3mondes.fr. (Large collection of African Maghreb, Asian, and Latin American films on video and zone 2 DVD at reasonable prices; some have English subtitles.)

New Yorker Films, Tel: 1-212-247-6110; Fax: 1-212-307-7855. Email: info@newyorkerfilms.com. Website: http://www.newyorkerfilms.com. (Distributes Sembène and Abderrahmane Sissako.)

Third World Newsreel, Noel Shaw, Distribution Department, 545 Eight Ave., 10th Floor, New York, NY 10018, United States of America. Tel: 1-212-947-9227, ext. 308; Fax: 1-212-594-6417. Email: twn@twn.org. Website: http://www.twn.org.

UC Extension Center for Media and Independent Learning. Berkeley, CA 94704, United States of America. Tel: 1-510-642-0460. Email: ucmedia@ucxonline.berkeley.edu. Website: http://www-cmil.unex,berkeley.edu/media/.

Women Make Movies, 462 Broadway, Ssuite 500E, New York, NY 10013, United States of America. Tel: 1-212-925-0606, ext. 360; Fax: 1-212-925-2052. Email: Orders@wmm.com. Website: http://wmm.com/catalog.

NOTES

1. For further information, see Nganang 2003 (in Resource Guide), pp. 15–25.
2. Sadoul 1960 (in Resource Guide). Also reprinted in Georges Sadoul, *Histoire du cinéma mondial: des origines à nos jours* (Paris: Flammarion, 1972), p. 499. Also quoted in Diawara 1992 (in Resource Guide), p. 24.

3. The historic 1965 confrontation between Jean Rouch and Sembène Ousmane appears as "You Look at Us As If We Were Insects," *CinémAction* 17 (1982): 77–78. Also see Okwui Enwezor (English trans.), *The Short Century: Independence and Liberation Movements in Africa 1945–1994* (Munich, London, and New York: Prestel, 2001), pp. 440–441.
4. Sembène's first recorded use of this term was probably in an interview by Guy Hennebelle and Catherine Ruelle in *Cinéastes d'Afrique noire,* a special issue of *Afrique Littéraire et Artistique* 49 (1978, 3rd Qtr.), p. 125, in which he says that African cinema is still in "the era of *mégotage*," defining the term by reference to *bricolage* or makeshift, handyman work, necessitated by lack of funds; others have suggested "crumbs" or "leftovers" as English equivalents. Hennebelle and Ruelle took up the term, titling their preface "The End of 'Mégotage'?" and it has been widely circulated since.
5. Boughedir 1981 (in Resource Guide), p. 31. Also quoted in Diawara 1992 (in Resource Guide), p. 31.
6. Mazrui 1986 (in Resource Guide).
7. Diawara 1992 (in Resource Guide), p. 35.
8. Hennebelle and Ruelle 1978 (in Resource Guide), p. 43. Also quoted in Pfaff 1988 (in Resource Guide), p. 218.
9. For further information, see Ellerson 2000 (in Resource Guide); her film, *Sisters of the Screen: African Women in the Cinema,* distributed by Women Make Movies, http://www.wmm.com; and her Website at http://www.founders.howard.edu/beti_ellerson/. See also Kenneth Harrow, *African Cinema: Postcolonial and Feminist Readings* (Trenton, NJ: Africa World Press, 1999).
10. Hondo 1979 (in Resource Guide). Also quoted in Pfaff 1988 (in Resource Guide), p. 161.
11. For further information, see Balogun 1987 (in Resource Guide).
12. Haynes 2000 (in Resource Guide), p. 10.
13. For further information on Portuguese African film, see Arenas (In press; in Resource Guide); Andrade-Watkins 1995 (in Resource Guide); and Moorman 2001 (in Resource Guide).
14. Tofatona Mahoso, "Unwinding the African Dream on African Ground," in Givanni 2000 (in Resource Guide), p. 219.
15. Ibid., p. 222.
16. Peter Davis's book and film, both titled *In Darkest Hollywood: Exploring the Jungles of Cinema's South Africa* (Athens: Ohio University Press, 1996), are essential sources for cinema under apartheid. See also Keyan Tomaselli, *The Cinema of Apartheid: Race and Class in South African Film* (Brooklyn, NY: Smyrna Press, 1988), Rob Nixon, "Cry White Season: Anti-Apartheid Heroism and the American Screen," in *Homelands, Harlem, and Hollywood: South African Culture and the World Beyond* (New York: Routledge, 1994), and *To Change Reels: Film and Film Culture in South Africa* (Detroit: Wayne State University Press, 2003), edited by Elizabeth Balseiro and Ntongela Masilela. The catalog for the *14th Milan Festival of African Cinema,* March 22–28, 2004 (Milan: Editrice Il Castoro, 2004), pp. 196–271, has a detailed retrospective of South African film from 1960 to 2004, in Italian, French, and English.
17. For further information, see two documentaries that include substantial portions of his work: *William Kentridge: Drawing the Passing,* directed by Maria Anna Tappeiner and Reinhard Wulf; and *William Kentridge: the End of the Beginning,* directed by Beata Lipman. Dan Cameron, Carolyn Christov-Bakargiev, and J. M. Coetzee, *William Kentridge* (London: Phaidon Press, 1999) contains still images from the animations, an essay by Nobel novelist J. M. Coetzee, and substantive comments by Kentridge himself.
18. *Chimurenga* (2003, February). http://www.chimurenga.co.za.
19. Balseiro and Masilela 2003 (in Resource Guide), p. 226.
20. Appiah 1997 (in Resource Guide).
21. Preconference document: "African Film Summit, Johannesburg, 3–6 April 2006," distributed by South African Film and Video Foundation, http://www.nfvf.co.za, or from Project Manager Lebone Maema, LeboneM@nfvf.co.za. After-summit reports include Dimitri Martinis, "Cinema of Crumbs," *Johannesburg Mail and Guardian* (2006, April 13); and Claude Haffner, "FEPACI at Tshwane" (2006, April 25), at http://www.africultures.com.

FOOD AND FOODWAYS

FRAN OSSEO-ASARE

Nkwan bɛyɛ dɛ a, efi fam

(The taste of the good soup comes from the good earth)

—Akan proverb, Ghana

There is no such thing as "*the* African kitchen," or "the African national dish," or even the "African word" for any specific recipe or ingredient or cooking technique. It makes more sense to talk about food in "regions" of Africa: northern, southern, eastern, western, and central. North Africa is discussed in the *North Africa and the Middle East* volume of this encyclopedia.

European colonizers imposed many national boundaries when carving Africa up according to European interests. Country borders often made little sense geographically or culturally. People with common cultural histories, languages, and allegiances may have been cut off from relatives assigned to other countries. Conversely, people sometimes ended up sharing a "nation" with former enemies.

This chapter first introduces factors across regions that have contributed to Sub-Saharan Africa's food culture since the beginning of the twentieth century. Secondly, it considers distinctive aspects of the foodways within each region.

Keys to understanding Sub-Saharan Africa's food and foodways include climatic and geographic features, historical factors, and demographic variables such as religion, degree of urbanization and population density, and economic development.

TRADE, MIGRATION, COLONIZATION, AND SLAVERY

Sub-Saharan Africa's history includes ancient kingdoms that left enduring marks on the food culture. The introduction of the camel revolutionized desert transportation and led to extensive trans-Saharan trade, facilitating movement of commodities and ideas ranging from Islam to salt.

Adoption of new foods had profound consequences. These foods included those spread by the trans-Saharan trade and by the trans-Atlantic and East African slave trades. Indian immigrants also carried spices and foods to Sub-Saharan Africa. The Portuguese brought New World foods, including Indian corn (maize), cassava (manioc), peanuts, sweet potatoes, tomatoes, pineapples, pumpkins, and chili peppers. Malaysians, Polynesians, Arabs, and Persians introduced bananas, plantains, ginger, mangoes, limes, black pepper, and cocoyams (taro).

European influence in the eighteenth and nineteenth centuries also had consequences stemming from shared languages and inherited cultural traditions. The main European colonizers were the British, French, Italians, Dutch, Portuguese, and Germans. As direct Dutch, German, and Italian influence waned, the primary European languages in Sub-Saharan Africa included English, French, and Portuguese. The sole Spanish-speaking country in Sub-Saharan Africa is Equatorial Guinea. Each colonizer developed certain agricultural commodities and fostered definite food preferences, from the British traditions of tea and baked beans and sausages to the corresponding French preference for coffee and baguettes.

SOCIAL CHANGE AND DEMOGRAPHIC VARIABLES

Social change and technology continue to affect the food culture. Today's communications technologies and changes in transportation allow faster (and perhaps more democratic) flows of information. Students travel to boarding schools in other parts of their countries, or to higher education outside, and return home. Workers migrate to other towns or countries to work while maintaining family ties. Information and ingredients flow both ways, including information about new foods and cooking techniques. Television cooking shows share information about recipes with oral audiences. Radios, magazines, newspapers, computers, and cell phones also widen access to information about cooking and eating.

Urbanization and the degree of socioeconomic development influence what people eat and how they obtain food. Some rural people may have a low income in terms of cash but eat well, while some unemployed urban dwellers may be unable to buy or grow subsistence food. Population density is related to urbanization, and it influences the types of crops grown and the type of agriculture that develops—for example, the intensely irrigated rice fields in densely populated Asian areas vs. the rain-based "swidden-fallow" ("shifting" or "slash and burn" agriculture) common in less populated tropical Sub-Saharan Africa.

The twentieth century was unkind to Sub-Saharan Africa. Political, social, and economic upheavals and dislocations coupled with natural disasters have challenged peoples' flexibility and ability to adjust to and re-create their futures while maintaining continuity with the past and the stability of identities rooted in traditions, including food.

SUB-SAHARAN AFRICAN COOKING AND CULTURE

Birth and death continue, as do marriages and harvest celebrations, initiations, rituals to honor and petition ancestors and God or gods, and the growing, harvesting, marketing and preparation of food. Many proverbs confirm that Sub-Saharan Africans value showing hospitality. However, generosity may be coupled with fear or hostility toward outsiders.

For centuries, Africans have placed three stones on the ground to support their cooking pots. Today's fire may still be on the ground, or it may be in a charcoal brazier, or a kerosene, gas, or electric stove may be used. Women likely still prepare the food, drawing on a rich female oral tradition.

Cooking tools include wooden mortars and pestles, grinding stones, stirring sticks, baskets, clay or metal pots, calabashes, and knives. Food preparation techniques include pounding, soaking, grinding, smoking, drying, fermenting, steaming, frying, baking, boiling, grilling, and simmering. Flavor principles and meal formats vary widely. In some areas, sugar is used in cooking and sweetened desserts are enjoyed; in others desserts are uncommon and sugar is not added to entrées. West African and Ethiopian food is reputed to be spicy, but food throughout the various regions is sometimes prepared simply, without pepper or spices.

Meals generally include a starchy carbohydrate, often a thick porridge made from millet, corn, rice, plantains or cooking bananas, or a root vegetable such as yam or cassava, that is eaten with a soup, stew, sauce, or relish. The accompanying one or more dishes contain some combination of oil, nuts, seeds, legumes, meat, fish, green leaves, fruits and vegetables (such as chili peppers and tomatoes), and seasonings such as salt, herbs, spices, or bouillon cubes.

The texture of food is important: *Fufu* should not be too soft nor rice too mushy; cormeal *ugali* or *sadza* should have the proper stiffness. Fried fish should be crispy, bean fritters not soggy, and so forth. Bitter flavors may be prized, especially in food cooked with green leaves, but the food should have the correct degree of bitterness.

Beverages include alcoholic drinks such as beer and wines made from honey, sorghum, bananas, or palm fruit, as well as nonalcoholic drinks from corn, or tropical fruits, leaves, berries, or coconuts.

Sub-Saharan African popular food features "street foods," snacks sold by urban street vendors. In the twenty-first century, leaves or newspaper wrappings are giving way to plastic, nonbiodegradable bags and bottles, which pose new environmental problems. Also, snacks now include canned or bottled sodas and beverages and Western snacks such as ice cream or frozen yogurt, frozen juice bars, cakes, crackers, and cookies.

Women are actively connected to food at all levels. In non-Muslim areas they are primarily responsible for household food farming as well as for processing food and preparing and serving meals. Women are engaged in smallholder agriculture, especially planting, providing likely over 70 percent of the food. In the last four decades, land devoted to food crops is estimated to have increased by 75 percent.[1] Men help clear and prepare fields, but women often do the weeding and harvesting. As men migrate to cities to work, a greater burden of food provisioning often falls on rural women. Population pressures are increasing while soil fertility is falling. Areas once self-sufficient in food now import it or substitute labor-saving crops such as maize (in Ethiopia) or cassava (in Ghana).

Spiritual considerations influence diets. Sub-Saharan Africans often have a strong connection to the soil and their ancestors and God, gods, or totems. To please or placate unseen forces, people have rules about what is allowable and what is forbidden to eat, and when. Fears of sorcery and witchcraft may influence what people eat; a belief in sympathetic magic sometimes exists, whereby characteristics are ascribed to foods based on how the foods look. While many food taboos are weakening, such as those against eating eggs, others remain.

Families once obtained food from subsistence farms or hunting and gathering, from bartering with neighbors, or through gifts exchanged among family and friends. As societies become more cash-based, food is purchased in small quantities from outdoor markets or house-to-house vendors, and from food stalls or shops in front of homes or alongside roads. Western-style grocery stores are appearing. A newer phenomenon is the rise of chain grocery stores and smaller franchise markets in Southern, East, and West Africa, catering to more than middle- and upper-middle class families.[2]

Food has traditionally been prepared by women within households, by caterers hired to deliver meals, or by vendors stationed strategically near schools, businesses, roads, or transportation hubs. "Guest house" kitchens sell sit-down meals to travelers or workers, as do small, informal eating places. These range from simple benches where men gather to drink beer from calabashes to sophisticated urban bars with bands, serving drinks and snacks. Urban dwellers are developing a taste for "fast food" or "exotic" cuisines such as Chinese food, pizza, fried chicken and "fries," or food from other parts of Africa. Sub-Saharan Africans increasingly travel as soldiers, workers, professionals, or students and carry new tastes in food back with them.

Advertising influences people, and new technologies facilitate the impact of marketing from both within and outside of Sub-Saharan Africa. Advances such as electric refrigeration allow improved food storage. Food processing, such as canning, freezing, and the development of convenience foods such as bouillon cubes, prepared mixes, and bottled sauces and juices, is increasing. People buy wild foods, from wild game to mushrooms, even though some undomesticated foods now face possible extinction. The imposition or adoption of such cash crops as rice, cocoa, peanuts, tea, and coffee has seen prime agricultural land reallocated to new crops, with negative consequences for food farming.

REGIONAL SUBSECTIONS

The following sections consider what food goes into the basket or calabash or cooking pot, where it comes from, how it is prepared, when and where and why it is eaten, and by whom, for West, Central, Southern, and East Africa.

West Africa

The strongest culinary links between Sub-Saharan Africa and North America are with West Africa, particularly eleven countries along the Guinea coast: Senegal, The Gambia, Guinea-Bissau, Guinea, Sierra Leone, Liberia, Ivory Coast, Ghana, Togo, Benin, and Nigeria. West Africa also includes Cape Verde (volcanic islands west of Senegal), and the countries sharing borders with the coastal nations (Mauritania, Mali, Niger, Chad, and Burkina Faso). From 1822 on, some 15,000 African-American former slaves migrated to Liberia. Beginning in 1957, all these countries (except Liberia, which had been free since its founding) regained their independence.

The links with the West were forged by the trans-Atlantic slave trade. The roots of southern regional cooking in the United States (such as slow stewing, deep frying, use of peanuts, chili peppers, corn grits, gumbo), as well as "soul food," are inextricably tied to the trans-Atlantic movement of people, techniques, and ingredients, part of a migration known as the "Columbian Exchange."

Salt was one item West Africans desired from the trade networks that had been crossing the Sahara Desert since 200–300 CE. Salt was scarce in West Africa. It was mined in the desert in large slabs, then exchanged for gold in equal weights, along with slaves, ivory, kola nuts, melegueta pepper, and other goods and food. Salt, called *sel indigène* in French-speaking countries, is traditionally obtained from the ashes of bark or leaves of trees such as the oil palm or baobab, or by evaporating seawater.

Agriculture developed around water sources, especially the Niger and Senegal River valleys and Lake Chad. Nilo-Saharan speakers probably first began cultivating pearl millet.

The Senegambia area developed production systems around African rice (*Oryza glaberrima*), fonio, and guinea millet, and sorghums were likely first grown around Lake Chad.

Cattle, sheep, and goats entered Africa in several waves from southwest and central Asian sources (or from the east), and indigenous cattle may have been domesticated, too. Fulbe (Fulani) groups specialized in cattle herding and remain pastoralists, along with such groups as the Serer and Wolof of Senegal and the Soninke of Mali.

Meals and Indigenous Foods

Wild tubers including African yams (genus *Dioscorea*) and oil palms were domesticated along the edges of the tropical forests. African yams are botanically unrelated to the "yams" or sweet potatoes, *Ipomoea batatas,* of the United States. Pigeon peas are probably native to western Africa, and sesame likely originated in tropical Africa.

Other indigenous foods of West Africa come from the ancient, massive baobab tree found in savanna areas throughout Africa. Its leaves provide stews with a prized slippery consistency, ashes from its wood have enough chlorides to make salt, and its astringent seeds make a tea and are dried, ground, and added to soups, roasted and eaten, or used as a baking powder.

Some indigenous foods such as African yam, rice, the Bambara groundnut, and melegueta peppers (also called "Grains of Paradise") have been largely replaced by Asian varieties of rice and yams, New World peanuts, and chili peppers, respectively. Onions and garlic have also been widely adopted.

Indigenous foods still important in the regional diet and daily life include red palm oil and palm fruit, kola nuts, shea nuts, okra, and melon seeds.

The red oil palm, *Elaeis guineesis,* has been called the most useful tree in West Africa. Its small, datelike orange-red fruits are found in everyday dishes and ritual dishes. Palm nut soup is integral to festivals, like the Ga thanksgiving festival Hɔmɔwɔ. Palm nut soup is served to pregnant or nursing mothers. Stews and sauces, including palaver sauce, traditionally include palm oil, and the oil palm is featured in Sierra Leone's official seal. The carotene-rich palm oil as well as palm kernel oil are found in many local medicines, and other parts of the tree also have medicinal as well as non-food-related purposes.

Palm oil imparts a distinctive red color and rich flavor to soups and sauces. In North America it has an undeserved negative reputation, partly because confusion exists between high-quality virgin red palm oil, palm kernel oil, coconut oil, and clear, refined palm oil. Palm oil and red palm fruits are available outside of Africa in jars (palm oil) or canned form (palm fruits). The canned pulp and oil are exported as palm butter, cream of palm, or palm fruits, or as *sauce graine* or *noix de palme.* Palm oil is also eaten in Brazil and the Caribbean, where it arrived along with African slaves and is called dendê oil.

Red palm fruits are processed by boiling and pounding, then straining them. Stews are often prepared from the oil. The pulp, or "palm butter," is added to soups, along with a combination of meat or fish, poultry, leafy greens or okra or eggplants, onions, tomatoes or chili peppers.

Okra is likely originally from West Africa. Often added to soups, stews, and sauces, either fresh or dried, whole, sliced or finely chopped, and sometimes seeded, it is prized for its mucilaginous thickening properties.

Oil, or "butter," from the indigenous shea plant, primarily known in North America for its cosmetic uses, also has a culinary role.

Grains such as sorghum, millet, and fonio have long been cultivated and eaten (see Table 1). They provide energy, protein, vitamins, and minerals to millions in Africa, thriving even in

Food Name	Region	Country	Typical Ingredients
Kenkey/dokono	West Africa	Ghana	Fermented corn dough steamed in corn husks or banana leaves
Banku	West Africa	Ghana	Fermented corn dough, stirred and cooked (soft)
Koko/akasa	West Africa	Ghana	Fermented corn dough porridge (thin)
Tuo zaafe	West Africa	Ghana	Thick sorghum or millet porridge
Ogi	West Africa	Nigeria	Fermented porridge from sorghum, millet, and/or maize
Gari (farine de manioc)	West/Central Africa	Various	Dried, grated, fermented cassava meal
Fufu (1) (in Nigeria, also called iyan or pounded yam)	West/ Central Africa	Especially Ghana, Nigeria, Cameroon	Peeled, boiled, pounded stiff but elastic dumpling, generally not chewed (yam, cassava, cocoyam, ripe or green plantain, single or combination)
Fufu (2)	Central Africa	Especially D.R.C., Central African Republic, Cameroon	A stiff porridge made from white corn flour, cassava flour, or a combination (similar to ugali, sadza, pap, nsima)
Lafun	West Africa	Nigeria	A fibrous, powdery form of fermented cassava similar to, but coarser than, fufu
Attiéké	West Africa	Ivory Coast	Steamed fermented cassava granules
miondo, (myondo), bobolo, bâton de manioc (*miondo* is a Duala word, *bobolo* is Ewando)	West Africa	Cameroon	Cassava roots soaked and fermented, peeled, mashed, drained, ground, wrapped in banana leaves, and boiled or steamed
Chickwangue (chicouangue)	Central Africa	Congo, Gabon	Similar to miondo

Bidia	Central Africa	D.R.C., Central African Republic	See fufu (2)
Injera (enjera)	Eastern Africa	Ethiopia/Eritrea	Fermented crepe/pancake commonly made from a type of millet called tef (teff), but also with sorghum or wheat
Canjeero	Eastern Africa	Somalia	See injera
Obusera	Eastern Africa	Uganda	Fermented millet porridge
Uji	Eastern Africa	Kenya, Tanzania	Swahili word for porridge, thin to thick, made from maize, millet, or sorghum
Ugali	Eastern Africa	Various, esp. Kenya, Tanzania	Swahili word for a thick porridge (or dumpling) commonly made from cornmeal, but also made with cassava flour
Posho	Eastern Africa	Uganda	See ugali
Atapa (atap)	Eastern Africa	Uganda	Ground dried sweet potato porridge, with ground millet/cassava and flavorings
Pap	Southern Africa	South Africa	Dutch word for porridge made from cornmeal flour or other staple grain
Bogobe	Southern Africa	Botswana	See pap
Sadza	Southern Africa	Zimbabwe	Stiff porridge (or dumpling) made from white field corn flour or red millet flour
Nsima/nhsima	Southern Africa	Zambia, Malawi	See pap
Xima	Southern Africa	Mozambique	Corn pap (see pap)
Amarhewu	Southern Africa	South Africa	Thin porridge made from slightly fermented cornmeal
Putu/phutu	Southern Africa	South Africa	(Zulu) A crumbly version of pap (see pap)
Umphokoqo	Southern Africa	South Africa	(Xhosa) A crumbly version of pap (see pap)

TABLE 1 Selected Representative Sub-Saharan African Carbohydrates/Starches

poor soils, resisting drought, and surviving without heavy applications of fertilizers. Wheat flour is prized, but bread and cakes are made primarily from imported flour.

Kola (or cola) nuts—seed kernels from an evergreen tree—contain stimulants including caffeine and are part of West African ceremonial and social life. They are offered to visitors as a sign of peace and hospitality. African Muslims, forbidden to drink alcohol, may chew them. Kola nuts have been important globally since they were used as a flavoring in Coca-Cola.

Seeds from a native African melon called *egusi* (*agushi, agusi, ogili,* or bitter apple) are ground to thicken and enrich soups or stews, made into cooking oil, and roasted to eat as snacks. Cowpeas, including black-eyed peas, are native to West Africa.

Adopted Foods

Many New World foods have been adopted and integrated into West African food and foodways. There exist controversies over whether Africans preceded Columbus to the New World and whether indigenous types of corn existed in Africa.[3] However, the Portuguese were crucial in introducing and facilitating the spread of such New World foods as maize (corn), cassava (manioc), peanuts, chili peppers, and tomatoes.

Other crops incorporated into the diet include bananas, plantains, coconuts, and tropical fruits such as pineapples, mangoes, lemons, limes, tamarind, and oranges, papayas, custard apples, and guava.

Meals

Meals in West Africa today are likely to begin with a breakfast of leftovers, or a thin porridge from ground or pounded corn or millet or sorghum, perhaps sweetened with sugar, and with tinned or powdered or fresh milk, possibly a beverage such as tea or coffee, perhaps a bread made with (imported) wheat. The heaviest meal is likely at mid-day, with snacks or a lighter evening meal.

The heavier meal is usually a soup, stew, or sauce, accompanied by a starchy carbohydrate such as West African *fufu* (a boiled, pounded form of African yams, plantains and cassava, or a combination, forming a springy, elastic ball that is eaten with soup). The soup is perhaps made with a combination of onions, possibly garlic, peppers, tomatoes, and fresh chili peppers; salted, smoked, or dried fish or meat; leaves, eggplant, pumpkin, or ground seeds. A thicker palmnut or peanut soup might be made with chicken or goat meat, guinea fowl, or wild game. Dried pulverized shrimp is a popular seasoning, as are salt, bouillon cubes, and herbs. Classic Senegalese dishes include *mafé,* in which meat or poultry are stewed in a creamy peanut and tomato sauce, or *thiebou dienne,* a marinated fish and rice dish. A popular one-pot meal is *garifoto* (also called *gari jollof*), in which a basic sauce is made from oil, onions, tomatoes, and peppers, then combined with a combination of meat, fish, seafood, or eggs and *gari,* a coarse cassava flour similar to the *farofa* of Brazil. Possibly African slaves returning from Brazil taught West Africans its preparation. *Gari* is a popular convenience food throughout West Africa. Mixed with water, it becomes an "instant" food to eat with a sauce or fried or canned fish. Ivory Coast features *attiéké,* a processed form of fermented cassava that is steamed much like North African couscous (see Table 1).

Throughout humid rainforest areas, the tsetse fly long prohibited cattle rearing, so milk and milk products were uncommon. Nonvegetable protein has come primarily from fish, shellfish, goats, sheep, pigs, poultry, wild game, insects, and snails. In drier northern regions, beef and milk products are more prevalent. In Mali, Mauritania, and Senegal a clarified butter, called *nebam sirme* in Pulaar (the Fulani language), is used. A yogurt drink, *kossam,* is a popular thirst quencher. Calcium comes from fish, poultry or animal bones, and green leaves such as kale and spinach, or pumpkin, cassava, and cocoyam leaves.

Cocoa plants arrived from Fernando Po in the late 1800s, and during the twentieth century West Africa became a leading commercial producer of cocoa beans. They were originally for export only, but today the domestic use of this product is increasing.

Eating Etiquette

Traditionally, family members in most West African families have not eaten together: Women, men, children, and adolescents may eat at separate times and places. Men commonly eat separately from children. Family and friends may share a common bowl or individual bowls. Hands are the most common eating utensils, properly washed before and after meals. The left hand, reserved for personal hygiene, was traditionally not used for eating or for handing items to someone. Water is the main beverage. In contemporary society, a wider range of beverages, and cutlery, are more common.

Meals are generally not served in courses. Snacks may precede or replace meals and include grilled meat kabobs and drinks.

A meal format might be a one-pot dish, like *jollof* rice (sometimes called the "national dish" of the Wolof people of Senegal but eaten throughout West Africa), or soup and pounded yam or fufu. Others label groundnut stew the national dish of Sierra Leone and *thiebou dienne* the national dish of Senegal, but these labels are misleading because versions of these dishes are served throughout West Africa and cannot be identified with a single place.

West Africa's humid tropical climate prohibits vineyards, but imported wines are becoming available. Palm wine, from the sap of palm trees, is occasionally bottled commercially. Hard liquor is often present and prized, especially in rituals. Nonalcoholic beverages include ginger beer, made locally throughout sub-Saharan Africa; fruit drinks; teas; coffee; and drinks from coconut, corn, millet, rice, sorghum, or tamarind or herbs such as lemon grass, mint, or hibiscus flowers.

Special Occasions and Eating Away from Home

It is difficult to capture the flavor, vibrancy, and spirit of West African cuisine when it is divorced from the context in which it is eaten, often involving feasting at social gatherings and ritual events such as engagements and weddings, funerals, or festivals. Foods may or may not be used symbolically. Western-style salads, vegetable side dishes, and desserts have not been eaten traditionally, though this is changing.

Urban West Africans like to snack, purchasing a variety of street foods including roasted plantain, or corn or yam, meat or fish pies, doughnuts, kebabs, fresh oranges, mangoes, bananas, pineapple, or coconuts, bean fritters, boiled or roasted peanuts, sugar cane, fresh coconuts, and water or other cold drinks. Restaurant-going has not historically been part of the culture, but socializing has been. Many gatherings include music and dancing. Bands play at funerals or celebrations such as weddings, festivals and parties, and large canopies may be erected outdoors to protect people from rain and sun.

Caterers prepare and serve foods at large gatherings. Several main dishes, starches, and beverages are served buffet style.

Western Africa is famous for its "market women" who dominate the sale of items in local outdoor markets and small-scale businesses.

In the evenings people gather to socialize, drinking and snacking, often at open-air clubs. Beer is a popular choice among non-Muslims, whether imported beers such as Guinness or

Heineken, commercially produced lagers such as Star, Club, or Flag, or locally produced beers made from millets, sorghum, maize, or plantains. Beer is brewed (heated before fermentation takes place), whereas wines are drinks made from the sap or juice of trees or plants that is fermented without heating—palm wine, for example. Such wines are usually best drunk within a day or two.

In parts of formerly "British" West Africa tea may be served to visitors, possibly with cookies (called "biscuits" in British English) or cake.

Diet and Health

The contemporary West African diet has seen some negative influences. Changing lifestyles mean that people may no longer need the quantity of fats, salt, and oils once required for hard physical labor or that were only available at special occasions. Cash and export crops have taken over land once allocated to food crops, and food crops that are easier or cheaper to grow, harvest, store, and process have sometimes replaced more nutritious crops.

Today's morning meal may be less nutritious than traditional breakfasts. Prof. Agyeman Badu Akosa, Director General of Ghana's Health Service, teaches that the Hausa food *koko* (porridge prepared from sorghum) and *koose* (bean fritters), or steamed bean balls, make up the ideal breakfast.[4] He advocates smaller serving sizes of carbohydrates such as fufu (usual servings being three or four times the optimal amount) and reduced consumption of oil and animal fats, plus increased consumption of vegetables.

A Ghanaian proverb proclaims, "It takes a heavy (or full) stomach to blow the trumpet." West Africans often feel they have not truly eaten unless they feel very full and satiated. The image of a literally "big man" or "big woman" has long been positive. A successful, generous, fertile, nurturing, energetic, wealthy person is often of large girth. Conversely, a thin person may be viewed suspiciously as stingy, sick, and selfish. To call a woman "fat" has long been a compliment to her and to her husband. Today, diabetes, hypertension, and high blood pressure are rising health concerns. Perhaps, given the limited dairy in the diet, West Africans are also frequently lactose intolerant. Protein–energy malnutrition (PEM), where people eat too little protein, is another concern, and there are efforts to introduce soy products into the diet, such as in infant weaning foods or as additions to traditional recipes. The Ga term *kwashiorkor* describes severe malnutrition in infants and children caused by a diet high in carbohydrates and low in protein.

Focus on Ghana and Nigeria

In 1957 Ghana, previously called the "Gold Coast" by its British colonizers on account of its gold resources, became the first Sub-Saharan African country to regain its independence. Neighboring Nigeria, with roughly 125 million people and 250 ethnic groups, is the most populated country in Sub-Saharan Africa. The four main ethnic groups in Nigeria include the Hausa, Fulani, Yoruba, and Ibo (or Igbo).

An "outdooring" is a West African ceremony held about a week after a child is born, at which the baby is brought outside, is introduced to the community, and publicly receives his or her name. Among the Akan of Ghana, a drop of water may be placed on the infant's tongue, followed by a drop of alcohol. The baby is admonished to always know the difference between the two, even though they look identical. The water and alcohol symbolize the need for integrity in life. Among the Ashanti, soup and fufu are likely to be part of the festive meal following the ceremony. The Akan and Ga people of Ghana are also likely to serve ɔtɔ, a sacred dish made with hard-boiled eggs, mashed yam, and palm oil.

GROUNDNUT SAUCE WITH PUMPKIN (SUB-SAHARAN AFRICA)

3 tablespoons peanut or other vegetable oil
1 onion, peeled and finely chopped (about 1 cup)
1 large or 2 medium cloves of garlic, peeled and crushed or minced (optional)
2 cups chopped tomatoes, fresh or canned
1 small can prepared pumpkin (vegetable variations are listed below)
1/2 cup creamy natural-style peanut butter
2–3 cup water (or more, if desired)
salt, black, white and/or cayenne pepper to taste

- Chop the tomatoes and set aside.
- Peel and chop the onion.
- Heat a skillet on medium heat, add oil, and sauté the onion until it is translucent, then add the chopped tomato and garlic and continue cooking for 5 minutes.
- Stir in the pumpkin.
- Stir the peanut butter with a cup or two of water until smooth and then stir it into the mixture on the stove.
- Lower the heat, cover the pan, and let the sauce simmer about 15 minutes for the flavors to blend. Stir occasionally to make sure the sauce does not scorch, and add more water if necessary.
- Add salt and pepper to taste.

Serve with rice, a boiled or roasted or mashed starchy vegetable, or any version of fufu, ugali, putu, or other traditional carbohydrate.

Sub-Saharan African cooking is flexible and forgiving and improvisational. This sauce has endless variations. Fresh, leftover, dried, canned, or smoked fish; meat; hard-boiled eggs; or poultry may be added (slice or cube any fresh meat or poultry and fry it with the onion). Stock, milk, or bouillon cubes may be added with or replace the water. Okra, eggplant, or any chopped greens can replace or complement the pumpkin. Tomato sauce may be substituted for the tomatoes.

In nearby Nigeria, during the public naming ceremony among Yoruba families, certain foods are introduced to an infant to symbolize qualities the child should have and how the child should live positively. For example, as water is important to people, so should the child be important to his or her family; as honey is sweet, so should the child be sweet to his or her family and community. Other symbolic foods include kola nuts, palm oil, and wine. Among the Yoruba, meals at an outdooring might include pounded yam with okra soup, rice with pepper soup, and mashed cassava (*eba*) with *egusi* soup.

Central Africa

Central Africa, the "heart of Africa," also known as Equatorial Africa or Middle Africa, is the region least familiar to North Americans even though many central Africans were carried to the New World as slaves. The Congo River basin dominates it and gives names to two of its countries: the Democratic Republic of the Congo (or DRC, formerly Zaire), with its capital at Kinshasa, and the Republic of the Congo, with its capital at Brazzaville. The list of countries included varies, but here, in addition to the DRC and Congo, it is considered to include Cameroon, Equatorial Guinea, the Central African Republic, Gabon, Angola, Burundi, and Rwanda. Cameroon is sometimes considered a part of West Africa, and Burundi and Rwanda are sometimes included in eastern Africa. Chad is sometimes included among the central African countries.

Bantu-speaking, iron-working agriculturalists and fishermen moved into the rain forests between 2000 and 1000 BC to cultivate food. They coexisted mostly peacefully with the hunter-gatherers deeper in the forests. Hundreds of Bantu-speaking ethnic groups inhabit the region. However, among the approximately 58 million people in the DRC, almost half the population comes from four groups: the Mongo, Luba, and Kongo (all Bantu-speaking) and the Mangbetu-Azande (from a different language family, formerly and imprecisely called "Hamitic," related to Semitic). Lingala, a Bantu language, is the *lingua franca* "trade language" of the DRC.

By the 1300s the Kongo had established a powerful kingdom on the southern bank of the Congo River. Portuguese explorers reached there by the 1480s and established friendly trading relations. By the mid-sixteenth century, however, Portugal wanted the Kongo's mineral resources and slaves for its sugar plantations in Brazil and Fernando Po. By the early 1800s Arab traders were also actively trading in ivory and slaves. The Kingdom of the Kongo became part of Portugal's Angola colony. Belgium later established the Congo Free State (the present DRC), and France, too, had a colony named Congo (the present Congo).

Apart from some foods eaten by forest hunter-foragers, the foods of Central Africa use ingredients similar to those in West Africa, perhaps with somewhat less complexity. The diets in highland areas such as Rwanda and Burundi share similarities with East Africa's, including reliance on maize, bananas and plantains, and sweet potatoes. Given the Belgian and French colonial influences, French is the most common Western language, and foods have French as well as local names. Thus, peanuts are *arachides,* and palm butter from the red oil palm is *sauce graine* or *noix de palme.* A version of chicken sauce (sometimes called the national dish of Gabon, but common throughout West and Central Africa) is *poulet nyembwe* (or *gnemboue* according to French phonetics). Green leaves are *feuilles.* The popular leaves from the cassava plant are *feuilles de manioc.* Other greens include those from okra, pumpkin, sorrel, sweet potato, cocoyam (taro), bitterleaf, *ndolé,* and the wild *gnetum africannum* (also known as *okok, koko,* or *eru*). Both okra pods and leaves (*ngumbo*) are eaten.

Several central African food words are linked linguistically to the New World. In Angola's Kimbundu language, peanuts are *nguba,* from which the term *goober* in English is derived. Likewise, the Brazilian word *dendê* for palm oil comes from its name in Kimbundu. Similarly, the word *ngumbo* for okra, mentioned in the previous paragraph, is the source for *gumbo*, the name of the famous Cajun soup often thickened with okra pods.

Cassava, or manioc, has been in central Africa since the seventeenth century, though originally it was cultivated for its leaves, not its roots. The Portuguese likely brought cassava to their colonies from Brazil. Similarly, they probably introduced the complex processing techniques for removing toxic cyanogenic glucosides from tubers to make the coarse cassava meal *gari.* Yams and rice are eaten less commonly than cassava and corn.

Like West Africans, Central Africans eat fufu (or *foo-foo* or *fou-fou,* or *foutou*). The Lingala name is *fufu*; the Tshiluba, *bidia.* It may be made of corn flour (*fufu de maize*), or cassava flour (*fufu gari* or *fufu de manioc*), or a combination. Fufu is pounded as in the common West African version, but is also made from a dry flour similarly to corn porridges in other parts of Sub-Saharan Africa (see Table 1).

Meats, fish, and fowl are eaten. Wild game (*viande de brousse*) includes antelope, buffalo, elephant (now often illegal), crocodile, hippopotamus, snake, monkey, and birds. Kola nuts are chewed.

Selling and eating street foods is popular. As societies shift to a money economy, some married women, previously confined to cooking "inside" for their husbands, now prepare and sell food on roadsides and in markets. One may purchase spicy brochettes eaten on skewers or in bread rolls with salad and dressing. Urban restaurants feature cuisines of former colonial powers, foreign immigrant groups, and other African countries, though Central African regional dishes are sometimes served. Exotic foreign dishes likely carry the fascination of being the foods of the powerful and prestigious. Modest restaurants in or near hotels and guesthouses provide sit-down meals for travelers.

A regional delicacy is the thumb-sized fatty larvae of the African palm weevil (*Rhychophorus phoenicus*). Found and collected in swampy lowlands of tropical forests, they are sold at high prices in urban areas such as Yaoundé and Douala, Cameroon. As in West Africa, large land snails are often prized.

Seeds from gourds, melons, and squashes (pumpkins) are dried and ground into flour to thicken and enrich soups and stews (e.g., *egusi* melon and wild mango seeds, *mangue sauvage*). Other starches include corn, sorghum, and millet.

The red oil palm and its fruits, along with beans (*haricots*), are sometimes identified as fertility symbols. Palm oil provides energy, lipids, calcium, phosphorus, and vitamin A.

Tomatoes, onions, peppers, and salt (including *sel indigene*) are important seasonings, as are local herbs and spices and bouillon cubes. Mineral salt (*sel gemme*), called *kanwa* in Cameroon, is used to soften *ndolé* leaves, meat, beans, and stockfish.

Alcoholic beverages such as palm and banana wine are important in many central African communities. Ngbaka and Ngando men in the Central African Republic traditionally collect palm sap every morning and before sunset. Red wine is prized not only for its intoxicating qualities but also its assumed healthy characteristics, such as "giving a person blood" and heating one up in the evenings.

Steaming or grilling foods in leaves is popular. *Kwanga* refers to cassava tubers that are soaked and steamed. Meat (*liboké de viande*) or fish (*liboké de poisson*) can also be processed into packages. Ingredients such as onion, tomato, okra, or crushed peanuts seasoned with lemon juice or chili pepper may be combined into a sauce, mixed with fish or meat, wrapped in leaves and steamed, or grilled over hot coals.

The Bangwa and Douala of Cameroon enjoy a bean pudding called *gateau de haricots, koki* (in the Duala language), *ekoki, haricots koki,* or *koki de niébé* that is similar to Nigeria's *moimoi.* Beans or cowpeas such as black-eyed peas are skinned, ground, and mixed with salt, palm oil, chili pepper, and tender young inner cocoyam leaves. The packets are wrapped in the sturdier outer cocoyam leaves and boiled or steamed until cooked. The pudding has many variations and is popular for special occasions such as dances, funeral gatherings, or meetings of men's or women's groups.

Other popular dishes include *miondo* or *bobolo,* fresh cassava that has been soaked, fermented, wrapped in leaves, and gracefully tied with a long string wound around the leaves (see Table 1). Cocoyam is also eaten, as in *ekwang* (or *ikwang*), grated cocoyam mixed with salt and a dash of palm oil, wrapped in leaves, and steamed.

The Central African version of palm oil stew is *moambé.* The stews use similar ingredients to West African palm oil stews (i.e., a little meat, fish or poultry, red palm oil, onion, tomato, okra, garlic, sorrel or other leaves, or chili pepper). A chicken stew that also includes pounded or ground peanuts could be called *moambé nsusu.* Two main soups are palmnut soup (*mbanga*) and bitterleaf soup (*ndolé*).

Sensitivity to bitter tastes and the ability to discriminate among degrees of bitterness are important culinary skills, whether in preparing stews or serving palm wine. Alkaloids in plants produce a bitter taste and are usually poisonous. Some types of cassava roots, and some leaves, must be carefully soaked or processed in several batches of water before being cooked or eaten.

Sweet foods have not traditionally been eaten as desserts at the end of a meal but rather primarily as snacks. These include fruits and berries, or wild honey eaten directly from the honeycomb. In urban Central Africa, people are developing a taste for sweet foods found in Western countries. Some Central African plants have chemicals that are very sweet, such as Gabon's *brazzeire,* a protein said to be 500 times sweeter than sugar. Obesity-plagued Western countries are anxious to learn more about such plants.

Historically there have been prohibitions against eating certain foods believed to foster unwanted characteristics. Thus, a pregnant woman avoided eating elephant meat for fear of bearing a child with a wide mouth and long nose, or wives refused gorilla meat to prevent their husbands from behaving like gorillas. Conversely, some foods were proscribed as helpful: a new mother might eat python meat to strengthen her back like the powerful snake's. Often only elders were considered strong enough to eat meat of dangerous animals such as buffalos or elephants.

Food plays a role in health and wellness in other ways. Disease may be seen as a result of sorcery and witchcraft, whereby a sorcerer symbolically devours victims. A parent's failure to obey a food prohibition may be divined to have caused a child's illness. Certain foods, such as palm wine, may be considered therapeutic and are considered to be helpful for treating spirit possession. Sharing food is also viewed as fostering fertility, solidarity, and harmony within families.

Alongside the desire for familiar staple foods that make one feel satisfied, there exists a desire for variation and novelty. In urban Central Africa, especially among the educated, new patterns are emerging. These include Western notions of time and dividing the day into breakfast, lunch, and dinner meals; the concept of light and heavy meals; nuclear family patterns of sharing meals together; and more consumption of Western prepared foods and techniques integrated into dietary patterns, though combined with the realities of large families and the need for very large cooking pots and traditional cooking equipment.

Special occasions include holidays such as New Year's Day and Christmas, national independence days, births, christenings, weddings, engagements, funerals, the end of mourning, adolescent initiation ceremonies, the end of the school year, and special rituals of men's and women's societies.

Food at such gatherings includes palm wine, cassava sticks (*bâtons de manioc*), fish, or meat as well as commercial beer, red wine, and spirits (hard liquor). Everyday foods are supplemented with prestige foods to help the hosts maintain their social status and demonstrate generosity, affluence, and masculinity. These items include expensive alcoholic drinks, thick stews rich with meat, and imported foods such as rice, pasta, and canned foods. The lavish show of food and drink honors the guests, even though the social expectation of lavishness is a hardship on poorer hosts.

Focus on Rwanda and Cameroon

Rwanda, the "Land of a Thousand Hills" (*pays des milles collines*), is a small, densely populated country between Uganda and the Democratic Republic of the Congo. In Rwanda sweet potatoes are often enjoyed boiled in their skins and mashed or roasted. Corn is eaten, as are bananas and plantains, called the "potatoes of the air," which may be steamed or boiled. Among forest

MBANGA SOUP (PALMNUT SOUP)

Many variations of palmnut soup exist throughout Central and Western Africa. The fresh palmnuts central to the dish are not available in North America; see the Africa Chop Website in the Resource Guide for online suppliers of canned palm fruits.

2 large onions, finely chopped
2 pounds stewing beef (or bottom round or chuck roast) or lamb, cut into chunks
1–2 pounds soup bones if meat is boneless (optional)
1 28-ounce can of pureed tomatoes (or blanch, peel, and puree fresh tomatoes)
1 large can palmnut cream concentrate (*sauce graine*) (29 ounces or 800 grams)
1 pound fresh mushrooms (portabella or any other type) (optional)
6 ounces smoked fish (such as mackerel or whiting)
1 pound fresh shrimp (optional)
3 king crab legs (optional)
1 10-ounce package frozen chopped okra (optional)
1 medium eggplant, peeled and cubed (3 cups) (optional)
1 fresh chili pepper chopped fine or ground, to taste (or ground red pepper to taste)**
1 clove garlic, crushed (optional)
2–3 large beef or shrimp bouillon cubes, such as Maggi (optional)
2 tablespoons dried shrimp or prawns, ground into powder (optional)
Salt to taste

**Always use *extreme caution* around fresh hot chili peppers. Avoid touching them directly, never touch your eyes or face after chopping peppers, and remember most of the "heat" in chili peppers is in the membranes on the inside. People are often advised to wear rubber gloves when handling peppers.

- Chop the onion. Remove excess fat or gristle from the meat and cut it into chunks, then add to a large heavy pot with 1/2 cup water and the rinsed soup bones, if used. Chop or grind the fresh pepper and sprinkle it or the dried pepper over the meat. Crush the garlic and add to the pot. Crumble the bouillon cubes and add. Stir all with a wooden spoon, cover, and put the pot onto the fire over a medium high heat to steam for about 15 minutes.
- If using eggplant, peel, cube, and cook it (bring the water to a boil, then lower to simmer) 10 minutes in a small covered saucepan. Puree the cooked eggplant in a blender, if available, and add to soup pot.
- Add the pureed tomatoes to the soup.
- Scoop or pour the cream of palm fruits into the soup.
- Add 4 to 6 cups of water. Allow the soup to simmer while preparing the vegetables and fish.
- Clean the mushrooms (if using) by rinsing them quickly, patting them dry with a paper towel, and trimming the ends of the stems. If they are small, add whole to the soup. If they are large, cut into halves, quarters, or slices.
- Rinse the smoked fish, remove and discard the bones and skin and add the flesh.
- Rinse and devein the shrimp, and rinse the crab legs and add.
- Add the pureed eggplant, powdered dried shrimp and frozen okra to the soup, and stir well.
- Cover and allow to cook for about 20 minutes for the flavors to blend and the okra to cook.
- As palm oil rises to the top, skim it off with a spoon and save to use in cooking stews.
- Just before serving, adjust the salt and red pepper to taste.

Serve with a thick porridge such as fufu, rice or rice balls (rice that has been mashed and formed into balls), or boiled African yam slices.

peoples, ripe banana beer or juices (*la bière de banane, umutobe, urwangwa*) play a role similar to palm wine, with a mild version served to women and children and a stronger one to men. Men drink *urwangwa* during important discussions and ceremonies.

Cameroon takes its name from the Portuguese explorers' name for the Wouri River, *Rio de Camarões*, meaning "The River of Prawns." The country peacefully combines a large French-speaking area with a smaller English-speaking region. Douala is its largest city. A special Sunday dish for a Douala family likely involves preparing *ndolé,* a dish made from *ndolé* leaves. First the leaves are washed, the tough center stems removed, and the leaves boiled in *sel gemme* until soft. Next, one person presses them in a sieve as a helper pours cold water over them. Then, other ingredients are added, such as beef, onions, tomatoes, peppers, and dried crayfish (*manjanga*). Sautéed fresh shrimp and a drizzle of heated oil, or freshly ground, blanched peanuts, may be added as a garnish.

In a traditional Yassa engagement ceremony in southern Cameroon, a prospective bridegroom offers food and drinks to his future in-laws in three steps: he brings palm wine or red wine to the girl's father, and the groom's maternal and paternal families give the future wife's family two cartons of cigarettes, two wads of tobacco, and two bottles of whisky. The woman's family responds by preparing a banquet at which to negotiate the bride price. Finally, at the "bringing in," the bride's mother receives drinks, meat, money, and presents to share among her family. The two families then feast together, the menu possibly including a roasted, smoked forest porcupine.

Southern Africa

Southern Africa includes the Republic of South Africa along with Namibia, Botswana, Zambia, Zimbabwe, Lesotho, Malawi, Swaziland, Mozambique, and Madagascar. South of the equator the climate and geography of Africa roughly mirrors that to the north: rain forests, semiarid savanna merging into true savanna, then deserts, culminating in a narrow band with a temperate, Mediterranean-like climate and great botanical diversity. There is great regional variation in climate and rainfall. Over three-quarters of Southern Africa is high plateau formed from mountains eroding over millions of years. Chains of mountains pass through Malawi, Lesotho, and South Africa. Eastern coastal plains are fertile, with a narrow western semiarid coastal band.

Indigenous southern African peoples were likely ancestors of the hunter-gatherer San (Sanqua) people, formerly and disparagingly called "Bushmen" by colonial settlers. The early San did not herd animals or raise crops, and never acquired metal-working skills. A related group, the more sedentary Khoikhoi (KoiKoi) or Kwena (whom the Dutch labeled "Hottentots," perhaps in mockery of the click sounds in their language) were cattle herders.

Metal-working, cattle-rearing Bantu-speaking people migrated into the region, eventually dominating it. Cattle, and the *kraal* in which they are penned, are central to southern African society. Descendants of the Bantu-speaking peoples include the Nguni (made up of the Zulu, Swazi, Xhosa, and Ndebele), as well as the Sotho, Vendi, and Tsonga. In the rural areas, women generally do the weeding and agricultural cultivation with their children's help, while men help clear the land in work parties.

Though the Spanish and Portuguese arrived in southern Africa by the end of the fifteenth century, Europeans took little interest in it until the mid-seventeenth century, when Cape Town became a port for supplying ships. Dutch settlers arrived, with French and German immigrants later joining them. The Dutch settlers, who came to be known as Boers or

Afrikaners, stayed on the coast and imported slaves to cook and work for them. Coming from the East, Madagascar, and Mozambique, most slaves spoke Malay and, along with other Easterners settling there, developed a type of cuisine called Cape Malay or Old Cape Cookery. Cape Malay cuisine combines European, especially Dutch, German, and French cooking with Malayan. In 1688, 150 Huguenots (French Protestants fleeing persecution) brought vine cuttings to the southwestern Cape and established vineyards. Indentured Indian and other Asian laborers came to eastern South Africa in the 1860s to work on sugar plantations, bringing their curries and recipes.

Dutch power in South Africa had passed to the British (in the Cape) by the early 1800s, a development that encouraged the Boers to migrate inland, on what was called the Great Trek, and form their own republics (the Transvaal and the Orange Free State).

The discovery of diamonds and then gold sparked conflict between the settler populations and led to the Anglo-Boer War (1899–1902), which resulted in the consolidation of British political power over both the Cape and the former Boer republics. The rise of the Afrikaner-led National Party in the 1940s, however, effectively reversed that political equation. The party enforced white minority rule through the system of *apartheid* or segregation, which oppressed the nonwhite population and ultimately sought to split them from the country in independent "homelands." After decades of pressure from the rest of the world, the apartheid system was brought to a relatively peaceful end, confirmed by the election of long-time resistance leader Nelson Mandela as President in 1994. Meanwhile, armed revolutionary movements gained power in Zimbabwe and the former Portuguese colony of Mozambique.

The evolution of food and foodways in southern Africa has reflected this complex history. For example, the Portuguese introduced corn, cassava, peanuts, tomatoes and hot peppers. Today hot chili peppers are available throughout much of Sub-Saharan Africa, including southern Africa. *Peri peri* is a Swahili word that denotes a very hot African birds' eye chili pepper from the *Capsicum frutescens* species. It gives its name to a famous dish, "*peri peri* chicken" (*Frango Piri-Piri* in Portuguese) or shrimp, or fish or meat, in which the poultry, seafood, or meat is marinated in a spicy sauce and grilled. The Portuguese also claim this dish, and helped spread it to their home country and to their colony of Goa on the west coast of India. "Peri peri" shrimp (or chicken) with rice is sometimes called Mozambique's "national dish." Today "peri peri" describes spicy African chili pepper-based sauces used as a condiment.

Nando's Chickenland is a growing chain of fast-food restaurants that began in South Africa in the late 1980s and has spread throughout Africa and even beyond. Its trademark dish is peri peri chicken, and Nando's claims to be the world's largest consumer of African bird's eye chilis.

The most common chili peppers used in Sub-Saharan Africa include bird's eye, habañero, and scotch bonnet (all 9–10 on the 10 hotness rating, or 100,000 to 300,000 SHU, Scoville Heat Units) and cayenne (8 or 30,000–50,000 SHU). By comparison, jalapeño peppers rate a 5 on the heat scale, paprika a 1 or 2.

Common foods among indigenous and black southern Africans include maize, curdled milk (*amasi*), millet, and sorghum prepared as porridges or beers; beans; and dried and fresh meat (*inyama* or *nyama*), including beef, goat, sheep, or wild game such as antelope, gazelle, ostrich, or hippo. Though wild game is increasingly hard to obtain, ostrich farms now raise the birds commercially. Chicken and guinea fowl are also used.

Green leaves are *morogo* in Swahili, *matapa* in Malawi, *cacani* in Mozambique, or *rape* in Zambia and Zimbabwe. Pumpkin leaves, leaves from beetroot, sweet potatoes, and bean plants are also cooked. An herbal tea is prepared from dried leaves from *rooibos* bushes

(Afrikaans for "redbush"). Lentils, peanuts, and cowpeas are popular. Other foods include tamarind, baobab, and tropical fruits. Mopane worms from the mopane tree are dried, roasted, fried, and cooked into stews. They are a delicacy among the Wenda, Tsonga, and Pedi peoples in northern Republic of South Africa, Botswana, and Zimbabwe. Insects such as locusts and termites are also eaten. Fish and seafood from the coast include kingklip, snoek, mackerel, hake, prawns, oysters, crayfish, and bream. A tiny anchovy-like fish called *kapenta* is popular in Zambia, Malawi, and Zimbabwe.

Maize's importance cannot be overstated. Around half of the arable land in South Africa alone is planted in maize, a mainstay of white and black South Africans. When eaten fresh, it is called "green" and boiled or roasted; when dried it is "stamped," or coarsely broken and known as "samp," or ground into various grades of maize meal from coarse to fine. Samp may be cooked with beans or combined with other seasonings, including peanuts, bouillon, butter, and milk powder.

Maize is most commonly used as flour to make porridges known variously as *sadza* (Zimbabwe) or *pap* (South Africa) (see Table 1). In Zimbabwe, *sadza* may also be made from red millet flour called *rapoko.* Maize itself is often called mealie or *meilie.* Often white corn is preferred.

Sub-Saharan African porridges (or pottages) cover a wider range of textures than is common in North America. Porridge may be made into flat layers (*vhutetwe* or *vhuswa*) and eaten once or twice a day with an accompaniment. Sometimes porridges are thin like a gruel or beverage, may have milk or sweeteners added, and may be prepared without salt.

Vetkoek ("fat cakes") of Dutch/Afrikaans origin have been embraced, and are called *amafekuku* by the Ndebele. Cape Cookery uses curry powder, onion, Indian and Malaysian spices like tamarind, ginger, cumin, tumeric, coriander, garlic, chili pepper, and allspice. It also features pickles, sambals, and chutneys combining sweet and sour flavors. Sugar is more integral to Southern African cooking than it is in West or Central Africa. Typical dishes include *bobotie* (a ground meat loaf), *sosaties* (marinated meat kebabs grilled on skewers), *bredies* (stews), chicken masala, curry (or *kerrie*) served with yellow rice (*geelrys*), *roti* (Indian flatbread), *boerewors* (sausages), *biltong* (dried meat often made from venison and using coriander seeds), and *atjars* (salads of grated or chopped fresh fruits or vegetables with spicy dressings).

Apart from men cooking meat over an open fire, women tend to be the cooks. The Malagasy of Madagascar have made a distinction between cooking in a pot and cooking over a fire, and they also distinguish a hierarchy of cooking liquids, where water is the least and milk the most prestigious.

Southern Africans value hospitality. A Zulu proverb proclaims, "A visitor's stomach is as small as the kidney of a bird"; a Swazi one, "When guests arrive, we eat." Visitors are expected to accept hospitality and considered rude if they refuse food.

Zulu men, as well as men throughout the region, favor grilled meat, especially chuck, steak, or brisket (*inyama eyosiwe*) served with pap or samp, eaten while sipping sorghum beer (*umqombothi*).

Men have traditionally dined separately from women and children, especially if visitors are present. The food is served in a common platter or bowl holding the starch with another for the relish or stew. A cleansed right hand is the common eating utensil, with cutlery now becoming more common.

The Zulu homelands are also home to Indian descendants of immigrants, many of whom worked on sugar plantations, and the Zulu have adopted spicy curries as their own, minus the ginger. A 1961 South African cookbook identifies curry and rice as a "national dish." Zulu curries are spicier than those of Cape Malay cuisine.

Mozambicans eat maize porridge, known as *nsima* or *xima,* but also are fond of rice, often combined with prawns or meat in *chiru,* a kind of pilau. Cassava and coconut milk are also common cooking ingredients.

Recent Social Changes

The twentieth and twenty-first centuries have witnessed many changes in southern Africa's foodways, reflecting the tumultuous history of the region. The San and Khoikhoi people have been displaced from their traditional lands and have adopted corn-based meals. The Herero rely less on dairy products such as curds and butter and now consume maize, meat, and black beans. In general, people substitute sheep and beef for wild game.

In landlocked Malawi people obtain roughly 70 percent of their animal protein from fish in Lake Malawi, Africa's third largest lake (formerly known as Lake Nyasa). Popular fish include bream, hake, and kapenta. However, population has climbed from 4 million at independence in 1964 to about 9.5 million by the close of the twentieth century. Overfishing and environmental degradation precipitated a 20 percent decrease in the commercial fish catch over four years (1988–1992), causing a food crisis.[5] More recent research indicates that global warming is further decimating the fish catch in Malawi as well as other East African Rift Valley lakes.[6]

Migrant labor experiences affect food preferences. Zimbabwe and South Africa rely heavily on migrant workers for their gold and diamond mines. Almost half of Lesotho's total male labor force works in the mining industry, leaving wives and families in rural areas. These men often eat food provided at workers' barracks or available from vendors—food that often differs from traditional dishes. A 1990s study of food habits in South Africa documents these shifts: from two meals a day to three, and different meals on weekends; more Western-style breakfasts; more desserts; more variety in meals (especially the main meal on Sunday); increased consumption of rice, potatoes, bread, meat, fruit, and spices; and increased preference for a sweet and sour taste such as in a drink made from beetroot, water, sugar, and vinegar.[7]

Ndebele diets blend food from the Zulu, Xhosa, and Swazi peoples. A popular Ndebele salad, *chakalaka,* is flavored with chili and curry powder, and combines cabbage, onion, tomatoes, and carrots.

In the South African study previously cited, fresh milk, sour milk (*maghew*), buttermilk, fruit juices and carbonated drinks were preferred beverages. Tea replaced *maghew* as a social nonalcoholic drink. Taboos on eggs and fish have weakened. British-style fish and chips, plus canned fish such as sardines, were now eaten, along with cakes, cookies, dried fruits, and peanuts. A few entrenched beliefs seem to remain, however, such as the Zulu idea that real men do not eat pumpkin or vegetables.

Migrant workers eat food sold by roadside vendors such as grilled meat, chips and fried cassava, roasted green corn, doughnuts, boiled eggs, cookies, cakes, and peanuts. Food or "tea" stalls provide lunch, such as rice or pap with stew or other side dishes, as well as morning tea with or without milk and bread.

Beer is the alcoholic drink of choice, and beer drinking is a main avenue for socializing, as it takes place in all-black male bars, not always legally licensed, called *shebeens* or *pungwe* (still segregated by race and class). Beer is produced commercially and locally and is an important staple and nutrient source. Women grow the grain and brew the beer that is included in many rituals and drunk on special occasions (as well as on a more casual basis). Thick local beers are brewed from corn, sorghum, and millet, and commercially brewed lagers continue gaining popularity.

Weddings, holy days, funerals, births and birthdays, initiations, and festivals marking the rhythm of nature are all important. Muslim Malay and Dutch communities have traditions such as eating yellow rice (geelrys) after a funeral.

Muslim fast days are important to Malay communities. Muslims abstain from alcohol and observe fasting, for example, during the month of Ramadan. *Lebaran* is the name the Cape Malay use for the feast of Eid al-Fitr at the end of Ramadan, which is celebrated with pies, puddings, curries, bredies (stews), geelrys, and kebabs.

Focus on Zimbabwe and South Africa

During colonial times, Zimbabwe was called Rhodesia. After independence, the country renamed itself with a Shona word meaning "houses of stone," after the huge stone building complex left by a powerful ancient kingdom. Zimbabwean women are often the potters, and they create containers ranging from undecorated vessels for brewing beer to chevron-decorated drinking bowls (*chipfuko*) with vertical strips of contrasting graphite black with hematite red ochres, or with patterns of bands, triangles, and vertical stripes cut into them. Traditionally a *shambakodze,* or sadza cooking pot, was a large clay pot with thicker sides and bottoms than other pots. Today's pots are made from aluminum, cast iron, or enameled iron. Homes also have spoons and ladles. The Shona word for a stirring stick is *mugoti.* A thinner stick, a *musika,* is first used to make thin porridges before the *mugoti.* Sadza is ladled into serving dishes using a *mugwaku,* and it may be smoothed to a pleasing finish with a *chibhako* (a flat smoothing spoon) or an empty corncob.

South Africa's cooking has been called a "rainbow cuisine" because of its many cultural influences. Nelson Mandela, a Xhosa and the country's most famous statesman, is reportedly fond of *amarhewu,* a thin porridge made from slightly fermented corn flour.

A popular social event in South Africa is a type of barbecue, the *braai* (i.e., "grilled"), or *braaivleis* ("grilled meat"). Originally a kind of rite of passage for white South African males, it now embodies the casual lifestyle of the region and has been adopted broadly by South Africans. The word *braai* variously refers to a grill, the act of grilling, and the get together or party itself.

A distinctive three-legged cast iron pot called a *potjieko* was likely introduced by early European traders and adopted by pioneering trek farmers. The pots cook slowly and evenly, can be huge in size in order to cook for many people, and are still common in contemporary southern Africa, especially for outdoor celebrations.

A typical *braai* includes steaks (cooked *very* well-done by men talking and drinking beer while grilling them), *boerwors* (sausages), pap, and a tomato and onion gravy, both possibly cooked in a *potjeiko,* maybe with a dessert of *melktert.* There might also be grilled fish or chicken, salads and other sauces/stews, vegetables and foil-wrapped baked potatoes, and plenty of beverages, especially beer. The outdoor setting can be anywhere from a backyard, park, kraal, or the "bush" to a beach or restaurant. The intimate, relaxed time with family and friends can last into the night, and the *braai* is said to symbolize the country and foster a sense of national identity.

Eastern Africa

Movies such as *The Lion King* present an image of Sub-Saharan Africa characterized by majestic wildlife, spectacular scenery with rolling savanna, vibrant forests, and breathtaking mountains. Such scenes are rooted in Eastern Africa. Also, the best-known Sub-Saharan African cuisine in North America, *injera* (a spongy crêpe-like bread on which stews are served), comes from northeastern Africa (specifically Ethiopia).

Eastern Africa has two parts. The phrase "East Africa" commonly refers to the former British colonies Kenya, Tanzania (formerly Tanganyika), and Uganda, whereas the "Horn of Africa" comprises the northeastern countries of Ethiopia, Eritrea, Djibouti, and Somalia. A broader definition of East Africa sometimes includes Rwanda and Burundi on the border between Uganda and the Democratic Republic of the Congo. The vast country of Sudan, which lies south of Egypt, west of the Horn countries, and north of the other East African countries, can be considered as part of this region as well.

Ethiopia and Eritrea share linked, turbulent, histories. Ethiopia, ancient Abyssinia, has a history also connected to its eastern neighbor Somalia. Tiny Djibouti is economically linked to its neighbors Ethiopia and Somalia. Half of Djibouti's population, the Issas, have ties to Somalia, and the other half, the Afars, to Ethiopia and Eritrea.

Eastern Africa has been influenced by Arabic, Indian, and European peoples as well as by Khoisan, Bantu, Cushitic, and Nilotic-speaking peoples.

The desert or semidesert areas became the territory of herding and nomadic peoples: camels for the Somali and Oromo, cattle for the Nilotes in the savanna grassland and interior plateaus. Nilotic-speaking migrants include the Masai and Samburu in Kenya and Tanzania; the Turkana, Pokot, Luo in Kenya; and the Langa, Acholi, Teso, and Karamajong in Uganda. The Bantu speakers (e.g., Kikuyu, Meru, Gusii or Kisii, Embu, Akamba, Luyha in Kenya; the Sukuma, Nyamwezi, Makende, Haya, Zaramo, Pane, and Chagga in Tanzania; and the Buganda and Busoga in Uganda) focused more on agriculture and tended to settle in upland areas.

In Ethiopia the Semitic-speaking kingdom of Axum (Aksum) flourished from 300 to 700 CE. Its king Ezana converted to Christianity, establishing the Ethiopian Orthodox Church, to which most of the Amhara and Tigrayan population in the present state of

GINGER BEER (FROM ANYWHERE IN SUB-SAHARAN AFRICA)

4–8 oz ginger root (depending on how strong you want it)
2 cups boiling water
2 cups cold water
1/2–3/4 cup sugar
2 tablespoons lime (or lemon) juice
6 cloves
About 1/4 of a short stick of cinnamon (optional)

- Peel ginger root with a vegetable peeler and grate it into a 2-quart glass or stainless steel bowl.
- Pound and mash the ginger well (with a potato masher, wooden spoon, or sturdy glass or jar), then pour 2 cups of boiling water over it and let it sit for at least 2 hours.
- Line a strainer or colander with cheesecloth that has been folded several times and place it over another bowl (stainless steel or glass). Slowly pour the ginger-water mixture through the strainer. Squeeze, twist, and press the cloth to remove most of the liquid. Discard the ginger in the cloth.
- Add 2 cups cold water to the liquid in the bowl and up to 3/4 cups sugar, stirring to dissolve it.
- Add the lime or lemon juice, cloves, and cinnamon and let sit at least an hour before removing the spices.
- Carefully pour the ginger beer into a pitcher, leaving most of the white sediment in the bottom of the bowl. Store the pitcher, covered, in the refrigerator.

Serve the ginger beer chilled over ice cubes, diluted to taste with water, seltzer water, or ginger ale. Use about 1/2 cup ginger beer per serving.

Ethiopia belong. The rock churches at Lalibela are monuments of this strict church, with its rigorous fast days and still-influential dietary proscriptions.

Food culture was also influenced by activities along the coast. From around 700 CE, Arab and Persian traders helped spread Islam. Their dhows (sailboats) traveled along the coastal cities exchanging goods, including wheat and wine, for slaves, gold, ivory, tortoise shell, and rhinoceros horn. While West and Central Africa had the trans-Atlantic slave trade, East Africa had the Indian Ocean slave trade. Between the eighth and twentieth centuries CE, about 14 million Africans were enslaved, often under horrific conditions. This slave trade facilitated the development of wealthy urban port city-states along the "Swahili Coast," extending from Somalia to Mozambique and including islands such as Zanzibar and Lamu. Arab traders and merchants frequently married Africans. The trade crossed the Indian Ocean to India and China, expanding the cosmopolitanism of the area. Swahili (meaning "of the coast"), a Bantu language with a heavy admixture of Arabic, continues as the *lingua franca* of trade in eastern and southern Africa today.

European Influences

When Portuguese explorers sailed to eastern Africa in the late fifteenth century, they received warm welcomes. Returning in the sixteenth century, they fought the Arabs for control of trade and became ruthless colonial rulers until the eighteenth century, when Arabic influence again became a major factor across the region. The Portuguese introduced numerous New World foods, including cassava, chili peppers, maize, peanuts, the sweet potato, and probably tomatoes.

In the nineteenth century European powers sought to regain control of eastern Africa. In 1832 the Omani sultan moved to Zanzibar and developed the clove plantations that later earned it the name "the spice island." A turbulent time began as Europeans carved up the region. The Germans initially claimed Tanganyika (today's Tanzania), then forfeited it to the British after World War I. The British also took Kenya and Uganda. Somalia was split into British, French, and Italian Somalilands. The French appropriated Djibouti. Italy briefly occupied Ethiopia just before and during World War II.

Each European colonizer left marks on the country; for example, the British set up a brewery for its soldiers and ended up popularizing beer within Ethiopia and Eritrea. Italians active in Ethiopia planted fruit orchards and vegetables, established a biscuit factory and salt and potash mines, and popularized pasta, pizza, pastries, and other Italian foods.

Asian and Southeast Asian Influences

Indian influence along the Swahili coast increased in the twentieth century, when 32,000 indentured laborers from Gujarat and Punjab were encouraged to settle there. Tensions remain between Indian descendents and black Africans, but Indian spices, herbs, and foods, from curries to *samosas* and *chapatis,* were widely adopted along the coast, along with sugar cane, coconuts, and the plantains and bananas likely introduced by Malaysian immigrants.

Foods

Coffee (*Coffea arabica*) probably originated in the Ethiopian highlands or its central plateaus. The beans spread from Yemen to Arabia, Constantinople, Europe and England, South America, and beyond. In the nineteenth century coffee circled back to Africa when British colonizers introduced Brazilian plants to their plantations in Kenya and Tanzania.

Coffee is woven into the social fabric of life in Ethiopia, Eritrea, Sudan, and Somalia as part of sociability and hospitality. Christian clergy originally denounced it as a Muslim drink, and in Ethiopia it was limited to Muslims and Oromo. In the nineteenth century, Emperor Menelik II popularized it as a drink for everyone. Coffee was originally flavored with salt, butter, or spices. The beans were roasted, ground, mixed with butter and honey, and shaped into small balls boiled in a pot. In the coffee-growing regions of Kaffa and Sidamo ground coffee beans are still mixed with ghee (clarified butter) to impart a buttery flavor. Italians introduced sugar as a flavoring in the 1930s, and Ethiopians enthusiastically embraced it.

Millet/Sorghum. There are several types of millet in East Africa, including pearl and finger millets, each with numerous varieties. East Africa's finger millet (*Corcorama abyssinica*) thrives in wetter and cooler climates than pearl millet and is the oldest domesticated tropical African cereal. It spread throughout Africa, India, and Indonesia, and millions of acres of millet are planted in Africa each year. It has long been a preferred staple food of the Padhola in Uganda, both for making a kind of millet bread (*kwon*) and for brewing beer.

Tef or *teff (Eragrostis teff)* denotes varieties of millet with small grains, popular for making the fermented dough used to prepare the large, spongy, crepe-like bread called *injera* and the spicy stews (*wats, watts*, or *w'ets*) or less spicy stews (*alechas* or *alichas*) served on it.

Tef is central to Ethiopia and Eritrea's cultural identities as well as a centerpiece of their diets. Despite its nutritional benefits, it is labor-intensive to cultivate. Recent times of war, drought, and uncertainty mean that maize has begun to play a larger role in the diet. Ethiopia now produces more corn than any other crop, including tef and finger millet.

At mealtime, the sauces/stews (fish, meat, chicken, or vegetarian) are ladled onto one of the *injera,* and other pieces are served alongside it. Small pieces are torn off and used to scoop up the stew. *Doro wat,* a spicy chicken and hard-boiled egg stew, is sometimes called the "national dish" of Ethiopia. In Somalia *injera* is called *canjeero* (see Table 1).

Maize (Corn). Maize consumption has dramatically increased to 30 percent in Ethiopian, Kenyan, and Tanzanian diets, and corn has become the most important cereal grain. Virtually all of the marketed corn is white. Initially Sub-Saharan Africans favored brightly colored flint and semi-flint and yellow corn. The preference shifted to white as a result of colonial agricultural policies, the taste migrant workers developed for it, and the closely related shift in the twentieth century from eating home-grown corn to its transformation to an urban food marketed as flour.

Maize is the main component of the thick porridge in the eastern Africa staple called *ugali* in Kenya, but other names in other parts of East Africa (see Table 1), such as *sadza* in Zimbabwe or *posho* in Uganda. Ugali-type porridges are also made from cassava flour or millet flour.

Other starchy carbohydrates eaten in East Africa include *ensete,* the "false banana," sweet potatoes, cocoyams (taro), potatoes, arrowroot, yams, and rice. Rice (*wali* in Swahili, *brees* in Somali) is most commonly eaten in Ethiopian, Asian, and Muslim communities, often flavored with coconut milk. Special occasions along the East African coast might feature a rice-and-meat one-pot dish (*pilau*), eaten alone or with *chapati* or a spicy stew.

Sugar cane, bananas, baobab, citrus fruits, melons, guava, passionfruit, custard apple, avocado pears, mangos, and tamarind are eaten. Sugar cane is chewed raw as a snack or made into beer. Baobab fruit can be eaten raw, in a sauce, or the seeds can be made into candy by coloring and sugar-coating them.

Milk and spiced ghee (a clarified butter, or butter oil, in which the water is evaporated and the oil separated from the milk solids) are integral to many dishes. Fermented, or sour, milk is drunk. Pastoralists pour milk from camels, cows, goats, or sheep into gourds or wooden containers to churn it, adding flavorings, spices, or herbs. Sweetened milk is eaten with porridge such as ugali, or milk may be mixed with blood.

East African pastoral peoples such as the Masai of Kenya and Tanzania and the Turkana of Kenya face hardships because of inadequate government support of their need to move animals around regions and across national boundaries to graze. Drought weakens their animals, making them more susceptible to disease and death, as well as encouraging overgrazing, which can lead to soil erosion.

Khat (also called Abyssinian tea or *miraa*) leaves are chewed as a stimulant, not a food. However, khat is important socially, particularly where Muslim law applies, prohibiting drinking of alcohol, as in Djibouti. Khat is important in the wedding ceremonies among the Somali and Boran of Kenya and Ethiopia.

Protein sources include legumes, kidney, hyacinth or lablab beans, cowpeas, chickpeas, lentils, peanuts, Bambara groundnuts, and milk products. Animal sources are meat, fish, seafood, poultry, and insects. When pastoral peoples consume fresh blood, they collect it from a special cut so that the animal does not bleed to death. Somali women may be given fresh goat blood after childbirth.

Salt is the most important seasoning, including salts from the ashes of plant materials such as banana peels or bean leaves. Other seasonings, such as curries, are common along the coast and in the northeast. *Berberé,* the signature seasoning of Ethiopia and Eritrea, is a complex and sophisticated blend of pungent spices, especially hot chili pepper. A woman's ability to prepare quality berberé was once considered a prerequisite for marriage.

Cooked greens from leaves such as cassava, pumpkin, or cabbage are common in stews, soups, and sauces. Eastern Africans are partial to collards or kale. These greens go by the same name as a popular "leftover" stew or gravy made from them in Kenya, known as *sukuma wiki,* Swahili for "push the week." Other greens include abundant and inexpensive spinach and Swiss chard. Additional popular vegetables include onions, tomatoes, pumpkins, eggplants, and okra.

People generally consider that they have eaten only when they have dined on their particular staple food. Often the word for "food" is the same as the region's staple carbohydrate dish (e.g., *irio* in Kikuyu, *isyo* among the Kikamba, *nyoyo* in Luo, *chakula* in Swahili). Popular dishes include an *irio* made from beans, corn, and potatoes and seasoned variously with onions, garlic, coriander leaves, tomatoes, salt, and ghee. Another type of *irio* is the Kikuyu *mataha,* including salt, mashed peas and beans, green (fresh) corn, green cooking bananas and potatoes, and possibly pumpkin leaves, onions, cooking fat, and curry spices.

Ugali (see Table 1) has been called the most important food in East Africa. It is the bland foil for a range of accompaniments, including fermented milk, grilled meat, peanuts, beans, cooked greens, and chicken or fish stews, sauces, gravies, and relishes. The proper etiquette for eating it includes washing hands before breaking off a small piece of the ugali with the thumb and first two fingers of the right hand and making a small indentation and scooping up some of the accompanying side dish.

Cooking bananas such as *matoke* are popular in Uganda, especially among the Baganda. *Matoke* is the name of a banana that is green when ripe, and also the name of a dish prepared from them.

Somali nomads sun-dry meat, such as camel meat, and then fry it in camel ghee to preserve it. Ethiopian *quanta* is made from meat cut into long strips and coated with hot spicy powder before drying. Ethiopians eat raw and very rare lean beef minced or cubed and spiced.

People may begin the day with a small meal of porridge, gruel, or cassava, though bread and tea are increasingly common. The main meals are usually eaten in the afternoon or evening.

The meal pattern varies during fasting times. *Saum* (or *Sawm*), the act of fasting, is one of the five pillars of Islam, a very important religious duty for serious Muslims. East Africa's large Muslim population takes this exercise in self-discipline seriously and fast regularly, especially during the month of Ramadan. During this time, children past puberty and adults neither eat nor drink from dawn to sunset, with exceptions for nursing mothers, travelers, and the sick and elderly. Younger children are encouraged to fast a half-day. People gather at sunset to eat light foods such as dates and *sambusi* (a type of samosa) before attending prayers, and again between midnight and dawn when a heavier meal of *sahur* food, which may include corn or rice, is eaten to fortify people for the coming day of fasting.

East Africans are generally quite sociable, and non-Muslim men gather to drink beer together and perhaps eat roasted meat (*nyama choma,* in Swahili). Muslims would likely gather and socialize over coffee or tea with their meat and ugali.

Snacking at food stalls or kiosks is also popular. Except among Muslims and Jews, pork is a popular "fast food." Roasted corn is eaten, as well as deep-fried foods reflecting Indian influences, such as samosas or a kind of donut called *mandazi* or *mahamri.*

Celebrations of rites of passage like marriages, new births, holy days, funerals, harvest days, and initiations are often organized seasonally. Agricultural societies prefer the end of harvest season, whereas pastoralists encourage courting, weddings and initiations during the rainy season, their time of abundance.

Efforts are ongoing to upgrade the nutritional qualities of some foods such as maize and sweet potatoes. There is also concern and controversy about the increased dependency on maize, including the potential dangers of genetically modified (GM) corn received as food aid in areas where drought or warfare have disrupted normal food supplies. The Republic of South Africa long ago embraced GM corn, but in 2002, despite widespread hunger and famine, Zimbabwe, Zambia, and Mozambique opposed receiving foreign aid in the form of unmilled corn, much of which was genetically modified and produced by U.S.-based agribusiness companies such as Monsanto and Syngenta. These African countries feared that some of the corn would be planted and contaminate other maize crops, eliminating their ability to sell maize to GM-phobic Europe, their main market. They also feared possible long-term health risks; still under-researched possible damage to the environment; the loss of biodiversity; and the possibility of the West "dumping" contaminated corn into their systems. Some NGOs (nongovernmental organizations) consider the issue of hunger in Africa not one of a lack of food but one of agricultural policies, inadequate food distribution systems, and the lack of support for small farmers.

Focus on Ethiopia and Kenya

Ethiopians have spent centuries perfecting the art of coffee drinking as a pastime. Red coffee berries are sun-dried, husked, washed and redried, then roasted over coals to a dark brown, and pounded to powder with a wooden pestle.

SUKUMA WIKI (EAST AFRICA)

1–2 bunches of fresh kale (or Swiss chard, collards, or spinach), finely chopped (if using frozen greens, defrost and drain them)
2 onions, chopped or thinly sliced
3 or 4 tomatoes, blanched, peeled and chopped (or substitute canned tomatoes, or 2–4 tablespoons tomato paste)
2 tablespoons vegetable oil
1–2 cloves of garlic, crushed (optional)
2 teaspoons coriander powder (optional) (or 1 heaping tablespoon finely minced fresh coriander leaves)
1 sweet green bell pepper, chopped (optional)
1/2 pound any leftover meat or poultry cooked or raw (optional), cut into small pieces
Salt and red or black pepper to taste

- If using fresh greens, wash and finely chop them and set aside.
- If using raw meat, cut it into small pieces and brown it in vegetable oil on medium heat. When nearly cooked, add the onion and other spices. If using cooked meat, add it when the onions are browned.
- Prepare the tomatoes or tomato paste and stir into the onions (and meat, if using).
- Stir in the greens and mix well.
- Allow the stew to simmer for a couple of minutes for the flavors to blend and the sauce to thicken. Add salt and pepper to taste.

In Kenya this would likely be served with ugali or chapatis. Rice or plantains can be substituted. This standby relies on leftovers. For example, it could include a couple of chopped carrots or chopped cabbage cooked with the kale.

Before a coffee drinking ceremony, the woman in charge prepares the house and builds up a fire in her stove, bringing a pot of water to a boil. After adding coffee powder to the water, she might cover the pot with sisal strands to trap the heat but not the steam as the coffee brews. The aroma attracts household members and guests to the room. Burning incense might add to the atmosphere. The coffee is poured into a coffee pot. Special tiny cups (*siniwoch*) are ceremoniously rinsed out and placed on a four-legged tray. The scalding coffee is poured (as a proverb says, *ye bunna sibatu, mefajetu,* "the pleasure of coffee is in its burning sensation"), and the first round, the "*abol,*" is sipped leisurely over conversation. Hot water is added to the pot for the second round, the *huletegna.* Repeated a third time, the final round is the *bareka* (blessing), when God's blessing is invoked on the house.

The largest and most powerful ethnic group in Kenya today is the Kikuyu. Europeans displaced the Kikuyu from the fertile highlands between Mt. Kenya and Nairobi, forcing them into overcrowded areas on poorer soil, and to become laborers on European farms.

Kikuyu kitchens typify those in many non-nomadic East African homes. Numerous traditional kitchen items are used alongside modern substitutions. A small stone or larger wooden mortar and pestle (*kinu* in Swahili) would be used to crush herbs and spices and pound grains. Modern equivalents include ceramic or stainless steel mortars and pestles or electric blenders and grinders; alternatively, pre-ground spices and flours may be purchased. For heating, a charcoal brazier (*jiko*) was used, now often replaced with gas and electric stoves and grills. Pasta was made with a wooden pasta maker (*kinu cha tambi*), though today packaged ready-made pastas are often used. Coconut was grated on a *mbuzi*, consisting of a portable folding wooden stool with a stainless steel blade, now often replaced by blenders or electric juice extractors; coconut may be purchased already desiccated and grated. Gourd and calabash containers and serving dishes (*kibuyu*) are now often replaced by plastic, glass, or ceramic cups, plates, or bowls. Sturdy wooden paddles with a flat blade (*mwiko*), of various sizes, were used for stirring ugali or stews. Wooden spoons are known as *mkamshi* or *kijiko*. A wooden blender for soup (*chombo cha kupigapiga*) is now often replaced by wire whisks or electric blenders. A grinding stone for spices (*jiwe la kusaga dawa*) or grains (*jiwe la kupazia*) can be found, comparable to the *kinu*. A clay water pot, with a spigot and lid (*mtungi*), can be used for cooling water, though bottles in refrigerators are often used today. A clay cooking pot (*chungu*) is now giving way to metal saucepans, crock pots, or pressure cookers. An aluminum pan (*sufuria*) finds use along with frying pans or deep-fat fryers. A winnowing basket is called the *kiteo*. For making coconut milk from grated coconut, a strainer (*kifumbu*) was used, for which nylon or muslin sieves are often substituted. A coconut shell ladle with a wooden handle (*upawa*) is often replaced by commercially made ladles. A woven palm basket (*kitanga*) to collect flour; and a chapati pan of heavy iron (*karai*), now yielding to nonstick or iron flat frying pans, may also be found in a Kikuyu kitchen.

CONCLUSION

Like language, food culture continuously borrows from and contributes to other cuisines, making the term "authentic cuisine" very slippery. Sub-Saharan African cuisines have borrowed freely from New World crops such as maize and cassava, pineapple, peanuts, and chili peppers. They have adopted and adapted coconuts and bananas and plantains and Indian spice mixtures. They have also contributed foods globally, including coffee, tamarind, cola, guinea fowl, okra, rooibos, and dendê oil. Their regional recipes vary to include East Africa's *injera* and *doro wat,* West Africa's *jollof* rice and creamy groundnut soups, Central Africa's palmnut and green leaf stews, and Southern Africa's curries and spicy *periperi*-marinated seafood and poultry.

Political realities and occupations by foreign powers have affected sub-Saharan African diets: for example, the Portuguese promoted gari-making in Angola, and the British promoted white corn in South Africa. Immigrant groups brought their foods and recipes, as did the Indians, Arabs, Malaysians, and Dutch. Sometimes ingredients seem to be adopted and spread spontaneously, like chili peppers.

This chapter identified similarities among and between regions (e.g., cornmeal porridges and stews made from greens, the importance of cooking techniques such as pounding and steaming), while acknowledging differences (e.g., the use or absence of milk and dairy products; the availability of ingredients such yams, plantains, palm oil, teff, rice, and coffee; and religious influences on diet).

New transportation technologies such as travel by camel and dhow once helped spread such foods as salt and melegueta peppers, bananas, and coconuts. In the twentieth and twenty-first centuries new forms of communication, transportation, and food processing technologies have added (and will continue to add) to the dynamic mix.

Alongside a need for the familiar, Sub-Saharan Africans long for novelty. They will try new foods in traditional ways (e.g., soybeans), traditional foods in new ways (e.g., instant fufu flour), or new foods in new ways (e.g., pizza, pasta). New foods are adapted to familiar tastes, such as adding smoked fish to pizza, or topping rice and beans with pasta. Sausages in South Africa now come in a range of flavors, and traditional drinks and herbs are being packaged commercially. In Ghana, Maggi flavoring cubes have expanded beyond chicken and fish to include *dawadawa* (locust beans) and *sheeto* (a traditional hot sauce).

Sub-Saharan Africa's food culture is inextricably intertwined with its political, social, and economic future. Poverty, instability, natural disasters, and health issues place unbearable burdens on many regions. These inhibit the creativity and freedom required to maintain culinary traditions and the ability to develop new ones.

Culinary knowledge remains largely an oral tradition. The richness of and variations in regional cooking have only sporadically been written down, and many nuances and complexities may disappear with the current generation of knowledgeable Sub-Saharan women. Scarce resources mean that even indigenous cookbooks from earlier times are disappearing.

As lifestyles have changed, there have been positive and negative impacts on the food culture. Today's fast foods often have an excess of fat, salt, or sugar. Disposable containers are introducing new litter problems. Nutrition education, however, is teaching the importance of eating fruits, vegetables and protein and reducing starchy carbohydrate consumption. Food science and processing advances have helped lessen food spoilage and improved sanitation and the nutritional values of foods.

Resilience, creativity, and ingenuity continue to flourish, along with growing respect for Sub-Saharan African cuisine. Contemporary Sub-Saharan Africans are posting recipes and information on the Internet and writing cookbooks. Today, they are growing, marketing, processing, and promoting their foods globally and making their cuisines newly accessible to North Americans.

APPENDIX: RECIPE WEIGHTS AND MEASURES CONVERSION TABLES

This chapter uses standard U.S. measurements. Table 2 gives metric equivalents.

Note, however, that "cup," "tablespoon," "teaspoon," and "pint" are not equivalent in U.S. and British measuring systems (and the systems of many African countries that were British colonies), as indicated in Table 3.

Standard U.S. Unit	Metric Equivalent
1/8 teaspoon	0.5 milliliter (mL)
1/4 teaspoon	1 mL
1/2 teaspoon	2 mL
1 teaspoon	5 mL
1 tablespoon (3 teaspoons)	15 mL
1/8 cup (2 tablespoons)	30 mL
1/4 cup (4 tablespoons)	50 mL
1/3 cup (5 tablespoons)	75 mL
1/2 cup (8 tablespoons)	125 mL
1 cup (16 tablespoons)	250 mL
4 cups (1 quart)	1 liter (L)
1 ounce (oz)	30 grams (g)
1 pound (lb)	500 g
2 pounds	1 kilogram (kg)
1/4 inch	0.6 centimeter (cm)
1/2 inch	1.25 cm
1 inch	2.5 cm

TABLE 2 Metric Equivalents for U.S. Measures

U.S. Unit/Equivalent	British Unit/Equivalent
1 U.S. cup (8 oz)	4/5 English cup
10 oz	1 English cup
1 1/4 U.S. teaspoons	1 English teaspoon
1 1/4 U.S. tablespoons	1 English tablespoon
1 U.S. pint = 16 fluid oz	4/5 English pint
20 fluid oz	1 English pint

TABLE 3 Equivalent Measures in British and U.S. Systems

As a further note, recipes in France and French-speaking areas tend to measure bulk materials such as flour by weight in grams rather than by volume in cups. Handy conversion calculators are available at the GourmetSleuth Website listed in the Resource Guide.

RESOURCE GUIDE

PRINT RESOURCES

Author's note: Many works consulted are not readily available, and are omitted from this list. A more comprehensive listing of sources is available in *Food Culture of Sub-Saharan Africa* (Osseo-Asare, 2005).

Appiah, Kwame Anthony, and H. L. Gates, Jr., eds. *Africana: The Encyclopedia of the African and African American Experience.* New York: Basic Civitas Books/Perseus Books Group, 1999.

Hamilton, Cherie Y. *Cuisines of Portuguese Encounters: Recipes from Portugal, Madeira/Azores, Guinea-Bissau, Cape Verde, São Tomé and Príncipe, Angola, Mozambique, Goa, Brazil, Malacca, East Timor, and Macao.* New York: Hippocrene Books, 2001.

Katz, Solomon H., and William Woys Weaver, eds. *Encyclopedia of Food and Culture.* New York: Charles Scribner's Sons, 2002.

Kiple, Kenneth F., and Kriemhild Coneè Ornelas, eds. *The Cambridge World History of Food,* vols. 1 and 2. Cambridge, UK: Cambridge University Press, 2000.

Kittler, P. G., and K. P. Sucher. *Food and Culture,* 3rd ed. Belmont, CA: Wadsworth/Thompson, 2001.

Kuper, Jessica, ed. *The Anthropologists' Cookbook.* New York: Universe Books, 1977.

McCann, James C. *Maize and Grace: Africa's Encounter with a New World Crop 1500–2000.* Cambridge, MA: Harvard Univrsity Press, 2005.

Osseo-Asare, Fran. *Food Culture in Sub-Saharan Africa.* Westport, CT: Greenwood Press, 2005.

Viola, Herman J., and Carolyn Margolis. *Seeds of Change.* Washington, DC: Smithsonian Institution Press, 1991.

COOKBOOKS

Hafner, Dorinda. *A Taste of Africa.* Berkeley, CA: Ten Speed Press, 1993.

Harris, Jessica. *The Africa Cookbook: Tastes of a Continent.* New York: Simon and Schuster, 1998.

Jackson, Elizabeth A. *South of the Sahara.* Hollis, NH: Fantail, 1999.

Mesfin, Daniel J., ed. *Exotic Ethiopian Cooking: Society, Culture, Hospitality and Traditions,* rev. extended ed. Falls Church, VA: Ethiopian Cookbook Enterprises, 1993.

Osseo-Asare, Fran. *A Good Soup Attracts Chairs: A First African Cookbook for American Kids.* Gretna: Pelican Publishing Company, 1993. (The black-and-white 2001 paperback edition is not recommended.)

Samuelsson, Marcus. *The Soul of a New Cuisine: A Discovery of the Foods and Flavors of Africa.* New York: Wiley, 2006.

van der Post, Laurens, and the editors of Time-Life Books. *African Cooking.* New York: Time-Life Books, 1970. Also see the companion booklet, *Recipes: African Cooking.* New York: Time-Life Books, 1970.

Warren, Olivia. *Taste of Eritrea: Recipes from One of East Africa's Most Interesting Little Countries.* New York: Hippocrene Books, 2000.

WEBSITES/PODCASTS

African Chop. http://www.africanchop.com.

BETUMI: The African Culinary Network. http://www.betumi.com. Podcast at http://www.betumi.com/media/podcast_xml.

The Congo Cookbook. http://www.geocities.com/congocookbook. Good information, but beware of clicking on the annoying popup ads.

GourmetSleuth. *Gram Conversion Calculator.* Accessed February 7, 2007. http://www.gourmetsleuth.com/gram_calc.htm.

Motherland Nigeria. http://www.motherlandnigeria.com/food.html.

FOOD AND FESTIVALS OF AFRICAN FOOD IN THE UNITED STATES

Atlanta, Georgia, Flavors of Africa: see http://flavorsofafrica.com/.
Chicago, Illinois, Ghanafest: http://www.ghananationalcouncil.org/.
Also, many African countries provide information about food at their official sites.

NOTES

1. *National Geographic* 208.3 (2005, September), Map Supplement ("Breadbaskets").
2. Dave D. Weatherspoon and Thomas Reardon, "The Rise of Supermarkets in Africa: Implications for Agrifood Systems and the Rural Poor," *Development Policy Review* 21.3 (2003): 333–355.
3. Doug Himes, "Central Africa," in *Encyclopedia of Food and Culture*, edited by Solomon H. Katz and William Woys Weaver (New York: Charles Scribner's Sons, 2002), p. 25.
4. Prof. Agyeman Badu Akoso, "Are You Eating Right?" *Food & Hospitality Business* (Ghana) 3 (n.d., probably 2006): 12–13; 22–23.
5. Joshua Nyambose, "Preserving the Future for Lake Malawi," *African Technology Forum* (1997). Accessed June 20, 2006. http://web.mit.edu/africantech/www/articles/Lake_Malawi.html.
6. Lidia Wasowicz, "African Lake Burned by Global Warming." Updated August 21, 2003. Accessed February 3, 2007. http://www.aegis.org/news/UPI/2003/UP030804.html.
7. Annemarie T. Viljoen and Gertruida J. Gericke, "Food Habits and Food Preferences of Black South African Men in the Army (1993–1994)," *Journal of Family Ecology and Consumer Sciences* 29 (2001): 100–115.

ARCHITECTURE

ARCHITECTURE: St. George's Church, carved out of solid rock at Lalibela, Ethiopia. © Images of Africa Photobank / Alamy.

ARCHITECTURE: Townships like this one in South Africa, originally designed to keep the local population away from the European settlers, provide simple housing for the poor. Courtesy of Shutterstock.

ARCHITECTURE: An interesting melding of architecture can be found in this photo from Lemu Island, just off the coast of Kenya. An Omani fort is in the background, a traditional sailing boat or jahazi is in the foreground, and the central Kenya flag is flying above the District Commissioner's office. © Images of Africa Photobank / Alamy.

ART

ART: *Mzee Yupokazi Akiwapeleka Wototo* by Georges Lilanga, 1992. © Contemporary African Art Collection Limited/CORBIS.

ART: A girl sells bogolan textiles on her rooftop overlooking the city of Djenne. Bogolan has recently reached a larger, global audience through prominent Western collections and museum shows. © Robert Estall Photo Agency / Alamy.

ART: This is a beautiful example of Tingatinga style. The style takes its name from Eduardo Saidi Tingatinga born in the 1930s in Tanzania. © Ariadne Van Zandbergen / Alamy.

FASHION AND APPEARANCE

FASHION AND APPEARANCE: Swathes of fabric on sale at a market in Kenya. Influenced by European missionaries, the kanga is a two-yard piece of fabric that is worn from the top of the breast to just below the knee. Courtesy of Shutterstock.

FASHION AND APPEARANCE: Detail of the sort of embroidery characteristically found on African boubous. Courtesy of Shutterstock.

FILM

FILM: Aissa Maiga plays a nightclub singer who has plenty to cry about in *Bamako*, Abderrahmane Sissako's 2007 critique of the IMF and the World Bank. Courtesy of New Yorker Films.

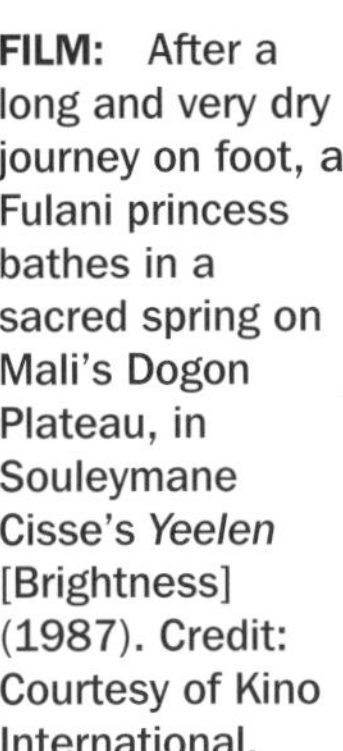

FILM: After a long and very dry journey on foot, a Fulani princess bathes in a sacred spring on Mali's Dogon Plateau, in Souleymane Cisse's *Yeelen* [Brightness] (1987). Credit: Courtesy of Kino International.

FOOD AND FOODWAYS

FOOD AND FOODWAYS: Preparing palmnuts (West and Central Africa). Courtesy of F. Osseo-Asare, BETUMI.

FOOD AND FOODWAYS: Plastic bags have often replaced leaves and newspaper for wrapping goods, causing new environmental problems in Sub-Saharan Africa. Courtesy of F. Osseo-Asare, BETUMI.

GAMES, TOYS, AND PASTIMES

GAMES, TOYS, AND PASTIMES: An artificial spider and web made of beads, inspired by Zulu art in South Africa. © Christa Knijff / Alamy.

GAMES, TOYS, AND PASTIMES: A game of bao in progress in Kenya. This popular pastime is a game that requires as much skill as chess. Courtesy of Shutterstock.

LITERATURE

LITERATURE: Former Senegal president and poet Léopold Sédar Senghor is applauded by his wife Colette during a ceremony to mark his 90th birthday in Verson, Normandy, 1996. Senghor was one of the originators of *négritude*, a literary movement that embraced and celebrated "blackness" without its potentially divisive ties to culture, language, or geography. © AP Photo/Remy de la Mauviniere.

LITERATURE: Nigerian author Wole Soyinka speaks to journalists at UNESCO headquarters in Paris after he was awarded the Nobel Prize for Literature in 1986. He is the first author from Africa to receive the prize. © AP Photo/Laurent Rebours.

GAMES, TOYS, AND PASTIMES

EVA NWOKAH AND CLARA IKEKEONWU

A variety of games, pastimes, and toys are found in different regions of Sub-Saharan Africa.[1] Many parts of Africa are in transition from traditional practices of folk games and pastimes and the use of locally made toy objects to the substitution of play ideas and materials from other continents, especially Europe, Asia, and the United States. Exposure to non-African materials has been increased through overseas travel by more educated or wealthier families; increased importation of foreign goods such as music, books, and toys; and exposure to television, magazines, video and DVD, computers, and radio. However, over 70 percent of families on the continent of Africa live in rural areas. Even when families live in urban areas, small towns or cities, most of them still have relatives in rural locations and they would be expected to visit them at special celebratory times of the year. They may have a grandparent or other older extended family member living with them who would help pass down traditions from one generation to another. How children spend their day, how they play, their playmates, and the type of play materials are all affected by the setting in which they live. The amount of time for play and recreation and the child-rearing beliefs and practices of the adults in the society have an additional impact. Such beliefs affect, for example, how much time children spend doing chores, whether they go to school, whether adults play with children, how much children are supervised, how age groups are formed, and what materials are available for play. Adult games and pastimes also vary by region.

In spite of the regional differences and variations between rural and urban areas, there are some striking similarities and common trends across all four regions (West Africa, Central Africa, Southern Africa, and East Africa) that reflect community values, childhood practices, and preferences. These characteristics create a unique genre of play experiences in African countries not found in Western cultures. David Lancy, in a study of Kpelle children in Gbarngasuakwelle in Liberia, identified eight main categories of play that he termed *playforms.* These were games, toys, and several pastimes consisting of make-believe (pretend play), hunting play, storytelling, dancing, musical instruments, and adult play. These categories can be found in all regions of Sub-Saharan Africa. Children's folk games teach social stories, values, and traditional customs. Games and pastimes reflect a strong oral tradition in which spoken language skills, such as rhymes, storytelling, speechmaking, and singing, are highly respected. Games, pastimes, and types of toys are affected by climate, setting, and available natural resources. Because the African continent is primarily a tropical or semitropical region, there is a similarity in the preponderance of outdoor play and in the characteristics of many of the games played in different regions. The separate roles of male and female and the importance of age group affiliation in African societies also affect the types of games played by one sex only and which age group plays certain games. Another commonality is the change occurring as a result of the influence of mass media, commercialization, and increased travel, apparent in the differences between rural and urban areas. Fruit and similar items have been used as balls to play football-type games for centuries. However, the media portrayal of soccer (association football, known simply as football in most African countries) as a national sport, its popularization as a school sport, and the availability of commercial balls in local markets contribute to the increased frequency of soccer as a pastime. The introduction of radio and television has also affected traditions such as *moonlight games*—on moonlight nights in the dry season, they used to be played from the early hours of the evening (6:30–7:30 PM) until midnight, when almost everyone had gone to bed, but now they are played less frequently or for a shorter duration.

Most activities in rural areas take place outdoors or under the shade of trees or thatched shelters when it is too hot. Villages typically have an open space where children can play and where important events and meetings may take place. In southeastern Nigeria, this is called the *ilo* (pronounced ee-lo). Children may play either in this large, open space or else in their compound, a smaller space surrounded by a few houses. The lack of traffic creates a safe environment, and, when several houses are structured around such an area, numerous adults or older children from different families are watching over the children. Children may move freely from one compound to another and may eat and sleep in a group rather than in their own compounds.

The link between what materials are available and the type of games played is obvious. Within Sub-Saharan Africa, a region may be predominantly rainforest, grassland, mountains, coast, or arid semidesert. The same game, such as *mancala*, may be played with pebbles and holes in the sand in one region but using a wooden board with seeds elsewhere. Access to certain natural materials is common to all regions, and items such as pebbles and bush twigs are two of the most readily available and frequently used objects. Many areas have a reddish type of earth that can be used to make clay blocks, models, and figures. Water play is less common because of the value of preserving water, but children play in sections of streams not used for drinking water and in the rain or mud in the rainy season, where they enjoy the creation of mud slides. The tropical climate provides for the presence of small insects, lizards, and even edible insects that may be caught and collected. Wood, in addition to clay, is readily available to carve. Other advantages in rural areas may be trees to climb, small animals to chase, and greater access to a variety of natural materials.

In addition to the climate, the amount of natural light affects children's activities. In the villages—as night falls quickly (sometimes by 6 PM) and only older children may use oil lamps—the degree of moonlight determines the type of play. With moonlight children will choose games that are more outdoor and physical, but, when it is dark or raining, they may tell stories, sitting on benches on a porch or indoors. They may enjoy listening to traditional folktales told by their parents, grandparents, or other adults during the moonlight activities.

Children in urban communities may be restricted in availability of play areas, especially if they live near a busy road. Apartment complexes are not typically built with consideration for children's play needs, but by landlords who are focused on profit. Overcrowding inside the houses or apartments also limits play spaces, and children are likely to play on the streets. Some children may attend local preschools and day care centers where they will also play games and play with toys. Children in urban areas are more likely to have access to imported toys and board games, children's television programs, the use of VCRs and DVDs, and children's books, comics, and magazines. Village markets have a few commercial toys, but, in towns and cities, there are many items for sale, especially imported from different countries in Asia.

Children grow up playing with children of the same age group. These groups are more clearly defined than in Western societies, and the close friendships and affiliations last throughout a person's life. Each age group consists of children within the age range of about five years. Children acquire knowledge by sharing conversations, games, and pastimes with those their own age. But much learning also happens when younger children observe older children and older children take care of younger ones. In some parts of Africa, older school children may be at boarding school during the semester, so they see their age groups only when they are back in their villages or towns during vacation. Many of the games and pastimes are differentiated by sex, much the same as in non-African societies. Jumping rope, playing house, and playing with wooden or plastic dolls are typical activities for girls, whereas wrestling, masquerades, and playing soccer are more usual for boys.

Most studies of play make a clear distinction between the concepts of play and work. Games, pastimes (or hobbies), and playing with toys are what children do during periods of leisure or playtime. This distinction is challenged by what we observe in the lives of African children, who may have work (chores) as well as play and school. Among the Kpelle of Liberia, for example, children participate in chores: for example, girls take care of babies, and boys chase birds away from rice farms. Some children also sell small-sized crops, such as peppers and peanuts, to other families. For such children, the dividing line between work and play is not clearly separate but could involve both kinds of activities. When children enjoy imitating adult activities, are they playing or working? Some games, such as hunting games, gradually become more like real-life adult pastimes or work until, eventually, as older children or teenagers, the children are doing adult work. Children in rural areas often start pastoral duties, such as taking care of young calves, by the age of 5 or 6 years. Selling small amounts of produce (including handling the money) can be done by a 5-year-old. In most African countries, it is common for boys and girls to participate in the same kinds of chores before the age of 4 years, but after this age, many chores become more specific to boys or girls. Chores done by both male and female Bamanan (or Bambara) children in Mali, for example, include running errands for older children and adults, scaring birds and monkeys from the fields, collecting firewood for the elderly, and taking care of young children. After age 4, only boys care for poultry and animals or learn hiving, mat weaving, and cutting thatch for roofing. Girls help with household responsibilities. Similar chores are done by young children in other African countries, such as in Zambia, where both boys and girls wash plates, get firewood, and run errands. Girls get water, pound food, bathe babies, and help with cooking, and boys do gardening. In Namibia, boys look after goats and cattle, collect and chop firewood, do plowing, and fetch water. Girls wash plates, do cleaning, pound grain, cook, and also fetch water. Wealthier families, and those living in towns, may have domestic help and not require the children to do as much to contribute to running the household. Given all of the chores and responsibilities of most children, only certain games and related play can be combined with chores, or else the children might neglect what they are supposed to do. For example, boys can kick an object, such as a can, to each other while carrying bundles of firewood on their heads. While caring for babies, girls may tie them on their backs or sides but still be able at the same time to play a game with pebbles in the sand. There may be time to play games with their friends between 3 and 6 PM, when chores are complete. When children also attend school (usually by age 6 or 7) and must still do chores, there is not much time for play, regardless of whether it is pretend play, pastimes, or games.

Games are forms of play with rules and procedures. Key aspects of a game include specific purposes or goals, roles of the players, number of players, equipment (if any), physical setting, winners or losers, and rewards or punishment. Not all games have winners or losers and may not, therefore, have rewards and punishments. Games are called folk games if they have a history of being passed down from one generation to another, from adult to child, or from older child to younger child. African children's folk games are multifaceted in that many include music, songs, rhymes, material objects, and, often, physical activity. Such games encourage group cooperation and competition. Games such as puzzles, rhymes, storytelling, and poetry support learning of mathematics, physical agility, music, and language skills. The folk games played in a society reflect the values and practices of the society. They are also a way for children to acquire knowledge of behaviors and beliefs that will be expected of them as adults. African songs and rhymes that accompany games focus on such topics as sharing and being kind to others; respect for one's elders, including children or siblings who are older than oneself; and being obedient to one's elders. Other themes are social values such as honesty and hard work. Songs and rhymes may include warnings about which animals or things to fear, along with those that are used as everyday threats to children for misbehaving. Songs and rhymes may retain old refrains or have a more modern twist, such as singing about popular politicians.

Although the social culture emphasizes that family, extended family, village or regional needs take precedence over the individual, much individual and group competitiveness remains. Games often have a leader who is the caller or catcher, just as children's dance groups may have a leader with a whistle, who sings the main refrain. In games there are often winners and losers. Another characteristic of African children's games is that some of the punishments for the losers can be a bit harsher than in Western societies. For example, in a shell game described in both Ghana and northern Nigeria, if the point of the shell does not come up when a boy spins it, he has to put his hand down in the sand and each child hits his hand with his or her fist (in Nigeria) or he puts the thumb of one hand down on the floor, with the other fingers off the floor, and the winner attempts to spin the shell to hit and cause pain on the knuckles of the loser (in Ghana). These punishments in games do not seem so harsh in a society where corporal punishment with a stick or switch may be commonplace as part of child rearing. Other punishments in games may include the loser being teased in a song, being hit on the head or the back of the hand, or being dumped on a pile of refuse.

Folk games (and the more modern games that children have learned from television or from others who have traveled) include many versions. There are games of physical skill that require using one's hands, whole body, or foot movement in an agile and skilful way. Games of strategy involve carefully planning a move or action and sometimes trying to anticipate an opponent's move. In games of chance, the outcome is determined by luck, as in throwing dice. There are string games, stone games, racing and catching games, pulling games, hiding games, ball games, mathematical games, games of alignment and configuration, games of memory and discrimination, board and card games, games with a jump rope, and games of dancing and clapping. Some games may involve both skill and strategy, and some may also involve an element of chance. Many African countries have similar games, but the games vary according to region, so the items used, the rules, and the ending of the game may be different. A clear example of this is the adult pastime of wrestling, which, in Nigeria, for example, depending on the location has different rules depending on the location in Nigeria. Children's language games, which include riddles, tongue twisters, song games, and puzzles are another example. They vary based on the language used. Many cultural groups use more than one language, and language games may be multilingual and include, for example, Pidgin English or Pidgin French as well as indigenous languages. Natural materials are often used in children's games. Most are usually pebbles or seeds, but others are bamboo sticks, banana leaves, gravel, palm fronds, orange peels, water, sand, palm kernels, African pear, cassava leaves, oil beans, rubber tree seeds, and sticks. Man-made materials used in games in southeastern Nigeria, for example, include cellophane, paper bags, nails, rubber-coated wire, local broomsticks and switches, plastic, rubber and steel balls, string, cans (including evaporated-milk cans and powdered-milk cans), thread, pen tops, rope, battery covers, tops for beer and soda bottles, empty sugar packets, pieces of glass, empty washing powder packets, and broken pottery.

Adult games include card games, board games, and physical games such as wrestling. Adult games are usually played by men and may be played in homes, outdoors, in local eating parlors, or meeting places; they are played in the evenings after the men have finished working in the fields or other occupations. They afford an opportunity to drink soft drinks (soda), beer, or palm wine and to share stories or discuss current affairs.

Although, for adults, playing games is clearly distinguishable from other activities, this is not always the case with pastimes or hobbies. Pastimes are a way of spending spare time pleasantly or doing something for recreation. Most definitions do not distinguish between a pastime and a hobby. A hobby is also something a person likes to study or do. However, the term *hobby* is often used to denote an individualized concept and can imply personal collecting of certain objects such as stamps or glass ornaments. Given the social and communal nature of African society, a personal hobby that is different from those of others, or to which a person devotes much training and money, is not common. Some people like to spend more time at a particular activity, such as drawing, drumming, storytelling, or wood-carving, and might become better at it than others.

A part-time activity may reflect a special skill or interest, but it may also generate essential family income, for example, a hobby or pastime of basket weaving for a subsistence farmer. His baskets may be sold alongside his produce in the local market. Women may do the same with broom making. Another example that provides additional income is the chasing and trapping of animals. The sale of trapped rabbits, rodents, or porcupines may also supplement family income.

Many outdoor pastimes exist for children. The frequency of such activities is enhanced by a climate conducive to playing outdoors, except during heavy rains or under the hot midday sun. If children live near the coast, playing on the beach, digging in the sand, or swimming in the water are common. Even inland, water play in rivers or streams may be permissible in areas not used for drinking water. Because sand is common in many African countries, playing and drawing in the sand are popular. School exercise books and writing utensils are relatively easy to obtain for those who can afford them, so some children enjoy drawing. Certain small rocks can be used as chalk to draw on clay, rock, or concrete surfaces. Pastimes related to animals include the chasing and trapping of animals such as rodents or the local variety of squirrel or rabbit, snake charming, bird watching, insect catching, and keeping animals such as dogs, lizards, or goats. Although keeping an animal as a pet may occur, these relationships are rarely the indoor kind found in Western countries where animals as pets are kept and treated as members of the family. This may be based on traditional views of humans versus animals or on a disdain for spending money on the care and feeding of an animal when there are always children with nutritional or medical needs in the extended family or village. There is also the risk of rabies and other diseases in the small dogs and other animals that roam the villages.

Children make take part in crafts such as basket weaving and broom making as pastimes, in imitation of adults or as part of contributing to household work. Children enjoy knocking

MASQUERADES IN SOME AFRICAN CULTURES

A popular community pastime or celebration is participation in or watching masquerades. These are performed primarily by male adults on special occasions in West and Central Africa. A masquerade includes a facial disguise; the body is also covered, elaborate costumes and face masks are used, and movement and music support the performance. The masked dancers may be disguised as animals, spirits, or ancestors. Some are thought to embody or become the actual spirit or ancestor during the ceremony, and certain types of masquerades may not be viewed by women or children. Children, especially boys, from about age 5, enjoy producing their own masquerades, with costumes and masks and dancing. Sometimes the activity is an imitation of adult masquerades and sometimes it is of the children's own creation. Cloth, straw, and sticks can be used to cover the face and hands. A mask can be made from a clay model covered with papier-mâché; when it dries, the mask is painted. Children dressed in masquerade attire may go door-to-door at special times, such as Easter and Christmas, similar to trick or treating rituals in the United States. They receive money, fruits, nuts, candy, or other food. Children's masquerades can be as informal as dressing up during pretend activity or as formal as an organized children's troupe. In some societies children are given some small roles in adult masquerade performances. The National Museum of African Art Website (see Resource Guide) shows children participating in child and adult masquerades in different countries.

oranges down from the tree or collecting other small fruits and edible seeds, many of which are considered food suitable only for children. They have to know which trees they are allowed to pluck fruit from. Tree climbing and exploring undergrowth are fun for children, who quickly learn what areas are appropriate to explore. Certain areas of bush may be considered unsafe for superstitious or other reasons. Older children or adults from other families watch out for small children in the community and make sure they do not wander into such places. Children typically play in groups. Physical pastimes, especially soccer for boys, are popular throughout Africa. Adult bicycles are made locally, and older children like to ride them. Skipping is popular with girls, as well as jump rope or the equivalent.

Pretend activity can be considered a pastime. Much of this play is imitating what is observed in real life. Girls may tie a piece of wood on their backs as a doll, pretend to cook on a wood fire, and use clay pots or empty cans as cooking utensils. Boys may use paper bags or sacks on their heads as masks or create toy machetes out of pieces of wood.

Social visiting, religious events, and community celebrations are aspects of African culture in which families spend much of their time. Children not only accompany their parents to such events, but adults are invited to a child's birthday party, considered more of a family event than just a children's event. There are family functions to attend most weekends, including birthday parties, funerals, christenings, and weddings. Social visiting is common for adults, who visit friends or relatives—often without notice—and may take their children with them. At all of these family functions, children typically join the company of other children who are present.

Language and movement are intertwined in the games and pastimes of African children. Dance, drama, songs, poetry, oral literature, folktales, and music are everyday occurrences in their lives. In African countries much of the population may not be literate in the indigenous languages or other languages. Sub-Saharan Africa has a long oral tradition, in which the spoken language is the primary medium for passing information down from one generation to another. Oral language skills are encouraged from a young age, especially in boys. Children learn quickly, however, when they are not supposed to talk, such as during adult conversation. Children are encouraged to sway to music and to dance before they can walk, and toddlers attempt to copy the dancing movements of older children. Children spend increasing amounts of time dancing in the evening when there is bright moonlight.

Songs can be classified based on themes such as heroes or heroines and villains, health, humor, animals, and threats, or based on the style of the song—solo, dialogue, rhyming, call and answer, and rhythmic formats. In songs that are dialogues, two children or groups of children alternately sing the words or phrases. Some songs are also a back-and-forth exchange, but one between a solo speaker and a group that forms the chorus. The chorus response is often brief. Songs occur in dance routines and as part of a game. Organized dance groups may consist of children of mixed ages, and boys and girls often dress in similar costume. Musical instruments such as drums, flutes, or metal gongs may be used. The girls may use handkerchiefs to wave, and the lead singer may have a whistle to blow to mark the main points of the refrain or rhythm. As children become older, they form separate male and female dance groups, and children who are exceptionally skilled may be selected for a high school group (similar to Western teenagers joining a choir or sports club).

Some instruments and objects used for dancing and singing are also considered toys. Toys are items associated with play, especially pretend activity. For infants, toys may be objects with bright colors that make noise and hold attention—objects that the infant can manipulate or watch. For toddlers, toys are items that can be stacked, banged, or carried, and may be miniature versions of adult objects. Older children may use toy items as parts of games or for pretending and acting out adult routines. Some toys are formal learning tools to encourage such skills as drawing or recognizing letter shapes. Most African children do not have manufactured toys. If toys are needed, they are created out of local materials and used for many kinds of play. The availability of raw materials for toys depends on whether the family lives in a rural environment that is forest, savannah, or rocky desert and on how much discarded material from cans and boxes is available. Whether children roll a bicycle wheel rim with a stick, for example, depends on how many old bicycle parts are nearby. Although commercial toys, such as plastic guns, dolls, infant rattles, and balls (imported mainly from China) are available in local markets and supermarkets in the cities sell more expensive imported toys, most families do not have the financial resources to purchase such toys. When commercial toys are available, they get broken or lost easily because of the number of children of different ages who access them. Many materials can be used to create handmade toys. They are made by the children themselves or by adults for children. Also, libraries in towns and in children's centers on university campuses have books for children, but in rural areas children's books are less common.

Natural materials for handmade toys may come from the ground, such as rocks and pebbles, or from plants and trees, such as palm fronds, plantain leaves, seeds, and palm fruit kernels. Other items are rope, rubber, clay pottery, coconut matting, and bamboo sticks. Musical instruments can be made of local materials, such as skins and wood. Propellers can be made by putting a stick into a certain kind of leaf that spins when the child pretends to be an airplane and runs with it. Game boards can be carved out of wood. Sticks are made into pestles for pretending to pound food in cooking play. Wooden and rag dolls are created from pieces of wood, raffia, or corn husks. There are also carved dolls and animals that are created for adult purposes, such as decoration, to symbolize the loss of a child, or for traditional religious practices. Sometimes they are mistaken for children's toys by writers and ethnographers. For example, with the high rate of mortality in twins in West Africa, when one twin survives in Nigeria, a carving may be made of the lost twin, which the family keeps or the remaining twin may sometimes carry. There are many man-made materials that can be adapted and turned into toys, including wire and cans to form miniature vehicles; boxes, paper, and cloth as masks; plastic bags rolled and tied with twine for balls; metal cans and sheets for musical instruments; dice bottle tops; and pen tops.

Most children in Sub-Saharan African countries are brought up in rural environments, with rich natural materials and open spaces to run and play in with freedom from the hazards of traffic and the discomforts of harsh, cold winters. But there are also many children whose lives have been tragically impacted by war, AIDS, or living on the streets. For these children, the opportunity for games and pastimes is limited. If they do not have their basic needs met—including clean water and medical care—they become sad and unwell and have little motivation to enjoy the play activities of most children or create toys.

Countries that have experienced armed conflict in the last 10 years include Chad, Rwanda, Guinea-Bissau, Democratic Republic of the Congo, Somalia, Liberia, Angola, and Sierra Leone. Thousands of children have experienced child soldiering, for which there is no traditional or cultural history. Children as young as five years of age are forced to be soldiers, have witnessed constant killing, and have killed others. Sometimes they have been forced to kill their own family or members of their community. Sierra Leone's deadly civil war (1991–2002) had a devastating impact on children, who then missed out on childhood by being abducted into the armed forces and, often, violently assaulted or mutilated.

A large number of children are orphans because they have lost their parents to AIDS. Some orphanages exist, but most of these children are taken care of by relatives or friends. According to information from the Integrated Regional Information Networks (IRIN) (2005), almost 4 million people in Nigeria were infected with HIV and almost 2 million children lost a parent due to AIDS-related illness by the end of 2003. In Kaduna, a city in the north of Nigeria, for example, almost every day a child tests positive for the virus. Pediatric medicine for AIDS is more expensive than adult medicine and costs approximately $80 a month. Since two-thirds of Nigerians earn less than $30 a month, this is too expensive even when it is available.[2]

A third group of children who also suffer considerably are adolescents and young children who live on the streets. In the 1980s "street children" were not such a serious concern, but now in most major cities they can be seen doing menial jobs, stopping cars, and selling wares or begging. They are often viewed as a nuisance, an eyesore, and as petty criminals. Street children are called a variety of names in different African countries. For example, in the Democratic Republic of the Congo, they are called *moineaux* or sparrows. Such children may live on the street either permanently as part of street culture or in the daytime but have somewhere to go at night where there is an older person responsible for them or acquainted with them. Street children may leave their homes for many reasons, including poverty, violence and abuse, and being orphaned or abandoned because of AIDS, handicaps, or birth history. Sometimes they leave because of torture or rape; occasionally older children are enticed by the excitement of a large town or city. Some children have families, but they are sent out by their families for several hours at a time to beg, perhaps because their families think the public is more likely to be charitable to children than to adults. However, several million children in Sub-Saharan Africa live without families, and many children in war-torn areas are unable to locate their families. Some children may be disowned, even by a family of professionals, because of their behavior. Families may also reject a child because the mother was a prostitute or because the child has an obvious physical or mental handicap. Fundamental social changes may have contributed to this crisis. In some regions there is an increasing trend for individual families to take primary responsibility for children rather than the whole community, which traditionally looked out for every child. This may be related to increased overall levels of poverty or to increased mobility in families moving to towns and cities.[3]

Other countries throughout the world have street children. But a major difference is that many of those children return home after six months or less, whereas more than half of the street children in African countries may still be on the street at least a year later, and some of the children may be as young as three years of age. These children are not likely to attend school, so their future is limited, and they may be picked up by the police and thrown in jail for a long time if no one claims them. In these street cultures older children take care of younger children, and the children look out for each other because, in most cases, they are their only family.

With the exception of orphans and street children, the common denominator in African societies is the role of the extended family. There is a wide discrepancy in lifestyle between wealthy families in Sub-Saharan African countries, who can obtain toys and electronic games, television, and other modern technological equipment, and those families from rural or poorer urban environments. Despite this difference, most children grow up with exposure to the rich African heritage that is passed down through different generations. The games, pastimes, and locally made traditional toys are passed on by other members of the extended family and community. Children also learn from their own age group. Music and movement, oral skills such as storytelling, songs, rhymes and proverbs, and numerous crafts permeate every aspect of society on an everyday basis as well as on special festive occasions. In a people-oriented culture, more time is spent in the company of others and less in individual play activities. Another feature of this region of the world is the blurred division between play and work. The following examples of games, pastimes, and toys in specific countries within different geographical regions illustrate such characteristics and also highlight some local variations.

REGIONAL SUBSECTIONS

West Africa

Nigeria

Dancing and clapping games are popular among girls throughout West Africa. In Nigeria, *oga* is the Igbo name for a hand clap and step game played by girls ages 3 to 16. The game encourages skills in lower body coordination, rhythm, counting, and addition. There are six possible moves: legs apart, left leg forward or backward, right leg forward or backward, and legs together. One girl is chosen as the leader and one or more girls face the leader. After a signal, they begin to clap, dance, or hop to a rhythm or song. At regular intervals that coincide with a clap, each girl must select one of the six moves. If her chosen move is the same as that chosen by the leader, that girl becomes the leader and scores a point. The game continues until someone reaches a particular score that the girls have previously agreed upon. Strategic skills may also be involved, in that girls learn to observe subtle cues from the leg movements of the leader to anticipate the leader's next move. The leader may try to disguise early signs of which leg she will put out in front, in order to score additional points and remain the leader.

String games are also played mainly by girls. *Omo ori odo* is a string game played among the Yoruba people in Nigeria. *Omo ori odo* means "pestle" (the upright wooden stick for pounding food); a piece of string is used to construct a typical pestle, such as that used by the Yoruba and Hausa peoples of Nigeria, with a "head" at each end (rather than a head at one end, the kind used by the Igbo people). To play the game, a string is carefully passed between the fingers of both hands after it has first been made into a circle. Two web-like

A YORUBA CALL AND RESPONSE GAME

An example of a lead speaker or singer and a response chorus can be found in a hide and seek game played by Yoruba children in western Nigeria:

Leader (who is covering his eyes and will look for the children): *Boju, boju* (Cover your face.)

Chorus: *Oh*
Leader: *Oloro m bo* (The *Oro* man is coming.)
Chorus: *Oh*
Leader: *E pa ra mo* (Hide yourselves.)
Chorus: *Oh*
Leader: *Se ki n si* (Should I uncover [my face]?)
Chorus: *Oh*
Leader: *Ng o si o* (I will uncover it.)
Chorus: *Oh*
Leader: *Si, Si, Si* (Uncover, uncover, uncover.)
Chorus: *Oh*

patterns emerge—one on each palm—and they are linked in a straight string. The web-like ends look like the two heads of the pestle. The girls sing while they make movements as if they are pounding food, placing their hands one on top of the other. The distance in between is occupied by the plain, non-webbed part. They sing

Omo ori odo po pa
Ome ori odo po pa

Po pa reflects the sound the pestle makes as it pounds on a surface.

Racing or catching games are also popular for both boys and girls. These games include various versions of the common game of hide and seek, which may occur as a moonlight game. Among the Urhobo people in Nigeria, the child who is the leader will call out a series of words to which the children respond and then calls, "Here I come, the one I catch I will eat with pepper," (meaning red pepper that is extremely hot and spicy) and chases the children until he or she catches one.

Some catch games involve both physical skill in running away and strategy in trying to avoid the chaser. These are often related to the combination of a weaker, slower animal and a faster, stronger animal. Among the Bini of Nigeria, such a game is called the Lion and the Goat. One team of children represents the goats and the other the lions. Children not on either team are the villagers, and an older child acts as the referee. The villagers form a circle. One of the children who is a goat goes inside the circle, and one who is a lion stays outside. The lion tries to break the circle to get inside. If the lion manages to get into the circle, the villagers allow the goat to go out. The lion becomes a goat if it is unsuccessful in catching the goat. The goat becomes a lion if it is caught by the lion. Children take turns at the end of each round between a lion and a goat.

Games of physical skill may involve the whole body or just hand-eye coordination. The pear game in Nigeria (*Oku-ube*) is typically played by boys and is an example of hand-eye coordination skill with some physical strength in throwing. A Nigerian pear, or oil bean, is tossed to the ground by one child and another child tries to hit it with his fruit. If he succeeds, he obtains the fruit, but if he fails, the other child picks up his fruit and tries to hit that of his opponent. Games similar to the pear game may be considered mathematical because they involve counting. For example, *Ghota guo* (catch and count) is played on a flat sandy surface. Up to four or five boys or girls sit or kneel in a small circle. Ten to twenty seeds or pebbles are placed in front of the first player. He or she must throw one up in the air about a foot high and catch it and proceed rapidly to do the same with the other seeds. While doing so, the other players count each seed that the player catches until one is missed and then another player has a turn. The winner is the player who successfully throws and catches all of the seeds. He or she is cheered and may be carried shoulder high.

Another game using small objects is well known as a game of strategy and has been popularized as a commercially available game in England and the United States. This is a game called *walae* in Ghana, *okwe-ala* in southeastern Nigeria, *ayo* in western Nigeria, and commonly known as *mancala* elsewhere. Variations of mancala are played by older children and adults in most African countries. It may be played using a wooden board with six holes in each side or by creating such shapes in the sand. Four stones or seeds are placed in each hole. Each player decides which group of stones to pick up and then drops one stone in each of the following holes in the board. Wherever he or she drops the last stone, all of the stones in that hole must be picked up and placed the same way in the following holes. The player stops when the last stone is placed in an empty hole. Good players are able to plan and anticipate where they could be at an advantage against their opponent, just as in planning moves in chess.

A favorite game for adult males in Nigeria is draughts or checkers, called *Draft* or *Draf*. There are thirty-two squares in two contrasting colors and twenty-four flat objects. The board is placed on a table or on the knees of the two players. Each player has twelve pieces on his or her side of the board, and both players try to capture as many of their opponents pieces as possible by jumping over with one of their pieces and taking them. Sometimes the players bet on who will be a winner and the winner collects the money. Card games are also popular, such as *Whot,* which is usually played by two to four players. The Whot game is thought to be the national card game of Nigeria. It was originally popular in Britain in the 1950s and 1960s and is similar to *Uno*. Players try to be the first to get rid of their cards.

Not all games involve a physical activity. Language games may be rhymes, riddles, and stories and sung or told. Some language games involve riddles that have a trick component. The following is an example of a fun trick tale from the Urhobo people in Nigeria:

Leader: *Itaye* (Here is a story.)
Players: *Ye* (Story)
Leader: *Asavwe* and *Ejavwevwo* (Mr. Pinch me and Mr. Leave me)
Aye towe kugbe (They dug a pond together.)
Ejavwevwo kowhuru (Mr. Leave me then died.)
Kono vwe awe na? (Who owns the pond now?)

Any child who did not understand the trick answer would say "Mr. Pinch me" and then get pinched by all of the other children. The safest answer would be "not Mr. Leave me."

Trick stories can also be in the form of a song, as in one in which the leader describes characteristics of particular objects or animals and the other children have to affirm the leader's statements only if they are correct. For example,

Leader: *Evwe ari sherio* (The goat has horns.)
Players: *Avi sherio* (It has horns.)
Leader: *Ogegede avi sherio* (The sheep has horns.)
Players: *Avi sherio* (It has horns.)
Leader: *Urhe avi sherio* (A tree has horns.)
Players (silence)

If a child forgets and automatically responds, he or she receives a light or heavy beating from the other children and is out of the game. Popular among Ibo children in Nigeria are different variations of these songs and rhymes, such as "What grows hair? Rats, goats, and lizards grow hair."

The manipulation of sounds and words in language and song to create emphasis and give different meanings is also found in, for example, songs that children combine with their frequent pastimes of dance, music, and movement. Children may dance and sing informally among themselves or in organized groups, with or without adult involvement. There are traditional children's songs that are meaningful in terms of everyday experiences and also describe what is considered morally correct behavior. For example, two songs heard in Ibo (Nigeria) girls' song and dance routines are about girls who went to fill their clay pots with water from the river or stream. One girl's pot broke, but the others did not wait for her and she asks "What kind of friend would someone be if she abandons her friend when this kind of problem occurs?" Another song is about an older girl who is too beautiful and the boys will not leave her alone. Perhaps she would prefer to be ugly.

Some popular children's television programs in Nigeria include storytelling shows, such as "Tales by Moonlight." Nigerian children also like to watch other children's programs such as "Funtime" and "Work it Out." In the latter program, children (about grades 5 and 6) are given mathematical problems to solve, and the winner receives a prize. Because Nigeria has the fourth largest television network in the world and each state in Nigeria has its own radio and television stations, there are many popular programs for children.

A pastime in which the actors may not sing and dance but may instead be silent is masquerading. The style of masks and costumes varies dramatically from one region to another. In Nigeria, there are many masquerades, and children are taught to dance and perform from a young age. The Okpella people in Nigeria, for example, have a masquerade that celebrates funerals and harvest, and there is an adult "Ancient Mother" who appears with a small child also dressed in costume. David Binkley and Allyson Purpura describe the role of children in the Gelede Yoruba festival in western Nigeria. This is a major festival that celebrates women and the power of women. It frequently has 4- and 5-year old boys perform first. Men and boys dress as women, to try to look big and beautiful. The small boys hold old discarded or borrowed masks to their faces to perform and then their performances are followed by those of teenage masqueraders.

Women belong to different women's groups who may sing and dance on special occasions, such as to celebrate the birth of a child, or in competitions. They do not have much time for many games and pastimes because they are busy with work and family commitments. Male adolescents and men, however, enjoy wrestling, especially in the rural areas. This is different from the organized sport of wrestling seen in Europe and the United States. The setting is usually in a village square or school playground. Teams of players may select contestants or one wrestler may challenge another by presenting his right palm to be slapped by the opponent. The two main rules are that no one should seriously injure their opponent or make him bleed and that the goal is to get the opponent flat on his back. This pastime is a competition of physical strength and skill. Also, some adult men in the north of Nigeria pursue the pastime of snake charming. Big snakes, usually pythons and cobras, are charmed and trapped in large calabash pots. Snake charmers display their skills at special events and gatherings and will entice the snakes out of the containers and twine them around the snake charmer's neck.

Ghana

In Ghana, the step and clap game popular with girls is known as *Ampe.* There may be several variations of the game. In Ampe, the two players are known as *Ohyiwa* and *Opare. Ohyiwa* scores a point when the player's left leg meets the right leg or the right leg meets the left leg of *Opare.* However, *Opare* scores a point when the left leg meets the left leg or the right leg meets the right leg of *Ohyiwa.* The first girl to get 10 points wins the game.

Some games may be a combination of racing and strategy. For example, *Anotoba,* a game played in Ghana, is like a game played in England or the United States known as "Drop the

Handkerchief." However, a beanbag or similar object is used and 10 to 20 players sit in a circle, with one performer running around the circle. He or she drops the beanbag quietly behind someone's back and runs around the circle. The player must find the beanbag before being by touched the performer or they switch roles and the player becomes the performer.

Hiding games may involve hiding people or objects. Finding hidden objects is a popular game throughout the world. In Ghana, near Kumasi, it is called *Pilolo.* The leader of a small group of children hides sticks or stones in different places, such as in palm trees or in the sand. Another child, the timekeeper, stands at a finishing place. Whoever can quickly reach the place where a stick is hidden and get to the end point is the winner of the game.

Also in Ghana, there is a game called *Kwaiara Franga* (Sunday's flag). It is similar to tic tac toe. Using chalk, the children draw a rectangle and two lines diagonally. Each child has three stones or marbles and has to place them appropriately until there is a row of three in order to win.

Tongue twisters are another type of language play, but one that emphasizes the skilful use of sounds. The Children's Folkgames Project includes examples of tongue twisters in Akan from Ghana. These are excellent examples because they show how a rapid succession of similar sounds can prove so difficult to pronounce. They can be quite humorous because errors in speech are very likely to occur the faster one tries to say the phrase or rhyme. Tongue twisters also reflect names of common objects and activities in the environment. The following tongue twister rhyme is a short narrative about *Mr. Kwaapaa* who went to the farm to remove stumps, and, when he saw a monitor lizard, he stopped and decided to chase it. When the lizard climbed a tree, a branch broke off and hit the man on the forehead.

Agya kwaa paa koo apaa
Kohunu mampam gyae apam
Kopaam mampam maa mampam

These are the first three lines of this tongue twister. It is tricky to say words that involve quickly switching back and forth from /k/ to /p/ and /m/ to /p/.

Pastimes include masquerades, which are popular in Ghana, as in other parts of West Africa. The Fante people in Ghana have a fancy dress masquerade at Christmas, Easter, and the New Year. The costumes are replicas of European costumes from the 1700s and 1800s and consist of masks bought from stores or made of wire mesh and painted. The costumes include gloves, hats, and other clothing. Some masqueraders are dressed as animals and some as people, such as an old man. Art and drawing are popular with children. In urban areas, there are numerous activities related to children's art. For at least ten years, the National Theatre of Ghana has held a children's arts festival with work submitted by children from all over Ghana. The children compete for prizes offered by corporate organizations.

Playing with marbles, and shooting birds with catapults, are other examples of pastimes in Ghana that involve either purchased or handmade objects. Numerous small toys are available for purchase in local markets, including molded dolls, made from red or green plastic, and plastic guns and small plastic and metal racing cars, mostly imported from China and Korea. Many children's toys are handmade from local materials. The wide availability of natural materials, such as sand, rocks, plants, and seeds, as well as discarded man-made materials, such as cans and wire, is used to create toys. In Ghana, a rattle would be a can with pebbles inside, with the open end banged to close it, and a pretend gun would be made from a stick. Examples of using everyday materials in Ghana include making a horn from a pawpaw leaf stick; a bow and arrow from a corncob, rubber strip, and palm branch; a helicopter from milk cans or from feathers on corncobs; a spinning top from a seed and broom straw; or a propeller from a pen top. A spinning top can also be made from a small gourd and wrapped with a string made from hemp.

Liberia

Storytelling is another language art and pastime. Among the Kpelle of Liberia, only boys tell stories, but the girls will listen. The art of story narration varies among boys of similar age and depends on how much they like listening to and telling these tales. Younger children prefer folktales known as *Meni-pele.* These folktales are simple and always contain a song. They include themes about the social values children will learn, such as how being greedy, lazy, and selfish goes against the concept of group cooperation and family reputation. As boys grow older, they may tell more fables and riddles than the simpler folktales.

Mali

Masquerading is also important for Dogon boys in Mali, and children's masquerades are an essential part of the adult rituals. The Dodo masquerade is performed during the Muslim holy month of Ramadan. The masqueraders go from one house to another. They sing and dance and are given money. The type of mask is unique because it is made out of a dried gourd and has horns made from palm stalks. The gourd is brightly painted, and older boys may also paint their bodies with white paint. One less usual feature is that girls participate in Dodo masquerades and may be musicians, dancers, or singers. Some children dress up as airplanes or cars, and different groups of children perform different songs and dances and wear different costumes. The leaf festival in Mali is a children's masquerade that must be performed before the planting of fields can occur. Some children wear leaf costumes and other are musicians.

Another pastime is drawing. All children like to draw pictures, and local markets have many school supplies, such as markers, pencils, and crayons and school notebooks, for children who can afford them. Enid Schildkrout compared children's art in several countries in West Africa. Based on her observations of Dogon children in Mali during four trips to that country between 1992 and 2002, she found that they drew three main types of pictures: masks and the costumes that went with them, local architecture, and traditional rituals and customs, such as shrines and sacrifices. The masks were those seen in theatrical performances, such as animal masks. The architecture included hillside villages and granaries. Traditional activities included drawings of elders and animal sacrifices. Sometimes such drawing books were sold to tourists.

Central Africa

Cameroon

Racing games are popular among children in Central Africa in rural and urban areas. In school playgrounds in Cameroon, up to ten girls may stand in a row and one girl standing a long distance away will hold up a handkerchief, mitten, or sock and, at the sound of a blown whistle, the girls run to the handkerchief. The girl who gets there first becomes the winner and is the one to hold the handkerchief for the others to race and reach first. Boys play a similar game but may run to a goal post or similar target.

Another game of physical skill popular in Cameroon and parts of the Congo is *Petit Poisson* (small fish). The game is played by boys and girls, usually of school age. Ten to sixteen players face each other in pairs and hold hands firmly. The boy or girl who has no partner becomes the petit poisson, who will leap up and land on the network of hands. Before leaping, this player shouts "petit poisson" and the other players reply, "Dans l'eau." The main player asks "Que je vien?" and the answer is "Oui." Then as the main player leaps up, lands, and crosses the firmly held hands to the end of the row, the players are all singing "Dans l'eau ici." After this player jumps off the end, he or she replaces one of those holding hands; then it is that person's turn to leap across. This is an example of a game where there are no winners or losers.

A game that involves physical skill and strategy and is popular in Central Africa is *Tabala*. This is a form of hopscotch and it is also seen in West African countries. Two girls or two boys play the game. A set of box-like shapes are drawn on the ground in two vertical rows with a dome shape at the top. The first player throws a piece of broken bottle or a piece of metal into one of the "houses" or "boxes." If the item successfully lands in a box, then she begins to hop on one leg through the boxes. She hops through all of the boxes except the one that contains the object thrown. Balancing precariously in the box nearest to the object, she stoops down to pick it up and then hops over it on her way out of the Tabala. If she does not fall down or miss her step, she has won the box where the object was thrown. The two players take turns, but the second player may not hop into the box that has been won by the other player. On subsequent rounds of hopping, the first player may hop and stand with two legs in the box that she previously won. The player who wins the most boxes can try to throw an object into the largest box or house, which forms a dome at the top. However, this throw is done while her back is to the Tabala, which makes it harder to do than in the previous throws. If her object lands in the dome, she is the winner.

Language games include telling riddles, and this is done mainly by children in their teens. In the Adamaoua Province in Cameroon, there is an introductory question-answer ritual before the actual riddle is given. The riddler says "*Ngengge*" and the players say "*Nang go.*" Then the interaction continues by the riddler offering the question and the player(s) giving an answer. Then the riddler says, "No, try again" and this occurs twice if the answers are wrong. By the third time, the player(s) must pretend to forfeit a village, part of a village, or members of the immediate or extended family. The riddler says, "Give me a village" and may respond to the offer by "It's not enough. Give me another." When he or she is satisfied with the offer, the player will tell the answer to the riddle.

The most popular pastime for boys is soccer. There are typically eleven boys to a team, but there may not be strict adherence to rules as in formal sports. If there are no balls available, grapefruits or balls made of rags are used. Girls enjoy many song and dance activities. In Yaoundé, Cameroon, a popular song play is known as *Kokorikoko.* Up to ten or more girls stand in a circle and there is a lead singer who stays in the middle of the circle. As they sing, the girls move around in a circle. The chorus goes as follows:

Lead singer	Response
Kokorikoko	Oya
O nana	Oya
O bilibili	Oya
O nana	Oya
O ti doo	Bambele

The climax of the song is "O ti doo" and, as the group members respond "Bambele," they stop and stamp their feet on the ground several times until the lead singer starts again.

Democratic Republic of the Congo (DRC)

Masquerading is popular in many parts of Central Africa, as in West Africa. Among the Kuba people of the Democratic Republic of Congo (formerly Zaire), as in many other regions, children may not see the more important, more powerful, and fiercer masquerades. Children are present and sing praises at the less significant masquerades performed by younger people. They may also play masquerades after the adults have performed and try to imitate some of the performances. The children will make and paint their own masks using pieces of material they find. Kuba men teach their sons how to make the masks and masquerade costumes.

In the Democratic Republic of the Congo, as in other African countries, children make toys out of wire, including airplanes, bulldozers, yachts, cars, helicopters, motorcycles, and tanks. The toys may be used by the children who made them or they may be sold in marketplaces. An extensive study of the Baluba and Basanga-Bayeke children's games, songs and dances was written by Centner in 1963. This work is thought to be the most extensive and detailed information on children's play in Sub-Saharan Africa. It includes descriptions and drawings of children's toys that can still be seen today, such as a vehicle with a long handlebar made out of bamboo sticks, and a wooden pull-along car (with a drawing of the boy who made it). With the same materials available, some traditions, such as making toys from natural objects, have not changed in the past forty years.

Southern Africa

Republic of South Africa

The Republic of South Africa has a unique combination of many different ethnic groups. The Afrikaans- and English-speaking communities include people of European, Asian, and Indian descent. Those of African origin also speak different languages, such as Xhosa. The different ethnic groups do not have the same preferences for games. For example, boys from families of African descent are more likely to participate in games that involve rhythmic jumping and singing than boys from families of European descent are. Indian children like to play Three Tins and Top. *Carrom* is a popular traditional game among Indian children, but not as popular as hide and seek, chasing, rhythmic, and challenging games such as Marbles and Top. Carrom is a game that has been played for nearly 200 years. It has been described as a combination of billiards or pool, marbles, and air hockey. A square board, usually made of wood, is used with pockets in each corner. Object pieces are used instead of balls, and there is a piece called the striker that is three times heavier than the object pieces. Players flick the striker against the object pieces from the other side of the board to try to get them into the corners. Carrom is played by adults and children. Substitutes such as bottle tops can be used for object pieces. Whereas the white children in the Republic of South Africa prefer hide and seek, rope skipping is more popular among black children. The South African Indigenous Games Research Project (2001–2002) found that over 500 different children's games are played in the Republic of South Africa, including at least 37 varieties of rope jumping, 18 varieties of hide and seek, and 13 varieties of hopscotch. Examples of the most popular games were blind man's buff and hide and seek, and the second most popular was rope skipping. Hopscotch was the fifth most popular game. Most children reported that they learned the games from other children rather than from adults. When children are younger, boys and girls play similar games that are physical and involve motor skills (such as tag, rounders, and street fighting). As they grow older, the physically challenging games, such as stingers, are just for boys, while the girls play clapping games or games such as Broken Telephone.

In the Republic of South Africa, as in other African countries, there are many variations of the game of tag or catch. It may be called "Crows and Cranes." Eight to twenty children form two groups in a large play area. One group are cranes and the other crows. They stand in a line facing each other. If the leader calls "crows," that team runs to a goal line behind them while the cranes chase them. If anyone is tagged before reaching the line, either that person is out of the game or a point is awarded to the other team. The team with the most points or the one with the most players left in the team is the winner. Another popular team game in the Republic of South Africa is African handball. Ten or more players are divided into two equal teams. The ball is thrown from one player to another on the same team. The purpose of the game is for the ball to pass only within the same team without the other team catching it. Whenever the ball is caught, the members of that team clap once and sometimes stamp their feet.

In countries that are multilingual, popular games may involve the use of more than one language. One example of this phenomenon is the use of Xhosa, English, and Afrikaans in the games of girls observed playing "rounders"(a game related to ball tag) and "wait" (a skipping game) in Khwezi Park outside Cape Town. In the wait game, one of the children uses an Afrikaans word and propose a particular chant or rhyme routine. This is followed by a player crossing over a rope made from twisted pantyhose, which is set at waist, knee, or ankle height. At each stage of the game, crossing the rope, the children call out the name of a color in English. The descriptions of the practice of these games also shows that, although the two games are similar to others in other continents, the use of rhymes, songs, dance, movement, humor, and teasing add a unique African and local modification.

Types of pastimes in southern Africa also depend on the characteristics of the environment, as in other regions. Children from affluent families may have private gardens and play with fewer children of the same age. Most children in rural areas always have friends or family to play with. Boys go out hunting, often with dogs, to find food such as birds or insects for themselves. They may play at boxing or wrestling with each other. Sometimes they collect materials such as clay and sticks to make toys. Children who are responsible for taking care of livestock use their animals to create pretend activity such as bullfights. If there is water nearby, swimming and water play are popular.

Zambia

Soccer is popular in southern African countries, as elsewhere on the continent. In 2003 in Lusaka, Zambia, a branch of PLAY SOCCER, a nonprofit organization, was started. This is an organization that supports soccer as a fun, recreational activity but combines it with informal educational activities to teach children about health, physical, and social concerns. This organization also exists in Ghana, Senegal, and the Republic of South Africa and it started branches in Cameroon and Malawi in 2005. In Zambia, 59 percent of children reported making toys themselves; other toys were bought or made by their parents. Three- to six-year-olds in Zambia play with balls, clay toys, wire toys, bottles, and cans.

Botswana

In the Okavango Delta of northwestern Botswana, where the primary adult occupations are hunting, fishing, and agriculture, children spend less time playing because their labor is in greater demand. Play pounding is the most common type of pretend play for girls, especially if their families obtain most of their nutrition from maize. They imitate the pounding of grain, usually with dirt and an imaginary mortar that could be made from a reed or stick. The girls continue this play until about age 10; it may be that play improves their skill for the adult labor of pounding. Children often play the cow game, which is a fantasy role-playing activity. Some children pretend to be oxen, and they are yoked or tied to a sled by others. Remnants of twine are used for the yoke, and the sled can either be one made by one of the fathers or an object they pretend is a sled. Dirt or a similar substance is piled on the sled to represent some other material, and then the oxen pull the sled, with one child as the driver. Part of the excitement of this activity is that the oxen may lose the load on the sled or rear up like real oxen. Another pastime is played with sticks; it is only played by boys until about age 12. One picks a spot on the ground and throws a stick at it and the other boys then also throw their sticks at the same spot. There are three groups of children in particular who have significantly less play time than other children in the Okavango Delta: those whose fathers are migrant laborers, children of junior wives (because there are more household responsibilities for them), and children who attend school (because sometimes they have to walk a long distance and also do chores or may be boarding during the week).

There is a well-established history of making wire toys in Botswana, as in other parts of southern Africa. Toys are made by children and by adults. Some toys are made for local consumption; these tend to be larger and less decoratively painted. The craftsmanship has become a cottage industry, with items sold to tourists in tourist markets and exported overseas. Although not well advertised until recently, images of the wire toys can be found in local paintings, on note cards, and on T-shirts. Children's simple toy push-cars made of crudely bent wires and basic wheels can frequently be observed being pushed by children along dusty paths and streets. The most popular design is based on the notion of a push-pull toy. Handles made of long scrap metal rods are connected with fragments of rubber bands to a bell-crank functioning steering system. The child can walk upright holding a big loop of metal and wire that represents and functions as a steering wheel. Sometimes the wire cars have a more complex design, with a headrest, windshield wiper, and radio antenna. Small model cars are made by snipping off the top and bottom inch of aluminum soda cans. The two ends are pushed together to make wheels and sometimes covered with rubber. Thin copper wire from recycled electrical appliance cord is also sometimes used. Older-style vehicles are mostly made of wood, and wire is used only for fittings, hinges, or axles. Modern styles have far more wire and may also use cork, rubber, and cloth. Some local carvers may make both metal and wooden crafts. They use shoe polish on the wood; then the empty shoe polish cans are used for wheels or other parts of metal toys. Small empty enamel paint containers are another source for metal toys. The innovative use of discarded items is typical of different regions of Africa, and the toy making in southern Africa not only reflects such creativity but emphasizes the blurred distinction between pastime activities and cottage industry income for older children and adults.

East Africa

Uganda

Racing and catching games are popular in Uganda, as in other African countries. An example of a catching game in Uganda is the "Dog and Hyena". The children divide into two groups behind their leaders. One leader is the dog and one is the hyena. The children dance and sing "*Chakity cha*" and try to grab the children who are lined up behind the other leader.

In Uganda, there is a version of a tug-of-war game where the teams are chosen by making choices. There are two leaders; they ask each child to choose between meat and rice, for example, and the child stands behind whichever leader is that choice. When the children have chosen teams, they grab hands and pull.

Songs may be combined with a dancing game, as in the game called *Nyaga Nyaga Nya.* In this game, the children sit in a circle and one person is the leader, who goes around the circle while the children sing the song. Whenever the song finishes, the child in front of whom the leader is standing must get up and dance and then becomes the leader. The children sing the song again. Another singing game is called *Kakopi.* The children sit in a line and extend their legs. While they are singing the Kakopi song, the leader taps each of their legs; the child whose leg the leader touches at the end of the song must bend the leg under himself or herself. As the game is repeated, whoever has both legs bent is out of the game. The last child who is left with an extended leg is called "the night dancer."

A counting game for young children in the Lango district of Uganda involves the children counting fingers around a group, while saying a rhyme about hens and the number of eggs they lay. In the Buganda region of Uganda, children count around the group, saying, "We are ducklings, one, two, three, four, five, etc." In Uganda, most pastimes for children are also group activities with friends. Although masquerades are not typical in Uganda, other pastimes include hunting for fun, especially for little rabbits and edible birds. Racing with goats is also popular. Another group activity is roasting sweet potatoes, using preheated mounds in which the potatoes are left to cook. Indoors, children like listening to radio or watching TV. There are several TV and radio programs for children in Uganda. *Emiti emito* (meaning "young trees") is filmed in schools or children's homes and is shown on WBS television, a local station. An example of a children's radio program is Capital Kids: children are asked to give their opinions on different topics. Local newspapers have children's columns or sections.

Toys in Uganda are available for purchase mostly in urban areas in supermarkets, outdoor markets (especially on market days), toy stores, gift shops, and from hawkers selling their wares on the streets or roadsides. The toys include toy cars, Barbie dolls, toy guns (including water guns), skipping ropes, yo-yos, bicycles and tricycles, Lego sets, doll houses, cartoon figures (such as Batman, Superman, and Tom and Jerry), toy soldiers, robots, stuffed animals such as teddy bears, tea sets and cooking utensils, and children's garden sets. Most of the toys come from China (and Hong Kong), but other sources are Dubai, Japan, Germany, the United Kingdom, the United States, and India. Such commercially available toys are too expensive for most Ugandan children, so they usually make toys out of local materials. In Budo, Uganda, a hula hoop for children to rotate around the waist by twisting their bodies is made from a stick that can bend in a circle. The two ends of the stick overlap. A strip cut from an old tire tube or other string is used to cover the overlapped edges so they cannot hurt the child. Small cars are made using wood or metal wire. The metal wire is obtained from old electricity cables that have wire inside, old fences, or nearby metalwork shops. The metal is bent and tied at different points using rubber bands. Wood is obtained from old tree trunks or pieces of firewood and cut and shaped into cars. Dolls are often made from dry banana leaves; the head of the doll is stuffed with cloth to make it bigger than the other body parts. Little clothes for these dolls are sewn by hand with needle and thread. Balls are also made from part of the banana tree. Soccer balls and smaller balls made of banana fiber are made firm by stuffing them with plastic bags or with paper. Skipping ropes are made from banana fibers, vines of climbing plants, or plants with long thin vines or stalks, such as sweet potatoes. Toy guns are popular with boys, especially those that look like AK47s; they are made of sticks and the leafstalks of yam plants.

Kenya

In rural areas, some games reflect the physical skills needed by adults in the environment, for example, among teenagers, the "spear" game among the Samburu, *Kiroroktet* among the Kalenjins, and the "cattle raiding" game among the Maasai. The goal in the spear game is to throw a willow stick, like a spear or javelin, into a rolling hoop to make it stop and also to find out how many spears can successfully be thrown into the hoop. A thin willow is made into a hoop and reinforced so that it will not be destroyed by being tossed and rolled. Instead of real spears, which might break, six eight-foot straight willow sticks are thrown within a wide-open space. The ground has to be the correct density for the willow to stick upright. The players form two teams. The first team stands in a row behind a throwing line marked on the ground while a member of the other team rolls a hoop in a line parallel to them. To gain points, the so-called spear has to stick in the ground. If the hoop is stopped by the first spear, the players can throw at a stationary object. The skills needed for this game are primarily physical strength and accuracy. Kiroroktet is another game involving physical skill, played by the Kalenjins in Kenya, usually among male teenagers, who create a large sisal rope net, made to look like a web tied between two trees or posts. Spaces within the web are both large and wide and narrow and small. Each of two teams has to maneuver its members through the spaces without touching the ropes. Although physical skill is involved, team cooperation and group problem-solving are also important. The cattle raiding game is also played by teenagers or preadolescent boys, and, unlike in the spear game, the real object is used—called a *rungu* (club). The rungu is 18 inches long; the game is to throw the rungu as far as possible.

In Kenya, there is a game similar to the games of jacks played in Europe and the United States. (It is also played in other African countries, using seven stones, and known as *Bia* or *Pombo* in Ghana.). Known as *Kora,* it is typically played by six to twenty-four schoolgirls or teenage girls. One of six stones is the queen stone. The girl player throws up the queen stone gently but high enough to give time to pick up the other stones while the queen stone is thrown. She tries not to drop any and to pick them up in different combinations. First one stone is picked up at a time until all five stones are caught and kept in the left hand. There are several rules for the sequence of picking up different numbers of stones after picking up all five stones. The next combination is two, two, then one or one, two, and then two. A turn is lost if any stone is not picked up in the correct sequence.

Some songs and rhymes also occur with skipping. They will often reflect everyday themes that children think about. For example, the first part of one skipping song by a boy who was skipping in Nanyuki, Kenya, goes like this:

> Mother told me to look after the chicks
> But I cannot look after the chicks,
> I have sat down idly
> In my mother's sorghum
> It is being eaten by birds.

Other themes may be playing truant from school, being stung by bees, telling lies to a parent about eating sugar, hiding under the shade instead of selling cassava, or getting lost.

As in other African countries, in Kenya rhymes occur as part of a game. One example is a rhyme that warns that if anyone speaks she will be "Mrs. Rat" and if anyone laughs she will be "Mrs. Lizard." This rhyme occurs as part of a hand game, with children sitting in pairs. The children hold the skin on the back of each other's hands and place their hands alternately on top of the other. At the end of the rhyme, each child pretends to put something into her mouth and swallow it.

The traditional game of mancala has its most complex form in Kenya. It is both a pastime and a game, requires as much skill as chess, and can also be played very quickly. In Kenya it is known as *Bao* and played mainly by older boys and men. Instead of two rows of holes, there are four rows of eight holes. When the last seed falls into an occupied hole on the inner row, the player is able to capture all of the seeds in the opposite inner row. One of the holes on each side is also a square instead of a round shape and involves additional rules of play. One of the greatest plays was forty-four moves by someone who was blindfolded.

CONCLUSION

How children throughout the world spend their time is of interest to scholars of many disciplines such as anthropology, child development, psychology, and recreation studies. Most resources on cultures in Sub-Saharan Africa that are meant to educate the public do not focus on or even mention children's activities and tend to describe adult sports and occupations rather than pastimes. Scientific information on particular regions has depended on the presence of someone with an interest in play and games who is prepared to spend time observing and meticulously reporting their findings. Therefore, available information is still limited, especially in countries ravaged by war. A recent upsurge of interest in children's games and play in the past ten years by such anthropologists as David Lancy, John Block, and Simon Ottenberg has provided a perspective on how children's play develops within an ecological and social context. Certain trends are notable in the description of different games and pastimes throughout Sub-Saharan Africa. Popular among all children are games of chase, which involve the excitement of anticipation or suspense, and games that involve physical skill, such as soccer by boys and skipping and hopscotch by girls. These appear to be universal games and pastimes that produce many regional variations and that can be found in other parts of the world. Unique to Central and West Africa is the pastime of masquerades. Unique to Southern Africa and parts of Central Africa is the practice of making toys out of wire and tin as a cottage industry. Mancala is probably the most well-known game played throughout Africa by older children and adults.

What is also common throughout the continent in games and pastimes is the frequency of how music, rhythm, and singing are embedded in so many activities. Such skills are encouraged early in life. The stories, rhymes, and riddles describe events and objects that are culture-specific and may be subject to change as societies become more modern and are changed by technology. Traditional games or folk games are also just one part of African culture that is subject to change and rapidly being influenced by other pastimes and more time spent in school. This kind of trend is not new. Traditional playground games gradually became less popular in Europe. Homemade toys common in the late nineteenth and early twentieth centuries in the United States also disappeared with the proliferation of cheap commercial alternatives. However, countries in Sub-Saharan Africa have fewer written records than other parts of the world; given the rapidity of change, more compilation of information on current games, pastimes, and toys is needed. What we see in present popular culture on the African continent is a wide range of games and pastimes combining folk games with more modern alternatives.

The way that games and pastimes are incorporated into children's chores challenges views about the dichotomy between work and play. Role playing and imitation of adult activities often slowly merge into adult work. As children gets older, it is sometimes hard to determine where play ends and work begins. The examples in this chapter demonstrate that children are creative and resourceful, both in terms of available materials and their allocation of time.

Play is embedded in chores, whether those chores involve carrying a younger child or tending animals, and children are able to perform multitasking at an early age. The toys they use can be made of any materials. Even in refugee camps, children scratch pictures in the sand with sticks and play chase. The lack of commercial toys does not imply impoverishment of play, provided that there are a variety of materials in the environment and opportunities to use them. Games, pastimes, and toys are found in every country and are an integral part of its culture. They contribute to sharing of values, learning new skills, developing relationships with others, and simply having fun.

RESOURCE GUIDE

PRINT SOURCES

Andreasen, Jude, and Cleve Overton. *Creative Recycling. Handmade in Africa.* Philadelphia: Xlibris, 2004.

Bock, John, and Sara E. Johnson. "Subsistence Ecology and Play among the Okavango Delta Peoples of Botswana." *Human Nature* 15.1 (2004): 63–81.

Butler, Francelia. *Skipping Around the World: The Ritual Nature of Folk Rhymes.* Hamden, CT: Library Professional Publications, 1989.

Centner, Th. *L'enfant Africain et ses jeux.* Lubumbashi, Zaire: CEPSI #17, 1963.

Cheska, Alice T. *Traditional Games and Dances in West African Nations.* Schorndorf, Germany: Verlag, 1987.

Corbett, Doris, John Cheffers, and Eileen Crowley Sullivan, eds. *Unique Games and Sports around the World. A Reference Guide. Part I Africa.* Westport, CT: Greenwood Press, 2001.

Delaroziere, MarieFrancoise. *Jouets des enfants d'Afrique. Regards sur des merveilles d'ingeniosité.* Paris: UNESCO, 1999.

Durojaiye, Susan M. "Children's Traditional Games and Rhymes in Three Cultures." *Educational Research* 19 (1977): 223–226.

Egblewogbe, Eustace Y. "Acquiring Traditional Knowledge through Games." Pp. 27–71 in E. Y. Egblewogbe, *Games and Songs as Education Media (A Case Study among the Ewes of Ghana).* Accra: Ghana Pub. Co, 1975.

Eisenhofer, Stefan. *Africa on the Move: Toys from West Africa.* Stuttgart, Germany: Arnoldsche, 2004.

Evans, Judith L. "Child Rearing Practices and Beliefs in Sub-Saharan Africa." Report of a workshop held in Windhoek, Namibia (October 26–29, 1993), sponsored by UNICEF.

Fayemi, A. Olusegun. *Voices from Within. Photographs of African Children.* New York: Albofa Press, 1999.

Lancy, David F. "The Play Behavior of Kpelle Children during Rapid Cultural Change." Pp. 84–91 in David F. Lancy and Bruce A. Tindall (eds.), *The Anthropological Study of Play: Problems and Prospects.* West Point, NY: Leisure Press, 1977.

———. *Playing on the Mother-Ground. Cultural Routines for Children's Development.* New York: The Guilford Press, 1996.

Leis, Philip E. *Enculturation and Socialization in an Ijaw Village.* New York: Holt, Rinehart and Winston, 1972.

Musah, William, and Christine Preston. "Using Natural Materials for Educational Toys: Examples from Ghana." *Australian Science Teachers Journal* 44.3 (1988): 41–45.

Nwokah, Eva, and Clara Ikekeonwu. "A Sociocultural Comparison of Nigerian and American Children's Games." Pp. 59–76 in, Margaret Duncan, Garry Chick, and Alan Aycock (eds.), *Diversions and Divergences in Fields of Play.* Greenwich, CT: Ablex, 1998.

Okanlawon, Tunde. "Games, Rhymes and Songs in Yoruba Children's Folklore." *Nigeria Magazine* 55 (1987): 77–82.

Onyefulu, Ifeoma. *Ogbo. Sharing Life in an African Village.* New York: Harcourt, Brace & Co., 1986.

Ottenberg, Simon and David Binkley. *Playful Performers, African Children's Masquerades.* Rutgers, NY: Transaction Publications, 2005.

Powell Hopson, Darlene, Derek S. Hopson, and Thomas Clavin. *Juba This and Juba That. 100 African-American Games for Children.* New York: Simon and Schuster, 1996.

Prinsloo, Mastin "Literacy Is Child's Play: Making Sense in Khwezi Park." *Language and Education* 18.4, (2004): 291–304.

Salamone, Frank A. "Children's Games as Mechanisms for Easing Ethnic Interaction in Ethnically Heterogeneous Communities: A Nigerian Case." *Ethnicity* 5 (1978): 203–212.

Schnildkrout, Enid. "Drawing Tradition: Dogon Children's Art in the Age of Tourism." *African Arts* (Spring, 2004).

———. "Young Traders of Northern Nigeria." *Natural History* (1981, June), 44–53. Accessed January 11, 2007. http://anthro.amnh.org/anthropology/research/hausa.htm.

Schwartzman, Helen B. *Transformations: the Anthropology of Children's Play.* New York: Plenum Press, 1978.

Uyovbukerhi, Atiboroko. "Moonlight Games in Urhobo Culture as Creative Dramatics." Paper presented at 5th Annual Conference of Urhobo Historical Society, Effurun, (October 29–31, 2004), Delta State, Nigeria.

William, Musah and Christine Preston. "Using Natural Materials for Educational Toys: Examples from Ghana." *Australian Science Teachers Journal* 44.3 (1998): 41–45.

WEBSITES

Abwenzi African Studies. Accessed May 11, 2006. http://lettersfromafrica.org/. Photos of children's play under "Games & toys" and under "Dances"; also a description of how to make a game of Bao out of an egg carton.

Access to Play a Thumb Piano, Make a Mask and See Pictures of African Children. Accessed May 11, 2006. http://pbskids.org/africa.

AfricanCraft.com. *Toys.* Accessed May 11, 2006. http://www.africancraft.com. Select "Exhibits" and then "Creative Recycling From Africa." Illustrates toys made in Senegal, Mali, Kenya, the Republic of South Africa, and then-Zaire purchased between 1985 to 2003.

Akuoko, D.A. *Children's Folk Games in Ghana.* Children's Folk Games Project. Accessed May 11, 2006. http://www.estcomp.ro/~cfg/ghana.html.

Binkley, David, and Allyson Purpura. *Playful Performers. Brochure to Accompany Exhibition of Research on Children's Masquerades, 2004.* Accessed May 11, 2006. http://www.nmafa.si.edu/exhibits/playful/index.html.

Boateng, Nuruddin. *Akan Tongue Twisters.* Children's Folk Games Project. Accessed May 10, 2006. http://www.estcomp.ro/~cfg/akantt.html.

Burnett, Cora, and Wim J. Hollander. "The South African Indigenous Games Research Project of 2001/2002." *South African Journal for Research in Sport, Physical Science and Recreation* 26.1 (2004): 9. Accessed May 11, 2006. http://www.sasc.org.za/ClientFiles/BURNETT%20462.doc.

Description of Mancala. Accessed May 11, 2006. http://www.oware.org.

Description of East and South African Variations of Mancala as Played in Kenya, Tanzania, Zambia and Malawi. Accessed May 11, 2006. http://www.msoworld.com/mindzine/news/classic/mancala.html.

Ghana: Children Drawing and Children Using Traditional Music Instruments. Accessed May 11, 2006. http://www.culturalcollaborative.org/w-childrenspottery.htm.

Gray, James. "The End of Innocence. Child Soldiers in Africa and International Assistance." M.A. thesis, Department of Political Science, Victoria University of Wellington, New Zealand, 2002. Accessed May 11, 2006. http://www.dev-zone.org/downloads/devnetabstract368.pdf.

How to Make Kenyan Musical Instruments, Jingles, Drum, Fiddle, Chivoli and Shaker. Accessed May 11, 2006. http://www.blissites.com/kenya/culture.html.

Illustration of a Toy Car Made from Wire and Rubber in Dakar, Senegal, a Toy Truck Made from Tin, Wood, Cord and Paint from Kano, Nigeria, and Toy Motorcycle and Bicycle Made in Mali. Accessed May 11, 2006. http://www.streetplay.com/playfulworld/recycledtoys.shtml.

International Bicycle Fund. *Africa Kid's Page.* Accessed May 11, 2006. http://www.ibike.org/library/africakids.htm. Lists children's nonfiction books on Africa. Lists other Websites on children's games.

International Foundation for Nigerian Children. Accessed May 11, 2006. www.ifnc.org/pictures.html.

IRINnews.org. *Nigeria: Children Orphaned By AIDS: Slipping through the Cracks.* October 6, 2005. UN Office for the Coordination of Humanitarian Affairs. Kaduna. Accessed May 10, 2006. http://www.irinnews.org/report.asp?ReportID=49393&SelectRegion=West_Africa&SelectCountry=NIGERIA.

Kopoka, Peter Anthony. "The Problem of Street Children in Africa: An Ignored Tragedy." Paper presented at the International Conference on Street Children and Street Children's Health in East Africa (April 19–21, 2000). Dar-es-Salaam, Tanzania. Accessed May 10, 2006. http://www.fiuc.org/iaup/esap/publications/dar/Streetchildren.pdf.

Kusaasira, Margaret. *Games from Uganda: Hoop.* Children's Folk Games Project. Accessed May 10, 2006. http://www.estcomp.ro/~cfg/uganda.html.

Motherland Nigeria: Kid Zone. Accessed May 11, 2006. http://www.motherlandnigeria.com/kidzone.html. Stories, games, proverbs, and other Websites listed.

Musical Instruments: Can Click on a Musical Instrument to Hear the Sounds They Make. Accessed May 11, 2006. http://www.lonker.net/art_african_2.htm.

Recycled Art & Toy Bazaar. Accessed May 11, 2006. http://www.indigoarts.com/store1_recycle.html. Shows items for sale, such as bugs from Burkina Faso made of tin and wire.

Sand, Jay. *The Jews of Africa: The Games.* Accessed May 10, 2006. http://www.mindspring.com/~jaypsand/games.htm.

MUSEUMS

American Museum of Natural History. Central Park West at 79th Street, New York, NY. Accessed May 11, 2006. http://anthro.amnh.org.

The Children's Museum of Indianapolis. Indianapolis, IN. Wire jumbo jet made in Zaire. Accessed May 11, 2006. http://www.childrensmuseum.org/themuseum/collcult.htm.

National Museum of African Art (Smithsonian). 950 Independence Avenue, SW, Washington DC. Accessed May 11, 2006. http://www.nmafa.si.edu/exhibits/playful/index.html. Playful Performers exhibit: includes The World of Childhood Masquerade and Exploring the World of Play. Examples of photographs: Democratic Republic of Congo: small girl with doll, constructing a small house of leaves, boy with handmade masquerade dolls; Zambia: drawing in the sand, masked dancers; Guinea-Bissau: masks; Nigeria: children with musical instruments-bamboo slit gongs and iron gongs. Advanced search on "toys and entertainment" shows a Yoruba gameboard and several dolls, including one from Liberia made of cans, plant fiber, and glass beads.

NOTES

1. We would like to acknowledge informants Mr. Sanmi Babarinde, Department of Linguistics and Nigerian Languages, University of Nigeria, Nsukka, Nigeria; Dr. Frida Mbunda, Department of English, University of Nigeria, Nsukka, Nigeria; and Mr. C. Felix Nnaji, Plano, Texas for videotape resources.
2. IRINnews.org 2005 (in Resource Guide, Websites).
3. Kopoka 2000 (in Resource Guide, Websites).

LITERATURE

GINETTE CURRY

The continent of Africa south of the Sahara is rich in linguistic traditions that date back to the empires of the Sudan, the kingdoms of the Lakes region, and those of southern and western Africa. African literature reflects this multiplicity of traditional and contextual cultures. A corpus of works of fiction, poetry, and non-fiction, it is also characterized by the impact of oral literature, which still plays an important role in African realities. In the past in traditional societies from West, East, Central, and Southern Africa, this expression was part of the fabric of everyday life. As a result, African literature south of the Sahara is not only the long and ancient heritage of oral literature but also a complex literary culture resulting from multiple ethnic, national, and regional traditions encompassing hundreds of languages.

African Literatures: Oral Traditions

Myths

Before the spread of African written literature in the Sub-Saharan region, oral traditions were pervasive and consisted of a body of ancient wisdom recorded in several forms. Among them, the creation myths of Sub-Saharan Africa are quite remarkable and are an enduring part of the African oral tradition. They can be defined as theological creative tales from specific African communities: imaginative expressions in a narrative form of the worldview or beliefs of the people they represent. They reflect the African people's belief about the world's beginnings. Traditional myths have had a major influence on contemporary African traditions. Multiple ethnic groups in Africa have their own myths about the creation of the world. Usually, in these stories, one all-powerful god creates the world and then leaves a group of lesser gods to oversee it. According to most African mythologies, a god first agreed to give humans eternal life, but his message was perverted through the stupidity or malice of the messenger. For example, in *The Palm-Wine Drinkard and His Dead Palm-Wine Tapster in the Dead's Town* (1952), Nigerian writer Amos Tutuola (1920–1997) drew his inspiration from his Yoruba tradition of creation myths. Tutuola's stories are based on traditional

Yoruba folktales, originally told in oral form, and are characterized by his unique style of narrative. *The Palm-Wine Drinkard* is the tale of a lover of palm wine who journeys into the Land of the Dead to bring back his favorite "tapster," or winemaker, who has died in a fall. Some of his other books include *My Life in the Bush of Ghosts* (1954), *Simbi and the Satyr of the Dark Jungle* (1955), and *The Brave African Huntress* (1958).

Creation myths from Sub-Saharan Africa not only originate from one country, but from a myriad of ethnic groups that constitute complex and diverse cultures. Some of these creation myths are part of African cultures such as the Yoruba of Nigeria, the Efik of Central Nigeria, the Ekoi of Southern Nigeria, the Mande people of Mali in West Africa, the Boshongo of Central Africa, the Zulu of the Republic of South Africa, the Washungwe of Zimbabwe, the Oromo of Ethiopia, and the Kikuyu of Kenya.

In Sub-Saharan Africa, myths and stories can be divided into creation myths, which are closely related to death myths, and stories about nature (the sun, the moon, and the sky). For example, the Boshongo of the Congo River region in the Democratic Republic of the Congo (formerly Zaïre) in Central Africa portray creation in generative terms in the oral tale "Bumba Vomits the World." On the other hand, the Krachi creation myths of Togo (West Africa), such as "The Separation of God from Man," convey the world's primordial unity between the sky and the earth and between gods and humans. In Yoruba culture (Nigeria), a story such as "How Humans Were Scattered" explains the diversity among human beings. On the other hand, the Bushmen of Southern Africa show in their creation myths that they believe in a good creator called god (Kaang, Khu), but also in an evil deity (Gawa or Gauna). They also reflect their belief in animal spirits (Cagn) in a story such as "Cagn Orders the World." Such mythical stories, no matter what African tradition they belong to, share some common themes, such as gods, evil creatures, beasts, the supernatural, salvation, and death, and they are characterized by the use of symbolism, metaphors, and beautiful allegories.

In addition, stories such as "Sa and Alatanga" from Guinea (West Africa) explain not only the making of the earth but also the reason why human beings die. In the Yao culture of the eastern shores of Malawi (Southern Africa), the story of creation involves a god (Mulling) and animals; man and woman emerge from water. Likewise, the Kikuyu from Kenya (East Africa) justify their existence through a god (Ngai) who used to live at Kirinyaga (Mount Kenya) and whose power wields the instruments of life and death. Furthermore, mythic stories about the sun, the moon, and the sky abound among the Wute of Cameroon (West Africa) and the Chaga in Tanzania (East Africa).

Oral Epics and Legends

Oral epics focus on heroic figures and celebrate their deeds. They are elaborate and can be performed on special occasions or in formal settings. They contain numerous references to songs and prophecies that show the reader that the epic is meant to be a spoken narrative. For example, in West Africa, the oral epic of Sundiata, founder of the kingdom of Mali, is still a rich part of the oral tradition of the Manding-speaking regions of Guinea, Burkina Faso, Mali, Senegal, and the Gambia. Traditional bards (*griots*) are the transmitters of these epics. Although the existence of the Manding empire of Mali is not in question, the epic of Sundiata tends to be more accurate in the details of the moral and social life of the Manding people rather than in those of history. Such epics can be read and enjoyed because they are full of accounts of heroism, the supernatural, suspense, pain, and success. The uniqueness of the oral epic of Sundiata is that, unlike most written literature, it has no single author. D. T. Niane wrote in his preface that he was inspired by the version of the griot Djeli Mamadou Kouyate, but, in reality, he reworked the epic into its present form.

Several themes characterize the African oral epic, including the important themes of destiny, the passing of time, and kings and kingdoms. Exile, war, glory, and the supernatural are also themes illustrated by imagery centered on emblems such as the lion and the buffalo (which represent Sundiata's father and mother). The Sundiata epic also underlines the presence of Islam in the region and is interspersed with many sayings that present a traditional view of African life. West African oral epics include the Soninke epic, related to the kingdom of Ghana, the Songhay and Zarma epics from the region of Gao, the Manding epics (including that of Sundiata) from the empire of Mali, which date back to the thirteenth to fifteenth centuries, and the Fulani and Wolof epics of the nineteenth century, which originate from the West African coast of Senegal; the Fulani epics are known all the way to Gabon, Chad, and the Central African Republic.

In Central Africa, the most famous oral epics are from Cameroon, for example, the epic of Jéki la Njambé Inono. The Mwindo epic originated from the Nyanga people of the eastern part of the Democratic Republic of the Congo (formerly Zaïre). In Southern Africa, Swahili epics go back to the thirteenth century; the only known classical epic, *Uandi Wa Mwana Kupona,* was composed in 1275 by a woman. In the twentieth century, Mazisi Kunene translated and reconstructed the nineteenth-century Zulu oral epics *Emperor Shaka the Great* (in 1979) and *Anthem of the Decades* (1981), works that convey the rich culture of the Zulu. Most important, the epics are celebrations of the richness and diversity of African cultures. They not only provide listeners with entertainment in different forms—music, songs, dance, group interaction—but they also have a strong didactic and moralizing influence on their communities.

Legends, on the other hand, are about events that occurred after the era of the gods. Like the epic, they focus on heroism and the establishment of dynasties. Oral epics are also usually a series of stories about past heroes and historical events, but legends are less elaborate in their literary forms. However, their setting is specific and usually refers to a period in history. Legends are associated with a particular locality or person. They are not restricted to being performed only on special occasions but are used in the context of everyday life. The stories are popularly regarded as historical although they cannot be verified. They blend fact and fiction but are presented as true. They may include supernatural beings, mythological elements, and explanations of natural events. For example, in Kenya (East Africa), the Kikuyu story of Mumbi and Gikuyu serves as a legend of origin and focuses on the sacred right of the Kikuyu to their land. It has been a source of unity and inspiration for its people. Likewise, in Uganda (eastern Africa), many legends circulate about Kintu, the legendary king of the Baganda people, who founded their nation. Through his various deeds, and his relationship with a shy god, Kintu brought both blessings and death to his people.

Folktales

Folktales help us understand the literary history of Africa and its customs. Originating from African oral traditions, many of them have been put in writing over the years. The number of folktales reflects the multiplicity of ethnic groups on the continent of Africa. According to Bascom and Waterman (in "African and New World Negro Folklore," *Funk and Wagnall's Standard Dictionary of Folklore, Mythology, and Legend*, 1972), there are about a quarter of a million African folktales. According to the general definition, folktales are generic in their setting. They are not presented as history or truth. They are didactic in nature and teach children as well as adults values and lessons in behavior. These stories are also used for social commentary and play a great role in affirming the cultural values of their communities. Good triumphs over evil in folktales, and they feature human and animal characters, separately or together, that are involved in quests or have tasks to accomplish.

Folktales are usually introduced by a phrase such as "once upon a time." The characters, which usually represent a single human characteristic that can be good or evil, are contrasted with each other. Many plots have more than one conflict and use magic as their canvas. Their narrative is enriched by rhymes, repetitions, dialogues, images, and vocabulary related to specific aspects of the culture.

African folktales are diverse. The most popular is the trickster tale. For example, in many parts of Sub-Saharan Africa, various animals represent the trickster. In East, Central, and Southern Africa, as well as in western Sudan, the trickster is most often portrayed as a hare. In Ghana, Liberia, and Sierra Leone, the trickster is a spider. In Benin and Nigeria, it takes the shape of a tortoise. In East Africa, the trickster is human and is represented by Abunuwas or Kibunwasi.

Sacred tales can be found among the Fon ethnic group in Benin: "The Gold Ring" and "The Prince and the Orphan" are representative. Cautionary tales such as "Pearl of Wisdom" from Gabon stress the importance of names in African cultures. Explanatory tales abound in the Igbo culture of Nigeria, such as "Why Hawk Preys on Chicks." Another tale from Cape Verde, West Africa, "Why Cat and Dog Are Always Fighting" belongs to this category as well. Also, African folktales convey several recurrent themes such as forgiveness, greed, friendship, wisdom, jealousy, and kindness.

Proverbs and Riddles

Proverbs, which can be defined as moral sayings about human defects or wisdom, are included in a number of African folktales. Contrary to folktales, however, proverbs are short and usually have a cause and result that show contrast. In the past, African proverbs were used in speaking, but nowadays they have been put in writing, either in African or European languages. For example, in the Swahili culture, proverbs have been passed down by the elders in an effort to convey wisdom to younger generations.

Proverbs have different functions. Some are warnings or criticism in order to correct bad behavior. Others recount the wisdom of what people say or provide consolation. Other proverbs, especially some Swahili proverbs, have religious (often Islamic) overtones. Superstition also plays a great part in this type of proverb. In East Africa, proverbs show the impact of indigenous beliefs and how they coexist with Islam.

In African societies, proverbs are used for many different reasons. Some express an eternal truth. For example, storytelling is an important part of the Wolof culture in Senegal (West Africa). The literal English translation of *Ku yaag ci teen, baag fekk la fa* is "A water pail will find the person who waits diligently at the well." The eternal truth that this proverb reveals is that God rewards those who diligently seek Him.

Proverbs are used to give a moral lesson to the story and to make it memorable. Some people like to quote proverbs in everyday conversation and circumstances. Proverbs are also used as warnings against foolish acts or as guides to good conduct. The Bassa proverb from Liberia (West Africa) *Nyana-so ni nyu do doun, key do za-nyohn de ke,* "Smoke does not affect only the honeybees; the honey gatherers are also affected," means that people must not ruin lives by malicious gossip. It admonishes troublemakers. Also, the Tonga proverb from Malawi (East Africa), *Chigau ndi ku mupozwa* ("Young growing cuttings determine a good harvest of cassava"), warns society that it should take care of its youth. Proverbs may also bring special meaning to certain situations. Among the Shona of Zimbabwe, the proverb

Kure ndokusina, kwachiri unofa wasvika "Far is where there is nothing; where something is, you will struggle to the death to reach it," means "Where there is a will, there is a way." This proverb applies to motivation and the desire to accomplish something of value for oneself whatever the situation may be.

Finally, some proverbs may solve problems. In Kenya (East Africa), the Bukusu people's proverb *Siemunda sisuta siekhumurwe* can be translated as "What is in the stomach carries what is in the head." It is a particularly therapeutic proverb because it means that good food is essential to healthy individuals (and a healthy society).

Although adults use proverbs in their daily lives, riddles are mostly the domain of children. Riddles are trick questions that may or may not have morality lessons. They are playful ways to stimulate a child's mind to figure out the solution. According to the *Encyclopedia Britannica,* the riddle is a form of guessing game that has been a part of the folklore of most cultures since ancient times.

There are two main types of riddles. The first type is descriptive and sometimes involves the use of metaphors. For example, riddles from the Sesotho (Republic of South Africa) are often questions; the listeners reply with the answer as the explanation. One such riddle is the following. Question: *Monna e molelele e mosweu*? [A tall white man?] Answer: *Tsela sa baeti* [A road for travelers]. Riddles also describe animals, plants, or objects in a puzzling way, sometimes to suggest an answer different from the correct one.

On the other hand, some African riddles are witty questions, such as the following Wolof riddle: Question: *Lou di djemantale te dou adou?* [Who teaches without speaking?] Answer: "*Tere!*" [A book!] Although riddles are sometimes introductions to proverbs, many of them are amusing material intended for children. Proverbs, on the other hand, are meant to change a person's behavior. Both have didactic purposes.

STORYTELLING AND AFRICAN RHYTHMS

A key originality of African proverbs is that they can be expressed not only in words, but also in the language of the drums. Therefore, storytelling is closely associated with African rhythms. For example, in Ghana and Senegal, storytellers beating the drums with their fingers, the flat of their hand, or their thumb can convey the proverbs' messages. In the past, this was the means by which they could be understood over long distances.

OVERVIEW: THE LATE NINETEENTH CENTURY TO THE PRESENT

In ancient times, various populations from Sub-Saharan Africa used stories as ways to perpetuate traditions and transmit history from one generation to the next. Unlike many literatures outside Africa, the peculiarity of African oral literature was and still is that it confounds the boundaries of fiction and non-fiction and that it sometimes blends aspects of reality and imagination. In the nineteenth century, written literature was rare in Africa. The main works at that time were the written texts of the Koran and the Bible, which spread with the Islamic conquests of West and East Africa and the increasing influence of missionaries in those same areas of the African continent. On the other hand, nineteenth-century oral literature was abundant and included stories, dramas, myths, songs, and proverbs that not only educated and entertained children, but also reminded African communities of their ancestors' heroic histories and their rich traditions. The African continent has a long-rooted history of storytelling. The griots, or bards, have always been at the center stage of this oral literature. Their role was essential in traditional societies as entertainers, historians, and the necessary translators of news in the African courts. The griots' role as carriers of African traditions is hereditary. In the nineteenth century, they were specifically attached to the rulers' courts, even though they became freelance professional bards over the years. Their performances were usually musically accompanied by the harplike *kora* and a type of xylophone called the *balafon*. This oral tradition of storytelling stems from African societies that had not been influenced by eighteenth- and nineteenth-century colonial encounters and their aftermath. Rich literary traditions in ancient African languages such as Arabic and Ge'ez developed in various parts of Africa long before the colonial period. For example, Ge'ez is an ancient literary and ecclesiastical language of Ethiopia. Its earliest inscription dates back to the third century AD; it was developed in the mountainous Ethiopian lands of the Horn of Africa. In the second part of the nineteenth century, the spread of colonialism triggered the appearance of written African literature. The increasing presence of primarily English, French, Portuguese, and Dutch influence on African populations led to the production of fictional texts written in the languages of the colonizers. Ironically, it is during the colonial period that written African literature developed. It not only revealed the richness of African cultures and traditions, but it also became a vehicle for African writers to denounce the negative political, cultural, and social effects of colonialism on African populations, mainly its imperialistic agenda.

Although the living heritage of oral literature represents a rich array of artistic expression that developed long before the beginning of colonialism, the first half of the twentieth century corresponds to the golden age of African nationalism on the continent. It is also a significant period in the development of African literary history. In Ghana, Joseph Ephraim Casely-Hayford (1866–1930) published *Ethiopia Unbound: Studies in Race Emancipation* (1911), a semi-autobiographical novel about a nationalist lawyer who is faced with the issues of modernity and the preservation of traditional customs in a colonial African environment. The book portrays the hypocrisy of European Christians in Africa and the subsequent effects of racism in maintaining traditional institutions.

Also, in Southern Africa, Thomas Mofolo (1873–1948) from Lesotho published his first novel written in Southern Sotho, *Moeti oa Bochabela,* in 1907. Its English title is *The Traveler of the East.* It is the story of a young Sotho chieftain's conversion to Christianity. The plot is inspired by traditional myths and praise poems. Three years later, in 1910, Mofolo published *Pitseng,* in which he describes the native mores in Lesotho and South Africa as well as the influence of Christianity on traditional marriage customs. In the same year, he wrote *Chaka,* a fictionalized account of the Zulu conqueror who built a powerful empire during the first quarter of the nineteenth century. Mofolo's historical novel was published in 1925.

In contrast, the 1950s and 1960s represent two decades of decolonization on the African continent south of the Sahara. During that time the majority of the African territories became independent from their European colonizers, and the number of African writers celebrating the coming of a new order for African nations and the assertion of a new identity increased.

During the late 1960s, African writers continued to be prolific. They published literary works in various genres that reflected the disillusionment created by the aftermath of decolonization. African literature as a whole started reflecting the conflicting political, social, and cultural situations resulting from the independence years. Far from being extinct, the institutions of colonialism persisted, and African countries were still dominated by Western political and economic interests. During that period, Senegalese anthropologist Cheikh Anta Diop (1923–1986) became famous for his theory about the ancient Egyptians being black (and thus African). He illustrated his discovery with historical, archaeological, and anthropological evidence in a series of books, *Antériorité des civilisations nègres: Mythe ou vérité historique* (1967) and *The African Origin of Civilization: Myth or Reality* (1983). Additionally, in *Pre-Colonial Africa* (1980), he compares the political and social systems of Europe and black Africa from antiquity to the modern age.

In West Africa, traditional forms of drama are still very much part of the contemporary literary scene. Nowadays, *Kotéba* is still very popular in countries such as Mali. Kotéba is adapted to all kinds of stages, but most particularly to the "round stage." The National Drama Group of Mali is commonly called the Kotéba of Mali. In the Kotéba Theater, everybody can be both spectator and actor at the same time. It can be used as a medium to expose the defects and misconduct of the leaders. As the traditional theater in Mali, the Kotéba Theater has always been a source of information. During the colonial period and later during the Moussa Traore dictatorship, the Kotéba Theater was banned. Today, after the first free democratic elections in Mali, the Kotéba is used in an entertaining way to disseminate information on new laws, rules, and types of behavior.

During the 1990s, a new wave of writers, a flood of private newspapers and magazines, and the formation of the Ethiopian Free Press Journalists' Association (EFJA) invigorated literary life in Ethiopia. In Nigeria, the Yoruba popular theater has been a major expression of culture in contemporary West Africa. It originated from the dramatization of biblical stories by various churches. For example, "Hubert Ogunde's Theater Party," which was created in 1945, consisted of songs written by Ogunde and improvised dialogues. Hubert Ogunde is the founder of a form of modern Nigerian theater that, from 1944 until 1960, was devoted to the anti-colonial and nationalist political struggle. Ogunde's theater was responding to the growing nationalist struggle for self-determination and independence that extended from the late 1940s through the 1950s and 1960s. For example, his play *Worse than Crime* (1945) was about the tyranny and exploitation of foreign domination in colonial Nigeria.

Another representative of Yoruba Popular Theater is E. K. Ogunmola's Yoruba "Opera." His best known play is *Love of Money* (1965), the story of a man who loses everything because of a woman. Finally, a major figure representative of that type of theater is Duro Ladipo. In his plays, Ladipo uses a language inspired by traditional Yoruba poetry. He also incorporates the songs and dances of Yoruba worshippers of Shango (the god of thunder), hunters, and masqueraders.

In Southern Africa, for decades Xhosa poetry has been deeply influenced by the *imbongi* (oral poet or praise singer) tradition. Samuel Edward Krune Mqhayi (1875–1945), a poet and novelist from the Cape Province of the Republic of South Africa, is famous for writing Xhosa praise poems and for being a pioneer of Xhosa literature. He became known as a traditional poet who was able to transcribe Xhosa oral praise poetry (*izibongo*) into written poetry. He brought Xhosa folklore, the Imbongi (oral poetry) tradition, into the modern age during the first half of the twentieth century, and his poems contributed to the development of Xhosa as a literary language. His deep concern with the history of his people explains why he did not agree with the official version of South African history in the textbooks.

In the Republic of South Africa, the descendents of the Dutch settlers speak the Afrikaans language, considered a dialect of Dutch until the late nineteenth century. In 1925, however, Afrikaans was classified as distinct and was recognized as an official language. The 1961 Constitution named the two official languages of the Republic of South Africa as Afrikaans and English. In 1976, the uprising in Soweto (Johannesburg) was triggered in part by the policy requiring that students be instructed in Afrikaans, which they justly argued was the language of their oppressors. Among influential Afrikaner writers, Etienne Leroux (Stephanus Daniël Petrus le Roux) is a novelist of an avant-garde literary group called the *Sestigers* (writers of the 1960s). He is one of the most important and controversial writers of this avant-garde group of writers whose common interests were their existential view of life and their dissatisfaction with apartheid and the authoritarian character of Afrikaner society under the ruling National Party. Leroux won several prestigious awards, including the Hertzog Prize for prose for *Sewe dae by die Silbersteins* (1964) and for *Magersfontein, O Magersfontein!* (1979).

In East Africa, the most famous contemporary writer is the Kenyan Ngugi Wa Thiong'o (b. 1938). He writes not only in English but also in his native tongue of Gikuyu, as a way of acknowledging and communicating Kikuyu culture. Ngugi is concerned with preserving the specificity of African languages and literary traditions. For him, language and culture are inseparable, and the loss of the former results in the loss of the latter. In 1980, *Caitaani Muthara-Ini* [Devil on the Cross] was the first modern novel written in Gikuyu. Both the Gikuyu and the English versions present a plot written in a manner that recalls traditional ballad singers. The novel is a realistic and fantastical account of a meeting between the devil and various villains who exploit the poor. Because Ngugi criticized the injustices of Kenyan society and championed the cause of ordinary Kenyans by communicating with them in the language of their daily lives, he was arrested and imprisoned without charge in a maximum security prison, where he wrote *Devil on the Cross.* In 1986, he published *Matigari-Nji Ruungi* (*Matigari*). He is the recipient of the 2001 Nonino Prize. Ngugi's works have been translated into more than thirty languages and continue to be the subject of books, critical monographs, and dissertations. Ngugi argues that literature written by Africans in a colonial language is not African literature, but "Afro-European literature." In *Decolonising the Mind: The Politics of Language in African Literature* (1986), he argues that African-language literature is the only authentic voice for Africans and explains his intention of writing only in Gikuyu or Kiswahili from that point on. He comments that African writers should use their native languages to write genuine African literature. Ngugi's criticism of colonial rule, Christianity, and postcolonial abuses earned him admiration from the general public despite his troubles with the Kenyan government. His first prize-winning novel, *Weep Not Child* (1964), was the first major novel in English by an East African writer. It is the story of a Kikuyu family drawn into the struggle for Kenyan independence during the state of emergency and the Mau Mau rebellion. *A Grain of Wheat* (1967) focuses on social, moral, and racial issues of the struggle for independence and its aftermath. *The River Between* (1965) is the story of lovers kept apart by the conflict between Christianity and traditional ways and beliefs. In 1977, *Petals of Blood* portrayed the social and economic problems in East Africa after independence and the exploitation of peasants and workers by foreign business interests and an indigenous bourgeoisie. In 1981, *Detained: A Writer's Prison Diary* described Ngugi's ordeal when he was imprisoned by the Kenyan government after the performance of *I Will Marry When I Want* in 1977.

Ngugi's latest work, *Wizard of the Crow* (2006), is, in many ways, his crowning achievement, a sweeping satirical condemnation of the corruption, hypocrisy, and brutality of the government of a fictional nation that is a thinly disguised version of his native Kenya (and the neoliberal world order in which it exists). With this work, he has reinforced his stature as one of Africa's—and the world's—leading literary figures.

Women Writers

Recently, one of the most important developments in African literature has been the emergence of African women writers. This new gender trend in African literature constitutes a change in perspective. Not only do women writers address African womens' coming of age, but they also reveal how patriarchal nationalism and colonialism continue to affect them. These works show that African women are both empowered and limited in today's African countries. A pioneer of this movement, Senegalese author Mariama Bâ (1929–1981), is one of Africa's most representative female literary figures of the twentieth century. In 1980, she obtained the Noma Prize for her first novel *Une si longue lettre* [So Long a Letter]. She died the following year, just before the publication of her second novel *Un chant écarlate* [Scarlet Song] in 1981. *So Long a Letter,* written in an epistolary form, is the story of a widow, Ramatoulaye, who writes to her childhood friend Aïssatou. Bâ's main themes are women's solidarity, the abuse of women in African patriarchal societies, polygamy, and the negative effects of other traditional practices on African women.

In Burkina Faso, Monique Ilboudo (b. 1959) is also a new female literary voice. She wrote two novels, *Murekatete* (2000) and also *Le mal de peau* (2001), which is about the theme of African identity. Her literary activities are not limited to writing novels, however. She also wrote articles in the *Revue Burkinabé de Droit* from 1997 until 1999; she started her career as a journalist by creating a column about African women's contemporary issues, called *Féminin Pluriel,* in the Burkinabe newspaper *L'Observateur Paalga* from 1992 until 1995.

In Ghana, Ama Ata Aidoo (b. 1940) is one of the major female literary voices. She has written *The Dilemma of a Ghost.* (1964) and *Anowa* (1970), which is, based on a Ghanaian legend.

In Nigeria, Flora Nwapa (1931–1993) is best known for her portrayal of Igbo life and customs from an African woman's perspective. She created Tana Press/The Flora Nwapa Company in order to publish African books in Nigeria. *Efuru* (1966), her first novel, is about a woman chosen by the gods. *Idu* (1970) also focuses on a woman who seeks her deceased husband in the Land of the Dead. In her subsequent publications, *This Is Lagos and Other Stories* (1971), *One Is Enough* (1981), and *Women Are Different* (1986), Nwapa portrays women in modern Nigerian society. *Never Again* (1975) and *Wives at War and Other Stories* (1980) are about the Biafran war in Nigeria. Her poems include *Cassava Song and Rice Song* in 1986. Buchi Emecheta (b. 1944) is another female novelist from Nigeria whose novels are about the unequal role of women in immigrant and African societies. Her autobiography, *Head Above Water,* appeared in 1986. Other emerging women writers, such as Nigerian Chimamanda Ngozi Adichie (b. 1977), are also making their voices heard in the new African literary landscape. Adichie's debut novel, *Purple Hibiscus* (2003), is about a young Nigerian woman going through adolescence at a time of drastic changes in her country. Her novel *Half of a Yellow Sun* (2006) is a powerful portrayal of the suffering and heroism of the besieged Biafran population during the Nigerian civil war.

Politics and Literature

The many aspects of African literature not only reflect the diversity of traditions in the African continent, but also show how politics and literature are intertwined and how aesthetics and politics are important components. African literature is as diverse as the many countries it represents.

A new wave of male writers is also making a major impact on the African literary scene. These writers focus less than their earlier counterparts on themes such as the conflict between the West and African cultures. Classic novels written from the 1950s to the 1990s, such as Nigerian author Chinua Achebe's *Things Fall Apart* (1958), Cameroonian Mongo Beti's *Poor Christ of Bomba* (1971), and Ferdinand Oyono's *Houseboy,* address issues pertaining to the impact of colonialism on African societies. They use the colonial experience as their departure point. The concerns of the new male African writers, on the other hand, go beyond the colonial legacy. In *Arrows of Rain* (2000), Nigerian author Okey Ndibe (b. 1960) writes about the political situation and the crisis of higher education in Nigeria today. Also, a new writer from Nigeria, Helon Habila (b. 1967) won the 2001 Caine Prize with his debut novel, *Waiting for an Angel,* which depicts the current despotic military dictatorship of his country. *The Heart of Redness* (2000) by Zakes Mda (b. 1948), which won the 2001 Commonwealth Writers Prize, is about the seeds of change in post-apartheid South Africa. His more recent book, *The Madonna of Excelsior* (2002), deals with issues of racial identity, rape, and revenge. Furthermore, there is almost no explicit reference to apartheid in the recent novel by South African Phaswane Mpe (1970–2004) *Welcome to Our Hillbrow* (2002). It is the story of a decaying urban landscape of Johannesburg called "Hillbrow," a symbol of the best and worst of South Africa. HIV and AIDS are common themes in his work.

Finally, Nigerian Ben Okri's (b. 1959) novels also seem representative of a new trend in African literature. He belongs to the younger generation of Nigerian authors. In 1991 he won the Booker-McConnell Prize for his novel *The Famished Road.* It is the story of Azaro, a spirit child who lives in a Nigerian village. Okri's originality is that his novels reflect an interaction between reality and the spirit world. This interaction is not only apparent in his first novel, but also in his other works, such as *Songs of Enchantment* (1993), a sequel to *The Famished Road,* and his most recent publication *In Arcadia* (2002), which is about the human quest for happiness. In his last novel, Okri borrowed the Greek myth of Arcadia to develop the theme of the human quest for happiness in nature. He is also known as a poet, storywriter, essayist, and critic. His novels are inspired by oral tradition as well.

In the Republic of South Africa, during the apartheid regime, as well as in other politically unstable African countries, many writers were forced to write from outside of their original country. This created a number of consequences related to authorship. Some writers were deeply involved in politics and therefore their works were banned by the regime that ruled their homeland. These authors went abroad and became, by virtue of their exile, cut off geographically and intellectually from their fellow countrymen., As time passed, they were no longer in tune with the current political scene (especially in the case of the Republic of South Africa). For example, South African writers living in England or the United States faced the dilemma of being the spokespersons of their community although they were no longer a part of it.

The main issue resulting from such a situation was that they were writing books that could be distributed in Western countries, but these works were not available to their (intended) African audience. Therefore, in the 1970s, South African protest literature had a hard time finding its way to a South African readership. In addition, many African writers wanted to write for an audience that was not necessarily, or primarily, African.

A Reading Culture in Africa

Unfortunately, despite a significant increase in literary production, Sub-Saharan Africa is still facing book shortages. Major policies still need to be implemented to develop a reading culture. In this respect, the student population as a whole still has only limited access to libraries with a broad selection of materials (to complement their learning process). Many schools do not have adequate materials, and what they do have is outdated or worn out. Despite the implementation of African library services that already share their resources with local schools, much work still needs to be done to develop literacy skills in Sub-Saharan Africa. Furthermore, many Africans cannot afford to buy books and therefore depend on libraries to access resources. However, Sub-Saharan African countries do not have enough funding for library services. Inadequacies and weaknesses still exist in the library services of a number of African nations. For example, Malawi's National Library Service received no funds to purchase books in 2003. However, one positive development is the transformation of some African libraries into centers that address the needs of their citizens in areas such as HIV/AIDS and other educational issues in their communities.

At present, there are many challenges surrounding the consumption, availability, and reception of literary works. The majority of African countries south of the Sahara are experiencing deteriorating economic conditions. The problem of low literacy levels, as well as the multiplicity of languages, is compounded by limited access to books and poor communication networks.

In recent years, more pan-African approaches have been implemented to address the many challenges publishers face in Africa. For example, The African Publishers Network (APNET), created in 1992, has been promoting activities that further African writers' literary production.

Likewise, both governmental and nongovernmental entities have helped fund professional training, book distribution, and resource material publications, to name a few initiatives. Furthermore, support for book and journal publishing by groups and networks is increasing.

Additionally, the Internet in Africa is growing and is increasingly a major tool to facilitate education and training. Since indigenous publishing and book distribution agencies in Africa are lacking, the Internet is a way to access information that is difficult to secure otherwise.

With the development of inexpensive publishing software, African writers have been able to self-publish their work or to publish, distribute, and market their books through print-on-demand companies. To date, however, most of the African book publishers who are involved in online and electronic publishing are based in the Republic of South Africa; this phenomenon has yet to take hold in a major way in the rest of the continent.

One positive aspect of the use of the Internet is the increase in public access facilities such as Internet cafés and business centers in many Sub-Saharan countries. An increasing number of national newspapers, such as *Le Soleil* in Senegal, offer online versions (including book review sections). Nevertheless, despite this tangible progress, the majority of the Sub-Saharan population still does not have Internet access.

REGIONAL SUBSECTIONS

West Africa

Nigeria

Chinua Achebe (b. 1930) is one of the most famous contemporary Nigerian novelists. He became known for portraying the social and psychological disintegration caused by the imposition of Western values on traditional African society. In 1967, he founded a publishing company at Enugu with the poet Christopher Okigbo (1932–1967), who died in the Nigerian civil war. Starting in 1970, Achebe was the director of two Nigerian publishers, Heinemann Educational Books Ltd. and Nwankwo-Ifejika Ltd. *Things Fall Apart* (1958), Achebe's first novel, is about traditional Igbo society at the time when the missionaries and colonial government arrived in Nigeria. *No Longer at Ease* (1960) depicts a newly appointed civil servant, struggling with maintaining the moral values he believes in when he accepts his new position. *Arrow of God* (1964) is set in the 1920s in a village under English administration. Furthermore, in *A Man of the People* (1966) and *Anthills of the Savannah* (1987), Achebe describes corruption and other aspects of postcolonial African life. Achebe has also published two books of poems: *Beware, SoulBrother* (1971) and *Christmas in Biafra* (1973).

Cyprian Ekwensi (b. 1921) started by writing novellas: *When Love Whispers* in 1947 and *The Leopard's Claw* in 1950. *Jagua Nana* (1961) is his most famous novel, about a prostitute tempted by the evils of city life in contemporary Africa. Another Ekwensi novel, *People of the City*, was published in 1954 and revised and edited in 1969. Its main theme is the corruption and abuse of power in Nigeria. *Burning Grass* (1962) depicts Fulani cattlemen in the north of Nigeria.

In 1986 Wole Soyinka (b. 1934) was the first black African writer to be awarded the Nobel Prize for Literature. He has been a major critic of Senghor's *négritude* movement. According to Soyinka, African people's assertion of their pride, color, and culture is a sign of weakness, as if they have to prove their worth to the world. He proclaimed that Africa does not have to be defensive, but proactive in its historical and cultural affirmation. His talent is characterized by a mastery of lyric and dramatic poetic forms. In the late 1950s, Soyinka founded an acting company and wrote his first major play, *A Dance of the Forests* (produced in 1960 and published in 1963). It is a strong criticism of modern Nigeria.

The Nigerian literary scene is characterized by other prolific writers, such as Gabriel Okara (b. 1921) whose poem "The Call of the River Nun" (1953), won an award at the Nigerian Festival of Arts. Some of his poems were published in the influential periodical *Black Orpheus*. His first novel, *The Voice* (1964), a direct translation from the Ijo (Ijaw) language, is about traditional African culture and Western materialism. His later work includes a collection of poems, *The Fisherman's Invocation* (1978).

Senegal

Léopold Sédar Senghor (1906–2001), mainly known for his famous poems, became the first president of Senegal in August 1960. In his earlier years, during the 1930s when he was a student in Paris, he started the literary *négritude* movement, which included not only French-speaking African intellectuals, but also Caribbean writers such as Léon Damas from Guyana (1912–1978) and Aimé Césaire from Martinique (b. 1913). Concurrent with the affirmation of African nationalism that developed during the 1930s, 1940s, and 1950s, this literary movement was born to reassert the values of traditional Africa, which had been devalorized by colonization and by the multiple effects of Western cultures on African societies. It proclaimed the richness of African history, traditions, and beliefs and had a great impact on the African literary scene of the 1930s, 1940s, and 1950s. Senghor's first volume of poetry, *Chants d'ombre* [Shadow Songs] (1945) reflects some of the main themes of négritude, focusing on African history, colonialism, African pride, identity, and sensuality. "Femme Noire" [Black Woman] (1945) was originally published in *Chants d'ombre* and is one the finest poems Senghor wrote during the late 1940s. It stresses the beauty and sensuality of the African woman as a source of inspiration. Senghor's literary career is also highlighted by a series of publications between the 1950s and the 1970s, consisting of volumes of poetry such as *Black Hosts* (1946), *Songs for Naett* (1949), *Nocturnes* (1961), and *Letters in the Season of Hivernage* (1972). Senghor was an innovator because he was able to use the French language to create a different form and rhyme and was therefore able to write about the African experience in an entirely new way and to create a new language of expression conveying African values and rhythm. He was the first African member of the Académie Française, the most distinguished French intellectual association. Senghor broadened the definition of *négritude* by identifying it with blackness in general, without specific reference to culture, language, or geography. Through his literary movement, he was able to affirm the racial heritage that black people share throughout the African diaspora.

In 1960 Birago Diop (1906–1989) published a book of poems entitled *Leurres et Lueurs* (1960) in which he shows his profound attachment to French culture, although his writing is also deeply inspired by his African cultural background. Diop also wrote short stories inspired by the Senegalese oral tradition. In 1947 he published *Les Contes d'Amadou Koumba*.

Sembène Ousmane's (b. 1923) commitment to the "indigenisation" of his writings and films is reflected by the fact that he was founder and editor of the first Wolof language monthly, *Kaddu* (1972). In *O Pays, mon beau pays!* (1957), Sembène writes about a small fishing village in Senegal. *Les Bouts de bois de Dieu* [God's Bits of Wood], published in 1960, is a novel depicting a strike in 1947–48 on the Dakar-Nigeria railway. It is the story of the railway workers, their families, and the heads of the railway company. This novel follows the tradition of socialist realism and ends with the victory of the workers. Later, in *L'Harmattan* (1963), the theme of independence is treated. This novel suggests that freedom for Africans can only be achieved through socialism. *Le Dernier de l'empire* [The Last of the Empire], published in 1981, is his criticism of the competing political parties in postcolonial Senegal.

Abdoulaye Sadji's (1910–1961) two famous novels, *Maïmouna: Petite fille noire* [Maïmouna: Little Black Girl] (1953) and *Nini, mulâtresse du Sénégal* [Nini, Mulatto Woman of Senegal] (1954), focus on heroines who become victims of urban society. Sadji's last novel is *Modou-Fatim* (1960), in which he describes the plight of a peasant who has to leave his land during the dry season to work in Dakar, the capital of Senegal.

Ghana

Ayi Kwei Armah (b. 1939) is a Ghanaian writer whose novels include *Two Thousand Seasons* (1973), *The Beautyful Ones Are Not Yet Born* (1988), *Osiris Rising: A Novel of Africa Past, Present, and Future* (1995), *The Healers* (2000), and *KMT: In the House of Life* (2002).

Kofi Awoonor (George Awoonor-Williams) (b. 1935) is another prominent Ghanaian novelist. His main works are *This Earth, My Brother,* (1971), *The Breast of the Earth* (1975), and *Comes the Voyager at Last* (1992). As a poet, his main collections are *Rediscovery and Other Poems* (1964), *Night of My Blood* (1971), *Ride Me, Memory* (1973), *The House By the Sea* (1978), *Until the Morning After* (1987), *Latin American and Caribbean Notebook I* (1992), and *Herding the Lost Lamb* (2002).

Kwame Anthony Appiah (b. 1954) is an internationally recognized philosopher and novelist. His *Avenging Angel* was published in 1990. In 1993 a major work by Appiah was published: *In My Father's House: Africa in the Philosophy of Culture*, and that year it was awarded the Herskovits Prize for African Studies in English. *Nobody Likes Letitia* appeared in 1994, and *Death in Venice* in 1995. Along with Henry Louis Gates Jr., he co-edited *Africana: The Encyclopedia of the African and African-American Experience,* an important reference work that appeared in 1999. He has also written *Thinking It Through: An Introduction to Contemporary Philosophy* (2003) and *The Ethics of Identity* (2005). His latest work is *Cosmopolitanism: Ethics in a World of Strangers* (2006).

Central Africa

Democratic Republic of the Congo (DRC)

Sony Labou Tansi (1947–1995) has written a significant play, *La parenthèse de sang* (1978), that reflects the humor and political commitment of his fiction. The philosopher Valentin Y. Mudimbe (b. 1941) wrote *Tales of Faith* in 1997, an intellectual and spiritual autobiography about the ideas of Central African intellectuals and their work in the twentieth century. He is also the author of nonfiction books and articles about African culture.

Rais Boneza (b. 1979) is a poet who published *Nomad, A Refugee Poet* (2003) and *Black Emerald* (2005), works inspired by his own experience as a refugee driven from his home by his country's authorities. His collections of poems reflect his views about the conditions prevailing in his motherland. He has also written a nonfiction work entitled *Peace by African's Peaceful Means* (2004).

Cameroon

Mongo Beti (1932–2001), also known as Alexandre Biyidi Awala, wrote his first novel, *Ville cruelle* [Cruel City], under the pseudonym Eza Boto in 1954. In 1956 *Le pauvre Christ de Bomba* [The Poor Christ of Bomba] created a scandal with its satirical description of the missionary and colonial world. Mongo Beti subsequently published *Mission terminée* (1957, winner of the *Prix Sainte Beuve* in 1958) and *Le Roi miraculé* in 1958. In 1978 he launched the bimonthly review *Peuples noirs, Peuples africains* [Black Peoples, African Peoples], which was published until 1991. This review chronicled—and tirelessly denounced—the evils brought to Africa by neocolonial regimes. In 1994, Beti opened the Librairie des Peuples Noirs [Library of the Black Peoples] in Yaoundé (the capital of Cameroon). In addition, in 1972 he published *Main basse sur le Cameroun, autopsie d'une décolonisation* [Cruel Hand on Cameroon: Autopsy of a Decolonization], which was banned until 1976 by the French Ministry of the Interior on the request of the Cameroon government.

Republic of the Congo (Congo-Brazzaville)

In 1979 Tchicaya U Tam'si (1931–1988) published his first novel, *La Vie et demie*, which won the Prix Spécial du Festival de la Francophonie. He has also received several other literary awards, such as the Grand Prix Littéraire de l'Afrique Noire, for *L'anté-peuple* [The Antipeople] (1983) and the Palme de la Francophonie for a collection of short stories, *Les sept solitudes de Lorsa Lopez* [The Seven Solitudes of Lorsa Lopez] (1985). In 1988 he won the Ibsen Foundation Prize. *L' anté-peuple* is partly based on the story of a refugee, the author's friend, who was falsely accused of the murder of a young woman. In 1988 U Tam'si published *Les yeux du volcan*. In *Qui a mangé Madame d' Avoine Bergotha* (1989), a dictator expels nearly all of the men from his country. In his poetry, U Tam'si also denounced the role of the Catholic Church, colonization, and Western education in Congo.

Another important literary voice hailing from Congo-Brazzaville is the novelist Emmanuel Dongola. In his latest work, *Johnny Mad Dog* (2002), he examined the life of teenagers caught up in the madness of civil war. His other works include *Jazz and Palm Wine, The Fire of Origins,* and *Little Boys Come from the Stars,* a tragicomic novel about childhood and coming of age in a troubled African society.

Angola

Artur Carlos Maurício Pestana dos Santos, commonly known as Pepetela (b. 1941) is a major writer of fiction. As a white Angolan writer, he fought in the long guerrilla war for Angola's independence. Much of his writing deals with Angola's political history in the twentieth century. In 1980, he published *Mayombe,* a novel that portrays the lives of a group of MPLA (Popular Movement for the Liberation of Angola) guerrillas who are involved in the anti-colonial struggle. In 1997 Pepetela won the Camões Prize, the world's highest literary honor for Lusophone literature.

José Luandino Vieira (b. 1935) is an Angolan writer of short fiction and novels. He is Portuguese by birth, but his parents immigrated to Angola in 1938, and he grew up immersed in the African quarters (*musseques*) of Luanda. He wrote in the language unique to the *musseque*, a fusion of Kimbundu and Portuguese. Vieira's works are inspired by the structure of the African oral narrative. His best known work was his early short story collection, *Luuanda* (1963), which received a Portuguese Writers' literary award in 1965. It is the examination of the oppressive rule of the colonial administration in Angola. His novella, *A vida verdadeira de Domingos Xavier* [The Real Life of Domingos Xavier] (1974), portrays the cruelty of the Portuguese administration and the courage of ordinary Angolans during the colonial period. Vieira also served as Secretary-General of the Union of Angolan writers, and in that capacity he helped get the works of other Angolan authors and poets published.

Southern Africa

The Republic of South Africa

The Republic of South Africa has been, and remains, notable for its rich and prolific literary output—on the part of both its indigenous African population and the descendants of its English and Dutch (Afrikaner) settler population. A testimony to its stature in the literary world is that, in recent years, two South Africans have been awarded the Nobel Prize for Literature: Nadine Gordimer (in 1991) and John Maxwell Coetzee (in 2003).

Among the pioneers of African fiction in the Republic of South Africa was Benedict Wallet Vilakazi (1906–1947), who wrote three novels during the 1930s. *Nje nempela* [Really and Truly] (1933) is based on events that happened during the Bambathi rebellion in 1906. In this novel, Vilikazi shows the conflict between traditional and Western cultures. *Noma nini* [Forever and Ever] (1935, but written in 1932 or earlier), won a prize in 1933 in the third competition of the International African Institute. *U-Dingiswayo ka Jobe* [Dingiswayo, Son of Jobe] (1939) is a historical novel about Dingiswayo, the king of the Mthethwa. Between 1933 and 1945, Vilakazi was best known for his collections of poetry in Zulu. In the early 1930s, he began to publish his poetry in various journals, including *ILanga lase Natal* [The Natal Sun], *UmAfrika* [The African], *The Bantu World*, and *The Star*. He also wrote scholarly articles in Zulu and English in such reviews as *African Studies*, *Bantu Studies*, *The Native Teachers' Journal*, and *Forum*.

Besides being a short story writer, S. E. K. Mqhayi (1875–1945) was also a novelist. In 1939, he wrote an autobiography, *U-Mqhayi Wase Ntabozuko* [Mqhayi of the Mountain of Beauty], which portrays his life (within the context of nineteenth-century Xhosa culture). Also, at the beginning of his writing career, he contributed to various Xhosa newspapers. Newspapers such as *The Izwi Labantu* [The Voice of the People] and *Imvo Zabantsundu* [African Opinion] had a great impact on the creation of Xhosa poetry and prose. Mqhayi wrote a story entitled "Ityala Lama-Wele" [The Lawsuit of the Twins] (1914) about a trial in a tribal court. Its aim was to show how the European courts threatened the customary judicial system in the Republic of South Africa.

Archibald Campbell Jordan (1907–1968) wrote his the novel *Ingqumbo Yeminyanya* [The Wrath of the Ancestral Spirits] (1940), a work that has been acclaimed as a great tragedy. It develops the theme of the unresolved conflict between traditional and Western ways. This work represents, together with Thomas Mofolo's *Chaka*, one of the major novels written in an African language in South Africa. Jordan published several of his poems in the newspaper *Imvo Zabantsundu* in 1936 and in *Ikhwezi lomso* in 1958. The poems were in Xhosa, some accompanied by English translations from Jordan himself. Also, his essays, which appeared in *Africa South* in the 1950s, represented the first theoretical system of African literature developed by a New African intellectual. They were later assembled posthumously as *Towards an African Literature: The Emergence of Literary Form in Xhosa*. This work is an important pioneering critical study; Jordan was a major literary figure who was ideologically committed to communism and belonged to the Non-European Unity Movement.

Yali Manisi (1926–1999) was the major Xhosa poetic voice of the second half of the twentieth century. Like his predecessor Mqhayi, he represents the living tradition of *izibongo* (praise poetry). His "Izibongo Zee Nkosi Zama Xhosa" [Praise Poems of Xhosa Chiefs] (1952) is a homage to Benedict Wallet Vilakazi, Zulu intellectual and poet. "Inkululeko" [Freedom] is an epic poem written in 1977. His poetry displays a historical sensibility and reflects the survival of Xhosa folklore into the twenty-first century.

Breyten Breytenbach (b. 1939) is one of the most famous South African novelists of his era. He was part of the Sestigers (Afrikaner writers of the 1960s). Although most of his poems were written in Afrikaans, he also published many novels in English, such as *Return to Paradise* (1993) and *Dog Heart* (1999). He wrote *'n Seisoen in die Paradys* (1976, [A Season in Paradise]) while he was incarcerated. His other prison writings were published as *Mouroir: Bespieelende notas van 'n roman* (1983, [Mouroir: Mirrornotes of a Novel]). Breytenbach was a leading Afrikaner poet and critic of apartheid (a position which led to his imprisonment). In 1965 he was awarded the A.P.B. prize for *Die ysterkoei moet sweet* (1964, [The Iron Cow Must Sweat]) and *Katastrofes* (1964). In 1984 and 1999 he received the Hertzog Prize for poetry. *The True Confessions of an Albino Terrorist* (1984) is a powerful account of his arrest and detention. Breytenbach's major themes are his suffering as a prisoner and as an exiled poet and his longing to return to his homeland.

André Philippus Brink (b. 1935) is another prominent member of the Sestigers. His novels in Afrikaans (and in English translation) were openly critical of the South African government. Like other voices of this literary movement, he aimed to portray sexual and moral matters as well as the inherent injustice of the apartheid system. In 1979 he published *'N Droë wit seisoen* (1979, [A Dry White Season]), which was made into a major film, and in 1982 his *Houd-Den-Bek: Roman* (*Chain of Voices*) appeared, which recounts, through many points of view, a slave revolt in 1825.

Athol Fugard (b. 1932) has made his mark as a novelist, playwright, director, and actor. He is of British and Afrikaner descent and is known for producing his first play, *No Good Friday,* in 1959 with his experimental theater group in Port Elisabeth. In his 1961 production of *The Blood Knot and Other Plays,* he focuses on the conflict between characters from different backgrounds. Fugard's plays explore the racism and repression of apartheid. Two of his plays in particular, *Sizwe Bansi Is Dead* and *Master Harold . . . and the Boys,* are regarded as masterful portrayals of the injustice, immorality, and, indeed, the insanity of the apartheid system. Although Fugard has enjoyed a long and distinguished career, perhaps his most well-known work at this point is his novel *Tsotsi* (1980), about the moral dilemma faced by a young South African gangster who suddenly and unexpectedly finds himself the custodian of a baby. In 2005 the South African director Gavin Hood made *Tsotsi* into a major film; this cinematic version has won an impressive array of international awards.

Mazisi Kunene (b. 1930) is an epic poet who won the Bantu Literary Competition Award in 1956. His early poetry was published as *Zulu Poems* in 1970. *Emperor Shaka the Great* (1979), an epic poem inspired by the rise of the Zulu empire, was followed by *Anthem of the Decades* (1981), a Zulu epic dedicated to the women of Africa. *The Ancestors and the Sacred Mountain* (a collection of poems) appeared in 1982. Kunene is a major voice in South African literature because of his commitment to his Zulu heritage.

Peter Abrahams (b. 1919) and Alan Paton (1903–88) were two of South Africa's most important literary voices of the 1950s. Both of these writers, one black (Abrahams) and one white (Paton), provided valuable perspectives on the cruelty and injustice of apartheid. Abrahams' most significant works are *Mine Boy* (1946) and his memoir, *Tell Freedom* (1954). Paton's emotionally powerful *Cry, the Beloved Country* (1948) brought international attention to the plight of the black majority in South Africa, and it was made into several major motion pictures. Another novel by Paton that attracted attention was *Too Late the Phalarope* (1953).

Nadine Gordimer (b. 1923) was awarded the Nobel Prize for Literature in 1991. A South African of European descent, she has used her talents as a writer to expose the hypocrisy of racism, turning her keen eye on the damage to the quality of human relationships done during the apartheid era and continuing in the present. Gordimer is primarily known as a novelist; her first novel, *The Lying Days,* appeared in 1953. Her major works include *The Conservationist* (1974), *Burger's Daughter* (1979), *July's People* (1981), and *A Sport of Nature* (1987), and, in the post-apartheid era, *None to Accompany Me* (1994), *The House Gun* (1998), *The Pickup* (2001), and *Get a Life* (2005). Gordimer has also been a prolific writer of short stories; over a dozen volumes of her work in this genre have been published.

The second South African writer to have been awarded the Nobel Prize for Literature is J. M. Coetzee (b. 1940). His novels, memoirs, and nonfiction pieces constitute an impressive body of work. His fiction, some of which is set within the troubled modern context of the Republic of South Africa, goes beyond the realm of the social and political and examines the pain and complexities of the human dilemma, and, in this sense, his writing is truly universal. His novels include *Dusklands* (1974), *In the Heart of the Country* (1977), *Waiting for the Barbarians* (1980), *The Life and Times of Michael K* (1983), *Age of Iron* (1990), *The Master of St. Petersburg* (1994), *Disgrace* (1999), *Elizabeth Costello* (2003), and *Slow Man* (2005). His autobiographical works are *Boyhood: Scenes from a Provincial Life* (1997) and *Youth: Scenes from a Provincial Life II* (2002), and his major nonfiction works include *White Writing: on the Culture of Letters in South Africa* (1988), *Giving Offense: Essays on Censorship* (1997), *The Lives of Animals* (1999), and two collections of his literary essays. In addition to the Nobel Prize, Coetzee has been awarded the Booker Prize twice, in 1983 for *The Life and Times of Michael K,* and in 1999 for *Disgrace.* Coetzee now lives and works in Australia.

The struggle against apartheid also produced a rich legacy of political writing. An essential document of the "Black Consciousness" movement of the 1970s is Steve Biko's *I Write What I Like: Selected Writings* (1978), the work of a brilliant young activist who was killed by the South African government while he was under detention. This anthology was reissued by the University of Chicago Press in 2002. Another work that provides invaluable insight into the long struggle for justice in South Africa, and an outstanding read, is *Long Walk to Freedom: The Autobiography of Nelson Mandela* (1995).

Zimbabwe

Zimbabwean writers are increasingly emerging as an important force on the African literary scene. Chenjerai Hove (b. 1956) is a young writer who has written the following novels: *Bones* (1988), *Shadows* (1994), and *Ancestors* (1996). He is a prolific poet as well. He is also the author of *Shebeen Tales* (1994) and *Palaver Finish* (2002), which has been translated into Shona as *Zvakwana!* and into Ndebele as *Akudle Inqondo.* Shimmer Chinodya (b. 1957) is another important Zimbabwean literary voice, whose *Harvest of Thorns* (1989) recounts the dangers and complexities of the armed struggle against the white minority government.

Chinodya was awarded the Commonwealth Writers Prize (Africa Region) for this novel in 1990. Other works by Chinodya include *Dew in the Morning* (1982), *Tales of Tahari* (2004), and his most recent novel, *Chairman of Fools* (2006).

Another important novel about the Zimbabwean freedom struggle is Alexander Kanengoni's (b. 1951) *Echoing Silences* (1999). Other works by Kanengoni that focus on this theme are two novels, *The Vicious Circle* (1983) and *When the Rainbird Cries* (1987), and a collection of short stories, *Effortless Tears* (1993).

Tsitsi Dangarembga (b. 1959) is a multitalented novelist, playwright, and film writer and director. Her major accomplishments to date are her novel *Nervous Conditions* (1988), which won the Commonwealth Writers Prize in 1989, and the film *Everyone's Child* (a work that she directed), a powerful commentary on the impact of AIDS.

East Africa

Tanzania

Euphrase Kezilahabi's (b. 1944) major contribution to contemporary African literature has been demonstrated by the publication of several of his Swahili novels over the past thirty years. His major works, among them *Rosa Mistika* (1970), *Kichwamaji* [The Nuthead] (1974), *Dunia Uwanja Wa Fujo* [The World is a Chaotic Place] (1975), *Gamba la Nyoka* [Snake's Skin] (1979), *Karibu Ndani* (1988), *Nagona* (1990), and *Mzingile* (1991), show the author's preoccupation with social change and the confusion created by the clash of tradition with modernity.

Julius Nyerere (1922–1999) was the father of Tanzanian independence and that nation's first president. A political thinker who tried to develop a variety of socialism based on traditional African social models, his *Uhuru na Ujamaa: Freedom and Socialism* (1968) is a major collection of his writings.

Kenya

For an overview of the work of Ngugi wa Thiong'o, a major figure not only of African but of world literature, see the introductory section of this chapter.

Emmanuel Kariuki's *Ngiri Mganga* is a collection of tales in Kiswahili about a bush doctor. In 2003, he won the Jomo Kenyatta Prize for Literature for *The Salem Mystery*, a children's book. In addition, Meja Mwangi (b. 1948) wrote about the challenges that contemporary Kenyan society faces in novels such as *Kill Me Quick* (1973) and *Going Down River Road* (1976).

Binyavanga Wainaina (b. 1971) won the Caine Prize for African Writing in 2002 and is working on his first novel, *The Fallen World of Appearances.* He has also written for the *East African, National Geographic, The Sunday Times* (Republic of South Africa), and *The Guardian* (UK). His publications include short stories such as *Discovering Home* (2001) and *An Affair to Dismember.* He is the founding editor of *Kwani*, the first important literary magazine from East Africa since *Transition.*

Rocha Chimera has written nonfiction works such as *Kiswahili: Past, Present and Future Horizons* (1998) and *Ufundishaji wa Fasihi: Nadharia na Mbinu* (1999) [The Teaching of Literature: Theory and Methods], co-authored with Kimani Njogu. The latter is a groundbreaking work praised for "addressing the tendency through globalization for African languages to be silenced, with English and other Western languages promoted as vehicles of literary expression."[1] In 2000 Chimera received the Noma Award for this study.

Somalia

In East Africa, Somali literature has a long tradition of religious verses composed in Arabic. Oral performance has been the main characteristic of such literature; poems are recited on the national radio and in other public venues. In the 1960s, the following two periodicals promoted the development of Somali writing: *Sahan* [Reconnaissance] and *Horseed* [Vanguard]. However, written Somali literature began after World War II and started flourishing after 1973. Today, Somalia's most well-known writer is Nuruddin Farah (b. 1945), a novelist concerned with the impact of civil war on his divided nation, the experience of exile, and the role of women in postcolonial Somalia. Farah is best known for his "Blood in the Sun" trilogy (*Maps*, *Gifts*, and *Secrets*), and his most recent novel, *Links* (2003). Farah was awarded the 1998 Neustadt International Prize for Literature.

CONCLUSION

In the 1980s and 1990s, African literature bore witness to the changing nature of African societies and their adjustment to a new economic order. At the dawn of the twenty-first century, new trends and new writers in African literature are emerging. Some of these authors do not live in Africa. They have either been forced into exile or decided to live abroad. For example, the 1986 Nobel Laureate for Literature, Nigerian author Wole Soyinka, was unable to return to Nigeria because the military dictatorship convicted him of treason for his writing and his activism. Some writers belonging to the new generation create narratives that oscillate between illusion and reality and that are imbued with magical realism, such as Sierra Leonean writer Syl Cheney-Coker (b. 1945), who won the Commonwealth Writers Prize for the publication of *The Last Harmattan of Alusine Dunbar* (1990). Other authors have synthesized Western and African influence in their works and reinvented their style, allowing them to be both "outsiders" and "insiders" in their vantage point on African culture. Finally, although some African writers are still rooted in the ethnic traditions, cosmologies, and legends of Sub-Saharan Africa, others write about the challenges that the new African states experience in contemporary Africa. In the past decade, leading literary figures have gained an international reputation for their work because they offer new and challenging images of the African experience. Thus, they confirm that African literature has now a central and prominent place in the wider body of world literature.

RESOURCE GUIDE

PRINT SOURCES

Abani, Chris. *Graceland*. New York, New York: Farrar, Straus & Giroux, 2004.

Achebe, Chinua. *Things Fall Apart*. London: Heinemann, 1958.

———. *Arrow of God*. New York: Anchor Books/Doubleday, 1969.

Aidoo, Ama Ata. *Anowa*. Harlow, England: Longman African Series, 1970.

———. *Our Sister Killjoy or Reflections from a Black-Eyed Squint*. London: Longman, 1977.

———. *Changes: A Love Story*. London: Women's Press, 1991.

Amadi, Elechi. *The Concubine*. Ibadan: Heinemann Books, 1993.

Appiah, Anthony. *In My Father's House: Africa in the Philosophy of Culture*. New York: Oxford University Press, 1992.

Armah, Ayi Kwei. *The Beautyful Ones Are Not Yet Born*. Boston, MA: Houghton Mifflin Company, 1968.

Awoonor, Kofi. *This Earth, My Brother*. London: Heinemann, 1972.

Bâ, Amadou H. *L'Etrange destin de Wangrin* (*The Fortunes of Wangrin*). Paris: Union Générale d' Editions, 1973.

Bâ, Mariama. *Une si longue lettre* (*So Long a Letter*). Dakar, Senegal: Nouvelles Editions Africaines, 1980.

Beti, Mongo. *Le Pauvre Christ de Bomba* [The Poor Christ of Bomba]. Paris: Robert Laffont, 1956.

———. *Mission terminée.* Paris: Buchet/Chastel, 1957.

———. *Remember Ruben.* Paris : Union Générale d'Editions, 1974.

———. *L'histoire du fou.* Paris: Julliard, 1994.

———. *Branle-bas en noir et blanc.* Paris: Julliard, 2000.

Boneza, Rais. *Nomad, A Refugee Poet.* Dundee, IL: Cook Communication, 2003.

Brink, André. *A Dry White Season.* New York: Penguin, 1984.

Bugul, Ken. *Riwan ou le chemin de sable.* Paris: Présence Africaine, 1999.

Cabral, Amilcar. *Unity and Struggle.* London: Heinemann, 1980.

Campbell, Jordan A. *Ingqumbo Yeminyanya* [The Wrath of the Ancestors]. Lovedale, Republic of South Africa: Lovedale Press, 1980.

Cheney-Coker, Syl. *The Last Harmattan of Alusine Dunbar.* Portsmouth, NH: Heinemann Educational Books, 1990.

Chimera, Rocha. *Kiswahili: Past, Present and Future Horizons.* Nairobi, Kenya: Nairobi University Press, 1998.

Coetzee, John Maxwell. *Life and Times of Michael K.* New York: Viking Press, 1985.

Curry, Ginette. *Awakening African Women: The Dynamics of Change.* London: Cambridge Scholars Press, 2004.

Dadié, Bernard B. *Climbié.* Paris: Seghers, 1956.

Dangarembga, Tsitsi. *She No Longer Sleeps.* Harare: College Press Zimbabwe, 1987.

———. *Nervous Conditions.* Seattle: Women's Press, 1988.

Diop, Birago. *Contes d'Amadou Koumba* (*Tales of Amadou Koumba*). Paris: Présence Africaine, 1988.

Diop, Boubacar B. *Murambi: Le livre des ossements.* Paris: Stock, 2000.

Diop, Cheikh Anta. *Antériorité des civilisations nègres: Mythe ou vérité historique?* Paris: Présence Africaine, 1993.

Dorkenoo, Efua. *Cutting the Rose: Female Genital Mutilation, The Practice and Its Prevention.* London: Minority Rights Group, 1994.

Emecheta, Buchi. *In the Ditch.* London: Barrie and Jenkins, 1972.

———. *Second-Class Citizen.* London: Allison and Busby, 1974.

———. *The Joys of Motherhood.* New York: George Braziller, 1979.

———. *Double Yoke.* New York: George Braziller, 1985.

———. *The New Tribe.* Portsmouth and Oxford, NH: Heinemann, 2000.

Farah, Nuruddin. *Maps.* Zurich, Switzerland: Ammann Verlag & Co, 1992.

Fugard, Athol. *The Blood Knot: A Play in Seven Scenes.* Cape Town, Republic of South Africa: Oxford University Press, 1992.

Gordimer, Nadine. *Burger's Daughter.* Harmondsworth, England: Penguin, 1979.

———. *The House Gun.* London: Bloomsbury, 1998.

———. *The Pickup.* London: Bloomsbury, 2001.

Hayford, Casely. *Ethiopia Unbound: Studies in Race Emancipation.* London: Frank Cass, 1969.

Head, Bessie. *A Question of Power.* London: Davis-Poynter, 1973.

———. *Serowe: Village of the Rainwind.* London: Heinemann, 1981.

———. *A Bewitched Crossroad: An African Saga.* New York: Paragon House Publishers, 1986.

———. *Tales of Tenderness and Power.* Johannesburg; London: Ad. Donker; Heinemann, 1989.

———. *A Woman Alone: Autobiographical Writings.* London: Heinemann, 1990.

Hove, Chenjerai. *Bones.* Harare, Zimbabwe: Baobab Books, 1986.

Isegawa, Moses. *Abessijnse Kronieken* (*Abyssinian Chronicles*). Amsterdam: Vertaling Ria Loohuizen, 1998.

Joubert, Elsa. *Die Swerfjare van Poppie Nongena* (*The Long Journey of Poppie Nongena*). Cape Town, Republic of South Africa: Tafelberg Publishers, 1996.

Kane, Cheikh A. *L' Aventure ambigüe* (*Ambiguous Adventure*). Paris: Julliard, 1971.

Karodia, Farida. *Daughters of the Twilight.* London: Women's Press, 1986.
———. *Coming Home and Other Stories.* London: Heinemann Educational, 1988.
———. *A Shattering of Silence.* Oxford: Heinemann, 1993.
Kenyatta, Jomo. *Facing Mt. Kenya: The Tribal Life of the Gikuyu.* London: Secker & Warburg, 1953.
Ki-Zerbo, Joseph. *Histoire de l 'Afrique noire: D'hier à demain.* Paris: Hatier, 1972.
Kourouma, Ahmadou. *Les Soleils des indépendances* (*The Suns of Independence*). Paris: Editions du Seuil, 1970.
Labou Tansi, Sony. *La vie et demie.* Paris: Editions du Seuil, 1979.
Laye, Camara. *L' Enfant noir.* Paris: Editions Plon, 1953.
Mama, Amina. *Beyond the Masks: Race, Gender, and Subjectivity.* London & New York: Routledge, 1995.
Mamdani, Mahmoud. *Citizen and Subject: Contemporary Africa and the Legacy of Late Colonialism.* Princeton, NJ: Princeton University Press, 1996.
Mandela, Nelson. *Long Walk to Freedom: The Autobiography of Nelson Mandela.* Boston: Little Brown & Co, 1995.
Marais, Eugène. *Die Siel Van Die Mier* [The Soul of the White Ant]. Johannesburg, Republic of South Africa: Jonathan Ball, 1990.
Mofolo, Thomas. *Chaka.* Oxford: Heinemann, 1983.
Mphahlele, Ezekiel. *Down Second Avenue.* London: Faber & Faber, 1959.
Mudimbe, Valentin Y. *The Invention of Africa: Gnosis, Philosophy, and the Order of Knowledge.* Bloomington, IN: Indiana University Press, 1988.
Mugo, Micere. *The Trial of Dedan Kimathi.* London: Heinemann, 1976.
———. *My Mother's Poem and Other Songs: Songs and Poems.* Nairobi, Kenya: East African Educational Publishers, 1994.
Niane, Tamsir D. *Soundjata ou l' épopée mandingue* (*Sundiata: An Epic of Old Mali*). Paris: Présence Africaine, 1985.
Njau, Rebeka. *The Scar: a Tragedy in One Act.* Moshi, Tanzania: Lobp Art Gallery, 1965.
———. *Ripples in the Pool.* Nairobi, Kenya; London: Heinemann, 1975.
———. *The Hypocrite.* Nairobi, Kenya: Uzima Press, 1977.
Nkrumah, Kwame. *Ghana: Autobiography of Kwame Nkrumah.* London: Panaf Books, 1957.
Nwapa, Flora. *Efuru.* London: Heinemann, 1966.
———. *Idu.* London: Heinemann, 1969.
———. *One Is Enough.* Enugu, Nigeria: Flora Nwapa Co., 1981.
———. *Women Are Different.* Enugu, Nigeria: Tana Press, 1986.
———. *Never Again.* Trenton, NJ: Africa World Press, 1992.
Ogot, Grace. *The Promised Land.* Nairobi, Kenya: East African Publishing House, 1966.
________. *The Strange Bride.* Nairobi, Kenya; London: Heinemann, 1989.
Okigbo, Christopher. *Labyrinths.* London: Heinemann, 1971.
Okoye, Ifeoma. *Behind the Clouds.* London: Longman, 1982.
————. *Men without Ears.* London: Longman, 1984.
Okri, Ben. *The Famished Road.* Peterborough, England: Anchor Books, 1991.
Oyono, Ferdinand. *Le vieux nègre et la médaille* (*The Old Man and the Medal*). Paris: Editions Juillard, 1967.
Paton, Alan. *Cry, The Beloved Country: A Story of Comfort and Desolation.* Harmondsworth, England: Penguin, 1977.
P'Bitek, Okot. *Song of Lawino.* Nairobi, Kenya: East African Publishing House, 1966.
Plaatje, Sol. *Native Life in South Africa.* London: P. S. King, 1916.
———. *Mudhi.* Cape Town, Republic of South Africa: Francolin, 1996.
Saro-Wiwa, Ken: *Sazaboy: A Novel in Rotten English.* Pueblo, CO: Passeggiata Press, 1986.
Schreiner, Olive. *The Story of an African Farm.* New York: Garland Publ., 1975.
Sembène, Ousmane. *Les Bouts de Bois de Dieu* (*God's Bits of Wood*). Paris: Le Livre Contemporain, 1960.
———. *The Black Docker.* London: Heinemann, 1987.
———. *The Money Order.* London: Heinemann, 1987.
———. *Niiwam and Taaw: Two Novellas.* Oxford, UK and Portsmouth, NH: Heinemann, 1992.

Senghor, Léopold S. *Oeuvre poétique*. Paris: Gallimard, 1957.
Serote, Wally M. *Third World Express*. Cape Town, Republic of South Africa: David Philip and Mayibuye Books, 1997.
Sofola, Zulu. *Wedlock of the Gods*. London: Evans, 1973.
———. *King Emene*. Ibadan, Nigeria: Heinemann, 1975.
———. *Old Wines Are Tasty*. Ibadan, Nigeria: University Press Limited, 1981.
———. *Memories in the Moonlight*. Ibadan, Nigeria: Evans, 1986.
———. *Song of a Maiden*. Ibadan, Nigeria: University Press Limited, 1986.
Sow Fall, Aminata. *La Grève des battus (The Beggars' Strike)*. Dakar, Senegal: Nouvelles Editions Africaines, 1979.
Soyinka, Wole. *Death and King's Horseman*. London: Eyre Methuen, 1976.
———. *Ake: The Years of Childhood*. London: Rex Collings, 1981.
Sutherland, Efua. *Playtime in Africa*. London: Brown Knight and Truscott, 1960.
———. *The Roadmakers*. Accra, Ghana: Ghana Information Services, 1961.
———. *The Marriage of Anansewa*, and *Edufa*. Harlow, UK: Longman, 1987.
Tadjo, Véronique. *Mamy Wata et le monstre* (*Mamy Wata and The Monster*). Abidjan, Ivory Coast: Nouvelles Editions Africaines, 1993.
Tlali, Miriam. *Amandla*. Johannesburg: Ravan Press, 1980.
———. *Between Two Worlds*. London: Longman, 1995.
Tutuola, Amos. *The Palm-Wine Drinkard and His Dead Palm-Wine Tapster in the Dead's Town*. London: Faber & Faber, 1952.
U Tam'si, Tchicaya. *Le mauvais sang*. Paris: L' Harmattan Collection Littératures, 1998.
Van Onselen, Charles. *The Seed is Mine: The Life of Kas Maine, a South African Sharecropper, 1894–1985*. New York: Hill & Wang, 1996.
Vera, Yvonne. *Under the Tongue*. Harare, Zimbabwe: Baobab Books, 1997.
———. *Butterfly Burning*. Harare, Zimbabwe: Baobab Books, 1998.
Vilakazi, Benedict. *Amal'ezulu*. Johannesburg: Witwatersrand University Press, 1962.
wa Thiong'o, Ngugi. *A Grain of Wheat*. London: Heinemann, 1967.
———. *Caitaani Mutharaba-ini* (*Devil on the Cross*). Nairobi, Kenya: Heinemann, 1980.
———. *Wizard of the Crows*. New York: Pantheon, 2006.

WEBSITES

African Educational Web Portal. http://www.africaresource.com.
African Review of Books. http://www.africanreviewofbooks.com. Independent publication publicizing African books.
African Writers Series. http://www.heinemann.co.uk/secondary/series/index.aspx?d=s&n=541&s=671&skey=2013.
African Writers: Voices of Change. http://web.uflib.ufl.edu/cm/africana/writers.htm.
Anglophone and Lusophone African Women's Writing. http://www.ex.ac.uk/~ajsimoes/aflit/default.htm
Bibliography of Lusophone African Women Writers (Jean-Marie Volet, University of Western Australia). http://www.arts.uwa.edu.au/AFLIT/FEMECalireLU.html.
Centenaire Amadou Hampaté Bâ, 1901–2001 (Mali, Ministère de la Culture, Bamako). http://w3.culture.gov.ml/a-culturelles/centenaire/index.html.
Ethiopiques: Revue négro-africaine de littérature et de philosophie (Dakar, Senegal). http://www.refer.sn/ethiopiques/.
Francophone African Poets in English Translation (University of Florida Libraries, Gainesville). http://web.uflib.ufl.edu/cm/africana/poets.htm.
H-AFRLITCINE Web Page (Humanities-Net, Via Michigan State University). http://www.h-net.msu.edu/~aflitweb/.
JENDA: A Journal of Culture and African Women Studies. http://www.jendajournal.com.
Mots Pluriels et les grands thèmes de notre temps (Archives of the School of Humanities—The University of Western Australia). http://www.arts.wwa.edu.au/MotsPluriels/index.html.

Noma Award for Publishing in Africa (sponsored by Kodansha Ltd., Japan) (Oxon, UK). http://www.nomaaward.org.
Post-Colonial Studies: African Literary Figures (Emory University, Atlanta, Georgia). http://www.english.emory.edu/Bahri/.
West Africa Review. http://www.westafricareview.com.

EVENTS AND FESTIVALS

African Vision 2005. "Think Africa: A Festival of African Literature, Culture and Politics." 96 Euston Road, London, NW1 2DB, England. http://www.bl.uk. In association with the British Library (The Africa Centre, London, UK). Explores the best new writings from Africa today.
Time of the Writer: International Writers Festival, Centre for Creative Art, University of KwaZulu-Natal, Memorial Tower Building, Howard College Campus, King George V Avenue, Durban, 4041, Republic of South Africa. http://www.nu.ac.za/cca/Time_of_the_writer.htm. Annual International Festival of African Writers since 1998. African writing from the global diaspora.
Zimbabwe's International Book Fair. ZIBF Head Office, P.O. Box CY 1179, Causeway, Harare, Zimbabwe. http://www.zibf.org.zw. Largest book fair in Africa, held annually during the first week of August.

ORGANIZATIONS

African Literature Association, Ithaca, NY, USA. Tel: 1-607-255-0534.
African Studies Association, Rutgers University, Douglass Campus, 132 George Street, New Brunswick, NJ 08901-1400 USA. http://www.africanstudies.org. Provides information and support services to the Africanist community.
Organization of Women Writers of Africa (OWWA), P.O. Box 652, Village Station, New York, NY 10014, USA. http://www.owwa.org. Based in New York and formed in 1991 by Ama Ata Aidoo from Ghana. Nonprofit organization that establishes links between women writers from Africa and the African diaspora.
US-Africa Literary Foundation, 1681 San Gabriel Avenue, Decatur, GA 30032 USA. Africanwriters@bowwaveo.org. Promotes the interests of African writers and makes African writings known and appreciated throughout the world.

NOTE

1. Population Communication International. Inc. *Telling Stories, Saving Lives.* http://www.population. org/newsarchive/archive_01winter_awards.shtm.

LOVE, SEX, AND MARRIAGE

ULRIKE SCHUERKENS

The family—and, in particular, the extended family—has traditionally played (and continues to play) an important role in Africa, although today powerful forces of change are challenging its centrality in African life. The number of household members is still often very high, as a husband, his wife, and their children frequently make up only part of the family unit. Often several generations and collateral parents live together. Taking care of the elderly and of poor and sick parents remains a common practice in African households. African families are also units of social and biological reproduction, and places where productive tasks and earnings are shared. Familial solidarity is still widespread despite difficult economic situations. Yet there are some changes insofar as men have lost powerful positions inside families because of the loss of jobs, retrenchment, or the loss of clients in the informal sector. Other significant developments have occurred. In recent years an increase in the number of couples who do not live together has taken place. Young women have begun to play a more important role in marriage discussions. Polygynous unions, in which a man has more than one wife, continue to be widespread, and unions founded on strong affective links between spouses are rather seldom. Marriage is the rule in Africa, except in some towns, where one can observe an increase of the number of unmarried women. Since the 1980s, households led by women have become more frequent as a result of migrations, divorces, and polygamous unions without coresidence.

HIV/AIDS has taken a serious toll on Africa. The African continent is the part of the world where most of the AIDS patients live: according to the World Health Organization (WHO), Sub-Saharan Africa has just over 10 percent of the world's population but is home to more than 60 percent of all people living with HIV—25.8 million. In 2005, an estimated 3.2 million people in the region became newly infected, while 2.4 million adults and children died of AIDS. In Africa, 55 percent of all infected people are women—contrary to the situation in Western countries, where men, particularly homosexuals, are most often infected. Ninety percent of AIDS orphans worldwide live in Africa. Since the beginning of the 1980s, when AIDS was first identified in the United States, the sickness has first spread through East Africa, then West and Southern Africa. In sixteen countries more than 10 percent of the adult population is infected; in the Republic of South Africa a fifth of the population; and in Botswana and Zimbabwe nearly one third, according to recent statistics.[1]

The reasons for this dramatic spread of AIDS are, in addition to poverty and urbanization, a poor medical infrastructure, a lack of medicine, civil wars, and political instability. Medical reasons such as the existence of nontreated sexually transmitted diseases favor the transmission of the virus. Other reasons are the rarity of the use of condoms, sexual promiscuity and prostitution, the unequal status of women and men, the limited decision-making power of women, and high age differences between the sexual partners. Furthermore, AIDS as a sickness linked to sexuality is submitted to cultural taboos that render a public discussion difficult. Thus, many countries have not tackled the problem from its beginning. In the 1990s, when AIDS was increasingly being considered a national catastrophe, governments began to support political measures and UN programs (such as UNAIDS, since 1996). A more informed approach to this disease in relation to the social dynamics of love, sexuality, and marriage is thus necessary to contribute to the development of the African continent.

LOVE IN AFRICA

In Africa the stability of marriage depends above all on fertility. Today, however, young women and men are increasingly defending notions of romantic love as important criteria for selecting a spouse. Nevertheless, in 1992, William Jankowiak and Edward Fischer found, as a result of an analysis of data collected from nearly 200 cultures, that the study of romantic love was nonexistent in Africa because of the assumption that "romantic love" is a feeling limited to the Euro-American culture.[2] But they underlined that Westernization and individualism are linked to the creation of such feelings. These scholars distinguish between romantic love and "companionship" love emerging in a long relationship. Scholars studying African cultures found that popular literature about love and romance began to emerge just after World War II in some countries, such as Nigeria. Today, young educated people expect to choose their spouses, but the extended family still has a large influence as their support and approval is important for the success of most marriages. A large number of studies on love have focused on urban groups and, in particular, elites. Some studies have taken a look at popular media, such as letters to editors and advice columns in popular African magazines.[3] As Daniel Jordan Smith found: "Courtship most often privileges the nature of a couple's personal relationship and is negotiated through interpersonal intimacy and expression of love. In contrast, marriage tends to be constructed within the framework of continuing ties and obligations to extended family and community, privileging fertility and the social roles of mother and father."[4] The same author also underlines the fact that "a tension between arranged marriage and personal preferences has long existed"[5] by referring to stories of runaway girls and men who defied their parents. Currently, video films, women's magazines, and newspapers express a growing fascination with romantic love. A personal relationship based on emotional intimacy and sexual attraction is, in Africa, a private affair and is displayed neither in films nor in public life. Another change that has taken place is the fact that younger women no longer tend to consider love, sex, or enjoyment as secondary to reproduction, whereas older women still stress that sex is a duty and not a pleasure.

These changes are linked to wider social transformations in African societies influenced by European colonial empires that were characterized by private property, economic competition, and the market economy (based on relations between owners of enterprises, the state, and individual workers). Intimate relations have thus been reconfigured in different socioeconomic contexts, and the waning importance of the extended family has contributed to re-create the relations between women and men. Some literary texts (written by men) describe current intimacy as a power struggle between the sexes where women try to live without depending on men in a male-dominated society.[6] These male authors show women who make choices: they divorce, they live without men, and they make a living themselves. The authors describe situations where men assert dominance over women in societies that do not permit women to gain self-respect but force them to accept difficult economic situations. Thus, intimate relations between women and men render explicit the character of social relations in a given society, and these writers have realized and expressed the inequality of gender roles in African society.

An article by Andrea Cornwall with the interesting title "Spending Power: Love, Money, and the Reconfiguration of Gender Relations in Ado-Odo, Southwestern Nigeria"[7] describes the role of money in gender relations. As one man says: "You can't ride a woman without giving her something."[8] These women may be young school or university students, unmarried women, or married wives. They need money for education, books, clothes, and sick children. They know that men are ready to give "gifts" in exchange for intimate relations. These women are not sex workers, but they find an answer to economic austerity that their body permits them to give. There are stories of "sugar mummies" or "sugar daddies" (wealthy women and men with a penchant for "toy boys" or "little girls"); and "senior girls" who remain unmarried, pursuing careers and having boyfriends. All these facts show that money has transformed intimate relations and has even contributed to a sexual culture that favors the spread of HIV/AIDS. There are voices that call for reconsidering intimate relations in Africa, but this requires also reconsidering other social relations. Intimate relations are thus the microcosm that reflects dynamics of the wider society (the macrocosm).

SEXUALITY IN AFRICA

Sexuality in Africa[9] is a very important topic, because it describes the relationship between women and men that is fundamental in the struggle against HIV/AIDS. Yet there are only few studies on sexuality, only in some countries and on very few ethnic groups. In fact, sexuality is an issue difficult for anthropologists, sociologists, and psychologists to investigate; in the reports in which they have tackled aspects of the topic, one can often find biased interpretations for different reasons, such as male researchers having difficulties in accessing female sexuality, or researchers interpreting according to a Western viewpoint that may not be adapted to an African context, where sexuality plays a rather different role than in Western countries. It is not the individual but the culture that determines how sexuality can be realized and what customs are accepted.

Scholars studying African societies have seldom published on sexuality, even if studies on marriage systems, female roles, and the changing roles of women and men are rather numerous. The findings are spread out over some hundred monographs on different ethnic groups. Most of them were produced in the 1960s and 1970s, and more recent studies are few and far between. According to Vangroenweghe, a large number of these findings can be classified as anecdotal and rarely representative of the whole group. Studies on sexuality are not realized by observing the activity, but through interviews, informal conversations, or questionnaires. Often, missions and administrative authorities introduced sexual habits during the twentieth century that differed from traditional practices, so people tend to give information reflecting accepted and expected norms, but not on real practices. Moreover, the gender of the interviewer and his or her personal beliefs influence the interview. In Europe, there are questions that will not be correctly answered, such as questions on income, housing, or sexuality. In

ABSTINENCE AFTER CHILDBIRTH

The Yoruba in Nigeria have practiced a long abstinence period after the birth of a child while the mother breastfeeds.[10] As a result, during 25 years of marriage producing several children, the wife may be renouncing the sexual union with her husband for up to 15 years. Therefore, a wife who breastfeeds needs other women—a fact that is socially accepted. These women may be parents, girlfriends, or prostitutes. Thus, given its nature, sexuality has rather different forms and may be conceived as a means of reproduction, a form of pleasure, a source of income, a means to define one's status in society, or as an aspect of male power.

Africa, people refuse to discuss the sexuality of parents and grandparents because these are topics that "cannot be addressed." These taboos also explain why sexual education is difficult to pursue in Africa.

The knowledge of certain aspects of sexuality (regarding the transmission of sexually transmitted diseases) among many Africans is insufficient. The high number of HIV-seropositive pregnant women and mothers in countries such as Botswana shows that sexual education is urgently needed. The sexual education provided by parents plays a rather small role in three types of relationships: father-son, father-daughter, and mother-son. Girls know less than boys, except for hygienic rules. In schools, sexuality is often a subject that is not tackled for political or religious reasons because of parental and religious pressure groups. Furthermore, there are high numbers of adolescent pregnancies, abortions, and rapes and high mortality rates for mothers caused by complications after abortions. In Africa, girls must often leave school if they become pregnant, but boys who are partly responsible can continue to attend. You can hear troubling stories about sexuality, such as young men who think they are ill at the moment of their first ejaculation, or young girls who consider nondesired sexual relations as normal (even if adult women may complain about violent behaviors).

Sexuality varies according to ethnic group, class, and working status. It may vary from region to region, and from country to country, and between communities experiencing differing levels of impact of Western influence. A universal characteristic is the greater sexual liberty of men than of women. There are more women than men living from sex work, more women who have been raped, and more women exposed to violence. This sexual inequality can be found in other sectors such as commercial and social activities, the right to land ownership, leadership, and succession rules.

CHARACTERISTICS OF SEXUALITY IN AFRICA

One of the general characteristics of sexuality in Africa is the fact that sexual relations exist without consideration of age categories and that sexual partners are not necessarily from the same age group. In Africa, the family system and the marriage system favor a social interaction of older men with younger and numerous women. Polygyny is one of the principal characteristics of certain regions of Africa. In western Africa, 30 to 40 percent of unions are monogamous. In 1989 31 percent of women in Uganda lived in polygynous families. This system is possible only with a large age difference between woman and man. A man can be 8 to 12 years older than the first wife and more than 15 years older than the second wife. The links between man and woman are feeble, although the woman forms an emotional and economic unity with her children. In the 1960s sometimes half of Ashanti women in Ghana had a household beside the house of their husband. Numerous women living in polygynous households express an ambivalent feeling about living in the same home with their husband. The stability of marriage is not high, and women have no difficulties finding another spouse.

A further characteristic of sexuality in Africa is that men have more sexual partners than women. The reasons for extraconjugal relations are the following: economic factors, a lack of sexual satisfaction, and revenge after sexual liberties taken by the spouse. Numerous Africans, including women, think that men need several sexual partners. Long-term sexual abstinence after childbirth is one of the explaining factors. But there is an ongoing change in sexuality in Africa caused by the spread of recent ideas about sexual behavior brought in with economic and educational development. These changes include a restriction on the period of breastfeeding, a lower age at first sexual intercourse, and the acceptance of sexual relations among women entering menopause.

Men who are polygynous have fewer extraconjugal relationships than monogamous men. Married men have more extra-conjugal relationships than married women. A study in Kinshasa, Democratic Republic of the Congo, revealed that 25 percent of married men had one or more extraconjugal partners, in contrast to 1 percent of their wives. The description of these women depends on the culture of the observer: prostitutes, sex workers, barmaids, and women with multiple partners. These networks seem to be responsible for the rapid spread of HIV/AIDS. The number of sexual relations inside the larger family has diminished, and commercial sexual relations have increased, so that the risk of passing sexually transmitted diseases is high.

In fact, the custom of extraconjugal relations *inside* the family was widespread, but declined as a result of the influence of missions and colonization that considered this practice incestuous. The Mongo in what is now the Democratic Republic of the Congo, the Masai in what are now Kenya and Tanzania, the Tswana in what is now Botswana, and other groups knew this practice. The Kikuyu of Kenya even had access to all women of the same male age cohort, who were initiated at the same moment. In other countries, such as Rwanda, Burundi, and Uganda, sons had sexual rights with the wives of their brothers and with the sisters of their wives. In fact, late marriage ages have begun to be a problem in societies where this practice of extraconjugal relations inside the family has been abolished.

A further characteristic of sexuality in Africa is the more or less invisibility of homosexuality. The subject is taboo and rather under-researched. In Eastern Africa, homosexuality is more frequent than in other parts of Africa south of the Sahara. In various regions, Muslims tolerate homosexuality before marriage, but homosexuality rarely forms the basis for an exclusive relationship for the entire life-period. It may be practiced during rituals or in certain circumstances (in prisons, armies, and boarding schools). Because of the fact that homosexuality is taboo, men who wish to live their homosexual identity often marry women and pursue discreetly their sexual relationships with men.

Another important issue is the fact that many women do not have control over their own sexuality with a partner who has risky relations. In Uganda and Zimbabwe, women often have no or little possibility of negotiating their sexual strategies. Women may risk repudiation if they refuse sexual relations or ask for protected intercourse. Early education and wider community norms require that women accept the sexual desires of men. The discussion of sexual topics by the couple is difficult, and negotiating rather impossible. In East Africa, women have less control over their sexuality than in West Africa, where the status of many women is higher. Yoruba women, for instance, may be economically independent and may return to their own family with their own children in case of divorce. Often, Yoruba women are traders or work other jobs. Despite this greater financial liberty, however, women in West Africa can only seldom refuse sexual relations (e.g., for one night), because refusal for longer periods may result in divorce. In East Africa, divorce very often means that women return to their families without taking their children. Yet women often choose to stay in towns, where they begin to make a living as sex workers, because this is one of their only survival strategies. In East Africa, an extraconjugal relationship is a reason for divorce. Therefore, most women are not attracted to preconjugal or extraconjugal sexual relations. This also means that there is much more prostitution in this region than in West Africa. In one in ten cases these involve sexual relations with women working in bars, hotels, and brothels.

In numerous African countries, if the man suffers from a sexually transmitted disease (STD), he accuses his wife. These diseases are known as "the disease of the woman". Often, women do not know that their husbands have acquired HIV/AIDS or another STD, and most of them ignore the danger that they have also been infected. In the Democratic Republic of Congo, neither elite women nor the wives of workers can refuse sexual relations with their husband on the grounds that he risks transmitting an STD, nor can they ask for the use of condoms. The very act of mentioning condoms would mean accusing the husband of having been unfaithful and admitting that his wife has some control over his extraconjugal contacts.

MARRIAGE SYSTEMS IN AFRICA

The principal elements of African marriage systems have largely been presented in ethnographic research during the second half of the twentieth century. In some rural and interior regions, marriage institutions can still be found that have changed little since 1900. Yet in most parts of the continent, urbanization, migration, modern education, and Christianity have influenced traditional African marriage practices. The most important factor has been European colonial influence since the middle and the end of the nineteenth century.

Traditional African Marriage

The first aspect of traditional African marriage is that marriage cannot be separated from the family institution. Marriage aims to raise the power, status, and number of family members. Marriage is thus a link between two families and not between two individuals. The importance of this institution is expressed via the dowry given by the family or the group—most often a bride price given by the groom's family, to that of the bride. The Ashanti, living in what is now the state of Ghana, practiced a rather low level of compensation and held a symbolic ceremony. By contrast, among the Nuer of the Sudan, the marriage aspirant had to give 40 head of cattle. The Nuer also practiced important ceremonies accompanying the wedding.

The importance of marriage as a means of acquiring rights in respect to the descendants of a woman is revealed by the fact that the final payments had often to be given after the woman had proven her reproductive capacity. In some societies, parts of, or the total, bride price had to be returned if the woman could not have children. Furthermore, the institution of sorority meant that if a wife died, her sister was expected to replace her in order to give birth to further children. The rights of the family were thus more important than the links between the couple.

African marriages are long-term processes. In societies where children are already engaged, several years may separate the ceremony and the actual life of the couple as husband and wife. During the whole period, mutual exchanges are practiced in order to express and solidify the link between both families. Subsistence economic systems favored an early economic independence and an early marriage that had to contribute to the group's wealth. Customs related to the residence patterns of husband and wife were various: residences could be in the husband's house, in the wife's house, in the homes of the husband's family or the wife's family, or in a new location, which was the most popular form of residence.

Contemporary Forms of Marriage or Unions

As Africa enters the twenty-first century, the institution of marriage is one that has experienced huge transformations. Even if marriage is still realized by customary rites, the form and the goal of these rituals have been widely modified. The sum of money paid and the sort of goods asked for have increased in value so that they now represent a serious handicap for those who intend to marry. In the olden days, in some societies, some cowrie shells were exchanged and a bottle of local gin was offered; today, in some cases, huge amounts of money, imported drinks, and costly presents are obligatory. The informal ceremony with friends and family, where people sang and danced, has been replaced in urban regions by public ceremonies, paid musicians, and official receptions.

A. F. Aryee[11] gives the example of a Peul (Fulani) marriage: the first payment had to be provided before the engagement, a ceremony that included the offering of two calves or two goats. At the marriage ceremony, presents in cash had to be given to the family of the fiancée, along with three heifers. It is thus understandable that the large family clan played an important role. In urban areas, many families and couples are obliged to take out a loan in order to pay for their marriage. In Nigeria, financial compensation may vary from 2,000 nairas for a young girl with a primary school education to 10,000 nairas for a university graduate.

It is astonishing how many different marriage forms exist in African societies. One can find customary forms of marriages beside civil or religious marriages: free agreeable unions (sometimes described as "legal cohabitation" or "mutual visits"), a church ceremony, or the combination of two or more ceremonies. The religious ceremony may take place in church, or, among Muslims, before the qadi or the djemaa.

In Liberia, a study showed that 38.3 percent of women able to bear children lived with partners in informal unions. In some countries, such as Nigeria (7.4 percent), Botswana (10.8 percent), and Uganda (13.5 percent), the rates were much lower.[12] Ceremonies may take place at different moments of the union; family pressures and an improvement of the financial possibilities of the couple can be followed by Western-style ceremonies at the church or the town hall. A church ceremony may intervene after several years of marriage in order to recognize the union. A study in the Ivory Coast found that unions in which the couple has celebrated the ceremony and has begun to live together involved 46.3 percent of women who were married or had been married, but nine other types of successive processes could be identified over various time periods. This study shows that religion, ethnic origin, and education were factors that contributed to the sorts of unions described by the interviewees.[13]

New Forms of Marriage

One of the essential characteristics of African marriages is the high frequency of casual unions, which one can also find on other continents. Even if a part of these unions is intended to be a transitional step before the official marriage, numerous couples do not plan further marriage rituals. One reason is the high cost of the marriage ceremony. Often, young men have difficulties acquiring this sum if their family or their parents cannot help them because of unemployment or insecure jobs. A poor man will lose interest or give up the union if he cannot secure the necessary means for an official marriage.

These informal unions without legal or customary support do not give wives and children the security that a formal marriage can provide. If the family or the parents refuse to recognize the legal character of these unions, the consequences for many people may be highly significant, especially in regard to questions related to heritage and family property rights. In many African regions, one can find spouses who cannot bury their wives or who see their children taken off by the wife's family because marriage rituals had not been accomplished.

The Ijaw of Nigeria, for example, according to a 1953 report, gave a man his biological children only if he had paid the total bride price. If he had paid half, he obtained the right to his sons, but his daughters became members of the family of his wife, and if he had paid only in palm wine, all the children belonged to the family of his wife.[14]

Even if a marriage ceremony was celebrated, the family could still express its dissatisfaction. At the death of one of the spouses the family could try to receive all of his or her belongings that had been accumulated during the marriage. These conflicts have been rather common because of the high frequency of interethnic marriages going into the twenty-first century. The rights of wives and children have not been guaranteed by many African legal systems, so unofficial unions have led to an increase in single-parent households or households headed by women (as well as an increase in street children). Studies in the 1990s showed that 36 percent of married women south of the Sahara had experienced divorce, separation, or widowhood. There were considerable regional and national variations in this regard: in Mali 7 percent, but in Ghana 61 percent, of women had faced this life experience.[15]

The ease of engaging in, and breaking, unions has contributed to the increase in casual marriages. In urban areas, the influence of parents and the family is rather insignificant. Moreover, disputes among generations have been a byproduct of modern formal education: illiterate or poorly educated parents have found it difficult to counsel youth, who have begun to ignore their guidance. The high amount of the dowry or bride price in West, East, and Southern Africa has been found to be at the origin of these widespread casual relationships. It may be that a change in these financial obligations might encourage more official marriages. In different West African countries (Mali, Senegal, Burkina Faso, and Niger) efforts have been made to limit the dowry or bride price and to register marriages in front of a state administrator. This has meant a lower divorce rate, for example, in Mali. In other countries, attempts to place legal limitations on the dowry or bride price have not worked as hoped for; for example, in Nigeria the legal limit on the amount of the bride price was considered to be too low by young men themselves, who refused to evoke the hostility of their future family-in-law by paying such a small amount.[16] In some African regions, churches try to regulate marriage ceremonies in order to avoid the consumption of alcohol and other unnecessary expenditures. All of these contemporary measures show that there are possible means for strengthening the marriage institution in Africa.

Polygyny in African Tradition

The widespread practice of polygyny is a particularity of current African marriage. Polygyny has been practiced in different historical ages and in different geographic regions of the world.[17] Polygyny is linked to the patriarchal system that is, with few exceptions, fundamental to African social organization. Wives and children still contribute to the wealth of a man and his clan. Those men who could afford to do so thus had to marry several women. In the traditional African community, the chief, the eldest, the rich, and the warrior married more women than other community members.

In the past, wars and conflicts between ethnic groups contributed to the death of men and the enslavement of women. The result was an excess of young women in most groups, which facilitated the practice of polygyny. Furthermore, the high age differences between spouses created a reserve of nubile women. The long period of sexual abstinence after the birth of a child and the ritual interdiction of sexual relations during menstruation contributed to the spread of polygyny. Moreover, the spread of Islam in Africa has added a religious support to the institution.

Polygyny in Africa Today

Even if the hypothesis is widespread today that polygyny is not functional in a modern society, polygynous practices have survived across the entire continent. Recent studies have shown that the rate of women age 15 to 49 living in polygynous unions lies between 7.5 percent in Lesotho and 46.6 percent in Senegal.[18] In West Africa, polygyny is prevalent (Benin 36.5 percent, Cameroon 37.2 percent, Ivory Coast 38.5 percent, and Ghana 30.8 percent). In East, South, and Central Africa, polygyny is limited, with rates of about 20 to 30 percent (and in Kenya 27.1 percent). Studies have shown that education is a factor that reduces the probability of contracting a polygynous marriage. For instance, in Cameroon, 44.8 percent of women with no formal education, as opposed to 18.8 percent of women with seven or more school years, live in polygynous unions (in Benin the rates are 38.7 percent vs. 24 percent; and in Kenya 34 percent vs. 22 percent).[19]

Marriage Age

Early marriage was favored in traditional African society. Physical maturity, symbolized by puberty rituals, was considered the time to think about marriage. Friends, parents, and age mates helped construct the house necessary for life as a young couple. In societies that honored a family with numerous children, an early marriage enabled the lengthening of the period of fecundity. Also, societies that had strict rules regarding sexuality and pregnancy before marriage considered early marriage a guarantee against undesirable sexual behavior. In most societies, young men married later than young women. The reason for this fact was the beginning of menstruation, which marked the transition from girl to woman and the puberty rites that announced to the community that the young woman was now able to marry. The transition age for boys (to the status of young men) was not easy to define and depended on the customs of the different ethnic groups. Men had to prove not only that they were physically mature but that they were ready to take over responsibility for their family. These factors explain the age differences between men and women at the time of marriage. Another factor was the number of girls or boys from the same family that married: the marriage of the sixth boy or the fourth girl could be a financial problem in a family when family resources had already been used for the other children.

Current Marriage Age

The transformation of African societies over the last half of the twentieth century has meant an increased marriage age, not only for girls having spent some years in school but also for men who have difficulties in affording the bride price. Economic changes have meant that the family has demanded more and more from the individual seeking to marry their child. Often the young man has to look for (and pay for) a convenient dwelling and household furnishings, and he also has to pay the bride price and sustain the family financially. And, as the couple is now required to assume its own financial responsibilities, the marriage age has become even higher.

For men, the marriage age is normally high. The difference between the spouses varies from three to eleven years, with still larger differences in West Africa. The higher marriage age for both sexes in Southern Africa contrasts with an earlier marriage age in West Africa and Central Africa, in particular for women. In East Africa the marriage age for women and men is at an intermediate level. Education is one of the most important factors in opting for a higher marriage age; after seven or more years spent in school, girls marry five to seven years later than girls who do not go to school.

In African societies marriage is a more or less universal phenomenon. Beside exceptions for slaves or priests, unmarried adults are rare. Social and religious sanctions were imposed upon people who did not marry. Studies show that by the age of 50, during the period 1975–1985, 100 percent of the interviewees were married in most of the African countries, with some exceptions in South Africa, Mauritania, Botswana, and Madagascar.[20] Of course, this statistic reflects the situation before the full impact of the AIDS epidemic.

There are some indications that, historically, sexual relations before or outside marriage were penalized. Recent changes in sexual behavior are thus the result of urbanization, anonymous social relations, and the economic factors that facilitate sexual liberty in a modern environment. The higher marriage age contributes to a disparity between physical maturity and the beginning of marriage, so youths are inclined to engage in premarital sexual activity. Pregnancies of young unmarried women constitute a major social problem, and abortion and the abandonment of babies are phenomena that follow. AIDS, and the associated deaths of young mothers and their children, are thus serious challenges to political elites in African countries.

The weakening of the institution of marriage has had a fundamental influence on the stability of families in African societies. The ability that people now have to marry and divorce without legal or social sanctions undermines the status of the African family. Because of this scenario, the father progressively disappears as the person responsible for the health and upbringing of the children, while the responsibility of the mother increases. Children are those most affected by this crisis.

REGIONAL SUBSECTIONS

West Africa

Ghana

In Ghana the power structure among the sexes favors men, who make the principal decisions within the household, in particular in relation to sexuality and reproduction. Even if women may obtain economic independence as market traders, they are most often still responsible at home for cooking, washing, and child care. Female-headed households can be found in increasing numbers in other African countries, according to a report by Augustine Ankomah.[21] Children are considered essential for a successful life, and childlessness is considered a tragedy. Ankomah reports that in Ghana "the ideal family size was found to be 6.1 children in 1979/80, but had dropped to 5.3 by 1988."[22] Parents do not necessarily have sex preferences for their children, but may prefer girls or boys depending on the matrilineal or patrilineal descent of the ethnic group. In Ghana, street children are an increasing social problem. These children originate from poor families or young mothers.

The socialization process is modeled along distinct sex roles, so every Ghanaian knows that it is the woman who takes care of the household tasks (even if she is educated beyond the primary level). Sexual topics can be found in conversation and gossip, but a serious debate about sexuality does not take place. Music, dances, and jokes evoke sexuality, but public exhibition of emotions by couples is unusual.

More than ninety ethnic groups can be found in the country, so there is much diversity in customs regarding sexual norms. The main ethnic group is the Akan, who comprise more than 44 percent of the total population of Ghana. The Akan are a matrilineal group: the other major ethnic groups are patrilineal. As Ankomah writes: In matrilineal societies, descent is traced through the mother's line and a person is therefore legally identified with his or her matrikin. A person inherits from the mother's line and thus children hold no claim whatsoever to their father's estate. As in many matrilineal groups, conjugal ties are weak and considered less important than blood ties. Conversely, in patrilineal societies, descent is traced from the father's line and children inherit from their fathers. While all the matrilineal Akan groups generally share similar sexual values and norms, within the patrilineal societies there are striking variations in premarital, marital, and extramarital sexual ethos.[23]

Sources of Sexual Knowledge. In most Ghanaian societies initiation and puberty rites instructed girls and boys in different aspects of sexual life, but these traditional channels of education have been undermined by rapid social change since the 1960s. The consequence has been a very limited access at home and in schools to education on sexual topics. Today, girls and boys rely on friends, parents, and teachers for their first information on sexuality. Magazines and books may serve as other sources of information in urban centers.

Heterosexual Behaviors. Sex games between children playing the roles of mother and father can be found in Ghana, but mutual examination of genitals may be punished. Boys and girls play together until puberty. The transition from infancy to adulthood was a social event in traditional Ghanaian societies, yet adolescence, as a distinct stage of life, did not exist. After the first menstruation, special initiation rites for girls were often performed, while boys' initiation ceremonies were not frequent.

At the end of the female initiation ceremony the girl was beautifully dressed, and she thanked everybody in her locality. She was then able to marry: if she had a "fiancé," he could take her as a wife after the marriage rites. If there was no promised husband, bachelors had a chance to have a look at her. During the initiation period, older women instructed the individual girl (and not a group of girls, as was practiced in East Africa) on menstrual taboos, pregnancy, personal hygiene, and sexual intercourse.

Akan groups in southern Ghana do not practice female circumcision. In northern Ghana and among migrant groups in the south originating from the north, however, this practice is quite common, and local people claim that female circumcision is "a precondition for marriage and a test of virginity."[24] There are reports of differences in male circumcision among the various ethnic groups in Ghana. Akan groups did not embrace it, but the Ga and Krobo practiced this ritual. Today, a great number of boys are circumcised some time after birth, while only few adults undergo this ritual.

Adult Sexuality. The acceptance of premarital sexual relationships differs according to ethnicity. In southern Ghana, girls were often married after their initiation ceremony and thus entered their conjugal life as virgins. Premarital sexuality was allowed among northern groups, such as the Kokomba, where pregnancy before marriage was frequent. Premarital sexual relations have become more widespread in the south as a consequence of modern urban life, and postpubertal and premarital chastity has changed substantially. According to Ankomah, the median age at first sexual intercourse for women in the late 1990s was 15 to 18 years.[25] The norm is "premarital serial monogamy with frequent partner switching."[26] Premarital sexual relationships of single women are often considered by these young women as means of obtaining material recompense, so that most Western researchers label this behavior as "prostitution." In fact, male–female relationships in Ghana are always sexual in nature, even if public displays of love are not the rule.

To live a life as a single man or woman is unimaginable in Ghana. Few single women decide to choose this lifestyle after a previous marriage and after having children (through the bearing of which they have demonstrated their fecundity). Moreover, single men are looked at with suspicion and regarded as irresponsible in the absence of a wife and children.

Marriage and Family. One of the most important social institutions in Ghana is marriage. Most women aged 15 to 19 live in marital unions. Marriage is a union between two families and not between individuals as in the Western tradition. Bride price in patrilineal groups may be higher than in matrilineal ethnic groups. One can find a variety of legal marriages: customary marriages, marriages "under the Ordinance" (Western-style monogamous marriages subject to divorce),[27] and Muslim marriages. According to Ankomah, "eight out of every ten marriages are under customary law, under which a man can marry many wives (polygyny)."[28] A small number of couples contract marriages under the Ordinance, which is a British colonial legacy. Often, marriage in church or in the mosque may follow customary marriage.

In Ghanaian ethnic groups, polygyny, with husbands having two or more wives, is accepted. It can be found in urban and rural areas, and among literate and nonliterate couples. Long periods of sexual abstinence after the birth of children (between three and thirty months) are a reason invoked for this institution. The pregnant woman often gives birth to her child among her kinsfolk, and she returns to her husband only when the baby is able to walk. Figures from 1960, 1980, and 1988 show that about 30 percent of all married men have more than one wife. But there is a difference according to age: younger women are more seldom in polygynous unions than older women.

Divorce is common and easily obtained under customary law. Grounds may include bad conduct, failure to provide monetary subsistence, and laziness, among other complaints. Women's adultery is a reason for divorce, but a woman cannot divorce because of her husband's adultery—the husband has to pacify her with money or gifts. The desire to divorce is discussed at an early stage by family arbitrators, and attempts are made to reunite the couple. Remarriages are high because of the bad reputation of single women.

As in other parts of Africa, a man, his wife or wives, and children do not form a family. The Western concept of the nuclear family can be found among some elite families, but it is the extended family that is matrilineally or patrilineally linked together that forms the basis of social organizations.

Homosexuality and Prostitution. Same-sex activities are seldom observed in Ghanaian society. They may exist as premarital forms of sexuality among young boys and girls, but rarely as a means of adult sexuality.

According to Ankomah, one has to distinguish in Ghana between sexual exchange and prostitution. Sexual exchange linked to material recompense rewards the relationship but not the sexual act. Prostitution paid for with money is illegal in Ghana, and women who practice it may have problems with the authorities. There are two groups of such women:

prostitutes who work in their homes and prostitutes who work in hotels. The former are often poorly educated elder women who have financial problems. The latter group is better educated, younger, and serve other social categories of clients.

Contraception, Sexually Transmitted Diseases, and HIV/AIDS. Ghanaian women in the 1990s could expect to have 6.4 children on average during their lives, and according to the census of 2000, 4.5 children. Even if knowledge about contraception is widespread, few women use any method of contraception. The pill and abstinence after birth are the most popular contraceptive methods. With the increase in HIV/AIDS, community and health institutions have intensified condom campaigns. There is a consensus among experts that sexually transmitted diseases are quite common in Ghana, and young people under 20 are more at risk than other age groups. In the 1980s the first cases of AIDS were reported in Ghana. In 1995 there were more than 10,000 reported cases. In 2002, 320,000 adults and children lived with HIV/AIDS. The adult rate was 2.3 percent.[29] Most people are infected through heterosexual contact. It is clear that the accepted practice of sexual exchange in order to obtain material gain favors HIV transmission. The disease is mainly reported in urban areas and can be found among women and men at the same rate.

Nigeria

Nigerian women have all the human rights stipulated in the constitution and thus they should not be discriminated against on the basis of sex. Yet there are some specific issues of sex discrimination, for instance, in the areas of inheritance rights and income taxes. There is a strong disapproval of the open discussion of sex, even if sexuality is publicly celebrated in festivities such as dance dramas.

Sources of Sexual Knowledge. There has been little or no teaching about sexuality in Nigeria. Youth have no access to sexual information and services, even though some NGOs try to give sexual education to marginalized groups. Most often children learn about sexuality from peers through storytelling. Discussing sexual topics is avoided because it is believed that it will result in promiscuity. Among the (Muslim) Hausa, parents and Qur'anic schoolteachers provide sexual education. "The curriculum for children and adults of both sexes includes lessons on the onset of puberty, menstruation . . . and ritual purifications after menstruation, sexual intercourse, and childbirth."[30] Boys are instructed on voice changes in puberty and purification baths after sexual intercourse. Both sexes are instructed on the virtue of abstinence for unmarried people. In 2002, the Catholic Church in Nigeria developed guidelines on sex education for engaged and married couples, adults, and youth. Increasingly, movies, books, and magazines give informal information on sexual matters.

Heterosexual Behaviors. In some regions of Nigeria, more than 80 percent of girls are married before age 14 and 98 percent before age 20.[31] However, social change and economic difficulties have led some young Hausa to adopt the nuclear-type family. 27 percent of married women are in a polygynous union.[32] Forced marriage is now waning or is limited to girls who do not attend school.

Adult Sexuality. Premarital chastity is highly valued in some ethnic groups and still is today. Twenty-five percent of urban females and 33 percent of rural females are virgins at marriage.[33]

Marriage and Family. Some ethnic groups consider sexual intercourse as appropriate only for procreation. Female sexual satisfaction is not considered important. The birth of male children is often preferred because they continue the family name. Women often avoid sexual relations while breastfeeding a baby. When a wife is childless, her husband can divorce. In most parts of Nigeria, customs recognize the husband's claim for damages or divorce after adultery. In the last two decades of the twentieth century, an increase in cohabitation was observed, but legal rules are still absent. Adultery is still permitted for the man, but not for his wife. In Muslim northern Nigeria, the Islamic law (Sharia), with its penalty of death by stoning for adultery, has been adopted, but has met with international protest.

Homosexuality and Prostitution. Homosexuality is frowned on, absent from, or forbidden in the different cultures of Nigeria. Child prostitution exists in Nigeria, even if it is illegal. It is not unknown for physically mature young girls to take "sugar daddies," who, in return for sexual intercourse, assist the girls by paying their school fees.

Contraception, Sexually Transmitted Diseases, and HIV/AIDS. Islamic custom recommends breastfeeding of babies for two years after birth or the use of condoms. Yet family planning needs the agreement of both spouses, who are free to use any suitable method. STDs are stigmatized, but clinics are underutilized, so data are limited. Nigeria has a national seroprevalence rate of 4.5 percent. Heterosexual intercourse spreads the disease in most of the cases. To date, government efforts have been rather limited: NGOs are involved in information campaigns and home-based care for sick people, yet behavioral changes are difficult to achieve and condom use is low. The estimated number of adults aged 15–49 living with HIV/AIDS is 3,200,000 (5.8 percent).[34]

Central African Region

Cameroon

The ethnic groups known as the Beti and the Bamiléké live in Cameroon and the Central African Republic; sexual life within these groups has been studied.[35]

Sources of Sexual Knowledge. Like other African groups, the Beti and Bamiléké practice initiation rituals for men and women.

Heterosexual Behaviors. Traditionally, when a Beti man wanted to marry, he undertook a definite courtship procedure. The first step was that the young man sent a friend or a parent to the young woman to inform her that he wanted to visit her. These first visits permitted the man to be presented to the family members of the young woman and to inform them about his own family. The following visits permitted the young couple to talk on topics of interest and provided an opportunity for the young woman to prepare meals whose quality expressed her feelings for the young man. The next step was to bring presents to the mother of the young woman in order to encourage a favorable attitude regarding his endeavors. The following step was that the young man could spend the night with the men of the girl's family before her mother permitted him to pass the night with her daughter and thus to begin their sexual relationship. After some nights, the young man had to propose marriage so that the two families could discuss the possible union and prepare the marriage ceremonial. If he did not discuss this topic, he would be denied any further access to the young woman.

Female premarital virginity is still highly valued in both groups.[36] The reasons are STDs, undesired pregnancy, and the impact of education and religion. By contrast, according to the common opinion of men and women, young men should have sexual intercourse before marriage.

Adult Sexuality. As in other African regions, sexuality is an ambivalent reality, valued for procreation in its beneficial aspects, but considered dangerous if practiced with bad intentions (it is thought to be able to disrupt the cosmic order). Sexual relations were forbidden for both sexes before activities requiring much physical energy or demanding spiritual concentration or manual dexterity. During activities linked to the preparation for, and conduct of, hunting, men had to avoid sexual activities in order to become more skillful and vigorous. Beti women knew the same interdiction on sexual relations before and during pottery making activities, since it was feared that the sexual act would diminish their capacity for concentration.

Adulterous relations were severely sanctioned. The Beti consider women and men who are known for their illicit sexual relations as social plagues, and if the group was (and is) faced with drought, poor harvests, or sterile women, these people are considered to be responsible. Separation, repudiation, an end of sexual relations, and the implementation of financial procedures are all measures that can be imposed to punish this behavior.

The preliminaries of the sexual act are extremely limited in African societies. The Beti do not favor kissing or stroking the body. This difference between African and Western societies lies in the fact that the secondary sexual organs of both sexes are not eroticized: lips, skin, and breast do not have the sexual value that they have in other civilizations.

The normal position of both partners seems to be facing each other lying on their sides, which is believed to favor the fertilization of the woman and to express an equal status of man and woman in the act of love.[37]This position seems to be rather common among African groups, and ethnologists such as Griaule, Dieterlin, and Lebeuf have also made note of it.

Nonmarital relationships are frequent among the Beti, with 20.7 percent of the women and 18.4 percent of the men questioned reporting this scenario, and rather seldom for the Bamiléké (1.4 percent for men and 3.5 percent for women).[38] Sexual relations with partners other than the regular partner have been more frequent among the Beti (39.4 percent) than among the Bamiléké (22.3 percent), but 89.1 percent of the Beti women and 77.1 percent of the Bamiléké women do not have this sort of sexual relationship, compared to 64.6 percent of the Beti men and 42.3 percent of the Bamiléké men.[39] Occasional sexual relations (among the Beti 30.1 percent and the Bamiléké 10.6 percent) have been more frequent for men (44.9 percent) than for women (11.6 percent).[40]

Marriage and Family. Traditionally the primary goal, when a man was looking for a woman, was to find a wife, a mother, and a child-feeding woman. Fertility was (and is) the most important aspect of marriage. A man who is looking for a woman tries to find out whether the couple can harmonize physically and affectively and whether the woman's parents will accept him. Polygynous unions are more frequent among the Bamiléké (28.1 percent) than among the Beti (13.6 percent).[41]

Homosexuality and Prostitution. The Beti did not know homosexuality and prostitution in their traditional society. Currently, sexual relations in exchange for money or gifts are seldom obtained by Bamiléké men (8.3 percent) and rather more important for Beti men (19.6 percent).[42]

Contraception, Sexually Transmitted Diseases, and HIV/AIDS. In the Beti group, the use of condoms is rather limited—20.5 percent, against 34.1 percent for the Bamiléké.[43] In Cameroon, at the end of 2003, 560,000 adults and children lived with HIV/AIDS. The adult rate was 6.9 percent.[44]

Gabon

The population of Gabon is formed of more than fifty ethnic groups. Family life is characterized by domestic units of five people or more, linked in rural areas to a larger group living in the same district.

Sources of Sexual Knowledge. Peer groups often give insufficient sexual information to young women. The topic is also addressed in schools, but often only after the first act of sexual intercourse has taken place. This event has taken place by 15 years of age among a quarter of the young women and half of the young men. Social class is also a variable in this case: young people of higher social class tend to have their first sexual intercourse later than those of lower social classes. The ethnic groups of Gabon do not require virginity until marriage. Premarital sexuality is the norm for both genders before the acceptance of a formal union, and this means high rates of undesired pregnancies, as parents do not discuss the topic of contraception with girls.

Heterosexual Behaviors. In a recent study, a high proportion of women (76 percent) and men (65 percent) declared that they were in love with their first sexual partner.[45] Yet the number of different partners during a lifetime is high: half of the women declare more than three partners and half of the men declare ten partners. Men are proud of their numerous sexual partners, a custom that is rather disapproved for women.

Adult Sexuality. The forms of unions have experienced large transformations in a society characterized by severe economic problems. Early sexual relations and multiple partnership are widespread phenomena. Women head 25 percent of households.[46] Often they are single, and only 39 percent of them form stable unions.[47] The factor of social class is linked to the choice of unions. Marriage is more frequent in higher social classes, and casual relationships are more frequent among the middle and lower classes. The number of men taking multiple female partners is high (50 percent) as older men sponsor young women,[48] and extramarital relations are socially tolerated.

Marriage and Family. In Gabon, all ethnic groups have adopted patrilocal residence, which means that the young bride has to leave her parents' village to go to that of her husband. Women can marry at age 15, men at age 18 with their parents' consent and both partners' mutual consent. A 1963 law has forbidden bride price, but one can still find this practice. Median prices amount to €400 to €500, depending on the ethnic group and the woman's level of instruction. Polygynous unions are accepted and can be chosen as a marriage form. Women who commit adultery can be punished with imprisonment that may last from one month up to two years, but condemnations have been seldom. Men can be punished only if they have had an extramarital relationship at the residence of the couple. Customary marriage is frequent (68 percent of women aged 15 to 49 and 67 percent of men aged 15 to 59); about 30 percent of men and women legalize their marriage, and 3 to 4 percent undergo a religious marriage.[49] Civil servants are often legally married because of the social advantages linked to their function. Thirty-three percent of women live in polygynous unions, and 14 percent of men have married more than two women.[50] Separations have been more frequent than divorces based on legally recognized unions, and the primary reasons have been adulterous relations or bad treatment. Violence against women has been widespread, with one woman out of five being forced into intercourse at some moment of her life.[51]

Homosexuality and Prostitution. Homosexuality is a taboo in Gabon and tolerated only if the partners do not display it in public, but, contrary to other African countries, homosexuality is not penalized. The incidence of prostitution is limited, and the phenomenon of street prostitution is especially uncommon.

Contraception, Sexually Transmitted Diseases, and HIV/AIDS. Postpartum abstinence of about 8 months is widespread. The pill and the condom are widely known, even though periodic abstinence is most often used (with mixed results because of lack of information). There is a high rate of infecundity linked to STDs. Frequent premarital and extraconjugal sexuality contributes to the spread of these diseases. The estimated number of adults (15–49 years) living with HIV/AIDS was 45,000 (8.1 percent) in 2003 for a total population of 1,351,000.[52]

Southern Africa

The Republic of South Africa

Within certain segments of the indigenous African cultures and communities, men are allowed to have more than one wife. After the fertile period of his wife, a man can take a younger woman still able to bear children. In urban areas, polygyny is less common, and men tend to form monogamous couples with women. Urbanized black women have begun to be more demanding in the realm of sexuality as a consequence of the women's liberation movement. Men continue to play the main role in decision making in the family.

Often, black men become migrant workers in towns or in mines, leaving their wives in the countryside, where they work on the farms and raise their children. The husband's visits are often limited to one or two a year, and frequently women are not allowed to visit their husbands in the town.

South Africa is notable for its cultural diversity. The white population is separated into Afrikaners (Boers) and the English-speaking groups. Afrikaners are mainly Calvinists, and sexuality is a topic that has been more or less taboo, yet two thirds of white women can discuss sexual topics with their mothers. Six million out of nearly 18 million black people are affiliated to independent Protestant churches. Among the Asian groups, Muslim and Hindu influences can be found.

Sources of Sexual Knowledge. Among the white groups, sexual education has been the responsibility of parents and family doctors, who often counsel and instruct youth about the use of contraception. There is no sexual education in schools because the church has been opposed to it, but private schools teach the topic.

Within the African community, there is little information on female initiation rituals. In the Pedi tribe, mothers and grandmothers conduct the girl's initiation and inform her on the subjects of menstruation and the duties and tasks of a woman related to men and sexuality.[53]

Heterosexual Behaviors. Forty percent of the country's population is under 15 years. Young children under 6 years attend nursery schools, where boys and girls are mixed. Within these institutions gender differences and gender-role models are reinforced. Children play "doctor-patient games" as an informal means of exploring their identity. In African communities children often sleep in the same room as their parents, which exposes them to parental sexual activities and can sometimes disturb their own sexual identity.

Puberty rites are frequent in African groups. Male circumcision is common and is seen as important for manhood. The age of circumcision varies according to the ethnic group (from 9 to 22 years). Complications from circumcision are frequent because of the lack of formal education among traditional healers. Female circumcision does not exist in South Africa, even though some ethnic groups "encourage the females at puberty to stretch the labia minora."[54]

Within African communities adolescents commonly experience their first sexual intercourse before their twelfth or thirteenth year. By age 13, most of them are sexually active to some extent, with peer pressure encouraging sexual encounters that involve full intercourse. Among white South Africans, 30 percent under age 17 were still virgins, according to one study.[55]

Adult Sexuality. Premarital courtship and dating are prevalent in the white community. The higher socioeconomic classes are less promiscuous because of their knowledge of sexually transmitted diseases. African men who are not members of Christian churches may have more than one wife. Nonreligious white couples may live together, but the churches disapprove of this practice. In African communities such as the Pedi, marriage establishes paternity and gives the right of sexual relations, and extramarital sexual activities are generally accepted.[56] As in other African countries, the practice of homosexuality is rather limited, even if there is a tendency to accept this phenomenon today more than previously.

Marriage and Family. In rural African communities a man who has many children is considered wealthy, so he has an incentive to marry a second woman. In these settings marriage is important in order to establish paternity and to provide the right to sexual intercourse, even though extramarital relations are possible and socially accepted. In the white society cohabitation is common but is not welcomed by the church, particularly by the Calvinist groups.

Homosexuality and Prostitution. Only in recent years has homosexuality begun to be more accepted socially. South Africa stands apart when it comes to the legal status of gays and lesbians in Africa, and in this regard it stands comparison with Western European countries. Not only is homosexuality legal and visible, but there are also national laws that ban discrimination on the basis of sexual orientation. Annual gay pride parades are held (with substantial participation). Yet the incidence of homosexuality in the black population is low compared to a much higher percentage of homosexual white men.

Prostitution was legalized in South Africa only in 1997.

Contraception, Sexually Transmitted Diseases, and HIV/AIDS. Family planning clinics are available and their services are often free, yet African men are often reluctant to allow their partners the use of contraceptive methods. Adolescent pregnancies are frequent because of the early age of first sexual intercourse and the lack of parental control in impoverished communities. Those with greater education try to limit family size and to use the pill.

Unemployment discourages marriage, and because of the high rate of unemployment—estimated at over 25 percent in the black population[57]—sexually transmitted disease is very widespread in South Africa. A survey in a township in Johannesburg estimated "that 20 percent of the population over the age of 15 is treated at least once a year for an STD."[58] Men are treated several times for the same diseases with multiple sexual partners. One scientist has reported "that there are upwards of three million new cases of STDs each year in our population of 26 million."[59] HIV infection is primarily spread through heterosexual relations. According to the UN-OCHA Integrated Regional Information Networks,[60] the adult rate of people living with HIV/AIDS was at 21.5 percent in 2005, meaning 5,370,000 adults. In 2003, South Africa had an estimated 5.3 million cases of HIV infection. Transmission of the virus from mother to child is frequent in South Africa. Homosexuality is a common form of transmission only within the white group. Unfortunately, the use of condoms is still not frequent in the black community because fertility is linked to social status.

Botswana

In Botswana, patriarchy is strongly entrenched, even though the constitution stipulates that there shall be no discrimination on the basis of gender. As in other African countries, anthropologists have documented gender-specific rites of passage preparing young people for appropriate sexual behavior upon marriage. In order to negotiate marriage, the groom's most important male relatives meet representatives of the bride's kinship group.

Sources of Sexual Knowledge. In Botswana, schools offer guidance and counseling on sexual matters: topics such as HIV/AIDS, STDs, teenage pregnancy, and family life are integrated into the curricula. Young people discuss sexuality with friends and members of the extended family, but there is a continuing reluctance to discuss the topic with parents. Youth have positive attitudes about condom use, and they currently engage in safer sexual practices than they did some years ago.

Heterosexual Behaviors. Formerly, puberty rituals included male circumcision and the formal instruction of girls, but this is now left to individual parents and institutions. Teenage pregnancies are considered a problem, and girls are often obliged to leave school when pregnant. For financial reasons, some girls engage in sexual relationships with elder men ("sugar daddies"), even though most sexual activities are between young persons in the same age group.

Adult Sexuality. As one study informs us, "Men are traditionally expected to initiate and control sexual activity."[61] In this realm, women are subordinate and possess little power to negotiate safe sex and the use of condoms.

Marriage and Family. From 1971 to 1991, the proportion of married people declined significantly, from 47.1 percent to 29 percent for men and from 42.9 percent to 27.2 percent for women. A large proportion of current families consist of mother-child formations. Cohabitation is also on the increase. A large percentage of the population has never married (44 percent in 1971 and 54.8 percent in 1991 for men and 37 percent and 49.5 percent, respectively, for women).[62]

Homosexuality and Prostitution. In Botswana, homosexuality is stigmatized and same-sex activity is illegal. However, prosecution for homosexual activity is rare. Mookodi et al. underline an interesting fact: "It is very common for homosexuality to be dismissed as a

'Western' disease and 'un-African.'"[63] Prostitution is outlawed but is nevertheless widely practiced in the country. There are some prostitutes who offer their services in the streets, while others frequent places where alcoholic drinks are sold.

Contraception, Sexually Transmitted Diseases, and HIV/AIDS. The use of contraception is high, with 44 percent of women aged 15 to 49 years taking advantage of it.[64] The pill is very popular. Condom use is low among women over 35 years, however. Postpartum abstinence is still important among rural women but is less favored among urban women. STDs present the third most important cause of attendance at public health facilities.[65] The population of 1.7 million has the highest HIV/AIDS infection rate in the world, both in rural and urban areas.[66] One of the reasons seems to be the fact that "many Botswana engage in short-term relationships and have other sexual partners subsequently."[67] In 2002 35.4 percent of pregnant women aged 15 to 49 years were infected with HIV. Consequently, there are many orphaned children, and many babies are born infected with HIV. The estimated number of adults aged 15–49 living with HIV/AIDS in 2002 was estimated at 300,000 (38.8 percent of the population).[68]

East Africa

Kenya

Gender roles are rather stable in Kenyan ethnic groups. Modern female role patterns have influenced a small group of women who exercise professions in Western medicine, in schools and universities, and in administration. As in other African societies, children are important, and resistance to population control is widespread. Life is organized according to age groups but varies among the different ethnic groups: the most common stages are childhood, initiation to young adulthood, marriage, family life, and life as an elder.

Sexuality is controlled within the kinship system. Nevertheless, in Kenya, "love is recognized and accepted as part of personal relationships. One may choose a marriage partner because of personal attraction, even though arranged marriages continue."[69]

Both sexes experience a rather large scope for sexual freedom. Unmarried boys and girls may sleep together in some groups and at certain moments. Nevertheless, sexual activity is not allowed in these scenarios, and pregnancy before marriage may be a cause of shame for the girl. Love as an acknowledged emotion, as in other African societies, was not a common phenomenon in many ethnic traditions. It was considered a "Western" idea. But "love," understood in the strictly limited sense as the will to choose a person, exists in some Kenyan ethnic groups.

Religion is very important in Kenyan society. Contrary to Roman Catholicism and mainline Protestantism, African independent churches allow polygyny, but they oppose abortion, contraception, sexual education, and equal social status between men and women. Kenyans are influenced both by the local value system and Western influences introduced by colonialism and missionaries. Other factors influencing sexuality are urbanization and the level of education. Unacceptable sexual behavior casts shame upon one's social group but is not necessarily a cause of personal guilt. When the influence of the ethnic groups diminishes, as is sometimes the case in urban areas, behaviors may appear that would be judged as promiscuous according to Western standards. The situation is a complex one. Virginity is highly valued in some groups and considered unimportant in others. Extramarital sex may be acceptable for married women in some groups and regarded as adultery in other groups. These value differences contribute to the cultural shock of living in urban areas, where Western media and ideas also influence behavior.

Sources of Sexual Knowledge. Sexual education was traditionally a part of initiation rituals. Parents do not educate their children in sexual questions: they generally avoid sexual topics. However, grandparents may be confidants of their grandchildren in sexual matters. Small children stay with their mother until the age of 7. Boys may then live with their fathers or older boys. In other groups, boys and girls go into separate houses with older children. These village buildings provide sex education and opportunities for secret sexual activities. Young men who reach puberty may live in private huts, where they can engage in sexual activities even before initiation ceremonies that normally take place every few years.

Heterosexual Behaviors. If, in villages, the boy lives together with other unmarried men, he has the possibility of listening to sexual discussions and to observe older boys with their girlfriends. But sexual intercourse is more or less strictly controlled depending on the ethnic group. Certain practices have changed in boarding schools, where nocturnal visits have, in certain cases, turned into rapes of female students not linked to the young men by clan ties. In urban areas children are kept in the family home.

A mixture of traditional initiation rituals and Western values characterizes Kenyan adolescence. In all groups, initiations included instruction on gender roles, marriage customs, and sexual behavior. Bantu-speaking cultures have practiced male (and usually female) circumcision. The Luo, however, do not practice circumcision. After initiation, young Masai and Samburu could choose a sexual partner among the unmarried girls. An uncircumcised man will have difficulties finding sexual partners. In fact, male circumcision is considered so important that doctors or clinicians will circumcise on their demand youths who live in urban areas.

Nilotic-speaking and some Bantu-speaking groups practice female circumcision. According to one authority, "its purpose is to reduce female sexual pleasure, and make women docile to their husbands and less likely to engage in adultery."[70] Some groups remove the clitoris during initiation; other groups remove the clitoris and the labia minora. Female circumcision was illegal during the colonial period. Then, after independence, it was permitted, and in more recent times it has been outlawed again. Today, there are some indications that the practice is waning.

In some groups sex play is institutionalized, but neither penetration nor touching of the genitals is allowed. Caressing the breasts and frottage are permitted. Youths who live in urban areas are pushed by peers to become sexually active. Age at first sexual intercourse is commonly 13 to 14 years in both rural and urban areas. Often women and men have multiple successive partners. Contraception is rarely used, even if better-educated girls and women of higher social status are trying to encourage this practice.

Adult Sexuality. Premarital sexual activities were traditionally controlled, and the father of a pregnant girl could ask her lover for the bride price. Groups who practiced female circumcision highly valued virginity at marriage. Courtship, whether in rural or in urban areas, included bride wealth. It was considered to represent compensation for the lost economic activities of the daughter. Bride price was formerly paid in cattle but today is usually paid in money. Various group members receive presents during a given time period in a practice that corresponds to a Western engagement. The amount of bride wealth depends on the status of the woman; for example, a single mother obtains a lower bride price than an educated woman. If the marriage fails, the bride price has to be returned. From these practices it becomes obvious that marriage is an alliance of two families and not a pact uniting two individuals based on love. Today, the emergence of huge slum areas around major towns has contributed to an increase in prostitution, STDs, and sexual abuse. Customs in urban areas have changed, often without the presence of corresponding measures of social control by clan or family members.

Marriage and Family. Most groups in Kenya are patrilineal, which implies that males bear responsibility for children in the families of their sisters. There are five recognized forms of marriage in Kenya: Christian, civil, and Hindu marriages, which are monogamous; and Islamic and African customary marriages, which may be polygynous. Yet polygyny is limited by financial considerations: a man must be able to sustain his wives. Indeed, a second wife may be an expression of wealth. Moreover, a polygynous husband has to be sexually active with all his wives in rotation. It may be the case that a man lives apart from his wives for a long time, for example when he is a migrant and lives in another region. Polygynous marriages are thus declining for economic reasons. Less formal arrangements, such as the "city wife" and one mistress supported by several men, have increased in number. These women are not prostitutes, as each man pays a part of the woman's expenses (rent, food, and clothes), and not a fee for sexual relations. In these arrangements, the woman's children are considered fatherless.

Caring for young children, having children who have reached the age of initiation, and becoming grandparents characterize the different stages of a marriage. In terms of sexuality within marriage, female orgasm is acceptable, but is not sought for, as childbearing is such a central aspect of female sexuality. By contrast, male orgasm is considered a sign of potency. Abstinence is observed during pregnancy until some time after birth, and during menstruation.

Approximately a dozen Kenyan ethnic groups allow marriages between two women. In these arrangements, a female husband replaces a man as the legal "father":

> the wife may bear children for her husband, in whose clan line they then belong. In other cases, women marry women to achieve economic independence, and bride price is paid. These autonomous female husbands are accepted as men in male economic roles. This dual-female marriage is economic, and illustrates the separation of sex and gender in African societies. There is no evidence of lesbianism in any of these marriages, and the wife is often provided with a male sexual partner to raise the children. The husband figure is henceforth forbidden to have sex with a man, because this would constitute homosexuality due to her legally male status.[71]

The Kenyan courts upheld these female marriages in 1986.

Homosexuality and Prostitution. Homosexual activities are infrequent, but tolerated as childish behavior. Among abandoned street children from age 7 to late adolescence, situational homosexuality is the norm. Gay Africans hardly exist in Kenya, however. Today, as in the colonial British penal code, homosexuality is illegal as a "crime against nature".[72] Expatriate white homosexuals avoid African partners, yet male prostitutes serving expatriates in international hotels exist.

Female prostitution is widespread; both tourists and Kenyans are clients. Even though prostitution is illegal, the state authorities tolerate it. Often, prostitutes are poorly educated women, single mothers, and poor women. In 1990, "almost 85 percent of Nairobi prostitutes tested positive for HIV."[73]

Contraception, Sexually Transmitted Diseases, and HIV/AIDS. USAID and other NGOs cooperate with government population control programs. Condoms are distributed in hospitals, but distribution in schools is forbidden. Because of cultural resistance to its use, Natural Family Planning has had only limited success. Moreover, methods requiring medical intervention and the pill are too expensive for most Kenyans and thus limited to the elites.

Sexually transmitted diseases, such as syphilis and gonorrhea, are widespread. Urban prostitutes, street youth, and residents of slums in Nairobi are heavily infected. AIDS was first diagnosed in 1984, but the government attempts to minimize the extent of the disease as tourism is one of the main income sources of the country. Urban youths seem to be affected at a rate of 12 percent. In 1994, there were 800,000 HIV-positive Kenyans; an estimated 100,000 had AIDS. In 2003, 1.2 million adults and children lived with HIV/AIDS, and the adult rate was 6.7 percent. Because promiscuity is widespread among the urban population and tourism is flourishing, HIV/AIDS rates are high within the middle class. Condoms are, however, available in clinics.[74]

Tanzania

Gender roles in Tanzania differ according to ethnic group but often reflect the dominance of men over women. The social structure is based on patrilineal and matrilineal systems. Eighty percent of Tanzania's ethnic groups are patrilineal (based on the father-son relationship). Sexual knowledge was traditionally part of initiation in adulthood for men and women. In some societies the circumcision of girls and boys was practiced, but the government of Tanzania has made female circumcision illegal. Data from 1996 indicate that 18 percent of Tanzanian women have undergone circumcision, often when they were between 6 and 20 years old.[75] In contrast to other regions, sexuality has three roles: "reproduction, expansion of kinship, and physical pleasure."[76] Yet sexual pleasure has to be achieved within the context of marriage, since adultery, homosexuality, and rape are considered violations of the social order. There are clear behavioral rules that apply to different ages.

Sources of Sexual Knowledge If knowledge is not conferred through initiation rites, mothers give some sexual instruction to daughters who are preparing for their marriage. Young girls also learn sexual techniques in discussions with each other or gain practical experience through interactions with young men.

Heterosexual Behaviors As a legacy of colonialism, patterns of sexual values and relations have changed. Family structures, as in many parts of Sub-Saharan Africa, have changed in the direction of a more nuclear model. An increasing number of adults remain unmarried or have temporary relationships. Today, it is common for marriage negotiations to involve the partners and no longer just the couple's parents and relatives.

Adult Sexuality The image of the ideal spouse varies according to ethnic group. Desirable characteristics for the man may include circumcision (or the lack thereof, depending on the culture); ability to support the family; loyalty to family, clan and in-laws; work ethic; and sexual virility. The ideal wife may be characterized as sexually attractive, able to bear children, able to care for the family, affectionate toward her husband, children and in-laws, and a good housewife and cook. In the case of women the desirability (or undesirability) of circumcision is also a culturally dependent variable.

Marriage and Family Behavioral norms for married people include courtship, weddings, sexual intercourse, polygamy, pregnancy, and childbirth. Unacceptable norms include adultery, child abuse, prostitution, abortion, and incest. Coitus usually takes place with no foreplay, and the male-above position is standard. "Dry-sex" (in which substances are used to dry up the woman's vaginal secretions) is widespread in various subequatorial African cultures; some men seem to regard it as more pleasurable, but it makes intercourse painful for women and increases the risk of infection. This practice is waning among educated urban youth. The implications of such practices, in the face of HIV/AIDS, are obviously important.

Homosexuality and Prostitution Male homosexuality is illegal in Tanzania. In practice, there are no punishments, as it is difficult to prove that someone is homosexual. Prostitution is mainly practiced in urban areas and it is confined to women. Men who take many sexual partners are allowed to do so if they can afford it. There are no brothels, and most prostitutes operate in their own houses, having a number of clients who visit them. Another form of prostitution involves barmaids, who may invite their clients to their own residences. A third variety involves young women who attract their customers in pubs, tourist hotels, or nightclubs. Their customers are people who have money but do not have time to look around for women (foreigners, tourists, and businessmen). The recent difficult economic situation has meant that poor urban women dominate the prostitution sector. Such relations provide economic and social security even though prostitution is illegal in Tanzania and the police intervene from time to time.

Contraception, Sexually Transmitted Diseases and HIV/AIDS Knowledge of contraception is widespread in Tanzania. The most popular methods are the pill and the condom. Yet only about 30 percent of men and 22.3 percent of women use these methods.[77] STDs are common; there were more than 28,000 cases in 1995 for an estimated population of over 37 million people.[78] In 2002 the estimated number of adults living with HIV/AIDS aged 15–49 was 1.3 million, a rate of 7.8 percent.

CONCLUSION

African gender relations are in transition. Factors that are contributing to this change are wars and internal conflicts, the HIV/AIDS epidemic, increased migration rates, poverty, and difficult economic situations. As wider societal needs change, gender relations also change. Traditionally, reference to the family meant the extended family comprising children, parents, grandparents, and great-grandparents. Yet the weakening of traditional values and behavioral changes are causing transformations in the shape of families. In large parts of Africa there is a decline in traditional systems of support for weaker people, such as children and the elderly. Female-headed households are widespread in rural regions that lose males to urban migration. An increase in street children has resulted in high rates of criminality in different regions. Peers, formal education institutions, and the media play an increasing role as factors of socialization for the youth. As the influence of parental socialization is waning and traditional means of imparting sexual education are disappearing, the rate of premarital and adolescent childbearing is reaching high levels in many African countries. Youth thus are lacking some of the behavioral and survival skills that were traditionally taught by parents.

From the literature reviewed in this chapter, it is clear that there are gaps in the research that has so far been undertaken on a number of topics. The impact of HIV/AIDS on gender relations and families is poorly understood. Divorce, separation, and remarriage are further important processes in discussing family transformations in Africa that need to be given high priority in relation to HIV/AIDS. The nuclearization of the family and the change in sexual behaviors seem to be linked to the spread of HIV/AIDS and needs to be studied. Another research gap concerns intergenerational relations between parents and their children that affect the family structure. African governments and NGOs need to learn more about gender relations (and related issues) so that they are better able to fight the HIV/AIDS epidemic and effectively assist weaker social groups.

RESOURCE GUIDE

PRINT SOURCES

Adeokun, A. Lawrence. "Marital Sexual Relationships and Birth Spacing among Two Yoruba Sub-Groups." *Africa: Journal of the International African Institute* 52.4 (1982): 1–14.

Adepoju, Aderanti, ed. *La famille africaine: Politiques démographiques et développement.* Paris: Karthala, 1999.

Ankomah, Augustine. "Premarital Sexual Behavior in Ghana in the Era of AIDS." *Health Policy and Planning* 7 (1992a): 135–43.

———. "The Sexual Behavior of Young Women in Cape Coast, Ghana: The Pecuniary Considerations Involved and Implications for AIDS." Ph.D. dissertation, Institute of Population Studies, University of Exeter, UK, 1992b.

Arnfred, Signe, ed. *Re-thinking Sexualities in Africa.* Uppsala: The Nordic Africa Institute, 2004.

Boni, Stefano. "Twentieth-Century Transformations in Notions of Gender, Parenthood, and Marriage in Southern Ghana: A Critique of the Hypothesis of 'Retrograde Steps' for Akan Women." *History in Africa* 28 (2001): 15–41.

Bungaro, Monica. "Male Feminist Fiction: Literary Subversions of a Gender-Biased Script." *Matatu* 29–30 (2005): 47–61.

Burman, Sandra, and Eleanor Preston-Whyte, eds. *A Questionable Issue: Illegitimacy in South Africa.* Cape Town: Oxford University Press, 1992.

Cornwall, Andrea. "Spending Power: Love, Money, and the Reconfiguration of Gender Relations in Ado-Odo, Southwestern Nigeria." *American Ethnologist* 29 (2002): 963–980.

Francoeur, Robert T., ed. *International Encyclopedia of Sexuality.* New York, London: Continuum International Publishing Group, 1997.

———, and Raymond Noonan, eds. *The Continuum Complete International Encyclopedia of Sexuality.* New York, London: Continuum International Publisher Group, 2004.

Hetherington, Penelope. "Generational Changes in Marriage Patterns in the Central Province of Kenya, 1930–1990." *Journal of Asian and African Studies* 36 (2001): 157–180.

Jahoda, Gustav. "Love, Marriage and Social Change: Letters to the Advice Column of a West African Newspaper." *Africa* 29 (1959): 177–190.

Jankowiak, William, and Edward Fischer. "A Cross-Cultural Perspective on Romantic Love." *Ethnology* 31 (1992): 149–155.

Molnos, Angela. *Cultural Source Materials for Population Planning in East Africa.* Nairobi: University of Nairobi Press, 1972–1973.

Monnig, H. V. *The Pedi.* Pretoria: L. van Schaik, 1983.

Mouvagha-Sow, Myriam. "Processus matrimoniaux et procréation à Libreville, Gabon." Ph.D. dissertation, University of Paris X, 2002.

Neequaye, Armon. "Prostitution in Accra." Pp. 175–185 in Martin Plant (ed.), *AIDS, Drugs, and Prostitution.* London: Tavistock/Routledge, 1990.

Olivier, L. *Sex and the South African Woman.* Johannesburg: Lowry Publishers, 1987.

Ombolo, Jean-Pierre. *Sexe et Société en Afrique Noire. L'anthropologie sexuelle beti: Essai analytique, critique et comparatif.* Paris: L'Harmattan, 1990.

Preston-Whyte, Eleanor M. "Half-Way There: Anthropology and Intervention-Oriented AIDS research in KwaZulu/Natal, South Africa." In Hans ten Brummelhuis and Gilbert Herdt (eds.), *Culture and Sexual Risk: Anthropological Perspectives on AIDS.* Amsterdam: Gordon and Breach Science Publishers, 1995.

———, and Maria Zondi. "Adolescent Sexuality and Its Implications for Teenage Pregnancy and AIDS." *South Africa's Continuing Medical Education Monthly* 9 (1991): 1389–1394.

Rivière, Claude. *Union et Procréation en Afrique. Rites de la vie chez les Évé du Togo.* Paris: L'Harmattan, 1990.

Rwenge Mburano, Jean Robert. "Les différences ethniques des comportements sexuels au Cameroun: l'exemple des Bamiléké et Beti." *African Population Studies* 19 (2004): 159–190.

Smith, Daniel Jordan. "Romance, Parenthood, and Gender in a Modern African Society." *Ethnology* 40 (2001): 129–151.

Tchak, Sami. *La sexualité féminine en Afrique.* Paris, Montreal: L'Harmattan, 1999.

Van Coeverden, H. A., S. de Groot, and E. E. Greathead. "Adolescent Sexuality and Contraception." *South Africa's Continuing Medical Education Monthly* 9 (1991): 1369–1379.

Van der Vliet, Virginia. "Traditional Husbands, Modern Wives? Constructing Marriages in a South African Township." *African Studies* 50 (1991): 219–241.

Vangroenweghe, Daniel. *SIDA et Sexualité en Afrique.* Bruxelles: Éditions EPO, 2000.

Veit-Wild, Flora, and Dirk Naguschewski, (eds.) "Body, Sexuality, and Gender: Versions and Subversions in African Literatures 1." *Matatu* (2005): 29–30.

WEBSITES

AIDES. Accessed February 26, 2006. http://www.aides.org. French NGO combating AIDS.

CAFS (Center for African Family Studies). Accessed July 16, 2006. http://www.cafs.org.

Feminist Africa. *Sexual Cultures.* 2005. http://www.feministafrica.org/2level.html.

IRIN (Integrated Regional Information Networks). *PlusNews, the HIV/AIDS News Service.* Accessed October 30, 2005. http://www.plusnews.org.

La Plateforme ELSA (Ensemble, Luttons contre le Sida en Afrique). Accessed February 26, 2006. http://www.plateforme-elsa.org/. French NGO combating AIDS in Africa.

UNAIDS (the Joint United Nations Program on HIV/AIDS). Accessed February 26, 2006. http://www.unAIDS.org/en/.

WHO (World Health Organization). *HIV Infections.* Accessed February 26, 2006. http://www.who.int/topics/hiv_infections/en/.

VIDEOS/FILMS

Bal Poussière [Dancing in the Dust] (Ivory Coast, 1988). Directed by Henri Duparc.

Dakan (Destiny) (Guinea, 1997). Directed by Mohamed Camara.

Guelwaar (Senegal, 1991). Directed by Ousmane Sembène.

Karmen Geï (Senegal, 2002). Directed by Joseph Gaye Ramaka.

Quartier Mozart (Cameroon, 1992). Directed by Jean-Pierre Bekolo.

Touki Bouki [The Journey of the Hyena] (Senegal, 1973). Directed by Djibril Diop Mambéty.

Visages de femmes [Faces of Women] (Ivory Coast, 1984). Directed by Désiré Écaré.

Xala [The Curse]. (Senegal, 1974). Directed by Ousmane Sembène.

NOTES

1. IRIN (in Resource Guide, Websites). Accessed April 12, 2006.
2. Jankowiak and Fischer 1992 (in Resource Guide), p. 149.
3. E.g., Jahoda 1959 (in Resource Guide).

4. Smith 2001 (in Resource Guide), p. 132.
5. Ibid., p. 134.
6. Bungaro 2005 (in Resource Guide).
7. Cornwall 2002 (in Resource Guide).
8. Ibid., p. 966.
9. This section and the following section are based on information given in Vangroenweghe 2000 (in Resource Guide), Chapter 4.
10. Adeokun 1982 (in Resource Guide).
11. A. F. Aryee, "L'évolution des modèles matrimoniaux," in Adepoju 1999, pp. 112–113.
12. Ibid., p. 113.
13. Ibid., p. 114.
14. Ibid., p. 115.
15. Ibid., p. 116.
16. Ibid., p. 117.
17. Ibid.
18. Ibid., p. 119.
19. Ibid., p. 118.
20. Ibid., p. 126.
21. Augustine Ankomah, "Ghana," in Francoeur 1997 (in Resource Guide), Vol. 1, pp. 519–546.
22. Ibid., p. 521.
23. Ibid., p. 524.
24. Ibid., p. 527.
25. Ibid., p. 529.
26. Ibid.
27. Christopher Kweku Rutledge, "African Traditional Religious Beliefs among the Akans." *GhanaWeb*. Accessed March 1, 2007. http://colanmc.siu.edu/BAS495/students/chris/ghweb.html.
28. Ankomah, "Ghana," p. 531.
29. UNAIDS (in Resource Guide, Websites).
30. Uwem Edimo Esiet et al., "Nigeria," in Francoeur and Noonan 2004 (in Resource Guide), p. 758.
31. Ibid., p. 760.
32. Ibid.
33. Ibid., p. 761.
34. Ibid., p. 778.
35. Principal sources for this section are Ombolo 1990 and Rwenge Mburano 2004 (in Resource Guide).
36. Rwenge Mburano 2004 (in Resource Guide).
37. Ombolo 1990 (in Resource Guide), p. 146.
38. Rwenge Mburano 2004 (in Resource Guide), p. 163.
39. Ibid., p. 170.
40. Ibid.
41. Ibid., p. 163.
42. Ibid., p. 171.
43. Ibid., p. 172. The result of this study seems to overevaluate the use of condoms, compared to other studies on this topic.
44. UNICEF. Accessed March 14, 2006. http://www.unicef.org.
45. Mouvagha-Sow 2002 (in Resource Guide), p. 127.
46. Ibid., p. 73.
47. Ibid., p. 79.
48. Ibid., p. 138.
49. Ibid., p. 182.
50. Ibid., p. 225.
51. Ibid., p. 461.
52. IRIN (in Resource Guide, Websites), accessed April 9, 2006.

53. Monnig 1983 (in Resource Guide).
54. Mervyn Bernard Hurvitz, "South Africa, 2nd Part, Another Perspective," in Francoeur 1997 (in Resource Guide), Vol. 2, p. 1121.
55. Ibid.
56. Monnig 1983 (in Resource Guide).
57. Hurvitz, "South Africa, 2nd Part, Another Perspective," p. 1124.
58. Ibid., p. 1126.
59. Ibid., p. 1127.
60. IRIN (in Resource Guide, Websites).
61. Godisang Mookodi, Oleosi Ntshebe, and Ian Taylor, "Botswana," in Francoeur and Noonan 2004 (in Resource Guide), p. 92.
62. Ibid.
63. Ibid.
64. Ibid., p. 94.
65. Ibid.
66. Ibid., p. 95.
67. Ibid.
68. Ibid., p. 96.
69. Norbert Brockman, "Kenya," in Francoeur 1997 (in Resource Guide), Vol. 2,. p. 846.
70. Ibid., p. 861.
71. Ibid., p. 862.
72. Ibid., p. 858.
73. Ibid., p. 861.
74. Ibid., p. 867.
75. Philip Setel, Eleuther Mwageni, Namsifu Mndeme, and Yusuf Hemed, "Tanzania," in Francoeur and Noonan 2004 (in Resource Guide), 1012.
76. Ibid., p. 1011.
77. Ibid., p. 1016.
78. Ibid., p. 1018.

MUSIC

GARY BAINES

Both musical production and reception are participatory processes. Musical performance invariably involves not only the mouth and ear but the entire body. Similarly, singing along or simply listening to music involves the use of the mouth and the ear, whereas grooving to its rhythms or marching to its beat involves the entire body. Music can empowering, even liberating, or merely entertaining. Whatever the case, it demands active engagement.

Music is the most fertile and resilient of all of Sub-Saharan Africa's cultural expressions. As such, it is a vital part of the lived experience of African community life—whether to mark rites of passage, celebrate ceremonial occasions, or as an accompaniment to leisure-time activities. Nowadays music is to be heard at church services, football matches, stadium concerts, or mass rallies. Although these are collective events, for the most part people choose to participate in such events as individuals. The element of choice that constitutes music patronage is demonstrated through individual acts of consumption such as buying, borrowing, or pirating recordings. Through the act of consuming a particular kind of music, individuals are able to emotionally and somatically "own" the music in a way that is not possible with any other art form.[1] Although identity is obviously not shaped by musical consumption alone, the act signifies something of how the individual sees him- or herself. For music is a primary site of the self-construction of the individual because of the singular place that culture, especially leisure activity, enjoys in a fluid and complex process of identity formation.

Music is also arguably the most widely appreciated and communicated form of cultural expression on the African continent. Most people are able to sing a song (or, at least, a chorus of one) or express a preference for an artist or musical style. However, they are less likely to be able to express opinions about books, artworks, films, or even television programs. Despite the impact of the mass media and new technologies on the continent, Africa is still primarily an aural and oral culture. Popular culture is sound-oriented, in contrast to the West, where it is primarily visual and textual.

POPULAR CULTURE AND MUSIC

The study of popular culture and music is now well established in academe. However, "popular" is a contested term, and the terrain of popular music is seldom defined to the satisfaction of all scholars. For some the term "popular" means simply appealing to the people, whereas for others it means something that amounts to an authentic expression of the people. For the purposes of this chapter, popular music will be defined generically as virtually any form of contemporary African music. The designation "pop" or "popular" actually is as much a statement about the means of musical production and promotion as it is about the aesthetics of the music. It includes any mass-produced recordings by professional musicians. It is music that has a popular audience that crosses categories of class, generation, gender, language, and rural-urban roots. Sometimes known as "Afropop," it is a synthesis of indigenous styles and global music idioms. These idioms range from Christian hymns and gospel music through to jazz, rhythm and blues, rock, and hip-hop.

A more problematical term is "traditional," for it presumes that musical styles are products of hermetically sealed cultures that exist in time warps. In fact, cultural exchange and musical cross-fertilization predates European colonization of Sub-Saharan Africa. And when European musical instruments arrived in the region, they were indigenized—meaning that they were appropriated in such a way as to adapt them for performing indigenous musics. The guitar is a case in point. From as early as the sixteenth century, this Iberian instrument was adopted in parts of West Africa at gatherings where revelers drank the fermented sap of palm trees, a traditional alternative to bottled beer. This music came to be called "palm wine music," and by the twentieth century virtually every village in West Africa had musicians who would provide music for patrons of informal bars who spent their afternoons relaxing in the shade of trees. Palm wine music eventually made the transition from bars to the recording studio. The music's greatest ambassador was Sierra Leone's S. E. Rogie, whose career stretched from the 1960s to the 1990s. His success encouraged many imitators throughout West Africa. These days, palm wine music is more likely to be found in archives than enjoyed in live performance. Although an artifact of a bygone era, it is still not, strictly speaking, traditional music.

Certain musicologists regard the term "traditional" as something of a misnomer. They reject the need to reference traditional African styles and instruments in order to lay claim to an African identity. Others believe that traditional music is part of an African heritage that should be preserved at all costs. The first group insists that African styles have been assimilated into global popular music to create new hybrids. They are more likely to pay tribute to the creativity of African musicians and their distinctive contribution to global pop than be committed to the preservation of tradition. The second group employs the term "traditional" to designate music transmitted by memory rather than by means of the written word or sound recording. Anonymous community compositions are regarded as expressing the collective spirit of preliterate or precapitalist societies. This discourse holds that unlike commercially produced popular music, traditional music is "authentic." But this discourse is premised on an essentialist understanding of identity that regards tradition as immutable and sacrosanct. It draws an unnecessarily rigid distinction between traditional and popular music and between "tribal" areas and the cities/townships. In emphasizing the traditional–modern, urban–rural dichotomy, these musicologists tend to overlook the extent of cultural exchange that has occurred throughout Sub-Saharan Africa.

Over the course of many centuries, Sub-Saharan Africa has been engaged in a lengthy cultural exchange with other continents. This pattern has been repeated over and over again and been referred to as a "long conversation" between Africa and other parts of the world.[2] Whereas some commentators see this relationship as symbiotic, for others it amounts to a form of cultural imperialism. Although there can be little doubt that the West benefits financially from the relationship, there is something of a two-way exchange or dialogue when it comes to the reception of music. Neither artists nor consumers slavishly imitate or adopt the music produced outside their countries or the continent. Rather, they tend to appropriate such styles selectively so as to make them their own. New musical hybrids emerge that draw inspiration from both Western music, which accentuates melody and harmony, and African music, which highlights rhythm. Thus, African music has made a significant contribution to many of the most popular styles in the West during the twentieth century.

Conversely, Western influences on Sub-Saharan African music have been equally profound. Christian mission work was partly facilitated by the colonization of the region. The assimilation of hymns was, in turn, facilitated by the rich vocal traditions of the continent. These twin processes can be illustrated with respect to the solemn and stirring "Nkosi Sikelele iAfrika" [God Bless Africa]. Composed in 1897 by a mission-educated teacher, Enoch Sontonga, it combined Protestant hymnody and African melody, harmony and rhythm. It was popularized in the idiom of the new black South African choral style known as *makwaya*, and its dissemination was made possible through Tonic Sol Fa notation. It resonated with the political and spiritual aspirations of a black modernizing elite and was adopted by the African National Congress as its anthem. "Nkosi Sikelele iAfrika" eventually not only became the national anthem of a democratic Republic of South Africa but was adopted and adapted by several other Sub-Saharan African countries as well. Aside from acquiring anthemic status, it has been become an artifact of popular culture as a result of being reinvented by the likes of Boom Shaka, who produced a *kwaito* version of the song.[3] Thus, post-colonial Africa has appropriated elements of its colonial heritage, in this instance specifically the musical influence of Christian missionaries, but refashioned and reinserted this into vernacular culture.

Whereas in most of Sub-Saharan Africa European and Latin American influences on popular music have been considerable, in the Republic of South Africa North American influences have possibly been more significant. Although South African blacks were never part of the slave trade that caused the African diaspora to the Americas, this has not diminished their ability to identify with the cultural expressions and political aspirations of African-Americans. They were exposed to a variety of American entertainment products such as records and Hollywood films, and such cultural products seemed to underscore an affinity between their own experiences and that of their African-American "cousins." But the cultural pollination that was a product of trans-Atlantic linkages has not been confined to any one region. Musical styles migrated across the globe with Africans and mutated into new forms in the "New World." Often these newly fashioned styles were transplanted back to Africa. It has been argued that the roots of the blues can be traced to West African traditional music. The blues has, in turn, fed back into contemporary West African music. Such musical "crossovers" can be illustrated by the collaboration between Mali's Ali Farka Toure and American guitarist Ry Cooder on the acclaimed *Talking Timbuktu* (1995) album.

Another instance of African influence on global pop is evident in the polyrhythmic percussive styles of numerous jazz and rock drummers. And the popularity of gospel music and jazz is perhaps indicative of shared cultural aesthetics and values between the indigenous people of Sub-Saharan Africa and African-Americans. All in all, the African diaspora has created a dynamic feedback relationship between Sub-Saharan Africa and the rest of the world.

Despite significant regional variations, Sub-Saharan Africa still remains largely undifferentiated for many Westerners. In global markets, the music of the region is invariably lumped together with other non-Western musical traditions collectively known as "world music." But it is precisely this distinction between the West and "the rest" that reinforces the

CROSS-CULTURAL COLLABORATIONS

Many international artists have looked to Africa for inspiration. Some have dabbled with the sounds of Sub-Saharan Africa in order to further their own careers, whilst others have become actively engaged in promoting it. The most (in)famous act of collaboration was Paul Simon's work with South African artists like Ray Phiri and Ladysmith Black Mambazo on the American's 1986 *Graceland* album. Deemed politically controversial because of Simon's violation of the UN cultural boycott that blacklisted international artists performing in South Africa, it was rightly regarded as a stunning crossover success. Peter Gabriel has collaborated with African artists such as Youssou N'Dour and Angelique Kidjo. He has also invested much time and money in WOMAD (World of Music Arts and Dance), an annual showcase of global culture. And Gabriel's RealWorld studio has been the venue of many other collaborative efforts. In 1993, the American slide guitarist Ry Cooder recorded a session with Mali's roots guitarist and singer, Ali Farka Toure. The resultant album, *Talking Timbuktu,* won a Grammy award in 1995. Collaborations have not been the prerogative of pop and rock musicians. A string of jazz musicians have worked with African counterparts. Even the classical ensemble, the Kronos Quartet, released *Pieces of Africa* (1992), which was a cooperative endeavor with African artists. These cross-cultural collaborations only represent the proverbial tip of the iceberg.

notion that the popular music of Sub-Saharan Africa is qualitatively different from its Anglo-American counterpart. Rather than render local and indigenous styles more accessible, this process of "othering" emphasizes its exoticism. On the other hand, the artists themselves are attempting to bridge this bifurcated market. Thus the Senegalese artist Youssou N'Dour admits to adopting a marketing strategy that emphasizes what is familiar rather than unknown to Western consumers so as to make an impact in markets outside of his own country. He has released different albums and even different versions of the same song for Western audiences and his Senegalese fans. African rhythms are toned down to appeal to audiences who might regard the sound as "raw." Although "purists" have regarded his albums such as *The Guide* (1994) and *Joko* (2000) as departures from his roots, N'Dour has no qualms about marketing himself as a "universal African" and exponent of Afropop. His marketing ploy trades on the idea that music is a universal language in the global pop village. But the emphasis on common denominators cannot gainsay the fact that culturally and regionally specific traits are countervailing currents against the forces of globalization and homogenization.

Notwithstanding the profusion of regional styles on the continent, Sub-Saharan African music is usually classified according to a performer's country of origin in the global marketplace. This is readily apparent on the shelves of any music store that stocks "world music." So whether the consumer is searching for the music of Mali's Salif Keita, Zimbabwe's Thomas Mapfumo, South Africa's Ladysmith Black Mambazo, or the Democratic Republic of the Congo's Papa Wemba, she is likely to find it under their countries of origin rather than categories such as *mbalax, chimurenga, isicathamiya*, or *soukous.* The only exceptions occur when African artists record music that already enjoys recognition as a distinct genre. So recordings by the Ivory Coast's Alpha Blondy or South Africa's Lucky Dube might be listed under reggae rather than their respective countries. This incongruity serves to highlight the fact that few African artists are recognized and enjoy extensive sales outside of their own countries. As popular as their music might be at home, such artists struggle to compete in a global market where they have had to play according to the rules of the international recording industry. They are at a comparative disadvantage with respect to artists based in the West.

Sub-Saharan Africa's female artists are doubly disadvantaged. Not only do they grow up in a patriarchal society, but they have to compete in an industry that judges women on the basis of appearance rather than talent. Yet the continent's latest diva, Angelique Kidjo, has overcome incredible odds to succeed in a man's world. Born in the small West African country of Benin, Kidjo has overcome not only gender discrimination but other enormous obstacles to carve out a niche for herself in world music markets. She grew up in a village situated at the crossroads of Islamic and black African cultures steeped in traditional religion. In the 1980s she relocated to Paris, where a large expatriate Francophone African musical community is to be found. It was her 1991 album *Logozo*, produced by American Joe Galdo, that launched her worldwide career and earned her commercial radio play in the United States. To charges of having "sold out" and abandoning her African roots, Kidjo responds that she regards herself as a global citizen. In so doing, Kidjo proclaims herself the "queen of African crossover pop." The precedent of female South African artists such as Miriam Makeba ("Mama Africa") and Yvone Chaka Chaka ("Princess of Africa") breaking through the proverbial glass ceiling has served as an incentive for Kidjo and the late Brenda Fassie. The latter has shaken up the industry's stereotypes more than any other artist in Sub-Saharan Africa. Fassie flaunted social conventions and was dubbed South Africa's own Madonna by a media that promotes the cult of celebrity. Her career was a roller coaster of highs and lows, but the sassy Fassie always seemed to land on her feet, and her demise has been much lamented. Not necessarily a role model (in the positive sense of the phrase), she has nevertheless made it easier for those who follow in her footsteps.

AFRICA'S MUSIC INDUSTRY

Sub-Saharan Africa is a peripheral player in the global economy, and the region's music industry functions as an attenuation of the international music industry. The South African industry, which is the oldest, most extensive, and sophisticated in the subcontinent, exemplifies this uneven relationship. The country's major record labels are subsidiaries of the "big five" international record companies: EMI, BMG, SONY, Universal Music Group, and Warner. These "majors" constitute an oligopoly of international companies that dominate sales and airplay because they own or distribute international as well as local artists through labels such as CCP (EMI) Colossal, Fresh (BMG), and Sheer Music (Sony). The "majors" concentrate their efforts on marketing well-established overseas artists by licensing them to local companies. The latter, for their part, invest relatively little capital in local acts. Thus the oldest and largest locally owned recording company, Gallo (Africa), has subsidized its local operation from the profits that accrue from distributing for the "majors." So the development of local artists has been left largely to small independent labels with limited resources. Only when the support of the independents has helped local artists break through into the South African music scene do the majors and their subsidiaries use their economic muscle to sign up such artists. This pattern is repeated—albeit on a smaller scale—throughout Sub-Saharan Africa.

If by African standards the South African music industry is significant, by world standards it is small. Figures released by the Recording Industry of South Africa (RISA) reported that sales amount to about 0.4 percent of total world sales, which makes the country the twenty-fifth largest market in the world. Another indicator of the relatively small size of the South African market is that total unit sales in 2003 were 16.9 million and that sales of only 25,000 and 50,000 units are necessary for the award of gold and platinum discs, respectively. A mere 20,000 people are employed in the music industry. Given these economies of scale, the music industry of Sub-Saharan African countries is negligible in global terms, but not necessarily as far as the generation of wealth in these countries is concerned. Still, a large proportion of the profits of the record industry are siphoned off to corporate headquarters by the majors. Thus much of the revenue from the sale of music in Sub-Saharan Africa accrues to beneficiaries outside the country. This trend has raised the concerns not only of the musicians, but of governments throughout the subcontinent.

The protection/promotion of cultural industries, including music, has been a concern of virtually all post-independent Sub-Saharan African governments. In South Africa, the ANC government has effected significant changes in the broadcast sector, especially radio. During the apartheid era, the South African Broadcasting Corporation (SABC) exercised an effective monopoly of the airwaves. But since 1996 the airwaves have been deregulated, and this has allowed privately owned commercial and community stations to compete with the public broadcaster. At the same time, the newly established Independent Broadcasting Authority (IBA) imposed local content quotas on radio and television stations. This meant that 20 percent of the music broadcast on the airwaves should be locally produced. Other Sub-Saharan countries such as Zaire adopted a heavier-handed approach and obliged radio stations to broadcast only local music. The introduction of quotas in South Africa was regarded as a means of leveling the playing field in order that local musicians could compete with international artists for air time. The authorities also invoked nation-building discourse by insisting that a thriving local music industry would aid the construction of a new national identity with greater pride in its artists and musical accomplishments. Although broadcasters expressed reservations about the appropriateness of quotas in an environment in which the broadcast sector was being deregulated and partially privatized, representatives of the music industry accepted the view that more could be done to promote the industry (notwithstanding their own poor record in supporting local artists). Although certain commercial stations, which target niche markets that consume primarily international repertoire, have ignored the quotas, radio audiences have generally become more aware of the output of local artists, and this, in turn, has convinced record companies to invest more in South African music. Consequently, there has been some growth of the country's music industry.

Exploitation in the African Music Industry

The bottom line for the recording industry is making profits, and it has had its fair share of unscrupulous executives, A&R men (artist and repertoire men, who determine a label's portfolio), talent scouts, and so on. The situation in Sub-Saharan Africa amounts to a difference of degree rather than kind. Relative levels of deprivation render artists even more susceptible to being exploited, as they have little likelihood of legal redress. Recording companies have preyed upon the ignorance of illiterate black artists who signed away ownership of their music in return for a flat fee. Most contracts signed made no provision for royalty payments. Stories abound of composers and performers being paid a few pounds for songs that have become "hits" and generated considerable revenue for recording companies. There have also been instances in which songs penned by African artists have become hits for international artists who have believed, sometimes in all ignorance, that these were "traditional" folk songs in the public domain. This can be illustrated with reference to the legal wrangle over the rights to the song "Mbube" by Solomon Linda.

Despite efforts by South African Recording Rights Association Limited (SARRAL) to recover royalties owing to composers (and their estates or families) who never received due credit for their works, such legendary artists as Simon "Mahlathini" Nkabinde have died in abject poverty.

And notwithstanding the attempts by certain companies in the industry to compensate artists exploited in the past, the trend is likely to continue until such time as there is a standard recording contract in the industry.

Aside from exploitation, the counterfeit trade also diverts money from the pockets of artists and performers. It is estimated that as much as half of the music sold in South Africa is pirated. Figures for other Sub-Saharan countries are reckoned to be even higher. Piracy takes the form not only of home taping or copying CDs with digital technology but the large-scale illegal importation of finished products from Asia, the Middle East, and Eastern Europe. Piracy has become particularly rife in the early twenty-first century and undercuts the sale of legal product. RISA figures suggest that that there has been a decline of 3.7 million units sold in South Africa between 2000 and 2004. The decline in sales has been ascribed not only to piracy but also to the downloading of music from the internet. Yet in contrast to countries where telecommunications and access to broadband is cheap, the cost of downloading MP3 and other digital formats in South Africa is prohibitively expensive. Moreover, only about 10 percent of South African households have access to the Internet, and it is probably the same group that purchases imported discs or locally manufactured recordings by international artists. Despite the decline of units sold, there has been no concurrent reduction of income for the record industry over the four-year period. The reason that profit margins have not been affected may be attributed to the stability and relative strengthening of the currency (the rand) without an accompanying decline in the price of CDs in retail outlets. In other words, the smaller volume of sales have been offset by improved profit margins on imported products and recordings by international artists reproduced in CD plants located in the country.

SOLOMON LINDA AND "MBUBE"

In 1939 Solomon Linda and his backing group the Evening Birds recorded a new melody in a Johannesburg studio. He named the song "Mbube" (Zulu for "lion"). Gallo Records paid Linda and his group a flat session fee for the recording, after which the company owned the song and did not have to pay any composer royalties, even though the record sold an estimated 100,000 copies over the next decade. In 1951 American folk musician Pete Seeger and his band, the Weavers, set the tune to English lyrics. They called it "Wimoweh" and it became a best seller in the United States. Then in 1961 it was recorded under the title "The Lion Sleeps Tonight" by the Tokens and became a worldwide hit. The song was copyrighted as an original by George Weiss, although the melody was identical to Linda's composition. In 1994 it was included in the soundtrack of the Disney film *The Lion King*. In the six decades since its release it has been covered by numerous artists and is arguably the best-known tune to have come out of Africa. *Rolling Stone* magazine estimated that it had grossed $15 million in composers' royalties by 2000. Its composer died a pauper in 1962. Linda's family recently filed a lawsuit against Disney to claim its share of the royalties to which it believed it is due. There is likely to be a similar case brought against Abilene, the New-York based company that administers the U.S. rights to "The Lion Sleeps Tonight." Only Pete Seeger has agreed to compensate the Linda estate, and a settlement has been negotiated without recourse to legal action. For a fuller treatment, see Rian Malan's article at http://www.3rdearmusic.com/forum/mbube2.html.

Radio and Recorded Music

Radio is still the most widely accessible form of mass media in Sub-Saharan Africa. Battery-operated transistor radios are cheap and portable. Television—including satellite transmissions—has made inroads on the continent as a purveyor of music. But the CD and DVD are out of the reach of most music consumers. The cassette tape, which is cheaper and easier to reproduce, is still the most popular music format. This is because cassette production requires a far lower initial investment—especially in cover design and packaging—and production can be tied more closely to actual rather than projected sales. The more sophisticated South African consumer market has recently begun to buck this trend. South African manufacturers ceased the production and importation of vinyl in 1994. In 1991 the value, but not number, of CD sales surpassed that of cassette. The trend has continued unabated, and the amount of international recordings sold in cassette format is now insignificant. Thus the growth in the value of sales of international recordings is not a result of the growth of total sales units but a result of the transference of consumer preferences from cassette to CD.

Most South African consumers still have little disposable income for items such as recorded music. The official unemployment rate might be given as 26.2 percent, but numerous sources put it as high as 40 percent. According to the World Bank, the country's per capita income was $3,630 (the equivalent of $10,000 purchasing power in the United States) in 2003, and the disparity in income between white and black was 5 to 1. Not only are there major gulfs between the incomes of whites and blacks, but the record market is racially segmented. More affluent white consumers tend to purchase international recording artists in CD format. An estimated 73 percent of the purchased CDs are imports or artists based outside South Africa available on the multinational record labels. Black consumers buy far more local product, and most still prefer the relatively cheaper cassette tape format. Cassettes comprise 35 percent of the units sold but only 20 percent of the total value of sales by the record industry. Over the past four years, the annual sale of imported artists' product declined from 13 million to 8.8 million units, while the sale of local artists' product increased from 7.2 to 8.5 million units. In other words, although sales of local artists (on both CD and cassette) make up only 27 percent of the value of recording industry sales, they account for 43 percent of the units sold. This implies that the sales of South African music are growing while those of international artists have declined substantially. This possibly reflects the growing purchasing power of the black middle class in post-apartheid South Africa.

Censorship of African Popular Music

Much of the popular music released in Sub-Saharan Africa conveys messages of either a moral or a political nature. African musicians are almost expected to use their privileged access to the media and other platforms to engage sociopolitical issues. Radio is usually under state control in many parts of the continent and therefore tends to broadcast music and political viewpoints sanctioned by the ruling elites. So social criticism is effectively disseminated through cassettes that are widely copied and pirated. This technology, as well as the Internet, has a subversive potential, which military dictatorships and one-party states have sought to control by means of censorship. Such governments that have reason to fear a groundswell of political opposition have sought to clamp down on music that is widely believed to have the capacity to empower people to resist controls. Nigeria's succession of short-lived democratic governments and repressive military juntas following independence was characterized by corruption and incompetence. When the popular musician Fela Kuti criticized the military regime in the 1970s, his commune-like compound, called the Kalakuta Republic, was raided by the army and razed to the ground. He responded by penning the song "Unknown Soldiers" in order to expose the failure of the regime to take responsibility for its illegal actions and violation of human rights. The military authorities resorted to continuous harassment of Kuti that culminated in his imprisonment on trumped-up currency smuggling charges in 1984. Similarly, the Zimbabwean musician Thomas Mapfumo's career has been dogged by showdowns with successive regimes in his native country. During the post-1965 UDI period in (then) Rhodesia, his music was so closely associated with resistance to Ian Smith's government that it was called *chimurenga*, which was the name given to the armed anti-colonial struggle. Since 1980, Mapfumo has continued to raise his voice in protest against the abuses of the Mugabe government. Both Nigeria and Zimbabwe's authoritarian regimes resorted to control and censorship of the media as an instrument with which to silence opposition. These are only two of numerous instances in which popular music has been a casualty of censorship Sub-Saharan Africa.

In South Africa during the apartheid era, independent recordings by artists who were critical of the regime struggled to find distributors and retail outlets to carry their repertoires. Moreover, such artists were often subjected to intimidation and harassment by the security police. More routine censorship was undertaken by the Directorate of Publications, which acted on public complaints about the content of books and record albums. Meanwhile, the SABC acted of its own accord to exclude "undesirable" songs from the airwaves. Any song that criticized the government, questioned moral and religious values upheld by the state, was deemed blasphemous, sexually explicit, used swear words, or otherwise occasioned offense could be declared "undesirable." Now a code of conduct is enforced by an independent body called the Broadcast Complaints Commission of South Africa (BCCSA). In one instance it ruled against Mbongemi Ngema's song "AmaNdiya," which was deemed to promote hate speech. The BCCSA was convinced that the song might exacerbate the already-tense relations between Zulus and Indians in KwaZulu-Natal and subjected its broadcast to certain conditions. Apologists for censorship invoked the experience of Rwanda, where the broadcast of the inflammatory music of Simon Bikindi was reckoned to be instrumental in fomenting genocidal violence. So even in the new political dispensation, in which the ANC government has committed itself to upholding freedom of expression guaranteed by the constitution, it has condoned censorship on the grounds of stabilizing the country's fragile democratic order.

Given the pressing problems faced by the postcolonial governments of Sub-Saharan Africa—many of their own making—it is not altogether surprising that most have steered clear of becoming involved in or regulating the music industry. There have been token efforts to combat piracy and infringement of copyright, but the state simply does not have the capacity or the political will to confront these problems. Although involvement in the music industry has proven lucrative for a few artists, the majority are unable to make a living off their music. If there is money to be made, it is invariably by the interlocutors between the artist and his or her audience: managers, A&R personnel, talent scouts, and so forth. This, of course, is not a problem unique to the region. But it is exacerbated in Sub-Saharan Africa, where buying CDs or patronizing live music at nightclubs or performances at larger venues is a something of a financial sacrifice by consumers. Although music has been integral to so much of the lived African experience, its commodification has undoubted disadvantages for the population at large. This is the contradiction at the heart of the music industry; it is the ultimate paradox of the consumption of African popular music.

Regional Subsections

The following survey of the popular music of Sub-Saharan Africa is necessarily selective and, accordingly, cannot do justice to the breadth and diversity of its musical idioms. It seeks to introduce readers to certain of the most significant regional styles and individual artists.

West Africa

West Africa is both a crucible and crossroads of cultural exchange. This is partly due to the region's strong oral traditions, which have been preserved by *griots* (the French term) or *jalis* (the Manding term), the traditional praise singers and historians. This goes hand in hand with West Africa's great musical traditions, which place a premium on percussion. These include Yoruba drums from present-day Nigeria; Ashanti and Ewe ensembles from Ghana; *sabar* stick drumming from Senegal; the *djembe* drum of Mali, Guinea, Senegal, and other countries; and various versions of the talking drum found throughout the region. It is also partly due to the region's long-standing cultural conversation with the New World, which begun with the slave trade. Many argue that West Africa nurtured the ancestral seeds of blues, jazz, rock 'n' roll, and reggae. And the region was colonized by European imperial powers: initially the Portuguese and Spanish, and then the French and British. This introduced new instruments, such as the guitar, to the region. Although the imperial powers have long since withdrawn from the region, their capitals—particularly Paris and London—continue to provide a point of departure for musicians in search of an international career.

Ghana

The first truly popular music of Anglophone West Africa was *highlife.* A dance music played mostly in the Gold Coast (later Ghana) and Nigeria, it represents one of the first fusions of African roots and Western music. It started life as a blend of Trinidadian calypso, military brass band music, Cuban *son*, and older African song forms. Then, following the return of veterans from World War II, elements of American big band swing jazz were added to the mix. The trumpeter E. T. Mensah formed the band the Tempos in Accra in 1948. His songs in English and West African vernacular languages gave his music broad appeal. Mensah's own career peaked in the late 1950s, and this happened to coincide with the independence of Ghana and the heyday of highlife. Highlife's golden era ended with the rise of Congolese music in the 1960s (discussed in the section on Central Africa), but it continued to reach audiences both in Sub-Saharan Africa and abroad until well into the 1970s.

The popularity of highlife afforded Ghanaian musicians opportunities to ply their trade abroad. In the early 1970s, the band Osibisa with its Afro-rock highlife fusion sound managed a succession of top ten hits in the United Kingdom. Combining highlife veterans with Caribbean musicians, they were harbingers of the world music phenomenon. And with the appropriation of reggae by African and western artists alike, it is not surprising that highlife exponents also climbed on the bandwagon. Pat Thomas' band Marijata merged highlife and reggae in the late 1970s. The same artist also became the first major Ghanaian musician to record in Germany, where he pioneered "burgher highlife," which sampled electronic keyboards and elements of disco. He eventually made his home amongst the Ghanaian expatriate community in Toronto, Canada, and continued to absorb an array of influences in his music.

Nigeria

Nigeria developed its own version of highlife. The electrified dance music grew out of acoustic Igbo blues and palm wine music. Most of Nigeria's highlife groups came from Igboland (the eastern region, which borders Cameroon) and it remains primarily an Igbo music. As in Ghana, the guitar-based sound caught on as a rock-informed alternative to the big band style pioneered by Mensah and his followers. Prince Nico scored a massive hit in

1976 with "Sweet Mother," which reportedly sold 13 million copies, making it the biggest selling African record ever. Another popular 1970s highlife outfit was the Oriental Brothers, who produced a complex, buoyant guitar and percussion sound with plaintive vocal harmonies. However, their feuding proved their undoing, and the three brothers formed their own bands that were unable to emulate the success of their original lineup. One of the most innovative highlife musicians was Sonny Okosun, who added reggae to his sound, which he called *ozzidi.* Although highlife remains popular in eastern Nigeria, nationally it has been eclipsed by *juju, fuji,* and Afro-reggae.

Juju has been described as deeply layered, percussive groove music. It took its first faltering steps in the 1920s as local bar music and developed over the years absorbing new technologies and influences. In the 1950s, amplification made it possible to combine acoustic elements, such as guitar melodies and solo singing from the older palm wine music, with unbridled Yoruba drumming to create the rich, dense sound of modern *juju.* It was the texture created by King Sunny Ade and his twenty-piece African Beats that defined the music's core: its percussion topped by eloquent talking drums and its harmonized call-and-response vocal mixing Yoruba proverbs and Christian themes. The choreography of Ade's live act, in which the bandleader's gentle, silky voice and subtle dance moves are mirrored by his four female backup singers, makes for mesmerizing performances. He leads his band like a consummate orchestral conductor and commands the attention of audiences wherever he has taken his stage show. Indeed, his world tours and albums released on the Island label have done more than anything to bring juju to the attention of the international music community.

Fela Anikulapo Kuti grabbed the headlines as much for his eccentricities and repeated confrontations with Nigeria's military authorities (mentioned previously) as for his musical prowess. On stage Kuti led his thirty-plus piece Afrobeat band through lengthy funk improvisations (à la James Brown). While drummers and guitarists laid down the groove, Kuti would preach in pidgin English, building the tension with a keyboard break or a blast on his tenor sax. The song would reach a crescendo to the accompaniment of blaring horns that seem to express indignation. Such performances provided Kuti with a platform to launch scathing broadsides against those he deemed responsible for the plight and oppression of Africa's urban poor. The publicity that followed the release of songs such as "Zombie" and "International Thief Thief," which are indictments of the conduct of Nigerian soldiers and multinational corporations such as ITT respectively, has occasioned retribution from the former. And his death from AIDS-related complications gave his enemies reason to dismiss him on account of his sexual proclivities and deviant lifestyle rather than have to acknowledge his contribution to the musical development of Sub-Saharan Africa.

Senegal

Francophone West Africa, and especially the Senegalese capital Dakar, has proved to be a mecca of popular music. Like most of the region, Senegalese pop of the 1950s and 1960s was heavily influenced by Latin American, especially Cuban, music. Under the patronage of President Leopold Senghor, an Africanization movement promoted the substitution of the indigenous language Wolof for French and Spanish lyrics. Traditional instruments such as the *tamar* (a small talking drum with variable pitch) and *sabar* (a big, standing, conga-like drum) were added to the customary lineup of guitars, drumkits, and brass. The most influential group of this period was the Star Band de Dakar, the house band of a popular nightclub, the Miami, owned by entrepreneur and talent scout Ibra Kassé. The competitive Dakar nightclub scene provided the launch pad for a crop of Senegalese groups. The first to achieve success abroad was Xalam, an eight-piece outfit that created a jazzy fusion style that borrowed liberally from Western and African influences.

One of those who passed through the ranks of the Star Band was the dynamic young vocalist Youssou N'Dour. With his own ten-piece band, he built on the platform of his mentors, but as a prodigiously talented musician and prolific songwriter, he came up with a new musical mix, which was dubbed *mbalax*. This label was subsequently applied to the whole new generation of Wolof pop with its modernized indigenous sound. N'Dour's seminal contribution was to replace the Latin American *pachanga* background with traditional rhythms. His high-pitched wailing voice overlaid traditional ceremonial rhythms provided by the guitars and the *sabar* and *tamar* drums. His residence at the Thiosane nightclub in Dakar, the frequent release of cassettes, and regular concerts in stadia won over a huge audience in his native country. In the 1980s he broadened his fan base to the expatriate Senegalese community in Paris through appearances in the French capital. But it was his guesting on Peter Gabriel's 1987 *So* album and his participation in the 1988 Human Rights Now Tour with Gabriel, Sting, and Bruce Springsteen that brought him to world attention. His 1994 album *The Guide (Womat)* had a mixed reception in Senegal but turned him into an African superstar.

While N'Dour turned increasingly to Europe to cement his reputation, a crop of new Senegalese singers emerged on the home front. These included Baaba Maal and Ismael Lô. Maal, like N'Dour, was an ethnic Tukolor but sang in the northern Pulaar language. He performed folkloric acoustic-based music, such as his famous *Djam Leelii* album with the guitarist Mansour Seck. With his group Dande Lenol, he played a key role in the incorporation of hip-hop, reggae and techno, notably on their landmark 1994 album *Firin' in Fouta.* He is a modern-day griot who celebrates village life in the same breath that he advocates contemporary causes such as women's rights in Africa. As with the griots, his work can be blatantly didactic without losing its melodic qualities. He sings of history and heroes, bringing the lessons of the past to the attention of today's audiences.

Ismael Lô also developed a high regard for the traditions of the Manding griots. He loved the deeply rhythmic and intricate *sabar* drumming of the Wolof people as well as the textures of those Manding instruments, the harplike *kora* and the *balafon,* a xylophone with resonators. But when he became a musician himself, Lô taught himself to play Western instruments such as the guitar and the harmonica. He played for five years in Super Diamono, a top *mbalax* band, which provided a musical apprenticeship of sorts. Then he opted to go solo and made a string of successful records with West Africa's premier producer, Ibrahim Sylla. Albums such as *Iso* exposed his elegant anthems and ballads to international audiences. Although the lyrics might have remained undecipherable to many in this audience, the sound textures of Senegalese popular music had become "familiarly different" by the 1990s.

Mali and Guinea

The euphoria of independence in Francophone West Africa was accompanied by attempts to reassert a pride in the achievements of its peoples, both past and present. In Mali and Guinea during the 1960s, this took the form of these governments pressing for the re-Africanization of local music. This entailed discouraging the ubiquitous Latin sounds and actually ordering bands to adapt folkloric or traditional material and instruments into their electric pop. This had unpredictable but spectacular spinoffs. The infusion of the region's melodic traditions transformed local dance music. The tinkling melodies of the *kora* and the *balafon* turned up in guitar and keyboard parts. The resulting sound, sometimes called

Manding swing, won a big audience for state-sponsored dance bands in these countries and laid the groundwork for crossover stars such as Salif Keita and Mory Kanté.

Salif Keita commenced singing professionally with the Rail Band of Bamako in the Malian capital in 1968. He abandoned the Latin-tinged sound of this legendary outfit in favour of a fusion-oriented group when he established his own band Les Ambassadeurs. He moved to Paris in 1984, and there he recorded the album *Soto*, which realized his ambition of producing work that combined traditional and progressive rock music. The brooding music was for listening rather than for dancing, which in itself was something of a departure in Afropop. Keita sings with the passion of blues shouters and R&B screamers. But the sound still manages to evoke the style of the Manding griots and their concern for the grand struggles and tragedies of history. The emotional intensity would seem to suggest that Keita was able to tap into the pain of his own life and to transcend it in cathartic song. These qualities became part of his trademark and were equally evident on follow-up albums such as *The Mansa of Mali.* Keita ranks amongst the most celebrated singers on the African continent.

Guinean vocalist and kora player Mory Kanté spearheaded the "electro-griot" sound, which spurred the trend of using keyboards and drum machines in Malian and Guinean pop. Growing up in an old griot family in eastern Guinea, Kanté commenced learning the balafon. He then went to Bamako to study the kora. There, he wound up taking Salif Keita's job as lead singer of the Rail Band. In 1981, Kanté moved to Paris, where he introduced electronic instruments and a strong horn section to accompany the kora in producing a new mélange of Manding pop. He simplifies the dense, intricate rhythms of Manding pop in favor of a strong backbeat. While this mix might be anathema to purists, Kanté achieved tremendous popularity throughout West Africa. In 1988, his version of the classic "Yeke Yeke" from the album *Akwaba Beach* topped charts in Europe. Kanté's career well illustrates that the popular music of West Africa has transcended national and even international boundaries.

Central Africa

The Congo is Sub-Saharan Africa's longest and most navigable river. It is a conduit of cultural influences. Early in the twentieth century, residents along its banks relaxed by dancing to *meringa*, which was a music produced by a combination of thumb piano with drum and bottle percussion. It was a hybrid style that drew from the musics of various ethnic groups: Kongo, Lulua, Luba, and others able to communicate in the newly emerged trade language of Lingala. When West Indian immigrants arrived with guitars and, later, when Cuban pop recordings flooded radio airwaves, Central Africans reappropriated music that Caribbean descendants of Congolese slaves had helped create. They, in turn, incorporated local elements and produced a variety of styles of Congo music such as *rumba* (distinct from the Caribbean form) and *soukous.* The region presents a compelling example of how internal and external influences interacted to produce a new musical elixir.

The Democratic Republic of the Congo (DRC)

The Congo is no ordinary country. It is a massive land mass that straddles Central Africa from the mouth of the Congo River on the Atlantic coast to Lake Tanganyika in the east. As the Belgian Congo, its populace suffered a particularly cruel colonial system that lasted until 1959. But independence was followed by political assassination and interethnic warfare. Then in 1965 Mobutu Sese Seko seized power and ruled the country he renamed Zaire with an iron fist for almost thirty years. Despite the venality of Mobutu's rule, massive corruption, and the desperate times, the Congo capital, Kinshasa, remained a vibrant music center until the 1990s, when the country descended into civil war and general anarchy.

From the 1950s Kinshasa's Matonge district was a bustling hive of musical activity with nighclubs that operated from dawn to dusk. Bands like Joseph Kabasele's African Jazz and Franco's OK Jazz played cha-chas, biguines, boleros, and rumbas. The sound they produced was probably more Cuban than African, but these pioneers of rumba provided the template for a musical style that was to become Sub-Saharan Africa's most influential pop music. Recordings made in the 1950s bore the imprint of the click pattern of the Afro-Cuban clavé, a pair of hardwood sticks struck together to produce a high-pitched sound. This gave the music its two-bar rhythmic pattern. This was overlaid with Lingala melodies that possess a unique cadence and flow that define a timeless vocal sound. But it was the modulating cyclical guitar patterns that suggested an infusion of African roots music. And it was this element that was increasingly highlighted as rumba mutated through the 1960s and 1970s. For instance, Franco (known offstage as Luambo Makiadi) expanded his small ensemble to a thirty-piece outfit that included batteries of guitars, horns, and vocalists layering musical conversation over bass, drums, and other forms of percussion. His own virtuoso guitar work earned him accolades, and he remained a firm favorite with the public until his death in 1989.

A younger generation of rumba players revolutionized the music and revitalized the Matonge music scene in the 1970s. Calling themselves Zaiko Langa Langa ("Zaire of our ancestors"), a group of students gave the music a makeover. They dropped the horn section and focused attention on three-guitar workouts, percussion, and shouting chants known as animation. A common chant was "*Pésa*! *Pésa*!" which means "Give it up!" Zaiko gave the music a rock 'n' roll edge and unprecedented youth appeal. Its tempo changes and sweaty, high-energy dance routines made it thoroughly modern electric pop. Yet, ironically, it dovetailed neatly with Mobutu's *authenticité* policy of the early 1970s. *Authenticité* encouraged modern expressions of ancestral traditions to redress the corrupting legacy of colonialism. Zaiko was not only politically correct but popular as well.

Congolese dance music came to be called *soukous* and came to the attention of African expatriates and European audiences at precisely the time world music was being marketed. It was to Paris that most of the Congo's purveyors of soukous went in the 1980s to promote their careers. These included Papa Wemba and Les Quatres Étoiles. They had to find a balance between their homegrown audiences and their fan bases overseas. Singer Papa Wemba had fronted a number of the different configurations of bands spawned by Zaiko. Known as much for his stylish dress sense as his vocal delivery, Wemba has chosen to cater to his different audiences by maintaining two bands: Viva le Musica for soukous and a group, including French session players, for his international pop. The musicians of Les Quatres Étoiles have not attempted to emulate Wemba's schizophrenic existence and have remained soukous loyalists. But they have had to make some concessions to European audiences by polishing the rough edges off the Congolese sound.

The turmoil that beset the Congo in the 1990s has forced many musicians into exile. The clubs of Matonge have been in a state of terminal decline. But the influence of Congolese musicians is still to be heard in East Africa, discussed subsequently.

Angola

This former Portuguese colony has been beset by innumerable problems since its independence from Lisbon in 1975. The MPLA (Popular Movement for the Liberation of Angola) government waged a relentless civil war against UNITA (National Union for the

Total Independence of Angola), which opposed the MPLA's pro-Soviet alignment and, until 1994, was backed by the apartheid regime. But even the Lusaka Accords brought precious little respite from the conflict, and so this vast country with significant resources still faces massive problems caused by a shattered economy and concomitant social dislocation. Obviously, cultural and leisure activities have been low on the list of priorities in a country in which most of its citizens are concerned with survival rather than entertainment and where, until recently, the MPLA government exercised a monopoly on musical production. Nonetheless, the Angolan capital, Luanda, has a well-equipped studio at the National Radio station and is the hub of the country's musical creativity.

Angola boasts a rich variety of musical styles. The bedrock of these is *semba*, which derives its name from the circling dance step associated with that rhythm and has historical ties to the Brazilian samba. There are also local variants of merengue (Latin American dance music) and pachanga (Afro-Cuban dance music). Such eclecticism is evident in the music of Orquestra os Jovens do Prenda, which blends the indigenous semba rhythm with Congolese rumba in a style they call *quilapanga.* Four guitars reproduce the textures of the two-person marimba xylophone, a five-piece percussive section provides the driving rhythm, and trumpets and saxophones interject a blast of big-band-style brass. Orquestra os Jovens do Prenda was formed in the mid-1960s and produced politicized lyrics critical of the colonial authorities before disbanding. In its post-independence incarnations it produced songs that dealt with the staple fare of pop music: love, lust, and so forth.

Angola's most acclaimed artist is Barceló De Carvalho, otherwise known as Bonga. Forced into exile for singing pro-independence songs, Bonga connected with musicians from other Portuguese-speaking countries in Europe. His repertoire continued to deal with political and social issues even after Angola's independence. His melancholy music mixes soukous and a softer, Brazilian-influenced sound behind his trademark raspy voice. He subsequently returned to Luanda, where he has continued to release music that showcases the variety of Angolan styles. Bonga's contemporary, Waldemar Bastos, has proved equally adept at airing his concerns with a pared-down backing of acoustic guitar, percussion, and bass. Musical activism has been and remains a feature of Angolan popular music.

Southern Africa

As is apparent from the Introduction, the Republic of South Africa has the most developed and sophisticated music industry on the African continent; hence it receives a rather more extensive treatment here than other countries have. However, neighboring states should not be regarded as attenuated echoes of South Africa. Zimbabwe, for instance, might share that country's strong vocal traditions, but its own cultural heritage makes it unique.

Republic of South Africa

Since the late 1920s, when Eric Gallo established the first local record company in Johannesburg, the "city of gold" has been the headquarters of South Africa's music industry. Gallo Records created a stable of labels that targeted black consumers while obtaining licenses from multinational record companies to distribute international music to predominantly white audiences. Historically, then, the country has had racially segmented markets, but there have been occasions when particular genres or styles have appealed to audiences across the racial divide. In keeping with the state's segregationist and apartheid policies, the national broadcaster reinforced ethnic cleavages by establishing radio channels for the different ethno-linguistic groups. The SABC delayed the introduction of television until 1976 because the government feared that foreign influences would undermine the insular and conservative culture dominated by white Afrikaners. However, this tunnel vision did not take cognizance of the infiltration of overseas fashions and trends on urban black culture. American influences on dress and street talk were particularly strong. And phonograph records and films had a significant impact on the development of popular music.

The first homegrown music to be commercially recorded was known as *marabi.* It was the quintessential music of the slumyards and the shebeens (illegal township taverns). It is usually associated with the keyboard (piano or pedal organ) although sometimes played on guitars. It has a cyclical harmonic structure that is typical of African indigenous musics but shows the influence of Dixieland jazz, especially in the syncopation. Marabi was the foundation of South African jazz, which enjoyed as much patronage among the black community as all the offshoots of rock 'n' roll music did amongst its white counterpart. Indeed, jazz became *the* popular music par excellence between the 1950s and 1970s. However, it has not managed to retain this status and has become, instead, a music patronized by an urban black elite and white aficionados.

Some of South Africa's most celebrated jazz artists spent some of their most productive years in exile. Yet they were able to build their careers on what they learned at home. For instance, Miriam Makeba had first sung professionally with the Jazz Dazzlers, the backing band of the top vocal combo the Manhattan Brothers. Then she fronted the Skylarks before being cast in the film *Come Back Africa* (1957) and the stage musical *King Kong* (1959). As with other members of the cast of the jazz opera, she opted not to return to her homeland after the show toured the United Kingdom and the United States. She was joined in exile by the trumpeter Hugh Masekela, to whom she was briefly married and who is best known in the West for his 1968 hit "Grazin' in the Grass." Masekela's apprenticeship had been with Father Trevor Huddleston's Band and the orchestra that performed *King Kong.* Masekela had also played alongside pianist Abdullah Ibrahim (also known as Dollar Brand) and trombonist Jonas Gwangwa in the Jazz Epistles. Both Ibrahim and Gwangwa established well-deserved reputations for themselves as virtuoso performers. The fourth major South African jazz musician to achieve international recognition was the saxophonist Dudu Pukwana. He arrived in the United Kingdom in the 1960s and played with Chris McGregor's Blue Notes and subsequently with the Brotherhood of Breath. Although the country was deprived of these and other talents for some thirty-odd years, and the homegrown jazz scene was that much poorer on account of their absence, South African jazz still remained fairly creative and vibrant but fell out of favor with the post-1970s generation.

The decline was partially arrested in the 1990s by a revival of the township swing jazz of the kind purveyed by the Elite Swingsters and the African Jazz Pioneers. Led by Ntemi Piliso, who had played with the best musicians in the 1950s and whose pedigree was unmatched, the AJP turned out a string of albums, one of which was recorded live at the jazz festival in Montreux, Switzerland. The retro revival proved a catalyst for the coming of age of a new crop of jazz instrumentalists. These included saxophonists McCoy Mrubata and Zim Ngqwana, and pianists Paul Hanmer and Moses Molelekwa. Although the emphasis in local jazz is once again on instrumental and fairly experimental jazz stylings, a few exciting female vocalists have emerged since the 1990s. The most noteworthy of these are Gloria Bosman and Sibongile Khumalo. But jazz struggles to compete commercially with international pop and other forms of homegrown music.

During the 1950s the tin whistle, or pennywhistle, became ubiquitous on the streets of South Africa's townships. Best known in the West in connection with Irish music, the pennywhistle is a cheap wind instrument played like the recorder but with very different tonal qualities. It was apparently adopted by township youths who used the pennywhistle jive bands as cover for illegal gambling games on street corners. As they sought to evade the police pick-up vans, which were dubbed *kwela kwelas*, the music came to be called *kwela*. Soon they were emulating skiffle bands and added homemade tea-chest basses and guitars to the lineup. The record companies realized the commercial potential of the pennywhistle jive sound following the success of the 1951 film *The Magic Garden*, which included the hit number "Pennywhistle Boogie" in its soundtrack. The simple plot celebrated the urban legend of the street urchin turned star. It was realized in real life in the person of Spokes Mashiyane, who was whisked off to the Gallo recording studio by the talent scout Strike Vilakazi while playing an impromptu street-corner session. In 1954 Mashiyane recorded a double-sided 78-rpm hit, "Ace Blues"/"Kwela Spokes." This proved to be the first of many kwela hits for Mashiyane and imitators such as Lemmy "Special" Mambaso and Thomas Phale.

Meanwhile, American rock 'n' roll artists like Elvis Presley and Bill Haley had become popular, particularly among white youths who embraced the music and subculture. As elsewhere, it was condemned by the country's self-appointed moral guardians. The reception of rock 'n' roll amongst blacks was rather more complex. A number of bands performed rock 'n' roll numbers that mimicked the American artists, although lyrics were either changed or sung in the vernacular. However, the unavailability of discs and lack of news coverage of African-American performers of rock 'n' roll meant that it was identified as a white product. Moreover, enthusiasm for African-American jazz and its local variants peaked in the late 1950s and early 1960s, when rock 'n' roll was at its most popular. And black musicians were forging an indigenous urban popular style, known as township jive or *mbaqanga*.

Kwela was superseded by *sax jive*. The beginning of this new style can be dated to Spokes Mashiyane's first recording on saxophone, "Big Joe Special" (1958). Many other untutored but musically gifted players such as Kippie Moeketsi and West Nkosi were instrumental in developing sax jive. It was usually built around very simple repeated melodic fragments with the musical accompaniment giving it variety and depth. By the 1960s, the rhythms had become heavier as the electric bass guitar was given emphasis in the mix. It now became known as *mbaqanga*. This is a Zulu word which literally means "dumpling," with connotations of "homemade," as the artists were invariably musically illiterate and could make "easy money" (i.e., bread or dough). Initially an instrumental idiom, *mbaqanga* soon developed into a vocal style called *mqashiyo*. The vocal component of *mbaqanga* developed directly from 1950s vocal troupes such as the Manhattan Brothers and the Skylarks. These styles had at first been copied directly from African-American models, but local artists developed an increasingly indigenized sound. A crucial phase in this development was the emergence of a lineup consisting of a male lead vocalist backed by five-part harmonies sung by female groups. The standard four-part harmony was extended by dividing the tenor into a high and low part, and the male vocalist sang in a very low bass range (*inkubodla*, literally "goat singing" or "groaning"). This style originated with Black Mambazo, but it is best exemplified by the recordings of Mahlathini and the Mahotella Queens. All the essential *mbaqanga* elements are to be heard in the eponymous track, in which the group claims to have "invented" the style. Mahlathini groans in counterpoint to the Mahotella Queens' five-part harmonies, underpinned by the rhythms of the Makhona Tsohle Band.

By the 1970s the groaner-plus-female-chorus formula of *mbaqanga* was being replaced by all male line-ups. This development is typified by the Boyoyo Boys, an outfit which had been originally assembled as a studio backing band for sax jive artist Thomas Phale. Led by principal composer Petrus Maneli, the Boyoyo Boys became successful in their own right. Their half-chanted harmonies and loping rhythms are showcased on their 1970s recordings. Another *mbaqanga* group that has become an institution in the South African music industry is the Soul Brothers. This three-piece outfit comprised Zulu vocals underscored by a deep, heavy bass sound and keyboards. The Hammond organ of Moses Mgwenya (suggestive of Booker T and the MGs), along with their rich, kwela-inspired brass section, is a hallmark of the Soul Brothers sound. They managed to continue scoring hits into the 1980s, and still exist, albeit with wholly new personnel.

In the wake of the 1976 Soweto uprising, the younger generation tended to distance itself from musical styles they associated with the old order—both neo-traditional and township jive. Instead, they embraced American soul music, funk, and disco. For instance, the Cannibals started out as a backing band for vocalist Jacob "Mparanyana" Radebe's impassioned delivery and monologues with backing of guitar, saxes, and female choruses which echoed the Stax sound of Otis Redding. After Radebe's death in 1979, the Cannibals evolved into Stimela, under the leadership of guitarist Ray Phiri, and changed direction. The band's incorporation of Afro-jazz influences is evident on its *Look, Listen and Decide* (1986) album.

One of the first bands to attract a multiracial following was Harari. Having started out as the Beaters, they changed their name after a successful tour of Zimbabwe. Their sound also underwent a transition from a fusion of American-style funk, soul, and pop to the addition of progressive rock influences. Only their occasional Zulu and Sotho lyrics, and their ethnic designer-chic outfits, set them apart from their overseas counterparts. Sipho "Hotstix" Mabuse was a drummer with both bands but embarked on a solo career in the 1980s, when he emerged as a talented multi-instrumentalist. He recorded such hits as "Jive Soweto" and "Burn Out" (1985), the latter becoming popular on the American dance club scene. These numbers achieved a seamless synthesis of *mbaqanga*, soul, and dance pop.

By the 1980s there had developed a slickly produced brand of township pop referred to by fans and detractors alike as "bubblegum". Electronic keyboards (i.e., synthesizers) replaced guitars, and the disco beat was produced by an electric drum box. Vocals were arranged in an overlapping call-and-response pattern, where one melodic phrase is repeated in traditional fashion. Lyrics were usually in English. Exponents included Yvonne Chaka Chaka and Brenda Fassie.

South African crossover music has assumed many forms. One of the most innovative has been the work of Johnny Clegg, who embraced Zulu culture. He teamed up with Zulu street guitarist Sipho Mchunu to form Juluka in the early 1970s. Live performances were highlighed by Zulu dance (*indlamu*) routines. Their repertoire included songs with English and Zulu lyrics and which combined the unique style of Zulu guitar work with Anglo-American rock. Their debut album was *Universal Men* (1979). With the departure of partner Mchunu, Clegg formed Savuka and the sound became increasingly Westernized as he sought to capitalize on his appeal as *Le Zoulou Blanc* overseas. Other crossover acts have included Mango Groove, Tananas, Malombo, Bayete, the Soweto String Quartet, Blk Sonshine and, more recently, Freshly Ground. These artists have successfully managed to bridge the racially segmented market.

White pop/rock artists have always struggled to compete in a relatively small (but affluent) end of the market, which has been saturated by Anglo-American products. They have also (sometimes deservedly) been criticized for producing imitative or derivative sounds. This is perhaps understandable, given the social conditioning of white audiences by the mass media during the apartheid era. Yet, some South African groups such as Freedom's Children, the Otis Waygood Blues Band, and Hawk (in the late 1960s and early 1970s) developed their own styles and original material that won them cult followings. By the late 1970s bands such as the Radio Rats and No Friends of Harry, from the unlikely place of Springs on the East Rand, were part of a thriving post-punk/new wave scene. Despite owing much to overseas inspiration, these bands produced lyrics that were responsive to the South African situation.

There were also a number of white artists who ran afoul of the apartheid regime because of the criticisms voiced in their music. For instance, the maverick "folkie" Roger Lucey's debut album *The Road is Much Longer* (1979) had four of its eleven tracks banned by the Publications Appeal Board. Other artists, such as James Phillips (who fronted the Cherry-Faced Lurchers), were capable of reflecting the lived experience of a section of South African society. Thus his "Shot Down in the Streets" (1985) or Bright Blue's "Weeping" (1987) were genuine expressions of white angst and guilt during the apartheid era.

There is a relatively large market for popular forms of Afrikaans music, such as their take on country and easy listening, which has always been apolitical. This mold was challenged during the 1980s, when a group of young Afrikaans artists articulated their disapproval of apartheid through their music. Christened the *Afrikaans Alternatief* movement, they embarked on their so-called *Voëlvry* tour in 1989. They were prevented from playing on certain university campuses and in towns controlled by supporters of the National Party government. The repertoires of the late Johannes Kerkorrel and Bernoldus Niemand (also known as James Phillips) included some scathing commentary on the hegemonic white Afrikaans culture. Perhaps the most important artist in this crop was the iconoclastic Koos Kombuis (also known as Andre le Toit). His earlier work included some poignant social criticism. His more recent work reflects the ambivalent attitudes of many towards the "new" South Africa. This is clearly evident in the title track of his album *Blameer Dit Op Apartheid* (1997). But his work also represents a search for a new Afrikaner identity in post-apartheid South Africa; one that distances itself from the stigma of Afrikaans being regarded as the language of the oppressor.

The biggest selling genre in South Africa is gospel music. It takes two forms: choral and contemporary, as per the categories in the South African Music Awards. The former category even distinguishes between choral gospel music rendered in the different official languages. Large choirs are a standard feature of black churches, especially the Pentecostal and Zionist ones. They combine elements from European hymns, African-American spirituals, and African traditional sources in enthusiastic renditions of gospel songs. Given that certain independent churches number their members in the millions, it is not surprising that recordings of their choirs sell thousands to this captive market. The latter category comprises a lead vocalist with the backing of an electric rock-type combo. The most successful contemporary gospel artist is Rebecca Malope, whose albums routinely become platinum. Working with producer Sizwe Zako, the diminutive vocalist has hit on a formula that guarantees good sales. In fact, she is reckoned to be the biggest-selling South African artist in any genre.

One of the few acts to rival the popularity of Malope is Joseph Shabalala's vocal troupe, Ladysmith Black Mambazo (LBM). Although LBM came to the attention of world music audiences as a result of their collaboration with Paul Simon on the American's controversial *Graceland* album, their a cappella style has deep roots in Zulu migrant culture, where it is known as *isicathamiya* or *mbube*—the latter name derived from the title of the 1939 song by Solomon Linda discussed earlier in this chapter. In the 1940s mbube passed through an aggressive-sounding phase called *isikhwela jo* (Zulu for "bombing") before evolving into the gentler harmonies of *isicathamiya* (Zulu for "tiptoeing").[4] LBM were awarded a Grammy for their album *Shaka Zulu* in 1987. Their growing popularity at home and abroad has continued into the new century.

South Africa's democratization has been accompanied by a musical "explosion" and profusion of styles. A new generation of artists has been influenced by rap, reggae, rock, and rhythm and blues. There are rappers such as Prophets of da City and Skwatta Camp, who perform their songs mainly in the Afrikaans street talk and slang of the Cape Flats. South Africa has its own dub poet in the person of Lesego Rampolokeng, who mixes Jamaican dub and American rap with Sotho oral poetry and delivers his social commentaries in a Johannesburg patois. Then there is Lucky Dube's reggae, which is inflected with the *mbaqanga* style on which he built his early singing career. There are a score of local acts such as Ringo who are producing a South African version of R&B. And, of course, Anglo-American influences are undoubtedly pervasive in the rock of the Springbok Nude Girls or Just Jinger. All these styles are eclectic or types of crossover that add to South Africa's rich musical and cultural diversity. They exemplify the wide spectrum of the hues and colors of the "rainbow nation" during the Mandela years.

The latest style to take hold in post-apartheid South Africa is *kwaito*, which is a form of black urban dance music. Kwaito emerged in 1992, when young local black music producers started to mix hip-hop, techno, and house music with local rhythms and basslines to create a fresh new style. Its tempo is slow, and its producers sample tunes indiscriminately from a wide range of musical sources. Popular kwaito hits of the late 1990s were usually short on lyrical content, with simple catch phrases in *tsotsitaal* (literally the language of the criminal elements) chanted over an electronically synthesized backbeat of house, hip-hop, and ragga beats. The pioneers of kwaito included Abashante, Boom Shaka, Trompies, Bongo Maffin, and Arthur Mofokate. Subsequently, kwaito came in for a lot of criticism because it celebrated a materialist consumer culture of a depoliticized generation of black youths. Its popularity was closely associated with the growth of the radio station YFM and Y magazine. It went hand in hand with the construction of a new identity among urban black youths, with its own dress codes and argot. It has even spawned its own designer label, known as *loxion kulca* (location culture). Kwaito is the music of the so-called "born frees" or "Y generation." Kwaito has been described variously as South Africa's take on hip-hop or a slowed-down version of house. It is neither. It is a unique and constantly mutating hybrid of a range of local and foreign influences.

Zimbabwe

During the independence struggle, or *Chimurenga*, Shona musicians created a new pop sound based on the chiming, cyclic melodies and rhythms of the *mbira,* a thumb piano used to communicate with ancestral spirits. This sound was popularized by Thomas Mapfumo and his band the Blacks Unlimited. He transposed the complex, sinewy lines of mbira music onto guitars and bass and backed it up with a solid bass drum pulse. He peppered his arrangements with quirky horn passages, added as many as three mbiras to the lineup, and overlaid the whole with chants and warbles. His songs became rallying cries for the struggle, with titles such as "Mothers, Send Your Children to War," and so his sound was called *chimurenga* (Shona for struggle). He has continued to speak out against the abuse of power by Robert Mugabe's ZANU-PF (Zimbabwean African National Union/Patriotic Front) with songs such as "Corruption" (1989). Thus Mapfumo has managed to raise the ire of both the Smith and Mugabe regimes with his brave stands against Zimbabwean authorities.

Mapfumo's only serious rival for the mantle of Zimbabwe's musical icon has been Oliver "Tuku" Mutukudzi. An accomplished guitarist in his own right, Mutukudzi pays a token tribute to Shona traditional music, but his music is thoroughly modern. His more obvious influences straddle South African jive and R&B. His soul-inflected style has been named after Mutukudzi's nickname, *tuku.* Like Mapfumo, Mutukudzi also laces his songs with social commentary and some sort of message.

The Bhundu Brothers epitomized the euphoric spirit of independent Zimbabwe. The quartet appeared on the scene in the 1980s with their breakneck *jit* sound, a catch-all term for the country's electric pop. Not only could they jive to rival Soweto's finest, but they were able to compress a languid rumba/soukous number into a three-minute blast. The guitar work was characterized by lively breaks and chunky bass lines and complemented by sweet vocal harmonies and a rhythm resting on a thumping downbeat characteristic of much southern African music. By the 1990s the group had dissolved, and like the country, its star quickly waned.

EAST AFRICA

Popular music in the East Africa region encompasses a wide range of styles of both local and foreign origin. The influence of Swahili culture, which is a fusion of African, Arab, and Indian elements, transcends its concentration on the East African Indian Ocean coastline. In fact, Swahili has become the language of wider communication across the region. Although the hinterland is the home of diverse ethnic and linguistic groups and many musicians make recordings in their mother tongues (such as Kikuyu and Luo), others prefer to record in Swahili so as to broaden their appeal beyond the ethno-linguistic market. Some of Kenya's best-known musicians are immigrants from nearby countries, most often from Tanzania and the Democratic Republic of the Congo. They occasionally sing in their own language but, more often than not, use Swahili so as to reach wider audiences. Thus language serves as both a bridge and a barrier to the marketing of East African musical styles.

Unlike much of the region, Ethiopia was not subjected to prolonged colonial occupation during the modern era and has endured periods of cultural isolation. Outside influences on the development of popular music were tempered accordingly. Thus, a unique pop music tradition has been fashioned by a unique configuration of indigenous and foreign elements. Ethiopian popular music, which once had little in common with other variants of Afropop, has since the 1990s become more generic.

Kenya

The Kenyan capital, Nairobi, is the musical melting pot of East Africa. It was here after the end of World War II that the African Broadcasting Service aired a mix of Cuban dance music, early Congolese rumba, and finger-style guitar, along with South African kwela and traditional sounds mostly from the country's Kikuyu and Luo peoples. It was here, too, where the first regional recording studio was established in 1947. And it was here that musicians performing in nightclubs developed a vibrant new sound that amounted to Kenya's first indigenous popular music, called *benga.*

Benga refers specifically to the dominant style of Luo pop music, which has been performed in the Lake Victoria region since the 1960s. But the term is also used in a generic sense of the other regional styles that have been influenced by the Luo version of benga. The music incorporates traditional elements, especially the mimickry by guitarists of the syncopated melodies of the Luo's eight-string *nyatiti* lyre. Benga is characterized by the interplay of bass, guitar, and vocal. Pulsating, staccato bass lines are prominent in the mix while the guitars repeat melodic lines or catchy riffs at the end of each vocal phrase. The best-known exponents of Luo *benga* were Shirati Jazz and the Victoria Kings. The former, under the leadership of D. O. Misiani, invoked Luo praise-singing traditions in their lyrics that relate stories and anecdotes about well-known individuals. The latter produced humorous love songs, laced with advice on morality and good living. The heyday of benga was during the 1970s, when the Voice of Kenya radio restricted the broadcast of Zairean-influenced music.

Congolese rumba music, or soukous (discussed under the Democratic Republic of the Congo), competed with benga for the ears and earnings of Kenyan consumers. Owing to deteriorating conditions in Zaire, several groups relocated to Kenya in the 1960s and 1970s and established a clientele in Nairobi's nightclubs. Bands such as Zaiko Langa Langa and Orchestra Shama Shama popularized the rousing, fast-paced rhythms and laid down the framework for *cavacha*, which is essentially a Kenyan version of rumba. This foundation was built upon by outfits such as Orchestra Virunga, Super Mazembe, and Orchestra Makassy, all of which were collaborations among Zairean, Kenyan, and Tanzanian musicians. Virunga's "Malako Disco" was one of Kenya's biggest-ever dance floor hits. Although expatriate Zaireans and Tanzanians were denied work permits in the 1980s by the Kenyan government, which wanted to boost local music, their contribution to cavacha was immensely important. The impact of the Tanzanian group Simba Wanyika exemplified the transition to a smoother cavacha style. Still guitar-driven, the sound blended the spare instrumentation of 1970s rumba-rock with the gentle rhythms and fullness of older rumba and warm Swahili vocals. There was less emphasis on snare drums with the rhythm being carried on congas together with clavés and hi-hat. Since the early 1980s the Swahili bands have experimented with stylistic innovations, but their music remains closely tied to their rumba origins. Swahili rumba remains one of the most popular sounds in Kenya.

The key sites of Swahili culture are the Kenyan ports of Lamu and Mombasa, as well as the northern Tanzanian city of Tanga and the island of Zanzibar. *Taarab* music grew out of a history of cultural interaction and features instruments such as the electric guitar, the *oud* (fretless lute), *rika* (tambourine), Indian tabla drums, accordion, and electronic keyboards. Its hybrid nature is evident from its component parts, which include long melodic lines, a style of singing influenced by Arabic traditions, dance rhythms influenced by traditional African drumming (*ngoma*), and stylized Swahili poetry dealing with romance and marriage. Taarab orchestras play for weddings and other important social occasions. In its recorded form, taarab has transcended its rather conservative Islamic roots and developed into a popular music style that has been well received beyond the coastal zone. For instance, vocalists such as Malika and Moreno Batamba achieved number one positions in the 1980s on the Kenyan pop charts with updated versions of taarab. And in the early 1990s, outfits called TOT Taarab and Muungano Taarab shook things up even further with a modern electric sound and provocative lyrics.

If taarab evinces Muslim Arab influences, the Christian gospel tradition is equally significant and assumes many forms in East Africa. It takes the form of large choirs that combine European harmonic elements and African rhythms and melodies. Choirs featuring a lead vocalist are sometimes backed by the standard rock instrumentation of guitars, bass, and drums. Gospel is also performed by small ensembles such as guitar bands that produce songs with inspirational or religious content. The popularity of gospel is such that the media produce a weekly chart of bestsellers alongside charts for African and international music.

Ethiopia

Ethiopian music derives its distinctive sound first and foremost from its plaintive, quavering vocals with their melancholy quality. Vocal delivery in the Amharic language follows the call-and-response pattern with trumpets and saxophones in the manner of American soul. It also marries traditional instruments such as the *masenko* (one-string fiddle) and the *krar* (lyre) with amplified Western instruments such as guitars and accordions. The time-honored *tchik-tchik-ka*—a fast, lopsided triplet beat—provides the rhythm for the physically sensuous *eskeuta* (or *iskista*) dance routines. This style was pioneered by artists such as Tilahoun Gessesse and Mahmoud Ahmed. These singers fronted a variety of backing bands, performed both traditional and popular songs, and generally diversified their repertoires. By the early 1970s, the capital, Addis Ababa, had a vibrant nightlife, and the Ethiopian music industry experienced its "golden years."

Things changed for the worse when Haile Selassie was ousted by the military dictator Mengistu Haile Mariam in 1974. During the late 1970s and 1980s the country was subjected to draconian laws that imposed strict censorship and restrictions on the import of tape recordings. Restrictions were also placed on travel so that musicians were unable to tour abroad. A number of recording artists such as Aster Aweke fled the repressive Mengistu regime and found audiences among expatriate Ethiopian communities abroad. A curfew stifled the live entertainment industry and drove musicians into studios, where session bands such as the Roha Band and the Wallias Band developed. The former backed already-established singers such as Mahmoud Ahmed, as well as a younger crop that included Neway Debebe. The Wallias Band backed, among others, the female vocalist Netsanet Melessa, who released a string of hits. The volume of sales of these artists increased exponentially as the cheaper cassette replaced the vinyl record as the format of consumer choice.

The demise of the Mengistu regime in 1991 proved to be a mixed blessing for Ethiopian musicians. Established artists were afforded the opportunity to tour and play for exiled communities abroad. A younger generation of artists embraced Kenyan pop and Congolese soukous as well as American rap and reggae. The introduction of the seven-note Western scale also challenged the traditional pentatonic scale. These developments have challenged the long-dominant Amharic music, which has been placed on a par with neo-traditional styles from regions beyond Addis Ababa and the central highlands of Ethiopia.

CONCLUSION

Sub-Saharan African music is as varied as the region's landscape, cuisine, and clothing. It is simultaneously unique and common, for it has elements that are both African and universal. This claim rests on the rejection of the culturalist argument that postulates the myth of an enclosed, traditional African culture. Indeed, Jean-Francois Bayart insists that "traditional culture does not exist; that culture is constantly being negotiated."[5] I share Bayart's suspicion of culturalist discourse that restrains "concrete historical societies in a substantialist definition of their identity by denying them the right to borrow, to be derivative."[6] In other words, culturalism emphasizes difference at the expense of the universal. This chapter has attempted to insert Sub-Saharan African into world music as well as celebrate the creativity of the region's artists.

RESOURCE GUIDE

PRINT SOURCES

Note: Some of these titles are out of print but are worth tracking down from second-hand book dealers, and libraries may still have them.

Andersson, Muff. *Music in the Mix: The Story of South African Popular Music.* Braamfontein: Ravan Press, 1981.

Ansell, Gwen. *Soweto Blues: Jazz, Popular Music & Politics in South Africa.* New York: Continuum, 2004.

Ballantine, Christopher. *Marabi Nights: Early South African Jazz and Vaudeville.* Braamfontein: Ravan Press, 1993.

Barlow, Sean, and Banning Eyre. *Afropop! An Illustrated Guide to Contemporary African Music.* Rowayton, CT: Saraband, 1995.

Bender, Wolfgang. *Sweet Mother: Modern African Music.* Chicago: University of Chicago Press, 1991.

Broughton, Simon, et al., eds. *World Music: The Rough Guide, Volume 1: Africa, Europe and the Middle East.* London: Rough Guides, 1999.

Cloonan, Martin and Drewett, Michael, eds. *Popular Music Censorship in Africa.* Aldershot: Ashgate, 2006.

Collins, John. *West African Pop Roots.* Philadelphia, PA: Temple University Press, 1992.

Coplan, David B. *In Township Tonight! South Africa's Black City Music and Theatre.* Braamfontein: Ravan Press, 1985.

Erlmann, Veit. *African Stars: Studies in Black South African Performance.* Chicago: The University of Chicago Press, 1991.

———. *Music, Modernity and the Global Imagination: South Africa and the West.* New York/Oxford: Oxford University Press, 1999.

Ewens, Graeme. *Africa O-Ye! A Celebration of African Music.* Enfield, Middlesex: Guinness, 1991. (Reprint, Da Capo Press, 1992.)

fRoots (formerly *Folk Roots*). A monthly magazine edited by Ian Anderson, who calls it the "essential worldwide roots music guide." Its Website, http://www.frootsmag.com/, has useful resources and some African content.

Graham, Ronnie. *The Da Capo Guide to Contemporary African Music.* New York: Da Capo Press, 1988. (Updated as *The World of African Music,* Pluto Press, 1992.)

Hamm, Charles. *Putting Popular Music In Its Place.* Cambridge: Cambridge University Press, 1995. Includes five pieces on South African music.

Kivnick, Helen Q. *Where Is the Way: Song and Struggle in South Africa.* Harmondsworth: Penguin, 1990.

Lems-Dworkin, Carol. *African Music: A Pan-African Annotated Bibliography.* London: Hans Zell Publishers, 1991.

Meintjies, Louise. *Sound of Africa! Making Music Zulu in a South African Studio.* Durham/London: Duke University Press, 2003.

Muller, Carol A. *South African Music: A Century of Traditions in Transformation.* Santa Barbara: ABC CLIO, 2004.

Ntama: Journal of African Music and Popular Culture. An online journal hosted by the African Music Archive at Mainz University, Germany. Articles, reviews, etc. by academics with text in English and German. http://ntama.uni-mainz.de/.

Palmer, Mai, and Annemette Kirkegaard, eds. *Playing with Identities in Contemporary Music in Africa.* Uppsala: Nordiska Afrikainstitutet, 2002.

Songlines. A quarterly world music magazine that provides good coverage of African artists. Amounts to an update of the *Rough Guide to World Music* (Broughton 1999).

Stapleton, Chris, and Chris May. *African All-Stars: The Pop Music of a Continent.* London: Paladin, 1989. (Published as *African Rock* by Obelisk/Dutton, 1990.)

Stone, Ruth., ed. *The Garland Handbook of African Music.* London: Taylor and Francis, 1999.

Taylor, Timothy D. *Global Pop: world music, world markets.* New York: Routledge, 1997.

Tenaille, Frank. *Music Is the Weapon of the Future: Fifty Years of African Popular Music.* Chicago: Lawrence Hill Books, 2002.

Thorsén, Stig-Magnus, ed. *Sounds of Change: Social and Political Features of Music in Africa.* Stockholm: Swedish International Development Cooperation Agency, 2005.

Waterman, Christopher. *Juju: A Social History and Ethnography of an African Popular Music.* Chicago: University of Chicago Press, 1990.

WEBSITES

Afribeat.com. June 2001. http://home.worldonline.co.za/~afribeat/. A South Africa–based site which profiles African artists, advertises events, and reviews music albums and films.

The African Music Encyclopedia. 2005. http://africanmusic.org/. African Music Encyclopedia with resources such as photographs and biographies of musicians, a glossary of African styles of music, a directory of distributors and places to buy music.

Afropop Worldwide. 2003. http://www.afropop.org/. Calls itself a guide to African and world music via public radio and the web. Includes comprehensive database and archive.

Amauzine. http://cd.co.za/. An electronic magazine with information on South African musical history and individual artists. Links to the South African Rock Encyclopedia.

fRootsmag.com. Southern Rag Ltd. http://www.frootsmag.com/. An electronic version of *fRoots* (formerly *Folk Roots Magazine*) that devotes a fair amount of attention to African popular music.

Fung, Karen. 2006. *Africa South of the Sahara.* SuLair: Stanford University Libraries and Academic Information Resources. http://www-sul.stanford.edu/depts/ssrg/africa/music.html. Directory of Sub-Saharan African internet resources hosted by Stanford University.

Making Music Productions (MMP). http://www.music.org.za/. Maintained by MMP as a reference and educational resource for musicians from South Africa and neighboring countries.

Music Industry Online. http://www.mio.co.za/. The site of MIO Entertainment, a South African company that seeks to educate musicians about how to get ahead in the industry through access to resources.

Paterson, Douglas. 16 May 2006. *East African Music.* http://members.aol.com/dpaterson/eamusic.htm. East African music site maintained by Douglas Paterson, who has been involved in promoting the music of Kenya and Tanzania.

VIDEOS/FILMS

Amandla! A Revolution in Four-Part Harmony (United States, 2002). Directed by Lee Hirsch. This documentary makes the case for protest music being integral to the struggle against apartheid in South Africa.

Rhythm of Resistance: The Black Music of South Africa (United Kingdom, 1979). Directed by Jeremy Marre. A documentary that records public performances and intimate moments of artists during the apartheid era. Now available on DVD.

Stopping the Music (Republic of South Africa, 2002). Directed by Michael Drewett. Relates the story of a South African musician and the special branch security officer who tried to silence him. Available from Freemuse.

RECORDINGS

Note: This select discography is intended to serve three purposes: (1) provide details for recordings mentioned in the text; (2) list some landmark recordings by individual artists; (3) list some compilations that might offer readers a primer for building a representative collection of Sub-Saharan African popular music. The list is arranged alphabetically with compilations at the end.

Ade, King Sunny, and His African Beats. *Juju Music.* Island, 1982. The first and best of the Nigerian's three albums to be made specifically for the international market.

Blondy, Alpha. *The Best of Alpha Blondy.* Shanachie. Peerless Afro-reggae by the Ivorian, who sings in his vernacular Dioula, as well as English and French.

Bonga. *Roça de Jindungo.* Vidisco. A good sample of Angolan samba, featuring Bonga's trademark growl and songs of oppression.

Franco and OK Jazz. *Originalité.* RetroAfric. A re-release of early recordings that mark the beginning of classic Congo rumba.

Kanté, Mory. *Akwaba Beach.* Barclay, 1988. Hi-tech music for the dance floor. The Malian's breakthrough album.

Keita, Salif. *The Mansa of Mali: A Retrospective*. Mango, 1994. Vocal performance of unsurpassed passion and intensity by the Malian master of the griot's art, descendant of a family of warriors and kings.

Kidjo, Angelique. *Logozo*. Mango, 1991. The breakthrough album of the Benin diva with the big heart and equally big voice.

Kuti, Fela Anikulapo. *Music Is the Weapon: The Best of Fela Kuti* (Wrasse Records, 2005) Two CDs and DVD hardly do justice to his repertoire, but this is a starting point.

Lô, Ismael. *Iso*. Barclay, 1994. Both ballads and up-tempo numbers convey the artist's cosmopolitan sophistication.

Maal, Baaba. *Firin' in Fouta*. Mango, 1994. A slickly produced pastiche of African modernist sounds.

Mapfumo, Thomas. *The Chimurenga Singles 1976–80*. Earthworks. The coded Shona lyrics of the Zimbabwean musician who gave the genre its name.

Mensah, E. T. *All for You*. RetroAfric. A collection of classic big band highlife tracks by the Ghanaian pioneer of the style.

N'Dour, Youssou. *The Guide (Wommat)*. Columbia, 1994. The Senegalese artist won deserved recognition in world music markets with this release.

Osibisa. *The Best of Osibisa*. The criss-cross rhythms of the Afro-rock highlife fusion of the Ghanaian group.

Rogie, S. E. *The Palm Wine Sounds of S. E. Rogie*. Stern's. A career overview of the Sierra Leone guitarist who devoted himself to the promotion of palm wine music.

Toure, Ali Farka, with Ry Cooder. *Talking Timbuktu*. Hannibal, 1995. Collaboration between the Malian and American guitarists in a wide variety of styles from hard Berber blues to sweet Bambara love songs to wild traditional riffs on the one-string fiddle.

Wemba, Papa. *Le Kuru Yaku*. Da Dass, 1971. Raw and unpolished, but the soukous star's superb harmonies command instant attention.

Various Artists. *Ethiopiques: The Golden Age of Modern Ethiopian Music 1969–75*. Buda Musique. Volumes 1 and 3. A nostalgic but judicious sampling of the biggest names and relatively unknown (to Western ears) artists from the twilight years of the Haile Selassie era.

Various Artists. *Gospel Spirit of Africa*. Gallo, 1998. Notwithstanding its name, it is a compendium of specifically South African gospel music.

Various Artists. *Guitar Paradise of East Africa*. Earthworks/Virgin, 1990. Showcases the guitar-based music of the region, including Swahili rumba styles and examples of taarab music.

Various Artists. *From Marabi to Disco*. Gallo. A chronological compilation covering the 1930s to the 1980s of styles that emanated from South Africa.

Various Artists. *The Nairobi Beat: Kenyan Pop Music Today*. Rounder Select, 1992. A sampling of benga styles from a range of Kenyan ethno-linguistic groups.

Various Artists. *The Rough Guide to South African Music*. World Music Network. A representative collection of tracks that samples the country's major musical genres.

EVENTS

All African Music Awards (aka Kora Awards). http://www.koraawards.co.za/. Introduced in 1994 in order to recognize artistic and musical excellence throughout Africa and its Diaspora. Modeled on the American Grammy Awards, the annual awards ceremony is now broadcast live by satellite to four continents.

Cape Town International Jazz Festival. http://www.capetownjazzfest.com/. Formerly the North Sea Jazz Festival, it is staged annually in South Africa's "Mother City." Lineup usually includes eminent African and international artists

Festival in the Desert. A celebration of Tuareg culture which features musicians from Mali, Niger, Mauritania and other countries. The annual gathering is held in the desert oasis Essakane, some 65 kilometers from Timbuktu, and is an alluring attraction for the adventurous, music-loving traveler.

National Arts Festival. http://www.nafest.co.za/. The premier event on South Africa's cultural calendar. This annual event is held in Grahamstown and usually boasts a range of musical performances from classical and opera through to jazz and contemporary music in all its forms. OppiKoppi.

An annual outdoor musical festival which stages a cross-section of South African performers. It has established itself as a household name and leader in the live music and festival industry in South Africa.

South African Music Awards. The annual ceremony recognizes achievements in the field of recorded music. Commencing in 1994 and coordinated by RiSA, SAMA has become a highlight on the calendar of the country's glitterati.

WOMEX. A WOMAD project, the World Music Expo is an annual showcase of third world music at first world sites. It also seeks to promote its presence in cyberspace through its virtual reality showcase of world music.

ORGANIZATIONS

Recording Industry of South Africa (RiSA). http://www.risa.org.za/risa.php. Successor to the Association of the South African Music Industry (ASAMI) which, like its predecessor, is committed to improving the state and promoting the interests of the industry. It hosts the annual South African Music Awards (SAMA) and fights to stamp out music piracy.

South African Music Rights Organization (SAMRO). Collects performance royalties for songs broadcast on radio or television ("needle time").

South African Recording Rights Association Limited (SARRAL). Collects the creator/songwriter royalties from the sale of products, including recorded music.

PROJECTS/INITIATIVES

Afrofile. A joint South African and Norwegian project focusing on the digital distribution of African music to major markets in the world.

Moshito. A private-public initiative to make South Africa a preferred destination for recording artists and to increase the presence of locally produced music in the global market. Holds an annual music conference and exhibition.

Music Industry Task Team (MITT). A forum of South African and international experts established in 2000 to investigate the state of the music industry and make recommendations to government.

NOTES

1. Lara Allen, "Music and Politics in Africa," *Social Dynamics* 30.2 (2004): 4–5.
2. Barlow and Eyre 1995 (in Resource Guide, Print Sources), p. vii.
3. David Coplan and Bennetta Julies-Rosette, "*Nkosi Sikelel' iAfrika* and the Liberation Spirit of South Africa," *African Studies* 64.2 (2005): 30.
4. See the article on Ladysmith Black Mambazo at Afropop Worldwide (in Resource Guide, Websites).
5. Jean-Francois Bayart, *The Illusion of Cultural Identity*, translated by Steven Rendell, Janet Rottman, Cynthia Schoch, and Jonathan Derrick (Chicago: Chicago University Press, 2005), p. 30.
6. Ibid., p. 245.

PERIODICALS

CHARLES MUIRU NGUGI

On August 20, 2005, the *East African Standard* published an extensive profile of Caroline Mutoko, a leading radio announcer in Kenya, describing her as Kenya's "fastest mouth." The article was generously illustrated with color photographs of her "liberally spaced, entirely tiled, three-bedroom apartment" where "parsimony meets stylishness." The apartment is in a "well-guarded" apartment block in a leafy section of Nairobi. The living room was described as being all of 7 meters across, and the kitchen was so large it had taken years to populate with choice accoutrements of modernity: a dining set, a lounge set, a card table with flowers, a drinks cabinet, and a glass-topped, round coffee table on which sat a chess board. She was photographed in different dresses, posing in different sections of her apartment. In one picture, she stood beside a mahogany-colored dining table in a navy-blue business suit; in another, she lounged, almost spread-eagled, on her green sofa, in a white dress, and in yet another picture, she sat cross-legged on the carpet in a black gown with gray fur trimming. Her car, we were told, is a Mitsubishi Outlander, a cross between a sedan and a sport utility vehicle. She works for the KISS 100 radio station, which commands 10 percent of the Shs. 8.4 billion ($116 million) advertising industry in Kenya. She was quoted as saying: "They call me the KISS 100 Rottweiler . . . I will make sure the money comes in . . . I'll kill everyone in order to deliver."[1]

This article clearly depicts a new, arriviste Africa—an Africa you are probably not used to seeing. It is certainly not the Africa of the *Egungun* masks and divination, of teeming wildlife, of the Maasai herdsman standing on one leg silhouetted against the setting sun in an African savannah of tall grass and acacia, of starving urchins and corrupt Big Men. This Africa is the product of the convergence of globalization, media freedom, and a certain resurgence of pride in things African, a kind of new Negritude. It may not be exactly representative of everyday life in Africa, but it is an Africa that is becoming increasingly common in many African periodicals. It is both existing and aspirational; although the African elite has attained it, the majority of Africans can only wish for it. In a continent where stars and celebrities have in the past meant the high achievers of other countries, the announcers, the rap and gospel musicians, celebrity pastors, athletes, sex therapists, the rich, and politicians are the new African celebrities, noteworthy for both their spectacle and role-model value. In three important categories—communication, transportation, and personal ornamentation—these new

African stars are setting the trend, by owning the latest gadgetry, driving the latest car models, and dressing to kill. They have become fodder for the African popular media. Periodicals all over the continent are focusing on them as never before and are using them as pegs to sell new lifestyles to African readers. Dele Momodu, the editor of Nigeria's *Ovation International* magazine, told a BBC reporter: "In the West they have established stars. For us, we are creating celebrities."[2]

Let us consider a few more examples to illustrate the lifestyle that these publications are selling and the kind of people being pointed out as role models. The September 18, 2005, issue of *Newswatch* magazine in Nigeria carried an article in its "Back of the Book" section headlined "The Magic of Fruits," with the following subhead: "Experts say those who eat a lot of fruits regularly enjoy greater resistance to diseases." The June 9, 2005, issue of the *Zenith* pullout magazine of *Le Soleil* of Dakar, Senegal, carried in-depth feature articles on the life, leadership style, and achievements of President Abdullahi Wade, and generous color pictures of leading musicians, including Youssou N'Dour and Baaba Maal, in full flight. The Nigerian magazine, *Ovation International*, in a 2004 issue, carried an extensive profile of "Jet Set pastor" Gabriel Oduyemi, showing off his palatial mansion and private jet. In its September 2004 issue, *Eve Magazine* of Kenya led with the story of Njeeri wa Ngugi, the wife of writer Ngugi wa Thiong'o, who had been raped by thugs in Nairobi. The same issue contained stories about how to eliminate secondhand clothes from your wardrobe. The June 2005 issue of *True Love East Africa* had a story about Kenyan TV personality Jimmy Gathu, giving advice on how to raise daughters, and another article titled "Too Shy to Undress: Your Body Image vs. Your Sex Life." And the *Saturday Nation* of June 4, 2005, had as its lead article, in its insert magazine, an article titled "Alpha Females," which profiled four ambitious women who succeeded in their careers despite considerable odds.

This consecration of African celebrities by the African media is fairly new. A decade ago, African publications were full of articles on Michael Jackson, Elizabeth Taylor, MC Hammer, Phil Collins, All-for-One, and others. Things have changed considerably since then. Today, it is the new tribe of African superstars, rap musicians, who stare at you from the pages of the periodicals, exhibiting their most threatening thug pose, wearing baggy, sagging pants, oversized T-shirts, chains a slave could ogle, gold teeth, and other "bling" accessories.

This chapter looks at periodicals and popular culture in Africa. It starts by giving an overview of the history of African periodicals. The next section deals with African periodicals and popular culture. This is followed by a second section dealing with African periodicals in four regional contexts: western Africa, central Africa, southern Africa, and eastern Africa. It is hoped that this article will add to our view of Africa. As Greg Garrett has observed: "Africa is still a dark continent. Not in the ways that the Victorians thought of it, to be sure, but today, even to most Westerners—scholars included—Africa remains largely a cipher, an empty outline in Western minds like the map consisting mostly of empty white in *Conrad's Heart of Darkness*, a map we fill in based on information or purest whimsy."[3] Popular culture in this article is taken to be culture that is widely accessible, assessed, disseminated, and widely viewed or heard or read. Periodicals are one of the main cultural influences in Africa, the others being other branches of the mass media including radio, television, films, and video.

TYPES OF PERIODICALS

Distinctions are often made by media scholars between the "popular" press and the "official" press. Although such distinctions could be made among African periodicals, the

African media scene presents interesting definitional issues of its own. Thus, we find numerous other categories of the press in addition to these two. The *official press* includes media that are owned by either the government or the ruling party. It articulates the view of the ruling class in a top-down manner, from the leader to the people at the bottom. The term *government press* refers to publications produced by the government for purposes of aiding its administrative function. This includes various gazettes or legal notices, as well as annual handbooks, parliamentary reports, and policy papers. The *private* or *independent press* consists of privately owned periodicals that pursue an independent editorial policy while operating openly. The *alternative* press, although independent, may or may not be privately owned. It might be owned by a political party, an underground movement, a rebel group, or a pressure group that may or may not be funded locally. The alternative press tends to exist underground, operating without license or registration of any kind.

All these periodical types must be treated together in discussions of popular culture in Africa because, separately, they are nearly insignificant as contributors to cultural change, yet, considered en masse, their impact is profound. Their content provokes debates and is circulated and recirculated. For instance, a piece of policy or law—such as a constitutional draft—published in an obscure official gazette often enters the public discourse, where it is then exchanged repeatedly between different peoples. In other words, it is made popular. It is this popular productivity that eventually turns an official publication into a part of the popular press. This example is particularly pertinent; the African press is not full of stories about fantastic space aliens who copulate with humans. Stories about vampires, devil worship, and *mami wata* tend to be transmitted more orally than through any form of modern mass media. As we shall see, the African press is essentially a political press.

For our purposes here, a popular periodical, while it can be a newspaper or magazine, can be identified by the following broad characteristics: it covers news or general human interest stories without providing footnotes or a bibliography, with any references or attribution being entirely in the text. Articles are written mostly by staff reporters or freelance writers. It is usually, but not exclusively, published by a commercial enterprise. Normally, it has a lot of photographs, but few graphs or tables. Most use topological devices such as headlines, subheads, and captions to attract attention to particular articles, as well as to aid readability and for general visual appeal. Finally, it targets a wide, diverse readership, even when its audience is conceived as limited for purposes of media planning.

Some media critics tend to differentiate between the popular press and the "quality" press, but this distinction is not used here. We take the view that all periodicals, popular or quality, contribute to culture. Moreover, in Africa, such distinctions are not often so pronounced. The gutter press did not even exist prior to the 1990s; whatever existed earlier was the underground press, which was more related to the quality press because it covered serious issues such as governance, politics, and economics. The distinction between the quality and the gutter or popular press is also often blurred by the treatment of stories in those two types of periodicals. Each tends to influence the other. For instance, the quality press tends to copy techniques such as the mobilization of the personal (the focus on personal narratives and experiences to evoke human interest) as an explanatory framework from the lifestyle and gutter press, which it then uses in its features or style sections.

Popular periodicals in Africa, therefore, include newspapers, lifestyle magazines, music magazines, and certain kinds of corporate media. The magazines in particular have glossy covers, often featuring happy-looking model couples or families, single men flaunting their muscles, or gorgeous single women of uncommon, hard-to-get vital statistics. Such periodicals carry advice on romance, marriage, health, sexuality, childbearing, cooking, religion, and travel. Some may carry a romantic fiction article in the centerfold or elsewhere. Some magazines, particularly those in countries such as Senegal, Kenya, Nigeria, Uganda, South Africa, and Ghana that have relatively better economies, carry colorful advertisements for all kinds of goods. An important segment of lifestyle magazines are corporate magazines that organizations publish exclusively for their members. Such periodicals resemble lifestyle magazines in their content and design. Airlines, credit card companies, hotel chains, hospitals, professional societies, churches, and other institutions have them.

Although the total number of publications in Africa is difficult to ascertain, Mette Shayne of the University of Chicago had by 1999 compiled a list of 503 publications that were being received by American libraries.[4] It is clear, however, that this is but a tiny fraction of the periodicals produced in Africa. One country alone, Ethiopia, has licensed more than 700 periodicals. The problem with African periodicals is that they are generally irregular and opportunistic. Many are produced to serve a momentary purpose and disappear as soon as the event or trend is over.

HISTORY OF AFRICAN PERIODICALS

The first newspapers in Africa appeared more than 150 years ago. The earliest periodicals were the *West African Herald*, which began publishing in Ghana in 1857, and *Iwe Irohin*, which appeared in Nigeria in 1859. During colonialism, periodicals edited by African nationalists were instrumental in anticolonial campaigns. Such nationalists as Jomo Kenyatta, Kwame Nkurumah, Julius Nyerere, Nnamidi Azikiwe, and Patrice Lumumba worked as journalists at one time in their careers.

After independence, Africans adopted what Dennis McQuail has called Development Media Theory, which placed heavy emphasis on the social responsibility role of the media without a concomitant stress being placed on media freedoms or rights.[5] Thus, the newly independent governments saw the media as part of the machinery of the state, not the independent Fourth Estate it is supposed to be. The media were subsequently deployed, using governmental fiat, in the role of facilitating development. Their main role was to provide news about development, which was seen as important in stimulating further development. The media were also enlisted in another important objective: to help forge cohesion and a sense of national identity from the disparate ethnicities that had been arbitrary cobbled together by European powers during colonialism.

The motivating force for transforming African societies emanated from the assumption that traditional or backward societies were ignorant of the benefits of modernity. These benefits needed to be pointed out, and the media was seen as being well suited to perform this role by academics such as Daniel Lerner, who had called for the illiterate, isolated, and traditional societies to be "motivated" by being given clues regarding the benefits of modernity.[6] Another scholar, Ithiel de Sola Pool, saw the media as capable of pinpointing for the Africans and others the opportunities existing for them to use the accessories of modernity[7]—soaps, over-the-counter medication, fashion, canned food, sewerage, tap water, electricity, consumer electronics, and cars.

Perhaps things would have been different if the majority of African countries had not embraced socialism and instituted *dirigiste* economies that nationalized the media and otherwise controlled them. For the better part of 40 years, the consequence of this ideological experimentation was to inhibit the media from carrying out its role of pointing out clues of modernity to its credulous masses. Many countries became so poor that there were no consumer goods worth writing about. Grinding poverty could not support advertising. Defamation and libel laws were misinterpreted to prohibit coverage of ostentation among the high and mighty, so that the majority of Africans remained ignorant of the extent to which their leaders wallowed in opulence, or came to regard such wealth as their leaders' birthright. The very ideology of development communication stressed that news had to have a development value. News was therefore reduced to a list of infrastructure-related development: roads, cattle dips, dispensaries, and schools. Coupled with this was the prevalence of the cultural imperialism view, which denigrated certain aspects of modernity as anti-African and therefore undeserving of being appropriated by self-respecting, patriotic Africans. A certain moralizing under the guise of protecting African culture also crept in, buttressed by antipornography laws. In this era, therefore, whatever contribution the media made to consumerism and cultural change was incidental and symbolic.

To perform the role ascribed to it, however, the African media had to be browbeaten into submission. Many journalists were detained, tortured, or killed and their publications banned, and printing presses vandalized by state agents. The condition of the African media prior to the 1990s is engraved in the views of Abodel Karimou, editor of *La Gazette* in Cameroon, who was quoted by Ghanaian journalist Baffour Ankomah in a famous article published in *Index on Censorship* in February 1988:

> When an edition of *La Gazette* is ready for press [I send] a photocopy of each page to the Ministry of Territorial Administration in Yaounde, the capital, which is three hours by bus from Douala, where *La Gazette* is printed. At the Ministry in Yaounde, the newspaper pages go through the bureaucracy—from the Reading Bureau, to the Director for Public Freedoms, to the Deputy Director for Political Affairs. Each official is permitted by law to make notes on the articles which are finally presented in resume form to the Minister for Territorial Administration. The big man goes through the resume, if he has time to spare. He orders each approved page to be stamped and signed by the Deputy Director for Political Affairs. Printers in Cameroon are not allowed to print material without the censor's stamp. From the printers, 10 copies of the approved newspaper pages are sent back to the Ministry for final approval and a second stamp. Newspaper vendors are forbidden to distribute any publication without the censor's second stamp.[8]

The situation improved after the so-called second liberation occurred in the early 1990s, when most African countries abandoned control not only of political rights, but of the economy as well. So many publications appeared that no directory has been able to capture them all.

The emergence of alternative press can partly be explained by the wave of political liberalization that swept Africa since the late 1980s. Most of these publications have been small newsletters and pamphlets that were easy and cheap to produce, but there are a number of magazines and newspapers. Most of these publications are virulently partisan, prescriptive, and preachy. An example of the aggressive periodicals aligned to political parties include *La Voie*, founded in 1991 in Ivory Coast, whose slogan is "a newspaper that will do combat for democratic values and human rights." These newspapers have broadened the agenda of issues available for public discussion in a continent in which dissent was disallowed by strongman, military, or single-party rule. Their rancor and cantankerousness, although fostering a culture of argumentation, has improved the bar for the tolerance of diverse opinion.

Because many of these publications are published on a shoestring budget, many have no schedule integrity to speak of. They are seen on the street whenever their proprietors manage to put enough money together to pay the printer. Many of the publications started in the last decade have folded up as soon as they were started, owing to a combination of inexperience on the part of the editors, bad management, and hostile governments. Some editors were forced into exile, and others abandoned journalism and joined politics. The professional weaknesses of those who remained in journalism as well as those who joined the profession during the transition to multiparty democracy has been noted by Lewis Odhiambo, a professor at the University of Nairobi's School of Journalism, who has remarked that political liberalization "brought to the fore what was hitherto latent, i.e., the degree of recklessness and unprofessional behavior that some participants in this sector can display."[9] Some are purely pornographic. Those that cover politics distinguish themselves by their parochialism, with many blindly supporting the tribal groups of their proprietors.

More recently, there has been a trend to establish publications that cater to groups of regional countries. In southern Africa, a regional newspaper, *Southern Times,* was established in 2004. It is a joint venture between Zimpapers and *New Era* of Namibia, both government-owned media houses. Media critics regard this venture as a clever attempt by Zimbabwe to control information outside of its borders. The *Southern Times,* headed by *The* [Zimbabwe] *Herald*'s assistant editor, Moses Magadza, has its editorial offices in Namibia and is printed in Zimbabwe. A Sunday paper, it was widely seen as an apparent attempt to counter the South African–based *Sunday Times,* which was seen as being anti-President Robert Mugabe of Zimbabwe. According to a joint statement issued by the publishers at its launch, a potential readership of millions across the region was envisaged. However, after the first 2 months, it had sold less than 20,000 copies. This is not the first time that a regional periodical had been established in southern Africa. During the heyday of the anti-apartheid struggle, members of the Southern African Development Coordination Conference (SADCC) established the Harare-based *Southern African Economist* in 1988.

In East Africa, the Nation Group of Newspapers launched the *East African* in 1994. It became the first regional periodical since the days of *Drum.* A quality weekly, it covers news throughout the entire East African region, with special emphasis on Kenya, Uganda, Tanzania, Rwanda, Burundi, Somalia, and southern Sudan. Since it was founded in Mombasa in 1902, *The Standard* has changed its name to *East African Standard* and back several times, suggesting confusion over its national and regional identity. In 2004, it was renamed *The Standard,* but it continues to have a special section for East African news.

West Africa does not have a regional publication that is based in the region, although some Nigerian magazines circulate in other West African countries. London-based *West Africa* magazine remains the foremost regional periodical covering West Africa.

Except in their coverage of political news, African publications often fail to capture the idiom of their society because they are too elitist. According to Kwame Karikari, a Ghanaian media analyst, "it can be argued that, therefore, both the state-owned and privately owned independent papers represent different and sometimes contending sections of the political and economic elite."[10] The quality press is often in English, French, or Portuguese and reaches but a small segment of the society. The number of people who speak the language of its publication, on the other hand, limits the reach of the vernacular press. The result is the formation of small concentric information communities overlapping international, national, regional, and ethnic boundaries. For instance, a Yoruba who reads the vernacular Yoruba press probably also reads the regional and national press.

AFRICAN PERIODICALS IN EXILE

The contribution of African periodicals based abroad to African popular culture also deserves mention. These periodicals are usually published in London and Paris. The practice of publishing periodicals in Europe started during the initial stages of colonization, when official publications were sent to the metropolis because no printing presses were available in Africa. *West Africa* magazine, perhaps the oldest publication in this category, first appeared in Liverpool in the 1890s but started appearing with regularity in London in 1917, where it is still published. However, in the 1970s, the number of publications published abroad increased dramatically, owing to a number of factors. The first was lack of state-of-the-art printing presses in Africa capable of printing color publications to satisfy the palates of an increasingly quality-conscious readership. At the same time, a need was felt for publications that could cater to the advertising requirements and business intelligence of foreign multinationals doing business in, or simply eying, the continent. These multinationals preferred a different kind of periodical: one that was pan-African in reach and possessing the requisite quality in production, editorial style, and content. Some publications were started to provide business and political intelligence vital to investing in a continent in which politics affected business and vice versa. The oil boom of 1970s resulted in a windfall that Nigeria used to subsidize the establishment of English-language magazines in Britain. The expulsion of editors and journalists by increasingly paranoid regimes throughout the continent beefed up the number of exiled African journalists. The likes of Ralph Uweche, Baffour Ankomar, Abdulah Rahman, Mohamed Babu, Kwasi Gyan Apenteng, Peter Enahoro, Abdullatif Abdullah, Ben Turok, and Donald Woods had found themselves either editing publications in London or simply cooling their heels there.

Examples of African publications included *New African*, *Africa Events*, *African Business*, *Africa*, and *Africa Now*, which joined *West Africa* magazine in London. In Paris, the main periodicals were *AfricAsia* and *Afrique Asie* as well as *Jeune Afrique*, which has been published in Paris for almost 50 years. These publications carried mainly business and political news on various African countries. Although they could have been expected to practice a kind of aggressive journalism, given their location away from the African state police, in reality, they practiced substantial self-censorship to be allowed into African countries. In spite of this shortcoming, African readers still found these periodicals interesting because they were often better written, designed, and printed than local publications. They carried extensive sporting news, stories about musical performances by Fela Kuti, Manu Dibango, Osibisa, Tabu Ley, Fela Kuti, Miriam Makeba, and other musicians of the day, and lifestyle end-of-the-book sections depicting the glitterati of the African diaspora at social functions, holding their wine glasses, resplendent in their business suits and expensive *agbadas*, next to their overdressed women wearing heavy makeup. These publications made African events abroad appear big and important, although they probably went unmentioned by the media of the country in which they took place. To many Africans on the continent, this "been-to" class was the class to aspire to.

Some of these publications, the notable ones being Enahoro's *Africa Now* and Uweche's *Africa*, folded up after the end of the Nigerian oil boom. The pro-Islamic *Africa Events*, which had been bankrolled by Middle Eastern financiers, also ceased publication. In Paris, *AfricAsia* and *Afrique Asie* also went belly-up because the socialist economies of Angola, Algeria, and Madagascar that they relied on could no longer support them financially. Gyan Apenteng founded *Africa Topics* after he left *West Africa*, but it ceased publication after a few years. *BusinessinAfrica*, which had been founded by Nigerian investors in London in the mid-1990s, relocated to Rivonia, South Africa, where it is still published. In addition to financial problems occasioned by the end of the oil boom and instability in Angola and elsewhere, African-owned periodicals also faced competition from publications such as *Africa Research Bulletin*, *Africa Contemporary Record*, and *Africa Economic Digest*. Some of these were newsletters, with lower production costs, relying more on dedicated subscribers than on advertising. They also tended to be edited by local hands, who knew the lay of the land in their own capitals better than the African exiles.

Today, few of these original publications remain. They include *West Africa* magazine, *New African*, and *African Business*, which are still published in London. Another notable publication is the weekly newspaper, *The Zimbabwean*, produced in London and distributed in Zimbabwe as an international publication and among Zimbabweans living abroad. Nigerian investors publish the *African Renaissance*. In addition, *African Soccer* is also based in London. In Paris, only *Jeune Afrique l'Intelligent* is still published of the original periodicals. It has been reconstituted as Groupe Jeune Afrique and now also publishes *Am-Afrique Magazine* and a host of corporate directories and books. To cater to Anglophone Africa, Groupe Jeune Afrique started the *Africa Report* and lured Patrick Smith, former editor of *Africa Confidential*, to edit it. Indigo Publications, also based in Paris, publishes *Africa Intelligence, Indian Ocean Newsletter, Africa Energy Intelligence, Africa Mining Intelligence, La Lettre du Continent*, and *Maghreb Confidential* newsletters. Another important publication is *Africutures*, which is published in Lyons and carries articles in both English and French. *Afrique Tribune*, published in Montreal, Canada, is another notable periodical published abroad.

AFRICAN PERIODICALS AND POPULAR CULTURE

That Africa's press is largely political is not a coincidence. It was conceived as such and it has always been so. For instance, in 1922, *La Presse Porto-Novienne*, a newspaper in Benin, described a journalist as "a man of talent, a soldier who fights neither with a rifle nor cannon but with ideas. He is a patriot who makes himself an ardent defender of just causes, of liberties, of rights; a public advocate, a propagator of light, a savior of the country, in turn the bitter enemy of those who commit injustice. The journalist is a militant, a politician who offers his life in defending private and general interests of people while taking on the hate of those whom he fights."[11] Obviously, this journalist was not a celebrity writer; he was a professional with a political agenda, an agenda that has proved to be rather enduring. Even today, acres of newsprint are still devoted to political news, analysis, commentary, and political cartoons.

A quick perusal of many of Sub-Saharan African periodicals indicates that media coverage is tilted toward coverage of men in prominent positions of leadership; rarely do women appear as news actors. The 2003 Gender and Media Baseline Study, an initiative of the Media Institute of South Africa and Gender Links, found that 83 percent of those who speak in the media are men, and women constitute only 17 percent of the sources in the media. Whenever women are portrayed in the media, they are overwhelmingly young and beautiful, working in such professions as beauty shops, nursing, teaching, airline hospitality, or as homemakers. They tend to carry their private labels with them—the wife of so-and-so, his daughter, his sister, his granddaughter. Older women are virtually absent in the media of Africa, and there is no significant difference between how women are represented in both the public and the private press. Media are staffed mostly by men, who occupy top positions in management, editorial, and reporter ranks. This gap is particularly acute in the print media; television and radio tend to attract more women, but the electronic media in Africa is seen as less rigorous and less academically challenging.[12]

A notable practice in African periodicals is what are called "real life" stories. Such articles are distinguished by their catchy headlines, as illustrated by the following: "Quarrels with my wife 'chased' me from home" and "Bitterness held me hostage for years," both of which appeared in Kenya's *Family Mirror* magazine.[13] The *Daily Nation* sometimes carries confessions of people who have been scammed by Nairobi's con artists. "True life confessions" are extremely popular in Kenya. One such confession was published as a book called *My Life in Crime* and was a bestseller.[14] It told stories of the exploits of bank robber John Kiriamiti, jailed for particularly violent bank robberies in the Nairobi of the 1970s. But perhaps the most ingenious innovation is the one by *Ovation International* magazine in Nigeria. This magazine is full of color pictures of smiling people in their best clothes. Do not be fooled; they are not national celebrities. They are just ordinary citizens who have paid to have their pictures published. This creates a situation whereby Nigerians buy the magazines to see people they know rather than read about celebrities they may never meet. It is a kind of reverse media intrusion, in which ordinary people pay to appear in the media rather than run away from the intrusion of it.

This technique of printing pictures of ordinary Africans was first used by *Drum* magazine in the 1960s and 1970s, with considerable success. For almost 30 years starting from 1951, *Drum* was one of the most popular magazines in Anglophone Africa. It was started by Jim Bailey, a white South African, and became unique for attracting a black readership by putting contemporary African culture at the center of its content. Its famous African editor, Henry Nxumalo, boasted in 1956 as follows: "From the coffee plantations of the Gold Coast to the jazz-stung nightspots of Nigeria, from the slow pomp of Uganda's royal ceremonies to the livid frenzy of Kenya's turmoils; in the dreaming hamlets of Zululand; among Cape Town's fun-filled coon life, and Johannesburg's teeming, thrilling thousands—everywhere, every month *Drum* is read and relished."[16]

Drum's content was varied: it typically printed entertainment, sports, letters to the editor, and political news concerning Africans and African Americans. It had a health advice column called "Dr. Drum," a heartbreak column called "Dear Dolly," a pen-pal section, and advertisements promoting correspondence colleges, radios, skin-lightening creams, weight-gaining tablets, and medicines for acne. On the cover were beautiful African girls. There were text and picture love stories in every issue. The magazine became so popular that Bailey serialized the magazine in Kenya, Nigeria, and Ghana, just on time to document the independence of most of Africa from colonial rule. The result was that its circulation rose to 300,000 copies. As Struan Douglas has observed: "*Drum* was a symbol of the new African cult, divorced from the tribal stereotypes, but urbanised, eager and proud."[17] Although it eventually disappeared from the

THE IMPORTANCE OF AFRICAN OBITUARIES

An important part of the content of some African periodicals concerns death. Obituary columns in such big newspapers as the *Guardian* of Lagos, the *Daily Nation* of Nairobi, the *New Vision* of Kampala, and *Ghanian Chronicle* are the equivalent of the birth and wedding pages in the *New York Times*. Obituaries and death notices have become an art unto themselves. Upon the death of a close relative, the family or clan, depending on their ostentatious inclinations, will take a quarter-page, half-page, or a full page of a newspaper to announce the death. It matters little that relatives who need to know can communicate via telephone or via word of mouth. As the Nigerian academic Dele Jegede has observed: "Because advertisement rates for obituaries are the highest, taking out a full-page ad to announce the passing away of a loved one or the thirtieth anniversary of the death of a grandparent is generally regarded as socially prestigious."[15] The design varies but little: the departed stares at you from an enlarged mug shot. Below it, details of the death are given, usually in a sentence that says whether the death occurred as result of a long or short illness, with all illness having been bravely borne. Then follows the names of the deceased's significant progeny: sons and daughters and grandchildren, their professional and sometimes educational accomplishments, and their locations all over the globe. Depending on the size of the advertisement, details of the professional or business accomplishments of the departed are provided, as are his philanthropic deeds while still alive. In Nigeria in particular, prominent people who sent condolences are thanked prominently. Finally, with variations among religious groups, God or another supreme power is beseeched to keep the departed in a nice place in the hereafter.

scene, it was restarted by popular demand, under different ownership. Today, Media24, a dominant player in the South Africa media scene, owns it.

Some African newspapers have entered into strategic alliances with major international newspapers, news agencies, and article syndicates in which they are allowed to carry opinions, analysis, and other articles. Some of these foreign articles are selected for their prurient characteristics. For instance, on September 22, 2005, the *Mail & Guardian* of South Africa carried a story sourced from AFP, headlined "Vibrators Fly off the Shelves in Hong Kong Pharmacies." The article said Hong Kong women had given up on waiting for their workaholic husbands and had welcomed a decision by a pharmacy chain to start stocking sex toys. On June 1, the advice column of another newspaper, the *Daily Nation* of Kenya, carried a letter to a Dr. Stuttaford, described as *The Times* (of London)'s doctor, headlined "I am losing my grip," from an English woman, whose husband had left her after the birth of her daughter because he was no longer experiencing sexual satisfaction with her, and another man had the same problem, presumably because the relevant part of her anatomy had become stretched and torn. Her question was accompanied by a graphic of a tall woman in a scanty, see-through nightgown, sewing a torn circular garment held in her lap.[18]

What these and similar articles show is that some African family newspapers will outsource from abroad prurient literature that appeals to the lowest common denominator when such articles cannot be written by in-house journalists, perhaps for fear of being seen as disrespectful. The African media have certainly realized that to attract the kind of massive audiences that are required by the market in keeping with free-market economics, they have to pander to the needs of the audience. The formula is simple: give the audience what they want. What readers show interest in, they get in droves. In Africa, this usually means politics and sex. But not every country considers this proliferation of sex acceptable. In Tanzania, for instance, porn-filled Swahili language publications such as *Chombeza, Arusha Leo, Kasheshia, Michapo, Cheka, Nyundo, Kombora, Majira, Watu,* and *Tingisha* were temporarily banned by the government between 1993 and 1999 for publishing obscenity and using profane language.

Another key feature of African media publications is the ubiquitous comic strip and satirical cartoons. The satirical cartoon almost always is a caricature of the political leadership, and is the best example of how far media freedom in Africa has come. Before the 1990s, the head of state in most African countries could not be cartooned, as this could result in the arrest of the cartoonist. Today, African politicians are perhaps the most caricatured of any leaders anywhere. In Nigeria, President Olusegun Obasanjo, a former military general, is often drawn with his generous girth protruding out of his military uniform, and President Robert Mugabe of Zimbabwe is always being drawn as a monkey and Mwai Kibaki of Kenya with an idiotic expression. An interesting innovation is what appears like a cross between a comic strip and an editorial satirical cartoon. It looks like a montage of satirical cartoons occupying prime newsprint real estate. Unlike the editorial cartoon, which appears next to the editorial, this montage appears on a single day every week, commenting on several issues at once and using different caricatures. An example is Paul Kelemba's "Madd, Madd World" in the *East African Standard*. Other leading cartoonists in Africa include Tanzanian Godfrey Mwangepamba (Gado), Nigerians Ebun Aleshinloye, Obi Azulu, and Ake Didi Onu, and South Africans Jonathan Shapiro, Nanda Sooben, and Al (Alphonse) Krok.

Many people in Africa cannot afford the price of periodicals, so they rely on the goodwill of the newspaper vendors, who in turn enjoy the goodwill and popularity emanating from this act. It is not unusual to see a vendor being surrounded by jobless people who read a publication from cover to cover and put it back on the stand. Nigerians, in their humor, have called them the "International Readers Associations" and "Free Readers Association of Nigeria" (FAN), hence FANatics. Some newspapers vendors charge a small fee to read a periodical, but they do so at the risk of being discovered by corporate inspectors, who see this practice as being inimical to their own interests. This communal reading of newspapers is a site of cultural production where discussions often ensue, arguments are picked, and lasting friendships struck. Those who are fortunate enough to read the newspapers for free then share their newly acquired information with those without access to newspapers. This results in hand-me-down news, a kind of informed gossip or third-party news, part of what John A. Wiseman called a "Chain of Communication."[19]

Once a publication has been paid for, however, its life has just started. Several people, as many as ten, may read it. When it is eventually discarded, what is left of it will be bought by a shopkeeper or butcher, who will use it to wrap meat or groceries. At the very end of its life, a periodical may be used as toilet paper in a pit latrine.

REGIONAL SUBSECTIONS

West Africa

Nigeria

Nigeria has a large media sector, probably only exceeded by South Africa. It is not clear how many newspapers there are in the country, but those that come out regularly exceed 100. They include well-respected dailies, popular tabloids, and publications that cater to specific ethnic interests. At least seventeen of these newspapers have a national circulation. These newspapers have an average print run of 45,000 copies daily. The main newspapers include *The Punch*, the most widely read daily newspaper in Nigeria, with a circulation of more than 100,000 copies. The *Guardian* has a circulation of 60,000. It is a darling of Nigeria's intellectual class, who respect it for its sober analysis and professionalism. The government-owned *Daily Times* sells about 45,000, and *Champion Daily* sells 38,000. Other newspapers include *Nigerian Tribune*, the *Daily Trust, The Comet, Vanguard, This Day,* and *The Daily Sun,* and the government-owned *New Nigerian,* which publishes separate editions in Lagos and Kaduna.

Nigeria also has more than fifty magazines, about twenty of which are circulated nationally, with the rest being regional. The magazine market is dominated by three giants, namely, *Tell, News,* and *Newswatch*, which have circulation figures of about 100,000, 80,000, and 50,000, respectively. *This Week* sells about 45,000 copies. The largest lifestyle magazine, *Ovation International,* founded in 1990 by Dele Momodu, is a phenomenon that sells more than 100,000 per issue. Other magazines include *Insider Weekly, City People, Society, Celebration, Vintage People, Prime People, Fantasy,* and *Romance International,* as well as soft-porn publications such as *Lolly, Ikebe Super* (meaning literally "Super Ass"), and *Fun Times.* Magazines are generally regarded as being geared to the elite, even more so than newspapers.

Lagos in particular, and southwestern Nigeria in general, have the lion's share of periodicals. There have been claims that the concentration of the media in this region skews national politics and imposes secularism on other parts of Nigeria, particularly the north, where Sharia (Islamic law) has been instituted. These charges, however, appear to be hollow. Ownership of other periodicals is varied and reflects the diversity of the large cosmopolitan commercial city that is Lagos. Abuja, the federal capital, has publications such as *Abuja Inquirer* and *Daily Trust.* Other large Nigerian cities such as Ibadan, Kano, Kaduna, and Enugu have their own thriving periodicals.

The Nigerian periodicals have always been critical of successive Nigerian governments, including military regimes. The history of the media in Nigeria is replete with detained and assassinated journalists, such as Dele Giwa, a famous *Newswatch* editor whom state agents killed with a letter bomb in 1986. However, it is dictator Sani Abacha's rule that remains a dark age for the Nigerian print media, not only because of detentions of journalists and tribulations of periodicals such as *Tell, News,* and *Tempo*, but also because of a poor economy and the introduction of a value-added tax for the print media sector. Many publications adopted cost-cutting measures, including downsizing and shelving capital development plans. A number of periodicals were unable to cope and simply folded up. These include *Financial Post, Evening Express, Lagos Life, AM News, Sunray, Guardian Express, Concord, National Interest, Tempo, The African Guardian, The African Concord, Anchor, Post Express, Eko Today, African Science Monitor, Banner, Classique,* and *Quality,* to mention but a few.

Under President Obasanjo, media freedom has improved. However, because of general insecurity, Reporters Without Borders still lists Nigeria as one of the most dangerous countries in Africa for journalists. Despite this, new publications have come up. Examples include *NewsAfrica* and *Breaking News,* which cover general news; *African Beatz,* which covers music; and *Smart* and *Market Today,* both of which are business magazines.

In the period since 2000 there appears to have been a slight drop in circulation of all publications, according to Nigerian scholar Oyo Olukoyun. This decline has been linked to the recent trend by radio stations of reviewing the content of periodicals for their readers. Consequences of this programming have been mixed, but, on balance, quite adverse to circulation. On days when there is no major news, there is low circulation as potential readers hold on to their money. However, whenever there is a major news item, the radio reviews spur circulation as people opt to buy newspapers for greater, in-depth coverage. A recent increase in the cover price of the *Guardian* and other publications has exacted a toll on the circulation of periodicals, forcing them to become even more elitist in their readership.

As in other parts of the world, globalization has been accompanied by increasing localization and the resurgence of ethnicity. In Nigeria, this is illustrated by the rise of the vernacular press. One newspaper in particular, *Alaroye,* a periodical published in Yoruba, has a circulation that rivals that of the national press. In the north, Hausa periodicals include *Al-Mizan,* which also sells widely.

Benin

Reporters Without Borders ranks Benin, the small West African republic of 6 million people, twenty-fifth in its worldwide index of press freedom. According to recent estimates, there are approximately 18 daily and 41 magazines in Benin. This is remarkable given that the country has been free of Marxist policies only since 1991. The papers, which are published Monday through Friday, are all tabloids with daily circulation of between 1,500 and 5,000 copies. All are found in the urban areas, particularly the capital, Cotonou. At least 60 percent of the population in Benin is illiterate, with most of them living in the rural areas, hence the concentration of the media in urban areas. Periodicals are linked to various political financiers, who exert their agenda on the newspapers. For instance, *Le Citoyen* is published by Christian Vieyra, a brother-in-law of former President Nicéphore Soglo. It began appearing in June 1996, soon after he lost his reelection bid.

A distinctive feature of the periodicals in Benin is that they tend to be owned or managed by very young people. Most of the top executives are men who have recently graduated from college. They have no specific training in journalism, because there is no journalism school in Benin, but a few have undertaken journalism training in Ghana, Senegal, and France. Perhaps because of inexperience and also because of lack of professional training, there is considerable sensationalism. At one time during the 1991 elections, for example, two newspapers, *Le Soleil* and *Tam Tam Express,* referred to then-President Soglo's wife, Rosine, as an "ugly witch." These excesses have invited antipress legislation, as well as self-regulation through the *Code de Deontologie de la Presse Beninoise,* a collection of twenty-six articles adopted in 1999 by all media outlets in Benin. Despite this problem, Benin appears keen to maintain the vibrancy of its media. Every year, it awards, through its High Authority of Audiovisual Communication, 4 million CFA francs (about $2,000 each) to periodicals that demonstrate increasing adherence to journalistic ethics.

Periodicals in Benin began their fascination with politics during the colonial era. Newspapers such as *La Voix's* and *Le Guide du Dahomey* played an important role in the emancipation of the country from colonial rule. However, the considerable press freedom enjoyed by the print media in Benin during the colonial era was greatly curtailed after independence, particularly during the reign of Mathieu Kérékou. Newspapers such as *Le Gon, Daho-Express, Kpanligan,* and *Ehuzu* were completely cowed by the Marxist regime. In the late 1980s, the Beninese started clamoring for political change. New periodicals emerged, notably *La Gazette du Golfe, Tam Tam Express,* and *Le Récade.* After political liberalization in the early 1990s, *Ehuzu,* which had served as the Marxist party newspaper, was renamed *La Nation.* Privately owned periodicals started to appear, but most of them disappeared as soon as they appeared. Ismaël Y. Soumanou, founder of contemporary Benin's first nonofficial newspaper, *La Gazette du Golfe,* in 1988, has boasted that it is the media that build the country's democracy. Today, the major newspapers include *Le Point au Quotidien, Le Point, Les Echos du Jour, Le Progres, La Nouvelle Tribune, Le Matin, La Pyramide, L'Aurore, Fraternite, L'Informateur, L'Evenement, Le Telegramme, La Cloche,* and *La Nation,* which is funded by the state.

CENTRAL AFRICA

Democratic Republic of the Congo (DRC)

It is not clear how many publications exist in the Democratic Republic of the Congo. However, two Central African journalists, Celestin Lingo and Suzanne Kala Lobe, told a media seminar in 2001 that there are 163 periodicals in the country, all of which are notable for their irregularity and low circulation.[20] A Fact-Finding Mission Report on the DRC by the Documentation and Research Service, Refugee and Nationality Commission of Belgium (CEDOCA), issued in October 2002, reported that there are 165 titles, but only about twenty appear regularly and only 8 newspapers are published daily.[21] The country is just emerging from armed conflicts between various forces under the control of the central Kinshasa government of President Joseph Kabila, local insurgents, and non-Congolese warlords and foreign powers, notably Rwanda, Uganda, Angola, and Zimbabwe. The government in Kinshasa lacks effective control of over half of the national territory. As a result, information about the media situation is scattered and localized, and media workers continue to be at the mercy of local officials who operate with impunity.

Free, privately owned media are a recent phenomenon in the country. Before 1990 the state was a one-party regime that tightly controlled the freedom of expression. In response to local and international pressure, Mobutu Sese Seko in 1990 relaxed restrictions on the country's civil liberties, and new periodicals emerged. These publications were met with abuses, which continued during the rule of Laurent Kabila, who overthrew Mobutu. The current president, Joseph Kabila, has relaxed media controls and has appointed Kikaya Bin Karubi, a former journalist, as information minister. However, abuses are still being reported. The U.S. State Department Report on Human Rights Practices for 2003 reported 50 abuses in which members of the press were detained, threatened, or abused by government agents.[22]

Newspapers are mainly published in Kinshasa, with few copies going to the rural areas. The main titles in Kinshasa are *La Reference Plus,* which sells 2,500 copies; *Le Potential,* 2,000; *Le Palmares,* 2,500; *Le Phare,* 1,000; *Le Soft,* 2,000; *Forum,* 1,000; *Demain Le Congo,* 1,000; *Salongo,* 1,000; *Elima,* 500; *La Tempete Des Tropiques,* 500; *Umoja,* 500; and *La Semaine de Reporter,* which sells 500 copies. Other periodicals appear irregularly in other cities such as Mbuji-Mayi, Lubumbashi, Mbandaka, Bukavu, Kisangani, and Goma. Most of these papers are eight pages of A5 size, and they are targeted only at people with a regular salary, mostly teachers and civil servants. The relatively high newspaper cover price of 300 Congolese francs (nearly US$1) is unaffordable for many Congolese. The poor economic circumstances and the small circulation prevent the periodicals from generating sufficient advertising revenue. This precarious financial situation impacts the quality of the writing. To minimize salary costs, the papers often employ students.

There are a lot of international organizations that are attempting to help the media in the DRC, but almost all of them are focusing on the electronic or New Media without realizing that even the print media needs resources and training. The main service provided by the government to the private media is the *Agence Congolaise de Presse.* This agency used to be extremely important during the years of *parti-état* (single-party) rule, when it was responsible for disseminating party news. Although it retains twenty-two bureaus nationwide equipped with telex machines and transmitters, most have stopped working. News dispatches are transported by road to newspapers.

Cameroon

The first newspapers to appear in Cameroon were produced by missionaries starting from 1900. Periodicals were started by African nationalists in the 1920s. An example that is often given is *Mbale* [The Truth], which was printed by Cameroonians in France and sent home. After the defeat of Germany in 1918, Cameroon was given to France and Britain to administer on behalf of the League of Nations. The country was divided into two, with each power administering its own territory. As French colonial policy changed after World War II, many publications emerged to agitate for political independence. When Cameroon became independent in 1960, the former British Colony of Southern Cameroons became united with the Eastern Cameroons, which had been under French control. This bilingual culture still remains, and periodicals are available in both languages, as well as in some of Cameroon's 250 indigenous languages. French-language papers have a higher circulation than English-language ones.

After independence, the government of Ahamadou Ahidjo tightened its hold on the press, adversely affecting periodicals such as *La Presse du Cameroun,* which had established a reputation for independence and objectivity. In 1966 the government passed a law that gave the Minister of Territorial Administration extensive censorship powers. Editors were required to submit their papers to the ministry before they could be printed, and all new publications had to be approved by the Ministry. Any editor breaking this law was liable to fine, jail, or both and his newspaper confiscated.

On December 19, 1990, new Liberty Laws came into effect and profoundly changed the media sector in Cameroon. The freedom of the press became guaranteed by the constitution. However, the media still faces problems associated with censorship, and Cameroonian journalists have made various protest speeches at international conferences. Libel laws are particularly used to obstruct press freedom.

Reports indicate that there are about thirty newspapers in Cameroon. Some of the larger newspapers include *Le Messager, Challenge Hebdo, Le Front Indépendant, Le Combattant, La Nouvelle Expression, Dikalo, La Gazette Provinciale,* and *The Herald. Le Messager* is the main opposition newspaper, and *Cameroon Tribune* is the main government-owned newspaper. As in other African countries, circulation is generally low, limited by poverty, illiteracy, and high cover price. To encourage growth in the media sector, the government has tried to reduce import duty on a variety of products needed in publishing. Other than this, there is no public assistance to the private press.

SOUTHERN AFRICA

Republic of South Africa

South Africa has the largest media sector of any country in Africa, which is hardly surprising given that it has the biggest economy on the continent. A perusal of sources such as the *South African Media Directory,* published by the Government Communication and Information System, and the list of media organizations compiled by the Media Institute of Southern Africa, reveal many periodicals published by diverse organizations in virtually all of South Africa's fifteen official languages.

During apartheid, media contribution to South African society was limited due to general fear and interethnic suspicion. The print media was ethnically divided. Rarely did ideas prevalent in one group find their way into the media of another group. The Afrikaans newspapers, regardless of whether they were conservative or liberal, supported the government. The English newspapers largely posed as the opposition press, a fact that concealed their support of the status quo. Although the English press covered events and news in black townships, the coverage was neither reliable nor reflective of the true situation on the ground. Manion Irwin, a founding editor of the *Weekly Mail* & *Guardian,* once remarked that his own English media tended to cover townships as "if they were foreign lands: exotic, remote, of sporadic interest."[23]

Fifteen years after the dismantling of apartheid, the freedom and diversity of the media has not closed the cultural chasm in South African society. According to Sandile Memela, a South African commentator, the dynamics of South African society, including economic domination by white South Africans, means that the media continue to distort and fragment black cultures while elevating the Eurocentric cultural experience. As a result, the African cultural experience exists independently of the mainstream media and white culture, and is "left stranded, strangled, and impoverished in the rural areas, beyond the fringe of absorption."[24] Eager to diversify its media, South Africa has established the Media Development and Diversity Agency, which began working in earnest in 2004. In January 2004, the agency approved payment of 3.6 million rand to 19 community media projects in the country.

South Africa's many publications reflect the diversity of its population. They include *Agenda,* a South African feminist journal started in 1987 by a group of women academics and activists, and *The Big Issue,* a leftist journal. Recently, there has been a rising popularity of men's magazines such *as Gentleman's Quarterly* (*GQ*), *For Him, Men's Health,* and *Maxim.* One of the main media owners in South Africa is Media24, which publishes more than thirty titles and controls more than 60 percent of the country's circulation. Media24's magazines include *YOU, Fairlady, Drum,* and *True Love,* which are sold as far afield as Kenya and Nigeria. The other media giant in South Africa is The Independent Group, which publishes the *Cape Argus, Sunday Independent, Daily News,* and *Isolezwe,* among others. Other notable magazines include *Chimurenga* and the government-owned *Bua.*

The down-market tabloid newspapers category has recently flourished, with spectacular gains in circulation, indicating that they have found a new market among people who appear not to have been newspaper readers in the past. *The Sun* offers sex, crime, scandals, and sports and has rapidly outstripped the established titles: its circulation has climbed through the 200,000 mark and was expected to hit the 400,000 mark by end of 2005. Some other big names in the South African periodicals list include *The Star* of Johannesburg, *The Sowetan, Beeld* (the largest Afrikaans daily), *Mail & Guardian,* and *Sunday Times. This Day,* an ambitious up-market daily started by a Nigerian proprietor, attracted a readership of 100,000 but crashed in 2004 because of financial problems and threats of legal action following its exposure of corruption in Parliament.

Angola

The state is a major player in the Angolan media and owns *Jornal de Angola,* the largest newspaper, with a circulation of 41,000. This state ownership of the media is a carryover from the socialist economic policies that the country has pursued under the MPLA party since it became independent in 1975. The country has been at war since independence, with the UNITA rebels fighting the socialist regime. Throughout the war, both the government and UNITA tightly controlled the media in their jurisdictions and used them for propaganda purposes. Today, the constitution provides for freedom of expression and of the press. However, there are reports of restriction on media freedom.

Following the liberalization of the media sector in the 1990s, the sector has grown significantly and a number of periodicals have emerged. There are a total of seven private weekly newspapers in Luanda, the capital: *Folha 8,* established in 1994; *Agora,* established in 1996; *O Angolense,* established in 1997; and *Semanário Angolense, Actual, A Capital,* and *A Palavra,* all established in 2003. The papers cost on average 120 kwanzas (approximately $1.50) each, and all have a combined circulation of 22,000 to 25,000 copies. This is extremely low given that the city has a population of 4 million, but low literacy levels and lack of disposable income can explain the low figure. It is estimated that less than 5 percent of the papers reach readers outside the capital, leaving the rural areas at the mercy of the government-owned press. The state-owned airline refuses to airlift private periodicals into the rural areas. The private independent press is therefore largely an urban phenomenon, where its growth has been spurred by advertising revenues from oil-related businesses.

Some of these new periodicals are expected to cease publication soon, according to *Associação da Imprensa Privada de Angola* (AIPA), the association that caters to the interests of the private periodicals. *Faro,* a weekly newspaper started in 2004 by a group of journalists, published only two issues and is no longer operational. Another group of journalists tried to revive *A Palavra,* a weekly that shut down in 2003, but this effort was also unsuccessful. *Actual,* one of the oldest private newspapers, is also said to be experiencing problems. It recently restyled itself as a business periodical, but this strategy appears to have been wrongly timed since there is probably no readership as yet to sustain a purely business publication. Apart from problems of limited advertising and readership, the private papers are struggling to find quality printing facilities at a price they can afford. Most printers decline to print periodicals because of fear of reprisals from the state.

EASTERN AFRICA

Kenya

Kenya has a diverse, vibrant media scene, with a sizable multiracial middle class and fairly well developed manufacturing, service, and agricultural sectors providing a base for substantial advertising revenue. The print media is dominated by two major publishing houses, the Nation and Standard. These two groups also have interests in other branches of the media, and some observers have expressed concern at the level of media concentration in Kenya.

The oldest newspaper in Kenya is the *East African Standard,* started in 1902. It catered to white settler interests throughout Kenyan colonialism, and was part of the Lonrho multinational corporation until the mid-1990s, when it was sold to Kenyan interests linked to former President Daniel arap Moi, with some shares being owned by the Kenyan public through the Nairobi Stock Exchange. The largest newspaper is the *Nation.* Started by the Aga Khan, head of the Ismaili Islamic sect in 1961, it is the largest newspaper in East and Central Africa. It also publishes *Sunday Nation, EastAfrican,* and *Taifa Leo* and owns the *Monitor* in Uganda and *Mwananchi* in Tanzania. During the days of single-party rule, the ruling party bought *Nairobi Times* from publisher Hilary Ngweno and renamed it the *Kenya Times.* In 1992, politician Kenneth Matiba founded *The People Daily.* These four are the only English-language daily newspapers in Kenya; they are supplemented by at least two Swahili dailies, *Kenya Leo* and *Taifa Leo.* The *Nation* sells 200,000 copies, with its Sunday edition selling over 250,000, making it the largest newspaper in East and Central Africa. The *Standard* has a circulation of 100,000, *The People Daily,* 45,000, and *Kenya Times,* 25,000.

There are many magazines as well, with a particularly large number of lifestyle magazines. They include *Parents,* the most successful magazine in Kenya, started by Eunice Mathu almost 30 years ago. Others include *Family Mirror, Couples, Today's Marriage, Step, We, Lady, Eve, True Love, Character,* and *Baby Times.* Recently, a magazine called *Kwani?* [So?] was started by writer Binyavanga Wainaina, the 2001 winner of the Caines Prize for literature. It is dedicated to the development of Kenyan writers. Political magazines have been on the decline. *The Weekly Review,* for a long time the leading political weekly, folded in 1999. Its rival, the *Economic Review,* had gone belly-up in 1995 when the taxman came after it. Other publications that have disappeared include *The Option, New Era, Economic Review, expression today, The Analyst, The Star, Weekend Mail,* and *Newsline.*

During the era of single-party rule, Kenya retained private ownership of the media, but journalists were still harassed by state agents. After political liberalization in 1991 many periodicals were started. However, most of them disregarded journalistic ethics and the government has been trying to rein them in without success. In 2001 a new unpopular media bill was passed. It requires publishers to purchase a bond for 1 million Kenyan shillings ($13,000) before publishing. The move scared off a number of small-time publishers, especially in the magazine sector, because they could not afford the bond.

Ethiopia

Ethiopia is one the very few African countries to have its own alphabet and numerical and writing system. Its written language, Ge'ez, was established in the fourth century AD. However, the first newspapers in Ethiopia are considered to be *Le Semeur d'Ethiopie* (1905–1911) and *Aimero* (1902–1903), although some historical evidence suggests that the handwritten sheet produced by Blatta Gebre Egziabhere around 1900 probably preceded both these and is therefore considered the first Amharic "newspaper" in the country. *Le Courier d'Ethiopie* was established in 1913, and *Yetwor Ware* [War News] was issued from the Italian mission from 1916 to 1918. *Berhanena Selam* [Light and Peace] was founded in 1925 but ceased publication with the Italian invasion in 1936. *Addis Zemen* [New Era] was started in 1941, followed by *Ethiopian Herald* in 1945.

Subsequently, there was a gradual increase in the number of periodicals, and by 1970, there were 6 dailies and 11 weeklies. Likewise, many magazines and journals emerged. After a military junta overthrew the monarchy in 1974, mass media institutions were converted into instruments of propaganda. Censorship became the norm and continued until the overthrow of the military by guerrilla forces in 1991. Under Public Enterprise Proclamation No. 25 of 1992, former state-owned printing houses were transformed into commercial enterprises.

Since 1992 790 organizations comprising 513 newspapers, 200 magazines, 3 news agencies, and 74 small electronic publishers have been given licenses, but only a tiny fraction of this number are operational. These publications cover the whole gamut of issues and topics: politics, economy, culture, sports, health, and recreation. Newspapers are available in Amharic, English, and Arabic. Media repression still remains a big problem. Media rights group Reporters Without Borders reported widespread media abuses after the violent protests that followed the 2005 elections.

Among the major newspapers are *Addis Zemen* and *Ethiopian Herald,* both state-owned dailies; *Menelik, Addis Admas, Seifenebelbal, Tobya, Wonchif, Tomar,* all private weeklies; and *The Reporter, The Sun, Addis Tribune,* and *Capital,* all privately owned English language publications.

CONCLUSION

African periodicals continue to influence popular culture on the continent. They add to the intensification of channels of information. They showcase local goods, services, and products. They purvey political messages. They subject global culture to a sieve, a gatekeeping process that valorizes sexual relations in global genres, while consecrating and engendering local discourses of romance, marriage, religion, funerary rituals, politics, and general lifestyles. What emerges is not a dominating Western popular culture, as is often feared, or a resurgence of an atavistic Africa, as is often portrayed by the Western media, but a contemporary African popular culture that is moderated by urbanization, globalization, and tradition. Global standards and genres are appropriated, inverted, or otherwise diluted and imbued with local narratives. Even the periodicals themselves succumb to these trends: we see ordinary citizens buying space to publish their own picture or those of their dead. And the irregular schedule of African periodicals is perhaps a reminder that they too are subject to African time; as the saying goes, there is no hurry in Africa.

With rising populations, increasing literacy levels, improving economies, and the establishment of more journalism schools, the future looks bright for periodicals on the continent.

Unless, of course, media convergence changes everything, in which case African periodicals will not die, but will be cannibalized by this process. In line with trends elsewhere, African media have been tending toward mergers, consolidation, and internationalization. Many African periodicals are now read across African borders, with some coming from abroad, but there has also been an increasing localization of the media. This creates widening informational communities, and it is in this sense that the media will aid African integration. The sharing of celebrities, political narratives, cartoons, lifestyles, and copying of journalistic conventions across boundaries are some of the ways in which periodicals contribute to the homogenization of African culture. The future will certainly see more trends in this direction, with increasing partnerships, as well as multiplatform and on-demand publishing. National markets are likely to be replaced by regional markets and eventually continental markets. This is already happening with respect to the electronic media. Although reaching only but a small segment of the African population, the print media will continue to serve as an important conduit of images and messages laden with a modernist appeal. The media are the principal tools for converting Africa into a consumer society, and African periodicals will continue to perform their part in this role.

RESOURCE GUIDE

PRINT SOURCES

Adeyemi, Adeyinka. "The Nigerian Press Under the Military: Persecution, Resilience, and Political Crisis (1983–1993)." In Lyn Graybill and Kenneth W. Thompson (eds.), *Africa's Second Wave of Freedom.* Lanham: University Press of America, 1998.

Barber, Karin, ed. *Readings in African Popular Culture.* Bloomington: Indiana University Press, 1997.

Bourgault, Louise M. *Mass Media in Sub-Saharan Africa.* Bloomington: Indiana University Press, 1995.

Campell, Joseph W. *The Emergent Independent Press in Benin and Côte d'Ivoire: From Voice of State to Advocate of Democracy.* New York: Praeger, 1998.

Eribo, Festus, and Enoh Tanjong. *Journalism and Mass Communication in Africa: Cameroon.* New York: Lexington Books, 2002.

Hachten, William A. *The Growth of the Media in the Third World.* Ames: Iowa State University Press, 1993.

———. *Muffled Drums: The News Media in Africa.* Ames: Iowa State University Press, 1971.

Hyden, Goran, Michael Leslie, and Folu F. Ogundimu. *Media and Democracy in Africa.* New Brunswick, NJ: Transaction Publishers, 2002.

Jegede, Dele. "Popular Culture in Urban Africa." Pp. 273–294 in Phyllis M. Martin and Patrick O'Meara (eds.), *Africa.* Bloomington: Indiana University Press, 1995.

Moroney, Sean, ed. *Handbook to the Modern World: Africa,* Volume 2. New York: Facts on File, 1989.

Mytton, Graham. *Mass Communication in Africa.* London: Edward Arnold, 1983.

Nwosu, I. E. *Mass Media and the African Society.* Nairobi: African Council for Communication Education, 1987.

Nyamnjoh, Francis B. *Africa's Media, Democracy and the Politics of Belonging.* London: Zed Books, 2005.

Odero, Mitch, and Esther Kamweru, eds. *Media Culture and Performance in Kenya.* Nairobi: Eastern Africa Media Institute–Kenya Chapter and Friedrich Ebert Stiftung, 2000.

Stokke, Olav. *Reporting Africa.* Uppsala: Scandinavian Institute of African Studies, 1971.

Switzer, Les, and Mohamed Adhikari, eds. *South Africa's Resistance Press: Alternative Voices in the Last Generation under Apartheid.* Athens: Ohio University Press, 2000.

Whiteman, Keye, ed. *West Africa over 75 Years.* London: West African Publishing, 1993.

Wilcox, Dennis L. *Mass Media in Black Africa.* New York: Praeger, 1975.

Ziegler, D., and M. K. Asante. *Thunder and Silence: The Media in Africa.* Trenton, NJ: Africa World Press, 1992.

Journals

Akwa, Christiane Dika Nsangue. "The Feedback Phenomenon in the Cameroonian Press, 1990–1993." *Africa Today* 86 (2004): 85–97.

Bastian, Misty L. *Mami Wata*. Encyclopedia Mythica. Accessed October 16, 2005. http://www.pantheon.org/articles/m/mami_wata.html.

Berger, Guy. "More Media for Southern Africa? The Place of Politics, Economics and Convergence in Developing Media Density." *Critical Arts* 18.1 (2004): 43–76.

Fabian, Johannes. "Popular Culture in Africa: Findings and Conjectures. To the Memory of Placide Tempels (1906–1977)." *Journal of the International African Institute* 48.4 (1978): 315–334.

Frederiksen, Bodil Folke. "Popular Culture, Gender Relations and the Democratization of Everyday Life in Kenya." *Journal of Southern African Studies* 26.2 (2002): 209–222.

Gondolar, Didier. "Dream and Drama: The Search for Elegance among Congolese Youth." *African Studies Review* 42.1 (1999): 23–48.

Journal of Popular Culture 32.2 (1998, Fall, Special Issue).

"Leisure in African History." *The International Journal of African Historical Studies* 35.1 (2002, Special Issue).

Mason, Andy. *Cartoon Journalism in Africa Puts Political Power into Perspective.* World Association of Christian Communication. Updated 2001. http://www.wacc.org.uk/wacc/content/pdf/1159.

Mutongi, Kenda. "Dear Dolly's Advice: Representations of Youth, Courtship, and Sexualities in Africa, 1960–1980." *The International Journal of African Historical Studies* 33.1 (2000): 1–23.

Olaniyan, Tejumola. "Cartooning in Nigeria: Paradigmatic Traditions." *Ijele: Art eJournal of the African World* 1.1 (2000). http://www.africaresource.com/ijele/vol1.1/olaniyan.html.

———. "The traditions of Cartooning in Nigeria." *Glendora Review: African Quarterly on the Arts* 2.2 (1997): 92–104.

Olukoyun, Ayo. "Media Accountability and Democracy in Nigeria, 1999–2003." *African Studies Review* 47.3 (2004): 69–90.

Perullo, Alex. "Hooligans and Heroes: Youth Identity and Hip-Hop in Dar-es-Salaam, Tanzania." *Africa Today* 51.4 (2005): 75—101.

Seda, O. "Understanding Popular Culture in Post-Colonial Africa." *Southern Africa Political & Economic Monthly* 11.6 (1998): 19–22.

Reports

Freedom of the Press 2004: A Global Survey of Media Independence. http://www.freedomhouse.org/template.cfm?page=15&year=2004.

Groupe de Recherche et d'Échanges Technologiques. *Media Status Report: Benin 2001.* http://www.gret.org.

Groupe de Recherche et d'Échanges Technologiques. *Media Status Report: Kenya 2001.* http://www.gret.org.

Jensen, Mike. *The African Internet—A 2001 Status Report.* http://www.digitaldivide.net/articles/view.php?ArticleID=322.

Maja-Pearce, A. "The Press in East Africa." *Index on Censorship* 7.21 (1992, special publication).

Media Institute of Southern Africa and Gender. *The Gender and Media Baseline Study.* 2003. http://www.misa.org/Gender/baseline-study.pdf.

Rhodes University Contemporary Debates on African Media. http://journ.ru.ac.za/amd/.

So This Is Democracy? Report on the State of Media Freedom in Southern Africa 2004. Media Institute of Southern Africa (MISA). http://www.misa.org/documents/STID2005.pdf.

Directories

African Newspapers Currently Received by American Libraries. http://www.library.northwestern.edu/africana/resources/97crlnews.html.

The African Publishers Networking Directory 1999/2000. London: African Books Collective, 1999.

International Women's Media Directory. http://www.iwmf.org/directory/.
Pearce, A. M. *Directory of African Media*. Belgium: Carpin, 1996.
South African Media Directory. http://www.gcis.gov.za/gcis/pdf/media.pdf.
Ulrich's Periodical Directory. http://www.ulrichsweb.com/ulrichsweb/. This comprehensive directory to periodicals worldwide requires a subscription, but most public and college libraries carry it.
Zell, Hans. *The African Publishing Companion*. London: Hans Zell Publishing Consultants, 2002.

Some Leading African Newspapers

The Addis Tribune (Ethiopia). http://www.addistribune.com/.
The Analyst (Liberia). http://www.analystnewspaper.com/.
Cameroon Tribune (Cameroon). http://www.cameroon-tribune.net.
The Cape Argus (South Africa). http://www.capeargus.co.za.
The Daily Champion (Nigeria). http://www.champion-newspapers.com/.
The East African Standard (Kenya). http://www.eastandard.net/.
Fraternite (Benin). http://www.fraternite-info.com/.
The Ghanian Chronicle (Ghana). http://www.ghanaian-chronicle.com/.
The Guardian (Nigeria). http://www.ngrguardiannews.com/.
The Herald (Zimbabwe). http://www.zimbabweherald.com/.
Jornal de Angola (Angola). http://www.jornaldeangola.com/.
Le Jour (Ivory Coast). http://www.lejourplus.com/.
Kenya Times (Kenya). http://www.timesnews.co.ke/.
Mail & Guardian (South Africa). http://www.mg.co.za/.
Mmegi (Botswana). http://www.mmegi.bw/.
The Monitor (Uganda). http://www.monitor.co.ug/.
The Namibian (Namibia). http://www.namibian.com.na/.
Nation (Kenya). http://www.nationmedia.com.
The New Vision (Uganda). http://www.newvision.co.ug/.
L'Observateur Paalaga (Burkina Faso). http://www.lobservateur.bf/.
Le Phare (DRC). http://www.le-phare.com/.
The Punch (Nigeria). http://www.punchng.com/.
Le quotidien Mutations (Cameroon). http://www.quotidienmutations.net.
Le Soleil (Senegal). http://www.lesoleil.sn/.
The Sowetan (South Africa). http://www.sowetan.co.za/.
Sunday Times (South Africa). http://www.sundaytimes.co.za.
This Day (Nigeria). http://www.thisdayonline.com.
The Times of Zambia (Zambia). http://www.times.co.zm/.
Vanguard (Nigeria). http://www.vanguardngr.com/.

Sample African Magazines

Agoo Magazine (Ghana).
Botsotso Magazine (South Africa). http://www.botsotso.org.za.
Chimurenga (South Africa). http://www.chimurenga.co.za/.
Drum (South Africa). http://www.media24.co.za/details.asp?category=magazines&publication=drum.
Eve (Kenya). http://www.oaklandmedia.com/eve/.
Fairlady (South Africa). http://www.women24.com/Women24/FairLady/FL_Template/.
Farafina (Nigeria). http://www.farafina-online.com/.
Foolscap (Nigeria). http://www.foolscap-media.com/.
Kwani? (Kenya). http://www.kwani.org/.
Let's Cook (Kenya). http://www.nationmedia.com/letscook/.

Momentum Magazine (Nigeria–USA). http://www.momentummag.com.
Nigerian Entertainment (Nigeria). http://www.nigerianentertainment.com.
Ovation International (Nigeria). http://www.ovationinternational.com/.
Stage Magazine (South Africa). http://www.stage.co.za/.
Uneek Magazine (Ghana).

A Sample of African Cartoonists

Godfrey Mwampembwa (Tanzania). http://www.gadonet.com/.
Nigerian cartoonists. http://www.cnenigeria.com/toons/index.htm.
South African Cartoonists. http://www.cartoonist.co.za/cartoonists.htm.

AFRICAN MEDIA ASSOCIATIONS

Benin: Union des Journalistes de la Presse Privée du Bénin (UJPB), 03 BP 2458 Cotonou. Tel: 229-32-50-55; Fax: 229-32-50-55. Contact: Célestin Akpovo.

Burkina Faso: Association des Médias Communautaires. Contact: André-Eugène Ilboudo. Email: aeugene@fasonet.bf.

Chad: Union des Journalistes Tchadiens (UJT), N'Djamena. Contact: Abakar Saleh, Secrétaire General. Tel: 235-52-51-36, 235-29-16-06. Email: asalehtd@yahoo.com.

Congo, Democratic Republic of: Journaliste en Danger (JED), 73, av. Maringa Kinshasa/Kasa-Vubu. Tel: 243-12-20-659; Fax: 243-12-20-659. Contact: M'BayaTshimanga, President. Email: jedkin@ic.cd; Email: direction@jed-congo.org.

Gabon: Association Professionnelle de la Presse Écrite Gabonaise (APPEG), BP 3849 Libreville. Email: wmestre@gabon-presse.org.url.

Gambia: Gambian Union of Journalists, 10 Atlantic Road, Banjul. Tel: 220-497-945; Fax: 220-497-946. Contact: Demba Jawo.

Ghana: West African Journalists Association (WAJA-UJAO), Ghana International Press Centre Accra, Tel: 233-21-31-56-52; Fax: 233-21-31-56-53. Contact: Kabral Blay-Amihere, Président. Email: waja@africaonline.com.gh.

Guinea: Association des Journalistes de Guinée (AJG), BP 1535 Conakry. Tel: 224-454-461; Fax: 224-454-461. Contact: Yaya Diallo, Secrétaire Général.

Ivory Coast: Union Nationale des Journalistes de Côte-d'Ivoire (UNJCI). Tel: 225-20-21-61-07. Contact: Honoratde Yedagne, Président. Email: unjci10@aviso.ci.

Kenya: Kenya Union of Journalists, Ukulima Cooperative House, Haile Selassie Avenue, PO Box 47035-00100, Nairobi, Kenya. Tel/Fax: 254-02-250-880. Contact: Ezekiel Mutua, Secretary General.

Liberia: Press Union of Liberia, Kiny Sao Bosso Street, Monrovia, Tel: 231-224-708; Fax: 231-227-838. Contact: Massaley Abraham, President.

Mali: Union Nationale des Journalistes du Mali (UNAJOM), BP 141 Bamako. Tel: 223-223-6-83; Fax: 223-234-3-13. Contact: Ousmane Maiga, Président.

Nigeria: Nigerian Union of Journalists, Area II, Garki Abuja, Tel: 234-09-234-30-17; Fax: 234-09-234-30-17. Contact: Lanre Ogundipe, President.

Senegal: Centre Africain des Femmes dans les Médias/African Women's Media Centre (CAFM/AWMC), Dakar Ponty, Tel: 221-823-86-87; Fax: 221-822-05-40. Contact: AmieJoof-Cole, Director. Email: awmc@metissacana.sn. Website: http://.www.awmc.com.

Senegal: Union des Journalistes de l'Afrique de l'Ouest (secrétariat general; UJAO-SG), BP 15578 Dakar-Fann. Tel: 221-820-47-46, 221-820-47-46; Fax: 221-820-17-60, 221-820-47-46. Email: synpics@telecomplus.sn. Contact: Alpha Abdallah Sall, Secrétaire Général.

Sierra Leone: Sierra Leone Association of Journalists (SLAJ), 31 Garrisson Street Freetown. Tel: 232-76-60-58-11, 232-76-601-716. Contact: Ibrahim El-Tayyib Bah, President. Email: tayyib19@hotmail.com; Email: slajalone@hotmail.com. Togo: Union des Journalistes Indépendants du Togo (UJIT), BP 81213 Lomé. Tel: 228-26-13-00, 228-21-38-21; Fax: 228-26-13-70, 228-21-38-21. Email: ujit@ids.tg.

Zambia: Southern African Broadcasting Association (SABA), Plot 2A/7/377a, Multimedia Centre, Bishop's Road, Kabulonga Lusaka. Tel: 260-1-263-595; Fax: 260-1-263-595, 260-1-265-018, 260-1-263-110, 260-1-254-317. Contact: John J. Musukuma, Secretary General. Email: pazasaba@zamnet.zm.

Zimbabwe: Zimbabwe Union of Journalists (ZUJ), 57 Whitecroft Building, Cnr Central and Sixth Avenue, Harare, Zimbabwe. Tel: +263-(0)4-795670, +263-(0)4-795609. Contact: Mathew Takaona, President. Email: admin@zuj.org.zw, info@zuj.org.zw.

NOTES

1. *East African Standard.* Updated August 20, 2005. http://www.eastandard.net/mags/style/articles.php?articleid=27597.
   The story, in the Style and Substance section, was headlined "Caroline off-air."
2. "Nigeria's Celebrity Class." *BBC* (2004, December 29). http://news.bbc.co.uk/2/hi/africa/4119365.stm.
3. Greg Garett, "Introduction: African Popular Culture and the Western Scholar." *Journal of Popular Culture* 32.2 (1998, Fall): 1.
4. Matte Shayne, *African Newspapers Currently Received by American Libraries.* Updated 1997. http://www.library.northwestern.edu/africana/resources/97crlnews.html.
5. Dennis Mcquail, *Mass Communication Theory: An Introduction.* London: Sage, 2000.
6. Daniel Lerner, *The Passing of Traditional Society: Modernizing the Middle East.* Glencoe, IL: Free Press, 1958.
7. Ithiel de Sola Pool, "The Role of Communication in the Process of Modernization and Technological Change." Pp. 279–293 in Bert F. Hoselitz and Wilbert E. Moore (eds.), *Industrialization and Society.* Paris: UNESCO-Mouton, 1963.
8. Baffour Ankomah, "Cameroon's Forbidden Topics." *Index on Censorship* 2 (1988): 24.
9. Lewis Odhiambo, "Eastern African Regional Perspectives." Background paper presented by Dr. Odhiambo at the seminar *Ten Years On: Assessment, Challenges and Prospects*, at Windhoek, Namibia, May 3–5, 2001. http://www.unesco.org/webworld/wpfd/2001_docs_rtf/odhiambo_en.rtf.
10. Kwame Karikari, "Africa: The Press and Democracy." *Race and Class* 34.3 (1993): 56–57.
11. Campbell 1998 (in Resource Guide), p. 35.
12. Media Institute of Southern Africa and Gender. *The Gender and Media Baseline Study.* Updated 2003. http://www.misa.org/Gender/baseline-study.pdf.
13. Frederiksen 2002 (in Resource Guide, Journals).
14. John Kiriamiti, *My Life in Crime.* Nairobi: Spear Books, 1980.
15. Jegede 1995 (in Resource Guide), p. 285.
16. Struan Douglas, "*Drum* Magazine." *Afribeat* magazine. http://home.worldonline.co.za/~afribeat/archiveafrica.html.
17. Ibid.
18. *Daily Nation* (2005, June 1).
19. John A. Wiseman, *The New Struggle for Democracy in Africa.* Aldershot, UK: Avebury, 1996, p. 56.
20. Celestin Lingo and Suzanne Kala Lobe. "Central Africa Regional Perspective, Summary Review, The Windhoek Seminar." Presentation at the seminar *Ten Years On: Assessment, Challenges and Prospects*, at Windhoek, Namibia, May 3–5, 2001. http://www.unesco.org/webworld/wpfd/2001_docs_rtf/central_africa_en.rtf.
21. Centre de documentation des instances d'asile (CEDOCA) 2002: *Rapport de mission à Kinshasa (République démocratique du Congo) du 16 juin au 5 août 2002.* Brussels, Belgium: Commissariat général aux réfugiés et aux apatrides.

22. Bureau of Democracy, Human Rights and Labor, U.S. State Department. *Congo, Democratic Republic of the, Country Reports on Human Rights Practices (2003)*. Published February 2004. http://www.state.gov/g/drl/rls/hrrpt/2003/27721.htm.
23. Irwin Manion, "Skirmishes on the Margins: The War Against South Africa's Alternative Press." *Index on Censorship* (1988, April 29).
24. *Changing Media for a Changing Society: The South African Experience*. Report of The International Communication Forum Conference held at Silvermist Mount Lodge, Cape Town, April 5–9, (2003), p. 10. London: International Communication Forum (ICF).

LOVE, SEX, AND MARRIAGE

LOVE, SEX, AND MARRIAGE: An AIDS awareness badge, inspired by Zulu bead work. Courtesy of Shutterstock.

LOVE, SEX, AND MARRIAGE: An expectant couple making a living in Soweto, a township in South Africa. Courtesy of Shutterstock.

LOVE, SEX, AND MARRIAGE: Dogon villagers in Mali watching an HIV/AIDS awareness video shown by a group of travelling government health advisors. © Neil Cooper / Alamy.

MUSIC

MUSIC: Senegal's singer Youssou N'Dour performs at a festival in Africa, 2005. © Lebrecht Music and Arts Photo Library / Alamy.

MUSIC: Congolese singer Papa Wemba performs during a concert at the New Morning Theater in Paris, 2006. © PIERRE VERDY/AFP/Getty Images.

PERIODICALS

PERIODICALS: A vendor sells newspapers at an intersection in Johannesburg, South Africa, 2003. Neighboring country Zimbabwe's continued suspension from the Commonwealth dominates the front pages. © AP Photo/Denis Farrell.

PERIODICALS: Luxury car pages partner with fashion pages on the production line at the magazine *True Love*, a women's magazine that targets black women. © Christophe Calais/Corbis.

RADIO AND TELEVISION

RADIO AND TELEVISION: Local programming plays on a television set in Soweto, the sprawling black township near Johannesburg. Courtesy of Shutterstock.

RADIO AND TELEVISION: Vusi Sixhaso, a founding member of Radio Zibonele, conducts a program in his Cape Town studio, 1995. © AP Photo/Sasa Kralj.

RADIO AND TELEVISION: Ghanaian soccer fans gather to watch Ghana play the Czech Republic on television during the 2006 World Cup. © AP Photo/Olivier Asselin.

SPORTS AND RECREATION

SPORTS AND RECREATION: Senegalese traditional wrestlers fight during an inter-village match in Hathioune, Senegal, 1998. For generations, young Senegalese men have wrestled to find their place in their culture, but modern wrestling—replete with flashy TV stars, punching, and big prize money—has left traditionalists struggling to hold on to their rituals. © AP Photo/David Guttenfelder.

SPORTS AND RECREATION: South Africa's Darryl Coeries, right, runs with the ball against Papua New Guinea's Leroy Muriki during the second round match at the World Rugby Sevens at Ballymore in Brisbane, Australia, 2003. © AP Photo/Steve Holland.

SPORTS AND RECREATION: A young man practices his skills on a makeshift football field in Namibia, Southern Africa. Courtesy of Shutterstock.

THEATER AND PERFORMANCE

THEATER AND PERFORMANCE: A woman passes the Market Theatre in Johannesburg carrying recyclable cardboard. From the day it opened in an abandoned fruit market, The Market Theatre has given voice to those whom the country's former white rulers sought to silence. © AP Photo/Denis Farrell.

THEATER AND PERFORMANCE: Actor Mpumi Shelemba performs with a cast of school children in this scene from the 1987 production of Mbongeni Ngema's *Sarafina* at the Market Theatre in Johannesburg. The Market Theatre celebrated its 30th year in 2006. © AP Photo/Ruphin Coudyzer.

TRANSPORTATION AND TRAVEL

TRANSPORTATION AND TRAVEL: A matatu minibus waits for passengers in downtown Nairobi, Kenya. Kenyans love the matatus because they're cheap and far more accessible than the spotty and unreliable city buses. © AP Photo/Khalil Senosi.

TRANSPORTATION AND TRAVEL: "Mammy-wagons," like this one in Madagascar carry large numbers, often packed in like sardines, to work in towns from the outlying shanty-towns and villages. Courtesy of Shutterstock.

RADIO AND TELEVISION

ALI N. MOHAMED

Radio and television have followed quite different paths in terms of their introduction, evolution, and diffusion in Sub-Saharan Africa. Whereas radio was quickly available on a fairly broad scale soon after the invention of wireless telephony, Africans have been slow in adopting television. Although radio was widely in use in the 1930s, 1940s, and 1950s—well before independence for most African states—television was still being introduced as recently as 1994 in Tanzania, 1996 in Rwanda, 1999 in Malawi, and 2000 in Botswana.

Several reasons are generally given for the delay in adopting television. Cost is one of them. Unlike radio, which is inexpensive but effective as a means of communication in poor societies with high illiteracy rates, television is considered a status symbol suited for the relatively comfortable urban lifestyles with modern amenities such as electricity—something not necessary in the case of radio. With majorities who cannot afford the cost of a television receiver, ownership and use of the medium remains a luxury enjoyed by a tiny minority across much of the continent.

Another major concern for countries that waited a long time to introduce television has been the feasibility of locally produced programming needed to cover air time. With the exception of newscasts and a few news-related feature programs, most of the air time on African television is covered with imported European, American, Middle Eastern, or Indian entertainment programs.

A third reason for the delay in introducing television in Africa has been political, at least in the case of some countries such as the Republic of South Africa. In spite of its status as the continent's most advanced country both economically and technologically, South Africa initiated television only in 1976. Leaders of the then-apartheid regime were concerned that television would expose white citizens of South Africa to casual and benign interaction between people of different races within Western societies. Scenes routinely depicted in imported programming from the United States and the United Kingdom were considered unacceptable by government officials because of the contradictions with core principles of the apartheid system that the programs presented. When television was finally introduced, therefore, white citizens were precluded by law from watching Channel 2 (for Blacks), which featured such popular shows as *Benson* that had both black and white characters.

Radio, on the other hand, has had a much less controversial reception on the continent. The quick embrace of radio was due to its technical character as the medium of the spoken word. In a continent known for its strong oral traditions, radio as a medium of mass communication was a perfect fit. Furthermore, the transistor radio receiver is portable and affordable, making it a favorite among the rural poor. Like television, however, radio broadcasting has been tightly controlled by national governments throughout Africa until the 1990s.

OVERVIEW OF BROADCASTING IN AFRICA

The Colonial Origins of African Radio

Radio broadcasting was introduced to much of Africa during the colonial period, mainly by Great Britain and France. In the 1920s and early 1930s, these two powers established small relay stations that transmitted British and French broadcast signals to their colonial personnel on the continent.

The Union of South Africa (later the Republic of South Africa) had fairly advanced technology in wireless telegraphy and telephony at the turn of the twentieth century, and so radio broadcasting in Africa first started there. In 1923, the government of South Africa issued broadcast regulations, and a few radio stations began operation that year. Soon, however, most of those early commercial ventures failed financially because of limited numbers of receivers and unwillingness by many clients to pay listener fees. In 1927, a businessman in the entertainment industry, I. W. Schlesinger, bought a ten-year license to establish the African Broadcasting Company (ABC), which proved financially successful thanks to the near-monopoly situation it enjoyed for a decade.

In 1936, the South African parliament passed the Broadcast Act, by which the South African Broadcasting Company (SABC) was founded. Both the early SABC and its predecessor, ABC, broadcast solely in English and Afrikaans, the language of the Afrikaner settlers of Dutch origin.

The first radio station in the rest of Africa was set up by the British in 1927 in Nairobi, Kenya, as a service to the settler community in the highlands and Rift Valley region of the country. Its main purpose was to provide a connection to the homeland for the settlers by offering a continuous menu of news and information from the United Kingdom.

The French started broadcasting on the continent in 1931, when a small 500-watt transmitter was built in Antananarivo on the Indian Ocean island of Madagascar. Most of that station's broadcast fare consisted of music and general information, which was read in French for an average of about two hours a day.

Although most of the earliest radio broadcasts in Africa were intended to bring news of home to European colonists, the British, especially, quickly initiated entertainment, news, and informational programs in various African vernacular languages. In 1931, the British East Africa Cable and Wireless Company took over management of the radio in Nairobi but would not produce programming for African listeners. In accordance with the British policy of cultivating African audiences, the colonial administration then bought transmitter time from the Cable and Wireless Company in order to broadcast afternoon programs to African audiences.

A limited number of vernacular languages—Kiswahili (Swahili), Gikuyu, Luo, and Kikamba—were used to broadcast short news and information bulletins. By 1954, the station was scheduling 41 hours' worth of programming per week divided among the four African languages. Programs in the vernacular included music (traditional African songs) as well as features on such subjects as the challenges of urban life for new city dwellers.

In northern Somalia, a small British military installation called Radio KUDU began service in the Somali language in 1941. After the war, the British installed a more powerful

10-kilowatt transmitter in order "to combat the growing influence of communism," according to one Somali historian.[1]

In Ghana, the British began training African broadcasters as early as 1937 and started offering services in four indigenous languages that same year. In Nigeria, radio broadcasts offering programs in the vernaculars were in full swing by the 1940s in Lagos, Ijebu-Ode, Enugu, Kano, Zaria, Kaduna, Jos, Sokoto, Maiduguri, and Katsina.

Belgium started broadcasting services aimed at indigenous African populations in 1939. In what was then the Belgian Congo (now the Democratic Republic of the Congo), the Belgians began a service that broadcast in French but also in four local African languages, namely Kikongo, Tshiluba, Lingala, and Kiswahili.[2] Meanwhile, Belgian missionaries operated a small radio station that broadcast religious services in French on Sundays.

By comparison, France was slow to set up broadcasting facilities in her colonies. When she finally did so, it was a much more highly centralized system than those established by the British and other colonial powers elsewhere in Africa. In 1931 the French started an ambitious radio service in Dakar, Senegal, that transmitted programming to several of her colonies in West Africa, including what are now Mali, Mauritania, and Guinea. Because of the regional focus of its coverage, this pioneer station in French West Africa was called *Inter-Afrique Occidentale Français.* The French were keener than the British on using radio to disseminate their influence and culture. Unlike the British, who encouraged the use of African languages and the propagation of African arts and culture, the French stressed the use of French and actively sought the transformation of Africans into black Frenchmen, termed *évolués.* The French found it convenient to offer their language and culture as a means of unifying their African subjects, most of who spoke different native tongues and represented rival indigenous cultures.[3]

Portugal's main colonial possessions in Africa, Angola and Mozambique, had a unique radio broadcasting experience, thanks to Portugal's peculiar laissez-faire attitude toward radio. As one observer put it, Portuguese policy in this area "constituted Africa's most diversified system of control, leaving room for private enterprise and advertising support."[4] Although Mozambique and Angola have relatively small populations, they were listed as having Africa's greatest number of separate broadcast services before either one of them gained independence in the mid 1970s. Mozambique got her first broadcast service in 1935 with the establishment of Lourenço Marques Radio. It was privately operated and relied almost entirely on advertising revenue generated from serving South African commercial interests. Until independence in 1974, Lourenço Marques Radio catered to young European and South African audiences by broadcasting in English and Afrikaans. But another prominent radio service, the privately owned *A Voz de Moçambique,* offered programming produced by the government's Information and Tourism Center that was designed for African audiences. *A Voz de Moçambique* aired entertainment and cultural programs in nine indigenous languages, although only two of those languages (Shangana and Ronga) got the largest share of air time.

By the 1940s and early 1950s, all other European colonial powers—Spain, Germany, and Italy—had established broadcast services aimed at African audiences in their respective colonies throughout the continent.

The cultivation of African audiences during the colonial period was part of a grand strategy to advance colonial interests. European powers initiated a process of cultural indoctrination that had three prominent support pillars: (1) an educational system that promoted European values and culture; (2) a missionary program that spread Christianity among Africans; and (3) radio broadcasting in the twentieth century that effectively cemented the influences of the other two institutions.

Radio was not only a useful tool for Christian missionaries to proselytize and gain converts, but more significantly, it transmitted music and other entertainment programs that spread and reinforced European cultural influences among the small but elite corps of African civil servants in urban centers who were very instrumental in the administration of the colonies.

With the exception of the Republic of South Africa, however, broadcast installations and communication technologies in many parts of colonial Africa were quite crude and frequently presented technical challenges for radio personnel. In Somalia, for example, reporters at KUDU Radio in Hargeisa had only one microphone in the one studio of the station. Even long after World War II in the early 1950s, the technical conditions of Somali radio remained woefully inadequate. In December 1951, for instance, the lead Somali broadcaster at KUDU Radio, Abdi Dualeh, decided to cover a live event: the opening session of the Protectorate Advisory Council. The occasion was quite festive and involved a police parade and performances by a Somali marching band. Dualeh was to report live from a window of the medical school and, as he would later recall,

> We possessed only one serviceable mic at that time. When R. C. Davis (the studio engineer) learned of my anxiety about trying the OB [Outside Broadcast], he produced a homemade microphone using the speaker from one of the "saucepan" radios as the principal component and he spent the preceding weekend anxiously testing lines so that my commentary could be fed to the radio transmitter which was less than a quarter mile away! [5]

This episode illustrated the many impediments that undermined the work of early African radio personnel. But it also reveals the determination and professionalism of the continent's pioneer radio broadcasters.

The Post-Colonial Period and Radio's Role in Social and Economic Development

In 1960 seventeen African countries gained political independence from Britain, France, Belgium, and Italy. Within five years, close to 85 percent of all Africans lived in free states. But the political freedoms of the 1960s brought tremendous challenges for which most of the newly independent states were ill prepared. Almost all Sub-Saharan African countries faced illiteracy rates of 75–95 percent, equally high proportions of rural populations, poor communication infrastructure, and a woefully inadequate civil service sector. Trained professionals, who were needed to run the affairs of the new states, were few and far between. For example, the Democratic Republic of the Congo had fewer than 10 college graduates at independence; Burkina Faso had one, while many others, such as Somalia, Tanzania, Uganda, and Gabon, had none!

Most likely, however, the thorniest issue for the majority of the new states was the problem of their ethnic composition. When European powers carved out the continent among themselves, they did not take into account traditional boundaries that separated ethnic groups, some of which had a history of hostilities and rivalries dating back centuries. Ethnic tensions have had a destabilizing effect, as civil wars in Nigeria, Sierra Leone, Ivory Coast, Zimbabwe, Ethiopia, Uganda, Burundi, Rwanda, and elsewhere have shown.

The leaders of Africa's independence movements, who later assumed leadership of the independent states, were aware of the power of radio in organizing society. They knew of the effective use of radio for propaganda purposes during WW II by both the Allied and Axis powers. Accordingly, Presidents Kwame Nkurumah of Ghana and Jomo Kenyatta of Kenya, Mwalimu Julius Nyerere of Tanzania, and Prime Ministers Abubakar Tafawi Balewa of Nigeria and Patrice Lumumba of the Democratic Republic of Congo all used radio for nation-building purposes by promoting the concept of national unity in their countries through frequent radio addresses. Furthermore, Africa's high illiteracy rates meant that radio was the only medium by which to communicate with masses in both rural and urban areas. This aspect of radio was widely cited as justification for nationalizing broadcast services throughout the continent in the 1960s and 1970s.

The utility of radio became quickly apparent also in its role in development—especially among Africa's rural populations. Influenced partly by the work of three American scholars[6] and the recommendations of UNESCO, many newly independent states used radio to promote national development goals. Radio was thus used to teach farmers how to increase their yields by rotating crops and using better irrigation methods; it was used to instruct women to boil stream water before letting children drink it; and it was used to teach men how to build latrines in order to improve sanitation and personal hygiene. To ensure wide diffusion of ideas that would foment change, these programs were transmitted in vernacular languages.

Some of the more ingenious radio campaigns for development may have taken place in Kenya and Tanzania in the 1970s and 1980s. When more than 26 percent of secondary school teachers were determined to be unqualified in Kenya, the government faced a tough dilemma: how to prepare more than 10,000 teachers before the start of the next school year? The teachers needed to take a course that would prepare them for the Kenya Junior Secondary Examination. The only option was to offer the course by correspondence over radio, and that is what Kenya did. Tanzania used a similar program to upgrade primary school teachers in the 1970s.

In Senegal, Ghana, Tanzania, and other countries, authorities organized rural radio listening groups, which were highly structured and designed to promote change and bring progress to rural communities. Following a radio feature program, such as one on an outbreak of rinderpest (a cattle disease), villagers would spend time discussing the contents and recommendations contained in the radio program. In Ethiopia, Somalia, and parts of Kenya, nomadic cattle and camel herders would come together in spontaneous radio listening groups and then spend hours discussing what they had heard and its possible implications for their lives. As one prominent African historian described it,

> It is a common, if amusing thing to come upon a group of nomads huddled excitedly over a short-wave transistor, engaged in a heated discussion of the literary merits of poems that have just been broadcast while they keep watch over their camel herds grazing nearby.[7]

Role of Radio in Propagating African Culture

In general, radio broadcasting in Africa has reflected a strong European influence mainly because of the inclinations of the educated and Westernized elites who are responsible for production of programming content. Their material is heavily colored by the legacy of colonial rule also because of the tastes acquired by modern urban audiences of radio, who are also highly Westernized.

Its important to note, however, that some political leaders, such as former presidents Julius Nyerere of Tanzania and Mobutu Sese Seko of Zaire (today's Democratic Republic of the Congo), made conscious efforts to promote traditional African culture through radio. Nyerere championed the cause of maintaining traditional African culture by promoting the use of Kiswahili throughout Tanzania. In 1965 Kiswahili was made compulsory in secondary schools and was declared the only language TANU members and candidates could use in their election campaigns. Furthermore, Tanzania enacted policies aimed at limiting

European cultural influence by requiring traditional music and other cultural programs to be given plenty of air time on radio.

In Zaire, Mobutu declared his "cultural authenticity" campaign during the 1970s to preserve Congolese culture. Many artists and musical groups were encouraged to produce music and entertainment programs that reflected the spirit of the "authenticity" campaign. The resulting songs and dances, based on traditional rhythms and sounds using traditional instruments, became a new musical form known as "l'animation politique."

The dances and musical output of some Congolese groups received a widespread following in neighboring countries including Kenya, Tanzania, Uganda, and Rwanda during the 1970s and 1980s. Some of the notable hits on radio in these countries included Dr. Nico's "Kiri Kiri," Tabu-Ley Rochereau's "Soum Joum," and OK Jazz's "Rumba Odemba."

In Senegal and Gambia, too, radio has been used to propagate African culture quite effectively. In both countries, radio frequently featured the work of griots, the ancient caste within the West African Manding ethnic groups that specializes in, among other things, traditional entertainment and performances at cultural events. Griots are highly regarded for mediating disputes and for arranging marriage terms between individuals of different ethnic groups. They are respected also for their skills in relating historical tales, accompanying themselves on traditional musical instruments such as the *balafon* (a kind of xylophone), the *ngoni* (a small traditional lute), and the *kora* (a cross between a lute and a harp).

In Senegal, the main government broadcast station aired a series called *Regards sur le Senegal d'autrefois* [A Look at the Senegal of the Past]. Ironically, this program, and others like it, was aired in Wolof but also in French!

In Somalia, where the Latin script was adopted to write the Somali language for the first time in 1972, the government created a national heritage and culture preservation agency that was charged with preserving traditional dances, songs, and other indigenous artistic forms. The work of this agency was frequently broadcast over the two shortwave radio stations in the country. Also, weekly programs such as *Ciyaaraha Hidaha iyo Dhaqanka* (traditional dances and games), *Dhaqanka Reer Guuraaga* (nomadic life and culture), and *Barnaamijka Suugaanta* (traditional literature) received considerable air time, while services in Italian, English, and French were cut back.

Burkina Faso (formerly Upper Volta) was an early promoter of African culture through radio programs in the vernacular. Some long-running programs include *Sous l'arbre à palabre* and *La Soirée en moore*, which stressed the importance of traditional African values based on respect for authority figures in the community, such as tribal chiefs, and within the family, such as husbands and fathers.

Oral Traditions and the Success of Radio

The tremendous success of radio in Africa can be attributed largely to the continent's strong oral traditions. Apart from the Latin and Arabic scripts, only the Amhara and Tigre ethnic groups of Ethiopia have had a centuries-old script for writing their language.

When radio came into the lives of Africans, it provided an instant means of expanding the reach and influence of traditional orators, poets, storytellers, and local bards. The mass audience effect was particularly pronounced where indigenous languages are spoken by millions of people spread over several countries. Thus, speakers of such languages as Hausa, Igbo, Kiswahili, Somali, Wolof, Luo, and isiZulu benefited from exposure to ideas, thoughts, and new cultural forms by poets, artists, and wordsmiths from a wide geographical area. Radio, therefore, was a medium that could integrate far-flung communities by providing a common cultural and ideological experience.

This is why, wherever possible, some African countries aggressively pushed for the adoption of a national language. Shortly after independence, Tanzania adopted Kiswahili as both the national and official language. Kenya's first president, Jomo Kenyatta, expended considerable political capital to get skeptical opponents to go along with his vision for Kiswahili as the national language of Kenya. In pushing the political decision to adopt Kiswahili over English as a national language, the president said:

> The basis of any independent government worth its salt is a national language. We are an independent nation and we can no longer continue aping our former colonial masters. We are lucky that today the majority of Kenyans can understand Kiswahili. . . . I know some people will start murmuring that the time is not ripe for this decision. To hell with such people! Those who feel they cannot do without English can as well pack up and go.[8]

In 1973, Somalia abolished Italian and English as official languages and replaced them with Somali and Arabic.

Early Television in Africa

The era of television in sub-Saharan Africa began with WNTV in Ibadan, Nigeria, in 1959. It was quickly followed by another television service in Enugu, Nigeria, also in 1959.

Along with Nigeria, less than a handful of countries in Africa began television service before independence. They include Kenya in 1962, and Northern and Southern Rhodesia (now Zambia and Zimbabwe, respectively) in 1961.

As previously noted, television got a slow introduction in much of Africa. After gaining independence in the early to mid-1960s, only a small number of countries moved to establish television services. They include Ghana, Ivory Coast, the Democratic Republic of the Congo, Senegal, Madagascar, and Niger. In this group, we can also count Ethiopia and Liberia, which were not colonized.

A few more countries introduced television in the 1970s: Benin in 1972, the Central African Republic and Togo in 1973, Uganda in 1975, Angola and South Africa in 1976, Guinea in 1977, and Swaziland in 1978.

During the 1980s the television club was joined by Namibia in 1981; Mali, Seychelles, and Somalia in 1983; Burundi and Mauritania in 1984; Cameroon in 1986; Chad in 1987; and Lesotho in 1988. In the 1990s Mozambique (1990), Tanzania (1994), Rwanda (1996), and Malawi (1999) introduced television.

In the immediate post-independence period, all African countries that had television sought to use it for educational and development-oriented programming, in addition to regular news, entertainment, and cultural content. In Nigeria, for example, early television concentrated on promoting science as a means of correcting perceived deficiencies in colonial educational policies. Through television, the state sought to popularize science among high school students as well as the general public. Some of the earliest locally produced programming in Ibadan and other western Nigerian cities included a series of half-hour broadcasts that featured outstanding physics and chemistry teachers. The shows were intended to fascinate and thus pique the interests of audiences, especially high school students. Other programs focused on world current affairs in which events were explained in great detail by placing them in historical and geographical contexts.

Another early Nigerian show was called *Spotlight*, and it featured playwright and Nobel laureate Wole Soyinka. According to one analyst, "The aim of *Spotlight* was to introduce what seemed to be the ordinary artistic manifestations of the period, probe their cultural origins through interviews with the artists and present them intimately to viewers."[9]

Elsewhere in Africa a similar commitment to using television for educational and development purposes was demonstrated. In 1965 Zambia moved quickly to replace the imported European content of its main television station in the mining center at Kitwe with locally produced educational programs consisting of variety shows, news, and public affairs programming that reflected real-life concerns of the African population.

In the Democratic Republic of the Congo (formerly Zaire), a nonprofit television production center, whose purpose was to facilitate program exchanges among French-speaking countries, was set up in the early 1960s. Known initially as STAR (*Service Technique Africain de Radio-Television*) and later as TELESTAR, the center was born out of the need to reduce production costs and to eliminate unnecessary duplication of programs in African countries facing identical challenges of development. A Ford Foundation study of the services provided by this center described it as follows:

> The essential aim of TELESTAR is to produce educational and socio-cultural programs presenting valid solutions to the vital problems which exist in Africa in general, and in the Congo in particular: close collaboration with government and private specialists in the different areas of interest—including health, education, agriculture education, emancipation of the African woman, and socio-cultural education.[10]

Because it served only French-speaking countries, TELESTAR was limited in its usefulness to many countries in the region, however. In 1962, with Nigeria leading the way, a group of pioneer African broadcasters met in Lagos and founded the Union of Radio and Television Organizations of Africa (URTNA). The founders of URTNA had two main concerns:

1. Recognition of a desperate need for regional collaboration in raising awareness about common socio-economic conditions and overcoming the challenges of geographic distances between African peoples affected by poor transport and communication links
2. Joint development of television programs that were "meaningful to the cultural and socio-economic aspirations of the newly independent African states"[11]

In spite of this apparent focus on cultural and educational programming, exchanges through URTNA involved a diverse range of content genres, including 35 percent that was entertainment, 32 percent development-related materials, 22 percent cultural programs, and 11 percent informational content.[12]

It should be noted that over time, the early enthusiasm about educational and development-oriented television content wore off and a larger proportion of programming time began to be filled with imported entertainment programs as Africa made a transition in the 1980s toward using television more as a source of entertainment.[13] Hours of transmission were increased as audience demands warranted. Increases in broadcast time allotted to entertainment inevitably led to increased importation of programming. This outcome was realized as local productions faced stiff competition from video cassette recorders and satellite dish services. UNESCO data reflect sharp increases in the mid-to-late 1980s in African consumption of imported entertainment materials, especially from the United States, the United Kingdom, and France. Reruns of U.S. serials such as *Dallas, Dynasty, The Jeffersons, The Six-Million-Dollar Man,* and *Championship Wrestling* were popular in the 1980s from Liberia and Nigeria in the west to Zambia and South Africa in the south. More recently, U.S. shows such as *Oprah, The Cosby Show, Everybody Loves Raymond,* and the daytime soap *Passions* attract large audiences throughout Africa.

Ironically, in most cases it is cheaper to import than to produce local cultural materials. U.S. distributors sell programming at such discounted rates that African markets can afford to purchase sufficient quantities of Hollywood entertainment fare every year.

Not to be outdone, the French have made deliberate efforts to maintain their cultural influence over former colonies through news, sports, and entertainment programs. At least four hours of programming are offered free to twenty-four national television organizations in Africa (including Arab North Africa), with the French government paying for satellite dishes and all affiliated costs of airing the programs.

Studies show that where French programs are shown, the proportion of imported content has exceeded locally produced programming.[14] Francophone African countries in which a majority of air time is covered with imported entertainment programs include Senegal, Togo, Ivory Coast, Gabon, and Djibouti. Because France has targeted Lusophone countries as well with free programming, we may include Angola and Mozambique in this list.

The United Kingdom exports television programs to Africa through the British Council and BBC Enterprises. British commercial productions are also available to African clients through the London-based International Television Enterprises.

Other European countries that supply Africa with television content to varying degrees include Germany, Belgium, and Italy. Before the collapse of the central government in Somalia, the lion's share of entertainment programming on the small television service in Mogadishu came from Egypt and Lebanon. Djibouti also imports much of its cultural programs from Middle Eastern sources such as Egypt.

A standard element in African television news coverage is the prominence accorded to political leaders such as presidents or prime ministers. Like radio before it, television is a source of constant information about the head of state and members of his cabinet. In nearly all African countries, television devotes disproportionate amounts of time to coverage of long-winded speeches and other ceremonial activities by the head of state. This is due in large measure to the reverence for authority that is deeply ingrained in the African psyche. Its also an aspect of Africa's oral traditions for which broadcasting furnishes a suitable extension. As Louise Bourgault described it,

> Electronic media function well in the communication of personalities. Moreover, oral thinking is close to the human life-world. In other words, it defines events in very personal or human terms.... The characteristics of the media fused with the orality of the audience and produced a solution for the political needs at hand. Herein lies the reason that so much airtime has been filled with the words, deeds, smallest movements, and activities of presidents.[15]

Although television is now available in various degrees of reach in all African countries, access is still severely limited by a combination of poor technical infrastructure and tough financial constraints. Lack of electricity in much of rural Africa, coupled with an insufficient number of transmitters, means that the overwhelming majority of Africans cannot have access to television service. Many more living in cities are too poor to afford television receivers and the monthly service fee that is charged by some state-owned and private service operators. Thus in 1965 there were 1.9 television receivers for every 1,000 people; in 1995 there were 28.2 receivers per 1,000 people; and today there are 32.7 receivers per every 1,000 people. According to UNESCO data, Sub-Saharan Africa still remains the most poorly served region in the world in terms of access to television.

Overview of the Broadcast Environment Today

The end of the Cold War at the start of the 1990s was a watershed moment for radio and television broadcasting in Africa. The collapse of Communism in Europe precipitated demands for political reforms and greater liberalization throughout the continent.

One of the more specific demands created by inside as well as outside pressures for reform was for more open and autonomous broadcast systems, hence the transition in the primary objectives of broadcasting from a *development* orientation to a new focus on *democratization.* The liberalization process came in the form of decentralization of broadcast authority throughout Africa. With few exceptions, most radio and television broadcasting in Africa originated in capital cities prior to the 1990s. This was a policy decision, as central governments were keen on keeping a tight lid on competing loyalties to regional authorities.

Although radio had a long history of broadcasting in vernacular languages, the flagship stations, where official resources and most professional personnel were concentrated, operated much like television and tended to broadcast mainly in French, English, or Portuguese. It has been during the post–Cold War era that Africa has experienced a proliferation of independent regional voices, many of them transmitting information in indigenous languages.

Three broad categories of independent radio can be identified with this latest phase of the African broadcast experience: (1) commercial private radio, found mainly in populated urban centers; (2) community radio, a combination of commercial and nonprofit ventures; and (3) rural radio, which is least professional in its outlook and entirely nonprofit.

Commercial Radio

Privately owned commercial radio stations are flourishing throughout Africa today. Many of these were started with the help of foreign investment capital. One of the earliest such ventures, FM 90 in Cotonou, Benin, was launched in 1991 by a partnership between Radio France Internationale and local Beninese investors. In other Francophone African states, local investors have had to compete with international entities for licenses to operate commercial radio stations. In 1992 the Ivory Coast issued five licenses for private FM stations, of which only one went to Ivorians. The successful foreign contestants were Radio France Internationale, the British Broadcasting Corporation (BBC), Africa No. 1 (owned largely by Gabon), and Radio Nostalgie, also of France. The winning Ivorian bidder was Jeune Afrique Musique (JAM), whose name gives away its primary format.

Although foreign investment capital is funding commercial radio operations throughout much of Africa, it is important to note that native investors own 100 percent share of private radio ventures in certain countries. In Somalia, where the absence of an effective central government has precluded the possibility of foreign investment, there are about half a dozen FM stations that operate commercially. One of the best known, Horn Afrik Radio, was started in 2000 in Mogadishu by two Somali-Canadians based in Ottawa. It has a serious format that emphasizes news, discussions, and interviews. Most Somali radio stations have overseas contributors who report on the approximately million-strong Somalis scattered throughout Europe and North America. Wadajir Radio of Galcaio in central Somalia, for example, has a two-hour discussion forum every Sunday that features diaspora Somalis and their involvement with the reconstruction of their homeland. The narrator of this program is based in Minneapolis, and the program is transmitted to Somalia via the Internet.

After delaying a decision for two years, the government of Ethiopia issued the first two licenses for privately owned FM radio stations in Addis Ababa in April 2006. The first license went to a former Voice of America reporter, Mimi Sebhatu, and her husband, Zerihun Teshame. The first program on Zami Public Connections Radio, as the station is called, was a debate between representatives of opposition political parties in Ethiopia. The second FM license went to two other Ethiopians, one of whom is the actor Abebe Balcha. So far, it appears that Ethiopia is not ready to issue licenses to would-be foreign investors.

The giants of private commercial radio in Africa, however, are South Africa and Nigeria. These two countries, with the best ratio of radio receivers per thousand population on the continent, have been quite successful at reaching millions of listeners beyond their borders.

In addition to the network of twenty stations that reach an average daily audience of 20 million, the South African Broadcast Corporation operates Channel Africa, an external service intended to cover the entire continent. Channel Africa prides itself on providing programming that is very African in its focus. The news and feature programs emphasize African angles to broader social, economic, and political issues of the day. Because it is intended to compete with the BBC and the Voice of America for African audiences, Channel Africa provides services in English, French, Portuguese, and Kiswahili.

In 1993 the Nigerian Broadcasting Corporation issued licenses for fourteen private radio operators. By the middle of 2002 twenty-nine more licenses had been issued. As of 2006, there were thirty-six private, commercial radio stations in Nigeria. Most of these target younger people with entertainment-oriented programming featuring Western music ranging from rap to country tunes. A popular format for musical programs in Nigeria and throughout Africa is the request line, whereby listeners call in to request a dedication song to be played.

A bill passed in 1991 provided for establishment of public radio modeled after both the BBC and America's National Public Radio (NPR). The bill allowed for the continued existence of government-owned radio stations, of which there were fifteen. Public radio stations number about eleven.

Rural and Community Radio

The terms "rural" and "community" radio are used interchangeably by some experts who have written about their role in African society. Certain distinctions between them can be drawn, however. Generally, its the geographic location of a station's service area that qualifies it as either a rural or a community-based medium. The purpose served by a radio station, too, affects what it is called. The mainstay of rural radio is development-oriented programming. Both kinds of radio are important cultural focal points for the communities they serve.

In South Africa the Independent Authority Act of 1993 envisaged community radio service to be based either on geographical zones or on "ascertainable common interest" such as professional cricket, rap music, or religion.

The concept of community radio gained currency in Africa with the liberalization movement that swept the continent during the 1990s, but it originated in Latin America in the 1960s and was widely adopted in Asia in the 1970s. Its appeal lies in its closeness to the grassroots, its cost effectiveness, and its independent character, which allows it to operate outside the control of the state.

According to Michael Delorme, former president of the World Association of Community Broadcasters (AMARC, by its French initials),

> Community radio is an act of participation in the process of community. It's controlled democratically by the population it serves . . . based on non-commercial relations with its audiences. Its mission is essentially one of community and group development. It is a local communication service. It informs, motivates discussion and entertains while broadcasting music and poetry that regenerate the collective soul.[16]

In 1985 AMARC listed only ten independent community radio stations in Africa. In 2006 South Africa alone had more than 150. One of the first countries to embrace the concept of community radio was Mali, which had eighty-seven such stations in 2006. One of them, Radio Benso, located in a rural part of southern Mali, is credited with reviving a community that previously could receive radio signals only from neighboring Ivory Coast. Now, villagers can readily obtain useful information about cotton farming, their main vocation, right in their own community. Radio Benso has enabled them to make announcements about important events to the broader community of about 300,000 people. Ordinary members of the community have been empowered to record and listen to their own songs, dance, and traditional music, thanks to community radio.

SOUTH AFRICA'S BUSH RADIO

In South Africa, the first community radio, Bush Radio, started broadcasting illegally in 1993 as an underground operation. Its objective was "to inform and educate the poor on issues they had little or no opportunity to learn about." Some of its earliest programs addressed rising crime among young people in the townships. Today, the station emphasizes programs intended to educate the public about issues that affect their lives. For example, each week, fourth- and fifth-year law students at the University of the Western Cape volunteer to air a program called "Community Law." The program explains legal matters affecting the poor and provides guidance to listeners about how to deal with specific legal issues.

Television

As previously noted, of all the regions of the world, Africa remains the most poorly served by television. Large differences in level of service exist between African countries, primarily as a function of economic development. Ethiopia, with a population of 70 million, has 300,000 television households, while South Africa, with one-third the population of Ethiopia, has twenty times as many television households.

Access to television for millions of Africans continues to be a challenge because of the scarcity of electricity in rural areas where most Africans live. Television transmitters are concentrated in populated urban centers where only a small percentage of urbanites can afford television service in their homes. The process of liberalization that swept the continent in the 1990s has had different effects on television service in different countries. With the exception of South Africa, all national governments in Africa have maintained close control over television while relaxing regulations for private ownership of radio services. Countries that permit independent commercial television include (but are not limited to) South Africa, Kenya, Ghana, Nigeria, Senegal, and Gabon.

Over the past decade, television programming has been influenced by two factors beyond the control of local television authorities: (1) the effect of transnational television services that are widely available to African television audiences and (2) competition for audiences and consequently, for advertising revenue, from alternative media sources such as satellite dishes and video cassette recorders.

One visible manifestation of the globalization phenomenon in Africa is the strong presence of transnational television services such as BBC World Television, CNN International, Visnews, Fox, Discovery, Canal France Internationale, MTV, and others. Surveys indicate that African audiences prefer the news, sports, and entertainment programming of these transnational sources either because of the quality of production and editing or simply because of newly acquired tastes.

The influence of international television services is apparent not only among audiences, but also among African television personnel. For instance, one analyst of CNN's impact on Nigerian newsmen and women observed, "Younger news people are often enchanted with much of the slick technical styles of CNN and the apparent diversity of the kinds of stories covered."[17]

Frequently, BBC, CNN, and Canal television material is reproduced and integrated into local news and feature programs. The newly acquired taste for "good" television content by African audiences, in turn, drives African television producers to mimic Western production techniques and dramatistic styles. In South Africa, many "local" entertainment programs are actually undisguised versions of well-known U.S. or British popular shows. The television network Kyknet, for example, airs *IDOLS*, a contest show "to determine the best young singer in South Africa."[18] The format is borrowed from the popular British show *Pop Idol.* In Nigeria, one of the most popular shows on television is *Rising Star,* another talent show aimed at showcasing undiscovered young Nigerian musical talent.

African television content is also affected by the availability of alternative sources of entertainment such as satellite dishes and video cassette players. Prior to the onset of the media globalization process, news and informational programs dominated African television screens. The French analyst of African media, Andre-Jean Tudesque, noted in 1992 that news took up 25 percent of television broadcast time in the Central African Republic, 35 percent in Uganda, and up to 53 percent in Burkina Faso.[19]

Although news featuring activities of political elites still gets plenty of air time, any extension of broadcast time goes to entertainment programs. This is the case in South Africa, Kenya, and Ghana, where both state-owned and independent television stations have increased their offerings of entertainment programs, both imported and locally produced. In Ghana, American soap opera serials (*Days of Our Lives, Touched by an Angel, The Bold and the Beautiful*, and *Passions*) are taking up more air time than news and informational programs.

REGIONAL SUBSECTIONS

West Africa

West African states such as Ghana and Senegal pioneered the use of radio for development purposes in Africa. It was in West Africa again that private commercial radio first flourished, in such places as Burkina Faso and Benin. But civil wars in Liberia, Sierra Leone, and Ivory Coast have interrupted progress toward full liberalization of broadcasting. In Liberia, the government of former President Charles Taylor shut down all private radio stations, allowing the government-controlled Liberian Communication Network to be the sole source of information for the people of Liberia. The government of Ivory Coast used state radio and television in 2004 and much of 2005 to disseminate virulent rhetoric against rebels fighting the government in northern regions of the country.

But encouraging signs of progress can be found elsewhere in the region. The latest country in Africa to allow private broadcasting is Guinea. In June 2006 *Radio Nostalgie* in Conakry became the first independent voice on Guinean airwaves. In this section, we will focus attention on Nigeria and Ghana.

Nigeria

Along with South Africa, Nigeria stands as Africa's media giant. In fact, the Nigerian Television Authority (NTA), with its 105 transmitters, qualifies as one of the world's five largest networks! On one level, broadcasting in Nigeria is well developed, with numerous public and private radio and television stations broadcasting in all major vernacular languages and spread evenly across the vast country of 130 million. On another level, her vast oil wealth and relatively high literacy rates notwithstanding, Nigeria struggles with most of the same problems facing lesser developed countries in Africa, such as the pervasive influence of Western culture through imported radio and television programs.

Broadcast services in Nigeria are regulated by the Nigerian Broadcast Corporation (NBC), which was created as part of a liberalization process in 1992. Although Nigeria's constitution of 1979 provided for "the federal and state governments or any other person or body authorized by the president, to own, establish or operate a television or wireless broadcasting station in the country," it was not until 1993 that privately owned broadcast stations began to appear in Nigeria. In June 1993 the Nigerian Broadcasting Corporation issued the first fourteen licenses to private radio operators. Today, thirty-six private stations are licensed in Nigeria. While NBC is the overall regulatory agency, direct administration of state-owned broadcast organizations comes under the Federal Radio Corporation of Nigeria (FRCN) and the Nigerian Television Authority (NTA).

Radio Nigeria. The Federal Radio Corporation of Nigeria (also known as Radio Nigeria) is the official national radio, owned wholly by the government and supervised by the Ministry of Information. The organization is more than seventy years old, making it one of the oldest in Africa. With its motto, "to uplift the nation and unite the people," Radio Nigeria uses powerful shortwave transmitters to beam cultural and development programs to all sectors of Nigerian society as well as to neighboring states such as Niger and Benin, where vernacular languages common to the different countries, such as Yoruba and Hausa, are spoken.

The FRCN has its facilities in five administrative zones, known as national stations. These are in Lagos, Ibadan, Kaduna, Enugu, and Abuja. Each zone operates with a significant level of autonomy, having its own staff, correspondents, and the freedom to initiate and produce original programming. The zones are convenient administrative units, as each roughly corresponds to one of the broad linguistic and geopolitical divisions of the country. Thus the Kaduna zone covers the northern states of Niger, Bauchi, Plateau, Sokoto, Kebbi, Zamfara, Borno, Yobe, and Katsina. The Ibadan station covers all Yoruba-speaking states of Lagos, Ondo, Oyo, Osun, Ekiti, and Ogun. The Enugu zonal station covers all Igbo-speaking states of Anambra, Enugu, Imo, Abia, Eboyin, Rivers, Bayelsa, and Akwa Ibom. The main network headquarters used to be in Lagos, the former capital, and now have been moved to the Abuja zonal station.

One of the enduring criticisms of state radio in Nigeria has been its limited focus on rural areas. Nigeria stands alone in West Africa for not having community radio as of 2006. The concentration on urban audiences with mostly news and entertainment programming is attributed to the inordinate influence over state radio on the part of powerful regional political interests throughout Nigeria.

More recently, however, competition from private commercial stations has forced the modernization of Radio Nigeria in two ways: (1) technically, by switching to digital FM and satellite technology, and (2) economically, by allowing greater commercialization of public radio. Reviews by an independent watchdog group in 2000 criticized Radio Nigeria for overcommercialization, especially in regard to news programs. The review charged that every bit of airtime (including news) was sold, so that news about corporate bodies or individuals was paid for in most instances.

National network stations broadcast mainly in English, while regional stations use a combination of English and vernacular languages. Public stations generally offer significant amounts of news and current affairs programming in addition to informational, cultural, and entertainment programs. Some stations specialize in specific content genres such as sports (e.g., Brilla FM in Lagos), music (e.g., Rhythm 93.7 FM in Port Harcourt), and news and talk (e.g., Spectrum FM in Lagos).

Public stations strive to comply with NBC rules to keep foreign-origination content at or below 40 percent. Therefore, much of the music and other cultural content is Nigerian or from other West African sources. Independent commercial radio stations, such as HOT FM 98.3 in Abuja, play more Western music and less African or Nigerian music. In the judgment of one observer, "listening to HOT FM 98.3 Radio feels like you had tuned to an American station with a rhythm and blues format hooked on the music of the 1980s and before."[21]

The autonomous Voice of Nigeria (VON) is a public station that has operated outside the mandate of the Federal Radio Corporation of Nigeria since 1991. Its history goes back to 1961, when it was created as the external service of the NBC. VON signals can be received throughout the world with programs in six languages: English, French, Arabic, Kiswahili, Hausa, and Fulfulde.

A SAMPLING OF PROGRAMS ON NIGERIA'S NTA

Following are some programs on NTA network stations:[20]

- *Fun Time:* a 30-minute children's program on Sundays that depicts children's activities through plays, cartoons, and songs.
- *Grassroots TV:* a 30-minute examination of official government projects that are designed for development of rural areas. The program airs on Monday evenings and is transmitted in Pidgin English.
- *Corruption Must Go:* according to NTA promotions, "an enlightenment program" that is sponsored by the Independent and Corrupt Practices Commission, "a government agency that promotes the virtues of honesty, probity, and accountability in all spheres of Nigerian life."
- *I Need to Know:* a drama show for teenagers who are wrestling with issues surrounding relationships, sex, and HIV/AIDS.
- *Today's Woman:* a 30-minute program on Wednesday evenings about women's contributions to society. The show is also an educational avenue for poor urban women juggling various roles within their families.

Local origination programs such as those described above are supplemented by rebroadcasts of BBC, CNN International, and Deutsche Welle news programs on many NTA regional stations.

Nigerian Television. Nigeria is home to Africa's largest public television network, with NTA operating sixty-seven stations and thirty-four new ones about to be added soon. The proliferation of NTA stations was precipitated by the rapid multiplication of states within the Nigerian federal system. Successive military coups in the 1960s, 1970s, and 1980s all added new states such that today Nigeria has thirty-six state governments, and one of the first symbols of prestige and power for state governments is to have its own radio and television service, albeit within the NTA framework.

In January 2004 the NTA switched to a zonal administrative system in which six big cities were designated as "Zonal Centers." These are: (1) South-South zone (Benin City), with eleven stations, (2) North-Central (Kaduna) with seventeen stations, (3) North-West (Lagos) with fifteen stations, (4) South-East (Enugu) with six stations, (5) North-East (Maiduguri) with sixteen stations, and (6) South-West (Ibadan).

According to its mission, NTA is committed to "enrich the life of the Nigerian by influencing positively his social, cultural, economic, political, technological thinking through a wide choice of programs."[22] Indeed, the range of programs offered on NTA stations, beside news and current affairs programs, include culture, public enlightenment, entertainment, education, religion, science and technology, fashion/styles, and recreation. NTA stations are on the air 76 hours a week with 41 hours devoted to network programs and 35 hours covered with local programming. Network programs consist of news (7 hours), sports (4 hours), current affairs (3 hours), drama/light entertainment (7 hours), youth/children (18 hours), and public enlightenment (2 hours).

Ghana

Ghana was the first Sub-Saharan African country to win independence, in 1957, and her first president, Kwame Nkrumah, placed much stock in radio as a tool for propagating his trademark pan-Africanist philosophy. Accordingly, the first external service of any radio network in Sub-Saharan Africa was launched by the Ghana Broadcasting System in 1961. A public television service, wholly funded by the state, began operation in July 1965, but two years later a commercial television service run by the government was introduced.

The road to the liberalized media environment of today's Ghana has been quite rocky and marked by numerous confrontations between media practitioners and government authorities. The 1992 constitution contains a provision that calls for the establishment of private media. But the government was reluctant to part with long-standing traditions of official control, especially over broadcast services. In 1993 a gathering of Ghanaian intellectuals in Accra, the capital, noted that social and economic development in Asia and Latin America were stimulated by independent voices in the press and on radio. They urged African countries to "free up the airwaves" by allowing private commercial broadcast services.

In May 1994 after the government had refused to loosen its grip, a pirate FM station called *Radio Eye* went on the air in Accra. It was the brainchild of Dr. Charles Wereko Brobbey, a strong advocate for independent broadcast voices in Ghana. Within 24 hours security agents shut down the station and arrested Brobbey and his associates. The government's actions sparked riots in Accra, presenting a serious challenge to the state monopoly over broadcasting.

In 1995 the first private radio station (JOY FM) was licensed to operate in Accra. Today, the city boasts sixteen private FM stations, with many more located in major cities across Ghana. Most of the private FM stations have mixed formats involving talk, discussions, interviews, and music. News bulletins are presented in English by most stations in Accra, but regional stations offer news in the various vernacular languages.

Unlike state-owned radio, private stations play Western music as much as they do African tunes. Certain stations, such as Atlantis Radio (87.9 MHz) in Accra, specialize in specific types of Western music (primarily American) such as country and jazz. Gospel music from the United States is quite popular among Christians in Ghana, and some stations play it on Sundays. Church-affiliated stations such as Channel R in Accra play American gospel music more frequently.

The government operates the two radio stations with the greatest reach: GBC 1 and GBC 2. GBC 1, popularly known as Radio 1, is the public service channel, and GBC 2 (or Radio 2) is the entertainment-oriented commercial channel. Radio 1 broadcasts in English as well in six vernacular languages of Ghana's largest ethnic groups: Akan, Dagbani, Ewe, Ga, Hausa, and Nzema. Radio 2 broadcasts in English only.

Ghana Television. The Ghana Broadcasting Corporation owns and operates the largest television service in Ghana: Ghana Television (or GTV). This is the only channel that beams its signal to all ten regions of Ghana.

Launched in 1965, this service was charged by President Nkrumah with the responsibility to "reflect and promote the highest national and social ideals of Ghanaian society."[23] Many of the earliest GTV programs were produced locally in collaboration with the Ghanaian Ministry of Education. The programs covered academic subjects—"Science" for secondary schools, "Teaching Methods" for teacher-training schools, "Auto Mechanics" for technical institutes, and so forth.

The policy of using television for educational and social development aims survived Nkrumah's ouster from power and continued through much of the 1970s. In the 1980s an increase in entertainment programming came at the expense of the science and education content of GTV. It was notable, however, that a daily 30-minute program in adult education aired in six vernacular languages. For example, every Monday at 6:30 PM an educational program in Akan would be aired, followed on Tuesday by one in Ga in the same time slot, and another on Wednesday in Ewe, and so so.

The 1990s and the first five years of the twenty-first century have seen a dramatic increase in imported non-African entertainment and news programming on GTV. On a random Saturday during the first five years of the 1990s, for example, a Ghanaian viewer of GTV could expect to listen to *Music for You* for an hour, followed in the early afternoon by about two hours of *Football Made in Germany*, a live broadcast of professional soccer games from the German leagues. At 4:30 PM, viewers could watch *Wheel of Fortune* from the United States, and at 8:00 PM they could watch the *Cosby Show*.

A SAMPLING OF PROGRAMS ON GHANA'S TV3

The following is a sampling of TV3 programs from Ghana:[24]

- *Sports Station* airs from 8:30 PM to 9:30 PM every Monday. It is a live presentation of the week's most interesting sporting events in Ghana, Africa, and Europe. The show features an interactive segment in which viewers can phone in their comments and questions to the two main anchors, Kojo Frempong and Victor Hagan.
- *Music Music* is a program that "promotes entertainment as a responsible social engagement to young adults," according to a station leaflet. It is not only a musical program but a cultural one, in that it affords Ghanaian artists a forum through which they can relate their personal stories and the important influences in their work. The program airs every Saturday from 7:30 PM to 9:00 PM.
- *Today's Woman* addresses contemporary issues surrounding the lives of Ghanaian women—from the challenges of motherhood for young professional women to the problems of raising adolescent kids. The show, which features interviews and discussions, is hosted by Doreen Andoh and airs for an hour on Saturday mornings.
- *The Promise* is a serial drama that revolves around the life of a young woman who is struggling with issues of love and betrayal in her interactions with neighbors and family members.

On any given week between 2000 and 2005, GTV viewers could watch about 50 imported news programs. Many of these are from CNN, Deutsche Welle, World Net, and South Africa's Channel O. GTV also imports about 20 programs a week in the soap/drama category, including *The Bold and the Beautiful, Touched by an Angel, Days of Our Lives,* and *Passions.* Imported sitcoms, which average about five a week, include *The Cosby Show, Everybody Loves Raymond, Damon, King of Queens,* and *One World.*

The proportion of airtime devoted to programs in the vernacular languages seems to have decreased from 1997 through the early part of 2003. While 180 programs were in English between 1997 and 2000, only seven programs were in native Ghanaian languages. In

2001 the number of English language programs increased to 195, while the number of programs in the vernacular remained the same at seven.

Ghana's TV3 station is a private free-to-air commercial channel. Its programs are produced in the slick technical styles of American and British productions, with the intended effect of holding audience attention. The channel offers news, sports, drama, music, and movies.

Central Africa

Over the last 15 years, almost every country in the central Africa region either has experienced civil war or has had to host hundreds of thousands of refugees fleeing from a neighboring country. Some of the blame for hostilities has been placed on radio stations that were used to incite hatred between ethnic groups. In 1994 Radio Tele Libre Mille Collines (RTLM), a private radio station in Kigali, Rwanda, spewed vicious anti-Tutsi venom that sparked genocide. In 2003 the International Criminal Tribunal for Rwanda sentenced one RTLM broadcaster to life imprisonment and sentenced his colleague to 35 years in jail.

Governments in the region have used this incident as pretext for placing limits on independent media. Although most countries in central Africa have private radio and television services, media operate under tight restrictions in the Democratic Republic of Congo, the Republic of Congo, Gabon, Chad, and Equatorial Guinea.

In this segment, we will focus on the Democratic Republic of the Congo and on Gabon.

The Democratic Republic of the Congo (DRC)

The largest Sub-Saharan African country, covering some 2.4 million square kilometers and stretching from the Atlantic Ocean in the west to the Great Lakes region of central Africa to the east, the DRC is a diverse country of 64 million inhabitants, who speak some 200 different languages.

The Congo has one of the most diverse media environments on the continent with 52 private television stations, 119 private radio outlets including commercial and religious stations, and 135 community radio stations. The state-controlled broadcasting network, Radio-Television Nationale Congolaise (RTNC), operates two television stations and six radio stations that transmit on shortwave, medium-wave, and FM. RTNC stations offer programming in French as well as the four national languages: Kiswahili, Lingala, Tshiluba, and Kikongo.

This nation, however, has a history of political instability that today is affecting the nature of its radio and television networks. An armed rebellion that simmered through most of the early 1990s eventually brought an end to the 32-year reign of President Mobutu Sese Seko in 1997. But the ouster of Mobutu led to greater instability when more ethnic groups sought to gain political clout through the barrel of the gun. Some new rebel groups were formed in response to what happened in the wake of the genocide in neighboring Rwanda in 1994, from which millions of refugees sought safety in the Congo.

In 2003 prolonged negotiations between the ethnically based factions of this country, called the Inter-Congolese Dialogue, were concluded in Pretoria, South Africa. Among other things, the negotiators established La Haute Autorité des Média (The Congolese High Authority on the Media), an agency that would regulate a free and democratic media system as set forth in the country's new constitution. But the many private radio and television stations were set up and used mainly as extensions of the formerly warring factions, thus enabling the continuation of hostilities, this time on the airwaves.

The government-owned stations of the Congolese National Radio and Television are also politicized, offering news, commentary, and educational programs designed to cast the party in power in the best light. This highly charged political environment has led to numerous arrests, beatings, and even deaths of reporters affiliated with opposing camps, especially in the territories still controlled by various rebel militias. It has also affected the quality of programming on both television and radio in the Congo. Many independent observers agree that a general lack of professionalism among practitioners has contributed to shoddy reporting and mediocre local programs.

Frequent harassment of enterprising reporters has further undermined morale. For instance, when the noted female journalist Simplice Kalunga wa Kalunga, producer and narrator of the television program about women, *Nouvelle Donne,* on the privately owned Channel Media Broadcasting, criticized omissions in a draft nationality bill before parliament, she was promptly arrested and interrogated at length in 2005 by the government prosecutor in Kinshasa. Consequently, journalists "opt for the simple way out—music. Radio and television focus on what is easy to broadcast—entertainment, music, and movies," as one observer put it.[25]

Both state and private television stations, therefore, rely on imported materials for entertainment and informational programming. The RNTC, for example, uses satellite feeds from Canal France Internationale. Other programs, produced in French by both BBC Television and the Voice of America, are routinely rebroadcast by Congolese television and radio stations.

Although radio, too, is heavily influenced by political rivalries between factions, there are exceptions that provide hope for a better future. One radio station that is notable for its professionalism and its broad audience profile is Radio Okapi. This station was established in February 2002 through a collaborative effort between the United Nations Mission in the Congo (MONUC, by its French initials) and the Swiss-based Fondation Hirondelle. The okapi, from which the station takes its name, is a rare and peaceful mammal that has no known enemies. It is well-liked throughout the Congo and is a protected species.

Radio Okapi broadcasts mainly in French, but through its predominantly Congolese staff it also provides services in four indigenous languages: Lingala, Tshiluba, Kiswahili, and Kikongo. The network center is in the capital, Kinshasa, but Radio Okapi has eight additional regional stations in Goma, Kisangani, Kananga, Mbandaka, Kalemi, Kindu, Bukaru, and Bunia. Some of these locations were selected because they are hotspots of rebel activity and civil strife.

The programs on Radio Okapi focus on peace, reconciliation, and democratization themes. One of the most widely acclaimed programs is called *Sisi Watoto* (Kiswahili for "We, the Children"). The various episodes of this program—all of them produced by young journalists who were former child combatants—emphasized themes that addressed the effects of war on children. The first episode, produced by the Bukavu branch of Radio Okapi, was about children forced to fend for themselves because of the war. Subsequent episodes focused on malnutrition among child victims of war and how to prevent it, rape of young girls, and young boys recruited into a rebel army either by coercion or through offers of food and money.

Another popular Okapi program is *Dialogue Entre Congolais* [Dialogue among Congolese]. It promotes conversations between various political leaders from all sectors of Congolese society. The program is aired live simultaneously from several regional stations and includes direct questions from listeners addressed to debaters and dialogue participants. Some programs invite guests from among local teachers, farmers, craftsmen, and merchants.

Radio Okapi is credited with defusing potentially dangerous situations such as the one on October 23, 2005, in Bunia. When a MONUC peacekeeping brigade arrested Mathiu Ngudjolo, commander of the Army of Patriotic Resistance of Ituri (FRPI), who was wanted for murder of a tribal chief from another ethnic group, rumors immediately spread among Ngudjolo's supporters that he was being tortured. Angry mobs began to congregate in the city center, and Radio Okapi reporter Basile Bukumbane decided to find out about the condition of the detainee, who, as it turned out, was being treated quite well. When Ngudjolo was informed about the rumors and the trouble they might provoke, he issued a statement: "I'm fine and well-treated. Remain calm. Do not respond to provocations." After the commander's words aired on Radio Okapi in Bunia, the crowds dispersed, tensions decreased, and bloodshed was averted.

The Hirondelle Foundation, which financially supports Radio Okapi, was created in 1995 as an organization of journalists that operates broadcast services in crisis areas. The Foundation is supported by Switzerland, the European Union, the United States, Sweden, the Netherlands, Great Britain, France, Canada, Germany, and Japan. While Radio Okapi is its largest project, similar Hirondelle programs in Central Africa include Radio Agatashya in the Great Lakes region and Radio Ndeke Luka in Bangui in the Central African Republic.

Gabon

Gabon has carved out a special niche for herself, especially in Francophone West and Central Africa, because of the world-class transnational broadcast services it inaugurated as early as 1980. The country's long-time leader, President Omar Bongo, has demonstrated a strong personal interest in the development of broadcast media in Gabon, and this has meant great opportunities as well as serious challenges for practitioners in the field.

Throughout the 1960s and 1970s, Gabon invested heavily in training a professional corps of reporters and other personnel who would staff the kind of pioneer broadcast service envisioned by President Bongo. Accordingly, hundreds of Gabonese journalists, producers, and managers received training at the *Studio Ecole* in Paris, at the *Organisation de la Radio et la Télévision Française* (ORTF), and at the *Institut Nationale de l'Audiovisuelle* (INA).

Until the 1990s all of Gabon's broadcast media were controlled by the government. The two radio networks, run directly by the Ministry of Information, are Radiodiffusion-Télévision Gabonaise and La Voix de la Rénovation. The latter is the national radio that specializes in news and current affairs, as well as scientific and cultural programs. The former is an entertainment network with several FM stations in the capital, Libreville, and in Post Gentil and Franceville.

In 1980 with technical assistance from Radio France Internationale, Gabon launched Africa No. 1, a radio service with five powerful shortwave transmitters that could beam news, entertainment, and cultural programs to the entire continent. Today, Africa No. 1 rivals the BBC, Radio France Internationale, and the Voice of America in terms of audience following, especially in Francophone Africa. The station generally plays contemporary music—about 75 percent of it African—that is directed at younger listeners. It also carries live broadcasts of major sporting events in Africa and Europe.

Over the years Africa No. 1 has adopted an aggressive marketing strategy that has enabled it to establish FM relay stations in several French-speaking countries in Africa, such as Senegal, Mali, and Ivory Coast. The station is heavily commercialized and has benefited from French investments in its infrastructure. The government of Gabon, however, holds a controlling share in Africa No. 1.

During the 1990s Gabon issued licenses to private radio operators for the first time. Today (2006) the country has five private radio stations, almost all of them entertainment-oriented: Radio Frequence 3, Radio Génération Nouvelle, Radio Mandarine, Radio Soleil,

and Radio Unité. Private radio operators have faced numerous challenges from a government that has not hesitated to take heavy-handed measures against independent voices. For example, in February 1994, Gabonese army tanks were dispatched to destroy the facilities of a private radio station, Radio Liberté. The government's explanation of the action was that the station was being used as a "propaganda mouthpiece" by opposition politicians.[26]

Television. Gabon is one of the earliest adopters of television on the continent, introducing it only three years after independence in 1963. By 1975 Gabon already had color television service.

Radiodiffusion-Télévision Gabonaise (RTG) operates two channels: RTG1 and RTG2, with Channel 2 specializing in entertainment programs consisting of music videos, movies, sports, and variety shows. RTG1 has a long history of production of original African television programming. As early as the mid-1960s RTG produced its own educational, cultural, and entertainment features. Some of these include a folklore program called *Bonne Nuit Village d'Afrique* [Good Night African Village], and an educational program called *Les Petits A's* [The Little A's]. Throughout much of the 1970s and into the early 1980s, Gabonese producers wrote the script for a cultural series called *Où vas-tu, Koumba?* [Where Are You Going, Koumba?], which addressed the problem of young people abandoning the land in favor of life in the city. Another show, *Tant qu'on a la santé* [While We Have Health], focused on health-related issues.[27]

A commercial television service, Tele-Africa, was introduced in 1988 and began broadcasting satellite news, sports, and other entertainment programming from France and the United States. After capturing a large part of the Gabonese television market during the 1990s, Tele-Africa is now poised to expand its service to other central African countries such as Cameroon and the Republic of Congo.

Southern Africa

The Republic of South Africa's broadcasting prowess envelops most of her neighbors in the region and has affected the communication policies of some countries. For example, South African television is available through satellite services in Botswana, and its growing popularity compelled the government in Gaborone to initiate its own television service in 2000. South African radio and television services are also widely available in Namibia, Lesotho, and the island of Mauritius. Most countries in Southern Africa allow independent broadcasting services to operate, although Malawi, Angola, Lesotho, and Swaziland do not yet have private television service as of 2006. In Madagascar, President Marc Ravalomanana owns one of the island's private television networks, Madagascar Broadcasting Service, while former Prime Minister Tantely Andrianarivo owns Amoron'i Mania Radio-Television in the southern city of Ambositra les Roses.

Zimbabwe stands alone in bucking the trend toward greater liberalization of radio and television in southern Africa. In 2002 the government of President Robert Mugabe shut down Joy TV, the only private television service in the country. The state-owned Zimbabwe Broadcasting Corporation (ZBC) runs all broadcasting inside Zimbabwe. But several overseas broadcast services target listeners in Zimbabwe. One of these is The Voice of the People, which was set up by former ZBC staff in Madagascar with financial support from the U.S.-based Soros Foundation. In 2003 the Voice of America began operating Studio 7, which broadcasts daily (weekday) programs in English, Shona, and Ndebele aimed at listeners in Zimbabwe.

In this segment, we will focus on the Republic of South Africa and Botswana.

Republic of South Africa

The Republic of South Africa is the continent's other media giant (besides Nigeria). Per capita, South Africa is the most media-rich country in Africa, with an impressive broadcast network that includes public radio and television stations, commercial radio and television, community radio stations, and transnational radio and television services. In 2000 the country's broadcast policy was overhauled when the Independent Communications Authority of South Africa (ICASA) was created. This new authority took over control and management of the state-owned South African Broadcasting Corporation (SABC). Within two years, ICASA issued licenses for more than ten private commercial stations. We will briefly review the audience profiles and sample programs of representative organizations from each category.

Public Radio Stations

South Africa has twenty public radio stations run by the SABC. Although SABC is state-owned, none of these stations receives any direct taxpayer funding. Instead, they depend on advertising revenue for 80 percent of their budgets and make up the balance from license fees charged to listeners.

Public radio stations provide news, entertainment, educational, and cultural programs in all the eleven official languages of South Africa (Afrikaans, English, Ndebele, Northern Sotho, Southern Sotho, Tsonga, Tswana, Swazi, Venda, Xhosa, and isiZulu). They also serve smaller communities who speak languages other than the official ones: German, Portuguese, Hindi, and the San languages.

The largest ethnic group in South Africa is the Zulus, who are served by Ukhozi FM, the largest public radio station in the country, with a weekly audience of 6.5 million. Ukhozi, which means "eagle" in isiZulu, is an adult contemporary station that offers news, music, current affairs, talk shows, education, sports, weather, and traffic information. Although one-third of Ukhozi FM listeners are young people between ages eighteen to twenty-four, much of the music it plays could be considered conservative and includes jazz, R&B, gospel, and African traditional. It also plays *kwaito,* a black South African pop music that uses slang in lyrics to reflect life in South Africa. Talk shows on Ukhozi typically address a broad range of issues, from AIDS to the environment and from politics to sports.

Ukhozi FM broadcasts on the 90.8 to 93.4 FM frequencies and can be heard in KwaZulu-Natal, Gauteng, Mpumalanga, northeastern Eastern Cape, eastern Free State, and southern Limpopo.

The Afrikaner and Coloured populations are served primarily by Radio Sonder Grense, which means "radio without borders" in Afrikaans. Its format is talk and current affairs, punctuated by soft pop and rock hits that are 60 percent English and 40 percent Afrikaans. Radio Sonder Grense has an average weekly audience of 1.8 million and is heard all over the country on the 100–104 FM frequencies.

Other public radio stations include SAfm (English), Lotus FM (the main station serving South Africa's Indian community, broadcasting in English), Umhlobo Wenene (Xhosa), Leseda FM (Southern Sotho), Thobela FM (Sepedi), Mungahana Lonene (Tsonga), Ikwekwezi FM (Ndebele), and Phalaphala FM (Venda).

It is important to note that regulations concerning content that ICASA passed in 2006 require that "every holder of a public broadcasting license must ensure that 40 percent of the musical works broadcast consist of South African music."

Commercial Radio Stations. Sixteen commercial radio stations are licensed by SABC. These stations generate more advertising revenue than public radio stations do, so by statute they are required to subsidize the latter.

As commercial organizations, these stations are subject to less stringent content regulations than their public radio counterparts are. ICASA rules state that 25 percent of the music broadcast over commercial stations should be South African, in contrast to 40 percent for public radio stations.[28]

The largest commercial radio station in South Africa, Metro FM, broadcasts in English and is based in Gauteng. The station targets young blacks in the twenty-five- to thirty-four-year-old age group who are "trendy, innovative, progressive, and aspirational,"[29] according to an SABC promotion. Metro FM is an entertainment channel focusing mainly on contemporary international music such as hip hop, R&B, and kwaito. Broadcasting on the 96.4 FM frequencies, this station has a weekly audience of 5.3 million spread over KwaZulu-Natal, Limpopo, Free State, Eastern Cape, and Western Cape.

A commercial station with a broader mission to cover all of Africa—the first of its kind on the continent—is SABC's Channel Africa. Broadcasting on shortwave, Channel's vision is to be "the voice of the African renaissance" guided by the values of *Mbuntu* (humanism).

Programs on Channel Africa cover a broad spectrum of subjects, from news and current affairs to cultural and scientific programs to music and entertainment. One of Channel Africa's weekly programs is called *37 Degrees,* a reference to what is considered the normal body temperature of a healthy human being on the Celsius scale. The name is a metaphor for gauging Africa's condition and that of her people with regard to specific issues. The program strives to evaluate what needs to be done in order to maintain "the temperature" at 37 degrees.

One episode of *37 Degrees* in December 2005 dealt with the problem of violence against women and children. The program was aired as part of the two-week international awareness-raising campaign that ran from November 25 to December 10. Through ceremonial functions around the world, the United Nations–endorsed campaign recognizes the dignity of victims of domestic violence, HIV/AIDS, and mental and physical disabilities.

Other programs on Channel Africa include *Musicians of Africa*, which features the work of musicians from across the continent; *Africa This Week*, a weekly round-up of top stories offering analyses and discussion by experts; and *Africa Rise and Shine*, a morning news bulletin with sports and economic news followed by interviews on current affairs.

Community Radio Stations. In addition to public radio, South Africa has a broad network of community radio stations that number more than 150. Their main purpose is to provide a forum for small communities bound not necessarily by geographic region or a common language but by other common interests, such as religion or a professional trade. Because community radios are so numerous and so diverse, their audiences are not large—generally averaging within the 75,000 to 150,000 range.

One of the best known community radios is Jozi FM Stereo, formerly known as Soweto Buwa Community Radio. Jozi FM is based in Soweto, the sprawling black township near Johannesburg, and it broadcasts in English. Its listeners are mainly blacks between the ages of 18 and 49. The station strongly emphasizes a multicultural theme that is reflected in both the music it plays and the topics it selects for its talk shows, to which it devotes half of its broadcast time. Using the 105–108 FM frequencies, Jozi FM reaches 450,000 listeners a week in Soweto and parts of the West Rand.[30]

Public Television. The SABC has two public television channels that are free-to-air: SABC 1 and SABC 2. Under mandate from ICASA, these two channels are required to "inform, educate, entertain, support and develop culture and education" through world-class programming.

As far as possible, public television programs are also asked to "secure fair and equal treatment for the various groups" that make up modern South Africa. Accordingly, SABC 1 and SABC 2 serve different audiences, and together they attract 89 percent of the total adult television viewing audience. SABC 1 is the most popular television service in South Africa with 14.5 million viewers. Its programs are heavily oriented toward entertainment and target younger viewers. On a typical day chosen at random (in this case, Tuesday, July 11, 2006), this is how a sampling of the program schedule was laid out:[31]

Midnight to 5 AM	*Sgubhu Sa Mampala* (compilation of the best music videos)
5–7 AM	*YO TV* (an entertaining and educational children's program in a vernacular language "done with an African flair")
8 AM	*The Bold and the Beautiful* (episode from U.S. soap opera serial)
8:30 AM	*Generations* (South African drama series)
9:00 AM	*Isidingo: The Need* (series "reflecting the needs, aspirations, conflicts and loves" of South African gold miners)
9:30 AM	*Zone 14* (local drama series about the lives of two families, the Sabiyas and the Molois, that unfolds in a township setting)
2:00 PM	*Rootz* (show featuring the work of local musicians)
5:30 PM	*Siswati/Ndebele News Headlines* (provides highlights of world news in vernacular language)
7:00 PM	*L'Attitude* (real-life series in which a reporter, Lebo Mashile, travels back roads of the country and relates stories about real people dealing with real-life situations)
7:30 PM	*Xhosa News* (local and world news, weather reports in Xhosa)
8:30 PM	*Soul City* (doctors and other health workers battle diseases afflicting the poor, yet the series offers comic relief through a romantic tale steeped in intrigue)

The programming on SABC 2 is more varied than that of its sister station, SABC 1, because the main target audience of SABC 2 consists of families from different ethnic and racial backgrounds. The channel features more infomercials as well as programs focusing on Africa and the rest of the world. Its July 11, 2006, program schedule included the U.S. talk show *Dr. Phil* and an episode from the U.S. soap opera serial *Days of Our Lives.* Locally produced programs on that day included *Agri TV* (program about the environment), *180 Degrees Live in Africa* (program that offers an introspective look at the African spirit), and *Muvhango* (an African soap opera). Programs for children included *Just Chill, Franklin* (in which the character of a turtle learns by making mistakes), and *Little Robot, Thabang Thabong* (a show about discoveries by children, targeting the 3- to 7-year-old age group).

SABC 2 airs news in six national languages: Sotho, Tswana, Sepedi, Venda, Tsonga, and Afrikaans.

Botswana

Botswana's broadcast service was begun in 1961 during the British Protectorate Administration. At that early stage of its development, the main facilities of the service, such as studios and transmitters, were located in Mafikeng, which was part of South Africa. From independence in 1966 to 1992, when Radio Botswana was restructured, the government kept tight control over all broadcasting (which was limited only to radio until 2000, when television was finally introduced).

The state-owned Radio Botswana is on the air for 18 hours each day, broadcasting in Setswana and in English. In 1992 Radio Botswana (RB) was split into two: a public station (RB1) and a commercial one (RB2) created in part to offset the increasing popularity of South African radio services among younger listeners. RB2 also competed for advertising revenue with foreign radio stations that had relays in Gaborone and other cities in Botswana. Radio Botswana modernized its facilities in the 1990s by setting up eighteen FM stations spread across the country in order to improve quality of reception.

While RB2 has made necessary adjustments for a market environment in determining suitable programming for younger listeners, RB1 continues to emphasize news, current affairs, and educational programming. One of the grim realities that educational radio in Botswana faces is the AIDS pandemic that has gripped the country of 1.7 million. In 2002, for example, 35.4 percent of all pregnant women in Botswana were HIV positive, according to the country's own National AIDS Coordinating Agency (NACA). The twin realities of these sobering statistics and high illiteracy rates meant that salvation had to be sought in educational programs on radio. Throughout the mid 1990s, therefore, Radio Botswana aired more than 150 episodes of *Makgabaneng,* a popular radio serial drama in Setswana focusing on AIDS from a variety of cultural and behavioral perspectives.

Other educational programs were intended to supplement the formal education received by children in rural schools, which were invariably served by less qualified teachers. With financial and technical support from Swedish Education Broadcasting, RB aired locally produced education programs targeting hundreds of rural schools. One such program, *English Time,* was designed to improve rural pupils' proficiency in the English language.

Better-educated professional urban listeners, on the other hand, receive news and informational programming from various transnational radio programs such as the BBC, the Voice of America, and South Africa's Channel Africa. In 1999 the first privately-owned radio station, *Yarona FM,* began operation in Gaborone. It is a joint venture between a consortium of local entrepreneurs, with 51 percent share, and South Africa's Union Alliance Media. *Yarona FM* is an entertainment channel that targets younger listeners. A second private station, *Gabz FM,* targets professional adults and broadcasts mainly in English.

Television. The government of Botswana put off introduction of television until 2000 because of insufficient supply of electric power in much of the Texas-sized country. The government also explained that it wanted to avoid the inequality television would engender, since only a few wealthy urban residents could afford access to the service.

The state-operated Botswana Television (BTV), with only one channel transmitting programs from the capital, Gaborone, offers news and current affairs programming in English and Setswana. The station goes on the air at noon and is on until midnight. On a typical day, the programming is dominated by entertainment fare. For example, on

Wednesday, August 30, 2006, the station opened at noon with an episode of *Sesame Street* and continued with other entertainment shows until 8:30 PM, when a sports and news show went on the air. BTV program schedules invariably include several American productions such as *Oprah, Seinfeld, Dr. Phil,* and the soap opera serial *Bold and the Beautiful.* BBC World News is regularly rebroadcast on BTV. The following paragraphs describe some locally produced programs.

Talk Back is a live show that began airing on March 18, 2003, with a view to preventing or mitigating the impact of HIV/AIDS in Botswana. The show is produced with technical assistance from Brazil and targets teachers in an interactive educational process intended to build educators' capacity to communicate effectively and competently with students and members of the community about AIDS prevention.

Mantlwaneng is a magazine program for children in elementary school. The word *Mantlwaneng* is Setswana for "children's playground." Children play by assuming different roles, such as imitating their parents as they solve problems. The show has different segments, including "Kids Star," which showcases children with special talents in music, dance, sports, or entrepreneurial skills.

Flavourdome is an international music show that airs on Friday evenings. The program is hosted by Sithandwa Mmopi, who regularly interviews local and international music personalities about their life and their work. Viewers get the opportunity to call in with a request to have their favorite music video played.

Sedibeng is a magazine program produced in Setswana that features conversations with people from all walks of life in Botswana. The word *sedibeng* means "at the well" and signifies the watering hole where people meet to exchange ideas and to talk about life and its challenges. Some past guests include the first female High Court judge, Unity Dow, and 1999 Miss Universe of Botswana, Mpule Kwelagobe. The show also features documentary films of interesting scenery and locations in southern Africa.

Botswana is served by three private television networks. Two of these, M-Net and Multi Choice, are owned and operated by South African interests. The third network, Gaborone Broadcasting Company (GBC), is owned by local investors and transmits about half of its programming in the Setswana language. Multi Choice also offers a cable service with twenty-three channels for those who can afford to pay the subscription fees.

East Africa

East Africa has long been a region of sharp contrasts, both between and within countries, when it comes to broadcast media cultures. The region includes Eritrea, the only country in Sub-Saharan Africa that has not allowed an independent broadcast voice. On the other hand, there is Somalia, with no effective central government and arguably the freest private media on the continent. Some radio stations in Mogadishu operate without any regulations whatsoever, and the outer limits of what they can broadcast is determined by what their listeners will tolerate. Other radio stations in Somalia, however, are tightly controlled by local or regional authorities.

Tanzania delayed introduction of television until 1994, when a private station began service. A state-operated television service was started in 2001, whereas neighboring Kenya has had a well-developed television service since the early 1960s. Another country that made a slow start is Ethiopia, where licenses to private broadcasters were first issued in April 2006. Today Ethiopia has three private radio stations. Uganda liberalized her media industry in 1993 and now boasts hundreds of private radio and television stations.

Both of the Indian Ocean island nations of Mauritius and Seychelles have multichannel television and radio services provided by transnational media companies such as South Africa's Multi Choice.

We will examine broadcast media in this region by focusing on Kenya and Ethiopia.

Kenya

The state-owned Kenya Broadcasting Corporation (KBC) is the main source of radio and television programming in Kenya. Most KBC programs are offered through its public radio and television services. A smaller number of commercial radio and television stations also operate under the KBC umbrella.

Through an act of parliament, KBC is charged with "development of local cultural values by facilitating the dissemination, preservation, and conservation of authentically indigenous values."

In addition to English and Kiswahili, the network of public radio stations in Kenya provides regional services in seventeen vernacular languages. Programs in indigenous languages are offered through three KBC regional services: KBC Central Services, KBC Western Services, and KBC Eastern Services. The Western Service broadcasts in eight languages (Luo, Kisii, Kalenji, Kuria, Teso, Luhya, Suba, and Pokot), while the Eastern Service broadcasts in five (Somali, Borana, Rendille, Burji , and Turkana) and the Central Services broadcasts in four (Meru, Embu, Masai, and Kamba).

The various vernacular services share the same transmission facilities and go on the air at different times, generally in a sequential order. For example, in the Eastern Service, the program in the Burji language goes on the air first from noon to 2 PM, Monday through Friday. It is followed by programs in Rendille, Borana, Turkana, and then Somali, all with a two-hour air time allotment.

Except for news and general educational features, each vernacular program offers its listeners a menu of entertainment and cultural programs determined by conditions peculiar to each subculture. For example, every week, the program in Rendille presents "Women on the Move," which deals with a myriad of challenges faced by Rendille women, such as domestic violence and the threat of HIV/AIDS. Eastern Service listeners have much in common as well, since all the ethnic groups targeted by the Service are cattle herders and thus subject to similar socioeconomic conditions. Consequently, vernacular programs broadcast in one service area tend to address similar topical issues.

By far the most popular KBC Radio programs, however, are those offered in Kiswahili and English. Each of these programs is on the air from 5 AM to midnight for a total of 19 hours a day.

According to internal KBC statistics, the Kiswahili service has the largest audience, averaging about 12 million a week. It offers news, current affairs, sports, and a heavy dose of entertainment programming. On a typical day, the Kiswahili service has seven 15-minute news bulletins: three in the morning and two each in the afternoon and evening. They are supplemented by thirteen or fourteen two-minute summaries of news headlines (*Mukhutasari Wa Habari*). There are also relatively frequent advertisements for a public radio station. In the morning, there is one 5-minute advertisement or announcement every hour or so. Advertisements become less frequent in the afternoon and evening, when an advertisement or announcement is run every two to three hours.

Entertainment programs include various music shows and request lines (*Salamu Za Vijana*). A sampling of the Kiswahili programs includes *Pamba Moto* (a music program that plays selections from central and southern Africa); *Ni Nini Maoni Yako* (a 30-minute talk show program that features experts on such matters as youth and drugs, environment and pollution, family life, and education); and *Kumepambazuka* (an eclectic program that presents music from around the world).

The English service of the KBC, with an average of 8 million listeners a week, is heavily entertainment-oriented. In the 19 hours the station is on each day, fifteen to seventeen music shows, ranging from 15 minutes to one hour, are played. The names of the shows generally indicate the kind of music played, such as *Soul Breakfast, The R&B Show, African Guitar, Kenyan Music, Rhythms of Congo,* and *Lingala Music.* The station maintains a balance between current affairs and educational programs. Some of the latter include *Child Survival, Water and Society*, and *Man and Medicine.*

In 1996 KBC commissioned Metro FM Radio to serve an area that is within a 100 kilometer radius of Nairobi, the capital. Metro is a 24-hour station devoted to music—Kenyan, African, and world. With its slogan, "Power in the Music," Metro FM appeals to young listeners in the 15–35-year age bracket, and according to KBC statistics it reaches more than 10 million listeners a week.

In addition to KBC-operated radio stations, Kenya has some privately-owned, commercial radio. These FM stations were established as a result of the liberalization of media laws in Kenya in 1992, when multiparty elections were also held. Some of these independent stations are Radio Citizen, which enjoys wide coverage, in part because it devotes one station each to the two largest ethnic groups in Kenya (Inooro FM for the Kikuyu and Radio Ramage for the Luo); Kiss FM, a pop music station in Nairobi; and Easy FM, owned by the Nation Media Group, which has relays in Nairobi, Eldoret, Kisumu, Mombasa, Nakuru, and Nyeri. Both Kiss and Easy FM broadcast in English.

KBC Television. KBC Television operates a free-to-air public channel (KBC Channel 1), a pay subscription channel (KBC Channel 2), and Metro Television, an entertainment channel that serves the metropolitan Nairobi area and is directed at young people. KBC Channel 1 transmits programming in both English and Kiswahili. For instance, the 7:00 PM news bulletin is read in Kiswahili, while the one at 9:00 PM is read in English. Other programs also alternate between Kiswahili and English. The stations, which go on the air from 5 AM to midnight, generally start with 30-minute rebroadcasts of BBC television's World News. After a break for "Morning Prayers," BBC News continues for another hour at 6 AM Throughout the day, BBC News is repeated at least two more times. KBC Channel 1 also retransmits news from the English service of the German network Deutsche Welle at 1:15 PM.

Entertainment programming on KBC 1 consists of a "Day Time Movie" at 11:00 AM and broadcast of sports events in the evening. During the last week of June 2006, for example, two World Cup soccer matches were shown regularly in the evenings.

In direct competition with KBC 1 since March 1990 has been the privately financed Kenya Television Network (KTN), which offers mostly a retransmission of CNN programming and some light entertainment. KTN is owned by the Standard Group and has transmitters in Kenya's five major cities: Nairobi, Mombasa, Nakuru, Eldoret, and Kisumu.

KBC 2, the pay channel, offers mostly entertainment programs consisting of American, British, and Indian films, U.S. soap opera serials, and some news and current affairs shows. The South African media company Multi Choice bought KBC 2 stock and now influences some of the entertainment programming choices on the channel.

Ethiopia

Until April 2006 when private broadcast licenses were first issued, all of Ethiopia's radio and television services were operated exclusively by the government. With the exception of two privately owned small FM stations in Addis Ababa, the government still maintains firm control over broadcast media. Radio and television services come under the Ethiopian Radio and Television Agency (ERTA). According to its charter, ERTA "transmits proclamations, policies, and strategies of the government."[32] Thus, broadcasting is an integral part of the official power structure and is used for promoting government initiatives in social and economic development schemes for rural and urban centers.

By far the medium with the widest reach in Ethiopia is radio. The government-owned Radio Ethiopia has a National Service that broadcasts daily programs in Amharic, Oromo, Tigre, Somali, Afar, Hararie, Agnuak, Nuer, and English on shortwave bands. Ethiopian radio listeners are treated to long news and interview programs that frequently feature high ranking officials of the central government as well as those from regional administrations, depending on the vernacular language of the program.

Although the ERTA charter calls for radio to "transmit entertainment programs on holidays and weekends," traditional Ethiopian music is a favorite of Ethiopian listeners, young and old, and tends to get plenty of time on the air. Among the best-known Ethiopian artists whose music is played on Internet radio stations for Ethiopians in the diaspora are Tilahun Gessesse, Alimayehu Eshete, Aster Aweke, and Mohamoud Ahmed.

Radio Ethiopia has an External Service that beams daily programs in English, French, and Arabic on shortwave bands. Programs on the External Service consist of information and educational content that is intended to promote Ethiopia's image by highlighting her unique culture and underscoring various social development projects. For instance, every Wednesday, the External Service features the *Guest of the Week*, followed by a program on *Ethiopia Today*. On Friday, *Press Review* is followed by *Introducing Ethiopia*. On Saturday, listeners can hear *Ethiopia This Week*. There is one music program on Thursday (Ethiopian music) and Sunday's lineup includes *Listeners' Choice*, another entertainment program for younger audiences.[33]

Ethiopian Television offers programming in Amharic and English and is on the air for a total of 8 hours during weekdays (noon to 2 PM and 5:30 to 11:30 PM), and for four hours on weekends. Its programming is heavily oriented toward news and features about local events. Officially, topics covered by ETV can be divided into four categories: politics, agriculture, sports, and the economy. Locally produced entertainment dramas with a development subtext are routinely shown. For younger audiences, Ethiopian music videos are played, mainly on weekends.

CONCLUSION

If Africa's short, post-independence history is any guide, the future of radio and television on the continent will be influenced by two factors, neither one of which is clearly predictable in its long-term implications.

Transnational Broadcast Services

Radio and television audiences throughout Africa are served by numerous international broadcast services. In the case of radio, this has been true since before independence, when African language programs were transmitted from the BBC in London and from Radio France Internationale in Paris, among other sources. Today, African-oriented programs are

Country	Radio households	Television households	Population
Angola	500,000	250,000	14,500,000
Benin	968,000	210,000	7,100,000
Botswana	380,000	63,000	1,800,000
Burkina Faso	1,150,000	120,000	13,800,000
Burundi	850,000	190,000	7,300,000
Cameroon	1,560,000	510,000	16,600,000
Cape Verde	62,500	38,000	482,000
Central African Republic	330,000	11,700	3,900,000
Chad	700,000	36,000	9,100,000
Comoros	90,000	17,000	812,000
Congo	200,000	38,000	3,900,000
Democratic Republic of the Congo	1,000,000	110,000	56,000,000
Ivory Coast	1,600,000	700,000	17,100,000
Djibouti	56,000	40,000	721,000
Equatorial Guinea	—	—	521,000
Eritrea	600,000	104,500	4,400,000
Ethiopia	2,694,000	310,000	74,200,000
Gabon	200,000	140,000	1,400,000
Gambia	112,000	19,000	1,500,000
Ghana	2,544,500	955,000	21,800,000
Guinea	650,000	110,000	8,800,000
Guinea-Bissau	49,200	46,000	1,600,000
Kenya	5,970,000	1,169,600	32,800,000
Lesotho	125,000	74,000	1,800,000
Madagascar	1,300,000	250,000	18,400,000
Malawi	1,350,000	56,000	12,600,000
Mali	1,250,000	260,000	13,800,000
Mauritania	245,000	100,000	3,100,000
Mauritius	279,000	288,300	1,200,000
Mozambique	1,949,000	265,000	19,500,000

Country	Radio households	Television households	Population
Namibia	318,000	140,000	2,000,000
Niger	600,000	100,000	12,900,000
Nigeria	15,249,000	6,286,400	130,200,000
Rwanda	950,000	58,000	8,600,000
São Tomé and Principe	15,050	10,000	169,000
Senegal	850,000	330,000	10,600,000
Seychelles	19,400	18,600	76,000
Sierra Leone	400,000	50,200	5,300,000
South Africa	8,324,000	6,134,000	45,300,000
Swaziland	95,000	30,000	1,100,000
Tanzania	3,631,000	996,000	38,400,000
Togo	700,000	416,000	5,100,000
Uganda	2,845,700	325,560	27,600,000
Zambia	1,291,000	550,000	11,000,000
Zimbabwe	1,687,000	700,700	12,900,000

TABLE 1 UNESCO Data on Radio and Television Receivers in Sub-Saharan Africa (2002)

beamed from all over the globe. In an era of independent, commercial radio, the full implication of these transnational services is yet to be determined. The effect of transnational television might be slightly more discernible. Surveys indicate that given a choice, African television audiences are drawn more toward Western news and entertainment programming. This trend worries cultural purists, who believe that it is incompatible with the desire to maintain distinct elements of Africa's own heritage and culture.

Independent Broadcasting and Ethnic Rivalries

Africa's post-independence leaders insisted on nationalizing broadcast services in order to bolster national unity and to forge a sense of new national identity. Almost 50 years later, interethnic conflicts sparked and fueled by radio or television seem to lend credence to concerns expressed by that first crop of leaders. Contemporary observers and rights groups have decried the role of radio in atrocities committed in Rwanda, Burundi, the Democratic Republic of the Congo, the Republic of Congo, Liberia, Sierra Leone, and Somalia. On the other hand, fear of government retaliation tends to limit the options for independent broadcasters, who invariably choose to offer entertainment-oriented programming. In the face of these impediments, it remains to be seen whether independent radio and television can flourish and at the same time contribute to the emergence of genuinely pluralistic and democratic societies in Africa.

RESOURCE GUIDE

PRINT SOURCES

Abdulkadir, Mansur. "Popular Culture in Advertising." Pp. 128–143 in Richard Fardon and Graham Furniss (eds.), *African Broadcast Cultures*. Westport, CT: Praeger, 2000.

Adam, Suleyman M. *The Development of Broadcasting in Somalia*. Mogadishu: Somali Ministry of Information, 1968.

Agunga, Robert, Solomon B. Aiyeru, and Festus Annor-Frempong. "Communication for Local Participation in Project Planning: A Study of Rural Development Workers in Ghana and Nigeria." *Journal of Development Communication* 16.2 (2005): 1–14.

Alozie, Emmanuel. "Development and Anti-Development Messages in Nigerian Advertising." *Journal of Development Communication* 15.2 (2004): 13–31.

Balit, Silvia. "The Future of Rural Radio in Africa." *Journal of Development Communication* 8.1 (1997): 64–71.

Banerjee, Indrajit, and Kalinga Seneviratne, eds. *Public Service Broadcasting: A Best Practices Sourcebook*. Paris: UNESCO, 2005.

Banks, Jack. "MTV and the Globalization of Popular Culture." *Gazette* 59.1 (1997): 43–60.

Berger, Guy. "Theorizing the Media-Democracy Relationship in Southern Africa." *Gazette* 64.1 (2002): 21–45.

Blake, Cecil. "Democratization: The Dominant Imperative for National Communication Policies in Africa in the 21st Century." *Gazette* 59.4 (1997): 253–269.

Bourgault, Louise M. *Mass Media in Sub-Saharan Africa*. Bloomington: Indiana University Press, 1995.

———. "Satellite Television Broadcasting in Nigeria: A Case Study in Media Globalization." *Journal of Development Communication* 8.1 (1997): 74–94.

Carver, Richard. "Broadcasting and Political Transition: Rwanda and Beyond." Pp. 188–197 in Richard Fardon and Graham Furniss (eds.), *African Broadcast Cultures*. Westport, CT: Praeger, 2000.

Chalaby, Jean K. "Television for a New Global Order." *Gazette* 65.6 (2003): 457–472.

Daloz, Jean-Pascal, and Katherine Verrier-Frechette. "Is Radio Pluralism an Instrument of Political Change?" Pp. 180–187 in Richard Fardon and Graham Furniss (eds.), *African Broadcast Cultures*. Westport, CT: Praeger, 2000.

Fardon, Richard, and Graham Furniss, eds. *African Broadcast Cultures*. Westport, CT: Praeger, 2000.

Gratz, Tilo. "New Local Radio Stations in African Languages and the Process of Political Transformation: The Case of Radio Rurale Locale Tanguieta in Northern Benin." Pp. 110–127 in Richard Fardon and Graham Furniss (eds.), *African Broadcast Cultures*. Westport, CT: Praeger, 2000.

Head, Sydney, ed. *Broadcasting in Africa: A Continental Survey of Radio and Television*. Philadelphia: Temple University Press, 1974.

Hyden, Goran, Michael Leslie, and Folu Ogundimu, eds. *Media and Democracy in Africa*. Uppsala, Sweden: Nordic Africa Institute, 2002.

Kabemba, Claude. "The State of the Media in the Democratic Republic of Congo." *EISA Occasional Paper No. 30* (2005). Accessed August 12, 2006. http://www.eisa.org.za/PDF/OP30/pdf.

Kivikuru, Ullamaija. "Different Means, Similar Goals, a Long Way to Go." *Journal of International Communication* 9.1 (2003): 113.

Lerner, Daniel, and Wilbur Schramm, eds. *Communication and Change in the Developing Countries*. Honolulu: East–West Center Press, 1967.

Minnie, Jeanette. "The Growth of Independent Broadcasting in South Africa: Lessons for Africa?" Pp. 174–179 in Richard Fardon and Graham Furniss (eds.), *African Broadcast Cultures*. Westport, CT: Praeger, 2000.

Nombre, Urbain. "Local Radio, Local Radio Culture and the Culture of Radios." Pp. 83–89 in Richard Fardon and Graham Furniss (eds.), *African Broadcast Cultures*. Westport, CT: Praeger, 2000.

Nulens, Gert, and Leo Van Audenhove. "An Information Society in Africa?" *Gazette* 61.6 (1999): 451–471.

Nuviadenu, Kekeli K. "Media Globalization and Localization: An Analysis of the International Flow of Programs on Ghana Television." *Global Media Journal* 4.7 (2005). Accessed July 28, 2006. http://lass.calumet.purdue.edu/cca/gmj/fa05/gmj-fa05-nuviadenu.htm.

Odame, Helen H. "Connecting Agricultural Research and Radio: New Opportunities for Communicating Innovation." *Journal of Development Communication* 14.1 (2003): 1–14.

Omatoyo, Akin, D. Chikwendu, and S.J. Auta. "The Use of Radio as a Source of Information among Rural Women in Selected Villages in Nigeria." *Journal of Development Communication* 8.1 (1997): 27–38.

Ramaprasad, Jyotika. "A Profile of Journalists in Post-Indepenedence Tanzania." *Gazette* 63.6 (2001): 539–555.

Richards, Paul. "Local Radio Conflict Moderation: The Case of Sierra Leone." Pp. 216–229 in Richard Fardon and Graham Furniss (eds.), *African Broadcast Cultures.* Westport, CT: Praeger, 2000.

Rogers, Everett M., ed. *Communication and Development: Critical Perspectives.* Beverly Hills, CA: Sage Publications, 1976.

Shah, Hemant. "Communication and Nation Building: Comparing U.S. Models of Ethnic Assimilation and 'Third World' Modernization." *Gazette* 65.2 (2003): 165–181.

Tawfik, M., G. Bartagnon, and Y. Courrier, eds. *World Communication and Information Report.* Paris: UNESCO, 2000.

Tomaselli, Keyan. "'Our Culture' vs 'Foreign Culture.'" *Gazette* 65.6 (2003): 427–441.

———, and H. Dunn, eds. *Media, Democracy and Renewal in Southern Africa.* Colorado Springs: International Academic Publishers, 2002.

———, and Arnold Shepperson. "Sociopolitical Transformation and the Media Environment: Writing Africa into Modernity." *Gazette* 62.1 (2000): 31–43.

Wedell, George, ed. *Making Broadcasting Useful—The African Experience: The Development of Radio and Television in Africa in the 1980s.* Manchester, UK: Manchester University Press, 1987.

WEBSITES

Africa No. 1. Accessed May 29, 2006. http://www.africa1.com/.

KBC English Service. Accessed August 12, 2006. http://www.kbc.co.ke/channel.asp?ID=2.

Nigerian Television Authority. *Welcome to NTA Programmes Online.* Accessed August 25, 2006. http://www.nta.com.ng/.

Radio Ghana. Accessed August 15, 2006. http://www.ghanaweb.com/GhanaHomePage/communication/radio.php.

Radio Okapi: Fondation Hirondelle MONUC. Accessed July 7, 2006. http://www.radiookapi.net/.

SABC 1. *Our Shows.* Accessed July 11, 2006. http://www.sabc1.co.za/portal/site/sabc1/.

UNESCO. *World Information and Communication Report, 2000.* Accessed June 26, 2006. http://www.unesco.org/webworld/wcir/en/index.html.

NOTES

1. Adam 1968 (in Resource Guide, Print Sources), p. 7.
2. Bourgault 1995 (in Resource Guide, Print Sources).
3. Arnold Gibbons, "Francophone West and Equatorial Africa," in Head 1974 (in Resource Guide, Print Sources), pp. 107–113.
4. Head 1974 (in Resource Guide, Print Sources), p. 158.
5. Quoted in Adam 1968 (in Resource Guide, Print Sources), p. 13.
6. The scholars were Daniel Lerner, Wilbur Schramm, and Everett Rogers through their seminal research studies on the role of communication in development: Lerner and Schramm 1967 and Rogers 1976 (in Resource Guide, Print Sources).

7. Said S. Samatar, "Somali Verbal and Material Arts," in Katheryne Loughran, John Loughran, John Johnson, and Said Samatar (eds.), *Somalia in Word and Image* (Washington, DC: Foundation for Cross Cultural Understanding, 1986), p. 30.
8. Peter Mwaura, *Communication Policies in Kenya* (Paris: Unesco Press, 1980), p. 29.
9. Segun Olusa, "Programme Building on a Limited Budget," in Wedell 1987 (in Resource Guide, Print Sources), p. 5.
10. Ford Foundation, *Telestar: Report on a Visit* (New York: Ford Foundation, 1970).
11. Kassaye Demena, "Progress in Program Exchange," in Wedell 1987 (in Resource Guide, Print Sources), p. 17.
12. Ibid., p. 24.
13. Bourgault 1995 (in Resource Guide, Print Sources).
14. Andre-Jean Tudesque, quoted ibid., p. 107.
15. Ibid., p. 77.
16. Quoted in Kivikuru 2003 (in Resource Guide, Print Sources), 113.
17. Bourgault 1997 (in Resource Guide, Print Sources).
18. Wikipedia, the Free Encyclopedia, "*Idols* (South Africa)." Accessed July 10, 2006. http://en.wikipedia.org/wiki/Idols_(South_Africa).
19. Quoted in Bourgault 1995 (in Resource Guide, Print Sources), p. 110.
20. *Welcome to the Special Sections at NTA Programming Online*. Accessed July 8, 2006. available from http://www.nta.com.ng/.
21. Akwani Obi, *Cultural Ambassadors: The American Voice of Abuja Radio*. Accessed June 26, 2006. Available from http://www.imdiversity.com/villages/global/arts-culture-media/culturalAmbassadors.asp.
22. Nigerian Television Authority, *Mission Statement*. Accessed July 8, 2006. http://www.nta.com.ng/.
23. Nuviadenu 2005 (in Resource Guide, Print Sources).
24. *TV3 Programmes*. Accessed August 24, 2006. http://www.tv3.com.gh/pages/programmes/default.asp.
25. Kabemba 2005 (in Resource Guide, Print Sources).
26. Eyoum Ngangue, "Africa: The Radio Scene Tells All." *The Unesco Courier*. April 2001. Accessed April 4, 2007. http://www.unesco.org/courier/2001_04/uk/medias.htm.
27. Bourgault 1995 (in Resource Guide, Print Sources), p. 122.
28. *SA Music Content Regulations 2006*. Accessed August 1, 2006. http://www.icasa.org.za/manager/clientfiles/documents/musiccontentregulation.
29. *METRO FM*. Audience profile online. Accessed July 6, 2006. Available at http://www.sabc.co.za/portal/site/corporate/menuitem.01b93ed679dcd7e48891f2e75401aeb9/.
30. *About Jozi FM*. Accessed July 23, 2006. http://www.abundantmedia.co.za/JoziFM.htm.
31. SABC 1 (in Resource Guide, Websites).
32. Ethiopian Radio and Television Agency, *Purpose*. Accessed May 26, 2006. http://www.erta.gov.et/etvprofile/aboutus.htm.
33. *ERTA Programs*. Accessed May 28, 2006. http://www.erta.gov.et/newscategory/entertainment/entertainment.htm.

SPORTS AND RECREATION

BEA VIDACS

Sports are among the major leisure preoccupations of people in the modern era. Researchers differ on definitions of sports and on what activities should be considered sports. However, there is general agreement that achievement or spectator sports are a modern phenomenon starting in the nineteenth century with the appearance of modern industrial society. We take a broader view of sports by taking into consideration the social significance of sports and sportlike activities in Africa and the ways in which they are part of popular culture. This can only be understood if we take sports to be a symbolic construct with meanings that go beyond immediate results and consider the larger role sports plays in the lives of the people involved with them either as athletes or spectators. What exactly is meant by sports depends on cultural factors. This chapter will concentrate on modern, Western ideas of sports, but it should be noted that this is not the only way to look at the topic. For example, among Swahili-speakers in Tanzania the word "sport" is translated as *michezo*, which encompasses such activities as dance, play, game, mockery, and pastime, indicating that sports is understood in a broader sense and not strictly differentiated from a series of allied activities as it is in contemporary Western languages.[1]

PRECOLONIAL PHYSICAL ACTIVITIES

The sports historian Allen Guttmann attributed seven characteristics to modern sports that distinguish them from earlier forms of athletic activity: secularism, equality of opportunity to participate, specialization of roles, rationalization, bureaucratic organization, quantification, and the quest for records.[2] These are also characteristics of the modern industrial era, and modern sports came into being concurrently with the Industrial Revolution. According to such a definition, we cannot speak of sports prior to the nineteenth century in Europe. However, this does not mean that there were no physical activities resembling sports prior to the appearance of modern sports, but rather that their organization, meaning, and social significance were usually quite different from those attached to modern sports. Traditional sportlike activities in Africa, such as stick fighting, wrestling, various forms of attempting to hit a target (spear or club throwing), running, and jumping were often part of the demonstration of male prowess (but wrestling in some African societies was practiced by women as well). These activities could be associated with the initiation ceremonies that marked a boy's official entrance into manhood and thus had ritual and social significance or else they were simply part of learning the activities necessary for physical survival, such as warfare or hunting. Because many of these activities were part of socialization, the process by which children gradually learn to become full-fledged members of their society, they usually started as children's games. The built-in competitive element was not standardized and records were not kept, although individual achievement brought honor and fame. Often winners gained more than just prestige: certain leadership positions were allotted to them as a result of their sporting success. For example, in Kenya among the Kikuyu people there was a two-mile competitive race associated with initiation ceremonies; a group of boys of roughly the same age competed, with the winner designated as the lifelong leader of the group. Jomo Kenyatta, Kenya's first post-independence president and an anthropologist trained in England, described the event (as it took place in the 1920s and 1930s) as follows:

> To start the race a ceremonial horn is blown.... The boys ... start running in a great excitement, as though they were going to a battle.... It is really considered a sort of fight between the spirit of childhood and that of adulthood. ... The one who reaches the tree first and throws his wooden spear over the tree is elected ... as the leader and spokesman of the age-group for life.[3]

Although the event was a race, its purpose had little to do with sporting success: rather its real significance was in the role it played in selecting the leader of the group, and thus it was an important part of how society was organized.

SPORTS IN THE COLONIAL ERA

Modern sports were introduced to African societies along with colonization. They originated in Britain and spread, similar to the Industrial Revolution itself, from there to Europe and to all other parts of the world, including Africa. Many of the actual games thus introduced had their roots in the preindustrial physical pastimes that had existed in Europe just as they had in Africa. These often took the form of competitions between communities associated with holidays and were free-for-alls that could last for several days. In Britain, with the beginnings of industrial society, these pastimes were increasingly curtailed and prohibited because they interfered with the discipline and general regimentation associated with industrial-era work processes. At the same time, private schools for boys (known in Britain as "public schools") took and transformed the very games that were being forbidden in the villages and on urban streets and adapted them to their own purposes. In their new incarnation, the games served to discipline the boys and to teach them fair play, teamwork, respect for rules, and leadership qualities. The sports ethic thus inculcated became a very important part of the British value system and was duly transmitted to all parts of the British Empire.

British colonizers and their close allies, the missionaries, carried these ideals with them to the colonies and tried to impart them to Africans. Missions often preceded colonization, so it was often in mission schools that Africans first became acquainted with sports. As colonies were established in the late nineteenth and early twentieth century, schools were in the forefront of spreading sports and inculcating the sports ethic into their students. Sports constituted an important part of the curriculum, especially in boarding schools. The graduates of these schools became part of the African elite, and in many places they were instrumental in spreading sports among the rest of the African population. In South Africa, for example, the game of soccer, or football as it is known outside the United States, was first played by the mission-educated elite, and when the sport spread to the masses they were among the leaders of the locally organized soccer clubs for the first few decades of the twentieth century.[4]

White traders, soldiers, and sometimes workers were the other agents spreading sports on the continent. In the French, Belgian, and Portuguese colonies sports spread somewhat later than in the British ones because the games ethic only became well established in the mother countries later on. This explains why in the British colonies the beginnings of soccer go back to the late nineteenth and early twentieth century, whereas in the French territories it appeared only in the 1920s. By contrast, in the British colony of Zanzibar, soccer, field hockey, and cricket were introduced as early as the 1870s by workers who laid the telegraph cables between Zanzibar and Aden. At the same time Zanzibar's St. Andrew's College began to train teachers and clergymen with a curriculum that included soccer and cricket: graduates of the school were to be sent all over East Africa and were instrumental in spreading these sports throughout the region.[5]

Outside of schools, team sports were usually practiced exclusively by whites for their own amusement and, apart from situations where there were not enough players to make up a team, Africans were not allowed to play with them. At a later stage, however, Africans began to form their own teams, but usually they were only allowed to play among themselves and not against Europeans. According to historian Laura Fair, the British colony of Zanzibar was an exception to this pattern, because there were competitions arranged between black and white teams on the island. This naturally gave rise to rivalries, where Africans vied to beat European teams to prove at least symbolically their equality with the colonizers.

Colonial practices also prescribed different sports for different segments of the local population. In Zanzibar young Arab and Asian men who were being groomed for positions of authority in the workforce were encouraged to participate in cricket, but those who were to go into lower-level administrative jobs were channeled into field hockey. Working class people of African descent were seen as suited for soccer and boxing.[6]

With the passing of time, sports became a popular pastime of all Africans. Foremost among them was football, which to this day is the most popular sport in the majority of African countries. The creation and running of soccer clubs was one of the most important forms of nontraditional associations in which Africans, who were otherwise excluded from decision making in the colonial world, could autonomously organize themselves. These sports clubs could be either multiethnic or ethnically exclusive, and in addition to organizing sports, they also functioned as mutual aid societies. In South Africa, for example, members of soccer clubs paid dues that not only helped defray the costs of travel to "away" games but, among other things, served to help members during periods of illness or to contribute to funeral costs.

Whites were ambivalent about encouraging sports among Africans. On the one hand they believed in the sports ethic and thought that the practice of sports would help inculcate European moral values that the "natives" were perceived to be lacking in—such elements of the sports ethic as discipline, fair play, and respect for the rules as discussed previously. On the other hand the colonial authorities also feared that African sports organizations could become hotbeds of anticolonial nationalist activity or of unruly behavior. A typical example of this sort of thinking is shown in the following letter by the lieutenant-governor of Brazzaville, Congo, to the governor-general written in 1932:

> The [Native Sports] Federation was created through a desire to develop sport. At the same time, however, requiring the native sports clubs to be affiliated with the official body will allow an additional means of surveillance, so that we can prevent undesirable elements who, under the cover of sport, get together for the purpose of political agitation and provoking disorder.[7]

Following an initial period of unregulated sporting activity, colonial governments, prompted by concerns such as these, attempted to impose their control over teams and sporting activities. Often they succeeded, most commonly through promises of equipment and the provision of white coaches and officials to the African teams, but also through the creation of various federations and associations where the leadership was in the majority white with only token representation of the local population. In Zanzibar one of the ways in which the autonomously organized teams were broken up was to recruit good football players into the police or other government-controlled work places and obliging them to play for the team of the agency in question. Although many players resented this, the job opportunity and accompanying regular salary were difficult to refuse. However, often they continued to play on their original teams as well as the new team and felt keenly the imposition. In the Republic of the Congo (Congo-Brazzaville), the co-opted teams resisted, and eventually the league organized by the colonial state had to disband because of the refusal of players to participate in it.

SPORTS IN THE POSTCOLONIAL ERA

Just before or immediately after gaining independence and sovereignty in the late 1950s and early 1960s, one of the first things the newly independent African countries did was to create sporting federations. Following the European model of sports organization, national federations were created to organize each sport and these federations were then affiliated with the appropriate worldwide governing body of the sport in question. Continental bodies were also formed. Because of the importance of soccer on the continent the most significant was the Confederation of African Football (CAF). Founded in 1957, it organized the first African Nations Cup in the same year with just three participants (Egypt, Sudan, and Ethiopia) because South Africa, the fourth co-founder of the organization, had been suspended by the other three because of the apartheid regime's segregationist practices. By 2006 the organization had 53 member countries, with 16 teams competing in the biennial finals of the African Nations Cup. Unfortunately, lack of funds can be a persistent problem for some member federations, causing them either to not field teams or to withdraw during the preliminary rounds of competition.

Other sports practiced on the continent have also created their own federations and united in continental confederations that are affiliated with the worldwide governing bodies of the sports in question. The tasks of these confederations include organizing and overseeing Africa-wide competitions and representing the interests of member federations in the worldwide body. Competitions organized by the confederations include the African Nations Cup in soccer, basketball, and other sports, as well as competitions for youth and women. It is also through the continental bodies that the elimination rounds are organized for worldwide events.

African countries also participate in the international Olympic movement. Most Sub-Saharan African countries began to participate regularly in the Summer Olympic Games only after gaining independence, from 1960 on. In 1976 twenty-five African nations and the South American nation of Guyana boycotted the Montreal games to protest the International Olympic Committee's refusal to ban the participation of New Zealand, whose rugby team had played in then-racially segregated South Africa despite the international boycott.

African participation in the Olympic Games is very uneven: the events in which Africans have left their mark are primarily track and field (particularly running) and, to a lesser extent, boxing. Practically all African medals have been won in these two fields. In addition, in soccer two West African countries, Nigeria and Cameroon, were the best in 1996 and 2000 respectively, and Ghana won the bronze medal in 1992. The uneven development of sports on the continent is further evident in the low number of medals won relative to population size when compared to other continents.

There is a gender disparity as well: between 1960 and 2004 African men won 130 medals (33 gold, 49 silver, and 48 bronze) and women won 35 (12 gold, 12 silver, and 11 bronze). This disparity is only partially explained by the fact that, overall, Africa sends only about half as many women to compete in the Olympics as men. The difference highlights a real gender imbalance in sports on the continent: women, despite a few outstanding exceptions such as Derartu Tulu of Ethiopia and Maria Mutola of Mozambique, lag far behind men. In fact, it was not until 1992, with Tulu's victory in the 10,000-meter race in Barcelona, that an African woman won a gold medal.

Participating in the Olympic movement also creates an opportunity for Africans to play important roles in the administration, organization, and decision-making processes of the Olympic movement. Every African country has its own National Olympic Committee affiliated first with the continental Olympic Committee (ANOCA) and through that to the International Olympic Committee.

LOCAL-LEVEL SPORTS IN AFRICA

Below the level of the continental federations are national federations whose main task is to oversee and regulate national or regional competitions as well as coordinate their sport's participation in international competitions. In the case of soccer this involves organizing a national championship and cup competition, which includes issuing licenses, assigning referees, and other administrative tasks. The national federations also oversee and support preparations for international competitions.

SCHOOL SPORTS AND YOUTH CHAMPIONSHIPS

In Africa, just as elsewhere, schools play an important role in exposing children to sports. However, in Africa the reach of the school system is not as wide as could be desired: not all children have access to an education and schools often lack resources for a comprehensive physical education program. Although in many countries there is a system of interschool competitions culminating in an annual nationwide meet, here, too, lack of resources or mismanagement often cause these events to be held irregularly.

Other forms of sports for youth outside the official system of sports organization can be found in neighborhood soccer tournaments held in many cities and also in the countryside. These lively events commonly mobilize the energies of an entire community and serve a diverse array of social functions that go beyond the obvious promotion of physical well-being. In different places such tournaments will have different meanings even within the same country. They can be seen as focal points for revitalizing a dispersed ethnic community or as part of the struggle for control over public spaces in urban slums, as preparation for being recognized as a player with potential and recruited into an official team, or they can be a way for young men to attract girls.

SPORTS IN THE DAILY LIVES OF AFRICANS

It is hard to get accurate information on sports participation in terms of numbers, but it is clear that the most popular sport on the continent is soccer, followed by boxing, basketball, wrestling, weightlifting, and track and field (among others). As elsewhere, fans and supporters are also part of sports in Africa, and their interest and involvement adds passion to sports on the continent. Most men have played soccer as youths and have participated in neighborhood tournaments or coached a team: many later become members of a club offering financial and moral support to the team.

Despite enormous interest and some world-class results, organized sports in Africa face many problems because of generalized poverty and frequent mismanagement of public goods. Sporting facilities are scarce, overused, not very well maintained, and consequently run down. The equipment needed is often not available, and makeshift arrangements for their provision are quite common, especially at lower levels of competition. In soccer, for example, despite the promises of club presidents, due to lack of resources players often have to use their own resources to obtain uniforms and proper footwear. Since this equipment is also a necessary prerequisite for participating in an official competition, hard-strapped teams sometimes resort to renting uniforms for each match, a procedure that, although ultimately more expensive, gives them the only possibility to play if they cannot afford the initial outlay for equipment. A range of other items, from health insurance to practice balls (taken for granted on a professional level in the West), are often missing or available in insufficient quantities.

The situation is somewhat better in cases of teams sponsored by local enterprises that may have superior financial resources at their disposal. However, the danger in such cases is that if one of these enterprises falls on bad times, support for the team can consequently dry up. In Zambia, for instance, football clubs as well as other sports were sponsored by the biggest employer in the country, the Zambia Consolidated Copper Mines (ZCCM), which financed facilities, built sports complexes, and gave jobs to players. When ZCCM was privatized in the late 1990s, the sponsorship of teams became uncertain and inconsistent, because only some of the successor companies were willing to continue the sponsorship, whereas others allowed facilities and equipment to deteriorate, with the result that sports declined in the country.

Elite sportsmen fare better than their lower-division counterparts, but unless they have joined the ranks of international superstars who practice their sport entirely abroad, it is only when competing at an international level that they have proper equipment. Sports in most African countries tends to be amateur in the sense that sportsmen and women and officials are not paid for their performance (at least not officially). Everywhere, however, there has prevailed for a long time a certain degree of hidden professionalism, especially in soccer, where players are given either monetary or in-kind bonuses. The crucial difference between regular remuneration and bonuses is that the latter appear as favors on the part of the team leadership rather than as the due of the players, and, of course, in times of economic hardship these can disappear entirely. Among these in-kind benefits are providing players with work opportunities (a substantial help in areas where unemployment is high) and paying for meals, housing, or school fees if they are students.

The majority of people in African countries are poor, and this determines in many ways what their aspirations are and how they conduct their lives. In addition to the honor and respect that achievement in sports can bring, it appears to many as a way out of poverty, and for these reasons people make enormous sacrifices to pursue sports as practitioners, coaches, or officials. Sometimes, as well, people are tempted to try to influence outcomes by other than sporting means. Referees can have an especially difficult time maintaining their integrity. Even if they are unwilling to take a bribe, they are frequently put into a position where they feel that they have no choice but to favor a particular team. In addition to the threat of physical violence in the course of a match, they may feel that they are under obligation.

If they must travel to an out-of-town game, this obligation is often unavoidable: because referees are usually not paid travel expenses (and certainly not in advance), they frequently must rely on the bounty of the visiting team for being transported to the venue of the match, and sometimes even for lodging, or alternatively their lodging and meals will be taken care of by the host team. In either situation referees can find it difficult to remain impartial. Corruption on a larger scale is also a problem, as when stadium constructions are stalled because the funds have disappeared or when the monetary means for the support of the national team do not reach those for whom they are intended.

THE MEANING OF SPORTS TO AFRICANS

The meaning of sports to Africans cannot be divorced from the socioeconomic and political realities of the continent. Sports are in part so important to Africans because they see in them one of the only avenues out of poverty. Even though only a tiny minority of African sportsmen become stars and millionaires, their example remains a powerful source of fascination, encouragement, and incentive to the millions who live in poverty and deprivation. In addition, there is also the transformative potential of sports on a group level in that the sporting glory achieved is seen as somehow proving the worth of the group—whether a village, an ethnic group, or a nation—vis-à-vis groups of similar nature. Thus sports is intricately intertwined with identity. Naturally, this is also the case on other continents: in most countries of the world sports performance is seen as an indicator of the worth of a people.

THE POSITION OF ATHLETES

Physical prowess has always been rewarded in human society and sports prowess is just an extension of this. Glory on the sports field translates into respect and an increased set of opportunities in life in Africa as well as elsewhere. As previously discussed, in precolonial societies in Africa leadership roles often went to people who were able to prove themselves in feats of physical prowess. Those who excel in modern sports on the local level tend to have a wider social network than their nonsporting counterparts. It is often the case that athletes come into contact with a larger number of people and from a greater variety of social and ethnic backgrounds, which means that sportsmen are often more able to transcend local ties and build relationships with people outside their own ethnic group and social milieu. Practitioners of team sports often play on multiethnic teams and form lifelong friendships with teammates that can help them get on in life. Popular players are local heroes and receive adulation and respect from everyone: international stars such as the Cameroonian soccer player Samuel Eto'o are known and revered all over the continent and serve as an inspiration to young people.

Sportsmen who excel on the international level also get recognition from the state. Because African governments wish to promote national unity through sports success, national teams or individual sportsmen returning victorious from international competition are given lavish receptions by the head of state and are decorated as well. In addition, athletes can be rewarded with substantial premiums (monetary or in-kind): for example, each member of the 1997 women's basketball team of Senegal, which won the African Championship in Nairobi, received a home.[8] Athletes also can be given honorary or real political functions upon completing their career. For example, the Cameroonian government named Roger Milla, the soccer star, its itinerant ambassador. In other cases they are asked to use their celebrity to popularize charitable causes: UNICEF in partnership with FIFA—soccer's international governing body—chose African football stars as its representatives to promote such causes as AIDS awareness and the protection of children.

For some sportsmen a sporting career can serve as a stepping stone to political prominence in their country. Among the most notorious of those who have risen to national or international political fame after an involvement with sports is Idi Amin Dada, Uganda's infamous ruler during the 1970s, who had been a boxer in the Ugandan army while a young man. A more positive example is George Weah, the Liberian soccer star, and FIFA's World Player of the Year in 1995. He both coached and financially sponsored the national team in its attempt to qualify for the 1998 World Cup during the civil war in Liberia. In 2005, he ran for president of his war-ravaged country; although ultimately his bid was not successful, his popularity was such that a runoff election had to be held with the eventual winner—a strong showing indicating the weight of sporting success in African society.

WOMEN ATHLETES

Women have been less successful and participate less often in sports on the continent (as shown by the gender disparity seen in the number of Olympic medals discussed previously). Perhaps the immediate cause of the disparity both on the level of Olympic competition and on the local level is that governments are unwilling to spend scarce resources on female athletes: available funds go disproportionately to the training of male athletes, and if cuts must be made, women's sports programs will always suffer in comparison to men's. These government choices, however, reflect deeper social attitudes that begin to work against women's sports participation much earlier. Girls have less disposable free time because they are expected to help out in the household at an earlier age than boys; and they generally lag behind boys in access to education, which handicaps them in sports because children often start practicing sports in school.

There may be other cultural factors hindering the development of women's sports. Islam can also be a significant cultural barrier to female participation in sports because it frowns upon women's appearance in public, and women's sports meet with strong social disapproval. Not all of Africa is dominated by Islam, however, and even within those areas that are, there is variation. For example, in the overwhelmingly Muslim country of Senegal, women's basketball is one of the most popular sports, and many young women aspire to become basketball players. In Nigeria women's soccer remains the best on the continent despite the banning of soccer in some parts of the Muslim-dominated northern part of the country.

Another measure of how involved women are with sports is whether they participate in its administration. There are female referees and coaches, and a few officials exist as well, but on the whole sports tends to be a male domain on the continent. Women are also involved in sports indirectly as supporters. Although they lag behind men in this activity, they nevertheless play an important role in the supporters' clubs, for example, in South African soccer; and women's adulation of sportsmen in general is an integral part of the social fabric of sport on the continent.

THE ROLE OF "MAGIC" IN SPORTS

Much has been written about the role of magic in the lives of Africans and often Western sports coverage also stresses this exotic aspect of sports in Africa. However, although there are beliefs in the supernatural in Africa that from a contemporary Western perspective seem like part of a bygone era, in fact the magical practices associated with sports have many Western counterparts. Because of the large role of chance or luck in sports, athletes everywhere tend to be superstitious and engage in various rituals—personal or communal—that they hope will enhance their performance or increase their luck. Viewed in this light, some of the practices African athletes engage in are not so unfamiliar: players use amulets or charms of various sorts, some of which have recognizable Western origins, whereas some can be considered more traditionally African (for example, praying individually or as a group before a match, players crossing themselves before entering the field, or the use of a small picture of the Virgin Mary wound up with the bandages a player puts on his feet). Other practices show more explicit continuity with traditional beliefs, but they are put to new uses in being thought to enhance sports performance. Some distinctly African practices reported are the burial of an amulet near the goal posts in soccer fields: when the players suppose that the entrance to the stadium has been magically "tied," they enter the stadium elsewhere than they were supposed to (for example, they climb the surrounding fences or walls instead of entering through the gate). It is hard to know whether these preventive measures are responses to actually-carried-out magical acts of aggression or merely presuppose that the opponent engaged in them; but, in any case, the preventive measures that are carried out show that people do believe in the efficacy of the magical acts and do try to counter their effects. Many sportsmen, however, do not think that it is possible to win by "magic" alone—in fact, there are lively debates among them as to whether magical practices work or not. Most sports practitioners think that magic can help enhance performance because of the psychological boost it gives players who perform better when they think they have powerful occult forces working on their side, and they leave unanswered whether magic can do anything beyond that. In fact, many Cameroonian soccer coaches use the phrase "work is my magic," implying that results cannot be achieved without hard work.

SPORTS AND POLITICS

Everywhere in the world sports is subject to political manipulation. Partly this is so because sports is intrinsically connected to the control of people (as seen already in the previous discussion of its early history). Partly, however, it is because sports express group identity: a sports team or an individual athlete can stand in the minds of the fans for the entire group. Because African countries came into being as a result of colonial conquest and borders incorporated ethnic groups that often did not have any commonality or even had a history of warfare and conflict, one of the main tasks postcolonial governments were faced with was the creation of national unity, of a shared sense of belonging among the diverse peoples enclosed within their borders. Sports was an obvious tool in the service of this endeavor and everywhere great emphasis was laid on promoting sports to foster national unity, and this remains a persistent theme of government rhetoric. Sports' success, especially in the case of team sports, is held up as an example for people to emulate. Although governments elsewhere make similar use of sports, Africa's pervasive underdevelopment renders sports one of the few avenues wherein an African nation can distinguish itself on the international stage: therefore, the propaganda associated with sports tends to be more strident than elsewhere.

Although it is true that the majority of African countries are ethnically divided and often there is distrust and ethnic rivalry among people, when it comes to international sports, in most cases the majority of the population puts this aside and, when the national team plays, roots for it and feels that the honor of the nation is at stake. This is particularly true if the team is victorious: when a national team wins, people do not question its ethnic composition—they support and celebrate it regardless of the origin of the individual players. However, in the case of a loss, ethnic rivalries frequently resurface: a particular ethnic group may be blamed for having betrayed the collectivity or the coach may be accused of having selected players from one group rather than another. The converse can also happen when members of a particular ethnic group claim that they have had a greater role in the victory than others.

The other widespread political use of sports in African countries occurs when a politician or political grouping identifies itself closely with a team or athlete, using them to gain legitimacy. Naturally, under these circumstances, victories and losses have political consequences, particularly losses. Everywhere in the world coaches are dismissed if a team performs below expectations, but the blame can go even further. To give just one example, after Senegal failed to qualify for the 2006 World Cup in soccer, the minister responsible for sports was relieved of his post. In cases of victory, governments often attempt to claim credit as if the victory had been the direct consequence of government policy supporting the sport and attempt, sometimes successfully, to exploit positive feelings to divert attention from social and economic problems. Direct interference by politicians with the day-to-day operations of a team is also not uncommon, and most often this takes the form of imposing players during the selection, a practice that is usually resented by coaches, players, and fans.

AFRICAN SPORTS IN THE INTERNATIONAL ARENA

For most of Africa international sports participation began when they joined international sports bodies following independence. Although it was a major step toward equality, the history of this participation also highlights the global inequalities Third-World peoples have faced. In many cases Africans have had to struggle for equal participation and representation in sports events and in the governing bodies of sports. For example, in the case of soccer, the Confederation of African Football fought a long battle within FIFA for an equitable number of places in the sport's premier event, the World Cup. Until 1970 the African continent shared one berth in the competition with Asia. In 1966 most African and Asian nations boycotted the World Cup to call attention to the injustice of this arrangement. The first time Africa had a place in its own right in the competition was in 1970 (with the qualification of the North African nation of Morocco) and from 1982 the number of representatives grew to two. In 1974 Zaire was the first Sub-Saharan nation to represent the continent in the World Cup, and following Cameroon's milestone quarterfinal finish in 1990 in Italy, Africa's allotment grew to three spots (1994) and then to the current five spots (1998).

Another bone of contention between African nations and the world governing body of soccer was the issue of apartheid in South Africa. As in all sports, soccer was segregated in South Africa under the white-controlled Football Association of South Africa (FASA). In 1957 South Africa was expelled from the Confederation of African Football by the other members, and pressure began to mount on FIFA to do likewise. The struggle culminated in 1974 with the unseating of Sir Stanley Rous, longtime president of FIFA and opponent of the expulsion, by João Havelange, a Brazilian businessman, who was elected as president on the basis of promises to expel South Africa from FIFA and to promote the development of soccer in Africa. Havelange's accession to the FIFA presidency was the first time that African countries—due to the one-country, one-vote policy—became a major voting bloc within the organization. They played a similar king-making role in the election and then reelection of Havelange's successor, Joseph Blatter, in 1998 and in 2002.[9]

Sports migration is another aspect of international sporting life, especially in Africa. Here again the decisive factor is African poverty, especially relative to Europe and the United States. Many African sportsmen on the elite level are plying their sport abroad. In the 2005–2006 season there were 764 African soccer players in the European first division alone and many more play in the lower divisions. Most often these athletes play for teams based in the countries of their former colonizers; however, some players have ventured farther afield to Asia, Eastern Europe, and Latin America.

This practice has several negative effects. Taking the cream of the crop leads to "deskilling"—players leaving their home countries for Europe or elsewhere as soon as they show talent, with the negative result of lowering the level of play at home. When players leave young, they may not be able to withstand the stress and hardship of relocation in a new culture and to adapt to circumstances they are completely unfamiliar with. Many young players, desperate to escape poverty and lured by the promise of huge sums, seize the first opportunity offered without really understanding the full implications and can end up rejected and abandoned without resources in a strange place. Their youth, inexperience, and status as aliens also make them particularly susceptible to exploitation at the hands of unscrupulous agents, who may take half or more of their earnings. Finally, if they do get a regular contract and attain a level of professional success, racism will always remain a potential problem. Even successful players who have gained acceptance and popularity within their clubs will always face potential racial abuse directed at them by supporters of the opposing team. In response, several European countries as well as FIFA have created organizations to combat racism in sports: for instance, one FIFA-run organization is "Let's Kick Racism out of Football."

DEVELOPMENT AND RECONCILIATION THROUGH SPORTS

Although sports can be a source of division between groups and countries there have been attempts to use it as a tool of development and reconciliation. The popularity of sports, especially soccer, in Africa has made it a vehicle to carry a wide range of social messages, from promoting reconciliation in war-torn areas to AIDS awareness. The British anthropologist Paul Richards has argued that part of the reason soccer can be used to carry the message of reconciliation is that it represents a culturally neutral area that, along with popular music, represents the larger world and does not belong to any particular group, thus comprising a realm where people of various backgrounds and interests can find common ground. He also stresses that especially in situations in which social order has completely broken down, such as in the case of civil war–ravaged Sierra Leone or Liberia, one of the main virtues of soccer is that it creates a space where, in contrast to the world outside the football field, people can agree on the rules and can abide by the decisions of the referee. In a prevailing climate of lawlessness this represents a very important avenue for learning a new set of behaviors.[10] Of course, it is questionable whether sports alone can cure all the ills of the continent.

REGIONAL SUBSECTIONS

West Africa

Senegal

The West African country of Senegal, a former French colony, has a variety of sporting traditions. Women's basketball and men's soccer are the most popular team sports, but wrestling, an individual sport, also mobilizes a large number of practitioners and fans. Unlike the two-team sports, which, although they have been enthusiastically embraced by Senegalese, are nonetheless foreign imports, wrestling as it is practiced in Senegal has grown out of a precolonial sportlike practice.[11]

The traditional form of wrestling commonly took place in association with the harvest festival. Under a variety of names, the most widespread of which was *mbapat*, this practice existed through most of the territory of present-day Senegal. The wrestling took the form of public contests, widely attended by members of surrounding communities and organized by young men under the supervision of their elders. The wrestlers were young adults who had already undergone circumcision and the initiation ceremony. Wrestling matches were an extension of the initiation ceremony in that they tested the manliness of the wrestler and demonstrated the power of the elders to control youth. In addition to personal honor, the honor of the entire community was seen to ride on the outcome of these bouts. Wrestling could also be regarded as a form of peacetime preparation for war, because the participants were precisely those young men who would have to defend the territory in case of attack. Contestants had to observe a number of taboos prior to the competition: for example, they had to abstain from sexual relations. Breaking the taboos carried supernatural sanctions. The bouts were accompanied by a variety of chants or songs, sung by the girlfriends or sisters of the combatants. These could be songs of praise and encouragement to the fighter being supported and songs of derision for his opponent, which questioned his virility by likening him to a woman, also showing that wrestling success represented the manliness of the wrestler.

With colonial conquest by the French, wrestling was gradually transformed. In the late nineteenth century a new form of wrestling, called *lamb*, came into being in the countryside and spread to the principal city, Dakar, where its form and functions changed significantly. Lamb evolved as a variant of mbapat, the principal difference being that in lamb the rules allowed for punches. During the 1920s lamb became very popular in Dakar. The season for wrestling lengthened to half a year from the beginning of the period of the sale of peanuts in December–January until the first rains in June–July, with the bouts being organized in towns on weekends and holidays. A variety of new techniques were introduced, and lamb incorporated additional elements from boxing and street fighting.

These new kinds of wrestling matches took place in enclosed spaces called arenas. Over time these venues became more and more commercialized: the first organized match with paying spectators took place in 1927 in a Dakar movie theater. Other paying venues, offering spectators' seats or standing room, rapidly proliferated after that. These arenas were among the most popular meeting places in town: they were lively and rowdy places where the crowd boisterously cheered its favorites and sometimes came to blows themselves. Between the two world wars the crowd could be in the thousands (the largest recorded was about three thousand). Such popularity also made the spectacle into a serious business that became quite lucrative for successful promoters and wrestlers.

Shortly before Senegal won its independence in 1960 the visibility and celebrity status of wrestlers rose: an official wrestling federation was created at the end of 1959. Politicians also began to take an interest in the sport and to use it for their own ends. They participated actively in ceremonies surrounding wrestling, such as by handing out trophies in the capacity of honorary or actual presidents of competitions. They often exploited these occasions to make political speeches in front of the assembled crowds. Another reason politicians took such an interest was that, by designating wrestling the principal sport of Senegal, they sought to use it to forge national unity.

Both mbapat and lamb continued to flourish in Senegal after independence, mbapat in the countryside and lamb in Dakar, with the two forms intermittently influencing each other. In times of hardship in the countryside, for example, during a drought in the late 1960s, new wrestlers reared on mbapat arrived in the city in great numbers, giving the sport a new impetus (and sometimes new champions). The sport continues to change in form as wrestlers of the 1990s have increasingly incorporated martial arts and weight-lifting elements into their repertoire.

There have been changes in social significance as well. After independence, the purses received by fighters began to rise, enabling successful practitioners to live exclusively from the sport. This process became more pronounced during the deepening economic crisis of the1970s, rendering the money-making aspect of wrestling paramount. By the late 1990s, the sums a first-class wrestler could receive rose to what amounts to astronomical sums in Senegalese terms: 15–30 million CFA francs (US$30,000–$60,000) in a country where a taxi driver earns US$100–$200 a month. Champions have huge entourages made up of trainers and various other helpers among whom are often included lawyers, *marabouts* (religious specialists), and *griots* (praise singers).

As in the West, wrestlers draw additional income from sponsorships. Among these sponsors are such companies as the national lottery, the national electricity company, and other commercial and manufacturing firms. During his heyday the image of the greatest champion of the 1990s, Mohamed Ndao, better known as "Tyson" (named after the American boxer), could be found on the cover of exercise books for school children, billboards in and around Dakar advertising the Nestle company brand, and in television commercials. This kind of opportunity and income, however, is only granted to a select few.

The relationship between politicians and wrestlers has continued to develop since the eve of independence. Politicians continue to appear together with wrestlers in the hopes of gaining popularity among the population, but wrestlers have started taking a more active role in politics as well: many support established politicians and one even supported an opposition candidate, and yet others have run in municipal elections. In fact, Tyson lost much of his popularity when he publicly appeared with the unpopular president, A. Diouf, during the latter's unsuccessful bid for reelection in 2000.

Nigeria

Football is the most popular sport in the former British colony of Nigeria. As elsewhere in Africa, football arrived in the country along with colonization. The first recorded soccer match in Nigeria took place in 1904 at Hope Waddel Training Institution between a team of Nigerian students and expatriate teachers against a team from a British ship, the *HMS Thistle*, and was won 3–2 by the home team. Besides being played in schools the game was also played in the army, and this, in fact, proved instrumental in spreading the game all over the territory. Government agencies and trading firms also contributed to the popularization of the game in the country: the Public Works Department (PWD) and Railway Institute were among the earliest organizers of league soccer and they ensured their success by hiring great players as their employees.

Hope Waddel was also the alma mater of Nnamdi Azikiwe, the leader of Nigeria's anti-colonial struggle and Nigeria's first president. In the 1930s he created his own sports organization including a soccer team, the Zik Athletic Club, and when the club toured various Nigerian towns to raise money for the war effort in the early 1940s Azikiwe adroitly used these occasions to make political speeches that openly criticized British colonial rule in front of the gathered crowds.[12]

Nigeria joined FIFA on the eve of independence in 1960. A national football league was begun in 1972, with a second and third division added later on. Several Nigerian clubs have been successful in such continentwide competitions as the African Cup Winners Cup and the CAF Cup. Although professionalism was introduced in 1990 the wish to test their mettle elsewhere and economic difficulties in their country have driven many talented Nigerian players to try their luck abroad. Nigeria, which is the most populous country in Africa, provides Europe and the rest of the world with the largest number of players from an African country. The national selection has also been successful: the junior team has won the world title twice and the senior team qualified three times for the World Cup and in 1996 won Olympic gold in Atlanta. Nigeria has dominated African women's soccer since the beginning of continental competitions in 1998, winning the African Championship for Women's Football four times, and their best finish in the Women's World Cup came with a fifth place in 1999.

Central Africa

Cameroon

Cameroon, a Central African country with a history of initial German (1884–1916) and subsequent French and English colonial domination, is best known in the world of sports for the 1990 achievement of becoming the first African nation to reach the quarterfinal stage of the FIFA World Cup.

As in many other African countries, soccer is the most popular sport in Cameroon. Soccer followed different trajectories in French and British-dominated Cameroon. It was introduced into French Cameroon during the late 1920s and early 1930s by the French, who played among themselves or with African migrants from other colonies who were in Cameroon as supervisory personnel. Cameroonians soon adopted the game, forming their own teams and initiating championships, first in Douala and subsequently in Yaoundé, the country's economic and administrative capitals, respectively; but as elsewhere in colonial Africa, they could only play with the permission and under the supervision of the colonial authorities. In the Western, British-dominated part of Cameroon most teams were organized on an occupational basis, with the support of various agencies of the colonial government: thus teams such as PWD (Public Works Department) Bamenda or Prisons Club of Buea were among the most prominent before independence.

The national football federation (FECAFOOT) was created in 1959 in anticipation of independence and became affiliated with the world body, FIFA, in 1962; it joined the Confederation of African Football (CAF) the following year. The country's national team, the Indomitable Lions, participated in an African record of five FIFA World Cups (1982, 1990, 1994, 1998, and 2002). In addition to its 1990 glory it also won the African Nations Cup four times (1984, 1988, 2000, and 2002), and the Lions became Olympic champions in 2000 in Sydney.

The national federation organizes first-, second-, and third-division championships, which operate respectively on national, regional, and district levels. In addition to the championship, there is also a National Challenge Cup, for which teams from all divisions compete, although it is most commonly won by first division teams.

When soccer was first introduced the players came from the ranks of high school students, who, by virtue of being educated, were part of the elite. Thus in the early phases of the history of soccer in Cameroon, recruitment did not take ethnic identity into consideration but rather elite status. As the sport became more broadly popular teams became ethnically homogeneous with leadership, coaches and players all coming from the same ethnic group. Well into the 1960s, transferring into a club of a different ethnic group than one's own was considered to be a betrayal. By the late 1980s this changed so that most teams participating in official championships—especially in large, multiethnic urban centers—recruited their players and coaches based on ability rather than on ethnicity to field the most efficient group of players. This does not mean that there is no ethnic dimension to teams, because people tend to identify a team with its leadership, which in most cases tends to be monoethnic. Smaller teams, where ethnic homogeneity is more striking, continue to exist as well, and such teams often have a vocal fan base that roots for them on the grounds of ethnic loyalty.

Cameroonians follow soccer avidly: everyone considers himself an expert and most men have on some level actively participated in soccer as licensed or unlicensed players, coaches, officials, organizers of neighborhood or village championships, and, of course, as fans. In urban centers there are also "old boys" teams, composed of men beyond competitive age who play recreational soccer on weekends. The "third half-time," which takes place in a neighborhood bar, is as important a part of the occasion as the match itself: membership of the old-boys teams is often multiethnic and members help each other out when the need arises. Soccer championships and cup competitions organized in urban centers by people descended from the same village or group of villages constitute another kind of communal activity that centers around soccer. These competitions are a means of maintaining ties with co-villagers and even the village itself because only descendants of the village can be on the roster of players. Far more women attend these matches as spectators than in the case of official championship matches, also showing that these village championships have important social functions that go beyond sport.

Cameroonians take great pride in the exploits of the Indomitable Lions and feel the sting keenly when they do not perform well. The Cameroonian government tries to claim credit for the team's victories, to boost its own popularity and to deflect attention from other issues, such as the economic crisis the country has been experiencing since 1987 and political unrest (which characterized Cameroon in the early 1990s). When the national team wins, the government declares a public holiday, and in the general upsurge of joy and pride, people seem to at least momentarily forget their discontent. These government maneuvers, however, can backfire because the population is aware that the government does not support the sport as it should. Among other things, football fields are not maintained, players do not get paid, there is corruption at all levels of the game, and the national stadium is left to deteriorate; and therefore when the national team loses they blame the government. During the 1994 World Cup when the Indomitable Lions were eliminated, several listeners of a call-in radio program demanded the resignation of the government. Thus although sports can be used by governments to garner support, the population can also turn against the government and challenge it through sports. When they do this they often use sports as a metaphor—when talking about the fate of sports they are actually talking about the fate of their country.

When the Indomitable Lions play against Europeans, and especially against the former colonial masters, the matches take on an extra-charged significance. They are seen as a way to redress the wrongs perpetuated by the colonizers against Cameroon during both the colonial and the postcolonial period. At such times the population supports the national team with special fervor, and they even celebrate other African teams when they manage to beat the former colonial power, as was the case in 2002 when Senegal beat the French national team in the World Cup in Korea/Japan. There can also be explosions of great bitterness: during the 1998 World Cup in France, when a questionable referee decision contributed to the elimination of the Indomitable Lions, there were riots in the major cities of Cameroon, protesting against what was seen as the blatant racism of the referee.

Democratic Republic of the Congo (DRC)

Football is also the most popular sport in the Democratic Republic of the Congo, formerly Zaire. The beginnings of the Congolese Football Association go back to as early as 1919, when Congo was a Belgian colony; but the federation only became formally affiliated with FIFA in 1962, following independence. The most important centers of soccer are the cities of Kinshasa and Lubumbashi, where the most famous teams of the country play (Daring Club Motema Pembe and Vita Club play in Kinshasa and Lubumbashi is home to Tout Puissant Mazembe).

The early years of independent Congo were characterized by political upheaval and ended in a coup d'état by Joseph Mobutu in 1965. In the early 1970s the Mobutu government dedicated substantial sums to the development of football to gain popularity and garner national pride. As a result the late 1960s and early 1970s were the heyday of Congolese football. Zairian teams won several continental trophies, and the national team, first named the Simbas (Lions) and later the Leopards, won the African Nations Cup twice: in 1968 (as Congo) and in 1974 (as Zaire). In 1974 Zaire was the first Sub-Saharan African nation to ever qualify for the FIFA World Cup; however, they were eliminated after the first round with the heaviest loss in World Cup history, 9–0 against Yugoslavia. This poor performance signaled the beginning of a downturn in the fortunes of Congolese football partly because of the withdrawal of presidential (and financial) support for the sport. As Mobutu's rule became increasingly autocratic, corruption grew and the economy of the country declined, and this was felt in all walks of life. The end of Mobutu's rule in 1997 found the country in disarray. After the fall of the Mobutu regime the Democratic Republic of the Congo underwent a five-year civil war, which left devastation in its wake and brought hardship for everyone, including sportsmen, and led to the further deterioration of sports facilities. Soccer still remains important to the Congolese, so much so that on April 1, 2006, veteran players staged a demonstration in Kinshasa to protest the mismanagement of the sport by the Federation (Fecofa) and the Ministry of Sports and Youth.[13] Despite these difficulties the men's national football team has qualified for the African Nations Cup several times in recent years and reached the semifinals in 1998, and the under-20 women's selection participated in the U-20 Women's Football World Cup in Moscow in 2006 for the first time.

Southern Africa

Republic of South Africa

Many commentators describe the Republic of South Africa as a "sports-mad" country, and this appears to be true of blacks and whites equally. The Dutch have been present in South Africa since 1652, but from the point of view of the spread of Western sports, the British presence in the region since the early nineteenth century has been much more important. British settlers and colonizers practiced sports such as cricket, rugby, and tennis among themselves from the 1820s onward, and sports spread to the African and the so-called Coloured population by the 1860s. By the 1870s British settlers had formed sporting associations and sport was an essential part of the social life of white South Africans.

As elsewhere in Africa, Africans and the other nonwhite groups learned these sports through mission schools, which wished to substitute "wholesome" pastimes for what they considered to be the "immoral" leisure activities of Africans. For both whites and nonwhites, these British imports represented respectability and Empire and thus were frequently equated with superiority and civilization. For English speakers, sports were part of British elite culture, and they were first seen as an expression of moral superiority and later of manliness. By the 1910s sports were serving to heal the rifts of the Boer War, which had been fought between white South Africans of Dutch and British extraction, and over time they became one of the most blatant symbols of South Africa's apartheid system. The strength that South Africa's national rugby team, the Springboks, showed in worldwide competition served to justify apartheid, at least in the eyes of its supporters, and further reinforced the association of the game with Afrikanerdom and white superiority. In the 1970s, when global public opinion turned against South African apartheid and the world began to observe a variety of sports boycotts, white South Africans felt the sting of being left out of international rugby much more keenly than being excluded from the Olympic movement or from other sports, because of rugby's central place in white South African self-validation.

Although during the last decades of the nineteenth century there had been a certain amount of interracial sport practiced in South Africa, by the early twentieth century *de facto* segregation had begun as whites increasingly feared competition from blacks and nonwhites. Although apartheid only became codified in 1948, the ground was prepared for it by earlier segregationist policies that confined nonwhites to segregated sports and limited and inferior sporting facilities. A set of stereotypical ideas came into being, and reflecting the racial hierarchy that whites were setting up in South Africa, different "races" were associated with different sports. Thus rugby was seen to be the domain of whites, cricket of the Coloured population (especially those of Asian descent), and soccer and boxing were left for the black population. In actuality, all peoples played all sports when given the opportunity: mission education had already spread Western sports to Africans, and mission-educated blacks had been enthusiastically playing cricket, rugby, tennis, croquet, and soccer since the 1860s. Sports became so important that by 1887 the first African newspaper had a separate sports section, and mission-educated Africans organized and ran sports clubs, often using sports to emphasize their status.

Nonwhite (mostly Asian) rugby has a long tradition in South Africa. The first Coloured rugby club was founded in 1886 in Cape Town, where it became especially popular in the working-class neighborhoods of District Six and Bo-Kaap. In addition to white-imposed discrimination, there were internal differences within the community; the two rugby unions of Cape Town were divided along religious lines, one admitting Muslims, the other not. Both neighborhoods were famous for their rough, often violent and intimidating playing styles, but nonetheless the lively animosity that characterized the game did not spill over into everyday life: on the contrary the Coloured community of Cape Town united around this pastime.[14]

Starting in the 1960s, a number of organizations—such as SACOS (South African Council of Sport), SASA (South African Sports Association), and SANROC (South African Non-Racial Olympic Committee)—came into being to combat apartheid by insisting on mixed teams and free competitions between the various racial groups of the country. These and like bodies maintained until the end of apartheid the principle of "no normal sport in an abnormal society." The apartheid sports establishment, in response to increasing criticism of its segregationist practices both within and outside South Africa, attempted to sidestep the issue by inviting black and Coloured sports associations to join the minority white sports federations, albeit on an unequal and segregated basis. This policy change was meant to reassure the international community that South Africa sanctioned multiracial competitions (although actually allowing segregation to continue unabated). It also exemplified the apartheid regime's perpetual strategy of creating divisions among its opponents and in this it was partly successful: although joining the white federations played into the hands of the apartheid regime, some teams did join, tempted by the promise of attaining better facilities.

Apartheid finally ended in South Africa in 1994, with free elections in which, for the first time, the black majority elected a government that was representative of the population.

Although it cannot be said that the sports boycott was the prime reason for the ending of the apartheid regime, the boycott, and especially the isolation of South Africa from world rugby, played a significant role in delegitimizing apartheid and undermining the confidence of white South Africans in their segregationist way of life.

Along with the dismantling of other aspects of apartheid, the ending of segregation in sports has been a major task of the new South Africa. Different sports have followed different trajectories in this process: in all cases integration necessitated serious rethinking and restructuring of the practice of sports nationwide. The new South African government, like other African governments, saw sports as one of the ways in which an overarching sense of nationhood could be forged that would enable the hitherto bitterly opposed and artificially separated population of the country to feel as one. Given South Africa's history this is not an easy task and it remains to be seen whether temporary successes can be made permanent. Perhaps the most striking example of the unifying aspect of sports was provided by the 1995 Rugby World Championship (RWC), which took place in South Africa and gave rise to several touching moments. Although rugby (as we have seen) had been a preserve of white supremacist ideas, on this occasion the entire population of the country stood behind its team. This was symbolically expressed by Nelson Mandela when he appeared in a Springboks jersey and cap to show his support for the team in the final and acknowledged when, after South Africa had won the tournament, François Pienaar, the captain of the team, graciously thanked 42 million South Africans for their support. However, despite these examples of interracial harmony during the RWC, the long history of rugby as the emblem of Afrikaner ideology is hard to change, and complete desegregation of rugby is still to be achieved. The primary problem is that the ending of apartheid and the passing of power from whites to the majority population cannot in itself cure the inequalities created by apartheid and the racist practices that preceded it for 50 years and more. To truly overcome the underdevelopment of most sports among nonwhites, significant resources and a clearly thought-out plan for development are needed.

Botswana

The Southern African country of Botswana gained its independence from Britain in 1966. Unlike most African countries it is relatively homogeneous ethnically. Botswana is one of the few countries in Sub-Saharan Africa that has a solid reputation for democratic governance and a relatively high level of economic performance. The development of sports, however, has not kept pace with the general development of the country. Sports are not a priority of the government: consequently, and until recently, Botswana has not registered any significant results in the international sporting arena. Botswana's first medal in a continentwide competition came in 1991, and the first Botswanan sportsman to win a medal in a major international sports event was runner California Molefe, who won silver in the 400-meter race in the IAAF World Indoor Championship in Moscow in 2006.

The relative unimportance of sports in Botswana is also shown by the fact that the Department of Sports and Recreation, which is charged with coordinating sports activities in the country, is not an independent body but rather a department of the Ministry of Labour and Home Affairs. The Botswana National Sports Council, established in 1975, is the agency that is responsible for the development of sports activities and programs and acts as an intermediary between the government and the national sports associations. The lack of relative weight in the government and the division of powers between the different agencies contributes to the underdevelopment of sports in Botswana. Often there is conflict between the sports associations for available resources. The most popular sports in the country are soccer and softball, but other sports such as volleyball and boxing are also practiced. Despite the popularity of soccer and softball the national selections often must struggle to get sufficient funding to participate in international sports events. The scarce resources devoted to sports are not enough to develop infrastructures, especially in the countryside. Most of the resources devoted to sports for youth reach only youngsters who are in school and leave those who are unable to attend school without the option of practicing sports. Botswana does not have a clearly stated sports policy and characteristically the training of physical education teachers at the University of Botswana only began in 1993. In 1999 a draft sports policy document was presented to the government. In recent years the country's growing AIDS problem (Botswana has one of the highest rates of HIV infection on the continent) has put further strain on the availability of resources in the country.

East Africa

Kenya

Kenyan athletes have gained worldwide fame for their exploits in track and field, especially running. The East African nation of Kenya was colonized by Britain. As elsewhere in Africa, Western sports spread along the lines laid down in missionary and colonial schools, where the future elite of Kenya acquired the "games ethic." Kenyan sportsmen, despite their later prominence in running, showed promise in other disciplines during the 1950s, particularly in the high jump. However, since the late 1960s, Kenya and running have almost become synonymous in the world of sports. Kenyans, along with Ethiopian athletes, have dominated long-distance running, and the depth of athletic talent in Kenya in these disciplines is such that several Kenyan runners have felt it necessary to change their nationality to avoid the problem raised by regulations for international sporting events that limit the number of entrants from a given country.

Much has been written about the special characteristics of African runners, attributing their outstanding performance to innate physical superiority. It is true that Kenyan runners dominate world long-distance running, with a significant majority of them coming from a single region and within that region from a single ethnic group, the Nandi. Despite this, caution must be exercised in attributing biological explanations to Kenyan athletic success. One of the most commonly cited factors used to account for the superiority of Kenyan runners is that their living at a high altitude enables them to run faster than others who hail from lower altitudes; however, this explanation is invalidated by the fact that numerous other groups in the world live at similar altitudes without producing similar-caliber runners. Another common theme that comes up in attempts to explain Kenyan running success is that Kenyan children become habituated to long-distance running over the course of childhoods in which they regularly run to faraway schools. According to John Bale and Joe Sang, this is a myth: there are enough schools in Kenya to make this practice unlikely.[15] Finally, Kenyan runners are often presented as biologically or naturally endowed with talent that makes them superb runners; such an explanation is impossible to prove because genetic factors cannot be separated from cultural factors influencing athletic performance. All these explanations are reminiscent of attempts during the 1930s and 1940s to account for the sweeping success of Scandinavian runners at that time, who were also depicted as having achieved their results effortlessly because of either environmental or biological factors. These explanations leave out the role of culture and expectations in determining the way people choose a particular sport and discount the dedication and rigorous training of the athletes.[16]

The international success of Kenyan runners does not mean that the circumstances of local athletes have improved significantly over time and hides the underdevelopment of other sports in the country. Despite the international attention the runners attract, the most popular sport in Kenya is not running, but soccer.

This popularity makes a very different kind of engagement with sports possible in the activities of the Mathare Youth Sports Association (MYSA) of Nairobi, Kenya. Mathare is a Nairobi slum with a population of about 500,000, making it one of the largest slums in East Africa. Its inhabitants are very poor and live under very harsh conditions. The settlement lacks basic amenities: water, electricity, and organized garbage collection. Unemployment is very high among the residents and most people live from the informal economy, mostly petty trading.

MYSA was created in this community in 1987 on the initiative of a Canadian consultant, Bob Munro.[17] Visiting a Nairobi slum, he noticed children playing soccer and started an organization that would combine sports and community service. The children were given soccer balls in return for participating in the cleanup of the neighborhood. This was the seed from which grew an organization that mobilizes thousands of people around youth football teams and community service. In 15 years MYSA has developed an extensive league system of about 100 leagues with a combined total of 1,000 teams of players between the ages of 9 and 18. The leagues are organized into 16 zones with the activities of each zone run by an elected sport council and a community service council. The executive council of the entire organization is elected from among the members of these councils.

MYSA functions along the principles of community participation and discipline. Members participate in sports activities, but since the beginning, community service has been equally important. One of MYSA's main foci continues to be the environment, but over time they have branched out into other directions. They established a scholarship fund to help pay for school fees, and they started a photography project and a Website creation and design project. In the area of community service they have initiated the "Jail Kid Programme," which helps jailed children by visiting them, providing them with food, and attempting to contact their parents. Other activities include an AIDS counseling program through which the 300 trained volunteers disseminate information to their peers about AIDS prevention.

Initially, MYSA only recruited boys, but since 1992 about 200 girls' teams have also come into existence. Involving girls in the activities of the organization helps in a small way to transform gender relations. For example, when girls were first admitted into MYSA, the community service tasks they were given often were traditional female ones, but by working consciously on the issue, the division of labor within the organization has been reshaped. Currently, girls and boys participate equally in all kinds of activities from washing soccer jerseys to driving garbage pickup trucks.[18]

The organization is supported to a large extent by Western donors, but it is remarkable for the degree of local involvement in the organization and day-to-day running of the Association. This is partly due to the high level of motivation and involvement of the membership and the fact that many who have participated in the football program as children remain with the organization in various capacities when they get older. One of the ways in which this became possible is that a team of adult players, Mathare United, has been created that participates in the national football championship and cup competition. The team has done extremely well on the national scene, having won the national cup competition several times since 1998, and having risen to the first division in a few seasons. It was founded by former participants in MYSA and all players as well as the technical and administrative staff have been members of the Association, either as players or as organizers. This lends a great degree of cohesion to the team, and players continue to perform community service, such as AIDS counseling and other volunteer work. Altogether the players contribute 80 hours of community work per month.

Originally the team, just as the Association, was funded by Western donors, but with growing success on the field it has gained sponsorship from local Kenyan enterprises.

MYSA has been recognized internationally, winning several international awards. Their environmental work, in particular, serves as a model for other organizations all over the world. In 1992 they participated in the UN Earth Summit on Environment and Development in Rio de Janeiro, where they were awarded the UNEP (United Nations Environmental Programme) Global 500 Award. In 2003 they won the Dutch Prince Claus Prize for their successful combination of confidence-building sports activity with environmental responsibility. They were nominated for the Nobel Peace Prize twice, in 2003 and 2004. In 2006 MYSA's team won the first Street Football World Cup, which was held in Germany during the FIFA World Cup.

Ethiopia

As mentioned previously, the other East African country famed for its runners is Ethiopia. Ethiopia was the only country in Africa (aside from Liberia) not to have been colonized by Europeans. Modern sports organization began in 1928, followed by a spread of sports clubs, which led to the establishment of the Ethiopian School Sport Association in 1938 and the National Sports Federation in 1940. The best sportsmen of the country were absorbed into the armed forces or the police, which provided them with better-than-average training opportunities and standard of living. This was the case for the marathon runner, Abebe Bikila, who was a member of the Imperial Guard of Emperor Haile Selassie. In 1960, at the Rome Olympics, Bikila became the first black African to win an Olympic gold medal with a world-best result. The memory of Bikila entering the Rome stadium barefoot has been etched into the minds of all those who saw it. Bikila immediately became a national hero in his native country and inspired many to emulate his example. He repeated this performance (in shoes this time) in the 1964 Tokyo Olympics, even though 6 weeks before the competition he underwent an appendectomy. When he died in 1973, following a tragic car accident four years earlier, thousands gathered to see his funeral procession. Other Ethiopian runners followed his example and along with the Kenyans they have dominated long-distance running events in the international arena. Among the most prominent have been Haile Gebreselassie, Kenenisa Bekele, and Derartu Tulu.

From 1974 to 1991 Ethiopia had a Marxist government and was under Soviet influence. The USSR provided aid in the form of sports equipment and the construction of sports facilities. It also sent coaches to Ethiopia and organized joint training sessions with Soviet sportsmen in the USSR. The earlier tendency to draft the best athletes into army sports clubs continued during the Marxist period and practically all of the top players were to be found in these clubs. Following the overthrow of the Marxist regime sports administration in the country was revamped. A National Sport Committee replaced the earlier structures in 1996 and is charged with overseeing the organization and development of sports in the country. Ethiopia remains a poor country, and since the end of communism much of the external funding the country received has dried up. The slack has only been partially taken up by the International Olympic Committee's Solidarity Fund and a few private companies.

CONCLUSION

There are commonalities across the continent in how Africa has fared in the postcolonial period: these are dictated primarily by political and economic conditions. Politics in Africa are frequently characterized by a lack of functioning democratic institutions and by autocratic governments that often do not hold the interests of the citizenry at heart. The resulting mismanagement and corruption determine people's lives and opportunities significantly. This, along with the unequal economic relationship of African countries to the developed world, contributes greatly to the poverty and underdevelopment prevailing on the continent. These circumstances are both reflected and reproduced in sports. They are evident in the deterioration or lack of adequate sports facilities and equipment, a chronic lack of funds for sports participation, and pervasive corruption on all levels. Often the success of a handful of athletes serves to hide the shortcomings of sports organizations and facilities and the harsh circumstances under which athletes, especially below the elite level, train.

Governments regularly try to take advantage of sports victories to forge national unity and to gain popularity and legitimacy. Sports do contribute to the development of national consciousness because national teams and individual athletes render the abstract idea of the nation concrete and are seen to symbolically stand for the nation in Africa, just as everywhere else in the world. With regard to political co-optation—because the majority of Africans are enthusiastic about sports and take great pride in the exploits of their athletes—to some degree this strategy works, but people are often able to see through the rhetoric of their leaders and can, and do, challenge them by attributing different meanings to victories or losses than those suggested by their governments.

International sports competitions are one of the few areas in which Africans can realistically feel equal or superior to the West. This is so despite that, due to underdevelopment, African athletes must prepare under conditions that are inferior to those of their counterparts in the developed world. But this structural inequality often motivates African athletes to do even better and sports victories take on great symbolic significance for their supporters, representing the triumph of the underdog. This is especially the case when the formerly colonized peoples meet the former colonizers in the sports arena.

The other reason international sports have great significance for Africans is that many athletes are inspired and motivated to surpass themselves because they see sports as one of the only avenues for breaking out of poverty. In recent years there has been an exodus of African sports talent to other parts of the world. Many African sportsmen and sportswomen seek their fortune as professionals abroad or even as naturalized citizens of other countries. Although this practice can perpetuate the underdevelopment of sports in their home countries, as long as the remuneration and training conditions are significantly better abroad than in Africa, athletes will continue to leave the continent.

RESOURCE GUIDE

PRINT SOURCES

Alegi, Peter. *Laduma! Soccer, Politics and Society in South Africa.* Scottsville: University of KwaZulu-Natal Press, 2004.

Armstrong, Gary, and Richard Giulianotti, eds. *Entering the Field: New Perspectives on World Football.* Oxford: Berg, 1997.

———. *Football in Africa: Conflict, Conciliation and Community.* New York: Palgrave Macmillan, 2004.

Baker, William, and James Mangan, eds. *Sport in Africa: Essays in Social History.* New York: Africana Publishing, 1987.

Bale, John, and Joe Sang. *Kenyan Running: Movement Culture, Geography and Global Change.* London: Frank Cass, 1996.

Black, David R., and John Nauright. *Rugby and the South African Nation.* Manchester, UK: Manchester University Press, 1998.

Brady, Martha, and Arjmand Banu Khan. *Letting Girls Play: The Mathare Youth Sports Association's Football Program for Girls.* New York: Population Council, 2002.

Broere, Marc, and Roy van der Drift. *Football Africa!* Translated by John Smith and Philip Watson. Oxford: WorldView Publishing, 1997.

Clignet, Remi, and Maureen Stark. "Modernisation and Football in Cameroun." *Journal of Modern African Studies.* 12.3 (1974): 409–421.

Darby, Paul. *Africa, Football, and FIFA: Politics, Colonialism, and Resistance.* London/Portland: Frank Cass, 2002.

———. "Africa, the FIFA Presidency and the Governance of World Football: 1974, 1998, and 2002," *Africa Today* 50.1 (2003): 3–24.

Fair, Laura. *Pastimes and Politics: Culture, Community, and Identity in Post-Abolition Urban Zanzibar, 1890–1945.* Athens and Oxford: Ohio University Press and James Currey, 2001.

Faye, Osseynou. "Sport, Argent et Politique: La Lutte Libre à Dakar." Pp. 309–340 in Momar-Coumba Diop (ed.), *Le Sénégal Contemporain.* Paris: Karthala, 2002.

Guttmann, Allen. *From Ritual to Record: The Nature of Modern Sports.* New York: Columbia University Press, 1978.

Kenyatta, Jomo. *Facing Mount Kenya.* New York: Vintage Books, 1965.

Leseth, Anne. "Michezo: Dance, Sport and Politics in Dar-es-Salaam, Tanzania." Pp. 231–247 in Eduardo P. Archetti and Noel Dyck (eds.), *Sport, Dance and Embodied Identities.* Oxford: Berg, 2003.

Martin, Phyllis M. *Leisure and Society in Colonial Brazzaville.* Cambridge: Cambridge University Press, 1995.

Saavedra, Martha. "Football Feminine—Development of the African Game: Senegal, Nigeria and South Africa." *Soccer and Society* 4.2–3 (2003): 225–253.

Vidacs, Bea. "The Postcolonial and the Level Playing Field in the 1998 World Cup." Pp. 147–158 in John Bale and Mike Cronin (eds.), *Postcolonialism and Sport.* Oxford: Berg, 2003.

WEBSITES

All Africa.com. Accessed August 24, 2006. http://allafrica.com/sport/. Provides a selection of sports-related news from all over the continent.

Athletics Africa.Com. Accessed August 24, 2006. http://www.AthleticsAfrica.Com. Maintained by Yomog Sports Media Company, Lagos, Nigeria. Provides sports-related news primarily from English-speaking countries.

Mots Pluriels. 1998. Accessed August 24, 2006. http://www.arts.uwa.edu.au/MotsPluriels/MP698 index.html. A special issue of *Mots Pluriels*, electronic journal (University of Western Australia) dedicated to soccer in Africa; guest editor: André Ntonfo (in French and English).

Sports in Africa: A Partnership for African Sports. Accessed August 23, 2006. http://www.ohiou.edu/sportsafrica/. This Website hosted by Ohio University gives access to *Impumelelo*, Interdisciplinary Electronic Journal of African Sport (Athens, Ohio), and to sports-related information on the continent from a social science perspective.

FILMS

The Ball (Mozambique, 2001). Directed by Orlando Mesquita; 5 minutes.

Le Ballon d'Or [The Golden Ball] (Guinea, 1994). Directed by Cheik Doukouré; 90 minutes.

Fintar o destino [Dribbling Fate] (Cape Verde, Portugal, 1998). Directed by Fernando Vendrell; 77 minutes.

Mr. Foot (Cameroon, 1991). Directed by Jean-Marie Teno; 20 minutes.

The Penalty Area (South Africa, 1993). Directed by Clifford Bestall; 26 minutes.

Yellow Card (Zimbabwe, 2000). Directed by John Riber; 90 minutes.

EVENTS

African Nations Cup (football). http://www.cafonline.org. Organized by the Confederation Africaine de Football. Held biennially since 1957 at differing venues, usually at the end of January or beginning of February.

All Africa Games. Also known as the Pan African Games, it is a multisport event held every 4 years on the continent since 1965 at varying venues.

Commonwealth Games. http://www.commonwealthgames.com. A multisport competition held every 4 years for the athletes of the Commonwealth of Nations, which is an association of Great Britain and its former colonial possessions. The Games have never been held on African soil.

Jeux de la Francophonie (Francophone Games). http://jeux.francophonie.org. A multisport competition held every 4 years for athletes from French-speaking countries. In 1994 and 2005 it took place in Sub-Saharan Africa (Madagascar and Niger, respectively). In addition to sporting events it also comprises a cultural competition with such categories as painting, literature, and dance.

ORGANIZATIONS

Confederation of African Athletics. http://www.webcaa.org. Stade Léopold Sédar Senghor, Route de Yoff, B.P. 88, Dakar, Senegal.

Confederation of African Football. http://www.cafonline.com. 3 Abdel Khalek Tharwat Street, El Hay El Motamayez, P.O. Box 23, 6th October City, Egypt.

Let's Kick Racism Out of Football. http://www.kickitout.org. Kick It Out, P.O. Box 29544, London, EC2A 4WR United Kingdom.

Mathare Youth Sports Association. http://www.mysakenya.org. Box 69038, Nairobi 00622, Kenya.

NOTES

1. Leseth 2002 (in Resource Guide).
2. Guttmann 1978 (in Resource Guide), pp. 15–55.
3. Kenyatta 1965 (in Resource Guide), pp. 134–135.
4. Alegi 2004 (in Resource Guide), pp. 32–34.
5. Fair 2001 (in Resource Guide), p. 236.
6. Ibid., p. 231.
7. Martin 1995 (in Resource Guide), p. 105.
8. Saavedra 2003 (in Resource Guide), p. 237.
9. Darby 2003 (in Resource Guide).
10. Paul Richards, "Soccer and Violence in War-Torn Africa: Soccer and Social Rehabilitation in Sierra Leone," in Armstrong and Giulianotti 1997 (in Resource Guide), pp. 141–157.
11. Faye 2002 (in Resource Guide).
12. Wiebe Boer, "The Story of Heroes, of Epics: The Rise of Football in Nigeria," in Armstrong and Giulianotti 2004 (in Resource Guide), pp. 59–79.
13. Enyimo, Martin. "Imminence de la reorganization du football congolais," *Le Potentiel* [Kinshasa] (2006, April 8). Accessed August 20, 2006. http://fr.allafrica.com/stories/200604100060.html.
14. Black and Nauright 1998 (in Resource Guide), pp. 47–55.
15. Bale and Sang 1996 (in Resource Guide), p. 155.
16. Ibid., pp. 138–162.
17. Hans Hognestad and Arvid Tollisen, "Playing Against Deprivation: Football and Development in Nairobi, Kenya," in Armstrong and Giulianotti 2004 (in Resource Guide), pp. 210–226.
18. Brady and Khan 2002 (in Resource Guide).

THEATER AND PERFORMANCE

UBONG SAMUEL NDA

"The performing arts" is a wide-embracing expression that encompasses drama, song, dance, and even storytelling. Theater and performance in Sub-Saharan Africa have been culture based. Performing arts in Africa have been veritable reflections of the cultures of the various peoples that make up the subcontinent. These artistic expressions have been encapsulations of the social thoughts, beliefs, and value systems of the people of the region. Paul Edwards cites Equaino as saying of the continent: "We are almost a nation of dancers, musicians, and poets."[1]

As an integral part of the people's way of life, performing arts in Africa do not possess the kind of conscious detachment that can be experienced in Western theater. Comparing the African verbal art of Ghana with Western drama, Charles Angmor states that indigenous drama is "the product of conscious art because it is generally a series of established customary or spontaneous acts. It does not operate as a rule on conflict and its resolution, but generally in consensus and consummation."[2] Performing arts in Sub-Saharan Africa are well embedded within the cultural matrix of the people. Its production is not based on a performer–audience divide, but as Adrian Roscoe puts it, one in which the "entire community is the cast and the village square the stage."[3]

Recent History of Theater and Performance in Africa

Drama, song, and dance in Sub-Saharan Africa have undergone three basic stages of existence. The first was the precolonial stage, when these indigenous cultural forms were in their original and authentic state. At this stage, they could only have been affected by some cross-cultural influences from other clans and neighboring ethnic communities. Many artistic performances in the region experienced modifications in content and style through such transfers. But it must be noted that such influences, as long as they were within the African worldview, did not have profound negative impacts on these forms. Rather, they enriched the aesthetic contents and accentuated the symbolic functionalities of these works.

By contrast, the colonial period was one of great upheaval on the African indigenous performance scene. Not only did the performances experience distortions and serious modifications that have affected them in form, content, and style; most of them also lost the sacredness of their enactments. Tar Ahura bemoans a situation where "the masquerade tradition among the Tiv started as a religious ritual but due to historical changes based on actual historical experiences . . . masquerade enactment[s] have shaken off the religious yoke and have become completely secular in content and purpose."[4] The postcolonial stage has not fared better, as it has been characterized by attempts to adapt these performances into forms that could suit the nuances of Western performance models. Not only have some of them been divested of their sociopolitical functions; a great number of them have now been taken from their natural performance venues to other stages and media in a bid to remodel them for other social contexts.

In spite of this historical intervention, indigenous theater and performance in Sub-Saharan Africa, especially those artistic expressions with fewer religiopolitical features, have been able to withstand the erosional forces of colonialism and Western culture. To their credit, the people have striven to preserve the essence, and in some cases the aesthetic authenticity, of these performances, even though their spirit and ritualistic significance may have been lost.

Interestingly, recent trends in the theater industry in the region have shown a revaluation of performance, in terms of taking the arts back to their original status—that of providing avenues for teaching societal morality. African theater was not merely for entertainment. It had indisputable social functions because, according to Bakary Traore, it was a "mirror of life. Every event is recorded therein."[5] Wole Soyinka further states that in Africa, "the artist has always functioned . . . as the record of the mores and experiences of his society and as the voice of vision in his own time."[6]

But the colonial period and the early years of the postcolonial era seem to have restricted the theater and its performances to the provision of entertainment for visiting dignitaries and fanfares at government ceremonies, divesting them of their great social functions. But in recent years, the emergence of the concept of theater for development (TFD) or community theater has led to the employment of performances, even in their adapted forms, for the developmental education of the people. Thus, the theater and indigenous performances of Sub-Saharan Africa, although having lost much in spiritual essence, seem to have regained much of their original relevance in relationship to the people.

The establishment of government and mission schools led to the emergence of Western–style proscenium concerts and plays in Africa. And, in Nigeria, it led to the rise of a new era of Nigerian theater exponents in the likes of James Ene Henshaw, Wole Soyinka, John Pepper Clark, and Ola Rotimi.

The University System and African Theater

The university system has been a crucial exponent of theater and performance in Africa. In Nigeria, apart from the triumvirate of Soyinka, Clark-Bekederemo, and Rotimi, the Nigerian universities have provided a beehive of artistic activities and provided opportunities for the emergence and success of another generation of great playwrights, directors, and actors. It is noteworthy that some of these "next" generation artists have been critical of their predecessors' treatment of the class structures within the African socioeconomic milieu. Prominent among these have been Femi Osofisan, whose socialist inclination has led to radical works such as *No More The Wasted Breed* (1982), *The Chattering and the Song* (1982), *Another Raft* (1989), *Yungba Yungba* (1993), and *The Dance Contest* (1993). About twenty-five universities in Nigeria offer degrees in performance-related courses at the undergraduate and postgraduate levels, and the production of plays, research, and experimentation in performance have been of great interest to these departments. Indeed, the theater departments of some of these universities, with their publicly acclaimed productions, have been valuable tools for engendering "town and gown" symbiosis between the institutions and their locations.

In Ghana, Efua T. Sutherland, the foremost of the nation's playwrights in the early post-independence years and an associate of Ghana's Pan-Africanist President Kwame Nkumah, started the Ghana Drama studio (an open-air performance venue) in 1957 in a bid to provide an incubating facility for budding playwrights and an avenue for the production of their works. She also assisted in the establishment of the School of Music and Drama in the University of Ghana in Legon as a center for experimentation and research in traditional cultural forms.

The Lubumbashi University in the Democratic Republic of the Congo has also done a great service to the performing arts through research into traditional theater forms and their performance techniques. The university's performing company, Catharsis, has devoted itself to the creation of plays with an indigenous base.

Again, in Uganda, as in most other countries studied, during the colonial period, government-sponsored drama competitions for schools and voluntary groups provided a boost to the performing arts. And at the higher educational level, Makerere University, through its dramatic society, which handled the first production of Ngugi wa Thiong'o's *The Black Hermit*, later ventured into the establishment of a Department of Drama, Music and Dance (which offered both undergraduate and graduate programs).

Governmentally owned establishments have also aided the development of theater and performance in Africa. In Nigeria, the governments of the thirty-one states have established Councils for Arts and Culture and sponsored viable performing companies that have ensured the survival of theatre and performance in the various states. The National Festival of Arts and Culture, a biennial assemblage of all the states to compete in the arts and culture-related events, has also boosted the performing arts in Nigeria. Apart from the National Theatre in Igannu, Lagos, various theater and multipurpose halls suitable for theater productions have sprung up in different parts of the country, providing venues for performances by resident and touring troupes.

In the Congo (later Zaire, now the Democratic Republic of the Congo), in 1965, the establishment of the national theater—the Theatre National Congolais—created an avenue for the production of plays by Congolese playwrights, notable among whom have been Guy Menga. Menga's plays include *The Oracle* (1968). Seven years after independence, the Mobutu government established the National Institute for Arts, which assumed the role of national theater.

In Kenya, a national theater was established in Nairobi by the colonial government in 1952. Even after independence, this theater continued under the control of, and was conducted in the interest of, the white settlers. But in 1968, Seth Adagala, a native Kenyan, was appointed as head of this theater. Adagala worked for the establishment of a drama school attached to the National Theatre, with the purpose of training professionals and performing plays that could be taken on tour to various locations.

The educational sector also did much to accelerate performance development. Schools were made to take part in drama festivals in which plays selected from the school curriculum were performed in competitions. Also, Nairobi University embarked on intensive research into indigenous forms and encouraged their fusion into their productions.

Uganda has a national theater, which was built in 1959, with a drama school established in 1963. The theater scene, which had witnessed tremendous growth in the early post-independence years with the productions of the National Theatre, the Free Traveling Theatre scheme of Makerere University, and the rise of other theater groups, soon faced a downward trend during the latter years of the Obote regime and throughout the Idi Amin totalitarian era. Indeed, many artistes who would not compromise their artistic muse with sycophantic political expedience were killed or forced into exile. There has, however, been a revival of theater activities over the last several decades.

In 1969, the University of Zambia established a Department of Drama and followed in 1971 with the Chikwakwa Theatre. Chikwakwa embarked on the vigorous production of plays based on indigenous culture and toured various parts of the country with them. The rehearsals were conducted in English, but the plays were presented in the language of the host community. This was an indigenous theater project through which local communities were assisted in developing their performance forms. This popularization of theater and performance led to the formation of the Zambian Theatre Arts Association and the emergence of other theater companies. One of them, the Theatre Circle (led by David Wallace), produced plays based on the local storytelling tradition. Another, the Kanyama Theatre, one of the professional troupes that sprang up in the 1980s, toured Zambia and other South African countries with its productions.

As already observed regarding many other African countries, the universities have been a remarkable launching pad for theater development. This has also been true of South Africa. For example, the theater department of the University of Zululand conducted a review of its curriculum to reflect the need for scholarship, at both the theoretical and practical levels, in indigenous performance. And as language barriers continued to constitute a bane for widespread understanding of indigenous performances, the dance form has become an increasingly important medium.

Community Theater

Another major development on the African performance scene has been the emergence of the "theater for development" or "community theater." In Nigeria, it started at the Ahmadu Bello University in Zaria in the 1980s as an attempt to use the social performances of the various communities—their representations of popular culture—as functional outlets of development information. Its foremost exponent has been Oga Steve Abah (of Ahmadu Bello University). This trend has spread to other universities and constitutes a major area of creativity among Nigerian university scholars.

Theater for development has also found great success in Zambia. The formation of the Zambian Popular Theatre Alliance in 1991 was the high point of the effort to employ the attractive and didactic propensities of the theater for the purpose of stimulating the development of the rural areas. The government of Zambia, in acknowledgment of the efforts by individuals and private organizations to promote Zambian culture through the theater, and in an attempt to consolidate these gains, established the Zambian Arts Council in 1994.

Also in southern Africa, in Zimbabwe a National Dance Company, established a year after independence, coordinated the national quest for the revival, preservation, and development of native dances.

Growing out of the ashes of the liberation struggle, the theater for development became a popular concept in Zimbabwe. Two of those who worked with Ngugi wa Thiong'o in the Kamariithu project in Kenya—Ngugi wa Mirii and Kimani Gecau—were hired by the Zimbabwean Ministry of Education and Culture to initiate and nurture the community theater program in the country. The theater for development methodology was so widely accepted that it attracted the hosting of a UNESCO-sponsored international workshop on this subject in Zimbabwe in 1983. A Zimbabwe Association of Community Theatre was formed in 1987, and a drama department was established at the University of Zimbabwe in 1984. Soon, this academic outfit became a leader in community theater activities in the country. As has been the case in many other African countries, school concerts with songs, sketches, and dances grew alongside the early attempts at the publishing and production of church-based plays by African artists. Adult performing groups such as Ama-Kwaya developed a repertory of concert features that they used in staging shows in churches and town halls. In the urban centers, groups of young talented singers got together to form troupes, some of which were influenced by black American musical groups.

PUPPETS AGAINST AIDS

One of the major preoccupations of the theater industry in South Africa since the attainment of majority rule has been the fight against HIV/AIDS. South Africa is one of the countries seriously hit by the spread of the virus and the theater has risen to the social challenge of providing information on the scourge. One of the programs in this direction has been "Puppets Against AIDS," initiated by the African Research and Educational Puppetry Program. It puts on the performance of sketches by manipulated puppets, with a narration that matches the action. The most popular and internationally recognized of such South African puppetry troupes is the Handspring Puppet Company, which was founded by Adrian Kohler and Basil Jones in 1981.

Videos and Theater Performance

The most recent development on the African theater scene has been the video film. In Nigeria, the high cost of film production did not deter practitioners of the Yoruba traveling theater, especially Ogunde and Adejumo (see Nigeria subsection), from venturing into film production. Their productions, mostly based on Yoruba folklore, became box office successes, causing pioneer film producers in Nigeria such as Eddie Ugbomah to change course and adopt the "Yoruba film tradition." Also at this time, Peter Igbo's success with the Nigerian Television Authority's *Cockcrow at Dawn* and the serialization of Chinua Achebe's *Things Fall Apart* on television inspired the production of various soap operas on national television. The success of this chain of events, especially given the use of video production facilities, motivated the emergence of video films. Many other artists and entrepreneurs have come out with works that have attracted great viewership and newspaper reviews. In his book *Nigerian Video Films*, Jonathan Haynes describes video films as "dramatic features shot on video and marketed on cassettes, and sometimes also exhibited publicly with video projectors or television monitors . . . [that] are being produced at a rate of nearly one a day."[7] He adds that the video boom is

> paradoxically, a consequence of general economic collapse, and the video effects reflect the ambient poverty; made on tiny budgets with insufficient equipment, training, and rehearsal, the quality of most of the videos is, it must be admitted, low. They provide little of the usual poetry of true cinema. But in the aggregate they contain a staggering amount of narrative energy.[8]

Moreover, he points out that "only the daily press rivals the videos as a medium for telling the story of Nigeria in the 1990s."[9]

Afolabi Adesanya traces this phenomenon (where it has gained prominence and has spread to other West African countries) to the failure of the conventional film industry and the problem of poor financing. It reflects a creative attempt to circumvent these barriers and forge a viable means of motion picture production:

> This happened in the mid-70s when, in spite of positive reviews, English language feature films by Nigerian film makers were not making the desired impact to stimulate constant market demand both at home and abroad. Ola Balogun's box office hit *Ajani Ogun*, which opened the flood gates, gave the much-needed impetus to local film production and led to a new career for travelling theatre troupes.[10]

This industry has witnessed such a boom that it has now been nicknamed "Nollywood," an acronym for Nigeria's Hollywood. Its products are popular all over West Africa and are well received by African audiences in various parts of Europe and America because they engage in the vivid capturing and representation of life in Nigeria.

Elsewhere, in East Africa, the theater for development method of communicating positive change became very popular in Tanzania in the 1970s. Its major exponents were Penina Mlama and Amandina Lihamba. Mlama, a former head of the Department of Theatre at the University of Dar es Salaam, has abandoned written scripts for indigenous expressions in her theater for development activities.

In West Africa, the establishment of French cultural centers in African colonies such as Senegal furthered theatrical development because these centers organized yearly drama contests in which the winners in each colony qualified for wider competitions. The competitive spirit they engendered continued even after independence because regional drama contests were held as part of the annual youth festivals.

In 1965, the Daniel Sorano National Theatre was established in Dakar, Senegal, under the leadership of Maurice Senghor, a relative of the nation's then-president, the poet Leopold Sedar Senghor. And in 1966, Senegal's striving for the preservation and promotion of African arts was recognized and rewarded with the hosting right for the first-ever Festival of African Arts and Culture. The country went on to be awarded the first Pan African Cultural Festival in Algiers.

In Cameroon, there has been a department of drama at the University of Yaounde, one of whose lecturers is Guillaume Oyani-Mbia. This artist, who had also once served as a minister in government, has to his credit plays such as *Three Suitors, One Husband* (1964), *Until Further Notice* (1970), *One Daughter Must Not Marry* (1971), *His Excellency's Special Train* (1979), and *Le Boubier* (1989). His plays are always created in both English and French to cater to the bilingual nature of the country.

REGIONAL SUBSECTIONS

It must be noted that although the zonal areas of Sub-Saharan Africa are divided into sovereign geopolitical entities (nations), ownership of theatrical activities cannot be ascribed to them. This is because these countries, products of the late nineteenth century Western scramble for Africa, witnessed the indiscriminate lumping together of "multiple language and ethnic groups within a single administrative territory . . ." (as Brocket and Hildy have aptly described it).[11] For instance, it is difficult to talk of a Nigerian song in the true sense of the term because the theatrical performance, primarily and essentially, belongs to the ethnic nationality from which culture it is derived. However, in the treatment of the indigenous forms from countries that constitute the zones of the subcontinent, this chapter shall strive to limit them to their countries and only refer to their ethnic origins (as the need arises) to portray their cultural significance.

West Africa

Nigeria

Nigeria, the most populous nation in Africa, is made up of more than 250 ethnic groups. Prior to colonialism, it was, in the words of Brocket and Hildy, "the site of several kingdoms"—and each of these ethnic kingdoms had performance traditions in dance, music, initiation rites, coronations, betrothals, the burial of dignitaries, and storytelling. Some of these expressions have been preserved till today, although in culturally adulterated states.

Yemi Ogunbiyi reports "the existence in many Nigerian societies of a robust theatrical tradition."[12] He further states that the "origins of the Nigerian theatre and drama lie in the numerous traditional, religious, and functional rituals to be found in practically every Nigerian society."[13]

One of the hotbeds of these activities has been the western part of Nigeria, the location of the Yoruba-speaking people. A highly artistic people with a rich cultural heritage, the polytheistic nature of their traditional religion provided for the celebration of many festivals in honor of their many gods and deities.

In the precolonial days, the egungun masquerade and its wandering troupes were prominent features in the Yoruba traditional theater scene. And from the egungun performance emerged the Alarinjo, the traditional traveling theater that became very popular among the Yoruba. Notable among the practitioners were Hubert Ogunde, Kola Ogunmola, and Duro Ladipo.[14]

As Christianity grew rapidly in the Yoruba west of Nigeria, dissatisfaction with traditional theater practice increased. As an alternative, church and secular concerts were staged to entertain the emerging elites and the European colonists. These concerts were tailored after the operatic performances of British and other European theaters. It is interesting that apart from the Alarinjo tradition, the concert party constituted another profound influence on Ogunde's productions. Indeed, his first play, *The Garden of Eden and the Throne of God* (1944), was staged for the benefit of the members of his church. As Ogunde launched his troupe into political commentary through the theater, his productions gained secularity. Thus, his *Strike and Hunger* (1945), a dramatic commentary on the plight of workers, was taken on a tour of various locations. *Yoruba Ronu* (1964), written and performed after independence, attacked the disunity foisted upon the Yoruba nation by political fragmentation and selfish political maneuvers. Ogunde's troupe performed more than 38 operas between 1944 and 1972.[15] He also pioneered the formation of the Association of Theatre Practitioners, and he worked for the formation of the National Troupe of Nigeria, of which he was the first director.

In the course of Ogunde's ascendancy, there also emerged other important theater artists in the Yoruba west. These include Duro Ladipo, whose operas *The Ghost Catcher* (1962) and *The King Did Not Hang* (1964) gained tremendous acceptance. There was also Moses Adejumo, who staged comic theatrical shows built around a comic figure—"Baba Sala." Whereas Duro Ladipo founded the Mbari-Mbayo Centre, a theater in which he also engaged in the training of artists, Adejumo is credited with the formation of the Alawada theater, a performing troupe that became very popular in Yoruba communities.

A major fallout from the concert tradition was the emergence of plays in the English language. The Glover Memorial Hall, which opened in Lagos in 1899, became the center for the production of plays based on Western culture. The first Nigerian play to be staged at the hall was D. A. Oloyede's *King Ejejigho and Princess Abeje of Kotangora* (1904). It is to the credit of mission schools that proscenium-staged halls such as Glover Memorial Hall were replicated through school assembly halls, and consequently young Nigerian men and women were brought up in the performance of Western masterpieces, especially those of

William Shakespeare. The product of this effort was the emergence of a new crop of theater artists and the beginning of another era in Nigerian theater.

It must be mentioned that although there was a flourishing of performance in traditional theater in precolonial and colonial times in the Yoruba nation, such was also experienced in the Ijaw nation of the Niger Delta among the Igbos and Efiks of the southeast and south, among the Tiv in the grasslands of Nigeria's Middle Belt, and among the Hausa and Fulani in the desert north. In each of these communities, the pure, unadulterated performances of the precolonial era experienced value modifications as a result of Western (and Islamic) influences and thus gave birth to their contemporary forms—a blend of the past with the irresistible aspects of the present. Commenting on Ekong, a popular performance format among the Ibibio of Akwa Ibom State in the south of Nigeria, Yemi Ogunbiyi states:

> The successful production of a performance depends largely on the joint effort of a team of professional actors who have to memorize their lines [and] rehearse them; a large orchestra whose instruments consist of slit gongs [and] hollow wooden drums; a team of community members who construct an arena-type stage, complete with dressing rooms; and the carver whose duty is to provide the props required for the performances.[16]

Elaborating on the Ekong performance, Ogunbiyi further states:

> The dominant features of Ekong are the skits and sketches which exploit family and social tensions, social types, behaviour types and disapproved individuals . . . Ekong also seeks, through the plays and songs, to impose a pervasive social control, not only over persons, kinship and political groups, but also over foreign missions and governments.[17]

The most prolific of the theater practitioners of this generation in Nigeria has been Wole Soyinka. Educated at the universities of Ibadan and Leeds, he had a professional experience at the Royal Court Theatre in London before returning to Nigeria to found a performing group known as the 1960 Masks. His first notable play was *A Dance of the Forests* (1960), a prophetic statement on the uncertainty of the then newly independent nation. Other plays from his stable include *The Trials of Brother Jero* (1964), *The Lion and the Jewel* (1964), *Kongi's Harvest* (1967), *The Bacchae of Euripides* (1973), *Death and the King's Horseman* (1975), *Opera Wonyosi* (1977), *A Play of Giants* (1985), *The Beatification of Area Boy* (1994), and *Document of Identity* (1999). His prowess in the literary and performance arts was internationally recognized when he was awarded the Nobel Prize for Literature in 1986. In *A Dance of the Forests*, Soyinka's futuristic look into Nigeria's turbulent independence period, there is a great feast of the tribes where the gods, instead of sending a grand delegation, send two accusers to predict a fearful future—which indeed was what happened to the newly independent nation in the Biafran War.

There is also J. P. Clark, now known as John Pepper Clark-Bekedereno, a contemporary of Soyinka who has made waves regionally and internationally with plays based on the culture of the Ijaw people of the Niger Delta. His plays include *Song of a Goat* (1964); *Masquerade* (1964); *The Raft* (1964); *Ozidi* (1966), based on a popular Ijaw mythological epic; *The Bikoroa Plays* (1981); and *The Wives Revolt* (1985).

Also in this set of notable Nigerian theater practitioners is Ola Rotimi, who like Soyinka and Clark-Bekederemo also rose in the professorial ranks (in teaching and research in the performing arts). Rotimi started at Yale University before returning home in 1968 to found the Ori Olokun Acting Company. He first drew public attention with his adaptation of the Greek classic *Oedipus Rex* by Sophocles into his native Yoruba language. The play was entitled *The Gods Are Not to Blame*. At his death in 2002, Rotimi had written and produced plays such as *Kurum* (1969), *Ovonranwen Nogbaisi* (1971), *If . . . The Tragedy of the Ruled* (1971), and *Hopes of the Living Dead* (1988).

Apart from the Society of Nigerian Theatre Artists (SONTA), which draws its membership from theater academicians and researchers, there is also the National Association of Nigerian Theatre Arts Practitioners (NANTAP), which caters to practicing artists. Also, the Nigerian video film industry has three major guilds that take care of the interests of actors, directors, and technical crew members.

Ghana

Ghana has been another interesting location for the expression of theater and performance in Sub-Saharan Africa. A former British colony that gained independence in 1957, it became at that time a launching pad for independence struggle activities for various other countries in the subcontinent.

Similar to Nigeria, Ghana is multiethnic and, according to Brocket and Hildy, has "a rich heritage of indigenous performance, especially dance-drama, storytelling, and ceremonies."[18]

The Ghanian concert party, similar to Yoruba operatic performances, has had a tremendous influence on theater and performance in the country. The emergence of the concert party could be credited to a school headmaster, Mr. Yalley, who, in 1918, started holding "mixed grill" concerts with dances, jokes, and songs during British Empire Day celebrations. This tradition was taken a step further by Bob Johnson, Yalley's former pupil, who increased the scope of the concert performance to include silent films and stories based on the traditional Ghanaian *anansesem* (spider) storytelling repertories.

The concert/operatic experience as well as the cantata renditions of clubs and organizations of the early Ghanaian churches (that were offshoots of European models) soon led to more literary productions. Kobina Sekyi's *The Blinkards* (1915) and J. B. Danguah's *The Third Woman* (1943) were the first attempts at literary productions by native Ghanaians. This era soon led to the post-independence period, which could be described as the "golden age" of Ghanaian theater and performance. It is interesting that, unlike the nearly all-male experience in the Nigerian scene at that time, the Ghanaian performance scene was pioneered by the efforts of two female playwrights, Efua T. Sutherland and Ama Ata Aidoo. In an effort to preserve and showcase the storytelling tradition of Ghana, Sutherland worked for the establishment of the "story house," known in local parlance as *Kadzidan*, with a space that suited the natural venues for storytelling in the Ghanaian mold. Prominent among her works are *Edufa* (1962), *Foriwa* (1962), and *The Marriage of Anansewa* (1975). *Edufa*—one of Sutherland's best works—shows how an emerging rich Ghanaian manipulates his wife to die in his place because of his craving for life and riches.

Ama Ata Adidoo worked with Efua Sutherland at the Ghana Drama Studio. Her plays include *The Dilemma of a Ghost* (1964) and *Anowa* (1970). Other prominent performing artists of the literary tradition have included Joe C. de Graft, with *Sons and Daughters* (1964), *Through a Film Darkly* (1966), and *Nuntu* (1975), as well as Mohammed Ben-Abdallah, whose works include *The Trial of Malam Iiya* (1991) and *The Land of a Million Magicians* (1991). Ben-Abdallah also played a frontline role in the construction of the Ghanaian National Theatre.

Senegal

Senegal is one of the prominent French-speaking countries in West Africa. It gained its independence from France in 1960 and has many ethnic and linguistic groups.

Senegal benefited from the William Ponty School, a college for the training of teachers that was established in 1930. According to Oscar Brocket and Frank Hildy, "between 1933 and 1948, stories from the various cultural groups of West Africa were dramatized and presented as end-of-the-year projects. The spoken part, rather stiff and elementary, was in French, while the sung text was in an African language. The play was further filled out with African songs and dance."[19] The Ponty School also played this developmental role in the theatrical development of other French-speaking West African countries such as Ivory Coast. The teacher–graduates of the school were trained and encouraged to replicate these Ponty end-of-the-year performances in their schools.

It should be noted that despite these strides in performance, Senegal has not produced many great playwrights. However, one of its best has been Cheik Aliou Ndao, whose works include *The Marabout* (1960), *The Exile of Albouri* (1968), *Almany's Son* (1973), and *Blood for a Throne* (1983). There has also been Abdou Anta Ka with works such as *The Amazulus* (1972) and *Pinthium Farm* (1972).

Noteworthy is that Senegal has been a great exponent of the Negritude philosophy, the founder and frontline advocate of which was its first president, Leopold Senghor. This philosophy was predicated on an admiration of and love for African arts, thought, and the past, and the need for their preservation. Although the concept met with criticism from some African artistic intellectuals such as Wole Soyinka, it no doubt enhanced the demand for indigenous performances in Senegal and other African countries.

The Gambia

The trend toward the perpetuation of traditional performance forms could be observed in the Gambia, where the Jali and Jalulu griots held sway as custodians of the people's history and genealogies, using them in musical performances in honor of prominent members of the Mandinka ethnic nationality. A Website report states the following about the historical role played by these cultural custodians:

> Formally the griots were the counsellors of kings and spiritual leaders: they conserved the constitutions of kingdoms by memory work alone and it is among the griots that kings used to choose the teachers for young princes.[20]

The quest to recapture the recitatory renditions of the griots has led to the emergence of young rap artists in Gambia, some of whom have gone on to record and mix their musical productions.

Central Africa

Cameroon

Like Nigeria, one of its closest neighbors, Cameroon is made up of about 250 different ethnic groups. Because the country experienced the colonial rule of both France and Britain, French and English are its two official languages. Cameroon formally gained its independence in 1961.

In contrast to the previously discussed examples in West Africa, the colonial governments did not directly or indirectly encourage the development of theater performance in this country, and the repressive government that took control after independence was no better. Autocratic governments always consider a free rein of artistic expression intolerable. Literary theatrical works underwent stringent censorship, leaving the scene open only for the performance of traditional dances.

Apart from the work of Guillaume Oyani-Mbia of the University of Yaoundé, there has also been Victor Musiaga, an Anglophone playwright and head of the Musiaga Drama Group. Among his popular works are *Madame Magrano* (1968), *Colofanco* (1970), *The Trials of Ngowo* (1973), *The Tragedy of Mr. No. Balance* (1975), and *The Director* (1978). Other artists include Werewere Liking, a woman who has written plays such as *The Power of Um* (1979), *The Sleep of Injustice* (1980), and *The Rainbow Measles* (1987), and Bole Butake, whose plays are highly critical of life in the country. They include *Lake God* (1986), *Palm Wine Will Flow* (1990), and *Shoes and Four Men in Arms* (1995).

The areas of music and dance continue to be strengths of Cameroon's performance profile. Its peculiar music, makossa, has become so popular in West and Central Africa that one of its greatest exponents, Awhilo Longumba, has become a household name in countries such as Nigeria.

Congo (Popular Republic of)

The Popular Republic of the Congo (Congo-Brazzaville, Republic of the Congo) is also multiethnic and gained independence from France in 1960. Apart from the precolonial traditional performances based on its ethnic festivals, its colonial years did not witness much theatrical activity. Apart from artists such as Guy Menga there have been others—for example, Antoine Letembet-Ambily, Tchuya U Tam'si, and Silvain Bemba. Letembet-Ambily wrote and produced *Europe Indicted* (1969). Tam'si, who is also notable as a poet, has to his credit plays such as *The Zulu* (1977), *Vwene, The Founder* (1977), and *The Glorious Destiny of Marshall Nnikon Nniku* (1979). Plays from Bemba's pen include *Hell is Orfeo* (1970), *The Man Who Killed the Crocodile* (1972), *Black Tarantula and the Devil* (1976), and *A Rotten World for an Over-Honest Laundryman* (1979). Some of these plays have used the storytelling method of traditional theater, where the griots provide the background to the story line and the link between the scenes.

Democratic Republic of the Congo (DRC)

The DRC, formerly Zaire, one of Africa's largest countries, became independent from Belgium in 1960. After World War II some measure of theatrical activity took place in the country, especially through the efforts of colonial theater entrepreneurs such as Albert Mongita. Mongita, who wrote *Thanks to Stanley* (1954) and *Ngumba* (1957), promoted many theatrical activities including indigenous festivals, and encouraged visits to such events by foreign nationals.

A major indigenous theatrical feature has been the expression of local folklore through storytelling, drama, music, and dance. Each of the various ethnic groups have their legends and stories, but the common characteristic has been the use of animal stereotype characters, most of which are assigned traits similar to the stock characters of the commedia dell'arte. This storytelling culture has been adapted to the mass media. One of the country's popular television programs is a storytelling slot where "grandpere" (grandfather), in the guise of the griots of old, tells stories from the people's cultural repertory and draws the attention of the viewers to the lessons embedded in them, especially as they illuminate the realities of everyday life.

Southern Africa

Zambia

Zambia, formerly called Northern Rhodesia, attained independence in 1964. A nation of six major linguistic groups, Zambia is rich in traditional performances. When its National Dance Company was established in 1969, many of its indigenous forms and features were adapted by its Sierra Leone–born director, Yulisa Pat Maddy.

The rise of copper-mining activities increased the number of European workers in the early 1950s. The mining companies embarked on the building of theaters for the recreational needs of their employees. As has been the case in many other African countries, some indigenous Zambians developed an interest in the foreign theatrical style that had permeated the school system. As the struggle for independence heightened, interest in the revival of African indigenous performance, and a desire to produce modern plays based on Zambian life and culture, developed and grew. The outcome of this impulse was the formation of the Zambian Arts Trust, which encouraged productions both in Swahili and in English.

The country has produced some notable playwrights, among whom are Kabwe Kasoma, Stephen Chifuoyise, and Masautso Phiri. Kasoma's plays include *Black Mamba* (a trilogy written in 1971). *Black Mamba* is based on the thoughts of former President Kenneth Kaunda, and it mostly uses the genres of dance and music to chronicle Zambia's independence struggles. Chifuoyise has written *I Resign* and *The District Governor Goes to the Village*. Phiri, the founder of the Tikwaza Theatre, has written *Soweto: Flowers Will Grow* (an experimental play produced in 1979), *Things Fall Apart*, and *Nightfall*.

Zimbabwe

Zimbabwe, a country of about six ethnic groups, had a protracted struggle for independence, which culminated in its attainment of majority rule in 1980.

Precolonial Zimbabwe had a wealth of interesting theatrical performances associated with the cultural life of the people, especially festivals, ceremonies of the traditional state, and human life cycle and agricultural rituals. These performances were unacceptable to the European settlers and therefore discouraged. But as could be observed in other countries, the white settlers introduced their own brand of theater entertainment, the participation in which, in Zimbabwe, was purely based on racial lines. Blacks were not only excluded from taking part in the productions; they were also barred as audience members. The settlers built many theaters and introduced theater groups that got together to form the Association of Rhodesian Theatrical Societies.

For their part, the African population had to make do with performances in schools, churches, and nonprofessional community and workers' clubs. The liberation struggle created the need to use local theater forms for the inculcation of independent consciousness in the people, and this effort invigorated indigenous performances. For instance, *pungwe*, a night performance of songs, dance, poetry presentation, and drama sketches, became popular among the freedom-fighting local communities.

The attainment of black majority rule in 1980 changed the state of things in the theater scene because Africans could now participate in the annual theater festivals.

Among the nation's playwrights has been Stephen Chifuayise, whose plays include *Ekesa* (1994) and *Strange Bedfellows* (1995). Others are Thompson Tsodzo, who wrote *The Storm* (1982) and *Changes* (1983), and Ben Sibenke, author of *My Uncle Grey Bhonzo.*

One reason for the scarcity of African written plays of note in this country is the emergence and popularity of the community theater method of play production, with its teamwork play creation procedure. According to Ross Kidd, as a country that experienced a long and difficult struggle for independence, Zimbabwe, since its independence in 1980, has been struggling to make optimum use of its rich cultural arts, "an activity which activated, politicized and boosted the morale of peasants during the liberation war and now offers a powerful means of maintaining the close two-way communication with the peasants."[21] The pungwe community performance method, which was based on indigenous cultural performance methods in the local areas and which served the ideological needs of the liberation war, has now been remodeled into a tool for development mobilization.

Republic of South Africa

South Africa was a hotbed of segregation and racial strife for many decades. Not until 1994 was a genuine and popularly elected democratic government sworn into office. Similar to most other African countries, South Africa is a multiethnic society with indigenous theatrical forms that predate the emergence of colonialism. B. L. Leshoai holds that the storytelling, poetry, dances, song, proverbs, and riddles that constitute the performance tradition of indigenous South Africa "provided entertainment, education, and spiritual therapy for all members of society."[22] Most of these performances have withstood the forces of Westernization and are still practiced, especially in the Zulu homeland, where cultural preservation has been a priority.

A European play was first performed in South Africa in the 1880s and performing companies from various parts of Europe started coming to present plays, especially in places such as Cape Town, from about 1900. One of the earliest playwrights was E. S. K. Mghaji, a Xhosa. His play *Itjiala La Maweles* [The Case of the Twins] was later translated into English. In spite of the general belief that Christianity sounded the death knell of African art, it should be acknowledged that two Christian publishing houses—Monja Publishing Depot and Lovedale Press—made an effort to publish works by black playwrights. One such playwright was Tashekisho Plaatje, who later became a founding member of the African National Congress (ANC). He translated Shakespeare's *Comedy of Errors* and *Julius Caesar*, the former as *Diphosphosho* and the latter as *Dintshonto Tsa Bo-Juliuse Kesara*.

The South African theater scene, in keeping with the obnoxious concept of apartheid, operated along segregated lines for many years. The Mixed Casts and Mixed Audiences Prohibitive Laws were passed in 1965, thereby making racially mixed production and watching of plays perilous experiences.

In the 1970s, the Black Consciousness Movement chose the theater as its medium of mobilization. In the process, the People's Experimental Theatre (PET) was founded in 1975. Its best known play, titled *Shanti*, was written by Mthuli Shezi, one of the founders of PET. In 1975, the founders of the project and prominent members of the movement were detained by the government.

In spite of this clampdown, the theater of the 1970s was a theater committed to experimentation in the forms that could bear the determined artistic protest against governmental policies. One of the theaters that sprang up to meet this challenge was the Space Theatre, founded in Cape Town in 1972 by the trio of Brian Astbung, Yvonne Bryceland, and Athol Fugard. Notable among the works produced at Space was *Sizwe Bansi Is Dead*, a joint creation of Athol Fugard, John Kani, and Winston Ntshona. Others included *Statements after an Arrest under the Immorality Act* and *The Island* by the same trio. Their partnership proved to be a successful experiment in collective creation. *Sizwe Bansi Is Dead* is a dramatic statement about the then–South African pass laws. In it, a man without a pass who goes into a town to obtain a job discovers a genuine pass in the pocket of a dead man and is persuaded to jettison his personal identity and assume that of the deceased in order to remain in the area and secure gainful employment.

The other theaters include the Market Theatre, located at a former fruit market in Johannesburg. It staged many productions, among them plays by Athol Fugard and black playwrights such as Matshemela Manaka, Maishe Maponya, and the community theater expert Zakes Mda. There were also Cape Town's Glass Theatre, Johannesburg's Nunnery Theatre, East London's Window Theatre, Port Elizabeth's Serpent Players, the Box Theatre, and The Junction Avenue Theatre Company. Although most of these companies were controlled and managed by whites, black performers were included through some tactical circumventions of the Mixed Cast Prohibition Act. Thus, even before the act was abrogated in 1977, collaborative creations had become notable features of the South African theater experience.

In the mid-1950s, a purely black effort in theater came about through the formation of the Syndicate of African Artists by Ezekiel Mphahlele and musicologist Khabi Mugoma. Productions based on indigenous features were produced in schools. Such efforts included *The Prodigal Son* by Bob Leshoai and Rudoff Mtimkutu's *Darkness Bears Light* (the authors were teachers at a high school in Pretoria). The syndicate's major objectives were to encourage the production of indigenous theater and to form a union that could act as a buffer against the exploitation of black artists by the European and Asian settler communities. As a consequence of his constant criticism of the apartheid government's program of "Bantu education," Mphahlele was relieved of his teaching appointment and had to leave South Africa to teach in Nigeria. Thereafter, the syndicate gradually faded into extinction.

The 1960 success of the opera *King Kong* was a result of the artistic multiracial collaborations that had started in the 1950s. The production had the popular Miriam Makeba as lead singer. It was based on a book written by a white lawyer, Harry Bloom, with music by Todd Matshikiza. The lyrics were by Pat Williams and Ralf Trewhela. The production was directed by Leon Gluckman, a white, with other whites as musical director, choreographer, décor and costume designers, as well as a selected cast of black actors, singers, and dancers including the saxophonist Hugh Masekela and the singer Letta Mbulu. This production ran for about six months in London and went on tour in many other locations in Britain. Interestingly, the opera was watched by mixed audiences in South Africa. The success of the production caused white audience members to invite black members of the cast to their homes for parties. This multiracial union of artists was soon followed up by other productions such as Eugene O'Neill's *Emperor Jones*, Athol Fugard's *The Blood Knot*, and some of Bob Leshoai's plays (*Morato of the Bataung*, *No Place to Hide*, *U-Notombinde*, and *The Tall Maiden*).

Mention must also be made of the success of another musical, *Ipi Tombi* (widely translated from Zulu as *Where Are the Girls*). The production was created by a white South African, Bertha Egnos, and her partner Gail Lakier. The play's musical record sold almost 50,000 copies in South Africa. The apartheid government was delighted with the success of this production, whereas blacks saw it as white exploitation of the talents of black performers.

Another influential event in the theater scene of South Africa was the founding of the annual Grahamstown Festival in 1970. It was initially a festival for white theater. In recent years, the festival has become a showcase for the South African performing arts. More than 500 theatrical activities are always lined up as part of the festival every year. Its popularity and its nonracial participation attest to the fact that South African theater is a flourishing and legitimate segment of the "rainbow nation's" socioeconomic life.

East Africa

Kenya

Kenya, similar to most other African countries, is a multiethnic nation. There are about forty major ethnic groups in the country. It was a British colony and was only able to gain its independence in 1963 after a protracted struggle. Similar to the West African countries, Kenya had a thriving theatrical scene before the advent of colonialism, but the differences in their colonial experiences have created contrasts in the transition from indigenous African performance to modern drama. The colonial experience of countries such as Kenya was much more severe than that of West Africa. In this regard, David Rubadiri says that colonialism in East Africa stifled any attempt at indigenous creative expression in the English language.[23]

However, as would be expected, the colonial rulers allowed for "safe drama" products such as were meant for the entertainment of the expatriates and their African elite collaborators. Such plays were not based on East African native cultures and could be said to have been irrelevant to the indigenous experience.

Another boost to drama performance came through an exile from South Africa, Ezekiel Mphahlele, whose Chemichemi Company, founded in 1964, performed plays in English and Swahili for audiences in various parts of the country.

It was not until 1962 that the first full-length play by a Kenyan emerged. Titled *The Black Hermit*, it was written by James Ngugi (who later became Ngugi wa Thiong'o). *The Black Hermit* deals with the dilemma of an educated African who must choose between an allegiance to his roots or to the new values. Ngugi, who has been noted more as a novelist, later came out with other dramatic works such as *This Time Tomorrow* (1998) and *The Trial of Dedan Kimathi* (1975), which he wrote in conjunction with Nicere Mugo. Ngugi also assisted in the creation of the Kamiriithu Community Educational and Culture Center, a theater for rural development programs. Its first production, *I'll Marry When I Want*, came from the collaborative effort of Ngugi wa Thiong'o, Ngugi wa Mirii, a professional in adult education, and the local performers. It was performed in the local Kikuyu language and made use of local songs and dances. The Kenyan government was uncomfortable with the issues raised in the play, especially the expression of betrayal of the Kenyan masses by the independent government. After banning further production of the play, the government clamped Ngugi wa Thiong'o into detention and relieved Ngugi wa Mirii of his public service appointment. The government later banned the Kamiriithu Center and destroyed its open-air theater.

But such profound experiences as the Kamriithu could not pass from the scene without inspiring some successors. Another public-spirited theater group—the Tamaduni Players—emerged in Nairobi, with a special interest in performances that highlighted the problems of the downtrodden. Its most notable production was the Swahili version of *The Trial of Dedan Kimathi*. Many other such theater groups emerged in various towns, and they came together to hold a performance festival for four days in Nairobi in 1986.

Kenya has also produced notable playwrights such as Micere Githae Mugo, who apart from coauthoring *The Trial of Dedan Kimathi* with Ngugi wa Thiong'o, also wrote *The Illness of Ex-Chief Kiti* (1976); Kenneth Watene, who wrote *My Son for My Freedom* (1973), *The Broken Pot* (1973), and *Dedan Kimathi* (1974); and Francis Imbuga, the author of *Betrayed in the City* (1976) and *Aminala* (1985).

In a critical summary of the theatrical situation in Kenya, Mike Kuria argues:

> Kenya is perhaps best known in literary circles because of Ngugi wa Thiong'o's and to a lesser extent Grace Ogot's fiction. In terms of drama, no Kenyan has risen to the ranks of Wole Soyinka in West Africa, Mbongemi Ngema in South Africa, Ebrahim Hussein in Tanzania, or John Ruganda in Uganda.[24]

Nevertheless, the emergence of more public professional performing troupes in the last two decades, and their emphasis on the use of indigenous features and forms, portend a popular demand for theatrical performances in a country that depends, to a considerable extent, on tourism for its revenue.

Uganda

Uganda was another British colonial outpost in Africa. It won its independence in 1962.

The country has about fifty major ethnic groups with rich cultura and indigenous performance forms. Like the Italian courts, which played a major role in the emergence of the Renaissance, the indigenous royal courts of Uganda are known to have played a key role in the preservation and development of traditional performance culture in the country. The kings had royal dancers, drummers, and singers in their retinues whose responsibility included participation in the rituals and ceremonies of the traditional state, as well as the entertainment of royal visitors.

As has been the trend so far, the advent of colonialism and the eventual fostering of Western values tended to replace indigenous Ugandan performance with European drama. It must be noted that, apart from Christian doctrinal declarations regarding some of the native performances, there was also a desire by the elites, and even the less educated, to emulate European performance styles in a psychological bid to be adjudged "modern." This accounted for the rapid growth of Western theater forms in most African countries.

Among the nations' frontline playwrights have been Robert Serumaga, John Ruganda, and Mukotani Rugyendo. Serumaga, the founder of the semiprofessional group Theatre Limited, which has participated in many international festivals, has to his credit plays such as *A Play* (1967), *The Elephants* (1970), *Majangwa* (1971), and *Renga Moi* (1972). Serumaga's *The Elephants* shows how characters in a university have reduced themselves from elephants to mice through their self-centered manipulations and dirty antics. Serumaga was interested in exploring the use of local performance techniques and the use of dance drama. Ruganda, an exponent of realism, wrote *The Burdens* (1972), *Black Mamba and Covenant with Death* (1973), *Music Without Tears* (1982), *Echoes of Silence* (1987), and *The Floods* (1988). Rugyendo, a one-time editor in Tanzania, has written plays such as *The Barbed Wire* (1977), *The Contest* (1977), and *And the Storm Gathers* (1977). Since 1994 there has been a working relationship between the Royal Court Theatre in London and the Ugandan theater. Ugandan theater practitioners have benefited from exchange programs with the Royal Court, especially in the areas of playwriting and directing.

Another aspect of Ugandan theater can be seen in the effort to adapt traditional folklore and legends into popular art works, as can be seen in the Nankassa and Muwogola folk dances of the Buganda Kingdom.

Mercy Mirembe Ntangaare, in her "Portrait of Women in Contemporary Uganda Theatre," summarizes the theater and performance scene in this country:

> During the last decades of the twentieth century uncertainties regarding the future of Uganda theatre have grown, mostly due to the impact of film and video and the development of [the]

> music-hall and the erotic dance enterprises, all of which have burgeoned in the wake of economic liberalisation. These developments have forced theatre proprietors to desire new means of survival . . . while others have expanded their comic repertoire and unusual gimmicks to arrest audiences.[25]

Tanzania

Tanzania, a country of about 120 ethnic groups, is made up of the former Tanganyika, which gained independence from Britain in 1961, and Zanzibar, which attained independence from British rule in 1964.

This nation, similar to many others in Africa, has a rich reservoir of indigenous performances. Until about 1940, the colonial rulers did not encourage these native expressions. Theater shows based on European stereotypes were allowed in schools and drama competitions were later introduced.

The Arusha Declaration of 1967, which was based on socialist principles, frowned on the production of foreign dramatic works and encouraged writings in Swahili—the country's official language. Interestingly, most of Tanzania's playwrights emerged after this declaration (to which they initially lent great support). But later they started questioning the relationship between the high pontifications of government officials and the level of corruption in the polity. One of the nation's foremost playwrights has been Ebrahim Hussein, from whose pen has come plays such as *Kinjeketile* (1970), *The One Who Got What She Deserved* (1970), *The Dock in the Village* (1976), and *Wedding* (1980). Hussein's *Kinjeketile* concerns the anti-German Maji Maji struggle in Tanganyika and how Kinjeketile mobilized the people into believing that the so-called magic water he sprinkled on them would make them invincible against the German guns. However, the efficacy of the water fails, bringing home to the people the fact that what they needed were weapons of genuine unity and reason in their fight against oppression.

Even traditional dancing was made to adapt its themes to suit the socialist ideology. Almost 30 dance troupes sprang up in Dar es Salaam alone. This boom in performance led to the emergence of a new form, Njongera, which was a mixture of poetic recitals with embellished movements, gestures, props, and costumes. This form seems to have been characteristic of the trend in the Sub-Saharan African performance milieu of the postcolonial era. The attempts to reach back to the rich cultural performances of the precolonial past, similar to the attempts by the Renaissance scholars to recapture the classical Hellenic and Roman past, have yielded forms that are not religiopolitical in essence but fairly new creations that are amalgams of the features of the old, tinged with the realities of the evolving society.

Mention must also be made of some Tanzanian playwrights who have written solely in Swahili and who have remained virtually unknown because many of their plays have not been translated into European languages. Such playwrights include Godwin Kaduma, author of *Pledge* (1980), and Emmanuel Mbogo, who wrote *The Dawn of Darkness* (1980) and *The Last Drop* (1985).

CONCLUSION

From the foregoing it can be deduced that theater performance has been a very vibrant segment of life in Africa before, during, and after the colonial experience. In the precolonial era, the performing arts in the Sub-Saharan region were in their pure state, only savoring the closely related influences of other clans and ethnic groups within the same geographical framework. When exposed to Western influences through the colonial experience, they faced an upheaval and the daunting task of either assimilating and absorbing these Western influences and adapting them to their own forms or witnessing their extinction. Indeed, many of these precolonial expressions are actually extinct. The postcolonial era has witnessed a sort of reawakening, as well as a leveling and sharpening process. This has involved leveling the various institutional and exclusivist aspects of the surviving performances, sharpening their contemporary significance through the addition of some aspect of the new influence, and using avenues provided by the new ways to preserve and propagate their societal meaning.

Theater and performance in Sub-Saharan Africa have been artistic mediums of social relevance. Because the theater is drawn from the culture of the people, even in their remodeled and adapted states and forms these performances still represent expressions of the totality of the people's experience and existence. And since African performances were designed to be "cultural teachers," most of the performances have found their way back to their original role of conveying messages of social and economic development and encouraging the collective good.

RESOURCE GUIDE

PRINT SOURCES

Adedeji, Joel. "'Alarinjo': The Traditional Yoruba Traveling Theatre." In Oyin Ogunba and Abiola Irele (eds.), *Theatre in Africa*. Ibadan: Ibadan University Press, 1978.

Adesanya, Afolabi. "From Film to Video." In Jonathan Haynes (ed.), *Nigerian Video Films*. Jos: Kraft Books Limited, 1991.

Ahura, Tar. "Origin and Development of the Masquerade Among the Tiv of Benue State of Nigeria." *Nigeria Magazine* 56 (1988).

Angmor, Charles. "Drama in Ghana." In Oyin Ogunba and Abiola Irele (eds.), *Theatre in Africa*. Ibadan: Ibadan University Press, 1978.

Brocket, Oscar, and Franklin J. Hildy. *History of the Theatre*. Boston: Allyn and Bacon, 2003.

Clark-Bekederemo, J. P. "Aspects of Nigerian Drama." In G. D. Killam (ed.), *African Writers for African Writing*. London: Heinemann, 1973.

Edwards, Paul. *Equiano's Travels*. London: Heinemann, 1967.

Fayose, P. Osazee. "The Influence of the Folktale on Written Fiction for Nigerian Youth." *Nigeria Magazine* 57 (1988).

Gbilekaa, Saint. "The Emergence of a New Radical Drama in Nigeria (1970–1986)." *Nigeria Magazine* 57 (1988).

Ibitokun, B. M. *African Drama and the Yoruba World-View*. Ibadan: Ibadan University Press, 1995.

Kidd, Ross. "Popular Culture for the Theatre for Development." In Ad Boeren and Kees Epskamp (eds.), *The Empowerment of Culture, Development, Communication, and Popular Media*. The Hague: CESO, 1992.

Kuria, Mike. "Contextualising Women's Theatre in Kenya." P. 47 in Martin Banham, James Gibbs, and Femi Osofisan (eds.), *African Theatre: Women*. Oxford: James Currey, 2002.

Leshoai, B. L. "Black South African Theatre." In Oyin Ogunba and Abiola Irele (eds.), *Theatre in Africa*. Ibadan: Ibadan University Press, 1978.

Ntangaare, Mercy Mirembe. "Portrait of Women in Contemporary Uganda Theatre." In Martin Banham, James Gibbs, and Femi Osofisan (eds,), *African Theatre: Women*. Oxford: James Currey, 2002.

Ogunba, Oyin. "Traditional African Festival Drama." In Oyin Ogunba and Abiola Irele (eds.), *Theatre in Africa*. Ibadan: Ibadan University Press, 1978.

Ogunbiyi, Yemi. *Drama and Theatre in Nigeria: A Critical Sourcebook*. Lagos: Nigeria Magazine, 1981.

Roscoe, Adrian. *Mother Is Gold*. London: Cambridge University Press, 1971.
Rubadiri, David. "The Development of Writing in East Africa." In Christopher Heywood (ed.), *Perspectives in African Literature*. London: Heinemann, 1971.
Soyinka, Wole. "The Writer in a Modern African State." In Per Wastbery (ed.), *The Writer in Modern Africa*. Uppsala: Scandinavia Institute of African Studies, 1968.
Traore, Bakary. *The Black African Theatre and its Social Functions*. Ibadan: Ibadan University Press, 1972.

WEBSITES

Camara, Momodou. *Gambian Culture and Art*. Accessed March 5, 2007. http://www.gambia.dk/cu.html.
Ogunba, O. *Nigeria Drama*. Accessed May 27, 2005. http://OnlineNigeria.com.
Trio Africa—Dance, Music and Drama of the Uganda People—East Africa. Accessed May 3, 2005. http://Uganda.com.

NOTES

1. See Paul Edwards, *Equiano's Travels* (London: Heinemann, 1967), p. 2.
2. Angmor 1978 (in Resource Guide).
3. Roscoe 1971 (in Resource Guide), p. 70.
4. Ahura 1988 (in Resource Guide), p. 12.
5. Traore 1972 (in Resource Guide), p. 2.
6. Soyinka 1968 (in Resource Guide), p. 60.
7. See Jonathan Haynes, preface to *Nigerian Video Films* (Jos: Kraft Books Limited, 1991), p. 8.
8. Ibid., p. 8.
9. Ibid., p. 14.
10. Adesanya 1991 (in Resource Guide), p. 14.
11. Brocket and Hildy 2003 (in Resource Guide), p. 580.
12. Ogunbiyi 1981 (in Resource Guide), p. 11.
13. Ibid., p. 13.
14. Adedeji 1978 (in Resource Guide), p. 27.
15. Ogunbiyi 1981 (in Resource Guide), p. 28.
16. Ibid., p. 28.
17. Ibid., p. 28.
18. Brocket and Hildy 2003 (in Resource Guide), p. 580.
19. Ibid., p. 582.
20. Camara (in Resource Guide, Websites).
21. Kidd 1992 (in Resource Guide), p. 26.
22. Leshoai 1978 (in Resource Guide), p. 115.
23. Rubadiri 1971 (in Resource Guide), p. 17.
24. Kuria 2002 (in Resource Guide), p. 47.
25. Ntangaare 2002 (in Resource Guide), p. 58.

TRANSPORTATION AND TRAVEL

FRED LINDSEY

Transportation in Sub-Saharan Africa has historically been a factor that slowed down the growth of much of this region. Transportation remains a key issue in the future of Africa's development, but because of poverty, diversity, and geographic variables, it may still be several decades before it meets the minimum of Western standards.

The major cause of the transportation predicament in Sub-Saharan Africa is the low population density on the continent compared with other locations. Although Sub-Saharan Africa has the greatest need for a good transportation system, given the spatial distribution of its population, overall, the area is underequipped relative to its needs, and one must deal with the fact that the infrastructure cannot be properly maintained, as it currently exists, because of the low per-capita incomes prevailing in its nations.

The effects of the deficient transportation system in Africa, particularly Sub-Saharan Africa, are rooted both in the colonial past as well as in some ill-considered interventionist policies of post-independence governments. During the colonial period, the transport infrastructure was heavily skewed in favor of the colonial enclaves and their connection to ports and mines, as massive railway building in sparsely populated Africa was considered uneconomical.

The limited rural road capacities that were built either during or after the colonial period are still heavily underused. Traffic consists mainly of pedestrians and "head porters" or "head loaders" (people carrying goods on their heads) as a result of the shortage of foreign exchange, which is necessary to buy spare parts for the available trucks and vehicles (as well as for many other reasons).

In Sub-Saharan Africa, transportation takes on an impoverished character and a quality typical of developing regions. It is technically and organizationally diverse and geographically unstable. According to the experts who have examined the problem, there appears to be an absence of both planning and regulation. Vehicle types range from jet aircraft to animal-hauled sleds. Many services are organized informally and are generally named according to the expressions of the local culture. The transportation infrastructure may include steel-and-glass airport terminal buildings or dusty, unmarked parking areas for trucks, buses, and taxis. Moreover, the spectrum of roads spans highways and footpaths, and lakes, lagoons, and rivers offer only limited opportunities for the development of waterborne transportation.

The most modern transportation is found in metropolitan areas, most of which are well linked by road, rail, and air across a vast and thinly settled subcontinent. However, within urban areas, the wealthy elite enjoy the highest levels of mobility and accessibility. The urban poor have a high level of transport deprivation, along with people in the rural areas.

TRANSPORTATION ISSUES FOR AFRICA

Although the condition and performance of transportation in Sub-Saharan Africa are most often judged according to Western industrial standards, it is nearly always perceived as a system that is "at the crossroads" or a system that is "severely restricted." It rates poorly in almost every category, and the system continues to deteriorate. The subcontinent has a small and declining share of global automobile, aviation, and shipping activities and fleets. Public transportation is generally ineffective, uncomfortable, inconvenient, and unreliable. Railway and road networks are basic in their construction, and sparse and poorly maintained. Many transport services are incoherent, with weak integration between different forms, fares, and routes. Car ownership is a luxury, and the serviceability, punctuality, and coverage of public transport are poor.

Although this loose and diverse collection of services that constitutes much of Sub-Saharan transportation appears to be wasteful and chaotic, this economic sector nevertheless offers affordable mobility and plentiful permanent and casual work. Furthermore, transport has not degenerated into an unproductive and nameless activity. Instead, it remains a significant forum for human initiative. It provides hope and gives meaning to many ordinary people's lives.

Geographic Variables

Africa stretches nearly 5,000 miles from north to south and 4,500 miles from east to west. It is larger than the United States, Europe, India, China, Argentina, and New Zealand combined.

"Africa south of the Sahara" is the term used to describe those countries that are not considered part of North Africa. "Tropical Africa" is the alternative modern label. Despite a few exceptions, Sub-Saharan Africa remains one of the most impoverished areas of the world. It is still suffering from the legacies of colonial conquest and occupation, neocolonialism, interethnic conflict, and political strife. The region contains many of the least developed countries in the world. Moreover, Sub-Saharan Africa has one of the world's fastest growing populations, and by 2025 it is expected to be the home of nearly a billion people. The high rate of population growth is likely to continue, although at reduced rates. High population will continue to put a strain on food and security and deepen poverty.

Africa is rich in raw materials: petroleum, diamonds, copper, uranium, and coal, among others. Agriculture is the primary occupation for most Africans, either for export or subsistence farming.

Poverty

Poverty is a widespread and persistent characteristic of all Sub-Saharan African countries. Furthermore, within most states there is a huge gap between a small, elite group, an emerging middle class, and an impoverished mass of peasants and urban poor. In the wake of the political independence of many African states, the former colonizers and other so-called advanced or developed states have initiated programs targeting the most deprived and poorer segments of these societies. Some improvements have been made in the fields of health care and education as well as economic development, but the material well-being of the vast majority of Africans has not improved substantially.

Indigence in Sub-Saharan Africa has increased substantially since the 1980s because many countries in the region have been hit by major economic problems. Experts suggest that the surge in poverty is primarily due to the inappropriate policies of the national leaderships and because the majority of the poor live in rural areas. Although there have been many initiatives against poverty in Sub-Saharan Africa, by and large they have not been effective. Poverty in Sub-Saharan Africa is especially pronounced in rural areas. For this region to experience rural economic growth there will have to be a reduction in social unrest, and domestic and foreign investment will have to be encouraged. There is also a need for land reform and changes in land tenure. Moreover, authorities will have to encourage rural development through increased investment in the human capital of the poor and by expanding the tax base for rural development.

A recurring theme is that human capital is the most important asset that African nations possess and that this asset is critical for vibrant growth in the lead sectors of agriculture and rural nonagricultural employment. Poverty remains the most pervasive feature in the lives of Africans, urban and rural alike. Furthermore, the AIDS pandemic has taken a major toll on the workforce and on African economies. In sum, there is a problem with underdevelopment in the rural areas of Sub-Saharan Africa and widespread poverty in the region because of low agricultural productivity, environmental degradation, unsustainable population growth, a poor rural infrastructure, low levels of investment in people, ethnic conflict, and high disease burdens (especially HIV/AIDS).

Lack of Adequate Investment and Development Aid

An effective transport infrastructure is a prerequisite for the viable economic development of a country, and it is necessary for any country to compete effectively in today's economy, and this is particularly true of developing countries. However, changes in the world economy have compounded the problems of transport adjustment in Sub-Saharan Africa. The terms of trade work against narrowly based export economies (which are the most common types on the continent). Declining commodity prices and the rising cost of imports have weakened African economies and diminished expenditure on transportation.

Along with these broader economic trends, revolutionary developments have occurred in global transport technologies and cargo handling that have further disadvantaged Africa. Few African seaports and airports have adapted to containerization and the increasing capacity, range, and capitalization of international shipping and aviation. New and costly demands are being made for more sophisticated navigational techniques and business management practices. High-capacity, long-range aircraft are unsuited to the slender market for passengers and airfreight in territory not straddled by major international air routes. Threats to the survival of small, undercapitalized African airlines include deregulation in the world airline industry, the emergence of powerful global airlines, and the imposition of stringent environmental controls at overseas airports.

Anxiety over the state of transport in Sub-Sahara Africa has manifested itself within the deliberations of world bodies. The first United Nations Decade for Transport and Communications in Africa was declared for the 1980s. Because its program was not completed, a second attempt was set for the 1990s. Initially, in the 1980s, technological modernization was the goal and the benchmark of progress. The notion lingered that advanced telecommunications would reduce impoverishment and marginalization. From the late 1980s onward, however, the emphasis in transport projects changed. The proliferation of new transport investments was curbed by the selective concentration by investors on principal transport corridors. Accordingly, Sub-Saharan countries are working toward multinational cooperation to avoid this duplicate transport effort.

A new policy feature in the 1990s was the desire to improve transport for the very poorest citizens. This implied concentrating less on the requirements of corporations and the public sector and attending more closely to the overlooked mobility needs of households and individuals. The transport handicaps of people living in densely populated but poorly served urban squatter camps and in inaccessible rural communities, it was believed, deserved special attention. The large number of off-road walking trips has largely passed unnoticed and uncounted in official transport surveys, and rural women shoulder an excessively time-consuming transport burden in this regard.

Another ingredient of the emergent transport initiatives appropriate to contemporary Africa was the rediscovery of intermediate technologies. Bicycles and donkey carts, for example, were being promoted to achieve self-reliance and to minimize the import of expensive vehicles. In a complementary development, labor-intensive techniques were being used increasingly to build and maintain roads. In some places this work was coupled with programs to relieve hunger and unemployment. Together, these initiatives reflected the decentralization and democratization of transport policies. They also signaled a shift to levels of transport investment and performance that were sustainable in impoverished economies, made the most effective use of local human and natural resources, harmonized with fragile African environments, and tapped into local energy sources. It is now generally recognized that significant advances in mobility and accessibility can be secured by incremental improvements in transport.

Transport is deeply implicated in the socioeconomic, cultural, and political transformation of Sub-Saharan Africa. In the early days of colonialism, transport was regarded as a civilizing force: subsequently, it has been widely viewed as essential to economic development. Yet transport plays various roles, and its impact is complex as well as sectional. It provides mobility but is also an avenue of work, a powerful symbol, and a social and personal activity. In all these respects, transport is not merely a passive or benign technology—it is also a lever and target for transformation. The constructive and destructive potential of transport requires watchful monitoring and debate.

Impact of Political Unrest

Throughout Sub-Saharan Africa, economic problems experienced by the railways have been compounded by political unrest. At times, civil wars have detrimentally affected railway operations in the Horn of Africa, Uganda, and Liberia. The greatest disruption has been experienced in southern Africa, where a combination of internal unrest and South African destabilization policies had a devastating effect on railway systems. Due to internal conflict, the Benguela rail line from the Copper Belt to the Angolan port of Lobito was closed in 1975. Throughout the 1980s, South African support of the Renamo rebels in Mozambique closed the railways linking Malawi, Zambia, and Zimbabwe to the ports of Maputo, Beira, and Nacala. Although Namibian independence and the dismantling of apartheid in South Africa have enabled rehabilitation to begin, the region has become reliant on international aid to reestablish its network.

Railways have had a profound impact on the development of Sub-Saharan Africa since the 1890s. Their establishment was intimately linked with the expansion of European power, and their subsequent development has mirrored many of the problems and opportunities apparent in African economies since independence. Because railways are capital intensive, they will be most viable where they are intensively used. Unfortunately, Sub-Saharan Africa, with its low population densities and its limited economic expansion, does not always offer the ideal conditions for railway development. The role of railways in the twenty-first century is likely to be less important than it has been in the twentieth century, but nevertheless, it will be significant.

TRANSPORTATION AND THE SPREAD OF DISEASE

In Sub-Saharan Africa, the AIDS epidemic has hit with particular force. It contributes to the deepening poverty in many communities because the burden of caring for the vast majority of victims, especially orphans, falls on already overstretched extended families of women and grandparents. The overall situation has reached alarming proportions, and women have moved from the periphery to the epicenter of the HIV/AIDS epidemic in Sub-Saharan Africa. Meanwhile, constraints on their access to education and treatment, coupled with their inability to find paid employment, are causing rural households, often headed by women, to slide further into poverty.

Over and above the personal suffering that accompanies HIV infection, wherever it strikes, HIV, in Sub-Saharan Africa, threatens to devastate whole communities, rolling back decades of progress toward a healthier and prosperous future. The transport sector is especially vulnerable to AIDS and important to AIDS prevention. Building and maintaining a transport infrastructure often involves sending teams of men away from families for extended periods of time, increasing the likelihood of multiple sexual partners. Also, the people who operate transport services (truck drivers, train crews, and sailors) spend many days and nights away from their families, a scenario that places them at heightened behavioral risk.

Governments face the dilemma of improving transport as an essential element of national development while protecting the health of the workers and their families; and with AIDS-ravaged economies starting to crumble, urgent national strategies are needed for strengthening government, community, and family capacities to cope and for multiplying international cooperation to reverse the tide of this global calamity.

Often overlooked is the ripple effect that the epidemic will have on future governance. Dramatically high mortality rates will result in the depletion of much of the labor force, in both urban and rural areas, with the losses having a profound impact on the very foundation of economies and state administrations.

RECENT TRANSPORTATION HISTORY

The contemporary conditions of African transport originated partly in the colonial period. Initially, the incorporation of Africa into the world economy required local skills and knowledge. Subsequently, colonial settlement was accompanied by major changes to indigenous transport. Mechanized transport gradually replaced canoeing, overland head porterage, and animal-drawn transportation. Steam shipping, railways, and the motorization of road transport introduced greater speed, capacity, and predictability to transport and lengthened its geographical reach. Transportation also became less constrained by the harsh physical environment, animal diseases, and the seasonality of the river flow. Similarly, the restricted availability of raw materials for constructing transport vehicles became less of a limitation.

Transport modernization in nineteenth and twentieth century Sub-Saharan Africa allowed trade to widen and created unprecedented increases in personal mobility, but these

TRANSPORTATION DEVELOPMENT: THE PRICE PAID BY AFRICANS

Technological succession in transport necessitated the engagement of thousands of Africans as unskilled laborers in railway, road, and harbor construction. The work was harsh and severe, and the men often resisted forced recruitment by a combination of European officials and indigenous chiefs. Many had their first taste of wage labor on the docks and railways, and these sites became key sites of African trade unionism, strikes, and political struggle. Few local manufacturing plants were established to serve the growing transport industry, and career prospects in transport were limited by the absence of training and by racism. Africans were effectively prevented from learning about transport entrepreneurship except in the road transport industry. In this sector, limited capital requirements enabled them to launch small bus and taxi businesses. Taxi driving and ownership persists as a prime career route into commerce.

Colonial transport initiatives were designed to serve particular patterns of settlement, administration, production, and consumption. In the process, transport modernization created new levels of indebtedness and dependence. It was also coupled with urbanization; the growth of migrant labor economies; and social, racial, and occupational stratification.

benefits accrued to only a small segment of the population and were confined to only a few places. Colonial traders and overseas suppliers of transport hardware gained most from the rail and road transport that was installed to facilitate the export of mineral resources and agricultural produce.

Postcolonial Transportation

The transition to independence in Sub-Saharan Africa starting in the 1960s was accompanied by considerable flux in transport. In some districts, years of warring necessitated the rebuilding of wrecked infrastructures, and serious effort was given to design transport for economic renewal. The redirection of the historic north–south orientation of rail systems became a priority. The goal was to create an internally oriented transport strategy that would serve the needs of these newly independent states. Sources of capital funding were multilateral and came from international agencies rather than colonial powers. Road construction, and therefore motorization, was highly favored. One aim was overcoming the inaccessibility of rural districts not penetrated by railways (to boost agricultural production). Other aims were to spread links away from the historic axes that pivoted on seaports and to establish a network of Pan-African highways that would tie together previously unconnected countries. Funds were also spent on new seaport terminals and railway projects. Airports were among the prized transport projects, partly because they symbolized modernity. The reflagging and renaming of airlines represented a celebration of African pride and a visible signal of independence. Although the West continued to be influential in postcolonial transportation, efforts were made to develop transport independently and to use it for wider political purposes. In southern Africa, in particular, this project was part of a lengthy effort to end the historic dependence of newly independent countries on the transport services of minority-ruled states.

MODES OF TRANSPORTATION

The need for public transportation in Sub-Saharan Africa has reached crisis proportions. The gap between supply and needs is increasing, which threatens the efficiency of cities. One development is that many public and semipublic bus companies have disappeared, as has been the case in Douala and Yaounde (Cameroon), Conakry (Guinea), and Pointe Noire (Congo).

In Abidjan (Ivory Coast) and in Dakar (Senegal) semiprivate companies are involved in a privatization process. This approach has been adopted in each of these cities, where the right to operate a transport service has been granted to a private company. This approach increases the participation of private operators in operating and financing the urban transport sector.

In some African cities, the public transport crisis has generated the development of motor taxis as substitutes to mini-buses or taxis. This has been the case in Contonou (Benin) since the 1980s and in Lome (Togo) and Douala since the 1990s, and this trend is spreading. The fleet of motor taxis is now very large. They rank as the first mode of transportation in their cities. Their popularity is attributed to such factors as door-to-door service, speed, the lack of adequate public transport, a dilapidated state or the lack of road networks in the outskirts of the town, and to unemployment, particularly among the youth. The last factor is significant because it explains why this mode of transport is tolerated and accepted by authorities. The viability of the motor-taxi mode of transport is questionable, however, considering its social costs, which threaten its sustainability. The rate of accidents is high, as is the number of victims. Also, drivers are young and not well trained, and passengers have no protection. Another social cost is air pollution due to the bad state of some vehicles, the lack of maintenance, and the poor quality of gasoline.

In many Sub-Saharan cities, trekking is the main mode of transport, sometimes over very long distances. There seems to have been an increase in travel by foot in the 1990s following the imposition of structural adjustment policies. Unfortunately, private modes of transport (personal cars, bicycles, etc.) are not affordable to a large majority of the population.

The current status of transport systems in Sub-Saharan Africa will likely prevail for many years before a balance is struck between the various modes of transport (and the organization of this economic sector is rationalized and improved). There are many options for the cities in Sub-Saharan Africa and there can be many sustainable solutions, depending on the context and on history.

Roads and Bridges

Most Sub-Saharan African countries have the basic building blocks of a transport infrastructure, this infrastructure is far from efficient.

At the end of the 1980s, it was estimated that Sub-Saharan Africa had nearly 2 million kilometers of accessible roads representing nearly $150 billion of infrastructure assets. However, as a result of poor infrastructure management and inadequate maintenance, many of these assets (in particular, primary access roads) were depleted.

In 1991, the World Bank had estimated that, just to restore and sustain that part of the road network that was economically viable, Sub-Saharan Africa would have to spend a minimum of $1.5 billion annually for the next ten years. Currently, far less than this amount is being spent on roads. Sub-Saharan African nations clearly need to reform the transport infrastructure and become competitive in the world economy. In particular, these countries must take some drastic measures in the way that the infrastructure is owned, financed, and operated, if this region is to progress in the new century. Such policies have stifled local attempts to develop transport means suited to the regions' technological capabilities (in particular, means of transport in between head-porterage and motorized vehicles, such as bicycle trailers, handcarts, or motorized rickshaws). Such deficiencies in the transport system, coupled with poor information, inhibit the production and distribution of market surplus, especially food items, and impair food security in food-deficit areas. Such deficiencies prevent the effective integration of small rural communities into the market system, the creation of new markets, and the ability to create a set of semitradable commodities with relative prices being determined by local conditions rather than by international price movements.

Railways

Railways provide an important means of modern transport throughout Sub-Saharan Africa, and their distribution and operation have been closely related to both political and economic developments. Their initial impact was profound, because they offered the first real alternative to head porterage, which was slow and labor intensive. In contrast to the traditional system, railways increased efficiency, reduced the cost of transport, and were particularly suited to the transport of bulk goods. They facilitated the opening of a modern commercial economy and initiated many of the development patterns that are still apparent today.

It is now widely accepted that railways are a necessary condition for development, although their existence is not a guarantee that this will always occur. The advent of railways has not always been beneficial or neutral in its effects. The construction and financing of railways was often a highly political issue and, according to some, contributed to African underdevelopment and poverty. Despite the debate over their role, it is widely accepted that modern railways face a number of problems. They enjoyed a near monopoly during the early part of the twentieth century but faced increasing competition from road transport toward the end of the century. In meeting this competition today, they often operate under considerable constraints. Many state systems depend on outdated technology, and the financial problems of national governments, which own and operate the majority of the networks, have resulted in serious underfunding. Moreover, railways in Sub-Saharan Africa have been a major victim of the political unrest that has afflicted many parts of the continent.

The majority of African railways were built during the late nineteenth and early twentieth centuries as essential elements of European colonial policy. The motives for railway construction were both political and economic. Initially, they allowed European powers to demonstrate the effective political control required to justify a claim to territory under the terms of the Berlin Conference of 1884–85. They also stimulated economic development through the promotion of cash crops and by facilitating mineral exploitation on a large scale. They established their principal objectives—exporting raw materials and importing capital goods—purposes they have retained to the present day (but purposes that have been seen as major contributors to African dependency and underdevelopment).

The pattern of railway construction resulting from these colonial policies was quite spatially unequal. Landlocked African countries—including Chad, Central African Republic, Niger, Rwanda, and Burundi—have no direct access to rail transport within their boundaries. Most other tropical countries have one or two major lines, usually linking a major port to an interior core economic region. Such patterns are very evident in eastern and western Africa, with only Nigeria, Kenya, Uganda, and Tanzania having a skeletal network. South Africa possesses the most comprehensive railway network: its 20,000+ kilometers (13,000 miles) of track, much of which is electrified, accounts for nearly one-third of the total trackage in Sub-Saharan Africa. It is the only railway system to have a grid rather than a linear pattern, and its importance is further enhanced by its links with neighboring systems, which extends its reach north to the Zaire (Congo) River.

Table 1 provides a sense of the distribution of railway assets in Sub-Saharan Africa.

Ports

In the development of modern Africa, ports and port cities have played a large part, both as gateway settlements for colonizing powers and as windows on a wider world for the

Country	Trackage (km)
Angola	2,762
Benin	578
Botwsana	888
Burkina Faso	622
Cameroon	1,104
Congo	510
Djibouti	100
Ethiopia	681
Gabon	649
Ghana	953
Guinea	662
Ivory Coast	660
Kenya	2,652
Lesotho	03
Liberia	267
Madagascar	883
Malawi	789
Mali	641
Mauritania	704
Mozambique	2,988
Namibia	2,382
Nigeria	3,505
Senegal	904
South Africa	20,005
Sudan	4,764
Swaziland	301
Tanzania	2,600
Togo	525
Uganda	1,241
Zaire	4,772
Zambia	1,273
Zimbabwe	2,759

Source: G. Freeman-Allen and James Abbott, *Jane's World Railways, 1996-1997.* 1996, Jane's Information Group, Sentinel House, 163 Brighton Rd., Coulsdon, Surrey CR5 2YH, United Kingdom.

TABLE 1 National Railways in Sub-Saharan Africa: Trackage

societies and economies of coastal and interior Africa. Imperial port cities were critical nodes in the establishment of both transport networks and urban systems. Unfortunately for modern Africa, they helped to create dependent territories within a global economy.

The cost of overcoming the restrictions imposed by distance is one of the basic factors affecting African development. Transport systems provide a framework for integration at various levels, thereby facilitating development and promoting cooperation. A port, as one part in a multifaceted transport system, fulfills critical functions, and the relative efficiency with which it does so can be a positive, neutral, or negative factor in development.

Ports reflect changing economic, political, and technological circumstances over time and on different scales. The independent countries of modern Africa are deeply concerned with the improvement of the international economic and political relationships that affect national development strategies; overseas trade is vital in this context, and African economies remain strongly oriented to distant overseas markets. The role played by ports in African development is thus very important.

Access to the sea, which depends on distance and available transport infrastructure, is also very unevenly distributed. Inland countries such as Niger and Uganda, and political enclaves such as Lesotho, depend upon neighbors for access to ocean ports. This is partly a result of the way in which the modern political map of Africa was created, and partly due to Africa's general lack of good harbor sites. Many landlocked countries in the interior of Africa find that the problem of access to ocean ports is difficult and expensive to resolve. In western Africa, Mali uses Dakar (Senegal) and Abidjan (Ivory Coast) as port outlets. In southern Africa, there is keen competition between Durban (South Africa) and the Mozambican ports of Maputo, Beira, and Nacala for traffic to and from a hinterland that includes Malawi, Zimbabwe, and Zambia.

The number of major seaports serving Africa is relatively small. Many are "primate" (that is, more than twice the size of the next largest seaport) in a national context, and few countries can claim a national seaport hierarchy. Reflecting global trends, primate ports, similar to cities, increase their national dominance. There is a close association between major seaports and primary development zones, partly for economic and political reasons, but also as a result of historical and environmental factors. The major seaports of Africa are also, for the most part, the continent's major coastal urban centers. A port city is the primate city in most African coastal countries. The primate city port thus fulfills a dominant role in the urban and transport geography of the continent, although there is generally no direct correlation between the size of the urban population and the volume of trade ("throughput") handled by the port.

The association between port traffic and city size suggest several distinct types of African ports and port cities. Unifunctional exporters of crude oil or mineral ores—such as Nouadhibout (Mauritania), Saldanha Bay (South Africa), and Bonny (Nigeria)—are of little general importance as ports or as urban centers, although their export traffic tonnages are very high. By contrast, numerous small or medium-sized multifunctional cargo ports, such as Freetown (Sierra Leone), Dar es Salaam (Tanzania), and Takoradi (Ghana) are also significant urban centers. The general cargo giants of Africa—such as Abidjan (Ivory Coast), Cape Town (South Africa), Dakar (Senegal), Durban (South Africa), and Lagos (Nigeria) —are distinctive in that the concentration of urban population and volume of cargo throughput involves a complex range of port-city functions.

The growth of ports is basically affected by four factors: the land situation and the water situation, and the land site and the water site. The water site (the physical conditions of the harbor) often provides the initial stimulus to development, but unless conditions in the other three categories are favorable, the settlement is unlikely to prosper. Table 2 provides an indication of the relative volume handled by the major African ports.

Country	Port	Million Metric Tons
South Africa	Richards Bay	69.7
South Africa	Saldanha Bay	30.0
South Africa	Durban	23.0
Nigeria	Lagos	13.3
South Africa	Cape Town	11.8
Guinea	Kamsar	11.5
Ivory Coast	Abidjan	10.3
Medium-Sized General Cargo Ports		
The Congo (Brazzaville)	Pointe Noire	9.1
Kenya	Mombasa	8.3
Senegal	Dakar	5.3
Tanzania	Dar es Salaam	4.4
Ghana	Tema	3.9
Cameroon	Douala	3.6
Gabon	Libreville	0.4
Togo	Kpeme	3.1
Mozambique	Maputo	2.5
Mozambique	Beira	2.4
Small Unifunctional Terminals		
Democratic Republic of the Congo	Moanda	1.5
Ghana	Takoradi	1.5
Zaire [now Democratic Republic of the Congo]	Matadi	1.3
Djibouti	Djibouti	1.3
Sierra Leone	Freetown	0.4
Mozambique	Nacala	0.2

Source: Adapted from Sharon Jones (ed.), *Lloyd's Ports of the World.* 1997, Informa Maritime and Transport Publisher, London, UK. The data in this table relate to the early 1990s. They are not comprehensive, because methods of data collection and presentation vary widely, but give a general indication of throughput levels.

TABLE 2 Selected Ports in Sub-Saharan Africa: Throughput Levels

Air

There are usually two specifics about Sub-Saharan Africa when it comes to discussing air transport. First, the world's air transport industry has been radically restructured since the 1970s through the combined forces of competition, privatization, and deregulation, and the simultaneous emergence of panglobal alliances of the world's most powerful airlines. Second, the historical development of air transport in Africa, combined with widespread contemporary poverty in the region, ensures that many of the factors impacting on the demand for, and supply of, airline services continue to be external to the continent.

Sub-Saharan air transport remains largely isolated from global trends. South Africa and Nigeria are primarily the states to have moved toward a largely deregulated domestic aviation policy. By early 1997, only South African Airways (SAA), Kenya Airways, and the South African regional carrier, Comair, were integrated into global alliances, but other countries are taking note and are making attempts to have their airlines available for such combinations.

In most instances, however, Sub-Saharan national carriers remain wholly or partially state owned, although privatization is a constant theme, not least because of World Bank and International Monetary Fund pressures. KLM Royal Dutch Airlines has taken a stake in the partially privatized Kenya Airways, which some commentators regard as a possible model for other African carriers. But, for the most part, many African airlines are both unprofitable and heavily indebted and thus are unlikely targets for foreign investment.

Sub-Saharan Africa's air transport networks largely evolved under colonialism. In West Africa, the earliest air routes were forged by French mail services during the late 1920s and early 1930s, and in East Africa, the impetus was provided by the Cairo–Cape route, operated by Britain's Imperial Airways. Such pioneering services established a geography of air transport in Sub-Saharan Africa that has yet to be substantially challenged. Although the fragmentation of the colonial empires into independent states led to the creation of a plethora of small national carriers, the balance of demand for air transport remains located outside the continent, reflecting the continued importance of former colonial linkages in tourism and business.

There is evidence to support the idea that Africa, in general, fulfills a capillary role in the major east–west intercontinental air routes that link North America, Europe, and Asia and the Pacific, but the airlines registered in Sub-Saharan Africa countries account for only a small percentage of all the global passengers. Travel for leisure reasons and tourism is the primary generator of air traffic into, and within, Sub-Saharan Africa. If tourism provides the bulk of demand, air service in Sub-Saharan Africa is also shaped by a limited business market. Given its economic status, it is not surprising that the Republic of South Africa is, by far, the dominant destination for business travelers.

POPULAR MODES OF TRANSPORTATION

Human transport is a routine African reality, because both adults and children are carriers of transport burdens, loads that in the developed world are transported by motorized transport or delivered and removed by pipelines, such as water, power, and sewage. When men perform the transport function, they typically do so with the aid of technology, such as carts and wheelbarrows, whereas women are substitutes for transport technologies and carry loads on their heads or on their backs. In much of Africa, particularly Sub-Saharan Africa, there are substantial cultural differences between the transport function of male and female porters.

Walking

In many African cities, "trekking" is the main mode of transport, sometimes for very long distances. As noted previously, there seems to have been an increase in travel by foot since the 1990s as a result of the structural adjustment policies imposed on African nations by (Western dominated) global economic institutions. Private modes of transport (personal cars, bicycles, etc.) are not affordable to a large majority of the populace. Generally, in Africa, women can spend up to three hours a day just fetching water, expending more than a third of their daily food intake because deforestation forces them to walk farther and spend more time and energy collecting wood for fuel. In Sub-Saharan Africa, the poor, particularly women, often expend large amounts of time and effort on transportation to meet basic subsistence, economic, and social needs. Much of these transport activities are done by head-loading, and on foot, mainly along village paths and tracks. Not surprisingly, walking is still the most common means of transport.

Animal Transport

With the steady (if uneven) progress of some Sub-Saharan African countries in the development of transport infrastructures, the use of oxen, donkeys, and other animals for transport has been reduced, but improvements in transport are still essential to rural development and future prosperity. In most of these countries, from the Sahel to the Zambesi, the cost and the inconvenience of transport is very high, and the animal cart remains the most widespread and accessible form of transport in rural areas.

Animal power is not only used for family-level farming, but it is also used for local transport in every conceivable way. The transport role of animals is important for carrying farm inputs (seed, fertilizers, etc.) and outputs (harvested crops and animal products). Pack animals and carts facilitate the marketing of produce. Animals also can be very important for carrying domestic water and fuel, particularly for women, by releasing time that can be used in other productive or socially important tasks. Animal power is normally more available and affordable to people in rural areas and fragile environments.

Access to animal transport is widespread, and, depending on the region, the donkey, the camel, and equines play a significant role in human mobility. Most communities have systems for borrowing or hiring animal transport to spread its costs and benefits. Historically, men have tended to control animal power for transport, and that still appears to be the prevailing trend, but women are making inroads in this regard.

Privately Owned and Operated Mini-Buses ("Mammy Wagons")

Some Africans use motorized and nonmotorized two-wheel bicycles because they are much more affordable than cars and they provide flexibility and convenience to their users in crowded traffic conditions. Bicycles offer a higher load-carrying capacity and increased travel speed. However, bicycles are usually monopolized by men. Men often use bicycles to fetch water from very long distances, and although they are usually supportive of women riding bicycles if there is a direct income benefit, there are cultural barriers to women's cycling in some regions. At first glance, the bicycle would appear to be ideal means of transportation in many African cities, particularly as a short-distance convenience for people short on money, but in many cases bikes are underused because they carry a stigma associated with poverty. Moreover, in some cases, Africans would rather walk because so many

African roads are not bicycle-friendly. Many Sub-Saharan Africans rely on major transport to travel significant distances. "Mammy wagons" carry large numbers of people, often packed in like sardines, to work in towns from the outlying shantytowns and villages. A mammy wagon consists of a wooden frame on a truck chassis. They look like open, midsize trucks and are usually filled to capacity, often carrying a name—a marker of identity—on their head boards. In some urban settings, mammy wagons are being replaced by coaches and buses, and taxis often play a significant role in carrying people around towns and cities.

Public Bus Systems

The status of public transport in Sub-Saharan African cities has reached crisis proportions as collective mobility needs have increased (because of the continued growth in urbanization). Although the demand for transport has continued to grow, public bus systems have continued to decline. Several public or semipublic bus companies have disappeared simply because there are not enough people who can afford to ride them, as has been the case in Douala and Yaounde (Cameroon), Conakry (Guinea), and Pointe Noire (Congo), or, as in other cities such as Abidjan (Ivory Coast) and Dakar (Senegal), where bus systems have been privatized.

REGIONAL SUBSECTIONS

Transportation is a vital element of every healthy economy and is crucial to any strategy that addresses poverty. Sub-Saharan Africa, a region struggling to alleviate rampant poverty, will have its success dictated in part by the effective development of its transportation sector. In Sub-Saharan Africa, as in other parts of the world, a planning process that does not adequately consider and seek to understand the transport needs of its users is rendered far less effective than one that is based on a more comprehensive and inclusive strategy.

It is truly unfortunate that women, who are responsible for most transportation demands in Africa, have been largely ignored by the current process. Both rural and urban women carry out a variety of tasks that often require trips of great distance. Most of these women, members of Sub-Saharan Africa's impoverished majority, cannot afford motorized transportation. In many places, work requiring transportation is carried out using carts, shoulder poles, and bicycles. Nevertheless, transportation planners, development professionals, and policy makers continue to address mobility needs with old policies that are based on motorization. If the intended outcome of a transportation system is based on motorization, then policy and planning efforts must find a way to include everyone.

To this end, the Sub-Saharan African Transport Policy Program (SSATP), a unique partnership of countries, regional economic communities, international organizations, and development companies, was created—dedicated to the goal of ensuring that transport plays its full part in achieving the development objectives of Sub-Saharan Africa. Conceived in the late 1980s by the World Bank and the United Nations Economic Commission for Africa, it is currently engaged in the implementation of its Long-Term Development Plan (LTDP) for 2004–2007, a strategy designed to respond to the pressing needs of road management, the financing of transport services, and regional integration, as well as the related issues of road safety, gender equity, employment, environmental protection, and the impact of HIV/AIDS.

It is important to reemphasize and direct all who are interested in transportation in Sub-Saharan Africa to the report by the United Nations Conference on Trade and Development (UNCTAD) 2003 Review of Maritime Transport, which said that the economic performance of African countries was generally below average compared to the rest of the developing world. Political turmoil and conflict in some regions of the continent have resulted in the retraction or reversal of economic growth and development as witnessed in countries such as Sierra Leone, Ivory Coast, Burundi, the Democratic Republic of the Congo, Rwanda, Chad, Liberia, and others.

The following are examples of countries that aptly indicate the vast differences among nations, and the persisting problems with transport, in Sub-Saharan Africa.

West Africa

Nigeria

Years of neglect have reduced the capacity and utility of the Nigerian railroad system. A project to restore this railway system is now under way. Moreover, even though a large number of roads, particularly in large cities, are paved, the vast majority are not, and as a consequence, transportation suffers much outside of metropolitan areas. As of 1991, the Nigerian Railway Corporation declared bankruptcy and it still faces operational difficulties. At last count, Nigeria has three airports that handle international flights (Murtala Muhammed International at Lagos, Amince Kano International at Kano, and Port Harcourt airport). There are twenty-nine other airports, with paved runways, in Nigeria.

There are three major ports, the foremost being Lagos, which handles the majority of cargo, and several more, which are based on Nigeria's river systems. Nigeria is also known for its oil, although its benefits have not really improved the lives of the general population, a fact that has reinforced the political leadership's reputation for corruption. This failure helps explain why there are still so many unpaved roads and a lag in transportation. In recent years, Nigeria has been one of the largest recipients of global and U.S. investment, principally in the petroleum, mining, and manufacturing sectors, but it remains to be seen whether this development will contribute to an improvement in the status of the nation's transportation system.

Ghana

Often referred to as the "Gateway of Africa," Ghana is moving toward becoming a hub for commercial activity in West Africa. The country is aiming to become a "middle-income" country by 2020. Ghana is one of Africa's largest markets in Sub-Saharan Africa, and it is a beneficiary of the (U.S.) African Growth and Opportunity Act (AGOA). Ghana is a leading country in Africa in terms of import and export volume, and it is an emerging market for telecommunications equipment, computers, and so forth. The transportation system, however, is in need of a considerable upgrade.

Ghana has a rail network of nearly ten thousand kilometers. This network connects Sekondi-Takoradi to Kumasi and Accra, with branch lines to Prestea, Arvaso, Kade, Tema, and the Shari Hills. Despite this grid, however, it has a poor rural infrastructure that has been blamed for problems in agriculture, partly because the transport system accounts for about 20 percent of the difference between farm prices and retail prices. Furthermore, only about one-third of the feeder road network can carry vehicular traffic, and the roads are bad in Ghana.

Ghana has two deep artificial harbors, one at Tema and the other at Takoradi. The plan is to improve Ghana's physical infrastructure, beginning with the expenditure to rehabilitate the port of Tema, a plan that is designed to increase its ability to handle dry tonnage by 50 percent.

In 1958, the Ghanaian government established Ghana Airways (GA) to replace the former African Airways Corporation. By the mid-1990s, Ghana Airways had begun an international scheduled passenger and cargo service to numerous European, Middle Eastern, and African destinations, including London, Dusseldorf, Rome, Abidjan, Dakar, Lagos, Lome, and Johannesburg. The airline has suffered from chronic financial problems and has had difficulties meeting its foreign debt obligations. As a consequence, it is unable to purchase new aircraft to bolster its domestic and regional routes.

Ghana has eleven airports. The most important are Kotoka International Airport at Accra and airports at Sekoni-Takoradi, Kumasi, and Tamale that serve domestic traffic. Overall, transportation has seen some limited improvement, but although Ghana has other pressing economic objectives, it cannot afford to ignore this particular economic sector.

Central Africa

Chad

Transportation in Chad is almost nonexistent, both within the country and in relation to outside markets. As a landlocked state, Chad's transport infrastructure is very limited, particularly in the north and east of the country. Chad has no ports, and the nearest ports are located on the Atlantic Ocean. Douala, Cameroon, at 1,700 kilometers from N'Djamena, is the closest.

There are no railways, and river transport is limited to the southwest corner of the country. Roads are mostly unsurfaced and are likely to be impassable during the rainy season, especially in the south. In the north, roads are merely tracks across the desert, and because of chronic civil war, land mines are still a danger. Fuel supplies can be erratic, even in the southwestern section of the country, where infrastructure is most advanced. Elsewhere, it is even more limited. Chad's economic development clearly depends on the expansion of its transport facilities. As it stands now, during the rainy season, the economy slows down almost to a standstill. There are only a limited number of passenger cars and commercial vehicles in use, including trucks and buses. The main export routes are to the Nigerian railhead of Maiduguri and the Cameroonian railhead of Ngaoundéré. Two ancient land routes connect Chad to the Mediterranean Sea and the Red Sea. Neither route has been used for commercial traffic in modern times, however.

Chad had forty-nine airports and airstrips several years ago, seven with paved runways. Air Tchad (state owned) provides internal service to twelve locations, but generally suffers from a lack of fuel and equipment. The international airport at N'Djamena was damaged during the war of 1981, but is now served by several international carriers, including Air Afrique.

Rwanda

Notwithstanding the 1994 genocide in Rwanda, it is a country where transportation is improving rapidly. Most of the principal cities in the country are now connected by paved roads. In addition, Rwanda has several links by road with other countries in East and Central Africa. Despite these assets, there is a basic safety concern for drivers of motor vehicles because they use excessive speed and many vehicles lack adequate safety equipment. Night driving is discouraged.

Roadways are often not marked, and the streets lack lights and shoulders. Although the main roads are considered safe, during the rainy season even they are sometimes accessible only via four-wheel drive. Public transportation can be dangerous due to overloading, inadequate maintenance, and careless drivers. Rwanda has an international airport at Kigali, its largest city, serving one domestic and several international destinations, but there is only limited transport between the port cities on Lake Kivu. At Lake Kivu, the largest of the Rwandan lakes, there is a boat service that is shared with the Democratic Republic of the Congo (DRC) that provides service between the ports of Cyangugu, Kibuye, and Gisenyi.

The government has made a large investment in transport infrastructure since the 1994 genocide. It has received aid from several sources, including the European Union, Japan, China, and a number of other countries. The main forms of public transport within Rwanda are shared taxis (which pick up and set down passengers) and express taxis (which run between major towns, generally at Kigali and major regional centers). There is also a limited national bus service run by a company called Onatracom, an affiliate of the Rwandan government. The government is also trying to implement a regular public bus system. Despite its past political problems, Rwanda is making tremendous strides toward modernity with its transportation effort.

Democratic Republic of the Congo (DRC)

In this vast nation, formerly known as Zaire, road transportation is a problem because only a small portion of the roads are paved. The vast interior is virtually devoid of roads. Its entire network was in serious disrepair as of 1990, and there has been very little improvement since then (in large measure because of an ongoing civil war). There are three discontinued rail lines, one linking Kinshasa and Matadi, another in the northeastern region, and one in the southeastern section of the country that, at one time, combined the rail and river transport within the copper-mining region of Shaba. At present, this entire system is in need of repair.

The nation's most significant waterway for passengers and freight—between Kinshasa and Kisangani—is barely usable. Ports are limited because the DRC has a very small coastline. Matadi, on the lower Congo River, is its principal port, but it is not accessible by large vessels. There is also the Atlantic port at Boma and inland ports at Kinshasa and at Ilebo (on the Kasai River).

The principal airport at Kinshasa is still recovering from war-related looting and damage, and consequently it is used by few foreign airlines. Travelers can fly to Brazzaville in the Congo and continue to Kinshasa by ferry across the Congo River. Domestic air services deteriorated in the late 1980s and early 1990s, and no major repairs have been made. Moreover, the international carrier, Air Zaire, went bankrupt. Little improvement in the transportation system of the DRC can be expected until the persistent problem of war and political instability in the nation (and region) is effectively addressed. With some recent democratic movement, including elections in late 2006, the future is looking up for the DRC.

Southern Africa

Republic of South Africa

Arguably, South Africa has the best transportation system on the continent of Africa. It is a product of more than a century of government investment. The South African Railway and Harbors Administration was established in 1910. For decades, it managed the operations of most of the nation's transportation network. In 1985, it became the South African Transport Service (SATS). In 1990 SATS was reorganized as a public commercial company. This system has six business divisions. Spoornet operates the railroads; Portnet manages the country's extensive port system; and Autonet is a comprehensive road transport service. Petronet manages the petroleum pipelines; there is also a parcel delivery service, known as PX, with assets of several billion dollars; and there is also South African Airways (SAA).

When the Union of South Africa was formed in 1910, railroad authorities had to unify and coordinate the operations of the four separate provincial railroad systems. Rail transport was always a critical element in economic development because it linked mining and agricultural centers to urban areas and moved unprocessed raw materials to the coast for export. South Africa was already a major regional axis of railroad transportation at the beginning of the twentieth century.

South Africa's railroads are now vital to the economies of several neighboring countries, especially landlocked Lesotho and Botswana, and also Mozambique, where existing railroads were sabotaged and destroyed in warfare. By the 1990s, the general managers from eight national railroads (South Africa, Botswana, Mozambique, Nambia, Swaziland, Zambia, Zimbabwe, and Zaire) formed a joint operational working group to integrate rail service in the region. Suburban commuter trains are important to many industrial and urban workers who live in the townships and rural areas, but the commuter lines are the least cost-effective rail service. The South African Rail Commuter Corporation (SARCC) relies on government subsidies to manage these trains. Much of the rolling stock is still in poor condition, in part because of the consequences of the racial violence of the 1990s, but the SARCC has begun refurbishing and modernizing coaches for their current use. Even with these problems, South Africa's transportation system is well ahead of that of most Sub-Saharan countries and is on a par with many of the industrial nations.

Zimbabwe

Zimbabwe is another country with a troubled transportation system. The cost in human lives, injuries, and psychological trauma because of political conflict and war has taken a heavy toll on the populace and the infrastructure, in particular on the transport and communications systems. Too often, limited rolling stock and vehicle resources have been taken over by the military for its transport requirement, and, as a consequence, they have been lost to an economy that is already seriously disrupted because of conflict and turmoil. However, the main road system is considered excellent because it generally follows the old line of white settlement. The main arteries of years ago, with two branches north to Victoria Falls and Kariba and a network fanning from Nyanda, close to the Zimbabwe ruins, are much improved. Much of the transportation resources have been diverted away from war-torn or unstable areas to other corridors.

Zimbabwe has one of the densest rail networks in Sub-Saharan Africa. The railway closely follows the main road network. The country has rail links with South Africa in the south and Zambia to the north. Two lines connect with lines through Mozambique to give landlocked Zimbabwe access to the ports of Maputo and Beira.

Air Zimbabwe, which replaced Air Rhodesia, is a government-backed company that has operated only within Rhodesia and to and from South Africa. The international airport at Harare has one of the longest civil runways in the world. There are seven other airports (at Bulawayo, Kariba, Gweru, Masvingo, Hwange, Buffalo Range, and Victoria Falls) that can accommodate medium-sized jet aircraft.

East Africa

Ethiopia

In Ethiopia, a lack of resources coupled with political instability has retarded the growth of a transportation infrastructure even though development of such a system traditionally has been a government objective.

Ethiopia is landlocked and was, by agreement with neighboring Eritrea, using the ports of Assab and Massawa, but since its border dispute (and war) with this nation (and former territorial possession), Ethiopia has used the port of Djibouti for nearly all of its imports. Between 1957 and its overthrow in 1974 the Haile Sellassie regime organized the development of transportation via three five-year plans. In 1975, after the Provisional Military Administrative Council (PMAC) seized power and articulated its socialist economic policy, the government assumed control of all transportation and communication facilities. The military government continued to expand and improve the transportation infrastructure by using its own funds and by securing loans from international organizations such as the World Bank.

By 1971, the transportation system included 13,000 kilometers of all-weather roads, a 781-kilometer railroad connecting Addis Ababa and Djibouti, twenty-five airports, and another twenty airfields.

Unfortunately, Ethiopia's two original rail systems, the Franco-Ethiopian railroad and the Akordat-Mitsiwa Railroad, were damaged by the early 1960s because they were the object of natural disasters or attacks by antigovernment forces. The government closed the Franco-Ethiopian line in 1976 and it was partially destroyed in later fighting (thirty years later, it was still in disrepair). In addition to the major ports, there is a limited inland water transportation system. The Baro River is navigable and is used as transport to Sudan. Traders also transport local goods on Lake Tana in the northwest part of the country and on Lake Abaya and Lake Chamo in the south. Serious problems persist, but in general, considering all of these factors, Ethiopia has started to improve its transportation system (within the limits of its resources).

Kenya

Kenya has experienced a rapid growth rate in the transport industry since its transportation policy (and industry) was liberalized. This change has provided a boost to the domestic economy and has also assisted many of the landlocked countries in East Africa.

In Kenya, transportation is divided into three sectors. Buses and mini-buses are the largest and most popularly used mode of transport, closely followed by water transport, which is mainly concentrated in the coastal area (and lake regions). Roads provide the most commonly used form of transport in Kenya. The present road transport network comprises a variety of roads that range from forest and farm tracks to multilane urban and suburban highways. The system is divided into classified and nonclassified roads with a total network of 151,000 kilometers.

Mini-buses, known as *matatus*, are the most popular mode of transport within the capital city of Nairobi. These vehicles also service the outskirts of Nairobi, and there are upcountry routes as well. Unlike the train service, the matatu industry is privately owned and has become a thriving business.

The only bus service that operates urban routes is the Kenya Bus Service, which runs a modern fleet of buses and features upcountry routes as well. The only train service in Kenya is run by the Kenya Railways, which is a government (parastatal) firm. Kenya Railways operates more than 150 stations where freight and passengers are collected and delivered. Their trains run six days a week on some routes, and unlike road transport, the train service does not experience traffic jams.

Water transport is the least used method of transportation in Kenya and it lacks a riverine component. Kenya Railways operates an inland waterway service on Lake Victoria for the movement of freight and passengers (within the Kenyan section of the lake). It also operates one wagon ferry route connecting Jinja and Port Bell (Uganda), Mwanza and Musona (Tanzania), and Kisumu (Kenya).

Kenya has a relatively well-developed air transport system. Air transport started in Kenya with the formation of East African Airways in 1946 (under the then East African High Commission, an economic union linking Kenya, Uganda, and Tanzania). More than thirty foreign airlines operate to and from Kenya through the country's international airports, namely, the Jomo Kenyatta International Airport (JKIA) in Nairobi, the Moi International Airport (MIA) in Mombasa, and the Eldoret International Airport (in Eldoret). The Kenya Airports Authority oversees the management and administration of these airports.

Pipeline transportation is one of the lesser known transport modes, and this is because its performance is hidden from view. Pipeline systems are of great significance to an economy. The nation's only pipeline company, Kenya Pipeline, is a government parastatal corporation that operates a pipeline that carries petroleum products. It runs from the Port of Mombasa (at the petroleum refinery) to Eldoret through Nairobi.

CONCLUSION

According to many experts, the future of Sub-Saharan Africa is difficult to predict. The massive social and economic implications of the AIDS problem are being more fully appreciated by African leaders and the international community. It is likely that HIV medication will become more available to all Africans and the tide will eventually turn against this epidemic.

But in other respects the outlook is cloudy. There is the grim possibility that the social and economic foundations of African nations will continue to deteriorate as continuing (and emerging) problems prove to be overwhelming. According to this scenario the elite classes will continue to safeguard their privileges through authoritarian rule, thus controlling an impoverished majority and causing continued repression, environmental destruction, and misery.

The more hopeful scenario is that market-driven global development will begin to lead Africa toward economic progress, as it has in other developing regions. The success of this possibility is dependent on the spread of education for women, poverty-reduction programs, and, some would argue, on the widespread use of birth control methods, leading to a significant slowing of population growth rates. But such progress is unlikely unless there is a coordinated effort by the international community to actively participate in this effort through significant financial contributions (taking care to include environmental considerations and policy in such efforts).

The continuing impact of political unrest, war, and civil strife is conducive to the rapid spread of HIV/AIDS as well as other stressful and disruptive situations such as the massive displacement of people. In January 2002 more than 6 million people in Sub-Saharan Africa fell under the mandate of the United Nations High Commission for Refugees (UNHCR).

What role will transportation play in the future of African development? Transport authorities feel that definite measures should be taken to improve certain systems in Sub-Saharan Africa. These measures include an increased investment in rural transport systems that are less capital intensive; improvement in the overall social infrastructure, especially schools and health facilities (especially in rural areas); and fostering local participation in, and control over, rural institutions. And these efforts must be complemented by a determined effort to reduce Africa's very high transport costs, which in real terms are often twice as high as elsewhere in the developing world for comparable items and distances.

Realistically, this latter goal cannot be achieved without a significant improvement in the quality of physical and institutional infrastructure, especially in the rural areas, including (but not exclusive to) the transportation sector itself. In the final analysis, the growth objective for Sub-Saharan transportation cannot be met unless transport costs are significantly reduced and public access for the general population is increased.

RESOURCE GUIDE

PRINT SOURCES

Aryeetey, Attoh S. *Geography of Sub-Saharan Africa.* Upper Saddle River, NJ: Prentice Hall, 2002.

Bryceson, Deborah F., and John Howe. "Rural Household Transport in Africa: Reducing the Burden on Women." *World Development* 21 (1993): 1715–1728.

Dawson, Jonathan, and Ian Barwell. *Roads Are Not Enough: New Perspectives on Rural Transport Planning in Developing Countries.* Bourton-on-Dunsmore, UK: Intermediate Technology Development Group Publishing, 1993.

Freeman-Allen, G., and James Abbott. *Jane's World Railways 1996–1997.* Coulsdon, UK: Jane's Information Group, 1996.

Godard, Xavier. *Les Transports Urbains en Afrique a l'Heure de l'Ajustement: Redefiner le Service Public (Villes et Citadins).* Arcueil, France: INRETS, 1992.

Graham, Brian. *Geography and Air Transport.* Chichester, UK: John Wiley and Sons, 1995.

Hanes, W. Travis III. "Railways Politics and Imperialism in Central Africa, 1889–1953." Pp. 41–70 in Clarence B. Davis and Kenneth E. Wilburn, Jr. (eds.), *Railway Imperialism.* Westport, CT: Greenwood, 1991.

Hilling, David. "The Evolution of the Major Ports of West Africa." *Geographical Journal* 135 (1969): 365–378.

———. *Transport and Developing Countries,* London: Routledge, 1996.

Manning, Patrick. *Francophone Sub-Saharan Africa, 1880–1995,* 2nd ed. Cambridge, UK: Cambridge University Press, 1999.

Mbwana, John. "Transport Infrastructure in Sub-Saharan Africa." *Africa Notes* (1997, November). Center for Strategic and International Studies, Washington, DC. Accessed March 5, 2007. http://www.einaudi.cornell.edu/africa/outreach/pdf/Transport_infrastrucuture.pdf [*sic*].

Njoh, Ambe J. "Transportation Infrastructure and Economic Development in Sub-Saharan Africa." *Public Works Management and Policy* 4 (2000): 286–296.

Pankhurst, Richard. *Economic History of Ethiopia, 1800–1935.* Addis Ababa: Haile Sellassie I University Press, 1968.

Peace, Adrian. "The Politics of Transporting." *Africa: Journal of the International African Institute* 58 (1988): 14–28.

Philpott, J. *Women and Non-Motorized Transport: Connection in Africa between Transportation and Economic Development.* Washington, DC: Transportation Research Board, 1994.

Pirie, Gordon H. "Southern African Air Transport After Apartheid." *Journal of Modern African Studies* 30 (1992): 341–348.

Setel, Philip W., Milton Lewis, and Maryinez Lyons. *Histories of Sexually Transmitted Diseases and HIV/AIDS in Sub-Saharan Africa,* Volume 44. Westport, CN: Greenwood, 1999.

Taaffe, Edward J., Richard L. Morrill, and Peter R. Gould. "Transport Expansion in Underdeveloped Countries: A Comparative Analysis." *Geographical Review* 53 (1963): 503–529.

Wiseman, John A. *Politics in Sub-Saharan Africa: Democracy and Political Change.* London: Routledge, 1995.

GENERAL BIBLIOGRAPHY

Appiah, Kwame Anthony. *In My Father's House: Africa in the Philosophy of Culture.* Oxford: Oxford University Press, 1993.

———, and Henry Louis Gates, Jr. *Africana: The Encyclopedia of the African and African American Experience.* New York: Basic Books, 1999.

Askew, Kelly. *Performing the Nation: Swahili Music and Cultural Politics in Tanzania.* Chicago Studies in Ethnomusicology. Chicago: University of Chicago Press, 2002.

Atkins, Keletso E. *The Moon Is Dead! Give Us Our Money! The Cultural Origins of an African Work Ethic, Natal, South Africa, 1843–1900.* Portsmouth, NH: Heinemann, 1993.

Barber, Karin. *Readings in African Popular Culture.* Bloomington: Indiana University Press, 1997.

Conteh-Morgan, John, and Tejumola Olaniyan. *African Drama and Performance.* Bloomington: Indiana University Press, 2004.

Curtin, Philip D. *The Image of Africa: British Ideas and Action, 1780–1850.* Madison: University of Wisconsin Press, 1964.

Davidson, Basil. *The African Genius.* Athens: Ohio University Press, 2004. Reprint of *The Africans,* New York: Longman, 1969.

Diawara, Manthia. *African Cinema: Politics and Culture.* Bloomington: Indiana University Press, 1992.

Eltis, David, Stephen D. Behrendt, David Richardson, and Herbert S. Klein. *The Trans-Atlantic Slave Trade: A Database on CD-ROM.* Cambridge, UK: Cambridge University Press, 2000.

Erlmann, Veit. *African Stars: Studies in Black South African Performance.* Chicago: University of Chicago Press, 1991.

FESPACO. *Les Cinemas d'Afrique: Dictionnaire.* Paris: Karthala, 2000.

Gates, Henry Louis Jr. *Wonders of the African World.* New York: Knopf, 2001.

Gillow, John. *African Textiles.* San Francisco: Chronicle Books, 2003.

Glassman, Jonothan. *Feasts and Riot: Revelry, Rebellion, and Popular Consciousness on the Swahili Coast, 1856–1888.* Portsmouth, NH: Heinemann, 1995.

Gugler, Josef. *African Film: Re-Imagining a Continent.* Bloomington: Indiana University Press, 2003.

Harney, Elizabeth. *Ethiopian Passages: Contemporary Art from the Diaspora.* Washington, DC: National Museum of African Art, Smithsonian Institution, 2003.

Harrow, Kenneth W., ed. *African Cinema: Postcolonial and Feminist Readings.* Trenton, NJ: Africa World Press, 1999.

Haynes, Jonathan, ed. *Nigerian Video Films.* Athens: Ohio University Press, 2000.

Hickey, Dennis, and Kenneth C. Wylie. *An Enchanting Darkness: The American Vision of Africa in the Twentieth Century.* East Lansing: Michigan State University Press, 1993.

Hunter-Gault, Charlayne. *New News Out of Africa: Uncovering Africa's Renaissance.* New York: W. E. B. Du Bois Institute/Oxford University Press USA, 2006.

Jewsiewicki, Bogumil. *A Congo Chronicle: Patrice Lumumba in Urban Art.* New York: Museum for African Art, 1999.

Mazrui, Ali A. *The Africans: A Triple Heritage.* Boston: Little, Brown, 1986.

Meredith, Martin. *The Fate of Africa: From the Hopes of Freedom to the Heart of Despair.* New York: Public Affairs, 2006.

Nixon, Rob. *Homelands, Harlem and Hollywood: South African Culture and the World Beyond.* London: Routledge, 1994.

Osseo-Asare, Fran. *Food Culture in Sub-Saharan Africa.* Food Culture Around the World Series, ed. Ken Albala. Westport, CT: Greenwood, 2005.

Pfaff, Francoise, ed. *Focus on African Films.* Bloomington: Indiana University Press, 2004.

Rabine, Leslie W. *The Global Circulation of African Fashion.* Dress, Body, Culture Series. Oxford: Berg, 2002.

Reader, John. *Africa: A Biography of the Continent.* New York: Knopf, 1999.

Richburg, Keith B. *Out of America: A Black Man Confronts Africa.* New York: Basic Books, 1997.

Soyinka, Wole. *Myth, Literature, and the African World.* Cambridge, UK: Cambridge University Press, 1976. Reprint, Cambridge, UK: Cambridge University Press/Canto, 1990.

Steiner, Christopher. *African Art in Transit.* Cambridge, UK: Cambridge University Press, 1994.

Thornton, John. *Africa and Africans in the Making of the Atlantic World, 1400–1800.* Cambridge, UK: Cambridge University Press, 1998.

Turino, Thomas. *Nationalists, Cosmopolitans, and Popular Music in Zimbabwe.* Chicago Studies in Ethnomusicology. Chicago: University of Chicago Press, 2000.

Ukadike, Nwachukwu Frank. *Questioning African Cinema: Conversations with Filmmakers.* Minneapolis: University of Minnesota Press, 2002.

Vansina, Jan. *Art History in Africa.* London: Longman, 1984.

Welsh-Asante, Kariamu, ed. *African Dance: An Artistic, Historical, and Philosophical Inquiry.* Trenton, NJ: Africa World Press, 1997.

White, Luise. *Speaking with Vampires: Rumor and History in Colonial Africa.* Studies on the History of Society and Culture. Berkeley: University of California Press, 2000.

ABOUT THE EDITORS AND CONTRIBUTORS

THE VOLUME EDITOR

DENNIS HICKEY is Professor of History at Edinboro University of Pennsylvania. He is the coauthor, with Kenneth C. Wylie, of *An Enchanting Darkness: The American Vision of Africa in the Twentieth Century* (1993) and co-editor, with Mikhail Vishnevskiy, of *African Security: International and Regional Problems* (2006).

THE GENERAL EDITOR

GARY HOPPENSTAND is Professor of American Studies at Michigan State University and the author of numerous books and articles in the field of popular culture studies. He is the former president of the national Popular Culture Association and the current editor-in-chief of *The Journal of Popular Culture.*

THE CONTRIBUTORS

GARY BAINES is an Associate Professor in the History Department, Rhodes University, Grahamstown, South Africa. His research interests in South African history and culture include film, literature and music. He has published numerous articles in these areas, as well as a monograph on the history of Port Elizabeth.

GINETTE CURRY has a Ph.D. in Post-Colonial Literatures from the Sorbonne University, Paris III and teaches at Florida International University. She is the author of *Awakening African Women: The Dynamics of Change* (2004). Her upcoming book is entitled: "*Toubab La!*" *Literary Representations of Mixed-Race Characters in the African Diaspora.*

MARTHA DONKOR is Assistant Professor of History at Edinboro University of Pennsylvania. Her research interests include African women's history, African women and education, immigrant education, and the African immigrant and refugee experience in Canada and the United States. She is currently working on a manuscript on Sudanese refugees in the United States.

CLARA IKEKEONWU is Professor of Linguistics at the University of Nigeria, Nsukka. Her research interests and numerous publications cover the areas of Phonetics, Phonology, African languages, and cultures. She was the Head of the Department of Linguistics and Nigerian Languages, University of Nigeria, Nsukka, 1995–1998 and 2002–2004.

GEORGE WILLIAM KOFI INTSIFUL is a Senior Lecturer of Architecture at the Department of Architecture at the Kwame Nkrumah University of Science and Technology (KNUST), Kumasi, Ghana. He has designed various buildings and written on architectural issues. Dr. Intsiful has taught in universities in Ghana, Liberia, the United States, and Zimbabwe.

FRED LINDSEY is Assistant Professor of Culture Studies at John F. Kennedy University, Pleasant Hill, California. He has written extensively on African, African American, and Native American history. He is currently completing articles for the *African-American National Biographies* for Harvard University Press.

ALI N. MOHAMED is Professor of Journalism and Mass Communication and Media Studies at Grambling State University and at Edinboro University of Pennsylvania. His research interests include the history of the civil rights movement from the mid-nineteenth century to the 1960s; as well as the effect of transnational media on the world's indigenous cultures, especially in Africa and the Islamic world. He is co-editor of *Brown and Black Communication: Latino and African-American Conflict and Convergence in Mass Media* (Praeger, 2003).

UBONG SAMUEL NDA is the Head, Department of Theatre Arts, University of Uyo, Uyo, Nigeria. He has authored articles on theater history, theater for development, and media. In 2002, he was one of the six African scholars awarded the Claude Ake Scholars Award by the Africa-America Institute.

CHARLES MUIRU NGUGI is a Doctoral candidate in the Program in History, Culture and Theory, Emory University, Atlanta. His research interests include cultural theory, media, nationalism, and constitutionalism. He has published several book chapters and contributed articles in academic journals.

EVA NWOKAH is Associate Professor of Communication Sciences and Disorders, University of North Carolina, Greensboro. She has written extensively on play, language, and emotion and has worked in England, Canada, the United States, and Nigeria. She is a Board member of TASP (The Association for the Study of Play).

FRAN OSSEO-ASARE is the founder of BETUMI: The African Culinary Network (www.betumi.com), a sociologist, food historian, award-winning instructional designer, and author of numerous books and articles, including *Food Culture in Sub-Saharan Africa* (2005), *A Good Soup Attracts Chairs* (1993, 2001), and *A New Land to Live In* (1977).

ULRIKE SCHUERKENS is senior lecturer at the École des Hautes Études en Sciences Sociales, Paris, France. She has doctorates in both sociology and social anthropology and ethnology. She received the diploma "Habilitation à diriger des recherches" from the University of Paris V. She has published extensively on migration, multiculturalism, social transformations, and development.

CHARLES SUGNET is Associate Professor of English at the University of Minnesota. He has published on literature and film in *Transition, The French Review, Village Voice, The Nation,* and elsewhere. He served as 1995–96 Fulbright professor at Cheikh Anta Diop University in Senegal, and recently held a fellowship from the American Institute for Maghrebi Studies for film research in Tunis.

MATTHEW EVANS TETI is an art dealer, curator, critic, and historian who lives and works in Chicago. He currently runs a contemporary fine art gallery called TETI and does research on Asian, African, and Pre-Columbian art for the Douglas Dawson Gallery.

BEA VIDACS is Visiting Professor of Anthropology at the University of Pécs, Hungary. She has written extensively on the social and political significance of football in Cameroon. She has been a Fulbright Visiting Lecturer in Hungary and in 2005 received the Richard Carley Hunt Fellowship from the Wenner-Gren Foundation.

INDEX